FAMILY LAW

FAMILY LAW

By

P. M. BROMLEY

M.A. (OXON.), LL.M. (MANCHESTER)

of the Middle Temple, Barrister;
Professor of Law in the University of Manchester

FOURTH EDITION

LONDON
BUTTERWORTHS
1971

ENGLAND: BUTTERWORTH & CO. (PUBLISHERS) LTD.
LONDON: 88 KINGSWAY, WC2B 6AB

AUSTRALIA: BUTTERWORTHS PTY. LTD.
SYDNEY: 586 PACIFIC HIGHWAY, CHATSWOOD, NSW 2067
MELBOURNE: 343 LITTLE COLLINS STREET, 3000
BRISBANE: 240 QUEEN STREET, 4000

CANADA: BUTTERWORTH & CO. (CANADA) LTD.
TORONTO: 14 CURITY AVENUE, 374

NEW ZEALAND: BUTTERWORTHS OF NEW ZEALAND LTD.
WELLINGTON: 26-28 WARING TAYLOR STREET, 1

SOUTH AFRICA: BUTTERWORTH & CO. (SOUTH AFRICA) (PTY.) LTD.
DURBAN: 152-154 GALE STREET

Fourth Edition	. . . .	July 1971
First Reprint	. . . .	August 1972
Second Reprint	. . .	November 1973

© BUTTERWORTH & CO. (PUBLISHERS) LTD.
1971

ISBN Casebound: 0 406 56003 X
Limp: 0 406 56004 8

MADE AND PRINTED IN GREAT BRITAIN
BY COMPTON PRINTING LTD, LONDON AND AYLESBURY

Preface

In the preface to the second edition of this book in 1962 I wrote: "More Acts of Parliament relating to family law must have appeared on the statute book since the first edition of this book was published in 1957 than during any other period of five years in the history of English law." During the past five years the number has been even greater. Some of the Acts in question, like the Rent Act 1968 and the Guardianship of Minors Act 1971, have merely consolidated earlier legislation; the alterations made by some others, like the Family Provision Act 1966 and the Family Allowances and National Insurance Acts, have been of detail rather than of principle (although of importance to those whom they affect). But many, like the Matrimonial Homes Act 1967, the Family Law Reform Act 1969, the Divorce Reform Act 1969 and the Matrimonial Proceedings and Property Act 1970, have introduced changes of the most profound significance. These are the inevitable consequences of the social revolution that we have been experiencing in this country for many years; that so much has been achieved in such a short period of time is due mainly to the establishment of the Law Commission and its particular interest in family law. Further reforms are likely in the near future. Two Bills now before Parliament (the main provisions of which I have summarised in Appendix E) will affect the law relating to nullity of marriage and the recognition of foreign divorces and legal separations when they get on to the statute book. The Law Commission have produced *inter alia* a Report on Polygamous Marriages (Law Com. No. 42) and a Working Paper on Jurisdiction in Matrimonial Causes, and they are also giving active attention to the whole question of matrimonial property and to the matrimonial jurisdiction of magistrates.

These statutory provisions together with a number of important decisions of the House of Lords and the Court of Appeal have necessitated the re-writing of a very large part of this book. At the same time I have cleared out some dead wood, particularly in the section dealing with children where the approach was becoming hopelessly out of date. I have also taken the opportunity of substantially rearranging the contents. Critics in the past have very properly drawn attention to the fact that the subject of financial provision was dealt with in a number of different places. It is much more logical to treat the questions of property and financial provision together, as they compose the economic aspects of family law, and I have placed both these subjects in Part III. Parts I and II are therefore now devoted entirely to the personal (or non-economic) aspects of the legal relationship of husband and wife and parent and child respectively. The passing of the Divorce

v

Reform Act has enabled me for the first time to carry out the plan I originally conceived of subdividing Part I; I can now deal with the formation and legal consequences of marriage separately from its breakdown, and finish, as I believe logically, with the termination of marriage by death and divorce.

Three other changes may be noticed. Section 1 of the Law Reform (Miscellaneous Provisions) Act 1970, which makes engagements legally unenforceable, has rendered the former chapter on contracts to marry obsolete. There is now a short section on this subject at the beginning of the chapter on marriage and I deal with the property of engaged couples in Part III. Next, I have deleted the chapter on illegitimate children. In view of the further assimilation of their legal position to that of legitimate children, I prefer to note the differences under the various headings of custody, education, financial provision, and so forth. Finally, I have scrapped the chapter on marriage settlements. These are now rarely entered into in practice and the problems they present can more properly be dealt with in books on trusts and revenue law. I still deal with the court's power to vary ante-nuptial and post-nuptial settlements in chapter XV, but many of these transactions of course are not marriage settlements in the conveyancer's sense of the term at all.

Once more I should like to express my debt to reviewers, friends, colleagues, students and correspondents who have drawn my attention to errors. I am particularly grateful to my friend and colleague, Mr F. R. Davies, who has again given me great help with the sections dealing with income tax, and to my former research students, Mr T. K. Earnshaw and Mr P. J. Pace, whose research in the fields of matrimonial property and custody respectively has been of considerable value to me. Finally, it is a great pleasure to place on record my thanks to the publishers for their unfailing help and co-operation in rushing the book through the press—a task made much heavier by my late delivery of the manuscript.

I have endeavoured to state the law as it stands on 1st May, 1971, except that I have managed to include references to the Attachment of Earnings Act 1971 and I have anticipated the coming into force of that Act, the Administration of Justice Act 1970, Part III of the Family Law Reform Act 1969, and all the provisions of the Children and Young Persons Act 1969.

May, 1971.   P.M.B.

Table of Contents

Table of Statutes

In the following Table references to "Stats" are to Halsbury's Statutes of England (Third Edition) showing the volume and page where the annotated text of the Act will be found.

Table of Cases

A

C

PAGE

P

PAGE

PAGE

PART I

HUSBAND AND WIFE

(1) MARRIAGE

SUMMARY OF CONTENTS

CHAPTER 1

Introduction

A. THE SCOPE OF FAMILY LAW

The word " family " is one which it is difficult, if not impossible, to define precisely. In one sense it means all blood relations who are descended from a common ancestor; in another it means all the members of a household, including husband and wife, children, servants and even lodgers. But for the present purpose both these definitions are far too wide. The fact that two persons can claim descent from a common ancestor does not *per se* affect their legal relations at all; it is relevant for only one purpose, that of intestate succession, and even here the remotest relations who can claim are the intestate's grandparents and their issue[1]. Similarly, the legal relationship between the head of a household and his servants and lodgers is essentially contractual and as such lies outside the scope of this book.

For our purpose we may regard the family as a basic social unit which consists normally of a husband and wife and their children. It is not necessary that all of these should be members of the family at the same time. A husband and wife can be considered as constituting a family before the birth of their first child or after all their children have left home to marry and establish families of their own, and some spouses will remain childless throughout their lives. Conversely, some families will consist of a child or children living with only one parent, for example when the other has died or where an unmarried woman is living with her illegitimate children. We must therefore consider the legal effects of two relationships: that of husband and wife and that of parent and child. Further, we must examine two other concepts: adoption, by which a child ceases legally to be a member of one family and becomes a member of another, and guardianship, by which one person is placed *in loco parentis* to another but which does not involve the latter's ceasing to be legally a member of his own family. Many of the rights and duties which flow from these relationships are personal and not proprietary. But they may affect rights in property as well. For convenience, therefore, the subject will be broken up into the following three main parts:

Part I. *Husband and Wife.* Here we must consider:

    (1) The contracting and annulment of marriage and the legal effects of coverture[2]; and

---

[1]See *post*, p. 506.

[2]*Coverture* technically means the condition of a married woman or *feme covert*. " Marriage " is an ambiguous word, and coverture is deliberately used here because it connotes the *state of being married* as distinct from the *act of marrying*. *Cf. Moss* v. *Moss*, [1963] 2 All E.R. 829; [1963] 2 Q.B. 799.

(2) The legal consequences of the breakdown of marriage.

Part II. *Parent and Child*. Here we must consider the legal rights and duties flowing from the relationship of parent and child (both legitimate and illegitimate), adoption and guardianship.

Part III. *Property and Financial Provision*. Here we must consider those rights in property which are created and affected by membership of the same family, together with the duty to support owed by members of the family to one another.

It is clear that marriage is usually the basis of the family. Not only does the relationship of husband and wife arise directly from it, but the legitimacy of children, which still partly determines their legal relationship with their parents, also depends in most cases upon whether their parents were married.[3] Before beginning to discuss the question of marriage, however, it will be convenient to consider some other matters, knowledge of which is indispensable to the understanding of much of family law: the courts administering family law, and the concepts of residence and domicile.

B. THE COURTS ADMINISTERING FAMILY LAW

Sometimes a question of family law arises in a case of contract or tort or in a criminal prosecution. For example, it may be necessary to determine whether a husband is liable on a contract made by his wife, whether he can be sued by her in tort, or whether the accused's spouse is a competent or compellable witness. Each of these cases will, of course, be tried in the ordinary civil or criminal courts and no special problem arises. What we are concerned with here are the courts which hear and determine causes raising issues solely of family law, for example the annulment or dissolution of marriage, the custody of children, and financial provision. As one would expect, the High Court has jurisdiction in almost all these matters,[4] but a considerable concurrent jurisdiction has now been given to county courts and magistrates' courts.

The High Court.—The greater part of the jurisdiction of the High Court is derived historically from the ecclesiastical courts. Although they had no power to dissolve a valid marriage, they had exclusive jurisdiction to grant decrees of nullity of marriage, divorce *a mensa et thoro* (equivalent to the modern judicial separation), and restitution of conjugal rights. Obviously this could not long survive the nineteenth century attitude to religious toleration. The Matrimonial Causes Act of 1857 transferred the ecclesiastical jurisdiction in matrimonial causes to a new statutory Divorce Court, which was also empowered to grant divorce by judicial process. In 1875 this jurisdiction was in turn transferred to the High Court and assigned to the Probate, Divorce and Admiralty Division.[5] In addition to the power to make orders relating to financial relief and the custody and education of children by way of

---

[3] See *post*, chap. 9.

[4] The most noticeable exception is that it has no power to make an affiliation order by which the mother of an illegitimate child can obtain maintenance for the child from the father.

[5] Supreme Court of Judicature Act 1873, s. 34.

ancillary relief in other matrimonial causes, this Division was later given jurisdiction to order financial provision if either spouse was guilty of wilful neglect to provide reasonable maintenance for the other or for the children of the family.

The second principal source of the jurisdiction of the High Court in family matters derives from the Court of Chancery. This court, exercising the prerogative power of the Crown as *parens patriae*, had a general supervisory jurisdiction over infants and, in particular, could make orders with respect to their custody and education, could appoint guardians for them and, by making them wards of court, could exercise a continuing control and supervision of them. This jurisdiction was vested in the Chancery Division when the High Court was created in 1875.[6] In view of this jurisdiction it was natural to add to it the power to make adoption orders when this became possible in 1926.

The Family Division.—The fact that two divisions of the High Court possessed the power to make orders with respect to children was really an historical anomaly. It became a positive embarrassment when the two jurisdictions came into conflict as they could, for example, if an order was sought in divorce proceedings with respect to a child who was already a ward of court. The position was made even more complicated by the fact that custody of a minor could also be claimed in the Queen's Bench Division by habeas corpus. The same confusion is seen if one looks at appeals from magistrates' courts. In proceedings under the Guardianship of Minors Act or the Adoption Act, they went to the Chancery Division; in affiliation proceedings, to the Queen's Bench Division; and in proceedings under the Matrimonial Proceedings (Magistrates' Courts) Act, to the Probate, Divorce and Admiralty Division.

It is obviously desirable to concentrate in one Division jurisdiction to deal with all matters likely to arise when a marriage breaks down. With this object in view, and as a first step perhaps to establishing a new court which could deal with all aspects of family law, section 1 of the Administration of Justice Act 1970 has renamed the Probate, Divorce and Admiralty Division as the Family Division of the High Court.[7] All the matters mentioned above, both at first instance and appellate, have been transferred to the Family Division together with a number of other aspects of family law. The complete list of business assigned to the Division will be found in Appendix A, *post*.

County Courts.—The first jurisdiction to deal with family matters vested in county courts was in relation to children, and they were given power to make orders under the Guardianship of Infants Acts in 1886 and to make adoption orders in 1926. Further powers followed,

---

[6] *Ibid.*

[7] The section comes into force on a date to be appointed by the Lord Chancellor: s. 54 (4). No order has yet been made, but it is expected that the section will be brought into operation during 1971. Of the other matters formerly assigned to the Probate, Divorce and Admiralty Division probate business (other than non-contentious and common form business) is now assigned to the Chancery Division and admiralty and prize cases are assigned to the Queen's Bench Division: s. 1 (3), (4).

mainly to make orders with respect to property.[8]   But the most
important extension of county courts' jurisdiction was conferred by
the Matrimonial Causes Act of 1967.   The enormous increase in the
number of divorce petitions during and immediately after the Second
World War made it impossible for the High Court judges in London and
on assize to get through the cases themselves.   Consequently Divorce
Commissioners (who were mainly, but not exclusively, county court
judges) were appointed to try matrimonial causes in London and certain
provincial towns.   When it is realised that about two-thirds of all cases
were heard by commissioners and over 90% of all cases were undefended, it will be appreciated that an enormous number of undefended petitions were being tried by county court judges.   But as they
were technically sitting as a part of the High Court, the proceedings had
none of the advantages of county court proceedings: for example,
solicitors could not settle pleadings and had no right of audience.   This
anomaly was removed by the Matrimonial Causes Act 1967, which
empowers the Lord Chancellor to designate any county court as a
divorce county court to hear any *undefended* matrimonial cause.[9]   The
following are matrimonial causes for this purpose:[10]

> petitions for divorce, nullity, judicial separation and jactitation of
> marriage;
> applications for leave to present a petition for divorce within the first
> three years of the marriage;
> applications for maintenance under section 6 of the Matrimonial
> Proceedings and Property Act 1970;
> applications to alter maintenance agreements during the lives of both
> parties.

All matrimonial causes must now be commenced in a county court or
in the Divorce Registry in London (which is a county court for this
purpose).   If the respondent or any other party enters a defence, the
case *must* be transferred to the High Court; a county court judge *may*
also order an undefended case to be transferred if he thinks this desirable
having regard to all the circumstances including the difficulty or
importance of the case or any issue arising in it.   If a defended case
subsequently becomes undefended, it may be transferred back to a
county court.[11]

All undefended cases which have not been transferred to the High
Court are now tried by county court judges, but they can be tried only
in divorce county courts specially designated as courts of trial.[12]

A county court seised of a matrimonial cause may also make any
ancillary order, *i.e.* those orders mentioned in Appendix D, *post*.[13]   The

[8]*E.g.*, under s. 17 of the Married Women's Property Act 1882 (*post*, p. 357) and the
Matrimonial Homes Act 1967.
[9]Section 1 (1).
[10]Sections 2 and 10 (1); Supreme Court of Judicature (Consolidation) Act 1925,
s. 225; Matrimonial Proceedings and Property Act 1925, s. 225; Matrimonial Proceedings
and Property Act 1970, Sched. 2, para. 2.
[11]Section 1 (3), (4); Matrimonial Causes Rules 1968, rr. 27 and 32.
[12]Section 1 (1).
[13]Section 2. The court may also make an order avoiding or restraining a transaction
intended to defeat a claim for financial relief (*post*, pp. 454-455).

fact that an application for ancillary relief is contested does not make the case a defended one, but a county court judge may independently order such an application or any application for maintenance to be transferred to the High Court if he thinks this desirable.[14]

Magistrates' Courts.—The oldest jurisdiction possessed by magistrates in the field of family law relates to affiliation orders, by which maintenance for illegitimate children can be obtained from the father. Historically the purpose of such orders was to relieve the poor law authority of the burden of maintaining the child themselves, and this was merely one example of the magistrates' powers to enforce this branch of the law. Their second head of jurisdiction derives from the administration of the criminal law. In 1878 a criminal court was empowered to make an order relieving a married woman from the duty of cohabiting with her husband if he was convicted of an aggravated assault on her. Out of this developed the powers now found in the Matrimonial Proceedings (Magistrates' Courts) Act 1960 to make separation and maintenance orders in favour of a spouse and custody and maintenance orders with respect to the children of the family.[15] Their jurisdiction over children was increased in 1925 and 1926, when they were given power to make orders under the Guardianship of Infants Acts and adoption orders respectively.

The fact that the proceedings are relatively cheap, speedy, informal and private and that the bench usually consists of laymen has doubtless led to the increasing popularity of the magistrates' court as a tribunal to resolve domestic litigation. Since 1937 there have been special statutory provisions relating to the constitution and procedure of magistrates' courts when they are hearing " domestic proceedings " These include proceedings under the Matrimonial Proceedings (Magistrates' Courts) Act, the Guardianship of Minors Act and the Affiliation Proceedings Act.[16] The court must consist of not more than three magistrates (including, so far as is practicable, both a man and a woman),[17] and no one may be present in the court except the officers of the court, the parties, solicitors and counsel, witnesses, representatives of the press, and any other person whom either party desires to attend or whom the court may specially permit to be present[18]. The powers of newspapers to report domestic proceedings are also considerably curtailed.[19]

Proposals for Reform.—This fragmentation of jurisdiction produces some undesirable results. It is not uncommon for a wife to take proceedings in a magistrates' court and then to petition for divorce in a county court, so that two sets of orders in different courts may be in

---

[14]Matrimonial Causes Rules 1968, rr. 80, 97, 99 and 100 (7), as amended by the Matrimonial Causes (Amendment No. 3) Rules 1970.

[15]See further *post*, pp. 147-148.

[16]Summary Procedure (Domestic Proceedings) Act 1937, now repealed and re-enacted by the Magistrates' Courts Act 1952, ss. 56-62. For the full definition of "domestic proceedings", see *ibid.*, s. 56 (1), and the Legitimacy Act 1959, s. 5.

[17]Magistrates' Courts Act 1952, s. 56 (2). For the powers of stipendiary magistrates, see *ibid.*, s. 121 (2).

[18]*Ibid.*, s. 57.

[19]See *ibid.*, s. 58.

force with respect to the same family. Consequently pressure has been building up for the past few years for the establishment of a unified Family Court (or perhaps, more precisely, a unified set of family courts) in which High Court judges, county court judges and lay magistrates would all play a part. Detailed proposals lie outside the scope of this book, but at least the formation of the Family Division of the High Court can be seen as the first step in this direction.

C. RESIDENCE AND DOMICILE

Residence.—Residence is relevant in family law for a number of reasons. For example, persons wishing to marry must normally have banns published in the parish in which each of them resides or give notice to the superintendent registrar of the registration district in which at least one of them resides. Again, a woman who is not domiciled in this country may petition for divorce here after three years' residence. The meaning of the concept was recently discussed by the Court of Appeal in *Fox* v. *Stirk*.[20] LORD DENNING, M.R., accepted the definition given in the Oxford English Dictionary

" to dwell permanently or for a considerable time, to have one's settled usual abode, to live in or at a particular place "

WIDGERY, L.J., again stressing the need for a degree of permanence, referred to

"the place where a man is based or where he continues to live, the place where he sleeps and shelters and has his home".[1]

It will thus be seen that two elements must be present: physical presence and an intention to remain in the same place, at any rate for more than a short period of time. The contrast between the permanent resident and the temporary visitor is an easy one to see; what may be difficult on the facts of a particular case is to decide whether the length of time a person proposes to remain is long enough to give his stay the quality of residence. Obviously there need not be an intention to remain permanently or even indefinitely; perhaps the best test is to ask oneself whether the person can be regarded as being based at the place in question rather than somewhere else.

There is no doubt that a person can have two or more places of residence and can reside in both or all of them or, alternatively, in each of them at different times. In *Fox* v. *Stirk* it was held that students of the University of Bristol who lived in a hall of residence during term time were resident there for the purpose of the Representation of the People Act and thus entitled to be placed on the electoral register. It cannot be doubted that they were also resident at their parents' homes if that was where they spent their vacations.[2]

Just as there must be a degree of permanence to constitute residence, a temporary absence will not deprive a person of his residence.[3] Hence

---

[20][1970] 3 All E.R. 7, C.A.; [1970] 2 Q.B. 463. See also McClean, *The Meaning of Residence*, 11 I.C.L.Q. 1153.

[1]At pp. 13 and 477, respectively.

[2]See also *Levene* v. *Inland Revenue Commissioners*, [1928] A.C. 217, H.L., at pp. 223, 232; *Morgan* v. *Murch*, [1970] 2 All E.R. 100, 104, C.A.

[3]*Fox* v. *Stirk*, (*supra*), at pp. 12, 475 and 13, 477, respectively.

spouses who are normally resident in their matrimonial home will continue to reside there whilst they are physically absent on, say, a month's holiday.

Domicile.—The concept of domicile and the difficulties which it may give rise to are primarily subjects of Private International Law and cannot be dealt with here in any detail.[4] But domicile is of importance for two reasons in family law: first, many problems in family law (such as capacity to marry and jurisdiction to grant a decree of divorce) are intimately bound up with the law of a man's domicile (or *lex domicilii*) and cannot be resolved without reference to it, and secondly, in certain cases a person's domicile depends on that of another (for example, husband or parent). The subject therefore falls within the scope of this book.

Domicile is completely unconnected with nationality, and a man can only be domiciled in a place which has a separate legal system; thus a man cannot be domiciled in the United Kingdom but must be domiciled in, say, England or Scotland (which have different legal systems), and he may be domiciled there even though he is not a Citizen of the United Kingdom and Colonies. The reason for this is that many rights and capacities are governed by the *lex domicilii* and hence it is essential that domicile itself be defined by reference to a legal system.

In accordance with this, two principles were early established, the need for which is self-evident. First, every person must have a domicile, and secondly, no person may have more than one domicile at any time.

Domicile of Origin.—Domicile of origin is an artificial concept in the sense that its acquisition depends in no way on the will of the person on whom it is conferred and that, if a person has no other domicile at any given time, his domicile of origin automatically revives. It is obviously essential in order to satisfy the condition that everyone (including a newly born child whose legitimacy, for example, will depend on his domicile) must have a domicile. In the case of a legitimate child, his domicile of origin is that of his father at the time of his birth; in the case of an illegitimate child it is that of his mother.[5] If a woman changes her domicile between the death of her husband and the birth of a posthumous child, it is not settled whether the child's domicile of origin is the last domicile of his father or that of his mother at the time of his birth, but most writers assume the latter to be correct.[6]

---

[4]Reference must be made to textbooks on Private International Law for a fuller discussion of the law of domicile and for the authorities for many of the propositions stated here. For criticisms of the present law and proposals for reform, see the First and Seventh Reports of the Private International Law Committee, 1954, Cmd. 9068, and 1963, Cmnd. 1955.

[5]*Henderson* v. *Henderson*, [1965] 1 All E.R. 179; [1967] P. 77; *Udny* v. *Udny* (1869), L.R. 1 Sc. & D. 441, 457, H.L. (*per* LORD WESTBURY). It is easy to see that this may give rise to circuity: whether a child is legitimate is a question for his *lex domicilii*, but his domicile may be different according to whether or not he is legitimate: see *post*, p. 242. If an illegitimate child is later legitimated *per subsequens matrimonium*, it is generally assumed, in the absence of authority, that this will not affect his domicile of origin.

[6]A foundling is normally presumed to have a domicile of origin in the place where he was found.

Domicile of Choice.—Any person over the age of 18 other than a married woman may acquire a domicile of choice.[7] This can only be acquired *animo et facto,* that is, the person intending to acquire it must assume residence in the country in question[8] and must have the intention of remaining there permanently or, at least, indefinitely.[9] It is lost in the same way, that is, by leaving the country with the intention of not returning there permanently or indefinitely.[10]

If, when a person loses his domicile of choice, he does not acquire another domicile, his domicile of origin automatically revives and will remain his domicile until he acquires a fresh domicile of choice. The artificiality of the domicile of origin is emphasised by its liability to reappear many years after the person in question has had any connection with the country in question.[11]

Dependent Domicile.—In English law neither a married woman nor a minor is capable of acquiring a domicile of choice, but their domicile in each case depends at all times upon that of another.

Married Women.—On marriage a woman automatically acquires her husband's domicile and retains it throughout her coverture.[12] This will not occur, of course, if the marriage is void; but if it is voidable, she will retain her husband's domicile until the marriage is annulled.[13] She is incapable of acquiring a separate domicile of choice even though the spouses separate by agreement[14] or under a decree of judicial separation.[15] Similarly, if the husband deserts his wife and acquires a fresh domicile abroad, her domicile still automatically follows his.[16]

Although it is generally essential that the marriage should be governed by one law and that the spouses should therefore share the same domicile, in a case like the last it is artificial in the extreme to insist that the wife should have thrust upon her a domicile in a state which she has never visited, which she has no intention of visiting and with which she has no connection whatsoever. Consequently, the Private International Law Committee in their Reports on Domicile[17] recommend that a wife who has been separated from her husband by

---

[7]A lunatic may not be able to acquire a domicile of choice because of his inability to form the necessary *animus.*

[8]Hence if a person leaves England with the intention of settling in New York and dies on the high seas, he will not have acquired a domicile in New York.

[9]See Cheshire, *Private International Law,* 8th Ed., 154-159.

[10]Cheshire, *op. cit.,* 173. Dicey and Morris, *Conflict of Laws,* 8th Ed., 105, consider that it is sufficient not to have a definite intention of returning, and this view was preferred in *Re Flynn,* [1968] 1 All E.R. 49, 58, and *Qureshi* v. *Qureshi,* [1971] 1 All E.R. 325, 328. It is very doubtful, however, whether indecision is enough to shake off a domicile of choice: see Cheshire, *loc. cit.*

[11]If indeed he ever had any connection with it at all, since he need not have been born there. The Private International Law Committee recommended that a person should retain a domicile of choice until it is lost by the acquisition of another domicile of choice.

[12]*Harvey* v. *Farnie* (1882), 8 App. Cas. 43, H.L.

[13]*De Reneville* v. *De Reneville,* [1948] 1 All E.R. 56, C.A.; [1948] P. 100.

[14]*Dolphin* v. *Robins* (1859), 7 H.L. Cas. 390, H.L.

[15]*A.-G. for Alberta* v. *Cook,* [1926] A.C. 444, P.C.

[16]*H.* v. *H.,* [1928] P. 206.

[17]1954, Cmd. 9068; 1963, Cmnd. 1955. For a critical discussion, see Graveson, *Reform of the Law of Domicile,* 70 L.Q.R. 492.

the order of a court of competent jurisdiction should be free to acquire a domicile of her own; but the difficulties which might ensue led them to the conclusion that the law should remain as it is if there is no such order, even though she has been deserted.

Once the marriage is terminated, the wife is free to acquire another domicile of choice. But until she does so, she is presumed to retain her former husband's domicile.[18]

Minors.—It is generally accepted that a minor is incapable of acquiring a domicile of his own, and that that of a legitimate child follows his father's and that of an illegitimate child follows his mother's.[19] The only exception to this rule is that a girl who marries will *ipso facto* acquire her husband's domicile.[20] Thus, if a father goes off to Bermuda with the intention of retiring there, leaving behind a married son, aged 17, the domicile of his son, his daughter-in-law and his grandchildren (if any) will automatically become Bermudan too. To prevent this absurd situation from arising, the Private International Law Committee recommend that male minors should be capable of acquiring their own domicile of choice on marriage.

In *Potinger* v. *Wightman*[1] it was held that, after the death of a legitimate child's father, his domicile will *prima facie* change with that of his mother. To this rule GRANT, M.R., himself predicated the possible exception that a mother cannot change her children's domicile fraudulently—in other words if her object in so doing is to obtain an advantage for herself, as it might be if the law of succession were more favourable to her in the country in which she acquires her new domicile of choice. But this rule (even with the exception grafted on it) is not invariable, as is shown by *Re Beaumont*.[2] In this case a widow, whose domicile (like that of her deceased husband) was Scottish, remarried and later moved to London with her second husband, thereby acquiring a dependent domicile in England. She left her infant daughter in Scotland with an aunt who brought her up. It was held that this girl never lost her Scottish domicile. STIRLING, J., held that a widowed mother has the *power* to change her infant children's domicile which the mother had never exercised in this case, as was evidenced by her leaving her daughter in Scotland. This power, he said, must be exercised for the child's welfare, and on this assumption the apparent exception in *Potinger* v. *Wightman* is completely explained.

If the mother's power to change her children's domicile in these cases derives from the fact that she has custody of them after the father's death, a divorced woman who is given the custody of her minor children could similarly change their domicile if she acquired a different domicile

---

[18]*Re Wallach*, [1950] 1 All E.R. 199, distinguished in *Re Scullard*, [1956] 3 All E.R. 898; [1957] Ch. 107, where the wife, *who had been separated from her husband for 47 years, was held to have acquired a fresh domicile even though she was ignorant of her husband's death*. See Graveson, *Domicile on the Ending of Dependence*, 6 I.C.L.Q. 1; Webb in 20 M.L.R. 177.

[19]*Henderson* v. *Henderson*, [1965] 1 All E.R. 179; [1967] P. 77.

[20]It is uncertain whether a widow under the age of 18 will retain her late husband's domicile or re-acquire her father's domicile.

[1](1817), 3 Mer. 67.

[2][1893] 3 Ch. 490.

from her former husband. There is no English authority on the point,[3] and although there is much to be said for the view that a father should cease to have the capacity to change his children's domicile if he has lost all legal rights with respect to them, English courts have been slow to deprive him of his powers in the past and may well cling to the view that the concept of dependent domicile is an absolute one based on status and is quite separate from the question of custody.

Although there is no authority on the point, it seems in keeping with general principles that an adopted child should acquire by the adoption the domicile of his adopter or adopters but that his domicile of origin should not be affected by the adoption.

---

[3]In Scotland it has been held that a divorced wife cannot change her children's domicile: *Shanks* v. *Shanks*, 1965 S.L.T. 330; in Northern Ireland it has been held that she can: *Hope* v. *Hope*, [1968] N.I. 1.

CHAPTER 2

Marriage

A. THE NATURE OF MARRIAGE

Quite apart from its abstract meaning as the social institution of marriage, " marriage " has two distinct meanings: the ceremony by which a man and woman become husband and wife or the *act of marrying*, and the relationship existing between a husband and his wife or the *state of being married*.[1] This distinction largely corresponds with its dual aspect of contract and status.

Marriage as a Contract.—In English law at least, marriage is an agreement by which a man and woman enter into a certain legal relationship with each other and which creates and imposes mutual rights and duties. Looked at from this point of view, marriage is clearly a contract. It presents similar problems to other contracts—for example, of form and capacity; and like other contracts it may be void or voidable. But it is, of course, quite unlike any commercial contract, and consequently it is *sui generis* in many respects. In particular we may note the following marked dissimilarities.

(1) The law relating to the capacity to marry is quite different from that of any other contract.

(2) A marriage may only be contracted if special formalities are carried out.

(3) The grounds on which a marriage may be void or voidable are for the most part completely different from those on which other contracts may be void or voidable.

(4) Unlike other voidable contracts, a voidable marriage cannot be declared void *ab initio* by repudiation by one of the parties but may be set aside only by a decree of nullity pronounced by a court of competent jurisdiction.

(5) A contract of marriage cannot be discharged by agreement, frustration or breach. Apart from death, it can be terminated only by a decree of dissolution (or divorce) pronounced by a court of competent jurisdiction.

(6) Provided that they do not offend against rules of public policy or statutory prohibitions, the parties to a commercial contract may make such terms as they think fit. But whatever agreement they may

---

[1]Graveson, *Status in the Common Law*, 80-81. Compare the use of the word " marriage " in the following two sentences: " The marriage took place yesterday between X and Y " and " A wife retains her husband's domicile during marriage ".

come to cannot *as such* confer rights or impose duties upon any other person. But the fact that marriage creates a status limits the parties' power to make their own terms and also may affect their legal rights and duties with respect to other persons.

Marriage as creating Status.—This second aspect of marriage is much more important than its first. It creates a status, that is, " the condition of belonging to a particular class of persons [*i.e.*, married persons] to whom the law assigns certain peculiar legal capacities or incapacities."[2]

In the first place, the spouses' mutual rights and duties are very largely fixed by law and not by agreement. Some of these may be varied by consent; for example, the spouses may release each other from the duty to cohabit. But many may not be altered; thus the wife may not contract out of her power to apply to the court for financial provision in the event of divorce.

Secondly, marriage may also affect the rights and duties of third persons. Thus a husband has an action against anyone who by committing a tort against the wife thereby deprives him of her consortium, and it is not open to the tortfeasor to argue that the marriage is *res inter alios acta*.

These illustrations are not intended by any means to be exhaustive and many more examples of both aspects of marriage will be found in this book. Amongst other matters which may be mentioned here are the ways in which marriage affects (or may affect) the parties' nationality, domicile and right to participate in the distribution of a deceased spouse's estate if he or she dies intestate.

Definition of Marriage.—The classic definition of marriage in English law is that of LORD PENZANCE in *Hyde* v. *Hyde*:[3]

"I conceive that marriage, as understood in Christendom, may . . . be defined as the voluntary union for life of one man and one woman to the exclusion of all others."

It will be seen that this definition involves three conditions.

First, the marriage must be *voluntary*. Thus, as we shall see,[4] it can be annulled if there was no true consent on the part of one of the parties.

Secondly, it must be *for life*. If by marriage " as understood in Christendom" LORD PENZANCE was referring to the view traditionally taken in Western Europe by the Roman Catholic Church and some other denominations, his statement is of course unexceptionable. But it does not mean that by English law marriage is indissoluble: divorce by judicial process had been possible in England for over eight years when *Hyde* v. *Hyde* was decided. The gloss put on the dictum by the Court of Appeal in *Nachimson* v. *Nachimson*[5]—that it must be the parties' intention when they entered into the marriage that it should last for

---

[2]Allen, *Status and Capacity*, 46 L.Q.R. 277, 288. In this article Sir Carleton Allen critically discusses a number of other definitions of status and analyses this elusive legal concept. See also Graveson, *op. cit.*

[3](1866), L.R. 1 P. & D. 130, 133. See further *post*, p. 43.

[4]*Post*, pp. 79 *et seq.*

[5][1930] P. 217, C.A.

life—is unsatisfactory. If, say, two people enter into a marriage for the sole purpose of enabling a child to be born legitimate, intending never to live together but to obtain a divorce by consent at the earliest opportunity, it cannot be doubted that their union is a marriage by English law. The only interpretation that can be put on LORD PENZANCE'S statement is that the marriage must last for life unless it is previously determined by a decree or some other act of dissolution.[6] If one may draw an analogy (perhaps not very happy) from the law of real property, marriage must resemble a determinable life interest rather than a term of years absolute.

Thirdly, it must be *monogamous*. Neither spouse may contract another marriage so long as the original union subsists.

B. AGREEMENTS TO MARRY

A marriage is frequently, although by no means invariably, preceded by an agreement to marry or " engagement ". At common law such agreements amounted to contracts provided that there was an intention to enter into legal relations (as there probably would not be in the case of an " unofficial engagement "). Because of their highly personal and non-commercial nature they possessed certain peculiar characteristics, but as a general rule they were governed by the general principles of the law of contract. Consequently if either party withdrew from the contract without lawful justification, the other could sue for breach of contract. Such actions became rare after the Second World War and were never brought by men at all—partly no doubt because of the difficulty of proving damage, but probably largely as the result of a change in social views.[7]

The fact that actions for breach of promise of marriage were still occasionally brought raised the question of their utility. If either party to an engagement was convinced that he (or she) ought not to marry the other, it was highly doubtful whether public policy was served by letting the threat of an action push him into a potentially unstable marriage or by penalising him in damages if he resiled. The Law Commission therefore recommended the abolition of these actions[8] and this recommendation was implemented by section 1 of the Law Reform (Miscellaneous Provisions) Act 1970. This provides that no agreement to marry shall take effect as a legally enforceable contract and that no action shall lie in this country for breach of such an agreement, wherever it was made.

Property of Engaged Couples.—The action for breach of promise of marriage might occasionally fulfil a social function by permitting a party to recover expenses which he had incurred in contemplation of the marriage. To take one or two examples: the woman might have travelled a considerable distance to marry and live in this country; the man might have bought furniture which he no longer needs; both

---

[6]*Nachimson* v. *Nachimson*, (*supra*), at pp. 225, 227 (*per* LORD HANWORTH, M.R.), 235 (*per* LAWRENCE, L.J.), 243-244 (*per* ROMER, L.J.).

[7]The civil judicial statistics do not disclose how many actions were brought. Nor do we know how far the existence of the action led to settlements out of court.

[8]Law Com. No. 26 (Breach of Promise of Marriage) 1969.

parties might have spent money and labour in securing a mortgage on the proposed matrimonial home, decorating it and carrying out repairs on it. There is now no remedy at all for the first two types of loss. Engaged couples acquiring property for use in their married life together are in a position little different from that of a newly married couple and consequently section 2 (1) of the Law Reform (Miscellaneous Provisions) Act 1970 seeks to give them some protection by enacting:

> " Where an agreement to marry is terminated, any rule of law relating to the rights of husbands and wives in relation to property in which either or both has or have a beneficial interest . . . shall apply, in relation to any property in which either or both of the parties to the agreement had a beneficial interest while the agreement was in force, as it applies in relation to property in which a husband or wife has a beneficial interest."

It therefore follows, for example, that if a man purchases a house in his own name partly with money provided by his fiancée and they enhance its value by doing work on it, the use of her money and her contribution to the improvement of the house will give her the same interest in it as she would have acquired had the parties been married at the time.[9]

In order to bring this sub-section into play it will be seen that there must have been an agreement to marry and at least one of the parties to it must have had an interest in the property whilst the agreement was in force. Now that such agreements are no longer legally enforceable, it is not clear what arrangements are caught by these words: is it sufficient, for example, that there was an " unofficial engagement " between the parties? It will be seen that the cause of the termination is irrelevant: it may be by agreement, by repudiation by one of the parties or by the death of one of them. The fact that the parties' proprietary rights are no longer to turn on their culpability[10] may be a weakness in the Act. If, say, a husband is responsible for the breakdown of the marriage, the court can take this into consideration in making financial provision for the wife and might, for example, order him to transfer his interest in the matrimonial home to her;[11] the court has no power, however, to make a comparable order against a man whose conduct has brought about the termination of an engagement.[12]

To enable parties to an engagement that has been terminated to settle disputes over property more expeditiously, either of them may now bring summary proceedings under section 17 of the Married Women's Property Act 1882 within three years of the termination of the agreement.[13]

Gifts between Engaged Couples.—At common law a gift made by one party to an engagement to the other in contemplation of marriage could not be recovered by the donor if he was in breach of contract. This meant, for example, that if the man broke off the engagement without legal justification, he could not recover the engage-

---

[9]For the interests taken by spouses in each other's property, see *post*, pp. 359 *et seq.* and 375 *et seq.*

[10]See Law Com. No. 26, paras. 35-42.

[11]Under s. 4 of the Matrimonial Proceedings and Property Act 1970. See *post*, p. 434.

[12]See Cretney, 33 M.L.R. 534.

[13]Law Reform (Miscellaneous Provisions) Act 1970, s. 2 (2). See further, *post*, p. 357.

ment ring, but he could do so if the woman was in breach of contract.[14]

In conformity with the principle that the parties' rights with respect to property should not depend upon their responsibility for the termination of the agreement, section 3 (1) of the Law Reform (Miscellaneous Provisions) Act 1970 now provides:

> "A party to an agreement to marry who makes a gift of property to the other party on the condition (express or implied) that it shall be returned if the agreement is terminated shall not be prevented from recovering the property by reason only of his having terminated the agreement."[15]

Whether a particular gift was made subject to an implied condition that it should be returned if the marriage did not take place must necessarily be a question of fact to be decided in each case. Normally property intended to become a part of the matrimonial home (for example, furniture) will fall into this category, and it is suggested that the general test to be applied should be: was the gift made to the donee as an individual or as the donor's future spouse? If it is in the latter class, it will be regarded as conditional, whereas if it is in the former, it will be regarded as absolute and recoverable only in the same circumstances as any other gift—for example, on the ground that it was induced by fraud or undue influence.

The engagement ring is specifically dealt with by the statute. The gift is presumed to be absolute but this presumption may be rebutted by proving that the ring was given on the condition (express or implied) that it should be returned if the marriage did not take place for any reason.[16] One would have thought that by current social convention an engagement ring was still regarded as a pledge and that the presumption ought to have been the other way. As it is, the ring is likely to be recoverable only in the most exceptional circumstances, for example if it can be shown that it was an heirloom in the man's family.

If a gift in contemplation of marriage is made to one or both of the engaged couple by a third person (as in the case of wedding presents), it is, in the absence of any contrary intention, conditional upon the celebration of the marriage and must therefore be returned if the marriage does not take place for any reason at all.[17] A contrary intention will clearly be shown if the gift is for immediate use before the marriage.

Undue Influence.—It was formerly believed that the fact that an engaged woman would probably place the greatest confidence in her fiancé raised a presumption in equity that he had exercised undue influence over her with respect to any gift that she made to him or any

---

[14]*Cohen* v. *Sellar*, [1926] 1 K.B. 536; *Jacobs* v. *Davis*, [1917] 2 K.B. 532. There is no direct authority for the position if the agreement was terminated otherwise than by breach, *e.g.*, by agreement or death. It was generally assumed that the donor (or his personal representatives) could recover conditional gifts: see *Cohen* v. *Sellar*.

[15]This is an unfortunately worded provision. If the man behaved in such a way as to justify the woman in breaking off the engagement, he could not recover conditional gifts at common law. But as it is she who has strictly terminated the agreement, it is arguable that the statute has no application and he still cannot recover the gift: see Cretney, 33 M.L.R. 534.

[16]Law Reform (Miscellaneous Provisions) Act 1970, s. 3 (2). See further Cretney, 33 M.L.R. 534.

[17]See *Jeffreys* v. *Luck* (1922), 153 L.T.Jo. 139.

contract or other transaction that she entered into at his request; consequently if she later sought to set the gift or transaction aside on this ground, the burden immediately shifted to the man to prove that there was in fact no such influence. But the change in relationship between engaged couples during the past century has recently led the Court of Appeal to reconsider the question in *Zamet* v. *Hyman*.[18] All the members of the court were of the opinion that the same rules must be applied today whether it is the man or the woman who secures the benefit. DONOVAN, L.J., said simply that the transaction could be set aside only if the party seeking to do so proved affirmatively that he or she had imposed confidence and trust in the other and that the disposition resulted from the abuse of such confidence and trust.[19] LORD EVERSHED, M.R., (with whose observations DANCKWERTS, L.J., agreed) stated the rule more fully in the following words:[20]

> " In any transaction of the kind of a deed or arrangement or settlement . . . made between an engaged couple which upon its face appears much more favourable to one party than the other, . . . the court may find a fiduciary relationship . . . so as to cast an onus on the party benefited of proving that the transaction was completed by the other party only after full, free and informed thought about it."

Thus the majority of the Court of Appeal were of the opinion that once a fiduciary relationship has been established, the burden shifts on to the party who might be expected to have exercised undue influence to prove that he or she did not do so—a burden which can usually be discharged only by showing that the other received genuinely independent advice.[1] In *Zamet* v. *Hyman* a woman aged 71 became engaged to a man aged 79. Both had children by previous marriages and three days before the marriage she executed a deed by which she relinquished all rights she might have on the husband's intestacy and under the Inheritance (Family Provision) Act in consideration of a sum of £600 payable to her out of the husband's estate on his death. Three years later the husband died intestate and left an estate worth about £10,000. In view of the vast discrepancy between the rights that she had relinquished and the sum she had gained and the fact that she had received virtually no legal advice, all the members of the court were of the view that the deed could not stand and that she was not bound by it.

C. THE CONTRACT OF MARRIAGE

In order that a man and woman may become husband and wife, two conditions must be satisfied: first, they must both possess the capacity to contract a marriage, and secondly, they must observe the necessary formalities.

A century ago the view was that the law of marriage in all its aspects was governed by the *lex loci celebrationis* on the ground that those

---

[18][1961] 3 All E.R. 933, C.A.
[19]At p. 942.
[20]At p. 938.
[1]*Cf.* the position where it is alleged that a parent has exercised undue influence over his child: *post*, pp. 459-460.

administering the law could not be expected to be familiar with any other rule. But this was decisively rejected by the Court of Appeal in 1877 in *Sottomayor* v. *De Barros*.[2] In the words of COTTON, L.J.:[3]

"The law of a country where a marriage is solemnised must alone decide all questions relating to the validity of the ceremony by which the marriage is alleged to have been constituted; but . . . personal capacity must depend on the law of the domicile."

The rule may therefore now be stated that, generally speaking, capacity to marry is determined by each party's *lex domicilii* whilst the formalities to be observed are those required by the *lex loci celebrationis*. Hence if a man domiciled in England marries in Scotland a woman domiciled in France, he must have capacity by English law, she must have capacity by French law and the marriage must be solemnized in a manner recognised by Scots law.

Capacity.—Despite some earlier doubts[4] it now seems to be accepted that capacity to marry is governed by the parties' ante-nuptial domicile. The vital test is: did each have capacity to marry the other by his or her *lex domicilii* at the time of the ceremony?[5] This may involve a further reference to the conflict of laws of the *lex domicilii*. In *R.* v. *Brentwood Superintendent Registrar of Marriages; ex parte Arias*[6] an Italian national who was domiciled in Switzerland and who had obtained a divorce in that country wished to marry in England. By Swiss law capacity to marry is governed by the law of the party's nationality and, as Italian law did not recognise the Swiss divorce, he lacked the capacity to marry in Italy and, therefore, in England too. Although the English court accepted the Swiss rule that made Arias a single man lacking capacity to marry, it is doubtful whether we should permit the *lex domicilii* to ignore the effects of an English decree. Suppose, for example, that a married woman, domiciled abroad, obtains a divorce in this country after three years' residence here but that this decree is not recognised by her *lex domicilii*. Although she lacks capacity by the law of her own domicile, it is submitted that the decree must be conclusive for all purposes in England that she is no longer married to her first husband and consequently the existence of a prior marriage cannot be a bar to her remarrying here.

English courts have insisted that, wherever the marriage is celebrated, a person domiciled in this country can contract a valid marriage only so long as he has capacity according to English law, and they have

---

[2]3 P.D. 1, C.A.
[3]At p. 5.
[4]Voiced particularly by Cheshire, who was formerly of the view that capacity should be determined by the law of the intended matrimonial domicile. This is supported by dicta in *De Reneville* v. *De Reneville*, [1948] 1 All E.R. 56, C.A., at pp. 61 and 65; [1948] P. 100, at pp. 114 and 121-122, and *Kenward* v. *Kenward*, [1950] 2 All E.R. 297, 310-311, C.A.; [1951] P. 124, 144-146. Cheshire himself now appears to be abandoning his position: *Private International Law*, 8th Ed., 308 *et seq.*
[5]*Padolecchia* v. *Padolecchia*, [1967] 3 All E.R. 863, 873; [1968] P. 314, 336, following *Schwebel* v. *Ungar* (1963), 42 D.L.R. (2d) 622; affirmed (1964), 48 D.L.R. (2d) 644; *Szechter* v. *Szechter*, [1970] 3 All E.R. 905. See further Dicey and Morris, *Conflict of Laws*, 8th Ed., 254 *et seq.*; Graveson, *Conflict of Laws*, 6th Ed., 268 *et seq.*
[6][1968] 3 All E.R. 279; [1968] 2 Q.B. 956.

D

consistently declared marriages void where that capacity has been lacking, even though the person concerned would have had capacity by the *lex loci celebrationis*.[7] But they have not applied this principle consistently in the case of a marriage in England of a person domiciled abroad. Where *neither* party is domiciled in England, they will admittedly regard the marriage as void if the parties lacked capacity by their *lex domicilii* even though they would have had capacity had they been domiciled in England; but where one of the parties is domiciled in England, the courts will not take account of any incapacity imposed by the *lex domicilii* of the other party which is not recognised by English law. Hence, if both parties are domiciled in a country where marriage between first cousins is prohibited, such a marriage will be void if celebrated in this country;[8] but if one of them is domiciled in England, the marriage will nevertheless be valid.[9]

This distinction has been judicially justified on the grounds that English courts are bound to protect their own nationals and that " no country is bound to recognise the laws of a foreign state when they work injustice to its own subjects ";[10] but the fact that such a marriage may be regarded as void in one country and valid in another is liable to produce greater hardship than it avoids. The social undesirability of producing these so-called " limping " marriages has been recognised by the departure from the common law rule in the provisions of the Marriage (Enabling) Act 1960. This Act relaxes the stringent rules relating to marriages within the prohibited degrees of affinity by permitting a person to marry certain relations of a former spouse even though the latter is still alive,[11] but it is provided that the Act shall not validate a marriage if *either* party to it is domiciled at the time of the celebration in a country outside Great Britain and the law of that country prohibits the marriage.[12]

There may be two further exceptions to the rule that capacity to marry is a question for the parties' *lex domicilii*. It is possible that their marriage will be void if they lack capacity by the *lex loci celebrationis*. So far as marriages celebrated in England are concerned, we will not permit a polygamous union to be contracted,[13] and it is hardly con-

---

[7]*Brook* v. *Brook* (1861), 9 H.L. Cas. 193, H.L. (prohibited degrees of affinity); *Pugh* v. *Pugh*, [1951] 2 All E.R. 680; [1951] P. 482 (nonage); *Sussex Peerage Case* (1844); 11 Cl. & F. 85, H.L. (Royal Marriages Act 1772).

[8]*Sottomayor* v. *De Barros* (1877), 3 P.D. 1, C.A.

[9]*Sottomayer* v. *De Barros* (1879), 5 P.D. 94, approved by the Court of Appeal in *Ogden* v. *Ogden*, [1908] P. 46.

[10]Per COTTON, L.J., in *Sottomayor* v. *De Barros* (1877), 3 P.D. at p. 7. But an English court will apparently not reciprocally recognise the validity of a marriage contracted between a domiciled Englishman and a person domiciled in the country where the marriage is solemnized if the former lacks capacity by English law, even though the incapacity is not recognised in that country: *Re Paine*, [1940] Ch. 46. See also Webb, *Some Thoughts on the Place of English Law as* Lex Fori *in English Private International Law*, 10 I.C.L.Q. 818, at pp. 825-829.

[11]See *post*, p. 25.

[12]Section 1 (3). A further attempt to prevent these "limping" marriages was made by the legislature in the Marriage with Foreigners Act 1906, under which a foreigner marrying a British subject in the United Kingdom can be required to produce a certificate that there is no impediment to the marriage by foreign law. But the attempt has been wholly ineffective as no Orders in Council have yet been made under the Act.

[13]See *post*, p. 48.

ceivable that we should permit our marriage laws to be used to enable a marriage to be contracted between persons under the age of 16 or related within the prohibited degrees. This seems to be amply justified on the grounds of public policy. The second possible exception is that English law will disregard any incapacity imposed by the *lex domicilii* if it is penal. It is not clear what incapacities are caught by this rule. It has been held to cover prohibitions against marrying outside one's own caste[14] and against the remarriage of a divorced person;[15] it is submitted that it is really a further example of public policy and would also include prohibitions against marrying persons of a different race and, perhaps, against the marriage of those who have taken vows of celibacy. Clearly, if the marriage was celebrated in England to a person domiciled here, we should disregard the prohibition anyway, and the so called exception may be merely a particular application of the principle we have already discussed. But in *Warter* v. *Warter*[16] HANNEN, P., referred to an incapacity " penal in its character and as such . . . inoperative out of the jurisdiction under which it was inflicted ". This is wide enough to oblige us to disregard it wherever the marriage was celebrated and whatever was the domicile of the other party. In the absence of any authority it is submitted that on grounds of public policy we should do so unless the marriage was celebrated in the country of the parties' domicile, when it must be void by any test.[17]

Formalities.—English law has rarely departed from the rule that the formal validity of the marriage depends upon the *lex loci celebrationis*. This is so even though persons domiciled in England may deliberately have gone to another country in order to evade the English rules as to formalities. Hence, the courts of this country always recognised the validity of the " Gretna Green " marriages since, until the law was altered by statute in 1939, a valid marriage could be contracted in Scotland *per verba de praesenti* in the presence of a witness, who, at least till a residence requirement was imposed by statute in 1856, was by tradition frequently the blacksmith in the first town over the Border. Similarly, a person resident in England may validly contract a marriage by proxy in a country the law of which permits such marriages,[18] and if the marriage is initially formally invalid by the *lex loci*, English law will recognise the effect of a local statute retrospec-

---

[14]*Chetti* v. *Chetti*, [1909] P. 67.

[15]*Warter* v. *Warter* (1890), 15 P.D. 152, 155, explaining *Scott* v. *A.-G.* (1886), 11 P.D. 128. But this does not apply if the prohibition is purely suspensive to ensure that the decree is not appealed: *Warter* v. *Warter*.

[16](1890), 15 P.D. 152, 155.

[17]Dicey and Morris, *op. cit.*, p. 271, suggest that English law would regard the marriage as valid or void according to the view taken by the *lex loci celebrationis*. Whilst it may be illogical to regard as valid a marriage which is void both by the *lex domicilii* and by the *lex loci celebrationis*, it seems equally unacceptable to let another system determine whether English courts are to give effect to a prohibition which offends our ideas of public policy.

[18]*Apt* v. *Apt*, [1947] 2 All E.R. 677, C.A.; [1948] P. 83; *Ponticelli* v. *Ponticelli*, [1958] 1 All E.R. 357; [1958] P. 204.

tively curing the invalidity.[19] But it should also be borne in mind that
a state may recognise the validity of a marriage contracted within its
frontiers even though the municipal law as to formalities is not complied
with. Thus, by English law a marriage celebrated in a foreign embassy
in London may be valid provided that at least one of the parties is a
subject of that ambassador's state.[20] Conversely, the Foreign Marriage
Acts 1892 and 1947 permit a naval, military or air force chaplain (or
other person authorised by the commanding officer) in certain circumstances to solemnize a marriage in a foreign territory, provided that at
least one of the parties is a member of Her Majesty's forces serving
there. Subject to certain very stringent conditions these Acts also
empower a British ambassador or consul or a Governor, High Com-
missioner or Resident to solemnize a marriage at his official residence
between persons one or both of whom are British subjects. International comity is preserved and the possibility of limping marriages
reduced by the provisions that a marriage must not be celebrated under
the Acts unless the authorities of the country in which it takes place
will not object to it, that it will be recognised as a valid marriage by the
law of the country to which each party belongs,[1] and that either there
are no sufficient facilities for the marriage of the parties by local law
or the local law will recognise its validity.[2]

Recognition of Common Law Marriages.—Despite the general acceptance of the principle *locus regit actum* it is clear that English law will
exceptionally recognise a marriage which is valid at common law even
though it is not valid by the *lex loci celebrationis*.

As we shall see,[3] originally at common law no religious ceremony was
necessary and the parties could contract a marriage by a declaration
that they took each other as husband and wife. Later, however, the
rule was modified and a valid marriage could be contracted only in the
presence of an episcopally ordained priest. In the type of case we are
considering it may not be possible to secure the services of such a person.
This occurred in *Wolfenden* v. *Wolfenden*.[4] The marriage had taken
place before a minister (not episcopally ordained) at a mission in the
Province of Hupeh, China, and by local law it was valid provided that
it was valid by English law. Holding that this was a good common law
marriage, LORD MERRIMAN, P., expressed the opinion that " in such
a territory . . . there is . . . no obligation that the ceremony shall be

---

[19] *Starkowski* v. *A.-G.*, [1953] 2 All E.R. 1272, H.L.; [1954] A.C. 155. *Quaere* whether
the retrospective operation would have been recognised if either party had remarried in
the meantime. See further Mendes da Costa, *The Formalities of Marriage in the Conflict
of Laws*, 7 I.C.L.Q. 217, at pp. 251 *et seq.;* Tolstoy, *The Validation of Void Marriages*,
31 M.L.R. 656.

[20]19 Halsbury's Laws of England (3rd Edn.) 777. *Quaere* whether *both* parties must be
subjects. The only authorities are very old, and now that the fiction of extra-territoriality
is relied on much less, it is possible that we might not recognise a marriage celebrated in
a foreign embassy in London.

[1]Presumably this means the law of each party's *domicile*, not nationality.

[2]The full conditions are contained in the Foreign Marriage Order, S.I. 1970, No. 1539.
For the detailed provisions, see Dicey and Morris, *op. cit.*, 244-247; Cheshire, *op. cit.*,
327-330; Graveson, *op. cit.*, 291-292.

[3]*Post*, p. 26.

[4][1945] 2 All E.R. 539; [1946] P. 61.

performed in the presence of an episcopally ordained priest ".[5] Similarly in *Penhas* v. *Tan Soo Eng*[6] the Privy Council, following *Wolfenden* v. *Wolfenden*, held that " in a country such as Singapore, where priests are few and there is no true parochial system, where the vast majority are not Christians, it is neither convenient nor necessary " that a marriage between a Jew and a non-Christian Chinese should be contracted in the presence of a priest. The rule that a priest's presence is necessary probably never applied outside England and Ireland; it certainly does not apply where compliance with it would be impossible, difficult or even inconvenient.

It seems that English law will recognise a common law marriage if no local form exists at all or if it would be impossible or unreasonable to expect the parties to comply with the *lex loci celebrationis* in the circumstances.[7] They would certainly be justified in not observing local formalities if, for example, the ceremony was offensive by English standards, if the only form available was a polygamous one, or if compliance would involve their participating in a ceremony contrary to their own religious convictions. A particular application of the same principle is to be seen in the rule, accepted by our courts, that members of belligerent forces occupying conquered territory cannot be expected to submit to the law of those they have conquered. So far as British forces are concerned, section 2 of the Foreign Marriage Act 1947 permits naval, military and air force chaplains and other persons authorised by the Commanding Officer to solemnize marriages in a foreign territory provided that at least one of the parties is a member of the British forces serving in that territory or is employed there in a capacity defined by Order in Council. The term " foreign territory " excludes any part of the Commonwealth but includes ships in foreign waters. The common law rule, however, applies generally and is certainly not confined to members of the British forces or even to persons domiciled in England. This is clear from a series of cases involving the marriage of members of the Polish forces and Polish civilians in Europe immediately after the Second World War.[8]

The first case we must consider is *Taczanowska* v. *Taczanowski*.[9] In 1946 the husband, who was then a member of the Polish forces in Italy

---

[5] At pp. 543 and 66, respectively.

[6] [1953] A.C. 304, P.C.

[7] A ship is regarded as part of the country whose flag it flies and it is generally accepted that marriages can be conducted on board if the law of the country permits it. Such authority as there is suggests that a marriage can be celebrated on board a ship registered at an English port if it is on the high seas, provided that there is a necessity. Whereas necessity could easily arise in the days when ships were at sea for weeks without putting into a port for a period long enough to enable the parties to comply with local law, this is hardly likely to arise today. See Dicey and Morris, *op. cit.*, 242. Cheshire, *op. cit.*, 342-343, and Graveson, *op. cit.*, 293, take the view that the marriage would be valid without adding the qualification of necessity.

[8] The problem arose particularly with respect to Poles because of the large number of Polish forces and displaced civilians in Central Europe who refused to return to Poland when it became controlled by a communist government after the War. Many subsequently settled in this country and acquired an English domicile.

[9] [1957] 2 All E.R. 563, C.A.; [1957] P. 301; followed in *Merker* v. *Merker*, [1962] 3 All E.R. 928; [1963] P. 283. Contrast *Lazarewicz* v. *Lazarewicz*, [1962] 2 All E.R. 5; [1962] P. 171, where the marriage was held to be void on the ground that the parties had intended, but failed, to comply with the *lex loci celebrationis*.

and the wife, who was a civilian refugee, were married in a church in Rome by a Roman Catholic priest. Both parties were Polish nationals and presumably were domiciled in Poland. The marriage was void by Italian municipal law because they had not complied with Italian civil regulations; by the Italian conflict of laws it would have been valid had they complied with their *lex patriae*, but this did not save the marriage because it was void by Polish law as well. On the wife's petition for nullity on the ground that the marriage was void as formally defective, it was held to be valid as a good common law marriage. As the husband was a member of a conquering army occupying Italy, he could not have been expected to submit to Italian law and consequently the marriage was not void merely because it failed to comply with the *lex loci celebrationis*. The suggestion that, failing the *lex loci*, the *lex domicilii* should be applied (which, as we have seen, would not have saved the marriage) was rejected on the fround that this was relevant only to capacity. The Court of Appeal fell back on the common law as the *lex fori* and upheld the marriage as a good marriage celebrated by the exchange of words before an episcopally ordained priest. This approach is open to the criticism that the application of the *lex fori* makes the validity of the marriage turn upon the accident of the court in which it is put in issue: it is difficult by any process of reasoning to see how a marriage celebrated in Italy between two persons domiciled in Poland can be governed by the English common law. A more acceptable explanation is that put forward by RUSSELL, L.J., in *Preston* v. *Preston:* [10]

> " Once the *lex loci* is rejected, . . . it may well leave it open to a court in this country to recognise as a marriage (in the context of the common law marriage) that which by the general law of Christendom was recognised as constituting the basic essence of the marriage contract—the contract *per verba de praesenti* without further formalities."

Taczanowska v. *Taczanowski* was followed by the Court of Appeal in *Preston* v. *Preston*. [11] The facts were identical save that the marriage had taken place in Germany and the court was therefore bound to find the marriage valid. The importance of the case is that it limits the application of *Taczanowska* v. *Taczanowksi* to those cases where one party is a member of a foreign occupying force or is " in a foreign country as part of the organisation necessarily or at least commonly set up when there is hostile occupation ". [12] Consequently civilians who have no connection with the occupying force cannot maintain that their marriage is valid as a common law marriage and must comply with the *lex loci* even though it might be equally unreasonable to expect them to comply with the law of a country whose nationals had been persecuting and harassing them for the previous six years. [13]

---

[10][1963] 2 All E.R. 405, 416, C.A.; [1963] P. 411, 436. *Quaere* how far the decision was really based on the social necessity of preserving the validity of over 3,000 marriages alleged to have been contracted in similar circumstances?

[11][1963] 2 All E.R. 405, C.A.; [1963] P. 411.

[12]*Per* ORMEROD, L.J., at pp. 411 and 427, respectively.

[13]The earlier decision to the contrary in *Kochanski* v. *Kochanska*, [1957] 3 All E.R. 142; [1958] P. 147, can no longer be regarded as good law

Characterisation.—It is sometimes difficult to decide whether a particular rule should be characterised as relating to capacity (in which case it is governed by the party's *lex domicilii*) or to formalities (in which case it is governed by the *lex loci celebrationis*). The problem arose in *Ogden* v. *Ogden*.[14] A domiciled Frenchman, aged 19, married in England a woman domiciled in this country without obtaining his parents' consent. By French law this meant that he lacked capacity to contract a valid marriage, but by English law parental consent is a question of formality and lack of it will not affect the validity; it therefore became vital to decide which law should govern the question. The Court of Appeal classified parental consent as a part of the ceremony (thus holding the marriage to be valid) apparently on the ground that English law would apply the *lex fori* to characterise a condition in the case of a marriage celebrated in England. It is submitted that the true *ratio* of the case is that we should ignore the effect of lack of parental consent on the husband's capacity as he married a woman domiciled in England in this country;[15] but in any event to fall back on the *lex fori* to characterise the matter is quite indefensible. In order to avoid a limping marriage, one should ask first of all what the relevant law relating to capacity is by the parties' *lex domicilii*; if this regards lack of parental consent as invalidating the marriage, we must accept and apply the rule. One must then ask what the relevant rule relating to formalities is by the *lex loci*. In the *Ogden* v. *Ogden* type of case, where consent is relevant by both systems, the marriage will be void if lack of consent deprives either party of capacity by his *lex domicilii* or if it renders the ceremony a nullity by the *lex loci celebrationis*.

We must now consider in greater detail the relevant English municipal law.

D. CAPACITY TO MARRY

In order that a person domiciled in England should have capacity to contract a valid marriage, the following conditions must be satisfied:

(a) one party must be male and the other female;

(b) neither party must be already married;

(c) both parties must be over the age of 16; and

(d) the parties must not be related within the prohibited degrees of consanguinity or affinity.[16]

---

[14][1908] P. 46 C.A., followed in *Lodge* v. *Lodge* (1963), 107 Sol. Jo. 437. In so far as the case also turns on the court's refusal to recognise a French decree of nullity, it is no longer good law: see *post*, p. 88.

[15]See *ante*, p. 18.

[16]A further prohibition is to be found in the Royal Marriages Act 1772, which was passed to prevent the contracting of highly undesirable marriages by the younger brothers of King George III. It provides that no descendant of King George II (other than the issue of princesses who have married into foreign families) may marry without the previous consent of the Sovereign formally granted under the great seal and declared in Council. Any marriage coming within the Act, consent to which has not been obtained, will be void; but if the descendant in question is over the age of 25 and gives twelve months' notice of the intended marriage to the Privy Council, it may be validly contracted unless both Houses of Parliament have in the meantime expressly declared their disapprobation of it. For a criticism of the Act and a discussion of how far (if at all) it has any force today, see Farran, *The Royal Marriage Act 1772*, 14 M.L.R. 53.

Sex.—A new problem, arising out of operations to effect a so-called change of sex, had to be considered by ORMROD, J., in *Corbett* v. *Corbett*. [17] The petitioner in this case was a man; before the marriage the respondent had undergone a surgical operation for the removal of " her " male genital organs and the provision of artificial female organs. After dealing at length with the medical evidence the learned judge (who is also a qualified medical practitioner) came to the conclusion that a person's biological sex is fixed at birth (at the latest) and cannot subsequently be changed by artificial means. That being so, the respondent, who was male at birth, was not a woman and the marriage was therefore void. [18]

Monogamy.—As a result of the English view of marriage as a monogamous union, neither party may contract a valid marriage whilst he or she is already married to someone else. If a person has already contracted one marriage, he cannot contract another until the first spouse dies or the first marriage is annulled or dissolved. [19] It follows that a mistaken belief that the first marriage has been terminated, for example, by the death of the spouse, is immaterial: what is relevant is whether it has in fact been terminated. Consequently, the second marriage may be void even though no prosecution for bigamy will lie in respect of it.

Age.—Both by canon law and at common law a valid marriage could be contracted only if both parties had reached the legal age of puberty, *viz.* 14 in the case of a boy and 12 in the case of a girl. If either party was under this age when the marriage was contracted, it could be avoided by either of them when that party reached the age of puberty; but if the marriage was ratified (as it would impliedly be by continued cohabitation), it became irrevocably binding. [20]

It is somewhat surprising that this remained the law until well into the present century. In the words of PEARCE, J.: [1]

> " According to modern thought it is considered socially and morally wrong that persons of an age, at which we now believe them to be immature and provide for their education, should have the stresses, responsibilities and sexual freedom of marriage and the physical strain of childbirth. Child marriages by common consent are believed to be bad for the participants and bad for the institution of marriage."

This change of thought led to the passing of the Age of Marriage Act in 1929. Section 1 (now re-enacted in section 2 of the Marriage Act 1949) effected two changes in the law. First, it was enacted that a valid marriage could not be contracted unless both parties had reached

---

[17][1970] 2 All E.R. 33.

[18]In this case the respondent was to be regarded as female by three independent biological criteria. There are persons, however, who are male by one test and female by another. ORMROD, J., deliberately left open the question of the effect of surgical operations in such cases but was inclined to give greater weight to the appearance of the genital organs. It is at least arguable that such persons are neither male nor female and consequently are legally incapable of marriage.

[19]But this does not apply if the first marriage was *void: post*, p. 59.

[20]Co. Litt. 79; Blackstone, *Commentaries*, i, 436.

[1]*Pugh* v. *Pugh*, [1951] 2 All E.R. 680, 687; [1951] P. 482, 492.

the age of 16, and secondly any marriage to which either party was under this age was made *void* and not voidable as before.

The provision that *both* parties must be over the age of 16 is important when the party under that age is not domiciled in England and has capacity by his or her own *lex domicilii*. This is illustrated by *Pugh* v. *Pugh*[2]. A man over the age of 16 and domiciled in England went through a form of marriage in Austria with a girl aged 15. She was domiciled in Hungary, by the law of which country the marriage was valid. It was nevertheless held that it was void since the man had no capacity by English law to marry her.

Prohibited Degrees.—Most, if not all, civilised states prohibit certain marriages as incestuous. The prohibited relationship may arise from consanguinity (*i.e.*, blood relationship) or from affinity (*i.e.*, relationship by marriage). Before the Reformation English law adopted the canon law in this respect, but one of the results of the break with the Roman Catholic Church was the adoption of a slightly modified table of prohibited degrees. The new law, which was Levitical in origin,[3] was to be found in a series of statutes,[4] but the vague reference in the statute 32 Hen. 8, c. 38, to marriages " prohibited by God's law " left the matter in considerable doubt, and the interpretation of this Act was still the subject of litigation as late as 1861.[5] But there was eventually little doubt that the prohibited degrees were those laid down by Archbishop Parker in 1563 and adopted in 1603 in the ninety-ninth Canon and set out in the Book of Common Prayer.[6]

Up till 1835 a marriage within the prohibited degrees was voidable merely, but the Marriage Act of that year made all such marriages void. By the end of the last century wide dissatisfaction was being expressed against the stringent rules relating to affinity, though it was only after bitter controversy that the Deceased Wife's Sister's Marriage Act was passed in 1907 permitting a man to marry his deceased wife's sister, and it was not till 1921 that he was allowed by statute to marry his deceased brother's widow.[7] In 1931 the principle of these two Acts was extended to eight other prohibited degrees of affinity,[8] and the Marriage (Enabling) Act 1960[9] has further relaxed the prohibition by enabling persons to marry within these degrees of affinity if the former marriage has been annulled or dissolved whether or not the previous spouse is still alive.

The degrees of relationship prohibited today are set out in the First Schedule to the Marriage Act of 1949 (see Appendix B, *post*). The

---

[2][1951] 2 All E.R. 680; [1951] P. 482.
[3]Leviticus 18.
[4]25 Hen. 8, c. 22, 28 Hen. 8, c. 7, and 32 Hen. 8, c. 38. All three of these statutes were repealed by 1 Ph. & M., c. 8, but 1 Eliz. 1, c. 1, revived 32 Hen. 8, c. 38, and thus by implication so much of the other two as it referred to. See *R.* v. *Chadwick* (1847), 11 Q.B. 173; 2 Cox C.C. 381; *Wing* v. *Taylor* (1861), 2 Sw. & Tr. 278.
[5]*Wing* v. *Taylor*, (*supra*).
[6]*Hill* v. *Good* (1674), Vaugh. 302, 328. But see *R.* v. *Chadwick* (1847), 2 Cox, C.C., at p. 406.
[7]Deceased Brother's Widow's Marriage Act 1921.
[8]Marriage (Prohibited Degrees of Relationship) Act 1931.
[9]Adopting the majority recommendation of the Morton Commission (1956 Cmd. 9678, Part XV). Three members thought that this would be socially undesirable

Schedule in fact reproduces Archbishop Parker's Table as amended by the four Acts passed between 1907 and 1960. It is drawn up in two columns, of which the left and right state the persons with whom a man and a woman respectively may not intermarry. Marriage within these degrees is prohibited at all times and in all circumstances:[10] thus a man may not marry his stepmother even after his father's death. A marriage will be prohibited whether the relationship is traced through the whole blood or the half blood,[11] and, despite the common law rule that a bastard is *filius nullius*, the eugenic basis of the prohibition also brings illegitimate relationships within it.[12] Consequently, a man may marry, for example, neither his half-brother's daughter nor his illegitimate son's widow. On the other hand a degree of affinity can only be created by marriage and not merely by the fact that two persons have had sexual intercourse; thus, whilst a man may not marry his stepdaughter, there is nothing to prevent his marrying his mistress's daughter.[13]

It should also be observed that the number of persons between whom marriage is forbidden by the Marriage Act is considerably greater than those between whom sexual intercourse is a criminal offence under the Sexual Offences Act 1956,[14] although, of course, all the relationships set out in the latter Act come within the prohibited degrees.

E. FORMALITIES OF MARRIAGE

1. HISTORICAL INTRODUCTION

The history of the English law relating to the formalities of marriage —and even the state of the law immediately before the passing of Lord Hardwicke's Act in 1753—is still a matter of considerable doubt.[15] Canon law emphasised the consensual aspect of the contract and before the Council of Trent in 1563 no religious ceremony had to be performed; all that was necessary was a declaration by the parties that they took each other as husband and wife, either *per verba de praesenti* (*e.g.*, " I take you as my wife [or husband] "), in which case the marriage was binding immediately, or *per verba de futuro* (*e.g.*, " I shall take you as my wife [or husband] "), in which case it became binding as soon as it was consummated. But it early became customary for the marriage to be solemnized *in facie ecclesiae* after the publishing of banns (unless this

---

[10]Marriage Act 1949, s. 1 (1). *Quaere* whether persons may intermarry if they are related by affinity through a voidable marriage which has been annulled. This depends on whether the decree operates retrospectively: see *post*, pp. 69-71.

[11]See the definitions of "brother" and "sister" in the Marriage Act 1949, s. 78 (1).

[12]*Haines* v. *Jeffell* (1696), 1 Ld. Raym. 68; *R.* v. *Brighton* (1861), 1 B. & S. 447.

[13]*Wing* v. *Taylor* (1861), 2 Sw. & Tr. 278. For the effect of adoption orders on the prohibited degrees, see *post*, p. 261.

[14]Ss. 10 and 11.

[15]*Cf.* the conflicting opinions expressed in *R.* v. *Millis* (1844), 10 Cl. & F. 534, H.L. See Swinburne, *Spousals*; Jackson, *Formation and Annulment of Marriage*, 2nd Ed., chap. 2; Pollock and Maitland, *History of English Law*, ii, 362 *et seq.*; the judgment of SIR W. SCOTT in *Dalrymple* v. *Dalrymple* (1811), 2 Hag. Con. 54; and the opinion of the judges in *Beamish* v. *Beamish* (1861), 9 H.L.Cas. 274, H.L.

was dispensed with by papal or episcopal licence) and with the consent of the parents of either party who was under the age of 21. The marriage would then be contracted at the church door *per verba de praesenti* in the presence of the priest, after which the parties would go into the church itself for the celebration of the nuptial mass.[16]

It is hardly surprising that the common law favoured the publicity of marriage *in facie ecclesiae*, for upon the existence of the union might depend many property rights and the identity of the heir at law. Consequently, there developed a curious rule that the wife was not dowable unless she was endowed at the church door,[17] and certain other proprietary disabilities may have followed as well.[18] But in the course of time the reason for the common law insistence upon such a marriage was forgotten. Neither the publishing of banns nor the presence of any other witness was any longer considered necessary; the emphasis shifted on to the presence of the priest (or, after the Reformation, a clerk in holy orders), so that eventually the rule was laid down that a valid marriage at common law could be contracted only *per verba de praesenti* exchanged in his presence.[19]

But the old marriage *per verba de praesenti* was not wholly ineffective. Until the middle of the eighteenth century a marriage could be contracted in one of three ways:

(a) *In facie ecclesiae*, after the publishing of banns or upon a licence, before witnesses, and with the consent of the parent or guardian of a party who was a minor. Such a marriage was obviously valid for all purposes.

(b) Clandestinely, *per verba de praesenti* before a clerk in holy orders, but not *in facie ecclesiae*. This, as we have seen, was as valid as if it had been solemnized *in facie ecclesiae*.

(c) *Per verba de praesenti* or *per verba de futuro* with subsequent sexual intercourse, but where the words were not spoken in the presence of an ordained priest or deacon. Whilst such a marriage would no longer produce all the legal effects of coverture at common law, it was nevertheless valid for many purposes. Such a union was indissoluble, so that, if either party to it subsequently married another, the later marriage could be annulled.[20] Moreover, either party could obtain an order from an ecclesiastical court calling upon the other to solemnize the marriage *in facie ecclesiae*.[1]

---

[16]The marriage service of the Church of England still preserves this ancient form. The first part of the service takes place in the body of the church and consists of the espousals (in which each party replies " I will ") followed by the contracting of the marriage *per verba de praesenti*. This concludes the civil aspect of the marriage: the remainder of the service, which takes place before the Lord's Table, is purely religious in character.

[17]Bracton, f. 303b.

[18]Swinburne, *op. cit.*

[19]*R.* v. *Millis* (1844), 10 Cl. & F. 534, H.L. During the Commonwealth, marriages could be celebrated before Justices of the Peace: Jackson, *op. cit.*, 59-60.

[20]*Bunting* v. *Lepingwell* (1585), 4 Co. Rep. 29a. This rule was abrogated by 32 Hen. 8, c. 38, in 1540 but revived in 1548 by 2 & 3 Ed. 6, c. 23.

[1]*Bunting* v. *Lepingwell*, (*supra*); *Baxtar* v. *Buckley* (1752), 1 Lee 42.

Lord Hardwicke's Act.—It needs little imagination to picture the social evils which resulted from such a state of law. A person who had believed himself to be validly married for years would suddenly find that his marriage was a nullity because of a previous clandestine or irregular union, the existence of which he had never before suspected. Children would marry without their parents' consent, and if the minor was a girl with a large fortune, the old common law rule that a wife's property vested in her husband on marriage made her a particularly attractive catch. The "Fleet" parsons thrived—profligate clergy who traded in clandestine marriages. By the middle of the eighteenth century matters had come to such a pass that there was a danger in certain sections of society that such marriages would become the rule rather than the exception.

It was to stop these abuses that Lord Hardwicke's Act was passed in 1753. The principle underlying this Act was to secure publicity by enacting that no marriage should be valid unless it was solemnized according to the rites of the Church of England in the parish church of one of the parties in the presence of a clergyman and two other witnesses.[2] Unless a licence had been obtained, banns had to be published in the parish churches of both parties for three Sundays. If either party was under the age of 21, parental consent had to be obtained as well, unless this was impossible to obtain or was unreasonably withheld, in which case the consent of the Lord Chancellor had to be obtained. If these stringent provisions were not observed, the marriage would in the vast majority of cases be void. Furthermore, the Act abolished the jurisdiction of the Ecclesiastical Courts to compel persons to celebrate the marriage *in facie ecclesiae* if they had contracted a marriage *per verba de praesenti* or *per verba de futuro* followed by consummation.

Marriage Act 1823.—Whilst Lord Hardwicke's Act effectively put a stop to clandestine marriages in England, it caused an almost greater social evil. For the new law was so stringent and the consequence of failing to observe it—the avoidance of the marriage—so harsh, that many couples deliberately evaded it by getting married in Scotland. This was particularly the case when one of the parties was a minor and parental consent was withheld; so that the 70 years following the passing of the Act saw an increasing number of "Gretna Green" marriages. It was in an attempt to prevent this that the Legislature in 1823 repealed Lord Hardwicke's Act and replaced it by a new Marriage Act. So far as the positive directions of the earlier Act were concerned, *viz.* the necessity of the solemnization of the marriage in the church of the parish in which one of the parties resided after the publication of banns or the grant of a licence, they were re-enacted with only a few minor alterations of detail; where the new Act differed largely was in the effect of non-compliance with these directions. A marriage was now to be void only if both parties *knowingly and wilfully* intermarried in any other place than the church wherein the banns might be published, or without the due publication of banns or the obtaining of a licence, or

---

[2]Marriages according to the usages of the Society of Friends (Quakers) and according to Jewish rites were exempt from the provisions of the Act.

if they *knowingly and wilfully* consented to the solemnization of the marriage by a person not in holy orders. In all other cases the marriage was to be valid notwithstanding any breach in the prescribed formalities. But where the marriage of a minor, whose parent or guardian had not given his consent, was procured by fraud, the Attorney-General, on the relation of the parent or guardian, might sue for the forfeiture of any property acquired as a result of the marriage by the party who had perpetrated the fraud.

This Act remained the principal Act governing the formalities of marriage in England for over 125 years. Naturally, it was greatly amended during that time. Thus, jurisdiction to make an order dispensing with parental consent was extended to county courts and magistrates' courts;[3] and in 1930 it became possible for the parties to be married in a church which was the regular place of worship of one of them even though it was the parish church of neither.[4] But two Acts introduced principles which were so radically different from those of the Acts of 1753 and 1823 that they must be mentioned separately.

Marriage Act 1836.—The principal criticism raised against the two earlier Acts was that they forced Roman Catholics and Protestant dissenters[5] to go through a religious form of marriage which might well be repugnant to them. The growth of religious toleration generally during the early years of the nineteenth century eventually led to the removal of this grievance by the Marriage Act of 1836.

This Act, together with the Births and Deaths Registration Act which was passed immediately after it, brought into existence the superintendent registrars of births, deaths and marriages, who were empowered to issue certificates to marry as an alternative to the publication of banns or the obtaining of a licence. But the real importance of the Act lay in the fact that it permitted marriages to be solemnized on the authority of a superintendent registrar's certificate (with or without a licence) in other ways than according to the rites of the Church of England. For the first time since the Middle Ages, English law recognised the validity of a marriage, which was purely civil in character and completely divorced from any religious element, by permitting the parties to marry *per verba de praesenti* in the presence of a superintendent registrar and a registrar of marriages and two other witnesses. The Act went even further by permitting places of worship of members of denominations other than the Church of England to be registered for the solemnization of marriages; and it now became lawful for marriages to be celebrated in these " registered buildings " in accordance with whatever religious ceremony the members wished to adopt, provided that at some stage the parties took each other as husband and wife *per verba de praesenti* in the presence of a registrar of marriages and at least two other witnesses.

---

[3]Guardianship of Infants Act 1925, s. 9.
[4]Marriage Measure 1930.
[5]Except Quakers who (together with Jews) were still permitted to celebrate their own marriages (see n.[2], *ante*).

Marriage Act 1898.—The Act of 1836 had removed the legitimate grievance of Roman Catholics and Protestant dissenters; the remaining disability under which they suffered—the necessity of having a registrar present at a religious ceremony—was removed by the Marriage Act of 1898. This Act permitted the trustees or governing body of a registered building to authorise a person to be present at the solemnization of marriages in that building, and henceforth a marriage could be lawfully solemnized there in the presence of an " authorised person " without a registrar being present at all. Normally, of course, this person would be a minister of the particular denomination, so that the combined effect of the Acts of 1836 and 1898 was to give to the ministers of all religious denominations the power of solemnizing marriages already enjoyed by clergymen of the Church of England.

Marriages Acts 1949-1970.—By 1949 the extremely complicated law relating to the formalities of marriage could be found only by reference to more than 40 statutes, quite apart from the case law which had grown up as the result of their judicial interpretation. The purpose of the Marriage Act of that year was to consolidate these enactments in one Act. As a result, nearly twenty of these statutes were repealed *in toto* and most of the rest were repealed in part. Few changes were made in the substantive law: the only notable exception was that the Attorney-General's power to sue for the forfeiture of property was taken away—a power which the married women's property legislation had, in any case, already made virtually obsolete.

The Act of 1949 has since been amended in minor details by a series of Acts,[6] one of which deserves special mention. The Acts of 1836 and 1898 had left those marrying according to the rites of the Church of England one privilege not shared by others: the power to marry in a private building on the authority of a special licence. This has now been extended by the Marriage (Registrar General's Licence) Act 1970, which permits the Registrar General to issue a licence authorising the solemnization of a marriage anywhere if one of the parties is suffering from a serious illness from which he is not expected to recover and cannot be moved to a register office or registered building. A much more important change in the law was the reduction of the age of majority to 18 by the Family Law Reform Act 1969, as a result of which anyone over this age may now marry without the consent of any other person.[7]

The above historical outline will have made it clear that the principles underlying the modern law cannot be understood unless it is appreciated that it is still based upon the desire to prevent the clandestine marriages which were the disgrace of eighteenth century England. In this respect, it is submitted, the law is now anachronous. Clandestine marriages are no longer the social evil that they were 200 years ago, neither does the

---

[6]The Marriage Act 1949 (Amendment) Act 1954; the Marriage Acts Amendment Act 1958; the Marriage (Enabling) Act 1960; the Marriage (Wales and Monmouthshire) Act 1962; the Marriage (Registrar General's Licence) Act 1970. These Acts (except for that of 1962) and the Marriage Act 1949 are collectively known as the Marriages Acts 1949-1970.

[7]Section 2 (1). This implements the recommendations of the Latey Committee on the Age of Majority, 1967, Cmnd. 3342.

modern law effectively prevent them. Provided that both parties are over the age of 18, a marriage can usually be lawfully solemnized on a common licence or a superintendent registrar's certificate and licence without the knowledge of the parties' friends and relations. A much greater social problem today is probably presented by the ease with which the parties can rush into marriage without giving due thought to the implications of their act. A superintendent registrar's licence may be obtained in 48 hours: an extreme case illustrating how a person may be married at literally five minutes' notice may be found in *Cooper* v. *Crane*.[8] It is this aspect of the law which may call for reform in the future.[9]

It will be convenient to consider the modern law under two heads: (a) where the marriage is solemnized according to the rites of the Church of England, and (b) where it is solemnized in some other wa. . Before doing this, however, we must consider the particular problem. presented if either party is under the age of 18, and finally it will be necessary to discuss marriages in naval, military and air force chapels.[10]

2. MARRIAGES OF PERSONS UNDER THE AGE OF 18

If either party to the marriage is over the age of 16 but under the age of 18, certain persons are normally required to give their express consent to the marriage or are given a power to dissent from it. These persons are the parents or guardians of the minor or the person to whose custody the minor has been committed by a court order: the full details are set out in the Second Schedule to the Marriage Act which is reproduced in Appendix C, *post*.[11] It should be noted that no consent is required at all if the minor is a widow or widower.[12] It will also be seen from what follows that, if it is impossible to obtain the necessary consent or, more particularly, if the consent is withheld, the consent of the court may be obtained instead. The " court " for this purpose is the High Court, a county court or a

---

[8][1891] P. 369. The respondent, who had unknown to the petitioner obtained a licence and arranged the wedding, took her out and, having got her to the church door, threatened to blow his brains out unless she went into the church and married him. It was held that the petitioner had not discharged the burden of proving that her will was overborne and that consequently the marriage was valid.

[9]The Latey Committee doubted whether the problem was as grave as is commonly supposed and were unanimously opposed to any kind of formal betrothal on the ground that this might encourage potentially unstable marriages rather than the reverse. See Cmnd. 3342, paras. 178-183.

[10]For the registration of marriages, see Part IV of the Marriage Act 1949 and the Marriage (Registrar General's Licence) Act 1970, s. 15.

[11] Although the Legitimacy Act 1959 has given the father of an illegitimate child a limited power to appoint a testamentary guardian (*post*, p. 323), it has not amended the Schedule of the Marriage Act so as to give that guardian any power to assent to or dissent from the child's marriage. Has this anomalous position been produced by an oversight ?

[12]Marriage Act 1949, s. 3 (1). If the minor is a ward of court, the court's consent must be obtained in addition to any other consents required by the Marriage Act: *ibid.*, s. 3 (6). See *post*, p. 338.

magistrates' court sitting as a " domestic court ";[13] in practice, almost all applications are made to a magistrates' court.

Marriages by a Superintendent Registrar's Certificate.—If the parties propose to marry on the authority of a superintendent registrar's certificate (whether by licence or without licence), the necessary consent or consents must be expressly given. If a person's consent cannot be obtained because he is absent or inaccessible or under any disability (*e.g.*, insanity), it is dispensed with entirely if there is any other person whose consent is also required (as will be the case where both parents must consent); where no other person's consent is required, however, either the Registrar General may dispense with the necessity of any consent or the consent of the court must be obtained. Where any person's consent is *refused*, then the consent of the court must be obtained in any case.[14]

Marriages by the Registrar General's Licence.—In this case the position is exactly the same as above except that the consent of a person who is absent, inaccessible or under a disability is never automatically dispensed with. The Registrar General has a discretion to dispense with it in all cases, whether or not there is any other person whose consent is required.[15]

Marriages by a Common Licence.—If the parties propose to marry on the authority of a common licence, the necessary consent or consents must be expressly given, and precisely the same rules apply as in the case of marriages by a superintendent registrar's certificate except that, where the only person whose consent is required is absent, inaccessible or under a disability, the necessity of obtaining any consent may be dispensed with by the Master of the Faculties and not by the Registrar General.[16]

Marriages after the Publication of Banns.—In this case express consent need not be given but

> " if any person whose consent to the marriage would have been required . . . in the case of a marriage intended to be solemnized otherwise than after the publication of the banns, openly and publicly declares or causes to be declared, in the church or chapel in which the banns are published, at the time of the publication, his dissent from the intended marriage, the publication of the banns shall be void."[17]

The Act does not expressly empower the court to consent to the marriage in this case. If the court's consent is obtained, therefore, it is

---

[13]*Ibid.*, s. 3 (5); Magistrates' Courts Act 1952, s. 56, as amended by the Family Law Reform Act 1969, s. 2 (2). For the meaning of " domestic court ", see *ante*, p. 5. There is no statutory right of appeal from an order of the court giving or withholding consent, so that there is no appeal at all from the decision of a magistrates' court: *Re Queskey*, [1946] 1 All E.R. 717; [1946] Ch. 250. Presumably this also applies in the case of a county court.

[14]Marriage Act 1949, s. 3 (1). Consent once given can be withdrawn at any time before the solemnization: *Hodgkinson* v. *Wilkie* (1795), 1 Hag. Con. 262, 265. *Quaere* whether a superintendent registrar could revoke a certificate on this ground: *cf. post*, p. 38, n. [17].

[15]Marriage (Registrar General's Licence) Act 1970, s. 6.

[16]Marriage Act 1949, s. 3 (2).

[17]*Ibid.*, s. 3 (3).

probably necessary for the parties to marry on the authority of a common licence or a superintendent registrar's certificate.[18]

3. MARRIAGES ACCORDING TO THE RITES OF THE CHURCH OF ENGLAND

There are two matters to be considered. First, certain preliminary formalities must be observed: a marriage may be solemnized according to the rites of the Church of England (which includes the Church in Wales)[19] only after the publication of banns or on the authority of a common licence, a special licence or a superintendent registrar's certificate.[20] Secondly, the law relating to the ceremony itself must be discussed.

Publication of Banns.—Since the purpose of publishing banns is to give publicity to the proposed marriage, they must normally be published in the parish church of the parish in which the parties reside, or, if they reside in different parishes, in the parish church of each of the two parishes.[1] But where a party resides in a chapelry (*i.e.*, a district attached to one of certain specified chapels) or in a parish in which the bishop of the diocese has licensed a public chapel or church building for the publication of banns and the solemnization of marriages (as he may do in a remote part of a parish covering a wide area or if the building is shared with other denominations), banns may be published either in that authorised chapel or building or in the parish church,[2] and if he resides in a district in which there is no church or chapel in which divine service is usually held every Sunday, banns may be published in any adjoining parish or chapelry.[3] Banns may be published in Scotland, Northern Ireland or the Republic of Ireland if either party is residing there,[4] or, provided that both parties are British subjects, in certain other parts of the British Commonwealth.[5] If one of the parties is an officer, seaman or marine on a Royal Naval ship *at sea*, banns may be published on board by the chaplain or, if there is no chaplain, by the captain or other officer in command.[6]

If the parties wish to be married in another church or authorised

---

[18]Although it is arguable that, if a person's consent is refused and that of the court is obtained instead, he is no longer " a person whose consent to the marriage would have been required " and therefore any subsequent dissent will be ineffectual.

[19]Marriage Act 1949, ss. 78 (2), 80 (3). A few technical provisions of the Act do not apply in Wales and Monmouthshire: see *ibid.*, 6th Sched., as amended by the Marriage (Wales and Monmouthshire) Act 1962.

[20]*Ibid.*, s. 5.

[1]*Ibid.*, s. 6 (1). There are special provisions dealing with changes in parish boundaries, the amalgamation of parishes and benefices, and cases where churches are being repaired or rebuilt or have been injured by war damage: *ibid.*, ss. 10, 18, 19 and 23; Pastoral Measure 1968, s. 27. For the meaning of " resides ", see *ante*, p. 6.

[2]Marriage Act 1949, s. 6 (1); Sharing of Church Buildings Act 1969 s. 6. See the definition of " authorised chapel " in the Marriage Act 1949, s. 78 (1), and see also *ibid.*, s. 21. For the licensing of chapels, see s. 20.

[3]Marriage Act 1949, s. 6 (3). See also s. 6 (2) and the Pastoral Measure 1968, s. 29.

[4]*Ibid.*, s. 13.

[5]Marriage of British Subjects (Facilities) Acts 1915 and 1916. See 17 Halsbury's Statutes (3rd Ed.) 35-38.

[6]Marriage Act 1949, s. 14.

chapel which is the normal place of worship of either of them,[7] banns must be published there as well as in their parish churches.[8]

Manner of Publication.—Banns must be published on three Sundays during morning service by a clergyman of the Church of England.[9] The form of words is prescribed by the rubric in the Book of Common Prayer.[10]

Names in which Banns should be Published.—Since the purpose of the publication of banns would be defeated if the parties could not be identified, they must be referred to by the names by which they are generally known. This will, of course, usually be their original Christian names and surname, or in the case of a woman who has been previously married, her married surname;[11] but if a person has assumed some other name by which he is generally known, the banns should be published in that name. An example of due publication under an assumed name is to be seen in *Dancer* v. *Dancer*.[12] The wife was the legitimate daughter of a Mr. and Mrs. Knight. When she was aged three, her mother went to live with a man called Roberts by whom she had five children. All the children, including the wife, Jessamine, passed as the legitimate children of Roberts and Mrs. Knight (who assumed the name of Roberts) and were known by the name of Roberts; and it was not till she was 17, when Roberts died, that Jessamine discovered that she was not his daughter. She continued to use the name of Roberts, and on the advice of the vicar who published the banns, she was named therein as Jessamine Roberts. It was held that the banns were duly published, for the wife was generally known by that name and the purpose of publishing the banns under it was not to conceal her identity but to avoid any concealment.

In all the cases where it has been held that the banns have not been duly published, there has been some fraudulent intention to conceal the party's identity.[13] The reason for the concealment is immaterial: thus it has been held that there was an undue publication where the parties' intention was to conceal the marriage from the man's relations,[14] and where the man was a deserter from the Royal Field Artillery and had assumed a false name to avoid detection and prosecu-

---

[7]As defined in the Marriage Act 1949, s. 72. The party must be enrolled on the church electoral roll. For marriages in guild churches in the City of London, see the City of London (Guild Churches) Act 1952, s. 22.

[8]Marriage Act 1949, s. 6 (4).

[9]*Ibid.*, ss. 7 and 9. If there is no morning service, banns may be published during the evening service (s. 7 (1)), and a lay reader may publish banns if there is no clergyman officiating (s. 9 (2)). A clergyman is entitled to a week's notice in writing before he publishes banns: s. 8.

[10]" I publish the banns of marriage between *M*. of   and *N*. of   . If any of you know cause or just impediment why these two persons should not be joined together in holy matrimony, ye are to declare it. This is the first [second, *or* third] time of asking."

[11]*Per* SIR R. PHILLIMORE in *Fendall* v. *Goldsmid* (1877), 2 P.D. 263, 264.

[12] [1948] 2 All E.R. 731; [1949] P. 147. See also *R.* v. *Billinghurst* (1814), 3 M. & S. 250. For the converse case of an undue publication under the original surname, see *Tooth* v. *Barrow* (1854), 1 Ecc. & Ad. 371.

[13]*Chipchase* v. *Chipchase*, [1939] 3 All E.R. 895, 899-900; [1939] P. 391, 398; *Gompertz* v. *Kensit* (1872), L.R. 13 Eq. 369.

[14]*Tooth* v. *Barrow* (*supra*).

tion.[15] A difficult case is *Chipcase* v. *Chipcase*.[16] A woman, whose maiden surname was Matthews, had married in 1915 a man called Leetch. He had deserted her in 1916 and she had not heard of him since. In 1928 she went through a form of marriage with the petitioner after the publication of banns in the name of Matthews, which she had used for some two years before the marriage and by which she was generally known in the district; her reason for having the banns published in this name was not that she was known by it but that it served to conceal, or at least not to emphasize, the fact that she had been married before. HENN COLLINS, J., holding that there had been an undue publication of the banns, said:[17]

> " The wife did not conceal her identity from the persons in her parish who knew her by that name, but I think that one of the purposes of the Marriage Act would be defeated if it was open to a person to have banns called in a name by which he was known in the parish when the use of his legal name might lead persons to make uncomfortable inquiries. In my view that is one of the very things against which the Act of Parliament was directed."

In so far as HENN COLLINS, J., held that there must be some intentional concealment before the court will hold that there has not been a due publication, his decision follows the earlier cases. The difficulty is to discover in what name the banns should have been published, for it is submitted that, if she was generally known by the name of Matthews, it would have equally defeated the purposes of the Act to publish the banns under any other name. The common sense answer to this problem is that the banns should have been published under both names in the alternative (*i.e.*, Matthews or Leetch), but there seems to be no precedent for doing this.

Common Licences.—Licences dispensing with the necessity of the publication of banns have been granted since the fourteenth century. They are now known as common licences (to distinguish them from special licences granted only by the Archbishop of Canterbury) and may be granted by the bishop of a diocese acting through his chancellor or one of the latter's surrogates.[18]

A common licence may be granted for the solemnization of a marriage only in the parish church of the parish, or an authorised chapel in the ecclesiastical district, in which one of the parties has had his or her usual place of residence for fifteen days immediately before the grant of the licence, or in the parish church or authorised chapel which is the usual place of worship of either of the parties.[19] The similarity between the granting of a common licence and the publication of banns is very close: the churches in which the marriage may be solemnized are the same, fifteen days is the period required for the publishing of banns on three successive Sundays, and there appears to be no significant

---

[15]*Small* v. *Small* (1923), 67 Sol. Jo. 277.

[16][1941] 2 All E.R. 560; [1942] P. 37.

[17]At pp. 562 and 40, respectively.

[18]Cripps, *Church and Clergy*, 8th Ed., 547-8.

[19]Marriage Act 1949, s. 15. If either party resides in a district where there is no church or chapel in which divine service is usually held every Sunday, the licence may authorise the solemnization of the marriage in any adjoining parish or chapelry.

difference between the word " resides " for the purpose of the publication of banns and the phrase " usual place of residence " for the purpose of the granting of a common licence.[20] On the other hand, the residence of the other party is immaterial.

Before a licence may be granted, one of the parties must swear (i) that he or she believes that there is no impediment to the marriage, (ii) that either the residence requirement is satisfied or the church in which the marriage is to take place is the regular place of worship of one of them, and (iii) if either of them is a minor, that all consents required by the Act have been obtained or dispensed with, or that the court has consented to the marriage, or that there is no person whose consent is required.[1]

Any person seeking to prevent the granting of a licence may enter a caveat stating the ground of his objection. In such a case the licence may not be granted until the caveat is withdrawn or the ecclesiastical judge with jurisdiction has decided that it ought not to obstruct the grant.[2] Although a caveat is rarely entered, the power to do so might be exercised, for example, by a parent who fears that his minor child may obtain a licence by falsely swearing that his consent to the marriage had been given.

Special Licences.—A special licence may be granted only by the Archbishop of Canterbury acting through the Master of the Faculties.[3] A special licence differs from any other authorisation to marry according to the rites of the Church of England in that it may permit the parties to marry at any time and in any place;[4] it is, therefore, the only way in which they may marry in a church or chapel in which their banns could not be published or for which a common licence or a superintendent registrar's certificate could not be issued,[5] or in any other building, e.g., a private house or a hospital, according to the rites of the Church of England.

Superintendent Registrar's Certificates.—A marriage may be solemnized on the authority of a superintendent registrar's certificate in any church or chapel in which banns may be published and which is within the registration district in which either party resides or which is the usual place of worship of either of them.[6] The issue of certificates will be discussed below; it should, however, be observed that a marriage in the Church of England may not be solemnized on the authority of a certificate *by licence*.[7]

---

[20]See *ante*, p. 6. But see McClean, *The Meaning of Residence*, 11 I.C.L.Q. 1153.

[1]Marriage Act 1949, s. 16 (1).

[2]Marriage Act 1949, s. 16 (2).

[3]By Roman Catholic canon law the dispensation had to be papal; the power was transferred to the Archbishop of Canterbury by the Ecclesiastical Licences Act 1533. The office of the Master of the Faculties is performed by the Dean of the Arches: Public Worship Regulation Act 1874, s. 7.

[4]Marriage Act 1949, s. 79 (6). The cost of a special licence is enough to deter most people from applying for one, and in practice they are granted only in special cases.

[5]But the marriage *ceremony* may be celebrated there after a marriage in a register office: see *post*, p. 39.

[6]Marriage Act 1949, ss. 17, 34, 35 (3). But the marriage may not be solemnized on the authority of a superintendent registrar's certificate without the minister's consent: *ibid.*, s. 17.

[7]*Ibid.*, s. 26 (2).

The Solemnization of the Marriage.—All marriages according to the rites of the Church of England must be solemnized by a clerk in holy orders of that Church in the presence of at least two other witnesses.[8] Except where the marriage is solemnized on the authority of a special licence, it must also be solemnized between 8 a.m. and 6 p.m.[9] In the case of a marriage after the publication of banns, the marriage may only be solemnized in one of the churches or authorised chapels in which the banns have been published; in the case of a marriage on the authority of a common licence or a superintendent registrar's certificate, it must take place in the church or chapel specified in the licence or certificate.[10] The marriage must also be solemnized within three months of the completion of the publication of the banns, the grant of the licence or the entry of notice in the superintendent registrar's marriage notice book, as the case may be.[11]

4. MARRIAGES SOLEMNIZED OTHERWISE THAN ACCORDING TO THE RITES OF THE CHURCH OF ENGLAND

All marriages otherwise than according to the rites of the Church of England may be solemnized only on the authority of a superintendent registrar's certificate, either without a licence or by licence, or on the authority of the Registrar General's licence. The difference between a certificate *simpliciter* and a certificate with a licence corresponds roughly to that between banns and a common licence, in that in the latter case the superintendent registrar is concerned with the residence qualification of one party only and the authorisation to marry may be obtained much more quickly. The Registrar General's licence corresponds to a special licence in that it enables the parties to marry elsewhere than in a building in which they could marry on the authority of a superintendent registrar's certificate. As with marriages in the Church of England, it will be necessary to consider separately the issue of certificates and the Registrar General's licence and the law relating to the marriage ceremony itself.

Issue of a Superintendent Registrar's Certificate without a Licence.—Notice of the proposed marriage must be given in writing to the superintendent registrar of the registration district in which the parties have resided for at least seven days immediately beforehand, or, if they have resided in different districts, then to the superintendent registrar of each district.[12] The person giving the notice must at the same time make a solemn declaration (i) that he or she believes that there is no impediment to the marriage, (ii) that the residence requirement is satisfied, and (iii) if either of them is a minor, that all consents

---

[8]*Ibid.*, ss. 22, 25. The precise words of the ceremony need not be spoken by the parties and consent may be given by signs, *e.g.*, in the case of a dumb person: *Harrod* v. *Harrod* (1854), 1 K. & J. 4. The marriage is probably contracted as soon as the parties have taken each other as husband and wife: *Quick* v. *Quick*, [1953] V.L.R. 224.

[9]*Ibid.*, ss. 4, 75 (1) (a).

[10]*Ibid.*, ss. 12 (1), 15, 25 (d).

[11]*Ibid.*, ss 12 (2), 16 (3), 33.

[12]*Ibid.*, s. 27 (1). For the matters which the notice must contain, see s. 27 (3). For the meaning of " resides ", see *ante*, p. 6.

required by the Act have been obtained or dispensed with, or that the court has consented to the marriage, or that there is no person whose consent is required.[13] The superintendent registrar must then enter the details of the notice in his marriage notice book and display the notice or a copy of it in a conspicuous place in his office for 21 successive days.[14]

As in the case of the granting of a common licence, anyone may enter a caveat against the issue of a certificate. The certificate may not then be issued until either the caveat has been withdrawn or the superintendent registrar or the Registrar General has satisfied himself that it ought not to obstruct the issue of the certificate.[15] Where the objection is that a consent to the marriage of a minor has not been obtained, any person whose consent is required may effectively prevent the marriage by the much simpler means of writing " forbidden " against the entry in the marriage notice book, in which case the certificate may not be issued unless the consent of the court has been obtained.[16]

If no impediment has been shown and the issue of the certificate has not been forbidden, the superintendent registrar must issue it at the end of the 21 days.[17]

As in the case of the publication of banns, a certificate may be issued where one of the parties resides in Scotland or Northern Ireland,[18] or, provided that both parties are British subjects, in certain other parts of the British Commonwealth.[19] Similarly, notice of marriage may be given by an officer, seaman or marine borne on the books of one of Her Majesty's ships at sea to the officer commanding the ship, who is empowered to grant a certificate.[20]

Issue of a Superintendent Registrar's Certificate with a Licence.—The law relating to the issue of a certificate with a licence is the same as that relating to the issue of a certificate *simpliciter* except in two important respects. First, notice is to be given to only *one* superintendent registrar—that of the registration district in which *either* party has resided for a period of *fifteen* days immediately beforehand.[1] The residence of the other party is irrelevant,[2] and conse-

---

[13]*Ibid.*, s. 28. *Cf.* the oath required before a common licence may be granted, *ante*, p. 36. The superintendent registrar is entitled to demand written evidence that the consents required have been given if either party is a minor: Family Law Reform Act 1969, s. 2 (3).

[14]*Ibid.*, ss. 27 (4), 31 (1).

[15]*Ibid.*, s. 29. A person entering a caveat frivolously is liable in damages to the person against whose marriage it was entered.

[16]*Ibid.*, s. 30.

[17]*Ibid.*, s. 31 (2). *Quaere* whether he can revoke the certificate before the marriage is solemnized if he discovers some impediment (*e.g.*, that one party is a minor and parental consent has not been given).

[18]*Ibid.*, ss. 37, 38. (But not when the other party resides in the Republic of Ireland.)

[19]Marriage of British Subjects (Facilities) Acts 1915 and 1916. See 17 Halsbury's Statutes (3rd Ed.) 35-38.

[20]Marriage Act 1949, s. 39.

[1]*Ibid.*, s. 27 (2).

[2]But it is arguable that both must reside in England or Wales, for the Act specifically states " whether the persons to be married reside in the same or in different districts " and thus implies that one of these two conditions must be satisfied.

quently the provisions relating to parties resident in other parts of the United Kingdom and the issue of certificates on board warships do not apply. Secondly, the superintendent registrar is not required to display the notice or a copy of it in his office, but, unless an impediment to the marriage has been shown or the issue of the certificate has been forbidden, he must issue the certificate and licence at any time after the expiration of one whole day after the giving of the notice.[3]

Solemnization of the Marriage.—A marriage on the authority of a superintendent registrar's certificate (whether by licence or without a licence) may be solemnized in a superintendent registrar's office, in a registered building, or according to the usages of the Society of Friends or of the Jews.[4] In any case the marriage must be solemnized within three months of the entry being made in the marriage notice book; and, unless it is a Quaker or Jewish marriage, it must also be solemnized between 8 a.m. and 6 p.m., with open doors and in the presence of at least two witnesses in addition to the superintendent registrar and registrar or, alternatively, the registrar or authorised person.[5]

Marriage in a Register Office.—The parties may marry in the office of the superintendent registrar to whom the notice of the intended marriage was given (or, if notice was given to two superintendent registrars, in the office of either of them), in the presence of the superintendent registrar and also of a registrar of marriages.[6] They must declare that they know of no impediment why they should not be joined in matrimony and then contract the marriage *per verba de praesenti*.[7] No religious service may be used in a superintendent registrar's office, but, if the parties so wish, the marriage there may be followed by a religious ceremony in a church or chapel. In this case the marriage which is *legally* binding for all purposes is that in the register office.[8] This provision is useful if the parties wish to be married in a private chapel in which banns may not be published (*e.g.*, the chapel of an Oxford or Cambridge college) without being put to the expense of obtaining a special licence or in a non-conformist place of worship which is not a registered building.

Marriage in a Registered Building.—Any building which is certified as a place of religious worship[9] may be registered by the Registrar General for the solemnization of marriages.[10] A super-

---

[3]*Ibid.*, s. 32. Hence, if notice is given on Monday, the certificate and licence may be issued on Wednesday.

[4]*Ibid.*, s. 26 (1). For marriages in the Church of England on a certificate without licence, see *ante*, p. 36.

[5]*Ibid.*, ss. 4, 33, 44 (2), 45 (1), 75 (1) (a).

[6]Marriage Act 1949, ss. 36, 45 (1).

[7]*Ibid.*, ss. 45 (1), 44 (3). The form of words to be used is: " I call upon these persons here present to witness that I, *AB*, do take thee, *CD*, to be my lawful wedded wife [*or* husband]." A Welsh form may be used: s. 52. As to marriages of dumb persons, see *Harrod* v. *Harrod*, p. 37, n. [8], *ante*.

[8]*Ibid.*, ss. 45 (2), 46.

[9]Under the Places of Worship Registration Act 1855.

[10]See the Marriage Act 1949, ss. 41 and 42, as amended by the Marriage Acts Amendment Act 1958, s. 1 (1). For church buildings shared by two or more denominations, see the Sharing of Church Buildings Act 1969, s. 6 and Sched. 1.

intendent registrar may normally issue a certificate or certificate and licence for the solemnization of a marriage in a registered building only within his own district, or, where the marriage is without a licence and the parties reside in different districts, within the district in which either of them resides.[11] In two cases, however, he may issue a certificate (with or without a licence) for the solemnization of a marriage in another district. First, he may do so if there is not in the district in which one of the parties resides a registered building in which marriages are solemnized according to the practices of the religious body to which one of them belongs.[12] Secondly, he may issue a certificate for the solemnization of the marriage in a registered building which is the usual place of worship of one of the parties.[13]

A marriage in a registered building may take place only if there is present a registrar of marriages or an " authorised person ".[14] It will be recalled that since the Marriage Act of 1898 the trustees or governing body of a registered building have been empowered to authorise a person to be present at a marriage there and thus dispense with the necessity of having a registrar in attendance.[15] The authorised person will, of course, normally be a minister of the particular faith or denomination. The marriage may be in any form provided that, at some stage in the ceremony, a declaration is made similar to that required when the marriage is in a register office, and the parties contract the union *per verba de praesenti*.[16]

Quaker Marriages.—The Act of 1949 preserves the right of the Society of Friends to solemnize marriages according to their own usages. Provided that the rules of the Society permit it, a marriage may be contracted in this way even though one or both parties are not members of the Society.[17]

Jewish Marriages.—The privilege of the Jewish community to celebrate marriages according to their own rites is also preserved. In this case, however, both parties must profess the Jewish religion.[18]

Marriages solemnized on the Authority of the Registrar General's Licence.—The Registrar General's power to issue a licence

---

[11]*Ibid.*, ss. 34 and 36.

[12]*Ibid.*, s. 35 (1), as amended by the Marriage Act 1949 (Amendment) Act 1954, s. 2. The registered building in which the superintendent registrar authorises the solemnization of the marriage must be in the registration district nearest to the residence of one of the parties in which there is a registration building where marriages may be so solemnized.

[13]Marriage Act 1949, s. 35 (2), as amended by the Marriage Act 1949 (Amendment) Act 1954, s. 1.

[14]Marriage Act 1949, s. 44 (2).

[15]See now the Marriage Act 1949, s. 43, as amended by the Marriage Acts Amendment Act 1958, s. 1 (2); the Sharing of Church Buildings Act 1969, Sched. 1. See also the Marriage Act 1949, s. 44 (5).

[16]*Ibid.*, s. 44 (1), (3). A slightly different form of words may be used if the marriage is solemnized in the presence of an authorised person without the presence of a registrar.

[17]*Ibid.*, s. 47. This privilege was first granted by the Marriage (Society of Friends) Act 1860. See the *Marriage Regulations* of the Society of Friends. The rule that the building in which the marriage is to be solemnized must be within the registration district in which one of the parties resides does not apply to marriages according to the usages of the Society of Friends: s. 35 (4).

[18]Marriage Act 1949, s. 26 (1) (d). S. 35 (4) (see n. [17], *supra*) also applies.

authorising the solemnization of a marriage elsewhere than in a register office or registered building is subject to two important limitations. In the first place, he must be satisfied that one of the parties is seriously ill and not expected to recover and that he cannot be moved to a place where the marriage could be solemnized under the provisions of the Act of 1949. Secondly, no such marriage may be solemnized according to the rites of the Church of England.[19]

No residence qualification is necessary, and notice must be given to the superintendent registrar of the registration district in which it is intended to solemnize the marriage. The person giving the notice must make the same declaration (except as regards the residence quali-fication) as that required when other notices are given to a superinten-dent registrar. In addition he must also produce such evidence as the Registrar General may require to satisfy him (i) that there is no impediment to the marriage, (ii) that all necessary consents have been given if either party is a minor, (iii) that there is a sufficient reason why a licence should be granted, and (iv) that the statutory conditions regarding the health of one party are satisfied and that that person can and does understand the nature and purport of the marriage ceremony.[20] The superintendent registrar must then enter the details in his marriage notice book and inform the Registrar General.[1] As in the case of a superintendent registrar's certificate, a caveat may be entered against the issue of a licence and the marriage may be forbidden by anyone whose consent to the marriage is required and has not been given.[2] If there is no impediment and the Registrar General is satisfied that sufficient grounds exist for the granting of a licence, he must issue it.[3]

The marriage must be solemnized in the place stated in the notice of marriage and within *one* month of the entry in the marriage notice book.[4] It may take the form of a civil ceremony in the presence of the superintendent registrar and a registrar,[5] or it may be according to any form or ceremony the parties choose to adopt (other than the rites of the Church of England) in the presence of a registrar. At least two witnesses must be present, and at some stage the parties must make the same declaration and contract the marriage in the same form of words as would be required at a marriage in a register office.[6]

---

[19]Marriage (Registrar General's Licence) Act 1970, s. 1. An unusual provision of the Act is that the Registrar General may remit the fee of £15 in whole or in part if he thinks that the payment would cause hardship to the parties: s. 17 (1).

[20]*Ibid.*, ss. 2 and 3. In the case of (iv) a registered medical practitioner's certificate is sufficient evidence.

[1]*Ibid.*, ss. 2 (2) and 4.

[2]*Ibid.*, ss. 5 and 7. A caveat may be entered with either the superintendent registrar or the Registrar General; in either case, however, only the Registrar General may decide that it should not obstruct the issue of the licence.

[3]*Ibid.*, s. 7.

[4]*Ibid.*, ss. 8 and 9. The marriage does not necessarily have to take place between 8 a.m. and 6 p.m.: see s. 16 (4).

[5]As in the case of a marriage in a register office, this may be followed by a religious ceremony which will be of no legal effect: *ibid.*, s. 11.

[6]*Ibid.*, s. 10. The provisions relating to the presence of a registrar and two witnesses, the declaration, and the form of words to be used do not apply if the marriage is solem-nized according to the usages of the Society of Friends or, if both parties profess the Jewish faith, according to Jewish rites. No clergyman of the Church of England may solemnize the marriage.

5. MARRIAGES IN NAVAL, MILITARY, AND AIR FORCE CHAPELS

Part V of the Marriage Act enables certain persons to marry in naval, military and air force chapels certified as such by the Secretary of State for Defence.[7] The purpose of this is to enable members of the Forces to marry in garrison churches, etc. Consequently, in order that a marriage may be solemnized in such a chapel, at least one of the parties must be a serving member or a former regular member of one of the armed forces, or a serving member of one of the women's services, or a daughter of any such person.[8] The privilege has since been extended to members of certain Commonwealth and N.A.T.O. forces and their daughters.[9] If the chapel has been licensed for this purpose by the bishop of the diocese, it may be treated as the parish church of the parish in which it is situated, and banns may be published and marriages solemnized in it provided that at least one of the parties resides in that parish.[10] The Registrar General may also register a chapel so as to enable the superintendent registrar of the district in which it stands to issue a certificate to marry in it (either with or without a licence) according to rites other than those of the Church of England.[11] Subject to these limitations and certain other modifications,[12] the same rules apply to marriages in these chapels as to other marriages.

6. RETROSPECTIVE VALIDATION OF MARRIAGES WHICH ARE VOID BECAUSE OF FORMAL DEFECTS

Although, as we shall see later,[13] failure to observe all the formal requirements of English law does not necessarily invalidate the marriage, certain defects in form will have this effect. The complexities of the English law on this subject have in the past led persons who were morally innocent to go through a form of marriage which has subsequently proved to be a legal nullity. Parliament has from time to time intervened to validate these marriages by curing the informality retrospectively.[14] Although the number of cases in which innocent parties contract a marriage that is void because of formal invalidity is not likely to be great today, nevertheless the situation might conceivably arise. Consequently, the Marriages Validity (Provisional Orders) Acts 1905 and 1924 have given the Home Secretary power to make orders for the purpose of curing retrospectively any formal defect in the

---

[7]Replacing the Marriage (Naval, Military and Air Force Chapels) Act 1932. See also the Defence (Transfer of Functions) Act 1964, s. 1 (2).

[8]For the detailed list, see the Marriage Act 1949, s. 68 and Sched. 3.

[9]Visiting Forces and International Headquarters (Application of Law) Order 1965, arts. 3 and 12 (2) and Sched. 3 (S.I. 1965 No. 1536).

[10]Marriage Act 1949, s. 69. But the parties may not marry in a chapel solely on the grounds that it is the usual place of worship of either of them: see Sched. 4, Part I.

[11]*Ibid.*, s. 70. " Authorised persons " may be appointed by the Secretary of State: Sched. 4, Part IV. It seems that the parties may marry there on the ground that no other registered building is available or that it is the regular place of worship of one of them: *ibid.*, Part III.

[12]See the Marriage Act 1949, Sched. 4, as amended by the Marriage Acts Amendment Act 1958, s. 1 (2).

[13]*Post*, pp. 72–74.

[14]A list of the public general Acts passed for this purpose will be found in 19 Halsbury's Laws of England (3rd Edn.), 811 (*o*). Many private Acts have also been passed.

marriage or of removing any doubt about the validity of a marriage due to informality.[15]

F. THE RECOGNITION OF FOREIGN MARRIAGES

The rapid development of international communications during the present century has made the question of how far English courts will recognise marriages entered into abroad much more burning than it was before. Four questions—selected more or less at random—will indicate the sort of situations in which the problem of recognition will be important.

> The husband, whilst in this country, deserts his wife and leaves her penniless. Can she take proceedings against him for maintenance?
> The husband is killed in this country as a result of another's negligence. Can his wife sue the tortfeasor under the Fatal Accidents Acts?
> Can the wife, whilst in this country, claim the benefits of social welfare legislation (*e.g.*, the National Insurance Act or the Family Allowances Act) *qua* wife?
> The husband dies intestate with respect to realty in this country. Can his wife claim it as widow of the intestate?

The Concept of the Christian Marriage.—Our discussion must necessarily begin with an examination of *Hyde* v. *Hyde*.[16] The petitioner, who was originally domiciled in England, embraced the Mormon faith and went out to Utah at a time when polygamy was still being practised by Mormons. He there married the respondent. Some years later he renounced Mormonism and, having returned to England, asked his wife to join him. This she refused to do, and since the excommunication which had followed the petitioner's renunciation left her free to remarry by Mormon law, she went through a form of marriage with the co-respondent. The husband then petitioned for divorce on the ground of the respondent's adultery. LORD PENZANCE held that this marriage was polygamous and therefore not a marriage within the definition cited earlier,[17] and consequently held that he had no jurisdiction to entertain divorce proceedings.

Non-Christian Monogamous Marriages.—Although LORD PENZANCE referred to " marriage as it is understood in Christendom ", it must not be supposed that this is synonymous with " a Christian marriage ". If the marriage satisfies the three conditions he laid down, it will be recognised by English courts even though neither party professes the Christian faith provided that each had capacity by his or her *lex domicilii* and they complied with the formalities laid down by the *lex loci celebrationis*.[18]

---

[15]Orders made under these Acts are subject to special parliamentary procedure under the Statutory Orders (Special Procedure) Acts 1945 and 1965: S.I. 1949 No. 2393. There is no power under these Acts to legalise a marriage which is void because of the incapacity of either party.

[16](1866), L.R. 1 P. & D. 130. See further *ante*, p. 12.

[17]Page 12.

[18]*Brinkley* v. *A.-G.* (1890), 15 P.D. 76 (marriage between a man domiciled in Ireland and a woman domiciled in Japan before the civil authority in Tokio recognised as a valid marriage). Otherwise all marriages celebrated between Jews in this country would be invalid. For capacity and formal requirements, see *ante*, pp. 16-23.

Most of the cases dealing with the recognition of foreign marriages have in fact been concerned with polygamous unions. It is still an open question how far English courts will recognise monogamous unions which fail to satisfy the other requirements laid down by LORD PENZANCE or which would have been void for some other reason if they had been contracted in England. It is submitted that the proper test to apply is that formulated by SIMON, P., in *Cheni* v. *Cheni*,[19] where he said:

> " I believe the true rule to be that the courts of this country will exceptionally refuse to give effect to a capacity or incapacity to marry by the law of the domicile on the ground that to give it recognition and effect would be unconscionable. . . .
> " What I believe to be the true test [is] whether the marriage is so offensive to the conscience of the English court that it should refuse to recognise and give effect to the proper foreign law. In deciding that question the court will seek to exercise common sense, good manners and a reasonable tolerance."

In that case the court gave recognition to a marriage between an uncle and niece which was valid by the law of the parties' domicile (Egypt) even though it would have been void by English law because they were related within the prohibited degrees.[20]   Likewise in *Nachimson* v. *Nachimson*[1] it was held that a marriage celebrated in Russia and intended to be entered into for life came within the *Hyde* v. *Hyde* definition notwithstanding that it could be dissolved by mutual consent declared before a registrar or at the will of either spouse by judicial process. On the other hand it seems inconceivable that English courts would recognise a union between two persons of the same sex; and it is very doubtful whether they would recognise a marriage contracted under duress[2] or a child marriage, at least unless the parties had ratified it when they were free agents or old enough to understand the nature and significance of marriage.

Polygamous Marriages.—For many years after the decision in *Hyde* v. *Hyde* the courts refused to recognise the validity of any marriage which did not satisfy LORD PENZANCE'S definition.[3]   In practice this meant the refusal to recognise polygamous unions—despite the fact that a large part of the civilised world permits polygamy and that the Judicial Committee of the Privy Council was upholding the validity of such unions on appeal from various courts in the Commonwealth. To fail to recognise a marriage which was valid by a man's *lex*

---

[19][1962] 3 All E.R. 873, 882-883; [1965] P. 98-99.

[20]See *ante*, p. 25. But would the court recognise a marriage if we regarded the relationship as criminally incestuous (*e.g.*, between brother and sister)?

[1][1930] P. 217, C.A. But the court implied that they would not have regarded it as a marriage had it been a mere cloak for casual intercourse, to be dissolved the next day, or if it had conferred no status on the parties (at pp. 233, 244).

[2]In *Szechter* v. *Szechter*, [1970] 3 All E.R. 905, SIMON, P., applied the *lex domicilii* when it was alleged that the marriage was void for duress. But this agreed with English law in permitting the court to annul the union.

[3]See *Re Bethell* (1888), 38 Ch.D. 220, and the remarks of AVORY, J., in *R.* v. *Naguib*, [1917] I K.B. 359, 360, C.C.A. *Re Bethell* is an unsatisfactory case because it is not entirely clear what the *ratio decidendi* was. A domiciled Englishman went through a form of marriage with Teepoo, a Baralong girl, according to the custom of the Baralong tribe in Bechuanaland. The Baralongs had no religion and practised polygamy. STIRLING, J., professing to follow *Hyde* v. *Hyde*, held that this marriage was void and that the child born of it was illegitimate.

domicilii (which is generally accepted as governing his status) seems the height of absurdity. Moreover, it is clear that LORD PENZANCE himself had intended no such result. At the end of his judgment he said:[4]

> " In conformity with these views the Court must reject the prayer for the petition, but . . . this decision is confined to that object. This Court [the Divorce Court] does not profess to decide upon the rights of succession or legitimacy which it might be proper to accord to the issue of the polygamous unions, nor upon the rights or obligations in relation to third persons which people living under the sanction of such unions may have created for themselves. *All that is intended to be here decided is that as between each other they are not entitled to the remedies, adjudication, or the relief of the matrimonial law of England.*"

But it was not until 1946 that the decision in *Hyde* v. *Hyde* was put in its proper context by the Court of Appeal in *Baindail* v. *Baindail*,[5] following earlier dicta of LORD MAUGHAM, L.C., in the *Sinha Peerage Case*.[6] In *Baindail* v. *Baindail* a woman domiciled in England went through a ceremony of marriage in England with a Hindu domiciled in India. She later discovered that he had a wife in India and petitioned for nullity on the ground that the marriage was bigamous and therefore void. The respondent was permitted by his *lex domicilii* to practise polygamy and the first marriage was therefore clearly polygamous. Nevertheless, it was held that this marriage was clearly valid by the law of the husband's domicile and that it must be recognised as valid here. The petitioner's contention was therefore sound and her marriage void.

It will be noticed that *Baindail* v. *Baindail* begs two questions: what marriages will be regarded as polygamous, and will a polygamous union be regarded as a marriage for all purposes?

What Marriages are Polygamous?[7]—It should be appreciated at the outset that English law regards a marriage as polygamous if it is possible for either party to take another spouse during its subsistence, whether he does so or not. Consequently, if the parties contract a marriage which is potentially polygamous, the mere fact that they intend to enter into a monogamous union will not without more create

---

[4]At p. 138. Italics supplied.

[5][1946] 1 All E.R. 342, C.A.; [1946] P. 122. See also *Srini Vasan* v. *Srini Vasan*, [1945] 2 All E.R. 21; [1946] P. 67, where on virtually identical facts BARNARD, J., came to the same decision as the Court of Appeal.

[6](1939), reported [1946] 1 All E.R. 348, H.L.

[7]The subject of polygamous marriages is dealt with at length in the standard textbooks on Private International Law and in many articles. Reference may be made *inter alia* to the following on which the present writer has drawn extensively and to which he is greatly indebted: Fitzpatrick, *Non-Christian Marriage*, 2 J. Comp. Leg. and Int. Law (2nd Series) 359; Vesey-Fitzgerald, *Nachimson's and Hyde's Cases*, 47 L.Q.R. 253, and *Mixed Marriages*, in *Current Legal Problems*, 1948, 222; Beckett, *The Recognition of Polygamous Marriages under English Law*, 48 L.Q.R. 341; Fleming, *The Conception of Marriage in English Law*, 11 Conv. 201; Bartholomew, *Polygamous Marriages*, 15 M.L.R. 35; *Recognition of Polygamous Marriages in Canada*, 10 I.C.L.Q. 305; *Recognition of Polygamous Marriages in America*, 13 I.C.L.Q. 1022; Morris, *The Recognition of Polygamous Marriages in English Law*, 66 Harv. L.R. 961; Mendes Da Costa, *Polygamous Marriages in the Conflict of Laws*, 44 Can. Bar Rev. 293; Hartley, *Polygamy and Social Policy*, 32 M.L.R. 155; Weston, 28 M.L.R. 484. See also Jackson, *Formation and Annulment of Marriage*, 2nd Ed., 131-144; Law Com. No. 42 (Report on Polygamous Marriages.)

a monogamous marriage: their reservations clearly cannot alter the legal effects of their act. This is illustrated by *Sowa* v. *Sowa*.[8] The parties, who were domiciled in Ghana, went through a form of marriage in that country which by tribal custom was potentially polygamous. The husband had previously presented his bride with a ring and a Bible, which symbolised his intention to turn the marriage into a Christian monogamous one, but he took no further steps to implement this. The Court of Appeal held that, as nothing had been done to change the initial character of the marriage, it must still be regarded as polygamous and consequently the wife was not entitled to matrimonial relief in the English courts.[9]

Whether a marriage is to be regarded as monogamous or polygamous must be determined in the first place by the *lex loci celebrationis*.[10] If the ceremony is designed to create a monogamous union, the marriage will at its inception be monogamous; conversely, if the ceremony is designed to create a polygamous union, the marriage will at its inception be polygamous. But this does not fix its character for all time: it is certainly possible for a potentially polygamous marriage to become monogamous, and it seems probable that an initially monogamous marriage may become polygamous.

An example of a change of the first sort is to be seen in *Cheni* v. *Cheni*.[11] The parties, who were Sephardic Jews domiciled in Egypt, went through a ceremony of marriage according to Jewish rites in Cairo. By Jewish and Egyptian law (as it then stood) the husband could take a second wife in certain circumstances if his wife bore him no child within ten years. In fact they had a child two years later and the marriage thereupon became irrevocably monogamous. SIMON, P., held that for the purposes of English law the marriage was now to be regarded as monogamous and consequently that he had jurisdiction to entertain a petition for nullity.[12] It would seem, however, that there must be some act or event to change the character of the marriage, such as the birth of the child in *Cheni* v. *Cheni*, a change of religious faith affecting the parties' legal status,[13] local legislation changing the character of the marriage,[14] or a second ceremony of marriage designed

---

[8][1961] 1 All E.R. 687, C.A.; [1961] P. at p. 80. LORD BROUGHAM's dictum to the contrary in *Warrender* v. *Warrender* (1835), 2 Cl. & Fin. 488, 535, H.L., can no longer be regarded as good law.

[9]See *post*, p. 50.

[10]This seems implicit in such cases as *Hyde* v. *Hyde* (1866), L.R. 1 P. & D. 130; *R.* v. *Hammersmith Superintendent Registrar of Marriages, ex parte Mir-Anwaruddin*, [1917] 1 K.B. 634, C.A.; *Re Bethell* (1888), 38 Ch. D. 220; *Sowa* v. *Sowa*, [1961] 1 All E.R. 687, C.A.; [1961] P. 70; *Cheni* v. *Cheni*, [1962] 3 All E.R. 873; [1965] P. 85.

[11][1962] 3 All E.R. 873; [1965] P. 85. Followed in *Parkasho* v. *Singh*, [1967] 1 All E.R. 737; [1968] P. 233. See Higgins in 26 M.L.R. 205.

[12]See further *post*, p 50.

[13]*Sinha Peerage Case* (1939), [1946] 1 All E.R. 348, H.L. (change of Hindu sect from one practising polygamy to one practising monogamy).

[14]*Parkasho* v. *Singh, (supra)* (Indian statute converting polygamous Sikh marriages into monogamous unions).

to create a monogamous union.[15] Similarly, it was held in *Ali* v. *Ali*[16] that the parties' initially polygamous marriage, which had remained *de facto* monogamous, was converted into a *de jure* monogamous union when they acquired a domicile in England, as the husband thereby lost the capacity to contract any further marriages so long as the first one was in existence.

Whether an initially monogamous marriage may be converted into a polygamous one is more doubtful. In *Cheni* v. *Cheni*[17] SIMON, P., said *obiter:* "there are no marriages which are not potentially polygamous, in the sense that they may be rendered so by a change of domicile and religion on the part of the spouses", but he added that it was more reasonable to presume that a polygamous union could be converted into a monogamous one than *vice versa*. This dictum was followed by the Privy Council in *A.-G. of Ceylon* v. *Reid*.[18] The respondent was domiciled in Ceylon and his capacity to marry depended upon his religious faith. Whilst he was a Christian he contracted a monogamous Christian marriage. He was then converted to Mohammedanism and went through a second ceremony of marriage without having the first dissolved. He was later charged with bigamy and the question of law raised by the relevant penal statute was whether the second marriage was valid or void. The Privy Council held that it was valid for, having changed to the Muslim faith, Reid was now permitted to practise polygamy by the law of Ceylon. The Judicial Committee deliberately left open the question whether this would be equally true in " a purely Christian country ":[19] a more important question may be the legal position of the first wife who, having contracted a monogamous marriage, now finds herself one of two or more. If the courts accept that the *ratio decidendi* of this case applies, say, to a woman domiciled in

---

[15]*Ohochuku* v. *Ohochuku*, [1960] 1 All E.R. 253. The parties, who had contracted a potentially polygamous marriage in Nigeria, subsequently went through a second ceremony in England. WRANGHAM, J., held that he could not dissolve the Nigerian marriage but that he could dissolve the English one. This decision is questionable on two grounds. As English courts will recognise the first marriage as a marriage, the second ceremony seems to have been of no legal effect at all (see *post*, p. 208, n.[12]) and the critical question is whether the marriage is polygamous or monogamous *at the time of the proceedings* (see *post*, p. 50). See the views of CAIRNS, J., in *Parkasho* v. *Singh*, (*supra*), at pp. 741 and 242, respectively; Mendes Da Costa, 44 Can. Bar. Rev. at pp. 310-311; Furmston, 10 I.C.L.Q. 180.

[16][1966] 1 All E.R. 664; [1968] P. 564. The case is criticised by Eekelaar, 15 I.C.L.Q. 1181, and Tolstoy, *The Conversion of a Polygamous Union into a Monogamous Marriage*, 17 I.C.L.Q. 721, on the ground that, as the *lex loci celebrationis* determines the character of the marriage, a subsequent change of domicile must be irrelevant. It is defended by Morris, 17 I.C.L.Q. 1014. See also Webb, 12 I.C.L.Q. 672; Cowen, *ibid.*, 1407.

[17][1962] 3 All E.R. 873, 877; [1965] P. 85, 90. See also *Russ* v. *Russ*, [1962] 3 All E.R. 193, 198, C.A.; [1964] P. 315, 326, where WILLMER, L.J., referred to a marriage between a man domiciled in Egypt and a woman domiciled in England as potentially polygamous.

[18][1965] 1 All E.R. 812, P.C.; [1965] A.C. 720. Strongly criticised by Koh in 29 M.L.R. 88.

[19]*Ibid.*, at pp. 817 and 734, respectively.

England before her marriage, they must apparently leave her remediless as she is now a party to a polygamous union.[20]

A polygamous marriage may be contracted only by persons whose *lex domicilii* permits polygamy.[1] Hence, if a man domiciled in England goes through a polygamous form of marriage abroad, the marriage will be void by English law.[2] There seems to be no justification for attempting to draw any distinction between a man and a woman in this respect, and a polygamous marriage contracted by a woman whose *lex domicilii* forbids polygamy would, it is submitted, be equally void.[3] On the other hand, however, a person who may practise polygamy by his *lex domicilii* may, by English law, lawfully contract a monogamous marriage. This is clear from *R. v. Hammersmith Superintendent Registrar of Marriages, ex parte Mir-Anwaruddin*.[4] Mir-Anwaruddin was a Mohammedan domiciled in Madras and by his *lex domicilii* he was permitted to take up to four wives. In 1913 he married X at a register office in England and two years later he executed a declaration of divorcement which by Mohammedan law dissolved his marriage to X by *talak*. He then applied to the Hammersmith Superintendent Registrar for a certificate and licence to marry Y, which the Superintendent Registrar refused to issue on the ground that the *talak* was ineffective to dissolve the first marriage by English law and that Mir-Anwaruddin was therefore still married to X. Mir-Anwaruddin thereupon sued for a writ of mandamus calling on the Superintendent Registrar to issue the certificate and licence. It was never for one moment doubted that Mir-Anwaruddin's marriage to X was valid although he could have contracted other marriages by Indian law, and the sole issue before the court was the validity of the *talak*. This was held to be ineffective[5] and so the mandamus was refused.

As the initial character of the union is determined by the *lex loci celebrationis*, any marriage celebrated in England must be monogamous at its inception.[6] Consequently if a person whose *lex domicilii*

---

[20]See *post*, p. 50. These cases run counter to the earlier case of *Mehta* v. *Mehta*, [1945] 2 All E.R. 690, where BARNARD, J., held that he had jurisdiction to entertain nullity proceedings because the marriage was monogamous at its inception and therefore remained a monogamous union despite the husband's ability to take a second wife by becoming an orthodox Hindu. But as was pointed out in *Cheni* v. *Cheni*, (*supra*), and *Parkasho* v. *Singh*, (*supra*), it in fact remained monogamous up to the time of the proceedings.

[1]*Risk* v. *Risk*, [1950] 2 All E.R. 973, 974; [1950] P. 50, 53. In *Kenward* v. *Kenward*, [1950] 2 All E.R. 297, 309-310, C.A.; [1951] P. 124, 144-145, DENNING, L.J., considered that a man, whose *lex domicilii* permitted mónogamy only, could contract a valid polygamous marriage if that was his intention, but there is no authority for this proposition and it does not seem in line with accepted principles: see Morris, 66 Harv. L.R. 984-986.

[2]*Cf. Re Bethell* (1888), 38 Ch. D. 220. But see Hartley, 32 M.L.R. 158-160.

[3]Morris, *loc. cit.*, 985-988, criticising the opposite view put forward by Beckett, 48 L.Q.R. 360-361. But if the woman goes to a foreign country with the object of marrying and remaining there, she will probably acquire a domicile of choice there as soon as she sets foot in the country and will thus have the necessary capacity at the time of the marriage.

[4][1917] 1 K.B. 634, C.A.

[5]See *post*, p. 51.

[6]See the *Hammersmith Marriage Case*, (*supra*); *Maher* v. *Maher*, [1951] 2 All E.R. 73, 39; [1951] P. 342, 346. But see also Jackson, *op. cit.*, 141.

permits polygamy has already contracted a valid polygamous marriage abroad, any marriage contracted in this country during the subsistence of the first will be void by English law even though it is valid by the *lex domicilii*.[7]

A further problem arises if a person who has already contracted two or more valid polygamous marriages acquires a domicile in England. In *Cheni* v. *Cheni*[8] the parties, who were uncle and niece, had contracted a valid marriage in Egypt where they were then domiciled. They later acquired a domicile in England and the wife petitioned for a decree of nullity on the ground that they were related within the prohibited degrees of consanguinity. SIMON, P., held that the marriage was valid by English law. If, as this case suggests, a change of domicile does not affect the validity of the marriage, are we to accept the fact that a man domiciled in England can have a plurality of wives? Such a view is startling; the alternative, that the change of domicile will automatically render all the marriages void, is equally unsatisfactory.

The Purposes for which a Polygamous Marriage will be recognised.—We have already seen that a polygamous marriage will be recognised so as to prevent the person so married from contracting a second marriage in England while the first marriage still subsists.[9] This is really a particular application of the wider rule that a polygamous marriage is now " recognised in this country unless there is some strong reason to the contrary ".[10] We must now consider one or two cases in which difficulty may arise.

Legitimacy of the Issue of a Polygamous Union.—Since legitimacy is primarily a question for the child's *lex domicilii*,[11] the real test to be applied here is not whether English law will recognise the validity of his parents' marriage, but whether the *lex domicilii* will regard the issue of it as legitimate. This may still be important in determining whether the child may take a gift under an English will or settlement in favour of the children of one of his parents.

The Privy Council has held that the offspring of a polygamous marriage are children for the purpose of the former English Statute of Distributions,[12] and there is little doubt that English courts will follow suit. But it seems that to inherit an entailed interest a child must be legitimate within the narrowest common law sense of the term and so the child of a polygamous marriage cannot be an heir.[13]

---

[7]*Baindail* v. *Baindail*, [1946] 1 All E.R. 342, C.A.; [1946] P. 122, *ante*, p. 45; *Srini Vasan* v. *Srini Vasan*, [1945] 2 All E.R. 21; [1946] P. 67.
[8][1962] 3 All E.R. 873; [1965] P. 85. See further, *ante*, p. 46.
[9]*Ante*, p. o. In *R.* v. *Sarwan Singh*, [1962] 3 All E.R. 612, it was held that a prosecution for bigamy would not lie in respect of the second marriage even though it was solemnized in England. *Sed quaere*? The point was left open in *Baindail* v. *Baindail*, [1946] 1 All E.R. 342, 347, C.A.; [1946] P. 122, 130. See further Bartholomew, *Polygamous Marriages and English Criminal Law*, 17 M.L.R. 344; Morris in 66 Harv. L.R. at pp. 991-993.
[10]*Per* LORD PARKER, C.J., in *Mohamed* v. *Knott*, [1968] 2 All E.R. 563, 567; [1969] 1 Q.B. 1, 13-14, citing Dicey and Morris, *Conflict of Laws*, 8th Ed., Rule 36.
[11]See *post*, pp. 241-243.
[12]*Bamgbose* v. *Daniel*, [1954] 3 All E.R. 263, P.C.; [1955] A.C. 107. See further Falconbridge, *Legitimacy or Legitimation and Succession in the Conflict of Laws*, 27 Can. Bar Rev. 1163, 1183 *et seq.*
[13]The point was left open by LORD MAUGHAM, L.C., in the *Sinha Peerage Case*, [1946] 1 All E.R. 348, 349, H.L.

E

Presumably either parent can apply for custody and maintenance of such children under the Guardianship of Minors Act if the children are within the jurisdiction.[14]

Matrimonial Causes.—We have already seen that *Hyde* v. *Hyde*[15] laid down the rule that matrimonial relief in English courts is not open to the parties to a polygamous marriage. For this purpose the important question is whether the marriage is to be regarded as polygamous at the time of the proceedings whatever its character was when it was contracted.[16] In *Hyde* v. *Hyde* LORD PENZANCE refused to hear a petition for divorce; in *Ali* v. *Ali*[17] CUMMING-BRUCE, J., went further and held that, when a potentially polygamous marriage became monogamous, the court had no power to grant a divorce on the ground of a matrimonial offence committed whilst it was still polygamous because at that stage the court will not concern itself with the marriage at all. *Hyde* v. *Hyde* was followed by BARNARD, J., in *Risk* v. *Risk*[18] where he refused to entertain nullity proceedings at the suit of a wife who had gone through a polygamous form of marriage with a Mohammedan in Egypt, notwithstanding that this marriage was probably void by English law because the wife had no power to contract a polygamous union. The same rule must clearly apply to petitions for judicial separation[19] and maintenance and also to proceedings under the Matrimonial Proceedings (Magistrates' Courts) Act,[20] although it is highly questionable whether it is socially desirable that a wife should be left without a remedy in such circumstances. It is also very doubtful whether we would recognise the spouses' duty to cohabit as sufficiently akin to our own concept of consortium to enable either of them to sue for damages for loss of consortium at common law. In *Shahnaz* v. *Rizwan*[1] WINN, J., went so far as to say:

> " Neither a husband nor a wife can be granted by the English court any right which inheres in the person seeking the assistance of the court specifically in the character of a husband or of a wife; and, by parity of reasoning, neither party coming to the court can enforce against the other any obligation which arises from, and specifically from, the capacity of the other party as wife or husband."

Nevertheless this does not prevent either from enforcing a contractual

---

[14]For the Guardianship of Minors Act, see *post*, pp. 282-283 and 478.

[15](1866), L.R. 1 P. & D. 130. See *ante*, p. 43.

[16]*Ali* v. *Ali*, [1966] 1 All E.R. 664; [1968] P. 564; *Cheni* v. *Cheni*, [1962] 3 All E.R. 873; [1965] P. 85; *Parkasho* v. *Singh*, [1967] 1 All E.R. 737; [1968] P. 233. For change of character of a marriage, see *ante*, pp. 46-48. This point was not considered in *Hyde* v. *Hyde*.

[17][1966] 1 All E.R. 664; [1968] P. 564. See Davis and Webb in 15 I.C.L.Q. 1185. The learned judge's approach seems unnecessarily restrictive, but if the case is to be regarded as correctly decided, the principle presumably still applies so that the petitioner cannot now rely on the respondent's adultery or behaviour or any period of desertion or separation occurring whilst the marriage was polygamous to show that the marriage has irretrievably broken down.

[18][1950] 2 All E.R. 973; [1951] P. 50. See also *Mehta* v. *Mehta*, [1945] 2 All E.R. 690, 693. But she could presumably sue for a declaratory judgment: see *post*, p. 56.

[19]*Cf. Nachimson* v. *Nachimson*, [1930] P. 217, C.A.

[20]*Sowa* v. *Sowa* [1961] 1 All E.R. 687, C.A.; [1961] P. 80. The Law Commission recommend that all forms of matrimonial relief should be available to the parties to a polygamous marriage: Law Com. No. 42.

[1][1964] 2 All E.R. 993, 996; [1965] 1 Q.B. 390, 397-398. Morris considers that an action would lie under the Fatal Accidents Acts: 66 Harv. L.R. at p. 1001. *Sed quaere?* Could, say, three wives all sue?

or proprietary right against the other even though that right can arise only as a consequence of the marriage, and in *Shahnaz* v. *Rizwan* the wife was permitted to enforce her husband's contractual promise to pay her dower made on the occasion of their entering into a potentially polygamous marriage in India.

Applying the converse of the rule in *Hyde* v. *Hyde*, it was held by SWINFEN EADY, L.J., in the *Hammersmith Marriage Case*[2] that a monogamous marriage cannot be dissolved by a process which is devised for polygamous unions. Here a marriage contracted in England was held not to have been dissolved by *talak*, a Mohammedan procedure designed to dissolve a polygamous Mohammedan marriage. In the later case of *Russ* v. *Russ*,[3] however, the Court of Appeal distinguished the *Hammersmith Marriage Case* on the grounds that in the earlier case it was not clear that the parties' *lex domicilii* would regard the marriage in question as dissolved by the *talak* (which consists of a threefold unilateral declaration of divorce by the husband) and that in any case the *talak* had been pronounced in a private room in London in the absence of the wife, whereas in *Russ* v. *Russ* there was evidence to prove that *talak* would dissolve all marriages by the parties' *lex domicilii* and this particular declaration had been made in the presence of the wife and an officer of the Egyptian court and had been entered on the court records.

Thus in *Russ* v. *Russ* the Court of Appeal rejected the ground of SWINFEN EADY, L.J.'s decision as too wide and it seems that the English courts will recognise a divorce which is valid by the spouses' *lex domicilii* even though this is designed to terminate a polygamous union and the marriage was monogamous at its inception. This was the view of SIMON, P., in *Qureshi* v. *Qureshi*[4] where he held that a *talak* pronounced in England had validly dissolved the marriage of parties domiciled in Pakistan. It should be noticed that in this case the proceedings were extra-judicial although, as SIMON, P., pointed out, had they been such as to offend the conscience of the court, the divorce might not be recognised for that reason. It is submitted that this is the only possible just solution and that the application of any other rule would put the parties into an impossible position. Let us suppose that a woman domiciled in England marries in this country a man who is permitted to practise polygamy. Both parties intend that this union shall be monogamous. They then return to his country and he subsequently divorces her for adultery by the only means open to him there—a process which is designed to dissolve potentially polygamous marriages. If the woman returns to this country, we should regard the divorce as ineffective and consequently she would be unable to remarry here even though she had capacity by what we should still regard as her *lex domicilii*.

---

[2][1917] I K.B. 634, C.A. For the facts, see *ante*, p. 48. See also *Maher* v. *Maher*, [1951] 2 All E.R. 37; [1951] P. 342, disapproved by WILLMER, L.J., in *Russ* v. *Russ*, [1962] 3 All E.R. 193, 200, C.A.; [1964] P. 315, 328.

[3][1962] 3 All E.R. 193, C.A.; [1964] P. 315.

[4][1971] I All E.R. 325, particularly at p. 345. See also Swaminathan, *Recognition of Foreign Unilateral Divorces in the English Conflict of Laws*, 28 M.L.R. 540, where a less restricted view is taken of the present application of the *Hammersmith Marriage Case*.

Social Welfare Legislation.—Refusals to allow benefit to a woman who had been married under a system allowing polygamy resulted in legislation to define the position of spouses in such cases. Now a marriage performed outside the United Kingdom under a law which permits polygamy is to be treated as a valid marriage for the purpose of the Family Allowances Act, the National Insurance (Industrial Injuries) Act and the National Insurance Act provided that it has in fact at all times been monogamous.[5]

The reason for this provision is that contributions and benefits are calculated on the assumption that a man has only one wife at a time. On the other hand, a man cannot be permitted to throw the burden of supporting his wife or wives on the taxpayer merely because his marriage is polygamous and consequently he is bound to support them for the purpose of the Ministry of Social Security Act even though the unions are *de facto* polygamous.[6]

Some Other Problems.—The following questions have been left open in cases in the past but may ultimately have to be decided.

> Do the surviving disabilities and privileges resulting from the doctrine of unity of legal personality apply to the parties to a polygamous marriage?[7]
> What interest do, say, two wives take on the intestacy of a husband leaving realty in England? Do they take £8,750 (or £30,000) each or as joint tenants or as tenants in common?[8]

G. PRESUMPTION OF MARRIAGE

It has long been established law that, if a man and woman cohabit and hold themselves out as husband and wife, this in itself raises a presumption that they are legally married.[9] Consequently, if the marriage is challenged, the burden lies upon those challenging it to prove that there was in fact no marriage and not upon those alleging it to prove that it has been solemnized. This may be important, for example, if the parties have been married abroad and have no written or other evidence of the solemnization, or if the validity of the marriage is called into question indirectly when the parties can no longer give evidence, as it may be if the legitimacy of their children is put in issue after their deaths.

A closer examination will show that there are really two presumptions: first, that at some time or other the parties went through a valid form of marriage, and, secondly, that, when they did so, they both had

---

[5]Family Allowances Act 1965, s. 17 (9); National Insurance (Industrial Injuries) Act 1965, s. 86 (5); National Insurance Act 1965, s. 113 (1) (re-enacting the Family Allowances and National Insurance Act 1956, s. 3). For the recommendations of the Law Commission, see Law Com. No. 42, paras. 125-134.

[6]*Din* v. *National Assistance Board*, [1967] 1 All E.R. 750; [1967] 2 Q.B. 213. For the Ministry of Social Security Act, see *post*, p. 413.

[7]This question was left open in *R.* v. *Caroubi* (1912), 7 Cr. App. R. 149, 151, C.C.A. (presumption that a crime committed by a wife in her husband's presence was committed as a result of coercion by him); *Mawji* v. *R.*, [1957] 1 All E.R. 385, 387, P.C.; [1957] A.C. 126, 135-136 (criminal conspiracy).

[8]This was left open in *Coleman* v. *Shang*, [1961] 2 All E.R. 406, P.C.; [1961] A.C. 481, where it was held that the *sole* relict of a man whose marriage was potentially polygamous was a widow for the purpose of the former English Statute of Distributions.

[9]But in a prosecution for bigamy the presumption of the prisoner's innocence outweighs the presumption of marriage to be drawn from cohabitation and the marriage must be strictly proved by the prosecution: see Archbold, *Criminal Pleading*, 37th Ed., s. 3769.

the capacity to marry. This distinction is important when the standard of proof necessary to rebut the presumption is considered.

Presumption of Formal Validity.—The presumption that the parties went through a valid form of marriage may always be rebutted, of course, by proving that they never contracted any marriage at all, and although this will usually be difficult to do by direct evidence, it may be possible to do so by inference.[10] Even if it is not disputed that the parties went through a form of marriage, it may still be alleged that owing to some formal defect the ceremony was a legal nullity. But in this case *omnia praesumuntur rite esse acta*, and the generally accepted view is that the presumption will not be rebutted unless the evidence to the contrary satisfies one beyond reasonable doubt that there has been no valid marriage.[11] The number of cases in which this has been done is in fact extremely small.

Presumption of Capacity.—The difference between the standards of proof required to rebut the presumptions of formal validity and of capacity was clearly stated by SIMON, P., in *Mahadervan* v. *Mahadervan*.[12] Earlier in *Tweney* v. *Tweney*[13] PILCHER, J., had said:

> " The petitioner's marriage to the present respondent being unexceptionable in form and duly consummated remains a good marriage until *some* evidence is adduced that the marriage was, *in fact*, a nullity."

This raises the question: What evidence will suffice for this purpose? Although this point still has to be decided, it is tentatively submitted on the present state of the authorities that, if any evidence is adduced showing that either of the parties lacked capacity, the presumption in favour of the validity of the marriage disappears and the question has to be decided on the balance of probability in the light of all the available evidence. It will usually be easy to determine whether either party was at the time of the marriage under the age of 16 or whether they are within the prohibited degrees of consanguinity or affinity; difficulty may arise when one of the parties has been previously married and it is alleged that this earlier marriage was still subsisting when the later union was contracted. The common problem is therefore this: A marries X and they later separate; A then marries Y without having the former marriage dissolved and not knowing whether X is still alive. Is the marriage between A and Y to be presumed to be valid?[14]

Whether X was still alive at the time of A's marriage to Y is a question of fact.[15] If X was suffering from a fatal disease when A last heard

---

[10]As in *Re Bradshaw*, [1938] 4 All E.R. 143, where the presumption was rebutted by evidence that the parties had subsequently intermarried.

[11]See *Mahadervan* v. *Mahadervan*, [1962] 3 All E.R. 1108, 1117; [1964] P. 233, 246, and the cases there cited, particularly *Hill* v. *Hill*, [1959] 1 All E.R. 281, 285, P.C.; *Piers* v. *Piers* (1849), 2 H.L. Cas. 331, H.L., at pp. 362, 370. But in *Re Taylor*, [1961] 1 All E.R. 55, 63, C.A., HARMAN, L.J., was of the opinion that the evidence in rebuttal should be *firm and clear*.

[12][1962] 3 All E.R. 1108, 1116-1117; [1964] P. 233, 245-246. See also *Re Peete*, [1952] 2 All E.R. 599, 601. But CAIRNS, J., apparently ignored it in *Taylor* v. *Taylor*, [1965] 1 All E.R. 872; [1967] P. 25, and required decisive evidence in a case dealing with capacity.

[13][1946] 1 All E.R. 564, 565; [1946] P. 180, 182. (Italics supplied.)

[14]The question in dispute may be alternatively whether a previous marriage was validly dissolved: *Gatty* v. *A.-G.*, [1951] P. 444.

[15]*Chard* v. *Chard*, [1955] 3 All E.R. 721; [1956] P. 259.

of him, he may be presumed to have died within a relatively short time; the converse is true if X was a young person in good health. But if X has been absent for seven years or more and has not been heard of during that time, this may of itself raise a presumption of law that he is dead provided that certain conditions are satisfied. The nature of this presumption was thus stated by SACHS, J., in *Chard* v. *Chard*:[16]

> " Where . . . there is no acceptable affirmative evidence that he was alive at some time during a continuous period of seven years or more, then if it can be proved first, that there are persons who would be likely to have heard of him over that period, secondly, that those persons have not heard of him, and thirdly, that all due inquiries have been made appropriate to the circumstances, [X] will be presumed to have died at some time within that period."

Thus, in *Tweney* v. *Tweney* the second marriage was presumed to be valid where the period of absence had been 12 years and A had made exhaustive enquiries.[17] In *Re Peete*[18] on the other hand the presumption that the second marriage was valid was rebutted. W had separated from her first husband some time before 1916. In that year she was told by his sister that he had been killed in an explosion in a factory where he was employed but that she (the sister) had been unable to identify his body. In 1919 W went through a form of marriage with H. In an application under the Inheritance (Family Provision) Act by W as H's widow, it was held that she could not succeed. Although there was an initial presumption that the marriage between H and W was valid, there was some evidence that she had not at that time the capacity to marry him, *viz.* the existence of the previous marriage. The sister's statement that the first husband had been killed was clearly inadmissible as it was hearsay; hence W had remarried only four years after last seeing her first husband and there was no admissible evidence to rebut the presumption that he was still alive after that short period.

Similarly, if any of the three conditions laid down by SACHS, J., is missing, the presumption cannot be invoked. In *Chard* v. *Chard* the husband went through a form of marriage with the respondent 16 years after last seeing his first wife. He had spent almost the whole of that time in prison, and there was some evidence that his first wife had also contracted a bigamous marriage. That being so, the husband was not likely to have heard of her during the intervening period and so the first of the three conditions was not satisfied. Hence no presumption was raised that the first wife was dead at the end of the 16 years, and as she would be only 44 years old at the time of the second marriage, the court inferred that she was still alive and granted a decree of nullity in respect of the second marriage. Again, in *Bradshaw* v. *Bradshaw*[19] it was inferred that the first husband was still alive after 19 years'

---

[16][1955] 3 All E.R. 721, 728; [1956] P. 259, 272; criticised by Nokes in 19 M.L.R. 208. See also Treitel, *Presumption of Death*, 17 M.L.R. 530.

[17]See also *Re Watkins*, [1953] 2 All E.R. 1113 (25 years' absence: second marriage presumed valid); *Bullock* v. *Bullock*, [1960] 2 All E.R. 307 (14 years' absence during which police had sought husband: second marriage presumed valid).

[18][1952] 2 All E.R. 599. *Cf. MacDarmaid* v. *A.-G.*, [1950] 1 All E.R. 497; [1950] P. 218 (first wife presumed to be still alive after three years).

[19][1956] P. 274, n.

absence. In this case the presumption could not be invoked because the third condition was not satisfied, as the wife had failed to make obvious enquiries about her husband (who, when she last saw him, was a regular soldier) from his Corps records.

These cases were distinguished in *Taylor* v. *Taylor*,[20] where the question in issue was whether a *previous* marriage was to be presumed to have been valid. W went through a form of marriage with G. She later left him and, having discovered facts which led her to conclude that this marriage was void because G was already married to another woman, she went through a form of marriage with H whilst G was still alive. H then petitioned for a decree of nullity on the ground that his marriage to W was void as she had been married to G when it was celebrated. These facts gave rise to conflicting presumptions and CAIRNS, J., resolved the problem by " leaning towards the preservation of existing unions " rather than " towards the avoiding of existing unions in favour of doubtful earlier and, to all intents and purposes, dead ones . "[1] He accordingly held that the presumption that W was validly married to H was not rebutted. It may be doubted, however, whether he was justified in coming to this conclusion. Had the sole question in issue been the validity of W's marriage to G, the court must have pronounced in its favour in the absence of any evidence to rebut the presumption. The facts indicated that the marriage to H was presumptively void and there was no evidence to rebut this presumption either. However practically convenient this decision may be, it seems to be logically unsupportable.[2]

H. JACTITATION OF MARRIAGE AND DECLARATORY JUDGMENTS

Jactitation of Marriage.—The decree of jactitation is a curious survival which is seldom sought today. The petitioner alleges that the respondent is not married to the petitioner but is wrongfully boasting or asserting that he or she is the petitioner's spouse. As an alternative to proving the marriage or denying the assertions, the respondent may raise as a defence the fact that the petitioner had authorised him or her to make the representations; and it seems that if the petitioner once gives an authorisation of this sort, he will be debarred from subsequently asking for the decree even though he has withdrawn the authority.[3] The decree, if granted, is in the form of an injunction restraining the respondent from making any further claims to be married to the petitioner. The decree may still be of use today in order to prevent a presumption of marriage being raised, although, of course,

---

[20][1965] 1 All E.R. 872; [1967] P. 25.
[1]At pp. 881 and 39, respectively.
[2]W could easily have petitioned for a decree of nullity with respect to her first marriage, and the hardship worked in *Re Peete* (*ante*, p. 54) was much greater. It is also submitted that CAIRNS, J., applied the wrong standard of proof: see *ante*, p. 53, n. [12].
[3]*Hawke* v. *Corri* (1820), 2 Hag. Con. 280; *Thompson* v. *Rourke*, [1893] P. 11; *ibid.*, 70, C.A.

it was of much greater importance before Lord Hardwicke's Act put a stop to clandestine marriages.[4]

Declaratory Judgments.—A spouse may petition for a declaration that his marriage was a valid one under the provisions of section 39 of the Matrimonial Causes Act 1965.[5] Such a judgment will bind the Crown and any other person joined as a respondent. In addition, the Court of Appeal held in *Har-Shefi* v. *Har-Shefi*[6] that the court has a general power to make an order declaratory of the parties' marital status without giving any other relief. This has introduced a new class of proceedings into the Family Division, but the tendency in recent cases has been to limit their scope and to restrict them to situations where no other relief is available.[7] Thus, the court has refused to make a declaration that a marriage was validly contracted (for which the proceedings mentioned above are available)[8] or that it was void (when the proper procedure is to petition for a decree of nullity).[9] Declaratory judgments are usually sought to determine whether or not a marriage is still subsisting as this is the only means of testing whether English courts will recognise the validity of a foreign decree of divorce or nullity.[10]

Jurisdiction to make Declaratory Orders.—In *Garthwaite* v. *Garthwaite*[11] the Court of Appeal held that it had no jurisdiction to declare that a marriage, celebrated in England, was still subsisting when neither party was domiciled or resident in this country. Unfortunately, the court did not state clearly what the basis of jurisdiction is. Undoubtedly it exists if one or both parties are domiciled here. For the purpose of determining what the wife's domicile is, the court will assume that the allegations in the petition are true: hence if she claims that her marriage is still subsisting, she must *ex hypothesi* have the same domicile as her husband, whilst if she alleges that it has been dissolved, she is capable of acquiring a domicile independent of his.[12]

---

[4]Jurisdiction is vested in the High Court, and county courts can hear *undefended* petitions: Matrimonial Causes Act 1967, s. 1 (see *ante*, p. 4). A decree of jactitation is a judgment *in personam* only and therefore binds only the parties and their privies: *R.* v. *Kingston* (1776), 20 State Tr. 355, 573, H.L. The Law Commission are provisionally of the opinion that jactitation proceedings should be abolished as they no longer fulfil any purpose: Working Paper No. 34.

[5] See *post*, pp. 244-245.

[6][1953] 1 All E.R. 783, C.A.; [1953] P. 161.

[7]See particularly *Aldrich* v. *A.-G.*, [1968] 1 All E.R. 345; [1968] P. 281.

[8]*Collett* v. *Collett*, [1967] 2 All E.R. 426; [1968] P. 482.

[9]*Kassim* v. *Kassim*, [1962] 3 All E.R. 426; [1962] P. 224.

[10]As in *Har-Shefi* v. *Har-Shefi*, (*supra*). But ORMROD, J., has questioned whether the provisions of the Supreme Court of Judicature (Consolidation) Act 1925, s. 21 (b) do not prevent the court from declaring a marriage valid (as distinct from annulled or dissolved): *Aldrich* v. *A.-G.*, (*supra*), at pp. 350 and 293, respectively. The judgment does not change status and the court may grant a declaration even though the marriage is (or was) polygamous: *Lee* v. *Lau*, [1964] 2 All E.R. 248; [1967] P. 14.

[11][1964] 2 All E.R. 233, C.A.; [1964] P. 356. Criticised by Hooper in 14 I.C.L.Q. 264. See generally North, *Declaratory Judgments in the Divorce Court*, 14 I.C.L.Q. 579.

[12]*Garthwaite* v. *Garthwaite*, (*supra*); *Har-Shefi* v. *Har-Shefi*, [1953] 1 All E.R. 783, C.A. ; [1953] P. 161. *Cf.* the same problem in the case of nullity, *post*, p. 84. This produces the anomalous position that the court's jurisdiction may depend upon whether the wife puts her claim in the affirmative or negative.

It seems that jurisdiction can also be assumed if both parties are resident in this country on the ground that this was the basis of the ecclesiastical courts' jurisdiction which the High Court now exercises.[13] If the petitioner seeks a declaration that the marriage is still subsisting, the court can apparently also make the order if it has jurisdiction to pronounce a decree of judicial separation, for the decree incorporates a declaration that a valid marriage exists between the parties.[14]

---

[13]This seems to be the ground on which the court assumed jurisdiction in *Sammy-Joe* v. *Sammy-Joe* (1966), *Times*, June 9th, C.A. See also *Qureshi* v. *Qureshi*, [1971] 1 All E.R. 325, 340. Residence of the respondent alone is probably sufficient, for the petitioner *ipso facto* submits to the jurisdiction by invoking it: *cf. post*, p. 143, n. [5].

[14]*Garthwaite* v. *Garthwaite*, (*supra*). For jurisdiction to grant a judicial separation, see *post*, p. 143. In *Lepre* v. *Lepre*, [1963] 2 All E.R. 49; [1965] P. 52, where a wife sought a declaration that a foreign decree of nullity would not be recognised in this country and also a decree of divorce, SIMON, P., held that he had jurisdiction to make the declaration if he had jurisdiction to pronounce a divorce, for he could do the latter only if the marriage was still subsisting.

CHAPTER 3

Void and Voidable Marriages

A. THE DISTINCTION BETWEEN VOID AND VOIDABLE MARRIAGES

As in the case of any other type of contract, a marriage may be void or voidable. A void marriage is strictly speaking a contradiction in terms, for it is no marriage at all: to speak of a void marriage is merely a compendious way of saying that, although the parties have been through a ceremony of marriage, they have never acquired the status of husband and wife owing to the presence of some impediment.[1] In brief, a void marriage is never a marriage either in fact or in law. A voidable marriage, on the other hand, is at its inception a valid subsisting marriage; in this case the effect of the impediment is to empower one (or, occasionally, either) of the spouses to take steps to have it turned into a void marriage. But whilst, in the case of other contracts, a voidable contract may usually be avoided by a simple repudiation by one party, a voidable marriage may only be set aside by a decree of nullity pronounced by a court of competent jurisdiction. Once this has been done, the decree for some purposes has a retrospective effect, so that the parties are deemed in law never to have been married at all The distinction has been thus judicially explained by LORD GREENE, M.R.:[2]

> " A void marriage is one that will be regarded by every court in any case in which the existence of the marriage is in issue as never having taken place and can be so treated by both parties to it without the necessity of any decree annulling it: a voidable marriage is one that will be regarded by every court as a valid subsisting marriage until a decree annulling it has been pronounced by a court of competent jurisdiction."

It is the retrospective effect of the decree that distinguishes the annulment of a voidable marriage from a divorce. The latter brings an existing marriage to an end but it does not in any way alter the previous status of the parties; they are still regarded in law as having been husband and wife before the decree was made absolute. But like a decree of divorce, a decree of nullity of a voidable marriage effects a change of status, and it has therefore been argued that voidable marriages are today anomalous. The reason for the anomaly is basically

---

[1]But if the parties have never been through a ceremony of marriage at all, their union cannot even be termed a void marriage: it is concubinage and no more.

[2]*De Reneville* v. *De Reneville*, [1948] 1 All E.R. 56, 60, C.A.; [1948] P. 100, 111. Professor Newark considers that historically this distinction is incorrect: *The Operation of Nullity Decrees*, 8 M.L.R. 203 (1945).

historical. Decrees of nullity could originally be pronounced only by
the ecclesiastical courts which, before the Reformation, applied the
canon law of the Roman Catholic Church. The Roman Catholic doctrine
of the indissolubility of marriage prevented them from granting
decrees of divorce, but it did not prevent them from pronouncing that
there had never been a marriage at all, and the concept of the voidable
marriage was retained by the English ecclesiastical courts after the
breach with Rome. But the retrospective effect of the decree is none the
less artificial and confusing and " in truth perpetuates a canonical
fiction ".[3]

The law has recently been reviewed by the Law Commission.[4] A
Bill to reform the law was introduced at the end of 1970; its provisions
are summarised in Appendix E, *post*.

Decrees of Nullity.—The vital distinction between a void and a
voidable marriage, therefore, is that the former, being void *ab initio*,
needs no decree to annul it, whilst the latter is in all respects a valid
marriage until a decree absolute of nullity is pronounced. A petition
for annulment may be presented only by one of the spouses in the lifetime of the other, so that if one of them dies before the decree is granted,
a voidable marriage must be treated as valid for all purposes and for all
time.[5] On the other hand, for example, either party to a void marriage may lawfully contract a valid marriage with someone else without
having the first marriage formally annulled.

Even though, in the case of a void marriage, a decree of nullity can
only be declaratory and cannot effect any change in the parties' status,
there may be good reason for obtaining such a decree. In the first place,
there may be some doubt whether on the facts or the law applicable
the marriage is void: whether, for example, one party voluntarily consented to the solemnization of the marriage or there was a due publication of banns. Secondly, a decree of nullity is a judgment *in rem*, so that
no one may subsequently allege that the marriage is in fact valid.
Moreover, the court has power on granting a decree to make certain
ancillary orders, and the " wife " may therefore present a petition in
order, for example, to obtain financial provision for herself or her
children.[6]

Jurisdiction to grant decrees of nullity (whether the marriage was
alleged to be void or voidable) was transferred from the ecclesiastical

---

[3]*Per* LORD GODDARD, C.J., in *R.* v. *Algar*, [1953] 2 All E.R. 1381, 1384, C.C.A.;
[1954] 1 Q.B. 279, 288. If there are cross-petitions for nullity and divorce, the court
must try the nullity issue first (whether it is alleged that the decree is void or voidable)
for it cannot dissolve a non-existent marriage: *S. (otherwise P.)* v. *S.*, [1970] 2 All E.R.
251; [1970] P. 208.
[4]Law Com. No. 33, Nullity of Marriage, 1970.
[5]*Elliott* v. *Gurr* (1812), 2 Phillim. 16; *A.* v. *B.* (1868), L.R. 1 P. & D. 559. At one time
any other person might present a petition for nullity provided that he had an interest
in having the marriage annulled, even though the marriage was voidable only: *Sherwood*
v. *Ray* (1837), 1 Moo. P.C.C. 353, P.C. Although this is inconsistent with dicta in *A.* v. *B.*,
it seems to have been regarded as still good law by COLLINGWOOD, J., in *J.* v. *J.*, [1952]
2 All E.R. 1129; [1953] P. 186, and by ORMROD, J., in *Kassim* v. *Kassim*, [1962] 3 All
E.R. 426, 432; [1962] P. 224, 234. But in practice such proceedings now appear to be
obsolete: see Newark, *loc. cit.*, 209-10.
[6]The legal consequences of the annulment of a void marriage are further considered by Cohn, *The Nullity of Marriage*, 64 L.Q.R. 324, 533.

courts to the new Divorce Court set up by the Matrimonial Causes Act of 1857, and was vested in the High Court by the Judicature Act of 1873. Since 1968 divorce county courts have been able to hear *undefended* petitions.[7] The decree is made in two stages: the decree nisi, followed by the decree absolute. The rules relating to the application for a decree nisi to be made absolute (including the restrictions imposed where the welfare of children is involved) are exactly the same as they are in divorce.[8] The marriage is finally annulled when the decree is made absolute and a party to a voidable marriage may not remarry until then.

Whether the marriage is void or voidable, the court has power to make a number of ancillary orders in addition to pronouncing the decree. These will be dealt with in various places in this book; a list of them will be found in Appendix D, *post*.

Third Parties' Rights.—From what has been said about the necessity of obtaining a decree to annul a voidable marriage, it follows that no one but the spouses may challenge its validity; third parties must treat it as valid unless a decree has been pronounced. On the other hand, if it is alleged that a marriage is void, any person with an interest in so doing may prove as a question of fact that there has never been a marriage at all. Thus, suppose that property is settled on trust for A for life with remainder to his widow or, if he leave no widow, to B absolutely. A goes through a ceremony of marriage with W who survives him. Even though the marriage between W and A was voidable, B cannot dispute its validity to prove that W is not A's widow; but he can show, even after A's death, that the marriage between them was void and that consequently the remainder over to him takes effect, for W, never having been A's wife, cannot now be his widow. But if a decree of nullity had been pronounced before A's death, then, whether the marriage was void or voidable, everyone is bound by it and W may not now assert that she is A's widow. It is easy to imagine other cases in which the validity of a marriage might be impeached: others interested in property might wish to prove that the children were illegitimate or that the alleged marriage had not revoked the will of one of the parties to it.[9]

Conversely, it might be in the interest of one of the parties to the marriage to prove that it was void. Suppose that a testator devises property to W so long as she remains his widow and, if she remarry, to X. W subsequently goes through a ceremony of marriage with K. In the event of a dispute between W and X over the beneficial interest in the property after the ceremony, W clearly succeeds if she can show that the marriage between herself and K is void.[10]

Bars to Relief.—Although the parties to a void or voidable marriage may be estopped *per rem judicatam* from denying its validity,[11]

---

[7]Matrimonial Causes Act 1967, s. 1. See further, *ante*, p. 4.
[8]See *post*, p. 208.
[9]*Cf. Harrod* v .*Harrod* (1854), 1 K. & J. 4; *Re Peete*, [1952] 2 All E.R. 599; *In the Estate of Park*, [1953] 2 All E.R. 408, C.A.; [1954] P. 89.
[10]*Allen* v. *Wood* (1834), 1 Bing. N.C. 8.
[11]See *post*, pp. 67-69.

a void marriage, being void *ab initio,* cannot on principle be turned into a valid marriage by any ratification by the parties.[12] In canon law and in some Continental legal systems a void marriage may be validated by continued cohabitation in certain circumstances;[13] although it may be socially desirable that a party who has, say, been induced to go through a ceremony to which he has not consented should not be able to assert that the marriage is invalid if he subsequently freely adopts it, this is an argument for holding such marriages voidable, not for enabling the parties to make a valid marriage out of an initial nullity.

But, as in the case of any other voidable contract, a party to a voidable marriage may effectively put it out of his power to obtain a decree of nullity by his own conduct. The older reports speak of the petitioner's " insincerity " in this connection, but the word is both ambiguous and infelicitous.[14] The modern view was first clearly stated by the House of Lords in *G. v. M.*[15] LORD SELBORNE, L.C., speaking of the old doctrine of insincerity, said:[16]

> " I think I can perceive that the real basis of reasoning which underlies that phraseology is this, and nothing more than this, that there may be conduct on the part of the person seeking this remedy which ought to estop that person from having it: as, for instance, any act from which the inference ought to be drawn that during the antecedent time[17] the party has, with a knowledge of the facts and of the law, approbated the marriage which he or she afterwards seeks to get rid of, or has taken advantages and derived benefits from the matrimonial relation which it would be unfair and inequitable to permit him or her, after having received them, to treat as if no such relation had ever existed. . . . The circumstances which may justify it are various, and in cases of this kind many sorts of conduct may exist, taking pecuniary benefits for example, living for a long time together in the same house or family with the status and character of husband and wife, after knowledge of everything which it is material to know. I do not at all mean to say that there may not be other circumstances which would produce the same effect; but it appears to me that, in order to justify any such doctrine as that which has been insisted on at the bar, there must be a foundation of substantial justice, depending upon the acts and conduct of the party sought to be barred."

Similarly, LORD WATSON said:[18]

> " In a suit for nullity of marriage there may be facts and circumstances proved which so plainly imply, on the part of the complaining spouse, a recognition of the existence and validity of the marriage, as to render it most inequitable and contrary to public policy that he or she should be permitted to go on to challenge it with effect."

---

[12]See *Miles* v. *Chilton* (1849), 1 Rob. Ecc. 684, (petitioner aware that respondent was already married); *Bateman* v. *Bateman* (1898), 78 L.T. 472, (continued cohabitation after discovery of facts).

[13]See Lasok, *Approbation of Marriage in English Law and the Doctrine of Validation,* 26 M.L.R. 249.

[14]See *G.* v. *M.* (1885), 10 App. Cas. 171, H.L., at pp. 186, 197, 201; *Tindall* v. *Tindall,* [1953] 1 All E.R. 139, 146-147, C.A.; [1953] P. 63, 76.

[15](1885), 10 App. Cas. 171, H.L.

[16]At p. 186.

[17]*I.e.,* the time between the date of the marriage and the ascertainment of the facts and the law on the one hand and the date of the petition on the other: *Nash* v. *Nash,* [1940] 1 All E.R. 206, 210; [1940] P. 60, 65.

[18]10 App. Cas. at pp. 197-198.

It would seem, then, that the doctrine is one of public policy which resembles the rule in the general law of contract that a party may lose the power to repudiate a voidable transaction by his own affirmation of it or by his laches. Although the ecclesiastical courts seem to have regarded the bar as an absolute one, the modern judicial tendency has been to regard it as discretionary, so that even though the petitioner has approbated the marriage, it is still within the court's power to grant a decree.[19] In practice, however, once approbation has been established, it is rare for the decree to be granted.

The passage cited above from LORD SELBORNE'S speech in *G. v. M.* indicates that there can usually be no approbation if the petitioner is ignorant of the facts or the law. This means that he must be aware not only of the existence of the grounds upon which the petition is based but also of the fact that these grounds will entitle him to petition for nullity, and any acts alleged to constitute approbation before he became aware of this must be disregarded. This is certainly true when the facts relied on constitute an overt adoption of the marriage, but it is doubtful whether the rule applies if the alleged approbation takes any other form.[20] In any case, as the Court of Appeal held in *Pettit v. Pettit*,[1] different considerations apply if the petitioner relies upon his own impotence (or, presumably, his own mental disorder, insanity or epilepsy). In such a case it is manifestly inappropriate to talk of his acquiescing in his own shortcomings and, what is more important, the respondent is as aggrieved as the petitioner. It would therefore be wholly inequitable to look solely at the petitioner's acts and to disregard the respondent's position even though the former did not realise that he had a remedy.

In the case of three of the four new grounds of nullity there is a sort of statutory doctrine of approbation in the sense that the decree may only be granted if the petitioner commences proceedings within a year of the marriage and has not voluntarily had marital intercourse after discovering the existence of the grounds for a decree.[2] The doctrine that we are considering is particularly relevant where the petition is based upon impotence or wilful refusal to consummate the marriage, although it is applicable in the other cases as well. We must now discuss some of the more important examples of it.[3]

---

[19]*Scott v. Scott*, [1959] 1 All E.R. 531, 535; [1959] P. 103, n., 108. *Cf.* BUCKNILL and COHEN, L.JJ., in *Clifford v. Clifford*, [1948] 1 All E.R. 394, 399, C.A.; [1948] P. 187, 197. But PHILLIMORE, J., expressly dissented from this view in *G. v. G.*, [1960] 3 All E.R. 56, 60-61; [1961] P. 87, 94.

[20]*Cf.* the conflicting opinions in *Pettit v. Pettit*, [1962] 3 All E.R. 37, C.A., at p. 44 (where WILLMER, L.J., doubted whether the rule applied in such circumstances but DONOVAN, L.J., was of the opinion that it did); [1963] P. 177, at pp. 189 and 191. See also *Tindall v. Tindall, (ante)*, and *Slater v. Slater*, [1953] 1 All E.R. 246, C.A.; [1953] P. 235. In the absence of evidence to the contrary the petitioner will be presumed to know what the law is: *W. v. W.*, [1952] 1 All E.R. 858, 863-864, C.A.; [1952] P. 152, 162-165.

[1][1962] 3 All E.R. 37, C.A.; [1963] P. 177. For the facts, see *post*, p. 66. See also *Mogridge v. Mogridge* (1965), 109 Sol. Jo. 814, C.A.

[2]Matrimonial Causes Act 1965, s. 9 (2). See *post*, p. 79.

[3]For a full discussion, see Lasok, *loc. cit.* The Law Commission suggest that approbation should be replaced by an absolute statutory bar: Law Com. No. 33, paras. 39-45.

Approbation by overt acts.—If a party, knowing that he may obtain a decree of nullity, acts in a way which is consistent only with his treating the marriage as valid, he may not subsequently treat it as voidable. A clear example of this is to be seen in *W.* v. *W.*[4] The parties were married in 1941, and although the wife underwent an operation in 1943 to remove the cause of her impotence, she remained unable to consummate the marriage. In 1944 the parties adopted a child which unfortunately died soon afterwards. In 1945 they adopted a second child at the instigation of the husband. He later petitioned for nullity on the grounds of his wife's inability to consummate the marriage, but it was held that by initiating the adoption proceedings in 1945 he had clearly approbated the marriage. At that time he must have realised that the chances of the marriage ever being consummated were extremely slender, and the adoption proceedings not only had the effect of severing the legal relations between the child and its natural parents and vesting them in the adopters but also involved the applicants' holding themselves out as husband and wife.[5] Since the husband had initiated these proceedings, he could not now assert the invalidity of the marriage.

Another example of the same type of case is to be found in *Tindall* v. *Tindall.*[6] The wife, after stating that she proposed to commence nullity proceedings on the grounds of her husband's impotence, unsuccessfully took proceedings against him in a magistrates' court, charging him with desertion and persistent cruelty. She then appealed to the Divisional Court and obtained an order that the husband should pay £15 into court as security for the costs of the appeal. When she eventually did petition for nullity, it was held that she had approbated the marriage by seeking an order that could only be made on the assumption that she was married to the respondent, and that it would therefore be contrary to public policy to permit her to succeed on a petition in which she sought to have the same marriage annulled. *A fortiori* an agreement between the spouses that the petitioner shall not institute proceedings for nullity will be a good defence to a petition.[7]

Other cases can easily be imagined, but reference should be made in particular to the problems that may be raised in this connection by artificial insemination. It is of unusual importance here because of the probability of the parties' resorting to it when one of them is impotent and a child cannot therefore be conceived in the normal way. If the parties by their act not only admit that the marriage is never likely to be consummated but also imply that any child which may be conceived will be born into a normal family where the husband and wife are validly married, it is difficult to resist the inference that they have necessarily approbated the marriage.[8] The inference seems to be even stronger

[4][1952] 1 All E.R. 858, C.A.; [1952] P. 152.
[5]See *post*, chap. 10.
[6][1953] 1 All E.R. 139, C.A.; [1953] P. 63. For proceedings in magistrates' courts, see *post*, chap. 7.
[7]*Aldridge* v. *Aldridge* (1888), 13 P.D. 210.
[8]The question was canvassed but left unanswered by the Court of Appeal in *W.* v. *W.*, [1952] 1 All E.R. 858; [1952] P. 152.

if the wife is inseminated by the seed of the husband as distinct from
that of some other donor.

Both artificial insemination and adoption raise a further problem
which still remains to be solved. If the impotence is psychological, the
parties occasionally resort to one of these means in the hope that the
birth or presence of the child may remove the impediment. If this
is their avowed motive, can it be said that the petitioner has approbated
the unconsummated marriage when his or her purpose is to achieve
consummation? It may be said straight away that, even if a private
understanding of this sort could ever rebut the inference of approbation,
it will not do so unless the petitioner makes his intentions clear to the
respondent at the time. He may not later rely upon a mental reservation " locked in his bosom and not declared " to the respondent.[9] In
W. v. W.[10] the husband sought to prove that there was no approbation
by showing that his motive in initiating the adoption proceedings was
to overcome the wife's fear of intercourse, but his argument failed
because he had not stated this to the wife and his declared purpose at
the time (to be inferred from the correspondence which passed between
the spouses) was to help his wife to overcome the grief and anxiety
caused by the death of the first child. In the words of JENKINS, L.J.,
" his acts must be judged by reference to their own nature and by
reference to his declared intentions at the material time ",[11] and judged
by this test, there was, as we have seen, a clear approbation.

The Court of Appeal in *W. v. W.* deliberately left open the question
whether a petitioner by declaring his intention could preserve his right
to have the marriage annulled.[12] Whilst no injustice might be
worked on the respondent in such a case, it might still be considered
contrary to public policy to grant the petition in such circumstances,
particularly in view of the interests of the innocent child.[13]

Delay.—Mere delay in presenting the petition will not necessarily bar
the remedy.[14] Whether it does will depend on the reason for it and the
petitioner's attitude to the marriage, and he is likely to be unsuccessful
if he has cohabited with the respondent for some time apparently
acquiescing in an unconsummated marriage. Thus, in *Scott* v. *Scott*[15]
it was held that a husband could not obtain a decree after he had
been content with a marriage without sexual intercourse for some
five years and now sought relief in order to marry another woman.
But a much longer delay will not bar the petitioner if it can be
satisfactorily explained, particularly if there is evidence of continuing

---

[9]*Per* HODSON, L.J., in *W. v. W.*, [1952] 1 All E.R. 858, 866, C.A.; [1952] P. 152,
168. *Cf. Morgan* v. *Morgan*, [1959] 1 All E.R. 539; [1959] P. 92.

[10][1952] 1 All E.R. 858, C.A.; [1952] P. 152. For the facts, see *ante*, p. 63.

[11]At pp. 865 and 166. See also EVERSHED, M.R., at pp. 863 and 161, and HODSON,
L.J., at pp. 865-866 and 168 respectively.

[12]At pp. 863, 161 (*per* EVERSHED, M.R.), and 865, 165 (*per* JENKINS, L.J.).

[13]Hence the Royal Commission and the Departmental Committee on Human
Artificial Insemination both recommended that the spouses' consent to the artificial
insemination of the wife should always be a bar: Cmd. 9678, paras. 281-287; Cmnd. 1105,
paras. 104-108, 156.

[14]*G.* v. *M.* (1885), 10 App. Cas. 171, 189, H.L. But if the facts are in dispute, the
burden of proof on the petitioner will be heavier the longer the delay: *ibid.*

[15][1959] 1 All E.R. 531; [1959] P. 103, n. See also *W. v. R.* (1876), 1 P.D. 405.

complaints or separation. In *Clifford* v. *Clifford*[16] the husband did not petition on the grounds of his wife's incapacity or wilful refusal to consummate the marriage for 27 years. For the first 18 years he used every proper means to overcome his wife's aversion to the sexual act. He then left her, and the further delay was due to his saving up so that he would have enough money to commence the proceedings. He admitted that he had a further reason for petitioning when he did, *viz.* that he would be retiring in three or four years time and would not then be in a position to keep both himself and the respondent. It was held that there was no bar to his petition. The delay was reasonably explicable so long as the husband was still seeking to achieve consummation, and the further period of nine years was also explained by his having to save up to bring the petition. In these circumstances the fact that he had an additional reason for wanting to have the marriage annulled did not prevent him from obtaining the remedy that he sought.

Acceptance of material benefits.—If the petitioner, knowing that he can obtain a decree of nullity, continues to accept material benefits to which he would be entitled only on the assumption that the marriage is valid, he may then be estopped from asserting that it is voidable.[17] In *Tindall* v. *Tindall*[18] the husband's lodging £15 as security for the wife's costs on her appeal from the magistrates' court could be said to be a pecuniary benefit to the petitioning wife; a more obvious case would occur if a petitioning wife had continued to accept income from a trust in the wife's favour in a marriage settlement.

Decree inequitable or contrary to public policy.—It is frequently said that the decree will not be granted if to do so would be inequitable or contrary to public policy.[19] Whilst most of the cases would probably fall into one of the preceding categories, there might be some which do not and yet where the decree might be refused. Thus, although a pre-marital agreement between the parties that they shall not have sexual intercourse is contrary to public policy and therefore not binding on them,[20] it may nevertheless preclude either from obtaining a decree of nullity if the marriage is in fact never consummated;[1] and if one of them is old, infirm or seriously crippled, the marriage might well be on this understanding, express or implied. Again in *Clifford* v. *Clifford*[2] COHEN, L.J., expressly reserved the question whether the husband would have been barred if his sole

---

[16][1948] 1 All E.R. 394, C.A.; [1948] P. 187. See also *G.* v. *G.*, [1960] 3 All E.R. 56; [1961] P. 87 (decree granted after twelve years during which time husband never expressed satisfaction with the marriage and wished wife to have operation which would have enabled her to consummate it).

[17]*G.* v. *M.* (1885), 10 App. Cas. 171, H.L.; *Nash* v. *Nash*, [1940] 1 All E.R. 206, 215; [1940] P. 60, 72.

[18][1953] 1 All E.R. 139, 144, C.A.; [1953] P. 63, 73. For the facts, see *ante*, p. 63.

[19]*G.* v. *M.*, (*ante*), at p. 198; *Tindall* v. *Tindall*, (*supra*), at pp. 143, 147, 148, and 72, 76-78, 79, respectively.

[20]*Cf. Brodie* v. *Brodie*, [1917] P. 271 (*post*, p. 135, n.[5]).

[1]*Morgan* v. *Morgan*, [1959] 1 All E.R. 539; [1959] P. 92.

[2] [1948] 1 All E.R. 394, 399, C.A.; [1948] P. 187, 197. *Cf. W.* v. *R.* (1876), 1 P.D. 405. The petitioner's adultery is not necessarily a bar although it may be a relevant factor to be considered with others: *G.* v. *M.*, (*ante*).

motive had been to get rid of his financial liability to maintain his wife.

This is particularly relevant if the petitioner relies on his own impotence, for justice demands that the court should take into account the respondent's attitude and reaction to the situation for which he is in no way responsible. This occurred in *Pettit* v. *Pettit*.[3] The marriage had never been consummated owing to the husband's impotence, although a child had been born as the result of *fecundatio ab extra*. Some 20 years after the solemnization the husband left the wife and twelve months later, having discovered for the first time that a spouse may petition for nullity on the grounds of his own impotence, he commenced the present proceedings. Bearing in mind that the wife had given 20 years of her life to the petitioner and had brought up his child and that a decree would embarrass her on both financial and religious grounds, the Court of Appeal held that it would be inequitable to grant a decree even though the husband had acted promptly on discovering that he had grounds for having the marriage annulled.

Collusion.—Collusion is apparently an absolute bar to a petition for nullity although in practice it is very rarely pleaded. Until 1970 it was a bar to divorce and the law on the subject has been developed in this connection.

The essence of collusion is that the initiation or conduct of the suit has been in some measure procured or determined by an agreement or bargain between the parties,[4] and the reason that it is a bar is that the existence of such an agreement raises doubts whether the decree would be granted on the merits at all. It is immaterial whether the bargain is struck by the parties personally or through their agents,[5] but if there is no agreement there can be no collusion. Hence the fact that the respondent wants to secure his release too and therefore does not defend the proceedings will not amount to collusion in the absence of any agreement to that effect[6] for otherwise the petitioner would be prejudiced by the respondent's anxiety to see the decree granted. Nor can there be collusion if the parties never come to an agreement but one acts independently of any bribe or inducement held out by the other.[7]

An agreement is clearly collusive if its purpose is to enable the petitioner to obtain a decree for which there are no grounds at all, for example if the respondent agrees not to defend a petition based on his inability or refusal to consummate the marriage when it has in fact been consummated. In most cases the basis of the bargain will be a monetary consideration, and there has been held to be collusion if the respondent pays the petitioner a sum of money to prevent the latter's abandoning the petition,[8] or if the respondent husband agrees not to

---

[3][1962] 3 All E.R. 37, C.A.; [1963] P. 177. See further, *ante*, p. 62. Contrast *Mogridge* v. *Mogridge* (1965), 109 Sol. Jo. 814, C.A.

[4]*Gosling* v. *Gosling*, [1967] 2 All E.R. 510, C.A., at pp. 513-514 and 520; [1968] P. 1, at pp. 11 and 22.

[5]As in *Lowndes* v. *Lowndes*, [1950] 1 All E.R. 999; [1950] P. 223, where the sum of £2,000 was paid not directly by the husband to the wife but by his brother to her friend.

[6]*Gethin* v. *Gethin* (1861), 31 L.J.P.M. & A. 43, 45.

[7]*Beattie* v. *Beattie*, [1938] 2 All E.R. 74; [1938] P. 99.

[8]*Lowndes* v. *Lowndes*, (*supra*).

defend in consideration of the wife's undertaking not to ask for financial provision.[9] It is not necessary that the benefit should be conferred on one of the parties personally and there will be collusion if the petitioner is induced to bring the proceedings by the respondent's promise to settle a sum of money on a child.[10]

When nullity proceedings are pending, the spouses will often wish to make arrangements about such matters as the maintenance of the wife and the disposal of the matrimonial home and its contents. It is the policy of the law to enable them to save time and costs by coming to an agreement themselves if possible,[11] but it is in respect of these very matters that the danger of collusion is highest because an unscrupulous spouse may well hold out a financial inducement to the other to bring a petition or not to oppose it. An agreement of this sort will not be collusive if it does not affect the conduct of the suit, so that if a wife proposes to petition anyway, the husband's agreeing to pay her £5 a week by way of maintenance is not objectionable. Even if it does affect the parties' conduct, earlier cases emphasised the necessity of establishing dishonesty or a corrupt intention before the bargain could be called collusive,[12] but there seems to be no need for such an element to be present.[13] If a husband agrees to pay the wife an agreed sum (which the court would accept as a proper figure) by way of financial provision if she petitions for nullity, it cannot be said that there is any attempt to deceive the court, but the agreement will nevertheless be collusive as it prompts the initiation of the suit.

If collusion is established,[14] it is still an absolute bar to the granting of a decree as it was in the ecclesiastical courts. But if the effect of the agreement was entirely spent before the proceedings were begun, so that the parties' conduct was in no way influenced by it, a petition may still be brought.[15] Similarly, even though the petition is dismissed on the ground of collusion, there is nothing to prevent another petition being presented later free from collusion.[16]

Estoppel.—Some controversy has recently arisen over the question how far the parties to a marriage, which may be proved *aliunde* to be void or voidable, may be estopped from asserting its invalidity: a

---

[9] *Emanuel* v. *Emanuel*, [1945] 2 All E.R. 494; [1946] P. 115; *Mulhouse* v. *Mulhouse*, [1964] 2 All E.R. 50; [1966] P. 39.

[10] *Churchward* v. *Churchward*, [1895] P. 7.

[11] *Cf.* the provisions enabling them to refer agreements to the court in divorce proceedings, *post*, pp. 217-218.

[12] *Per* Bucknill, L.J., in *Scott* v. *Scott*, [1913] P. 52, 54 (" dishonest purpose "); *per* Willmer, J., in *Lowndes* v. *Lowndes*, (*supra*), at pp. 1005 and 231, respectively (" tending to pervert the course of justice "); *per* Scarman, J., in *Noble* v. *Noble* (*No. 2*), [1964] 1 All E.R. 577, 581; [1964] P. 250, 257 (" corrupt intention ").

[13] *Gosling* v. *Gosling*, [1967] 2 All E.R. 510, 521, C.A.; [1968] P. 1, 22-23, *per* Sachs, L.J. *Cf.* Willmer, L.J., at pp. 515 and 13-14, and Danckwerts, L.J., at pp. 520 and 21, respectively.

[14] There is a presumption of innocence so that the petitioner is not bound to prove absence of collusion unless the pleadings or evidence points to the contrary: *Emanuel* v. *Emanuel*, (*supra*).

[15] *Watkin* v. *Watkin* (1919), 122 L.T. 225.

[16] *Churchward* v. *Churchward*, (*supra*), at p. 31; *Sandler* v. *Sandler*, [1934] P. 149, C.A., at pp. 157, 160. Now that collusion is no longer a bar in divorce proceedings, the Law Commission recommend that it should be abolished as a bar to a petition for nullity: Law Com. No. 33, paras. 37-38.

problem that is in some respects akin to that of approbation. Suppose, for example, that a married man goes through a form of marriage with a woman after representing to her that he is a bachelor or a widower; if he leaves her unsupported, may he raise the nullity of this marriage as a defence to any action brought by her for maintenance? Alternatively, if previous matrimonial proceedings have been brought between the same parties on the assumption that the marriage is valid, may either subsequently petition for nullity or put the validity of the marriage in issue in subsequent proceedings?

It is submitted that a distinction must be drawn between estoppel by conduct and estoppel *per rem judicatam* for this purpose. In the former case the better view seems to be that the parties by their own conduct cannot prevent the court from enquiring into the real state of affairs and declaring what their true status is. In *Miles* v. *Chilton*,[17] where the husband petitioned for nullity on the ground that the wife was already married at the time of the ceremony in question, DR. LUSHINGTON held that the wife's averment that the husband had deceived her into believing that she had already been divorced by her first husband was no answer to the petition. The position with respect to estoppel *per rem judicatam* is more complicated. Decrees of nullity, divorce and judicial separation are all judgments *in rem* and bind not only the parties but the whole world. Hence nobody can assert the validity of a marriage after a decree of nullity has been pronounced or deny its validity after a decree of judicial separation.[18] If a petition for nullity, divorce or judicial separation is dismissed, this will create an estoppel *inter partes* only. If, for example, H unsuccessfully petitions for a decree of nullity on the ground that the other party to the marriage, W, was married to another man at the time of the ceremony, neither H nor W can now assert that the marriage is void for this reason, although a third person who was not a party to the proceedings or privy to them could still do so.[19] If the outcome of any other proceedings between the parties in the High Court rests on the validity of their marriage, this will presumably also create an estoppel *inter partes*, so that neither of them could assert that the marriage was void if, for example, successful proceedings for maintenance had been previously brought under section 6 of the Matrimonial Proceedings and Property Act.[1] It has been held that proceedings before magistrates cannot create an estoppel in the High Court[2] or, presumably, in a county court. Although

---

[17](1849), 1 Rob. Eccl. 684. The contrary view stated obiter by the Divisional Court in *Bullock* v. *Bullock*, [1960] 2 All E.R. 307, at pp. 309 and 313, does not seem to be supported by the authorities there cited.

[18]See Tolstoy, *Marriage by Estoppel*, 84 L.Q.R. 245, and the authorities there cited, particularly *Woodland* v. *Woodland*, [1928] P. 169.

[19]The problem arose in an acute form in *Wilkins* v. *Wilkins*, [1896] P. 108, C.A. On the wife's petition for divorce the respondent husband's answer had been that the marriage was void because the wife's first husband was alive at the time of his marriage to the petitioner. This fact was expressly found against him. The first husband later returned to England and the second husband then petitioned for nullity. It was held that the first judgment estopped him from doing so, but the Court of Appeal solved the problem by giving him leave to apply for a new trial on that issue.

[1]See *post*, p. 427.

[2]*Hayward* v. *Hayward*, [1961] 1 All E.R. 236, 243; [1961] P. 152, 161.

non-matrimonial proceedings in a county court have been held to create an estoppel in a magistrates' court, it has been stated obiter that they cannot bind the High Court in matrimonial proceedings.[3]

When questions of status are involved, estoppel inevitably creates difficulties. There may be little justification for permitting either party to assert the invalidity of a marriage when he or she has already had an opportunity of doing so but, as PHILLIMORE, J., said in *Hayward* v. *Hayward*,[4] public policy demands that, when status is in issue, the courts should declare the truth unencumbered by technical rules. At the moment a man may be validly married to one woman but estopped from denying that he is also married to a second: a result no less absurd than the fact that a stranger may be able to show that a marriage is void whilst, as between themselves, the parties are prevented from doing so.

Retrospective Effect of Decrees of Nullity.—As we have already seen, a decree of nullity is merely declaratory where the marriage is void *ab initio*. Hence, all children of the union are illegitimate at common law (although they may now be legitimate by statute)[5] and if, for example, money has been paid or property has been transferred to one of the parties on the assumption that he or she is the spouse of the other, it may be recovered on the ground that the transaction was void because of a mistake of fact. Where the marriage is voidable only, the decree again declares the parties never to have been married at all. The consequence is that before the decree the parties are regarded as husband and wife both in law and in fact, whilst after the decree absolute they are deemed in law never to have been married at all. The logical application of this anomalous doctrine has produced somewhat startling results. At common law the children of a voidable marriage were automatically bastardised by the decree, although their status of legitimacy is now preserved by statute.[6] All the trusts under a marriage settlement also automatically fail and the interest of the person entitled before the solemnization of the marriage revives.[7] Similarly, if a widow remarries and this second marriage is annulled, she reverts to the status of her former husband's widow and may therefore claim an annuity payable to her *dum vidua*.[8]

A most striking example of the application of this doctrine is to be found in the decision of LORD MERRIVALE, P., in *Newbould* v. *A.-G.*[9]

---

[3] *Whittaker* v. *Whittaker*, [1939] 3 All E.R. 833, 837. Presumably undefended matrimonial proceedings in a county court will raise an estoppel in all courts; they have been held to create an estoppel in non-matrimonial proceedings in the High Court: *Razelos* v. *Razelos*, [1969] 3 All E.R. 929.

[4] [1961] 1 All E.R. 236, 241-242; [1961] P. 152, 158-159. It is submitted, however, that the learned judge did not sufficiently differentiate between estoppels *per rem judicatam* and estoppels *in pais*. In *Taylor* v. *Taylor* [1965] 1 All E.R. 872, 875; [1967] P. 25, 29, it was conceded that no estoppel of any kind would bind the court but the point was not argued.

[5] See the provisions of the Legitimacy Act 1959, s. 2 (*post*, p. 237).

[6] See *post*, pp. 238-239.

[7] *Re Wombwell's Settlement*, [1922] 2 Ch. 298; *Re Ames' Settlement*, [1946] 1 All E.R. 689; [1946] Ch. 217. *Cf. P.* v. *P.*, [1916] 2 I.R. 400.

[8] *Re D'Altroy's Will Trusts*, [1968] 1 All E.R. 181. The point had been left open by the Court of Appeal in *Re Eaves*, [1939] 4 All E.R. 260; [1940] Ch. 109.

[9] [1931] P. 75. See Jackson, *Formation and Annulment of Marriage*, 2nd Ed., 92 *et seq.*

F, who was at the time married to K, had a son by M. The marriage between F and K was subsequently annulled on the grounds of K's inability to consummate it and F then married M. It was held that the marriage between F and M legitimated the son notwithstanding the former provision in the Legitimacy Act that no one could be legitimated under that Act if either parent was at the time of his birth married to a third person, for the effect of the decree was that F was now regarded as never having been married to K at all.[10]

But after the decision of the Court of Appeal in *De Reneville* v. *De Reneville*,[11] there was a judicial tendency to regard decrees of nullity in respect of voidable marriages more like decrees of divorce. In *R.* v. *Algar*[12] after a decree had been pronounced on the ground of the husband's impotence, it was discovered that he had been drawing on the wife's bank account by forging cheques in her name, and he was prosecuted and convicted of forgery. The wife gave evidence against him which she would have been incompetent to do had the marriage been dissolved and not annulled.[13] By analogy, the Court of Criminal Appeal held that she was incompetent after the decree of nullity. Similarly in *Wiggins* v. *Wiggins*,[14] W obtained a decree nisi of nullity on the ground of her husband's impotence. Before the decree was made absolute, she went through a form of marriage with X. It was held that this marriage was void on the grounds of bigamy and that this defect was not retrospectively cured by the decree absolute. Later, however, a swing back to the earlier view was to be seen in *Re D'Altroy's Will Trusts*.[15] A testatrix left a life interest in her residuary estate to L, so long as he remained her late daughter's widower. L remarried before the testatrix's death but this marriage was annulled on the ground of L's impotence before the estate was distributed. PENNYCUICK, J., held that the decree operated retrospectively so that L reverted to his former status and was entitled to the bequest.

At the moment the courts are clearly applying two inconsistent principles. Although, it is submitted, the cases relied on in *R.* v. *Algar* are all distinguishable,[16] it is significant that neither this case nor *Wiggins* v. *Wiggins* appears to have been cited to the court in *Re D'Altroy's Will Trusts*. It remains to be seen whether they will apply the strict logic of the latter or follow the more realistic approach of the former in the future. A possible compromise is to hold that the

---

[10]For legitimation *per subsequens matrimonium*, see *post*, pp. 239-241.

[11][1948] 1 All E.R. 56, C.A.; [1948] P. 100 (*post*, p. 84).

[12][1953] 2 All E.R. 1381, C.C.A.; [1954] 1 Q.B. 279.

[13]See *post*, p. 101.

[14][1958] 2 All E.R. 555, not following the Northern Irish case of *Mason* v. *Mason*, [1944] N.I. 134, where on similar facts ANDREWS, C.J., held that the second marriage was valid.

[15][1968] 1 All E.R. 181, followed in *Re Rodwell*, [1969] 3 All E.R. 1363; [1970] Ch. 726 (daughter whose voidable marriage had been annulled before her father's death held to be " a daughter who has not been married " for the purpose of the Inheritance (Family Provision) Act). For a trenchant criticism, see Tiley, 32 M.L.R. 210.

[16]*Adams* v. *Adams*, which turned on a question of consideration in a separation agreement (*post*, p. 141); *De Reneville* v. *De Reneville*, where the court was considering the parties' status before a decree was pronounced at all (*post*, p. 84); *Re Eaves*, (see *infra*) where GODDARD, L.J., (as he then was) expressly left open the very point which he was called upon to decide in *R.* v. *Algar*, [1939] 4 All E.R. at p. 268; [1940] Ch. at p. 123.

parties must be regarded as having been married between the ceremony and the decree absolute but that, after the decree, they revert to their pre-marital status. In this way *R. v. Algar* (which was concerned with the wife's status at the time of the commission of the offence), *Wiggins v. Wiggins* (which turned on the wife's status at the time of her marriage to X) and *Re D'Altroy's Will Trusts* (insofar as it turned on L's status at the time of the application) could all be reconciled.[17] It must be confessed, however, that this solution is neither elegant nor logical.

Concluded Transactions.—There is one clear exception to the rule that a decree of nullity acts retrospectively. Before the marriage is annulled money may have been paid and property distributed on the assumption (valid at the time) that the parties to the marriage were husband and wife. To attempt to set these transactions aside might not only produce chaos but also work substantial injustice, so that the rule has been evolved that " transactions which have been concluded, things which have been done, during the period [of the voidable marriage] on the footing of the existence of that status, cannot be undone or reopened ".[18] Thus, in *Re Eaves*[19] property was bequeathed to the testator's son subject to a life interest in favour of the plaintiff so long as she remained the testator's widow. Six years after the testator's death the widow remarried, and on the eve of her second marriage she permitted the son to sell the property and to use the proceeds for his own purposes on the assumption that her own interest would cease. The second marriage was subsequently annulled on the grounds of the husband's impotence, and the widow then claimed a life interest in the proceeds of the sale. It was held that she must fail, for the sale was a concluded transaction carried out on the footing that the second marriage was valid.

What " transactions and things " are included in this category are not clear, but it is submitted that any out and out payment of money (whether capital or income) or assignment of property would come within the exception.[20]

B. GROUNDS ON WHICH A MARRIAGE WILL BE VOID

Lack of Capacity.—Obviously lack of capacity to marry will *ipso facto* render the marriage void. Whether there is such a lack of capacity must be determined by reference to the pre-marital *lex domicilii* of each

---

[17]*Quaere* whether the issue in *Re D'Altroy's Will Trusts* should not have been L's status at the testatrix's death. The Law Commission suggest that this solution should be adopted by statute: Law Com. No. 33, para 25. If it were adopted, *Re Rodwell* would also be correctly decided, but *Newbould* v. *A.-G.* would have to be regarded as wrong.
[18]*Per* CLAUSON, L.J., in *Re Eaves*, [1939] 4 All E.R. 260, C.A.; [1940] Ch. 109, 117.
[19][1939] 4 All E.R. 260, C.A.; [1940] Ch. 109, following *Dodworth* v. *Dale*, [1936] 2 K.B. 503. This case is complicated by the fact that the widow, having acquiesced in the sale of the property, could not be permitted in equity to go back on the transaction
[20]In *Dodworth* v. *Dale*, (*supra*), it was held that an income tax marriage allowance was not recoverable by the Crown after the marriage had been annulled. In *Re D'Altroy's Will Trusts*, (*ante*), where the trustees held both the capital and the accumulated income, PENNYCUICK, J., ordered the whole of the accumulated income to be paid over to the beneficiary whose marriage had been annulled.

party. If the relevant law is English, the marriage will be void if either party is under the age of 16 or is already married, or if the parties are related within the prohibited degrees.[1]

Formal Defects.—Whether failure to comply with the formal requirements relating to the marriage ceremony will make the marriage void must be determined by reference to the *lex loci celebrationis*.[2]

If the marriage is solemnized in England, it is not every defect in the formalities laid down in the Marriage Act that will render the ceremony a nullity. Whilst public policy requires that these formalities should be strictly observed, the consequences of avoiding any marriage where there was some technical defect, however slight, would be socially even more undesirable. English law has effected a compromise between these conflicting demands of public policy with the result that some formal defects will not render the marriage void at all, whilst in the case of the rest the marriage will be void only if *both* parties contracted it with knowledge of the defect. In other words, it is impossible for a person in England innocently to contract a marriage which is void because of a formal defect. The real sanction is afforded by the criminal law, for if a party knowingly fails to comply with the Marriage Act, he will normally have to make a false oath or declaration which is punishable under the Perjury Act of 1911.[3] This should adequately safeguard the marriage law without prejudicing the position of the innocent spouse.

Defects which will never invalidate a Marriage.—The Marriage Act 1949 specifically enacts that a marriage shall not be rendered void on any of the following grounds:[4]

(a) That any of the statutory residence requirements was not fulfilled (whether for the purpose of the publication of banns or of obtaining a common licence or superintendent registrar's certificate);

(b) That the necessary consents had not been given in the case of the marriage of a minor by common licence or a superintendent registrar's certificate;[5]

(c) That the registered building in which the parties were married had not been certified as a place of religious worship or was not the usual place of worship of either of them; or

---

[1] See *ante*, chap. 2, sec. D. In *Corbett* v. *Corbett*, [1970] 2 All E.R. 33, a decree was pronounced when the parties were of the same sex (see *ante*, p. 24). *Quaere* whether there is even the simulacrum of a marriage to be annulled. See further Law Com. No. 33, paras. 30-32. A marriage may also be void under the Royal Marriages Act 1772, see *ante*, p. 23, n.[16].

[2] See *ante*, pp. 19-22.

[3] S. 3. If a material alteration is made to any document (*e.g.*, the date on a superintendent registrar's certificate), this will be punishable under the Forgery Act 1913. See also the Marriage Act 1949, s. 75, and the Marriage (Registrar General's Licence) Act 1970, s. 16 (punishment of offences relating to the solemnization of marriages).

[4] Ss. 24 and 48. See also s. 47 (3) (authorisation of marriage according to the usages of the Society of Friends), s. 71 (evidence of marriages in naval, military and air force chapels) and s. 72 (usual place of worship), and the Marriage (Registrar General's Licence) Act 1970, s. 12 (marriages solemnized on the Registrar General's licence).

[5] The Act refers to consents only where the parties are married on the authority of a superintendent registrar's certificate, but the same is true where they are married by common licence: *R.* v. *Birmingham* (1828), 8 B. & C. 29.

(d) That an incorrect declaration had been made in order to obtain permission to marry in a registered building in a registration district in which neither party resided on the grounds that there was not there a building in which marriages were solemnized according to the rites of the religious belief which one of them professed.

Although these are the only formal defects which the Act says shall not invalidate a marriage, it is a general rule that, if the irregularity is not one of those which the Act expressly states may invalidate it, the defect will never make the ceremony a nullity.[6] Hence, for example, even though the parties are aware that two witnesses are not present at the ceremony, the marriage will still be perfectly valid.[7]

Defects which may invalidate a Marriage.—In the following cases only will a failure to comply with the provisions of the Marriage Act make the marriage void, and then only if *both* parties were aware of the irregularity at the time of the ceremony.[8]

In the case of a marriage according to the rites of the Church of England (otherwise than by special licence), the following come within the rule:[9]

(a) That the marriage was solemnized in a place other than a church or chapel in which banns may be published.

(b) That banns had not been duly published, a common licence obtained or a superintendent registrar's certificate duly issued. Since failure to comply with the residence qualification will never invalidate a marriage, an undue publication of banns will usually occur when one or both of the parties have been wrongly named or where there has been no publication at all.[10] But the object of giving publicity to the intended union (which is the purpose of the publication of banns) does not apply to a licence or certificate; so that provided that either of these was issued for the marriage of the parties which in fact took place, the marriage will not be void even though one of the parties was designated by a wholly false name.[11]

(c) That, in the case of the marriage of a minor by banns, a person entitled to do so had publicly dissented from the marriage at the time of the publication of the banns.[12]

(d) That more than three months had elapsed from the completion of the publication of the banns, the grant of a common licence or the entry of the notice of marriage in the superintendent registrar's marriage notice book, as the case may be.

---

[6]*Campbell* v. *Corley* (1856), 28 L.T. O.S. 109.

[7]*Campbell* v. *Corley*, (*supra*); *Wing* v. *Taylor* (1861), 2 Sw. & Tr. 278.

[8]The Act speaks of " knowingly and wilfully " intermarrying, and it is not clear whether it is sufficient that both parties should know as a question of fact that the formality is not complied with or whether in addition they must know as a question of law that the defect will invalidate the marriage. The point was left open by LORD PENZANCE in *Greaves* v. *Greaves* (1872), L.R. 2 P. & D. 423, 424-425.

[9]Marriage Act 1949, s. 25.

[10]But there would presumably be an undue publication, *e.g.*, if the banns were not published by a clergyman or authorised lay reader.

[11]*Bevan* v. *M'Mahon* (1861), 2 Sw. & Tr. 230; *Plummer* v. *Plummer*, [1917] P. 163, C.A.; *R.* v. *Lamb* (1934), 50 T.L.R. 310, C.C.A.

[12]Contrast the position where the marriage of a minor is by common licence or a superintendent registrar's certificate: see *supra*.

(e) That, in the case of a marriage by superintendent registrar's certificate, the ceremony was performed in a church or chapel other than that specified in the notice of marriage and certificate.

(f) That the marriage was solemnized by a person who was not in Holy Orders.

In the case of other marriages, the following come within the rule:[13]

(a) That due notice of marriage had not been given to the superintendent registrar.[14]

(b) That a certificate and, where it is necessary, a licence had not been duly issued.

(c) That more than three months had elapsed since the entry of the notice in the superintendent registrar's marriage notice book.

(d) That the marriage was not solemnized in the building specified in the notice and certificate.

(e) That the marriage was not solemnized in the presence of a superintendent registrar and a registrar or (if it was solemnized in a registered building) in the presence of a registrar or an authorised person.

C. GROUNDS ON WHICH A MARRIAGE WILL BE VOIDABLE

The cases in which a marriage will be voidable can be divided into two: those where it has not been consummated owing to one party's impotence or the respondent's wilful refusal, and those where the marriage, although consummated, is voidable on some other ground laid down by statute.[15]

I. NON-CONSUMMATION

Meaning of " Consummation ".—Even in canon law a marriage was not always finally and irrevocably indissoluble until the union had been consummated by the sexual act. A marriage is said to be consummated as soon as the parties have sexual intercourse after the solemnization.[16] The distinction between the act of intercourse and the possibility of that act resulting in the birth of a child must be kept clear: once the parties have had intercourse the marriage is consummated

---

[13]Marriage Act 1949, s. 49. The same rules apply *mutatis mutandis* if the marriage is solemnized on the authority of the Registrar General's licence: Marriage (Registrar General's Licence) Act 1970, s. 13. In particular, such a marriage will be void if the parties knowingly and wilfully intermarry more than *one* month after the entry of notice.

[14]*I.e.*, in the due form. Notice in a false name does not invalidate the notice or the marriage: see *supra*.

[15]The possibility of a further ground, *viz.* the failure of an essential condition of the marriage contract, rests solely upon the judgment of DENNING, L.J., in *Kenward* v. *Kenward*, [1950] 2 All E.R. 297, C.A.; [1951] P. 124. In that case the condition was that the parties should cohabit and it had failed because of the refusal of the Russian authorities to permit the wife, who was resident in Russia, to join her husband in England. The other members of the Court of Appeal did not consider this point as they held that the marriage was void owing to formal defects. Attractive as DENNING, L.J.'s views are, it is submitted that the necessity of relying upon events subsequent to the ceremony logically precludes them from being grounds for nullity in the absence of statutory authority.

[16]Not *before* the solemnization. Hence the marriage is not automatically consummated by reason of the fact that the parties have had pre-marital intercourse: *cf.* *Dredge* v. *Dredge*, [1947] 1 All E.R. 29.

even though one or both are sterile,[17] and conversely, if they have not
had intercourse, the birth of a child as the result of fecundation *ab extra*
or artificial insemination will not amount to consummation.[18]

In order to amount to consummation, the intercourse must, in the
words of DR. LUSHINGTON in *D——E* v. *A——G*[19] be " ordinary and
complete, and not partial and imperfect ". Hence, as in *D——E* v.
A——G, there will be no consummation if the husband does not
achieve full penetration in the normal sense. The necessity of complete
intercourse has raised difficulties where the spouses use some form of
contraception. In 1945 the Court of Appeal held in *Cowen* v. *Cowen*[20]
that there had been no consummation where the husband had invariably
either worn a contraceptive sheath or practised *coitus interruptus*,[1]
but two years later the House of Lords in *Baxter* v. *Baxter*[2] overruled
at least the first part of the decision in *Cowen* v. *Cowen* by holding that
the marriage had been consummated notwithstanding the husband's
use of a sheath. As LORD JOWITT, L.C., pointed out, the possibility of
conception is irrelevant to the question of consummation and when
Parliament passed the Matrimonial Causes Act in 1937 (the statute on
which the petition was based) it was common knowledge that many
people, especially young married couples, used contraceptives and that
in common parlance this would amount to consummation.[3] The decision in *Baxter* v. *Baxter* obviously applies if either party uses any form
of mechanical or chemical contraception, but the House of Lords
deliberately left open the question whether *coitus interruptus* would
amount to consummation.[4] There have been three reported cases at
first instance since *Baxter* v. *Baxter*, in one of which it was held that it
did not,[5] and in the other two that it did and that since *Baxter* v.
Baxter neither branch of the decision of *Cowen* v. *Cowen* could any
longer be regarded as good law.[6] In the last of these, *Cackett* v.
Cackett,[7] HODSON, J., in holding that the marriage was consummated by *coitus interruptus*, stated that the court would be driven into
an impossible position if it tried further to define what normal sexual
intercourse was.[8] It has since been held that a marriage is consummated even though the husband is physically incapable of
ejaculation after penetration,[9] but not if he is incapable of sustaining

[17]*D——E* v. *A——G* (1845), 1 Rob. Eccl. 279; *Baxter* v. *Baxter*, [1947] 2 All E.R.
886, H.L.; [1948] A.C. 274. Otherwise, if the wife were beyond the age of child bearing,
the marriage could never be consummated.
[18]Cf. *Clarke* v. *Clarke*, [1943] 2 All E.R. 540; *L.* v. *L.*, [1949] 1 All E.R. 141;
[1949] P. 211.
[19](1845), 1 Rob. Eccl. 279, 298. See Webb and Bevan, *Source Book of Family Law*,
83-85.
[20][1945] 2 All E.R. 197, C.A.; [1946] P. 36.
[1]*I.e.*, deliberate withdrawal before ejaculation.
[2][1947] 2 All E.R. 886, H.L.; [1948] A.C. 274.
[3]At pp. 890 and 892, 286 and 290, respectively.
[4]At pp. 888 and 283, respectively.
[5]*Grimes* v. *Grimes*, [1948] 2 All E.R. 147; [1948] P. 323.
[6]*White* v. *White*, [1948] 2 All E.R. 151; [1948] P. 330; *Cackett* v. *Cackett*, [1950]
1 All E.R. 677; [1950] P. 253.
[7][1950] 1 All E.R. 677; [1950] P. 253.
[8]At pp. 680 and 258-9, respectively.
[9]*R.* v. *R.*, [1952] 1 All E.R. 1194.

an erection for more than a very short period of time after penetration.[10]
Perhaps inevitably the courts have tended to concentrate on the
husband's role during intercourse,[11] and on the authority of these cases
it is suggested that the marriage is consummated as soon as the
husband achieves full penetration (unless this is only transient) and
that ejaculation is irrelevant.

Inability to Consummate.—Inability to consummate the marriage may be due to physiological or to psychological causes and
may be either general or merely *quoad* the particular spouse. It has
long been accepted that in any of these cases inability of one spouse
to consummate the particular marriage makes the marriage voidable at
the option of the other and the Court of Appeal laid it down in *Harthan*
v. *Harthan*[12] that a spouse may petition in reliance on his own impotence. This decision is a natural corollary from the premise that one
of the objects in giving relief where the marriage cannot be consummated is to prevent the formation of an adulterous union[13] and the
recognition of the fact that a spouse may be impotent only *quoad*
the other.[14]

It is generally said that relief will be granted only if the impotence
is incurable, but today " incurable " in this context has received a very
extended meaning and it will be considered incurable not only if it
is wholly incapable of any remedy but also if it can be cured only by an
operation attended by danger or, in any event, if it is improbable that
the operation will be successful or the party refuses to undergo it.[15]
But where the petitioner relies upon his own impotence, it is submitted
that the court might well take the view that he should not be allowed
to complain of the situation if the impediment could be removed
without danger to himself.[16]

The petitioner's knowledge of the *respondent's* impotence before
marriage is not necessarily a bar to the petition,[17] although it is submitted that it should be strong evidence of approbation.[18] But if he
relies upon *his own* impotence, he will fail if he was aware of it beforehand and deceived the respondent, who may then plead the *suppressio*

---

[10] *W.* (*otherwise K.*) v. *W.*, [1967] 3 All E.R. 178 n.
[11] Thus there can be consummation even though the wife's vagina has been artificially
extended (or, perhaps, wholly constructed): *S.* v. *S.* (*otherwise W.*) (*No. 2*), [1962] 3 All
E.R. 55, C.A.; [1963] P. 37. But she must be biologically female to begin with: *Corbett*
v. *Corbett*, [1970] 2 All E.R. 33.
[12] [1948] 2 All E.R. 639, C.A.; [1949] P. 115.
[13] See *D——E* v. *A——G* (1845), 1 Rob. Eccl. 279, 299.
[14] See *C.* v. *C.*, [1921] P. 399. Hence if each is impotent *quoad* the other, either
may petition: *G.* v. *G.*, [1912] P. 173.
[15] *S.* v. *S.* (*orse C.*), [1954] 3 All E.R. 736, 741; [1956] P. 1, 11; *M.* v. *M.*, [1956]
3 All E.R. 769; [1957] P. 139. *Cf. L.* v. *L.* (1882), 7 P.D. 16; *G.* v. *G.* (1908), 25 T.L.R. 328.
[16] A wilful refusal to take treatment in such a case might amount to wilful refusal
to consummate the marriage: *S.* v. *S.* (*orse C.*), [1954] 3 All E.R. at pp. 743-4; [1956]
P. at pp. 15-16.
[17] *Nash* v. *Nash*, [1940] 1 All E.R. 206, 209; [1940] P. 60, 64-5; *J.* v. *J.*, [1947]
2 All E.R. 43, 44, C.A.; [1947] P. 158, 163, (overruled on another point by *Baxter* v.
Baxter, (*ante*)).
[18] *Cf. S.* v. *S.* (*No. 2*), [1962] 3 All E.R. 55, 63, C.A.; [1963] P. 37, 61.

veri as a bar, or apparently in any case if at the time of the marriage he knew that the respondent was also impotent.[19]

Sexual incapacity is a ground for avoiding the marriage only if it exists at the time of the solemnization and there is still no practical possibility of the marriage being consummated at the date of the hearing.[20]

Wilful Refusal to Consummate.—Before 1937 a spouse could not avoid the marriage if it remained unconsummated on account of the other's refusal to have intercourse,[1] although relief on this ground was probably in fact given in some cases in reliance on the presumption that, if the marriage had not been consummated after three years' cohabitation through no fault of the petitioner, the respondent must be impotent.[2]   The law was put on a more rational footing by the Matrimonial Causes Act 1937, which enacted that a marriage should be voidable if it had not been consummated owing to the respondent's wilful refusal to do so.[3] This connotes " a settled and definite decision come to without just excuse ", and the whole history of the marriage must be looked at.[4]   Thus in *Jodla* v. *Jodla*[5] the parties, who were both practising Roman Catholics, married in a register office on the understanding that they should not cohabit until they had gone through a ceremony of marriage according to Roman Catholic rites, and it was held that in the circumstances the husband's refusal without excuse to make arrangements for such a ceremony amounted to wilful refusal to consummate the marriage.

Refusal to have intercourse in any form will clearly come within the statute, and so may wilful refusal to take treatment (attended by no danger) to remove a physical or psychological impediment to consummation.[6]   As we have seen, there will not be a wilful refusal to consummate if one spouse insists upon the use of contraceptives or, probably, of *coitus interruptus*. But *Baxter* v. *Baxter*[7] has raised a difficulty

---

[19]*Harthan* v. *Harthan*, [1948] 2 All E.R. 639, 644, C.A.; [1949] P. 115, 129. In the latter case therefore he should petition on the ground of the respondent's impotence for the knowledge will not necessarily bar him. See Bevan, *Limitations on the Right of an Impotent Spouse to Petition for Nullity*, 76 L.Q.R. 267.

[20]*S.* v. *S. (orse W.)*, [1962] 2 All E.R. 816, C.A.; [1963] P. 162, approving *S.* v. *S. (orse C.)*, [1954] 3 All E.R. 736; [1956] P. 1. For if the party is cured or curable at the time of the hearing, he or she could not have been incurably incapable at the time of the solemnization. In Scotland it has been held that the party must have been incurable at all times since the solemnization: *M.* v. *W.*, 1966 S.L.T. 25. This is a logical extension of the rule.

[1]*Napier* v. *Napier*, [1915] P. 184, C.A.

[2]*G.* v. *M.* (1885), 10 App. Cas. 171, H.L., at pp. 189-190, 198-9. But impotence could always be proved *aliunde: ibid.* Cf. *S.* v. *S. (orse W.)*, *(supra)*, at pp. 818-819 and 171, respectively.

[3]See now Matrimonial Causes Act 1965, s. 9 (1) (a).

[4]*Per* LORD JOWITT, L.C., in *Horton* v. *Horton*, [1947] 2 All E.R. 871, 874, H.L. He left open the question whether the petitioner could succeed if he had originally refused to consummate but then changed his mind by which time the respondent had changed her mind and refused to let the petitioner have intercourse.

[5][1960] 1 All E.R. 625. *Cf. Boggins* v. *Boggins*, [1966] C.L.Y. 4041 (husband who deserted wife before consummating marriage held to have wilfully refused to do so).

[6] *S.* v. *S. (orse C.)*, [1954] 3 All E.R. 736, 743-4; [1956] P. 1, 15-16.

[7]*Ante.* For a contrary view, see Gower, *Baxter* v. *Baxter in Perspective*, 11 M.L.R. 176, particularly at 186-7.

which cannot be easily solved. Suppose the marriage is never consummated because the husband, H, refuses to use a contraceptive and the wife, W, refuses to let him have intercourse unless he does. It is difficult to see how either of them can be said to have refused to consummate, for W has been prepared to do so within the meaning given to the term by *Baxter* v. *Baxter*, and H has expressed his willingness to have intercourse in the natural way.

Once the marriage has been consummated, it will not be voidable if one spouse subsequently refuses to continue to have intercourse. In such a case, as in the case of the use of contraceptives or the practice of *coitus interruptus* against the other spouse's will, the latter's only remedy lies in divorce.

2. OTHER STATUTORY GROUNDS

The Matrimonial Causes Act of 1937 introduced three new grounds on which a marriage will now be voidable, and which are now embodied in section 9 of the Matrimonial Causes Act 1965. These are:

(a) That *either party* was at the time of the marriage (i) of unsound mind, or (ii) suffering from mental disorder within the meaning of the Mental Health Act 1959[8] of such a kind or to such an extent as to be unfitted for marriage and the procreation of children, or (iii) subject to recurrent attacks of insanity or epilepsy. The meaning of this provision was considered by ORMROD, J., in *Bennett* v. *Bennett*,[9] where he concluded that " unsoundness of mind " in (i) and " insanity " in (iii) both mean the same as " unsoundness of mind " as a former ground of divorce, namely that the party must be

> " incapable of managing himself and his affairs—provided that it is remembered that ' affairs ' include the problems of society and married life, and that the test of ability to manage affairs is that required of the reasonable man."[10]

He further held that " unfitted for marriage " in (ii) means " incapable of carrying out the ordinary duties and obligations of marriage " These grounds must be kept distinct from those on which a marriage will be void for insanity. Under the Act the petitioner is basing his petition on his own or the respondent's general state of mental health at the time of the ceremony; he may therefore obtain relief even though the party in question understood the nature of the contract he was entering into at the time.

(b) That *the respondent* was at the time of the marriage suffering from venereal disease in a communicable form.

---

[8] See the Mental Health Act 1959, s. 4.

[9] [1969] 1 All E.R. 539. The learned judge was unable to give any meaning to " unfitted for the procreation of children " except " unfitted to bring up children", which is not what the Act says.

[10] *Per Phillimore*, J., in *Whysall* v. *Whysall*, [1959] 3 All E.R. 389, 396; [1960] P. 52, 66. In *Bennett* v. *Bennett* ORMROD, J., thought that there was no appreciable difference between this and the degree of mental incompetence which makes a marriage void at common law (see *post*, p. 80). But this would make (i) redundant because either the party would have to be in that mental state at the time of the ceremony (in which case the marriage would be void) or the disorder would have to be recurrent (in which case it would come within (iii)). It is submitted that incapacity to manage one's affairs implies a less serious state of mental illness.

(c) That *the respondent wife* was at the time of the marriage pregnant by some person other than the petitioner.[11]

But the Act also imposes three important limitations on the petitioner's power to seek relief and has thus created a statutory form of approbation. First, he must have been unaware of the facts alleged at the time of the marriage. Secondly, the proceedings must be instituted within a year of the marriage. This period is arbitrary and runs automatically from the date of the marriage; there is no equitable principle to be applied to extend the period from the date of the discovery of the grounds for a decree, and if the petitioner does not discover them within the year, he will be left with no remedy in nullity at all.[12] Thirdly, no decree may be granted if the petitioner has voluntarily had sexual intercourse with the respondent since discovering the existence of the grounds for a decree. The test to be applied is objective rather than subjective in the sense that the Court of Appeal has held that the petitioner is barred if he had intercourse when in possession of facts from which a reasonable man would conclude that he had grounds for a decree even though he personally refused to draw the conclusion.[13] The wording of the Act indicates that the petitioner will be barred if he has intercourse in such circumstances even though he does not know that the law gives him any relief at all.[14]

D. LACK OF CONSENT

Since marriage is a contract, absence of consent will invalidate the ceremony. But a contract of marriage is not quite on the same footing as other contracts in this respect. In the first place, some factors which may vitiate a commercial contract (for example, fraud) will not necessarily affect a marriage at all. Secondly, whereas absence of consent will sometimes make a commercial contract void (for example, in the case of mistake) and sometimes voidable (for example, in the case of insanity), it will not necessarily have the same effect on a marriage. As marriage is a voluntary union, based upon the parties' consent, it is submitted that on general principle absence of consent (from whatever cause) should always make a marriage void.[15] This appears to have been the position in canon law, where, however, even though void, such marriages could be ratified by cohabitation after the party in question

---

[11]For the position before 1937, see *Moss* v. *Moss*, [1897] P. 263.

[12]See *Chaplin* v. *Chaplin*, [1948] 2 All E.R. 408, C.A.; [1949] P. 72. The Morton Commission recommended that the court should have a discretionary power to extend the time in special circumstances: Cmd. 9678, paras. 284-285.

[13]*Smith* v. *Smith*, [1947] 2 All E.R. 741, C.A.; [1948] P. 77. Presumably an objective test should be applied to determine whether the petitioner was aware of the material facts at the time of the marriage. A mere suspicion is not enough: *Stocker* v. *Stocker*, [1966] 2 All E.R. 147.

[14]Contra *Watts* v. *Watts* (1968), 112 Sol. Jo. 964, where LATEY, J., held that he would not be barred if he had intercourse not knowing that he had any relief at all but that he would be if he knew that the law gave him some relief even though he did not know what it was. The point was left open in *Stocker* v. *Stocker*, (*supra*). The Law Commission recommend that this limitation should be removed, that the period should be three years and that knowledge of the party's mental condition before marriage should not be a bar at all. They would also extend the three years' limitation period to marriages voidable for lack of consent. See Law Com. No. 33, paras. 76-86.

[15]This view was taken in earlier editions of this book.

recovered his sanity, discovered the mistake, or ceased to be subject to fear or duress.[16] Such a rule works justice, for in such circumstances it is wholly undesirable to permit, say, a man who has coerced a woman into marrying him to allege years later that the marriage is void or to allow a third person to impugn the legitimacy of the parties' children after their death. The anomalous rule by which an initial nullity could be turned into a valid marriage seems to have been forgotten or over-looked and—perhaps because of a desire to avoid injustice—there are an increasing number of *dicta* suggesting that, in some cases at least, absence of consent makes a marriage voidable only. At the moment, therefore, it seems safest to regard the law as doubtful and to leave open the question whether such marriages are void or voidable.[17]

We must now consider the various factors which may negative a party's consent.

Insanity.—This will affect a marriage if either party was so insane at the time of the ceremony as to be unable to understand the nature of the contract he was entering into. There is a presumption that he was capable of doing so and the burden of proof therefore lies upon the party impeaching the validity of the marriage.[18] The test to be applied was thus formulated by SINGLETON, L.J., in *In the Estate of Park*:[19]

> " Was the [person] . . . capable of understanding the nature of the contract into which he was entering, or was his mental condition such that he was incapable of understanding it? To ascertain the nature of the contract of marriage a man must be mentally capable of appreciating that it involves the responsibilities normally attaching to marriage. Without that degree of mentality, it cannot be said that he understands the nature of the contract."

Although insanity will render a commercial contract voidable only and there is an eighteenth century authority that the same is true of a marriage,[20] it is submitted that this is not good law today. There are many dicta to the contrary,[1] and in *In the Estate of Park* it was never doubted that the validity of the marriage could be put in issue after the death of one of the parties.[2]

---

[16]See Tolstoy, *Void and Voidable Marriages*, 27 M.L.R. 385, and *The Validation of Void Marriages*, 31 M.L.R. 656, and the authorities there cited.

[17]The distinction becomes vital, of course, if no steps are taken to annul the marriage. If it is ratified or approbated, it will become a valid marriage if it is voidable or if it is void and the old canon law rule is still applied in full but not if the courts hold it to be void and decline to apply the doctrine of ratification. The Law Commission recommend that they should be voidable: Law Com. No. 33, paras. 11 *et seq.*

[18]*Harrod* v. *Harrod* (1854), 1 K. & J. 4, 9. But if the person is proved to have been generally insane, there will be a presumption that he was insane at the time of the marriage and the burden of proof will consequently shift on to the party seeking to uphold its validity: *Turner* v. *Meyers* (1808), 1 Hag. Con. 414, 417.

[19][1953] 2 All E.R. 1411, 1430, C.A.; [1954] P. 112, 127. *Cf.* KARMINSKI, J. (in the Div. Court), at pp. 414 and 99; BIRKETT, L.J., at pp. 1434 and 134-5; HODSON, L.J., at pp. 1436-7 and 137 respectively; *Hunter* v. *Edney* (1881), 10 P.D. 93, 95; *Durham* v. *Durham* (1885), 10 P.D. 80, 82.

[20]*Ash's Case* (1702), Prec. Ch. 203. In *Hancock* v. *Peaty* (1867), L.R. 1 P. & D. 335, LORD PENZANCE questioned whether the petitioner could petition on the grounds of the respondent's insanity if he were aware of it at the time of the ceremony, but he expressly left the point open.

[1]*E.g., per* SIR JOHN NICHOLL in *Browning* v. *Reane* (1812), 2 Phillim. 69; *per* RONAN, L.J., in *P.* v. *P.*, [1916] 2 I.R. 400, 433.

[2]Nor was it in *Harrod* v. *Harrod, (supra),* or *In the Estate of Spier,* [1947] W.N. 46.

Drunkenness.—In the absence of any binding English authority, it is submitted that the effect of drunkenness will be the same as that of insanity and that the contract will therefore be void if the drunkenness induced temporary insanity of such a nature as to make the marriage void for that reason or otherwise rendered the party incapable of understanding the nature of the contract into which he was entering.[3] The effect of addiction to drugs would presumably be the same.

Mistake.—A mistake will affect the marriage in two cases only. First, a mistake as to the identity of the other contracting party will invalidate the contract if this results in one party's failing to marry the individual whom he or she intends to marry. In the New Zealand case of *C.* v. *C.*[4] W married H in the erroneous belief that he was a well known boxer called Miller. It was held that the marriage was not invalidated by the mistake because she married the very individual she meant to marry. Secondly, the marriage will be affected if one of the parties is mistaken as to the nature of the ceremony and does not appreciate that he is contracting a marriage. In *Valier* v. *Valier*[5] the husband, who was an Italian and whose knowledge of the English language was poor, was taken to a register office by the wife and there went through the usual form of marriage. He did not understand what was happening at the time, the parties never cohabited and the marriage was never consummated. It was held that he was entitled to a decree of nullity.

But if each party appreciates that he is going through a form of marriage with the other, no other type of mistake apparently can affect the contract.[6] Thus, it has been held that the marriage will not be invalidated by a mistake as to the monogamous or polygamous nature of the union,[7] the other party's fortune,[8] the woman's chastity,[9] or the recognition of the union by the religious denomination of the parties.[10]

Despite the dictum of LORD MERRIVALE, P., in *Valier* v. *Valier*[11] that a marriage which has been entered into when one of the parties was labouring under a mistake might subsequently be ratified, it seems that, on general principle and by analogy with the law of contract, such a marriage must be void *ab initio*.

---

[3]*Cf. Legey* v. *O'Brien* (1834), Milw. 325; *Sullivan* v. *Sullivan* (1818), 2 Hag. Con. 238, 246 (*per* SIR W. SCOTT).

[4][1942] N.Z.L.R. 356. But if A becomes engaged to B, whom she has never seen before, by correspondence, and C successfully personates B at the wedding, the marriage would be void because A intends to marry B and nobody else: *ibid.*, p. 359.

[5](1925), 133 L.T. 830. See also *Ford* v. *Stier*, [1896] P. 1, and *Kelly* v. *Kelly* (1932), 49 T.L.R. 99 (mistaken belief that ceremony was formal betrothal); *Mehta* v. *Mehta*, [1945] 2 All E.R. 690 (mistaken belief that Hindu marriage ceremony was ceremony of religious conversion).

[6]*Moss* v. *Moss*, [1897] P. 263, 271-3; *Kenward* v. *Kenward*, [1949] 2 All E.R. 959, 963; [1950] P. 71, 79 (*per* HODSON, J.); [1950] 2 All E.R. 297, 302, C.A.; [1951] P. 124, 133-4 (*per* EVERSHED, M.R.).

[7]*Kassim* v. *Kassim*, [1962] 3 All E.R. 426; [1962] P. 224.

[8]*Wakefield* v. *Mackay* (1807), 1 Hag. Con. 394, 398.

[9]Even though she is pregnant *per alium: Moss* v. *Moss*, (*supra*).

[10]*Ussher* v. *Ussher*, [1912] 2 I.R. 445.

[11]At p. 832. See also the doubts expressed by ORMROD, J., in *Kassim* v. *Kassim*, (*supra*), at pp. 429 and 229, respectively. But subsequent cohabitation might be evidence of there having been no mistake.

F

Fraud and Misrepresentation.—Unlike the case of a commercial contract, neither a fraudulent nor an innocent misrepresentation will of itself affect the validity of a marriage.[12] But if the misrepresentation induces an operative mistake (*e.g.*, as to the nature of the ceremony), the marriage will be avoided by the latter.[13]

Fear and Duress.—If, owing to fear or threats, one of the parties is induced to enter into a marriage which, in the absence of compulsion, he would never have contracted, the marriage can be annulled. The fear may be due to a number of causes. In *Buckland* v. *Buckland*,[14] for example, the petitioner, a youth aged 20 resident in Malta, was groundlessly charged with defiling the respondent, a girl of 15. Although he protested his innocence, he was twice advised that he stood no chance of an acquittal but would probably be sent to prison for a period of up to two years unless he married her. He did so and it was held that he was entitled to a decree of nullity. Nor is it necessary that the fear should have been inspired by any acts on the other party's part. In *H.* v. *H.*[15] the petitioner at the time of the marriage was a Hungarian national residing in Budapest. She came of a rich family and was therefore politically *persona non grata* with the communist government of that state. She reasonably entertained the fear that if she remained in Hungary she was liable to be sent to prison or a concentration camp if not put to death, and in order to get out of the country she married the respondent who was a French national. After the marriage she obtained a French passport and with it came to England. It was obviously understood by both parties that the marriage was being contracted solely for this purpose; they never cohabited and the marriage was never consummated. It was held that in these circumstances the presumption that the petitioner had consented to the marriage was rebutted.

As the Court of Appeal held in *Singh* v. *Singh*,[16] there must be a threat of immediate danger to " life, limb or liberty ". In the words of BUTT, J., in *Scott* v. *Sebright*:[17]

> " Whenever from natural weakness of intellect or from fear—whether reasonably entertained or not—either party is actually in a state of mental incompetence to resist pressure improperly brought to bear, there is no more consent than in the case of a person of stronger intellect and more robust courage yielding to a more serious danger. "

---

[12]*Swift* v. *Kelly* (1835), 3 Knapp 257, 293, P.C.; *Moss* v. *Moss*, (*supra*), at p. 266.

[13]*Moss* v. *Moss*, (*supra*), at pp. 268-9.

[14][1967] 2 All E.R. 300; [1968] P. 296. See also *Scott* v. *Sebright* (1886), 12 P.D. 21 (threats to make petitioner bankrupt, to denounce her and finally to shoot her); *Griffith* v. *Griffith*, [1944] I.R. 35 (fear of prosecution for unlawful carnal knowledge. All the earlier cases are collected and exhaustively discussed by Manchester, *Marriage or Prison: the Case of the Reluctant Bridegroom*, 29 M.L.R. 622.

[15][1953] 2 All E.R. 1229; [1954] P. 258. See also *Szechter* v. *Szechter*, [1970] 3 All E.R. 905 (marriage contracted in prison in Warsaw to enable woman to escape from Poland); *Parojcic* v. *Parojcic*, [1959] 1 All E.R. 1 (fear imposed by petitioner's father).

[16][1971] 2 W.L.R. 963, C.A. (arranged Sikh marriage held valid.). *Cf. Szechter* v. *Szechter*, (supra), at p. 915.

[17](1886), 12 P.D. 21, 24. See also *Cooper* v. *Crane*, [1891] P. 369, 376-7; *Buckland* v *Buckland*, [1967] 2 All E.R. 300, 302; [1968] P. 296, 301. Lanham, *loc. cit.*

Whether there was present a sufficient degree of fear to vitiate the party's consent is clearly a question of fact, and if he happens to be more susceptible to the pressure brought to bear upon him than another might be, the marriage may still be annulled even though a person of ordinary courage and resistance would not have yielded to it. In *Buckland* v. *Buckland*[18] SCARMAN, J., added that the fear must be reasonably entertained. It is submitted that the opposite view expressed in the passage from BUTT, J.'s judgment cited above is to be preferred, for if a person is in a mental state in which he is no longer capable of offering resistance to threats, it seems immaterial that it would be obvious to a reasonable person, similarly placed, that the other has no intention of carrying them out at all.

It also seems that fear will not vitiate consent unless it arises from some external circumstance for which the party is not himself responsible.[19] In *Buckland* v. *Buckland* the petitioner succeeded because his fear arose from the unjust charge preferred against him; presumably he would have failed had he actually been guilty of defiling the respondent.

The majority of dicta indicate that, as in the case of a commercial contract, fear and duress will make a marriage voidable and not void.[20]

"Sham Marriages."—The question has been canvassed whether a " sham marriage "—that is, where the parties go through the form of marriage purely for the purpose of representing themselves as married to the outside world with no intention of cohabiting—is to be regarded in law as a nullity. This problem may become more important in these days of political, racial and religious persecution and restricted immigration for (as in *H.* v. *H.*)[21] a woman who is a citizen of state X may go through a form of marriage with a citizen of state Y merely in order to escape from X or to enter Y on the strength of her husband's nationality or passport.

The question had to be decided by COLLINGWOOD, J., in *Silver* v. *Silver*.[1] In this case the wife, who was a German subject, had gone through a form of marriage with the respondent, who was a British subject, in order to be able to enter England and remain here. The spouses separated immediately after their arrival in this country, never cohabited, and in fact met only twice in the next 29 years, when the wife commenced nullity proceedings as she wanted to marry another

---

[18][1967] 2 All E.R. 300, 302; [1968] P. 296, 301. KARMINSKI, J., seems to have been of the same opinion in *H.* v. *H.*, [1953] 2 All E.R. 1229 1234; [1954] P. 258, 269.

[19]*Buckland* v. *Buckland*, (*supra*), at pp. 302 and 301, respectively, following *Griffith* v. *Griffith*, [1944] I.R. 35, 43-4, where HAUGH, J., held that the marriage could be annulled only if the fear was *unjustly* imposed. But see Law. Com. No. 33, para. 66.

[20]See *Parojcic* v. *Parojcic*, [1959] 1 All E.R. 1, 4-5; *Ross Smith* v. *Ross-Smith*, [1961] 1 All E.R. 255, 260, C.A.; [1961] P. 39, 57. A similar view is expressed in 12 Halsbury's Laws of England (3rd Ed.) 225. The opposite conclusion is reached by Tolstoy, *Void and Voidable Marriages*, 27 M.L.R. 385, and Lanham, *Duress and Void Contracts*, 29 M.L.R. 615.*Cf.* KARMINSKI, L.J., in *Singh* v. *Singh*, (*ante*), at pp. 965-966; *McLarnon* v. *McLarnon* (1968), 112 Sol. Jo. 419, where it was held that the marriage could be annulled notwithstanding that it had been consummated. See further Webb and Bevan, *Source Book of Family Law*, 82-83.

[21]See *ante*.

[1][1955] 2 All E.R. 614.

man. COLLINGWOOD, J., decided that, as they had freely entered into
the marriage contract with the intention of becoming man and wife,
the marriage was perfectly valid and could not be affected by any
mental reservations.   This is in keeping with earlier decisions and
dicta,[2] and it would be difficult to defend any other view.

E. NULLITY IN THE CONFLICT OF LAWS

This subject is a difficult one which still wants final settlement by
the House of Lords in certain respects.[3] Two problems have to be
considered:

(1) What jurisdiction have English courts when the case contains
a foreign element ?

(2) In what circumstances will an English court recognise the
validity of a decree of nullity pronounced by a foreign court ?

Jurisdiction of English Courts.—The three leading cases in this
field are now the decisions of the Court of Appeal in *De Reneville* v.
De Reneville in 1947[4] and *Ramsay-Fairfax* v. *Ramsay-Fairfax* in
1955,[5] and of the House of Lords in *Ross Smith* v. *Ross Smith* in
1962.[6]

Apart from statutory provisions there are at least two cases where
an English court has jurisdiction to pronounce a decree.   Clearly it has
jurisdiction if both parties are domiciled in England and, apparently,
if one of them only is domiciled here, on the principle that our courts
can always adjudicate on the status of a person domiciled within the
jurisdiction.[7]   In this connection it must be borne in mind that,
if the marriage is alleged to be *voidable*, the wife must *ex hypothesi*
be married to the husband at the time of the petition and hearing
and must therefore have the same domicile as he has, whereas if it
is *void*, she will not automatically have acquired her husband's
domicile but will either have retained her pre-marital domicile or have
acquired a fresh domicile by choice.[8]   Secondly, the court will have

---

[2]See *Bell* v. *Graham* (1859), 13 Moo. P.C.C. 242, P.C.; *Kelly* v. *Kelly* (1932), 49 T.L.R.
99, 101; *H.* v. *H.*, [1953] 2 All E.R. 1229, 1234; [1954] P. 258, 269.

[3]In addition to the standard works on private international law, see the Report of the
Morton Commission (1956, Cmd. 9678). The Commission were highly critical of the
existing anomalies and made extensive recommendations which are far too detailed to
be considered here. For a critical discussion of them, see Mann, *The Royal Commission
on Marriage and Divorce*, 21 M.L.R. 1; Grodecki, *Recent Developments in Nullity
Jurisdiction*, 20 M.L.R. 566.

[4][1948] 1 All E.R. 56, C.A.; [1948] P. 100.

[5][1955] 3 All E.R. 695, C.A.; [1956] P. 115.

[6][1962] 1 All E.R. 344, H.L.; [1963] A.C. 280. See Grodecki, Webb and Lewis
in 11 I.C.L.Q. 651; Latey, *Basis of Jurisdiction in Nullity of Marriage*, 78 L.Q.R. 417.

[7]*De Reneville* v. *De Reneville*, [1948] 1 All E.R. 56, C.A., at pp. 61, 64; [1948]
P. 100, at pp. 114, 122; *Mehta* v. *Mehta*, [1945] 2 All E.R. 690; *White* v. *White*, [1937]
1 All E.R. 708; [1937] P. 111; *Har-Shefi* v. *Har-Shefi*, [1953] 1 All E.R. 783, C.A.;
[1953] P. 161. The party or parties must be domiciled here *when the petition is presented*:
cf. Leon v. *Leon*, [1966] 3 All E.R. 820; [1967] P. 275.

[8]*De Reneville* v. *De Reneville*, (*supra*). Her domicile may *incidentally* be the same
as her husband's. It will be seen that this question of domicile may raise a preliminary
problem of classification, for the court may have jurisdiction if the marriage is void
(which may give the wife an English domicile) but not if it is voidable and the husband
is domiciled abroad.

jurisdiction if both parties are resident in this country (for this was the basis of the ecclesiastical courts' jurisdiction which the High Court now exercises)[9] but residence of the petitioner alone in England will not suffice, for there is no principle of international law which can require a respondent who is neither domiciled nor resident here and whose marriage was not celebrated here to appear in an English court to answer a petition which may affect his status.[10] The concept of residence in this context seems to have an unusually wide meaning as the result of the decision of the Court of Appeal in *Sinclair* v. *Sinclair*,[11] where SCARMAN, J., defined it as " a state of affairs which connects a man and his family sufficiently clearly with England to make it just that the court should intervene ".[12] In this case it was held that a husband was still resident here when he was living in the U.S.A. for business reasons but was continuing to maintain a matrimonial home in England, in which his wife (the petitioner) still resided with their children, to which he himself intended to return (at least from time to time) in order to keep in touch with his family, and in which he had left some of his personal property. The precise limits of the concept are now not at all clear; whilst it was agreed that a merely casual or transient presence in this country could not give the court jurisdiction, it seems that it will be sufficient if the respondent has some sort of home here (even though he has another residence elsewhere) and an intention to visit it occasionally. It looks as though the court may have gone back on the principle enunciated in earlier cases and is in danger of forcing a respondent to come to England to defend proceedings even though his connection with this country is very tenuous.

If the marriage is *voidable*, the court has no jurisdiction simply by reason of the fact that the marriage was celebrated in England,[13] for such a slight link with English law does not justify the court in pronouncing a decree changing the status of persons whose personal law may have no other connection with ours. This objection does not apply to the same extent where the marriage is *void*, however, for the decree is merely declaratory. The members of the House of Lords in *Ross Smith* v. *Ross Smith* were equally divided on the question whether in such a case the courts should continue to exercise a jurisdiction assumed over a century ago in *Simonin* v. *Mallac;*[14] but however anomalous the decision may be, SIMON, P., believed it to have stood too long to overrule and he applied it in *Padolecchia* v. *Padolecchia.*[15] It is reasonable to permit a petition to be brought if it is alleged that the marriage is void as a result of formal

---

[9]*Ramsay-Fairfax* v. *Ramsay-Fairfax, (ante).* In fact residence of the respondent alone would appear to be sufficient, for the petitioner *ipso facto* submits to the jurisdiction by invoking it: *Magnier* v. *Magnier* (1968), 112 Sol. Jo. 233, and *cf. post,* p. 143, n.[5].

[10]*De Reneville* v. *De Reneville, (supra).*

[11][1967] 3 All E.R. 882, C.A.; [1968] P. 189. The case was in fact concerned with jurisdiction to grant a decree of judicial separation but it is submitted that the same principle must be applied in both cases.

[12]At pp. 898 and 232, respectively.

[13]*Ross Smith* v. *Ross Smith, (supra).*

[14](1860), 2 Sw. & Tr. 67.

[15][1967] 3 All E.R. 863; [1968] P. 314.

defect, because English law will have to be applied as the *lex loci celebrationis;* but the facts of *Padolecchia* v. *Padolecchia* indicate how remote the connection with this country may be in other circumstances. H and W, who were both domiciled in Italy, married in that country in 1953.   In 1958 H, whilst in Venezuela, obtained a proxy divorce in Mexico. Neither he nor W ever set foot in Mexico and the divorce was not recognised in Italy.   In 1964 H went through a ceremony of marriage with X, who was domiciled in Denmark, whilst on a short visit to England. He later petitioned for nullity on the ground that his marriage to X was bigamous and therefore void. Clearly this was so because he lacked the capacity to marry X by his *lex domicilii,* but this appears to be of little concern to English courts. The argument that it is open to anyone to put the validity of a void marriage in issue in any proceedings (which suggests that there should be no limit to the court's jurisdiction to pronounce decrees of nullity in such circumstances) overlooks the point that they are judgments *in rem.* It seems contrary to principle and convenience to make X come to this country to defend the proceedings and it is submitted that *Simonin* v. *Mallac* and *Padolecchia* v. *Padolecchia* should be overruled.

In two cases jurisdiction has been extended by statute. By section 40 (1) of the Matrimonial Causes Act 1965 the court may pronounce a decree of nullity on the wife's petition:

> (a) . . . if the wife has been deserted by her husband or the husband has been deported from the United Kingdom under any law for the time being in force relating to deportation, and the husband was immediately before the desertion or deportation domiciled in England; *or*

> (b) . . . if the wife is resident in England and has been ordinarily resident[16] there for a period of three years immediately preceding the commencement of the proceedings, and the husband is not domiciled in any other part of the United Kingdom or in the Channel Islands or the Isle of Man.[17]

The former provision is designed to protect the wife who might otherwise be prejudiced by her husband's acquiring a domicile outside England. However convenient the latter provision may be to the wife who is permanently resident in this country, it is submitted that it is an unfortunate piece of legislation, for whilst much has been done to attempt to avoid limping marriages, the courts of the husband's domicile may refuse to recognise a decree of nullity based solely upon the wife's residence, and are even less likely to accept it if the grounds for the decree are unknown to the *lex domicilii.*

Choice of Law.—This is probably the most speculative aspect of nullity in the conflict of laws. Once it has been established that the

---

[16]The wife is ordinarily resident in England if she has her real home here: *Stransky* v. *Stransky*, [1954] 2 All E.R. 536; [1954] P. 428. *Cf. ante*, p. 6. The three years' residence must be continuous: *Hopkins* v. *Hopkins*, [1950] 2 All E.R. 1035; [1951] P. 116, but the period can begin before marriage: *Navas* v. *Navas*, [1969] 3 All E.R. 677; [1970] P. 159.

[17]Paragraph (a) was originally enacted by the Matrimonial Causes Act 1937, s. 13, and (b) by the Law Reform (Miscellaneous Provisions) Act 1949, s. 1. These statutory provisions do not entitle a husband to cross-petition if the court would not have jurisdiction to entertain a petition by him: *Russell* v. *Russell*, [1957] 1 All E.R. 929; [1957] P. 375.

court has jurisdiction, it must then decide whether it is to apply the substantive law of England or of some other country.

It seems indisputable that questions of formal invalidity (and its consequences) must be referred to the *lex loci celebrationis* by which alone they are governed.[18] Similarly, if the marriage is void as a consequence of either party's lack of capacity by his or her *lex domicilii* at the time of the marriage, we must apply that law and treat the marriage as void in this country.[19] Difficulty arises if some other ground for annulment is relied on. This problem arose in *De Reneville* v. *De Reneville*.[20] In this case the husband was domiciled at all times in France but the wife had been domiciled in England before the marriage, which had taken place in France. The parties lived together in France and the French Congo until the wife left the husband, returned to England and petitioned here for a decree on the ground of the husband's inability or wilful refusal to consummate the marriage. The Court of Appeal held that the validity of the marriage must be determined by French law either as the law of the husband's domicile at the time of the marriage or as the law of their intended matrimonial domicile. The same problem arose again in *Ponticelli* v. *Ponticelli*.[1] The husband, who was at all material times domiciled in England and had married in Italy a woman domiciled in that country, petitioned here for a decree on the ground of the wife's refusal to consummate the marriage. The choice lay between applying English law (by which the marriage was voidable) or Italian law (which probably afforded no remedy in the circumstances). SACHS, J., held that he should apply the former as the husband's *lex domicilii* or (should that be wrong) as the *lex fori* or the law of the intended matrimonial domicile.

It is submitted that in any case the *lex fori* is irrelevant and is to be avoided as it makes the outcome of the proceedings depend on the country in which the petitioner brings them. In both *De Reneville* v. *De Reneville* and *Ponticelli* v. *Ponticelli* the husband's domicile was the same throughout as the intended matrimonial domicile and so it was not necessary for the court to choose between them. As *ex hypothesi* the marriage will be voidable, both parties will have the same domicile and the effect of the decree will be to change their status; as this is a question for their *lex domicilii*, it is submitted that the best solution is to apply the law of their domicile at the time of the petition.[2]

In any case where the court has jurisdiction by virtue of section 40 of the Matrimonial Causes Act, it is expressly provided that the law applicable shall be the same as if both parties were domiciled in

---

[18]*Kenward* v. *Kenward*, [1950] 2 All E.R. 297, C.A.; [1951] P. 124. See *ante*, pp. 19-22.
[19]*Padolecchia* v. *Padolecchia*, [1967] 3 All E.R. 863; [1968] P. 314 (bigamy); *Szechter* v. *Szechter*, [1970] 3 All E.R. 905 (duress). See *ante*, pp. 17-19.
[20][1948] 1 All E.R. 56, C.A.; [1948] P. 100.
[1][1958] 1 All E.R. 357; [1958] P. 204.
[2]See Cheshire, *Private International Law*, 8th Ed., 396-400. Dicey and Morris, *Conflict of Laws*, 8th Ed., Rule 45 (2), prefer the husband's *lex domicilii* at the time of the marriage; Graveson, *Conflict of Laws*, 6th Ed., 361, prefers the intended matrimonial domicile; Morris, *De Reneville Revisited*, 19 I.C.L.Q. 424, at p. 428, prefers the *lex fori*.

England.[3]   But this will of course still necessitate reference to the *lex loci celebrationis* in the case of formal invalidity or to the *lex domicilii* of one of the parties in the case of incapacity.

Recognition of Foreign Decrees.—On the general principle of reciprocity, an English court ought to recognise a decree granted by a foreign court if that court assumed jurisdiction on some ground which *mutatis mutandis* would give an English court jurisdiction. In *Salvesen* v. *Administrator of Austrian Property*[4] the House of Lords recognised a decree pronounced by the court of the parties' domicile, and a decree pronounced by the *forum loci celebrationis* has also been recognised where the marriage was void.[5] In *Travers* v. *Holley*[6] it was laid down that an English court would recognise a decree of divorce pronounced by a foreign court even though the parties were domiciled in England, provided that the basis of jurisdiction corresponded with a basis of jurisdiction accepted by an English court, and it would seem to follow that the same argument should be applied in nullity cases and that the doctrine of reciprocity should be applied in all cases.[7]

Similarly, as in the case of divorce, an English court will recognise a decree pronounced by the court of another jurisdiction which is recognised by the court of both parties' domicile.[8] What is yet to be decided is whether the principle of *Indyka* v. *Indyka*,[9] under which an English court will recognise a decree of divorce provided that there is a real and substantial connection between one of the parties and the country in which it was granted, will be applied to nullity as well. In order to reduce the number of limping marriages, it is submitted that it should be and that we ought to recognise a decree pronounced, say, in a country in which the petitioner is resident and with which he has a real and substantial connection even though the respondent is not resident there, the parties are not domiciled there, and the marriage was not celebrated there.

It will be seen that recognition can give rise to a problem of classification in the same way as jurisdiction can. There may be some cases where we should recognise the decree if the marriage was void but not if it was voidable—for example, if it were alleged that the wife had acquired a separate domicile in the country where the decree was pronounced. It is submitted that the only workable solution is to refer the question of characterisation to the court pronouncing the decree. If that held the marriage to be void, we must assume it to be void for the purpose of the question of recognition.

---

[3]Matrimonial Causes Act 1965, s. 40 (2).
[4][1927] A.C. 641, H.L.
[5]*Merker* v. *Merker*, [1962] 3 All E.R. 928; [1963] P. 283.
[6][1953] 2 All E.R. 794, C.A.; [1953] P. 246. See *post*, p. 219.
[7]The principle of reciprocity was not followed in the earlier case of *Chapelle* v. *Chapelle*, [1950] 1 All E.R. 236; [1950] P. 134, on the ground that one of the parties was domiciled in England, but it is submitted that this case cannot stand with other authorities. For a detailed criticism, see Cross in 3 I.C.L.Q. 247.
[8]*Abate* v. *Cauvin*, [1961] 1 All E.R. 569; [1961] P. 29.
[9][1967] 2 All E.R. 689, H.L.; [1969] 1 A.C. 33. See *post*, pp. 220-223. On the question of recognition generally, see further Grodecki, *Recognition of Foreign Nullity Decrees*, 74 L.Q.R. 225; Webb in 24 M.L.R. 366.

But in any case, an English court will not recognise the validity of a foreign decree which has been obtained by collusion or fraud[10] or which offends against English ideas of substantial justice. In the past the courts have refused to recognise a decree on the latter ground only if there was some procedural shortcoming as a result of which, for example, the respondent had been unable to defend the proceedings. In *Formosa* v. *Formosa*,[11] however, the Court of Appeal apparently took the view that they would not recognise a decree when they considered that the substantive law applied produced a result contrary to natural justice. In that case the husband, whose domicile of origin was Maltese, acquired a domicile of choice in England and married the wife who was also domiciled here, in an English register office. He subsequently re-acquired a Maltese domicile and a Maltese court annulled the marriage on the ground that, as the husband was a Roman Catholic, he could marry only in a Roman Catholic church. The Court of Appeal refused to recognise the decree. Although the judgment of the Maltese court is indefensible, the decision of the Court of Appeal goes against the principle that an English court will not enquire into the substantive merits of a decree pronounced by a competent court abroad. The case stands alone and it remains to be seen whether it will be followed in other fields or, ultimately, accepted by the House of Lords.

---

[10]*Salvesen* v. *Administrator of Austrian Property*, [1927] A.C. 641, H.L., at pp. 663, 671-2; *Casey* v. *Casey*, [1949] 2 All E.R. 110, 117, C.A.; [1949] P. 420, 433.

[11][1962] 3 All E.R. 419, C.A.; [1963] P. 259. The case is strongly criticised by Lewis in 12 I.C.L.Q. 298 and by Blom-Cooper in 26 M.L.R. 94.

CHAPTER 4

The Effects of Coverture

A. INTRODUCTORY

The principal effect of marriage at common law was that for many purposes it fused the legal personalities of husband and wife into one. The clearest exposition of this doctrine of unity of husband and wife is probably that of BLACKSTONE, who said:[1]

> " By marriage, the husband and wife are one person in law; that is, the very being or legal existence of the woman is suspended during the marriage, or at least is incorporated and consolidated into that of the husband; under whose wing, protection, and *cover*, she performs everything; and is therefore called in our law-French a *feme-covert, femina viro co-operta*; is said to be *covert-baron*, or under the protection and influence of her husband, her *baron*, or lord; and her condition during marriage is called her *coverture*. Upon this principle of a union of person in husband and wife, depend almost all the legal rights, duties, and disabilities, that either of them acquire by the marriage."

The principle is enunciated in the *Dialogus de Scaccario* in the twelfth century and has been repeated by every leading common law writer since.[2] But it may be doubted whether this doctrine was ever a firmly established rule of the common law. One or two examples will suffice to show that it was but imperfectly applied. Thus it operated to prevent any action at common law between the spouses, but if a tort was committed either by or against a married woman both she and her husband were correctly joined as co-defendants or co-plaintiffs to the action, and notwithstanding the maxim *actio personalis moritur cum persona*, if the husband predeceased the wife, she could still be sued or sue in person. A woman on marriage *ipso facto* acquired her husband's domicile but not his nationality. Similar inconsistencies were to be found in the law relating to the interest taken by a husband in his wife's property. He acquired an absolute interest in her chattels, a similar interest in her choses in action but only provided that they were reduced into possession, a power to dispose of her leasehold interests during his lifetime but no power to dispose of them by will, and no more than an interest for his life in her inheritable estates of freehold. It is difficult to see on what single principle the common law could logically arrive at all these conclusions.

Neither equity nor the ecclesiastical law accepted this doctrine of unity of personality, and both gave married women access to their

---

[1]*Commentaries*, i, 442.
[2]See Williams, *Legal Unity of Husband and Wife*, 10 M.L.R. 16, at pp. 16-18.

courts and even permitted actions between spouses. But it was not until 1870 that the Married Women's Property Act of that year gave a wife an extremely limited right to maintain an action in her own name in the courts of common law.[3] Whilst a series of statutes extending over 65 years and culminating in the Law Reform (Married Women and Tortfeasors) Act of 1935 have to a very large extent put a married woman in the same legal position as her unmarried sister, it would be dangerous to assume that they have abolished the common law doctrine in its entirety. These statutes have been typical of so much English legislative reform in that they have created extensive exceptions to the old rules without striking at the root of the trouble by abolishing outright the fundamental principle on which the anomalies are based. Time and again the courts have reiterated that these Acts have not given a wife the legal status of a feme sole except in certain clearly defined and limited fields, and even these exceptions have been construed, if not narrowly, at least inconsistently. In only one case, *Rees* v. *Hughes*[4] does there appear to have been a departure from the strict wording of the statutes with a bold application of the maxim *cessante ratione legis cessat ipsa lex*, and even here the Court of Appeal did no more than hold that a husband is no longer under a legal duty to bury his deceased wife at his own expense if her estate is large enough to enable her personal representatives to do so themselves. As LUSH puts it:[5]

" It is untraversable that a married woman's position in law is anomalous and enigmatic. . . .
" The rule of unity . . . still prevails as a rule in those matters wherein it was established at common law and has not been abrogated by statute. The rule at the present day lifts its head hydra-like and is on occasions applied with surprising results."

These changes have of course affected the spouses' rights and obligations *vis a vis* third persons. For example, a married woman now has a capacity to enter into contracts which she lacked at common law and her husband is no longer liable for torts committed by her. But, what is of much greater importance, their rights and obligations towards each other have also been fundamentally altered. As we shall see, during the past century the wife's position has steadily changed from something in many respects inferior to that of a servant (who could at least quit her master's service by giving notice) to that of the joint, co-equal head of the family. Consequently in this chapter we shall first discuss the right to consortium and the corresponding duty to cohabit that each spouse owes to the other. We shall then consider how far marriage affects rights and duties in contract and tort both as between the spouses themselves and between the spouses and third

---

[3]But a woman judicially separated from her husband could sue and be sued as if she were a feme sole by the Matrimonial Causes Act 1857, s. 26.
[4][1946] 2 All E.R. 47, C.A.; [1946] K.B. 517.
[5]*Husband and Wife*, 4th Ed., pp. 21 and 58. See generally the whole of the first chapter of that work; Williams, *Legal Unity of Husband and Wife*, 10 M.L.R 16; Kahn-Freund, *Inconsistencies and Injustices in the Law of Husband and Wife*, 15 M L.R. 133, 16 M.L.R. 34, 148; *A Century of Family Law* (ed. Graveson and Crane).

persons. Finally we shall examine two matters of public law: the
problems created by the relationship of husband and wife in the
criminal law and its relevance in the law of nationality. The effect of
the relationship on rights in property and the duty of support will be
considered in later chapters.[6]

B. THE RIGHT TO CONSORTIUM

I. THE NATURE OF CONSORTIUM

Mutual Duty to Cohabit.—Consortium means living together as
husband and wife with all the incidents that flow from that relationship.
At one time it would have been said that the husband had the right to
his wife's consortium whilst the latter had not so much a reciprocal
right to her husband's consortium as a correlative duty to give him
her society and her services—a view which was not entirely obsolete in
the middle of the nineteenth century.[7] A clear illustration of the
wife's legal subjection to her husband can be seen in the old common
law rule that a woman who murdered her husband was guilty of petit
treason, like the vassal who slew his lord or the servant who slew his
master.[8] In BACON'S *Abridgement* in 1736 it was stated that a husband
might beat his wife (but not in a violent or cruel manner) and confine
her.[9] Whether he ever had a legal power to administer corporal
punishment is open to some doubt: HALE denied that he had,[10] although BLACKSTONE maintained that, whilst the practice had become
obsolete in polite society, " the lower rank of people, who were always
fond of the old common law, still claim and exert their ancient privilege ".[11] In any event, this is no longer law, and it would be no
defence today to a husband prosecuted for assaulting his wife that he
was doing no more than administering reasonable chastisement.[12]

But the husband's right to enforce consortium by confining her
remained longer in doubt. In 1852 the Court of Queen's Bench held
that they would not force a wife to return to her husband against her
will by enabling him to obtain custody of her by habeas corpus.[13]
But this decision did not determine whether he could enforce his right
extra-judicially by lawfully confining her once she was in his house.
More than a century earlier the Court of King's Bench had held that
he was entitled to restrain her only in order to protect his property or
his honour, for example if she squandered his wealth or went " into
lewd company ",[14] but in 1840 COLERIDGE, J., denied that there was

---

[6]See *post*, chapters 14 and 15.
[7]See the judgment of COLERIDGE, J., in *Re Cochrane* (1840), 8 Dowl. 630.
[8]The distinction between petit treason and murder was abolished in 1828 by
9 Geo. 4, c. 31, s. 2.
[9]Tit. Baron and Feme (B).
[10]*Lord Leigh's Case* (1674), 3 Keble 433, where he said that *castigatio* meant no
more than admonition and confinement.
[11]*Commentaries*, i, 445.
[12]*R.* v. *Jackson*, [1891] 1 Q.B. 671, C.A., at pp. 679, 682.
[13]*R.* v. *Leggatt* (1852), 18 Q.B. 781.
[14]*R.* v. *Lister* (1721), 1 Str. 478. *Cf.* Viner's *Abridgement*, Tit. Baron and Feme,
V, a, 11.

any such limitation on the husband's powers.[15] It was eventually not until the Legislature had accorded to a married woman a measure of financial independence of her husband by the Married Women's Property Act of 1882[16] that it was finally established that she had a similar right to her personal liberty by the decision of the Court of Appeal in *R. v. Jackson* in 1891.[17] In that case the wife had gone to live with relations whilst her husband was absent in New Zealand. After his return she refused to live with him again and failed to comply with a decree of restitution of conjugal rights. Consequently he arranged with two men that they should seize her as she came out of church one Sunday afternoon, and she was then put into a carriage and taken to her husband's residence, where she was allowed complete freedom of the house but was not permitted to leave the building. She then applied for a writ of habeas corpus and it was unanimously held by the Court of Appeal that it was no defence that the husband was merely confining her in order to enforce his right to her consortium. So ended the husband's right to treat his wife as he would a recalcitrant animal. In the words of McCardie, J.:[18]

> " From the date of their decision the shackles of servitude fell from the limbs of married women and they were free to come and go at their own will."

In *R. v. Jackson* both Lord Halsbury, L.C., and Lord Esher, M.R., left open the question whether a husband might not still be entitled to restrain his wife to protect his honour, for example if she was in the very act of going to meet her paramour,[19] but it is submitted that today even this conduct would not justify his using force to restrain her. It is important to remember that *R. v. Jackson* in no way altered the law relating to a husband's right to his wife's consortium; it merely decided that he is not entitled to resort to extra-judicial methods to enforce it. Hence it was still possible even thirty years ago to speak of the husband as the head of the family. But the movement for the equality of the rights of the sexes, which had begun in the middle of the nineteenth century and which had gained renewed impetus by women's work in the First World War, was now to be felt in the home. The victory gained in the field of public law in the Sex Disqualification (Removal) Act of 1919 was carried into the field of private law. In 1923 the Legislature equated the rights of the spouses to petition for divorce;[20] in 1925 it established the principle that they have equal rights with respect to their children;[1] and in 1967 it gave each of them the power to apply for an order regulating their rights to occupy the matrimonial home.[2] All these changes reflect the modern view that the wife is no longer the weaker partner subservient

---

[15]*Re Cochrane*, (*ante*). See Lush, *Husband and Wife*, 4th Ed., 24 *et seq.*
[16]*Post*, p. 353.
[17][1891] 1 Q.B. 671, C.A.
[18]*Place* v. *Searle*, [1932] 2 K.B. 497, 500-501.
[19]At pp. 679-680 and 683, respectively.
[20]*Post*, p. 204
[1]*Post*, p. 270.
[2]*Post*, p. 390.

to the stronger but that both spouses are the joint, co-equal heads of the family. This, it is submitted, is also the position today as regards consortium; so that it can be said: " It seems to be clear that at the present day a husband has a right to the consortium of his wife, and the wife to the consortium of her husband ",[3] and these rights must now be regarded as exactly reciprocal.

It follows, of course, that a wife has no greater right to force herself upon her husband than he has to compel her to cohabit with him. In *Nanda* v. *Nanda*[4] a wife, whose husband had deserted her, installed herself against his will in the flat in which he was living with another woman and their two children. It was held that she had no right to trespass on her husband's property which had never been the matrimonial home and that he was entitled to an injunction to restrain her from doing so again in the future.

The Incidents of Consortium.—As has already been stated, consortium primarily means living together as husband and wife. Normally this will involve sharing the common matrimonial home, but this is not absolutely essential. It may be possible for the spouses to cohabit only from time to time, as where the husband has to spend long periods away from home for reasons of business or where he is a member of the armed forces and consequently can live with his wife only when he is on leave. Yet intermittent cohabitation of this kind none the less amounts to consortium which can in fact exist in even more limited circumstances than these, for example where both spouses are in domestic service and reside with different families.[5] Moreover, so long as the spouses retain the intention of cohabiting whenever possible, the consortium is regarded as continuous. [6]

Consortium, then, connotes as far as possible the sharing of a common home and a common domestic life. It is difficult to go beyond this and to define with more precision the duties which the spouses owe to each other: this is, after all, a matter of common knowledge rather than a subject for legal analysis. The incidents of consortium are capable of considerable variation and clearly will depend upon such factors as the age, health, social position and financial circumstances of the spouses. In most families the husband's duties will be largely conditioned by the fact that he is the breadwinner; the wife will usually be primarily responsible for the running of the home, a duty which may take the form of supervising a large domestic staff or of doing the household " chores " herself, such as cooking, cleaning, mending and looking after the children; but today in many cases (particularly where both spouses are working) these tasks are shared by both. Jurisprudentially, in a sense consortium resembles ownership, for husband and wife enjoy " a

---

[3] *Per* SCRUTTON, L.J., in *Place* v. *Searle*, [1932] 2 K.B. 497, 512, C.A.
[4] [1967] 3 All E.R. 401; [1968] P. 351. The wife's position was, if anything, strengthened by her having obtained a decree for restitution of conjugal rights but this gave her no right to insist on cohabitation. Decrees for restitution of conjugal rights have now been abolished: see *post*, p. 102.
[5] *Huxtable* v. *Huxtable* (1899), 68 L.J.P. 83.
[6] *R.* v. *Creamer*, [1919] 1 K.B. 564, C.C.A.

bundle of rights some hardly capable of precise definition ".[7] Nevertheless it may be worth while to examine in a little more detail one or two of these rights which have been directly or indirectly the subject of judicial decision.

The Wife's Right to her Husband's Name.—By custom, on marriage a wife assumes her husband's surname and, if he is a peer, his title and rank. She is entitled to retain this name after the marriage has been terminated either by death or by divorce, and a man has no such property in his name as to entitle him to sue for an injunction to prevent his divorced wife from using it unless, at any rate, she is doing so for the purpose of defrauding him or some other right of his is being invaded.[8] If she is still holding herself out as his wife, he may of course restrain her from doing so by jactitation proceedings.[9]

The Matrimonial Home.—As we have already seen, it is the duty of the spouses to live together as far as their circumstances will permit. But differences may arise between them as to where the matrimonial home is to be. In accordance with the view that the husband was the head of the household, the earlier opinion was that he had the right to determine this and a judicial dictum to this effect is to be found as late as 1940.[10] The modern view, however, is that this, like other domestic matters of common concern, is something in which the wife too has a right to be heard and which the spouses are bound to settle by agreement—a view most clearly voiced by DENNING, L.J., in *Dunn* v. *Dunn*.[11] Such an agreement may be entered into before marriage[12] or after it, and will remain in force until a change of circumstances (for example, a change in the spouses' financial position or health or business interests) makes it necessary or desirable for them to change their home and thus come to a fresh agreement.

Where the spouses find it impossible to come to an agreement, it seems imperative that one of them should have a casting vote in order to resolve the deadlock. As a matter of law neither of them has an absolute right in this respect against the other and all the circumstances must be taken into consideration. This means that in a large number of cases the husband will be entitled to the last word for the simple reason that he will be the breadwinner and must be able to live near his place of work,[13] but it is easy to conceive of cases where the wife's

---

[7]*Per* LORD REID in *Best* v. *Samuel Fox & Co., Ltd.*, [1952] 2 All E.R. 394, 401, H.L.; [1952] A.C 716, 736.

[8]*Cowley* v. *Cowley*, [1900] P. 305, C.A.; affirmed, [1901] A.C. 450, H.L. *Cf. Du Boulay* v. *Du Boulay* (1869), L.R. 2 P.C. 430, 441, P.C. Thus, if she holds herself out as his wife after he has remarried, she may be guilty of libel or slander if the reasonable inference is that he is not legally married to his second wife.

[9]See *ante*, p. 55.

[10]*Mansey* v. *Mansey*, [1940] 2 All E.R. 424, 426; [1940] P. 139, 140. See also *King* v. *King*, [1941] 2 All E.R. 103, 110; [1942] P. 1, 8.

[11][1948] 2 All E.R. 822, 823, C.A.; [1949] P. 98, 103. See also *McGowan* v. *McGowan*, [1948] 2 All E.R. 1032, 1035; *Walter* v. *Walter* (1949), 65 T L.R. 680; *Hosegood* v. *Hosegood* (1950), 66 T.L.R. (Part 1) 735, 739, C.A.

[12]*King* v. *King*, (*supra*). *Cf. G.* v. *G.*, [1930] P. 72.

[13]*Per* DENNING, L.J., in *Dunn* v. *Dunn*, (*supra*), at pp. 823 and 103, respectively. *Cf.* HODSON, L.J., in *W.* v. *W.* (*No.* 2), [1954] 2 All E.R. 829, 840, C.A.; [1954] P. 486, 515.

considerations will come first—for example, where she is working and the husband is not.[14] Moreover, whatever arrangements the husband proposes must be reasonable from the wife's point of view; he cannot, for example, insist upon her living with his mother when the two women obviously will not be able to share the same house.[15] Similarly, if business requirements make it necessary for one spouse to move, the other will not be bound to go too if, say, the proposed removal would be liable to impair the latter's health or would be contrary to his or her own business interests.[16]

The practical importance of the question of the right to choose the matrimonial home lies in the fact that where the spouses separate as a result of their inability to agree on where the home is to be, it is the spouse who is acting unreasonably who will be in desertion. Where both act unreasonably (or, at least, where it cannot be said that either clearly has right upon his side), it would seem that neither can allege that the other is in desertion.[17]

Sexual Intercourse.—We have already seen that each spouse owes the other a duty to consummate the marriage and that (with certain exceptions) the incapacity of either or the wilful refusal of the respondent to do so will entitle the petitioner to a decree of nullity.[18] This mutual right to intercourse continues after the marriage has been consummated provided that it is reasonably exercised; but one spouse is not bound to submit to the demands of the other if they are inordinate or unreasonable or are likely to lead to a breakdown in health.[19] A wife is also entitled to fulfil her natural desire to bear children, so that her husband is not entitled to insist upon using contraceptives or practising *coitus interruptus* against her will.

An unreasonable insistence upon intercourse or the wilful refusal to have intercourse at all will entitle the party suffering as a consequence to leave the other and a course of conduct of this sort which injures the other's health will amount to cruelty.[20] Supervening impotence, on the other hand, like any other deterioration in a spouse's health, would appear to be no cause of any matrimonial relief at all.[1]

By marriage a wife consents to intercourse with her husband during coverture and she thus confers on him a privilege which she is not entitled to withdraw whenever she pleases.[2] It therefore follows as a general rule that a husband cannot be guilty as a principal of rape on

---

[14]As in *King* v. *King*, (*supra*).

[15]*Millichamp* v. *Millichamp* (1931), 146 L.T. 96; *Munro* v. *Munro*, [1950] 1 All E.R. 832, C.A. Contrast *Jackson* v. *Jackson* (1932), 146 L.T. 406.

[16]See *Walter* v. *Walter* (1949), 65 T.L.R. 680 (*post*, p. 176).

[17]*Post*, pp. 176-177.

[18]*Ante*, pp. 76-78.

[19]Either because of the state of the spouse's health or because of the manner in which the other insists upon intercourse (*e.g., coitus interruptus*). Similarly, a husband may not insist upon intercourse if he knows himself to be suffering from a venereal disease: *Foster* v. *Foster*, [1921] P. 438, C.A.

[20]*Post*, pp. 156-158 (cruelty) and 168-170.

[1]But see *post*, p. 157.

[2]*R.* v. *Clarence* (1888), 22 Q.B.D. 23, at pp. 53-54; *R.* v. *Clarke*, [1949] 2 All E.R. 448.

his own wife.[3]   But if the wife obtains a judicial separation or a separation order in a magistrates' court, this relieves her of the duty of cohabiting with her husband and accordingly BYRNE, J., held in *R. v. Clarke*[4] that in such a case a husband could be guilty of rape.   In *R. v. Miller*[5] LYNSKEY, J., stated *obiter* that a husband could also be guilty of raping his wife if the spouses had entered into a separation agreement, at any rate if it contained a non-molestation clause.   He declined to extend the exception further, however, and directed the jury that they must acquit a husband of rape who had had intercourse with his wife against her will when they were living apart, even though she had in fact already filed a petition for divorce.   It would therefore seem that before the husband can be guilty of rape upon his wife either they must have agreed to live apart or a court order must have been made.

LYNSKEY, J., nevertheless did hold that, following *R. v. Jackson*,[6] a husband cannot insist upon his right to have intercourse by force and that he could therefore in the circumstances be convicted of an assault on his wife, even though he used no more force than was necessary to effect his aims.   It is difficult to see logically how this can be, for if the wife is deemed to have given an implied consent to intercourse, she ought also to be considered to have given an implied consent to any acts connected therewith and her consent should clearly be a defence to the charge of assault.[7]   But even though logically unsupportable, the decision is clearly consonant with the changed views of the wife's status in the present century.

Mutual Protection.—Each spouse is entitled to use such force as is reasonably necessary to protect the other from attack or other physical harm and may lawfully kill an assailant if he or she believes that the act is absolutely necessary to preserve the other's life.[8]

Marital Confidences.—Referring to the relationship of husband and wife, UNGOED-THOMAS, J., said in *Argyll* v. *Argyll*[9]:

> " There could hardly be anything more intimate or confidential than is involved in that relationship, or than in the mutual trust and confidences which are shared between husband and wife. The confidential nature of the relationship is of its very essence and so obviously and necessarily implicit in it that there is no need for it to be expressed."

But if the marriage breaks down, bitterness and vindictiveness may lead one spouse to seek to break these confidences. Does the law offer the other any remedy in such circumstances?

In *Argyll* v. *Argyll* it was held that it did. Some two years after divorcing the plaintiff on the ground of her adultery, the defendant wrote a series of articles for a newspaper some of which contained information relating to the plaintiff's " private life, personal affairs and

---

[3] I Hale P.C. 629; *R.* v. *Miller*, [1954] 2 All E.R. 529; [1954] 2 Q.B. 282. But he may be guilty of aiding or abetting: *Lord Audley's Case* (1631), 3 St. Tr. 401, H.L.

[4] [1949] 2 All E.R. 448. *Quaere* if this would also apply if a decree nisi of divorce or nullity had been pronounced.

[5] [1954] 2 All E.R. 529; [1954] 2 Q.B. 282.

[6] [1891] 1 Q.B. 671, C.A., (*ante*, p. 93).

[7] He would of course clearly be guilty of assault if he used more force than was necessary (*e.g.*, by knocking her partly unconscious).

[8] *Anon.* (1695), 3 Salk. 46; *Leward* v. *Basely* (1695), 1 Ld. Raym. 62.

[9] [1965] 1 All E.R. 611, 619; [1967] Ch. 302, 322.

private conduct, communicated to the defendant in confidence during the subsistence of the marriage ". UNGOED-THOMAS, J., held that equity's general jurisdiction to restrain breach of confidence was sufficiently wide to enable him to grant an injunction to prevent the defendant from divulging these secrets and the newspaper from publishing them. The protection apparently extends only to confidential communications[10] and clearly the court will have to decide in each case whether the publication of the material in question will work the very mischief which the law seeks to prevent.

It is also probable that equity will assist the plaintiff only if he or she comes to the court with clean hands. An attempt was made to raise this defence in the *Argyll* case on the grounds that the plaintiff had herself published articles disclosing matrimonial secrets and that her own view of marriage, as exemplified by her adultery, could only be described as immoral. It failed, however, first because the defendant proposed to disclose much more intimate confidences so that his breaches would have been " of an altogether different order of perfidy ", and secondly because, however reprehensible the plaintiff's own adultery may have been, her subsequent conduct could only undermine confidence for the future and not retrospectively release the defendant from his duty to keep confidences already disclosed.

It is obvious, however, that two rules of public policy may come into conflict. Whilst on the one hand the law should protect marital confidences, on the other hand it is a fundamental principle that in any legal proceedings, civil or criminal, no relevant evidence should be excluded if it will help the court or the jury to arrive at the truth. If a person accused of a criminal offence has confessed his guilt to his wife, the prosecution may wish to call the wife to give evidence of the confession; similarly a statement made by a party in civil proceedings may be helpful to his adversary. A compromise must be effected and it will be convenient at this stage to consider how far the relationship of husband and wife affects the law of evidence generally.

Evidence in Civil Proceedings.—At common law neither the parties nor their spouses were competent witnesses in civil proceedings. The reason for excluding the testimony of the latter does not appear to have been based upon the fiction of unity but partly upon the fact that their evidence might be untrustworthy, partly on the wish to protect marital confidences, and partly upon the undesirability of having a witness giving evidence against his or her spouse and the consequent unfairness of permitting him or her to give evidence for the spouse. The rule was abolished with respect to the parties themselves by the Evidence Act 1851 and with respect to their spouses by the Evidence Amendment Act 1853,[11] so that now they are competent and compellable witnesses for any party to the action.

---

[10]At pp. 625 and 330, respectively.
[11]S. 1. But they were not competent to give evidence in proceedings instituted in consequence of adultery until the Evidence Further Amendment Act 1869 and (subject to certain exceptions) could not be compelled to answer any question tending to show they were guilty of adultery until the Civil Evidence Act 1968, s. 16 (5).

The Common Law Commissioners, on whose recommendation the Act of 1853 had been passed, had further advised that communications between spouses (which would now really for the first time become admissible) should nevertheless be privileged because, as they said, " so much of the happiness of human life may fairly be said to depend on the inviolability of domestic confidence ". Accordingly section 3 of the Act of 1853 provided:

> " No husband shall be compellable to disclose any communication made to him by his wife during the marriage, and no wife shall be compellable to disclose any communication made to her by her husband during the marriage."

This is a curious piece of legislation because it gave the privilege to the spouse *to whom* the statement was made and not to the maker of it. Hence, if the statement in question was made by the husband to his wife, *he* might be compelled to disclose it although his wife might not; but if she waived her privilege he had no power to prevent her from breaking his confidence. This was illogical and indefensible and for these reasons the privilege was abolished and section 3 repealed by the Civil Evidence Act 1968.[12] It will thus be seen that *in civil proceedings* the principle that relevant evidence should not be excluded has been allowed to oust completely the principle that marital confidences should be protected.

A married witness may, however, claim certain other privileges. The rule that a witness may not be compelled to answer any question or produce any document that tends to expose him to criminal proceedings has now been extended to questions and documents that might incriminate his or her spouse.[13] Furthermore no statement made by either spouse to the other or to a third person *with a view to effecting a reconciliation* may be put in evidence without the consent of the spouse who made it. The reason for this is, of course, that it is more important that spouses should be reconciled than divorced and complete frankness will not be obtained if the parties have at the back of their minds the fear that whatever is said may be given in evidence in matrimonial proceedings if the attempt at reconciliation fails.[14]

Evidence in Criminal Proceedings.—Until the passing of the Criminal Evidence Act in 1898, the accused could not give evidence in criminal proceedings except in a few isolated cases where there were statutory provisions to the contrary. It is not surprising that generally speaking the accused's spouse was equally incompetent, for it was considered contrary to public policy that a witness should give evidence either for

---

[12]Section 16 (3), implementing the recommendations of the Law Reform Committee contained in their 16th Report, Cmnd. 3472. The Committee was of the opinion that the judge's discretion to exclude evidence gave sufficient protection: see paras. 42-43.

[13]Civil Evidence Act 1968, s. 14.

[14]*Theodoropoulas* v. *Theodoropoulas*, [1963] 2 All E.R. 772; [1964] P. 311, and the cases there cited; *Pais* v. *Pais*, [1970] 3 All E.R. 491. It is immaterial whether the initiative was taken by one of the spouses or by a third person: *Henley* v. *Henley*, [1955] 1 All E.R. 590, n.; [1955] P. 202. See also the Matrimonial Proceedings (Magistrates' Courts) Act 1960, s. 4 (5).

or against his or her spouse in civil proceedings, *a fortiori* this would not be permissible in a criminal cause. To this rule there is one exception at common law, *viz.* that a spouse is a competent witness for the prosecution if the accused is charged with committing a crime of personal violence against him or her[15] or perhaps of any crime affecting the witness's liberty or health.[16] If the rule were otherwise, it might be absolutely impossible to prove the offence; hence in such a case the spouse is not only competent but also compellable.[17]

The Criminal Evidence Act 1898 has made the accused's spouse a competent witness for the defence subject to two limitations. First, the spouse may not be called except upon the application of the accused.[18] Secondly, the privilege formerly accorded to matrimonial communications by the Evidence Amendment Act in civil proceedings was extended to criminal proceedings.[19] This provision is still in force. It means that if a married man charged with, say, burglary calls his wife as a witness and she is asked in cross-examination whether her husband has confessed his guilt to her, it is she alone who decides whether or not to preserve his confidence. This rule, which prevents the accused from controlling whether statements made by him to his spouse should be disclosed or withheld, is even more illogical in criminal proceedings than it was in civil proceedings. It also illustrates the principle that such protection as exists is purely statutory and that no privilege attaches to the communication as such. Consequently the prosecution may always put the statement in evidence if they can prove it without calling the accused or the spouse. This occurred in *Rumping* v. *D.P.P.*[20] The police intercepted a letter written by the accused, who was charged with murder, to his wife and containing a virtual confession of guilt. It was held by the House of Lords that it had been properly admitted as evidence.

The principle that a spouse should not give evidence against the accused has been further eroded by statute. In certain specified crimes (mainly of a sexual nature or against children) the wife or husband of the accused is a competent (but not compellable)[1] witness

---

[15]This includes any form of violence, *e.g.*, causing grievous bodily harm (*R.* v *Lapworth*, [1931] 1 K.B. 117, C.C.A.), rape (*Lord Audley's Case* (1631), 3 St. Tr. 401 H.L.), sodomy (*R.* v. *Blanchard*, [1952] 1 All E.R. 114).

[16]*Per* PICKFORD and AVORY, JJ., in *D.P.P.* v. *Blady*, [1912] 2 K.B. 89, at pp. 90, 91. In *R.* v. *Verolla*, [1962] 2 All E.R. 426; [1963] 1 Q.B. 285, STEVENSON, J., admitted the evidence of a wife whose husband was charged with attempting to poison her, preferring these dicta to the decision in *R.* v. *Yeo*, [1951] 1 All E.R. 864, *n.*, where GORMAN, J., refused to admit the evidence of a wife whose husband was charged with sending her a letter threatening to murder her. But the cases are distinguishable on the ground that the same rule should apply to an attempt as to a completed offence but not to a mere threat. The spouse may also be a competent witness for the Crown on a charge of treason, but there is no authority.

[17]*R.* v. *Lapworth*, (*supra*).

[18]S. 1 (c). By analogy with *Leach* v. *R.* (*infra*), this does not make the spouse *compellable* on the accused's application, but there is no direct authority.

[19]S. 1 (d).

[20][1962] 3 All E.R. 256, H.L.; [1964] A.C. 814. The only protection given to the accused is the general discretion vested in the court to exclude prejudicial evidence improperly obtained.

[1]*Leach* v. *R.*, [1912] A.C. 305, H.L.

for the prosecution or the defence without the accused's consent.[2] A person is also a competent witness for the prosecution in any proceedings *brought by that person* against his or her spouse[3] and is also competent (but not compellable) to give evidence for the prosecution or the defence in any proceedings not brought by him in which his or her spouse is charged with any offence with reference to that person or to that person's property.[4] Only in the last case is the witness specifically given the statutory privilege to decline to disclose any communication made by the accused during the marriage.

If a spouse is incompetent to give evidence against the accused during the marriage, the incompetence continues in respect of matters which occurred during coverture after a decree of divorce and, apparently, after a decree of nullity where the marriage was voidable.[5]

2. LOSS OF THE RIGHT TO CONSORTIUM

The right to consortium can be lost, broadly speaking, in three ways.

First, if the spouses agree to live apart, the agreement divests each of them of the right to the other's consortium. But once the agreement comes to an end, the right will revive. Hence if, say, the husband entirely repudiates his obligations under the agreement, the wife will be entitled to treat it as at an end and, if she does so, may demand that the husband should resume cohabitation. Separation agreements will be treated more fully in the next chapter.

Secondly, a decree of judicial separation or a separation order made under the Matrimonial Proceedings (Magistrates' Courts) Act relieves the spouse obtaining the order from the duty of cohabiting with the other, so that, as long as the order is in force, the right to consortium ceases to exist. Separation by a court order will be discussed in greater detail in later chapters.[6]

Thirdly, matrimonial misconduct will also deprive the spouse misconducting himself of the right to the other's consortium. Clearly this term is sufficiently wide to include any conduct which would afford a defence to a charge of desertion brought against the other spouse: it would obviously be absurd to say in the same breath that the latter owes

---

[2]Criminal Evidence Act 1898, s. 4 and Sched. (as amended); Sexual Offences Act 1956, s. 39. For a full list of the offences to which this provision applies (including those added by later statutes), see Phipson, *Evidence*, 11th Ed., 608.

[3]Theft Act 1968, s. 30 (2). It is doubtful whether the witness is compellable but the point will be academic in most cases as he is not likely to refuse to give evidence in proceedings instituted by himself unless there has been a reconciliation in the meantime.

[4]*Ibid.*, s. 30 (3). It is far from clear what offences can be regarded as committed " with reference to the person ". The spouse is already competent at common law if the offence is one of violence. The section probably includes such matters as the sending of the threatening letter in *R*. v. *Yeo*, (*supra*), living on a wife's immoral earnings and wilful neglect to maintain. The accused's spouse is also a compellable witness for the Crown or the accused in certain cases relating to public highways and proceedings instituted for the purpose of trying or enforcing a civil right: Evidence Act 1877, s. 1.

[5]*R*. v. *Algar*, [1953] 2 All E.R. 1381, C.C.A.; [1954] 1 Q.B. 279. See further, *ante*, p. 70. If the marriage is *void*, of course, either party to it may give evidence against the other: *R*. v. *Young and Muezzell* (1851), 5 Cox C.C. 296. Judicial separation does not affect the rules relating to marital incompetence: *Moss* v. *Moss*, [1963] 2 All E.R. 829; [1963] 2 Q.B. 799.

[6]*Post*, chaps. 6 and 7.

a duty to cohabit and yet is not in desertion if he breaks off cohabitation.[7] It must not be forgotten that this duty is mutual, and, as JEUNE, P., put it:[8]

> " Neither party to a marriage can, I think, insist on cohabitation unless she or he is willing to perform a marital duty inseparable from it."

Moreover, it would seem that a matrimonial offence committed by one spouse will deprive him of the right to the other's consortium whatever be the other's own conduct. Hence, a husband is not bound to cohabit with his wife if she has committed adultery, even though he has committed adultery too.[9]

3. BREACH OF THE DUTY TO COHABIT

Although the right to consortium has been likened to the rights attached to ownership, in one important respect this analogy breaks down, for as between the spouses the duty to cohabit is legally completely unenforceable. The doctrine of unity of personality prevented either spouse from suing the other at common law, and consequently the only remedy which a deserted spouse had before 1858 was to petition in the ecclesiastical courts for a decree for restitution of conjugal rights. This decree called upon a spouse in desertion to resume cohabitation with the petitioner, and if it was disobeyed, the respondent could be excommunicated. The power to excommunicate on this ground was abolished by statute in 1813 and was replaced by a power to commit for contempt,[10] but this was in turn abolished by the Matrimonial Causes Act of 1884, after which there was no direct sanction for failure to comply with the decree at all. The Act of 1884 compensated for this by enacting that disobedience to a decree for restitution should give the other spouse an immediate right to petition for judicial separation or, until 1923 in the case of a wife, for divorce if the husband had also committed adultery. For many years petitions were still brought by wives who wanted to take advantage of the court's power to make ancillary orders, particularly orders for maintenance, but the need to use this machinery was largely removed by the Law Reform (Miscellaneous Provisions) Act 1949, which gave her power to petition for maintenance in the High Court without bringing any other proceedings. The decree for restitution had obviously become a complete anomaly and it was eventually abolished by section 20 of the Matrimonial Proceedings and Property Act 1970.[11]

Although the duty to cohabit is not specifically enforceable, a breach of it may lead to other consequences. If there is a total breach, the spouse in default will be in desertion, and this will in turn enable the other to petition for divorce or judicial separation at the end of two years or

---

[7]For good cause for separation, see *post*, pp. 168-170.
[8]*Synge* v. *Synge*, [1900] P. 180, 195.
[9]*Brooking-Phillips* v. *Brooking-Phillips*, [1913] P. 80. C.A.
[10]Ecclesiastical Courts Act 1813.
[11]During the years 1965-1969 there were on the average 29 petitions for restitution a year and nine decrees. The courts still give *indirect* support to the right to consortium, *e. g.*by declaring void any condition attached to a bequest providing an incentive for the beneficiary to live apart from his or her spouse or to obtain a divorce: see *Re Johnson's Will Trusts*, [1967] 1 All E.R. 553; [1967] Ch. 387, and the cases there cited.

to make an application immediately for an order under the Matrimonial Proceedings (Magistrates' Courts) Act. If the wife is in desertion, the husband ceases to be under any obligation to maintain her.[12]

If there is only a partial breach of the mutual duties that the spouses owe each other, this may in itself give the innocent party the right to petition for divorce, judicial separation or nullity if it is sufficiently serious (*e.g.*, behaviour such that the other spouse cannot reasonably be expected to live with him or wilful refusal to consummate the marriage) or to apply for an order in a magistrates' court (*e.g.*, a husband's insistence on sexual intercourse if he knows himself to be suffering from a venereal disease).[13] If the conduct is something less than this, it may nevertheless still entitle the other to break off cohabitation completely without being in desertion (or even so as to put the defaulting spouse in constructive desertion) if it is such as to make married life together virtually impossible.[14]

C. REMEDIES FOR INTERFERENCE WITH THE RIGHT TO CONSORTIUM

I. DAMAGES FOR LOSS OF CONSORTIUM AND SERVICES

Scope of the Action.—At common law a husband had a writ of ravishment or trespass *vi et armis de uxore rapta et abducta*, under which he could obtain damages against a defendant who had taken away his wife, but this action is now completely obsolete. It was replaced by the much wider action for damages for enticement which emerged in the middle of the eighteenth century and which was available to both spouses.[15] The husband had two further remedies: an action for damages for harbouring his wife[16] and an action for damages for adultery. The latter began as the common law action for criminal conversation (or crim. con.) by which the husband could obtain compensation for the loss of his wife's comfort and society as the result of the adulterer's wrongful act. Crim. con. was abolished by the Matrimonial Causes Act of 1857 and was replaced by a statutory claim for damages in the divorce court which was almost always made on a petition for divorce. The reason that neither of these remedies was available to the wife was that they were based upon the quasi-proprietary interest which the husband had in his wife and her services at common law.

The common law actions were brought very rarely and even the claim for damages for adultery was becoming uncommon. It was anomalous that the latter should be confined to the husband, and it was doubtful whether it was any longer socially desirable to give either spouse

---

[12]See *post*, p. 403.

[13]For divorce, see *post*, chap. 8, judicial separation, *post*, chap. 6, nullity, *ante*, chap. 3, orders in a magistrates' court, *post*, chap. 7.

[14]See *post*, pp. 168-170 and 173.

[15]The earliest reported case seems to be *Winsmore* v. *Greenbank* (1745), Willes 577. It was established that the wife could sue in *Gray* v. *Gee* (1923), 39 T.L.R. 429.

[16]This was probably obsolete before it was formally abolished: see the judgment of DEVLIN, J., in *Winchester* v. *Fleming*, [1957] 3 All E.R. 711; [1958] 1 Q.B. 259.

a remedy if the loss of the other's consortium was due to the latter's voluntary act, even though the defendant had induced or encouraged it. Consequently the Law Reform (Miscellaneous Provisions) Act of 1970 abolished actions for enticement and harbouring and the right to claim damages for adultery.[17] This means that the plaintiff now has an action for damages for loss of consortium only if this was due to the defendant's breach of contract or tort.

Loss of Consortium due to Breach of Contract.—If as a result of a breach of a contractual duty owed by the defendant to the plaintiff the latter loses the consortium of his spouse, he may recover for this loss by way of damages for breach of contract provided that it was a foreseeable consequence of the breach and therefore not too remote. Thus in *Jackson* v. *Watson & Sons*,[18] where the plaintiff's wife died from food poisoning as a result of eating salmon which the defendant had sold to the plaintiff, the Court of Appeal held that he could recover for the loss of his wife's services.

Loss of Consortium due to the Defendant's Tort.—Loss of consortium due to the defendant's tortious act may arise in one of two ways.

First, it may be the result of a tort committed against the plaintiff himself. If, for example, the defendant tells the plaintiff's wife untruthfully that the plaintiff has been guilty of adultery with the intention of inducing her to leave her husband and succeeds in his purpose, the plaintiff could recover for this loss in an action for slander.[19]

Secondly, if a husband loses his wife's consortium as a result of a tort committed against *her*, he has a separate cause of action against the tortfeasor for loss of consortium. Thus, if as a result of X's negligence W (a married woman) is injured and has to spend a considerable time in hospital, X may be sued not only by W for her personal injuries but also by her husband for the loss of her consortium. This cause of action is entirely independent of the wife's; hence it was held in *Mallett* v. *Dunn*[20] that although the wife's claim for personal injuries had to be reduced because of her own contributory negligence, her husband's claim was not liable to be reduced at all and he could recover in full. Presumably, however, the husband could recover nothing if the wife's claim were barred completely, as it would be, for example, if the injury had been entirely due to her own negligence.

Action for Loss of Consortium by the Wife.—This last cause of action—that resting on loss of consortium due to a tort committed against the plaintiff's wife—is really an anomalous survival of the old common law concept that the husband's interest in the wife is quasi-proprietary, and in *Best* v. *Samuel Fox & Co., Ltd.*[1] the House of

---

[17]Sections 4 and 5 (a) and (c). This implements the recommendation of the Law Commission: Law Com. No. 25, paras. 99-102.

[18][1909] 2 K.B. 193, C.A.

[19]*Cf. Lynch* v. *Knight* (1861), 9 H.L. Cas. 577, H.L.; *Lampert* v. *Eastern National Omnibus Co., Ltd.*, [1954] 2 All E.R. 719.

[20][1949] 1 All E.R. 973; [1949] 2 K.B. 180.

[1][1952] 2 All E.R. 394, H.L.; [1952] A.C. 716. See Fridman, *Consortium as an " Interest " in the Law of Torts,* 32 Can. Bar Rev. 1065.

Lords refused to extend it so as to give the wife a similar cause of action. In that case the plaintiff's husband had been rendered impotent as a result of the defendant's negligence and she sued the defendant for the loss which she suffered as a consequence of being no longer able to enjoy normal sexual relations with her husband. The House unanimously held that no action of this sort would lie at the suit of the wife and expressed the view that if the rights of the spouses should be equalised in this respect, this should be done by abolishing the husband's right by legislation and not by extending the anomaly further. This clearly precludes the wife from suing for loss of consortium occasioned by a tort committed against her husband; what is not now clear is whether she may sue if the loss is due to a tort committed against herself or to a breach of a contractual duty owed to her. LORD GODDARD's speech (in which LORD OAKSEY and LORD REID concurred on this point) is sufficiently wide to preclude any action by a wife for loss of consortium,[2] but it must be borne in mind that loss of consortium due to a tort committed against the husband was the sole question before the House and LORD PORTER and LORD MORTON were clearly considering this point only.[3] In the earlier case of *Lynch* v. *Knight*[4] the House of Lords was divided on this matter; but it is submitted that on principle the wife should be able to recover provided that the loss is not too remote a consequence of the tort or breach of contract, since she can establish an independent cause of action.[5] This was the view of HILBERY, J., in the later case of *Lampert* v. *Eastern National Omnibus Co., Ltd.*,[6] where he held that the plaintiff, who had been badly disfigured in an accident for which the defendant's servant was partly to blame, could have recovered for the loss of her husband's consortium had she been able to prove that the disfigurement was the cause of his leaving her.[7]

Impairment of Consortium.—In *Best* v. *Fox*[8] the House of Lords left open the further question whether an action can ever lie for the impairment, as distinct from the complete loss, of consortium. LORD GODDARD took the view that consortium is an indivisible abstraction and that consequently no action will lie for its mere impairment— an opinion with which LORD PORTER was inclined to agree.[9] LORD REID (with whom LORD OAKSEY concurred) maintained that since consortium is a bundle of rights, a husband could recover if any of these rights were interfered with, even though he was only in part deprived of his wife's comfort and society.[10] LORD GODDARD'S and LORD

---

[2]At pp. 399 and 732-733, respectively.

[3]At pp. 395, 400 and 726, 735, respectively.

[4](1861), 9 H.L. Cas. 577, H.L.

[5]But if the tort is not actionable *per se* and the *only* damage which the wife can show is the loss of her husband's consortium, *quaere* whether she can succeed.

[6][1954] 2 All E.R. 719. See Fridman, *loc. cit.*

[7]In fact she failed because the spouses had been getting on badly together for a long time and the husband had merely used his wife's disfigurement as an excuse for leaving her.

[8][1952] 2 All E.R. 394, H.L.; [1952] A.C. 716. See further 18 M.L.R. 514.

[9]At pp. 399-400, 396 and 733-734, 728, respectively. This was the ratio of the decision of the Court of Appeal in this case: [1951] 2 All E.R. 116; [1951] 2 K.B. 639.

[10]At pp. 401 and 736, respectively. LORD MORTON expressed no opinion on this aspect of the case.

PORTER's objection to giving damages for the impairment of consortium is based upon the fact that in truth the husband's claim is
always for the expenses occasioned by the medical attention required
by his wife and by the loss of her services—in other words that he is
claiming for pecuniary loss rather than for any personal injury. But
expenses due to the impairment of consortium could be quite high, for
example if the husband had to hire a nurse or domestic help, and
consequently it is submitted that the action should lie. This argument
prevailed in *Lawrence* v. *Biddle.*[11]

Effect of the Spouse's Death.—Since the decision of LORD
ELLENBOROUGH, C.J., in *Baker* v. *Bolton*[12] it has been the accepted
rule in tort that " in a civil court the death of a human being could not
be complained of as an injury ". In that case the stage coach in which
the plaintiff and his wife were travelling overturned owing to the
defendant's negligence, and the wife died a month later in hospital. It
was held that the plaintiff could recover for the loss of his wife's consortium only until the time of her death, from which of course it follows
that if the wife dies instantaneously no action will lie at common law
for the loss of her consortium at all. In such a case the spouse's sole
remedy is that afforded by the Fatal Accidents Acts.[13]

In *Jackson* v. *Watson & Sons*,[14] however, the Court of Appeal held
that the rule in *Baker* v. *Bolton* has no application where the cause of
action is contractual, and consequently permitted the plaintiff to
recover for the loss of his wife's consortium due to her death as a result
of eating defective salmon sold to him by the defendant. The absurdity
of this distinction can be demonstrated by the fact that the plaintiff
would have had no remedy (other than that provided by the Fatal
Accidents Acts) if the defendant had sold the tin of salmon to the
plaintiff's wife instead of to the plaintiff, for in that case there would
have been no privity of contract between the parties.

Measure of Damages.[15]—The commonest head of damages is for
medical and nursing expenses[16] and for the pecuniary loss of the wife's
services, for example the cost of providing a housekeeper to look after
the husband and children whilst the wife is in hospital. Although it
seems that compensation can be recovered for loss of companionship,
damages are usually low.[17] In particular, the husband cannot claim

---

[11][1966] 1 All E.R. 575; [1966] 2 Q.B. 504, followed in *Cutts* v. *Chumley*, [1967] 2 All
E.R. 89. See also *Hare* v. *British Transport Commission*, [1956] 1 All E.R. 578. Damages
for impairment of consortium have also been awarded by the High Court of Australia
(*Toohey* v. *Hollier* (1955), 92 C.L.R. 618) but refused by the Supreme Court of Ireland
(*Spaight* v. *Dundon*, [1961] I.R. 201). See further Milner, *Injuries to Consortium in
Modern Anglo-American Law*, 7 I.C.L.Q. 417. For a full criticism of the law relating to
loss of consortium and service, see Williams, *Some Reforms in the Law of Tort*, 24,
M.L.R. 101.

[12](1808), 1 Camp. 493. The principle was affirmed by the House of Lords in
Admiralty Commissioners v. *S.S. Amerika*, [1917] A.C. 38.

[13]See *post*, pp. 108 et seq.

[14][1909] 2 K.B. 193, C.A. See *ante*, p. 104.

[15]See Street, *Principles of the Law of Damages*, 227-235.

[16]Unless, of course, the wife has already recovered them. It may be more
advantageous for the husband to sue, for if the wife has been contributorily negligent, her
damages will be reduced *pro tanto*, whereas the husband can recover *in toto* (*ante*, p.104).

[17]In *Sellars* v. *Best*, [1954] 2 All E.R. 389, PEARSON, J., awarded £100. The point was
left open by DEVLIN, J., in *McNeill* v. *Johnstone*, [1958] 3 All E.R. 16, 19. See also
Lawrence v. *Biddle*, (*supra*).

as such for loss of earnings occasioned by the injury to his wife;[18] if, for example, he and his wife were professional entertainers and as a result of her incapacity he could earn less than half the sum they jointly earned, he would have no claim for his loss any more than he could claim for injury to any other business partner. But there appear to be at least three cases in which loss of earnings may be claimed. First, if the loss arises directly and peculiarly out of the loss of consortium, the husband may recover for it. This occurred in *Behrens* v. *Bertram Mills Circus, Ltd.*,[19] where it was held that the plaintiff, a midget who earned his living by appearing with his wife (another midget) in exhibitions in funfairs and who stayed at home whilst his wife was incapacitated as a result of an accident for which the defendants were liable, could recover for his loss of earnings, as he was peculiarly dependent on his wife in that he could not easily mix with persons of a normal stature and that it was not reasonable to expect him to go on tour alone in his caravan and look after himself. Secondly, if the husband loses his earnings in order to be with his wife and thus speeds her recovery, he may recover for this loss if his action is a proper step taken to mitigate the damage sustained by the loss of consortium.[20] Thirdly, if, as a result of the injury she has suffered, the wife has to live away from her home and the husband's usual place of work and the latter elects not to be deprived of her consortium but to forgo his earnings instead, it would seem that he can claim for this loss instead of claiming for loss of consortium. Thus in *McNeill* v. *Johnstone*[1] the husband, who was an officer in the United States Air Force stationed at Margate, took unpaid leave to be near his wife who was in hospital at Swindon, and DEVLIN, J., held that he could recover such part of his loss of earnings and his expenses as were attributable to his preserving his consortium.

Proposals for Reform.—Insofar as the present law is based upon the common law view that a husband's interest in his wife's services and consortium is quasi-proprietary, it is clearly anachronistic and there is no justification today for refusing the wife compensation for any financial loss she suffers as a result of a tort committed against her husband. Consequently the Law Reform Committee would equate the rights of the spouses and propose that " where a husband or a wife is tortiously injured, the other spouse should be able to recover reasonable medical and nursing expenses and all other costs properly incurred in consequence of the injury, such as reasonable visits to hospital and the reasonable cost of providing domestic help to replace the injured partner ". Such a claim would include any loss of earnings reasonably

---

[18]*Kirkham* v. *Boughey*, [1957] 3 All E.R. 153; [1958] 2 Q.B. 338. *Cf.* the analogous rule under the Fatal Accidents Acts, *post*, pp. 109-110.
[19][1957] 1 All E.R. 583; [1957] 2 Q.B. 1.
[20]*Kirkham* v. *Boughey*, (*supra*). Hence the loss is not recoverable if the sole justification for the husband's action is the comfort or pleasure that it gives to the wife: *ibid.,* pp. 157 and 343, respectively.
[1][1958] 3 All E.R. 16. *Quaere* whether he can recover the full loss of his earnings if this sum is greater than that at which the court would assess the loss of consortium.

incurred by any action taken in consequence of the injury.[2]

2. THE FATAL ACCIDENTS ACTS

The rule in *Baker* v. *Bolton*[3] gave rise to the cynical maxim that it was cheaper to kill than to maim. The consequences of the fact that the dependants of a person who had been killed as the result of the negligence of another might be left penniless without recourse against the tortfeasor became much more serious with the introduction of heavy machinery and the invention of the railway in the early nineteenth century. The legislature eventually intervened to ameliorate the position by passing in 1846 the Fatal Accidents Act (commonly called Lord Campbell's Act).[4]

This Act introduced an action which is " new in its species, new in its quality, new in its principle, in every way new ",[5] for it permitted a claim to be made on behalf of certain dependants of any person who had been killed as the result of the defendant's wrongful act, neglect or default. The damages must accordingly be assessed in accordance with the financial loss suffered by the dependants as a result of the death.

For whose Benefit the Action will lie.—The action will lie only on behalf of persons standing in the following relationships to the deceased: wife, husband, parent, grandparent, child, grandchild, brother, sister, uncle, aunt and the issue of a brother, sister, uncle and aunt.[6] An adopted person is to be treated as the child of his adopter or adopters;[7] and (subject to this) any relationship by affinity is to be treated as a relationship by consanguinity,[8] any relationship of the half blood as a relationship of the whole blood, the stepchild of any person as his child, and an illegitimate person as the legitimate child of his mother and reputed father.[9]

---

[2]Eleventh Report (Loss of Services, etc.), 1963, Cmnd. 2017. In the analogous case of an employer's right to recover expenses incurred in consequence of a tortious injury inflicted on his employee, they recommend that the amount recoverable should be reduced in proportion to the latter's contributory negligence (para. 10). Presumably the same principle should be applied in the case of a spouse's claim.

[3]*Ante*, p. 106.

[4]This Act, the Fatal Accidents Act 1864 and the Fatal Accidents Act 1959 are together known as the Fatal Accidents Acts 1846-1959. For criticisms of the Acts, see Stone, *The Economic Aspects of Death in the Family* (1965), 8 J.S.P.T.L. 188.

[5]*Per* LORD BLACKBURN in *Seward* v. *" Vera Cruz"* (1884), 10 App. Cas. 59, 70-71, H.L.

[6]Fatal Accidents Act 1846, ss. 2, 5; Fatal Accidents Act 1959, s. 1 (1). A posthumous child (and presumably any other child *en ventre sa mere* at the date of the death) may claim: *The George and Richard* (1871), L.R. 3 A. & E. 466.

[7]Fatal Accidents Act 1959, s. 1 (2) (a), (3). Obviously an adopted child may claim on the death of his adoptive parent and *vice versa;* the wording of the Act is sufficiently wide to enable him to claim on the death of his adopter's natural parent (who would now become his grandparent for the purpose of the Act) and so on.

[8]There is an ambiguity here. A man may clearly claim on the death of, *e.g.,* his wife's father. He may presumably claim on the death, *e.g.,* of his sister's husband. May this process be extended to include relationships traced through two (or even more) marriages ? *E.g.,* may a man claim on the death of his wife's sister's husband ?

[9]Fatal Accidents Act 1950, s. 1 (2) (b), (c). Can a person claim on the death, *e.g.,* of his stepparent's natural parent and can an illegitimate person claim on the death, *e.g.,* of his mother's parent? (*Cf.* the same problem in the case of an adopted person, n. [7]).

The claimant must also have suffered some pecuniary loss as a result of the death, and no action will lie in the absence of any such loss.[10] Hence, a wife can claim nothing if her husband had ceased to pay her maintenance as a result of her adultery before his death.[11] Similarly she cannot recover anything if the sole support she had from him came from the proceeds of his criminal activities for *ex turpi causa non oritur actio*.[12] Where the claimant has been wholly or partly dependant on the deceased before his death, pecuniary loss is obviously easy to prove, as, for example, in the case of a wife who has been supported by her husband, a child supported by his parent, or an old person supported by his adult child. Benefits received in kind are also sufficient, provided that they are capable of being assessed. Thus, a husband has an interest in the domestic services performed in the house by his wife,[13] and it has been held that an action will lie by parents in respect of the death of a son who had from time to time given them presents of food as well as small sums of money[14] and of a son who had gratuitously performed services for which they were paid.[15]

Even though the deceased had made no contribution to the claimant's support before his death, an action will lie under the Fatal Accidents Acts provided that the latter had a reasonable expectation of pecuniary advantage in the future, had the other survived. This is particularly important in the case of a child who could have looked to the deceased to pay for his education or, conversely, in the case of a parent who had reasonable hopes of being supported by his child in his old age.[16] On the other hand, no action is maintainable where there is a " mere speculative possibility of benefit "[17] or a " bare chance of receiving some slight pecuniary help ".[18]   In *Barnett* v. *Cohen*[19] a father brought an action under the Act in respect of the death of his four-year-old son. The boy had been very bright and the plaintiff had had hopes of ultimately sending him to a university. In view of the fact that the son, who could not have been expected to contribute anything to his father's income for at least twelve years, would all that time have been subject to all the risks of illness, disease, accident and death, and that the father might not have lived so long because of the poor state of his own health, it was held that the chance of financial benefit to the father, had the son not been killed, was too remote and that the action must fail.

Furthermore, the financial benefit which the claimant has lost as a result of the death must derive from the relationship and must not be a mere business loss.   In *Burgess* v. *Florence Nightingale Hospital for*

---

[10]*Duckworth* v. *Johnson* (1859), 4 H. & N. 653.
[11]*Stimpson* v. *Wood* (1888), 57 L.J.Q.B. 484.
[12]*Burns* v. *Edman*, [1970] 1 All E.R. 886; [1970] 2 Q.B. 541.
[13]*Berry* v. *Humm & Co.*, [1915] 1 K.B. 627.
[14]*Dalton* v. *South Eastern Rail. Co.* (1858), 4 C.B.N.S. 296.
[15]*Franklin* v. *South Eastern Rail. Co.* (1858), 3 H. & N. 211.
[16]*Pym* v. *Great Northern Rail. Co.* (1862), 2 B. & S. 759, Q.B.; (1863), 4 B. & S. 396, Ex. Ch.; *Taff Vale Rail. Co.* v. *Jenkins*, [1913] A.C. 1, H.L.; *Hetherington* v. *North Eastern Rail. Co.* (1882), 9 Q.B.D. 160.
[17]*Per* McCARDIE, J., in *Barnett* v. *Cohen*, [1921] 2 K.B. 461, 471.
[18]*Per* STEPHEN, J., in *Stimpson* v. *Wood* (1888), 57 L.J.Q.B. 484, 486.
[19][1921] 2 K.B. 461. *Cf. Burns* v. *Edman*, (*supra*) (possibility of deceased husband's reforming and taking up honest work too remote).

Gentlewomen[20] the plaintiff and his wife had been professional dancing partners who, as a team, had earned more than twice the husband could expect to earn with any other partner. They had shared their income and also their expenses which, in view of the fact that they could live together in hotels, etc., were less than twice the husband's individual expenses. In a claim under the Act as a result of the wife's death, it was held that the plaintiff could recover nothing for his loss of income, for this benefit arose from a business partnership to which their relationship of husband and wife was, as it were, incidental; but that he could recover for the loss due to the increased expenses for this arose immediately from the fact that they were husband and wife. As the Court of Appeal pointed out in *Malyon* v. *Plummer*,[1] however, the matter must be viewed realistically, and if a benefit was in fact derived from the relationship, its loss will be recoverable even though it appears at first sight to be a business loss. In that case the plaintiff's husband had turned his business into a private company; he held 999 shares and the plaintiff held the remaining share. The spouses were both directors, but it was essentially a one-man business under the husband's control. The wife worked casually and intermittently in the office, and although she was paid sums varying from £600 to £800 a year as a director, the actual value of her services (which the husband would otherwise have had to pay someone else to carry out) was assessed at £200 a year. The husband was killed as a result of the defendant's negligence and the wife's attempts to keep the business going were unsuccessful. In an action under the Fatal Accidents Acts it was held that, as her directorship and the fact that her earnings were grossly in excess of their value were really due to the relationship of husband and wife and not to a business relationship, she was entitled to recover compensation for her loss based upon the difference between her actual earnings and the value of the work she had put in.

The action must be brought by the personal representatives on behalf of the dependants,[2] but if there are no personal representatives or the personal representatives do not commence proceedings under the Act within six months of the death, the action may be brought by any one or more of the dependants themselves.[3] In any event, the action must normally be brought within three years of the death.[4] Only one

---

[20][1955] 1 All E.R. 511; [1955] 1 Q.B. 349.

[1][1963] 2 All E.R. 344, C.A.; [1964] 1 Q.B. 330. *Cf. Saikaley* v. *Pelletier* (1966), 57 D.L.R. (2d) 394 (damages recovered for loss of mother who lived with son and daughter-in-law and did housework in return for board, lodging and pocket money). Cases like *Franklin* v. *South Eastern Rail. Co.* (*ante*) are clearly distinguishable, for there the deceased gave his services free as a result of the relationship between himself and the plaintiff.

[2]Hence personal representatives have no power to compromise the claim of any dependant unless the latter is *sui juris* and agrees to the compromise: *Jeffrey* v. *Kent C.C.*, [1958] 3 All E.R. 155.

[3]Fatal Accidents Act 1846, s. 2; Fatal Accidents Act 1864. If no personal representatives have been appointed, the dependants may sue in their own name even within the first six months: *Holleran* v. *Bagnell* (1879), L.R. 4 Ir. 740

[4]Law Reform (Limitation of Actions, &c.) Act 1954, s. 3. Where death results from a collision at sea, any action against the *other* vessel is normally barred after two years: Maritime Conventions Act 1911, s. 8; *The Alnwick*, [1965] 2 All E.R. 569, C.A.; [1965] P. 357; *The Niceto de Larrinaga*, [1965] 2 All E.R. 930; [1966] P. 80.

action may be brought, so that if any dependant is not included as a claimant, he has no remedy under the Act at all.[5]

Against whom the Action may be brought.—An action under the Fatal Accidents Acts will lie against any person whom the deceased could himself have sued in respect of the injury causing death had he not died.[6] The crucial test is therefore: could the deceased have maintained an action against the defendant at the date of his death? Hence no action will lie if the latter could have raised the defence of *volenti non fit injuria,*[7] if the deceased had already sued for his own injuries, if he had received during his lifetime compensation in full satisfaction[8] or if he died more than three years after the injury[9] so that his own claim would have been statute barred.[10] Similarly, no action will lie if the defendant had *wholly* contracted out of liability;[11] on the other hand, however, since the Fatal Accidents Acts give a completely new cause of action with an independent assessment of damages, the claim by the dependants will in no way be affected by a mere *limitation* of liability. In *Nunan* v. *Southern Rail. Co.*[12] the plaintiff's husband had been killed as a result of the defendant's servants' negligence. He had been travelling on a workman's ticket under which the defendant's liability was limited to £100. The plaintiff was awarded £800 damages under the Fatal Accidents Act, and it was held by the Court of Appeal that, since the deceased would have had a cause of action, the plaintiff was not limited to the sum which he could have recovered.

It is doubtful whether any action can be brought under the Crown Proceedings Act against the Crown for damages under the Fatal Accidents Acts.[13]

---

[5]Fatal Accidents Act 1846, s. 3. But if a dependant has been improperly excluded, he may have a remedy against the personal representatives or other plaintiffs: *per* LORD ATKIN in *Avery* v. *London & North Eastern Rail. Co.,* [1938] 2 All E.R. 592, 595, H.L.; [1938] A.C. 606, 613.

[6]Fatal Accidents Act 1846, s. 1. This is so whether the original cause of action was tortious or contractual: *Grein* v. *Imperial Airways, Ltd.,* [1936] 2 All E.R. 1258, C.A., at pp. 1275, 1287: [1937] 1 K.B. 50, at pp. 71, 88.

[7]*Senior* v. *Ward* (1859), 1 E. & E. 385.

[8]*Read* v. *Great Eastern Rail. Co.* (1868), L.R. 3 Q.B. 555.

[9]Unless material facts relating to the cause of action were outside the deceased's actual or constructive knowledge for a period of at least two years after the cause of action accrued. In this case the personal representatives can apply to bring the action within a year of the time when he knew or could reasonably have ascertained the facts or, if he died without this actual or constructive knowledge, within a year of the death: Limitation Act 1963, s. 3; *Lucy* v. *W. T. Henleys Telegraph Works Co., Ltd.,* [1969] 3 All E.R. 456, C.A.; [1970] 1 Q.B. 393.

[10]*Williams* v. *Mersey Docks and Harbour Board,* [1905] 1 K.B. 804, C.A. The better view (which is now generally accepted) is that provided the deceased's claim was not statute barred at his death, the original period of limitation ceases to be relevant and the new three years' period starts to run: *British Columbia Electric Rail. Co., Ltd.* v. *Gentile,* [1914] A.C. 1034, P.C.; *Venn* v. *Tedesco,* [1926] 2 K.B. 227. For the contrary view that no action will lie if the original limitation period has run out before the claim is brought under the Act, see *Markey* v. *Tolworth Joint Isolation Hospital District Board,* [1900] 2 Q.B. 454; and *cf.* the wording of the Limitation Act 1963, s. 3l (*supra,* n.[9]).

[11]*Haigh* v. *Royal Mail Steam Packet Co., Ltd.* (1883), 52 L.J.Q.B. 640, C.A.

[12][1924] 1 K.B. 223, C.A.

[13]See Street, *Torts,* 4th Ed., 421.

Assessment of Damages.[14]—Damages are to be measured solely by reference to the financial loss which the dependants have suffered as a result of the death, except that they may also be awarded in respect of funeral expenses if these have been incurred by any party for whose benefit the action is brought.[15] We have already seen that no action will lie at all if no financial loss has been suffered; similarly, no damages may be recovered for any wounded feelings or mental suffering which the death has caused the dependants.[16]

In order to arrive at the correct sum to award by way of damages, the court must first assess what the deceased was likely to have earned in the future had he remained alive. From this can be calculated the dependency, that is the annual benefit which the dependant or dependants would have received from the estimated earnings. There must then be applied to the dependency the appropriate multiplier based upon the number of years for which the dependency was likely to have continued if the deceased had not been killed. Suppose that the deceased's estimated earnings were £2,000 a year net, of which he was likely to have spent half on his wife and children; the dependency will then be £1,000. If the court applies a multiplier of twelve, the damages will be £12,000.[17]

Often the assessment of future earnings and the benefit which the dependants would have received from them must obviously be a matter of speculation. " In most cases the most reliable guide as to what would happen in the future if the deceased had lived is what did in fact happen when he was alive. "[18] It must also be realised that the dependency need not have been a benefit in cash: the value of services in kind may also be assessed. Hence, in the case of the death of a wife, the husband may claim for the loss of her services less the cost of maintaining her.[19]

It is perhaps even more difficult to arrive at the correct multiplier. Essentially this represents the number of years for which the dependency was likely to have continued if the deceased had not been killed. It is therefore frequently appropriate to start with his estimated working life; it must be remembered, however, that the dependency of a

---

[14]See generally Kemp and Kemp, *Quantum of Damages*, vol. 2, 2nd Ed.; Street, *Principles of the Law of Damages*, particularly pp. 148-166 and 179-183.

[15]Law Reform (Miscellaneous Provisions) Act 1934, s. 2 (3). Funeral expenses may be recovered even though the claimant cannot prove financial dependency, but in any case they must be reasonable: *Stanton* v. *Ewart F. Youldon, Ltd.*, [1960] 1 All E.R. 429; *Hart* v. *Griffith-Jones*, [1948] 2 All E.R. 729 (claim for embalming body of child allowed, but not £225 for a monument to place over the grave).

[16]*Blake* v. *Midland Rail. Co.* (1852), 18 Q.B. 93.

[17]See generally LORD WRIGHT in *Davies* v. *Powell Duffryn Associated Collieries, Ltd.*, [1942] 1 All E.R. 657, 665, H.L.; [1942] A.C. 601, 617; LORD DIPLOCK in *Malyon* v. *Plummer*, [1963] 2 All E.R. 344, 353, C.A.; [1964] 1 Q.B. 330, 349-350, and *Mallett* v. *McMonagle*, [1969] 2 All E.R. 178, 191, H.L.; [1970] A.C. 166, 176-178; LORD MORRIS and LORD PEARSON in *Taylor* v. *O'Connor*, [1970] 1 All E.R. 365, H.L., at pp. 370 and 377-378; [1971] A.C. 115, at pp. 131-132 and 141-142.

[18]*Per* DIPLOCK, L.J., in *Malyon* v. *Plummer*, (*supra*), at pp. 353 and 349, respectively.

[19]*Berry* v. *Humm & Co.*, [1915] 1 K.B. 627, 630. *Cf. Burgess* v. *Florence Nightingale Hospital for Gentlewomen*, [1955] 1 All E.R. 511; [1955] 1 Q.B. 349 (increase in husband's expenses due to wife's death); *Peacock* v. *Amusement Equipment Co., Ltd.*, [1954] 2 All E.R. 123 (loss of house in which dependant had been living with the deceased. Overruled on another point, [1954] 2 All E.R. 689, C.A.; [1954] 2 Q.B. 347).

child will normally cease when he starts earning his own living[20] and, conversely, a rich man can be expected to use his savings to provide for his family after his retirement and his death so that the basic figure is his widow's expectation of life.[1] The estimated duration of the dependency must now be reduced to take account of various contingencies, for example the possibility that the deceased might have died prematurely in any event (particularly if his expectation of life was not great),[2] that the dependant might die prematurely (again with specific reference to the particular dependant's expectation of life),[3] that the dependant (if she is the deceased's widow) will remarry[4] or that, if the marriage was unstable, it might have broken down.[5] Similarly, damages will be less in the case of the death of a son than that of a husband because a child is under no legal obligation to support his parents and, had he married, he might well have cut down the sum he was prepared to pay his mother or father.[6]

The multiplier must be further reduced to take account of the fact that the dependant is receiving a lump sum now representing annual payments in the future. As the House of Lords pointed out in *Taylor* v. *O'Connor*,[7] the dependant is expected to invest the damages prudently and to live on both income and capital; if one merely multiplied the dependency by the number of years it was likely to have lasted (reduced to take account of contingencies), no account would be taken of the income which this capital sum would produce.[8] Similarly, if the

---

[20]Or marries in the case of a daughter: see *Rawlinson* v. *Babcock and Wilcox, Ltd.*, [1966] 3 All E.R. 882.

[1]*Taylor* v. *O'Connor*, (*supra*).

[2]*Hall* v. *Wilson*, [1939] 4 All E.R. 85. But see *Bishop* v. *Cunard White Star Co., Ltd.*, [1950] 2 All E.R. 22, 26; [1950] P. 240, 248.

[3]*Williamson* v. *John I. Thornycroft & Co., Ltd.*, [1940] 4 All E.R. 61, C.A.; [1940] 2 K.B. 658. If the dependant dies before judgment the element of doubt disappears and the damages may be assessed more accurately: *ibid*. See also *Whittome* v. *Coates*, [1965] 3 All E.R. 268, C.A.

[4]*Curwen* v. *James*, [1963] 2 All E.R. 619, C.A. (where the widow remarried after judgment had been given but before the appeal was heard); *Goodburn* v. *Thomas Cotton, Ltd.*, [1968] 1 All E.R. 518, C.A.; [1968] 1 Q.B. 845. See Ogus, 31 M.L.R. 339.

[5]*Gadsby* v. *Hodkinson* (1966), 110 Sol. Jo. 834, C.A.

[6]*Dolbey* v. *Goodwin* [1955] 2 All E.R. 166, C.A.

[7][1970] 1 All E.R. 365, H.L.; [1971] A.C. 115. Wise investment will also take account of inflation: *ibid*., pp. 380 and 144, respectively (*per* LORD PEARSON). See also *Mallett* v. *McMonagle*, (*supra*), at pp. 190 and 175-176, respectively (*per* LORD DIPLOCK).

[8]The following example given by LORD PEARSON in *Taylor* v. *O'Connor*, (*supra*), at pp. 379 and 144, respectively, may make the point clearer. Suppose £45,000 is invested at 3% and it is required to give an annual sum of £3,750.

	Capital £	Annual sum to be provided £	Income at 3% £	Withdrawn from capital £
	45,000 2,400	3,750	1,350	2,400
After 1 year	42,600 2,472	3,750	1,278	2,472
After 2 years	40,128 2,546	3,750	1,204 .	2,546
After 3 years	37,582	3,750	1,127	2,623

The fund will be completely exhausted after 15 years.

G

award is large (as it was in that case), account must also be taken of the incidence of income tax and either the multiplier or the dependency must be increased to give the dependant the same net sum as she would have received had the deceased still been alive.[9] It is submitted that the question that ought to be asked is this: if the dependency is £x and its probable duration, reduced to take account of contingencies, is y years, what sum, invested at current rates of interest, will enable the dependant, using both capital and income, to receive £x a year net for y years? The sum is not difficult to calculate and ought to give a reasonably accurate assessment of the damages to be awarded; it seems, however, as though it does not commend itself to the judges who prefer to trust their own and practitioners' experience to give the correct multiplier.[10]

The principle that the purpose of the Fatal Accidents Acts is to compensate the dependants for their financial loss has been applied in a series of cases which have established the rule that any claim must be reduced by the amount of any gain which accrues to a dependant as a direct result of the death. Thus, a dependant must bring into account any part of the deceased's estate which devolves on him or her, if this represents a gain which would not have accrued but for the death.[11] But if the dependant acquires property of which he would have had the use had the deceased remained alive, this is clearly not a financial advantage resulting from the death, and so the value does not have to be taken into account. Thus in *Heatley* v. *Steel Company of Wales, Ltd.*[12] the plaintiff's husband, in respect of whose death the action was brought, had died intestate, with the result that the beneficial interest in the matrimonial home, which was valued at £750, passed to the plaintiff. It was held that her claim under the Fatal Accidents Acts was not to be reduced by this £750, for the net gain to her was nothing, as she still had to have a roof over her head.[13]

Conversely, it follows from the principle that the dependants are entitled to be put back in the financial position they were in when the deceased was alive that if, say, a widow decides to go out to work after

---

[9]*Taylor* v. *O'Connor, (supra).* It must be assumed that income tax will remain at its present rate. But the House of Lords refused (without giving reasons) to take into account the fact that the dependant's private income might mean that she will be paying surtax on the income at a much higher rate: see LORD REID at pp. 368 and 129 and LORD DILHORNE at pp. 376 and 139, respectively. This seems arbitrary and unsatisfactory.

[10]In *Taylor* v. *O'Connor, (supra),* both LORD GUEST (at pp. 373 and 135) and LORD PEARSON (at pp. 377 and 140, respectively) deprecated the use of actuarial tables as giving a false appearance of accuracy and increasing the length and expense of trials Sixteen years' purchase appears to be about the most that the courts are prepared to sanction: *Mallett* v. *McMonagle, (supra),* at pp. 191 and 177, respectively.

[11]*E.g.,* investments, for the dependants' interest in them is increased by the amount by which their present value exceeds the interest in expectancy: *Bishop* v. *Cunard White Star Co., Ltd., (supra),* pp. 26 and 248, respectively.

[12][1953] 1 All E.R. 489, C.A. *Cf. Daniels* v. *Jones,* [1961] 3 All E.R. 24, C.A.

[13]But if, contrary to obvious facts, it would seem that the dependant has lost nothing financially by the death, arithmetic must give way to common sense: *Daniels* v. *Jones, (supra). Cf. Kassam* v. *Kampala Aerated Water Co., Ltd.,* [1965] 2 All E.R. 875, P.C.

her husband's death, she does not have to bring her earnings into account.[14]

Since any damages awarded to the deceased's personal representatives under the Law Reform (Miscellaneous Provisions) Act 1934 for personal injuries to the deceased and for loss of his expectation of life go to swell his estate, it was finally laid down by the House of Lords in *Davies* v. *Powell Duffryn Associated Collieries, Ltd.*[15] that if the dependants took any interest in the damages, any claim made by them under the Fatal Accidents Acts must be *pro tanto* reduced.[16]

But where the gain to the dependant is not a benefit which could have been claimed as of right but is a gratuitous payment or transfer of property due to the charity or generosity of another, the position is not entirely clear. It has been held that a payment out of a fund launched to help the dependants of the victims of a railway disaster does not diminish a claim under the Act, for otherwise the generosity of the subscribers would merely benefit the defendant by reducing his liability and the springs of charity in the future might well dry up.[17] This is obviously a policy decision: in other cases the true test, it is submitted, is that formulated by SOMERVELL, L.J., in *Peacock* v. *Amusement Equipment Co., Ltd.*,[18] where he pointed out that the benefit must be brought into account only if there was some probability or reasonable expectation of it at the time of the death. In that case the plaintiff's wife had left all her property in her will to her two children by a former husband. The children later paid to the plaintiff a sum representing one-third of the value of the estate and it was held that this sum did not have to be brought into account in assessing the plaintiff's damages in an action under the Fatal Accidents Acts as it was paid solely as the result of the step-children's generosity and was not a benefit of which the plaintiff had any expectation when his wife died.

The same problem arises in a slightly different form in those cases where a widow remarries before the trial and her second husband treats the deceased's children as though they were his own. In this connection it must be remembered that a man is now under a legal duty to maintain his wife's children by a former marriage if they are members of the

---

[14]*Buckley* v. *John Allen & Ford (Oxford), Ltd.*, [1967] 1 All E.R. 539; [1967] 2 Q.B. 637 (no deduction made for rent received by widow from letting rooms in the former matrimonial home).

[15][1942] 1 All E.R. 657, H.L.; [1942] A.C. 601, following LORD WRIGHT in *Rose* v. *Ford*, [1937] 3 All E.R. 359, 375, H.L.; [1937] A.C. 826, 853.

[16]But not if the claim on behalf of the estate is for loss of or damage to property of which the dependant would have had the use had the deceased remained alive, on the principle exemplified in *Heatley* v. *Steel Co. of Wales, Ltd.*, *(supra)*: *Bishop* v. *Cunard White Star Co., Ltd.*, *(supra)*, at pp. 26 and 248, respectively. It is better to claim the damages under the Fatal Accidents Acts, for they do not then attract death duties and they cannot be taken by the deceased's creditors if the estate is insolvent: see *Hutchinson* v. *London and North Eastern Rail. Co.*, [1942] 1 K.B. 481, 491, C.A.

[17]*Redpath* v. *Belfast and County Down Rail.*, [1947] N.I. 167. *Cf. Baker* v. *Dalgleish Steam Shipping Co.*, [1922] 1 K.B. 361, C.A., at pp. 369, 380; *Bowskill* v. *Dawson*, [1954] 2 All E.R. 649, C.A., at pp. 655, 656; [1955] 1 Q.B. 13, at pp. 24, 26.

[18][1954] 2 All E.R. 689, 692, C.A.; [1954] 2 Q.B. 347, 353. See also *Green* v. *Russell*, [1958] 3 All E.R. 44, 47-48; [1959] 1 Q.B. 28, 39-40; *Voller* v. *Dairy Produce Packers, Ltd.*, [1962] 3 All E.R. 938; *Moore* v. *Babcock & Wilcox, Ltd.*, [1966] 3 All E.R. 882.

family;[19] consequently, if the second husband is a man whose financial position is such that he can reasonably be expected to provide for the children as well as their own father would have done, they will be able to recover for financial loss only up to the date of their mother's remarriage, for after that they have suffered none.[20] If on the other hand the second husband is financially worse off than the first, or if in any case his income is low so that he could not be expected to fulfil the obligations of a father and maintain the children to the same extent, they will clearly be entitled to recover for their loss under the Fatal Accidents Act.[1]

This rule as a whole may well be regarded as an unwarranted judicial fetter upon the operation of the Acts which serves no one but the tortfeasor. Its application was most hurtful to the dependants of a breadwinner who had had the foresight to take out a substantial insurance policy upon his own life or whose employer had provided for the payment of a pension to his widow and children. The position in this respect has now been considerably improved by the provisions of section 2 of the Fatal Accidents Act 1959, which enacts that in assessing damages under the Fatal Accidents Acts no account shall be taken of any insurance money,[2] benefit under the National Insurance Acts,[3] payment by a friendly society or a trade union for the relief or maintenance of dependants, pension,[4] or gratuity which has been or will be or may be paid as a result of the death. Although the term " gratuity " is not defined, it is submitted that it probably does not include all gratuitous payments but, like the other payments specified, presupposes an existing relationship between the payer and the deceased and would therefore not cover the types of payment or gain mentioned in the last two paragraphs.

Where the death was caused partly by the deceased's contributory negligence, the damages recoverable under the Fatal Accidents Acts must be reduced in proportion to the deceased's share of the responsibility for the damage causing his death.[5]

The court must apportion the damages amongst the claimants if there are more than one.[6] The normal practice today is for the court first to assess the total sum to be awarded and then to apportion it rather than to assess each dependant's claim and then to aggregate

---

[19]See *post*, pp. 472 and 474.
[20]*Reincke* v. *Gray*, [1964] 2 All E.R. 687, C.A.
[1]*Mead* v. *Clarke Chapman & Co., Ltd.*, [1956] 1 All E.R. 44, C.A. This case was decided before a step-father was placed under a statutory duty to maintain his step-children but it was distinguished on both grounds in *Reincke* v. *Gray*, (*supra*).
[2]Including a return of premiums. The money need not necessarily be paid or payable to the dependant or the deceased's personal representatives: see *Malyon* v. *Plummer*, [1963] 2 All E.R. 344, C.A.; [1964] 1 Q.B. 330, where it was held that insurance money paid to a company on the death of a director which benefited his widow by increasing the value of her shares was to be left out of account. See further *ante*, p. 110.
[3]These include death benefits under the National Insurance (Industrial Injuries) Act 1965 and widow's benefits, guardian's allowances and death grants under the National Insurance Act 1965.
[4]Including a return of contributions and any payment of a lump sum in respect of employment.
[5]Law Reform (Contributory Negligence) Act 1945, s. 1 (4).
[6]Fatal Accidents Act 1846, s. 2.

these amounts.[7]   This simplifies procedure and rests upon the assumption that apportionment is of only minor importance because the damages will be used to maintain the family however they are apportioned; hence if the dependants are the widow and children of the deceased, the bulk of the damages will be given to the widow as she can be expected to use them to maintain her children.[8] But this is not an invariable rule and the court will make a genuine apportionment if failure to do so might prejudice the claimant.   In *Moore* v. *Babcock & Wilcox, Ltd.*[9] the deceased left two dependants, his widow and a daughter.   The widow died before the action came to trial.   Had the bulk of the sum payable in respect of loss before the widow's death been paid to her estate, it would have received nothing because the sum was less than that awarded for loss of the deceased's expectation of life which had to be brought into account.   CHAPMAN, J., therefore made a genuine apportionment and gave five-sevenths to the widow and two-sevenths to the daughter.

3. THE CARRIAGE BY AIR ACT 1961

In the case of injury or death of a passenger on an aircraft, the application of the common law rules and the provisions of the Fatal Accidents Acts are modified by the Carriage by Air Act 1961.[10]   The carrier's liability is absolute unless he proves that he and his servants or agents have taken all necessary measures to avoid the damage or that it was impossible for them to take such measures;[11] but if the negligence of the person injured or killed contributed to the damage, the provisions of the Law Reform (Contributory Negligence) Act 1945 apply so as to reduce the damages awarded in proportion to the passenger's share in the responsibility.[12]

The Carriage by Air Act imposes two limitations upon causes of action arising out of personal injuries.   In the first place, the action must be brought within two years.[13]   Secondly, the carrier's liability is limited to 250,000 francs unless the contract of carriage fixes a higher maximum sum.[14]   Any provision in a contract of carriage relieving the carrier of liability or fixing a lower limit than 250,000 francs is void.[15] But there is no limit to the carrier's liability at all if the damage resulted from an act or omission of the carrier (or, provided that they were

---

[7]See *Jeffrey* v. *Kent C.C.*, [1958] 3 All E.R. 155, 157.

[8]See the Report of the Committee on Funds in Court, 1959, Cmnd. 818, para. 15. Money payable to a minor must be paid into court, as must money payable to the widow if the proceedings were also brought for the benefit of a minor: Administration of Justice Act 1965, s. 19.

[9][1966] 3 All E.R. 882. See also *Goodburn* v. *Thomas Cotton, Ltd.*, [1968] 1 All E.R. 518, C.A.; [1968] 1 Q.B. 845 (larger sums apportioned to children and less to widow because of the high chance that the latter would remarry).

[10]This Act gives effect to the Warsaw Convention as amended at the Hague in 1955. The Convention applies only to contracts of international carriage by air, but s. 10 (1) of the Act and the Carriage by Air Act (Applications of Provisions) Order, S.I. 1967 No. 480, extend it to non-international carriage.

[11]Carriage by Air Act 1961, 1st Sched., Arts. 17 and 20.

[12]*Ibid.*, s. 6 and 1st Sched., Art 21.

[13]*Ibid.*, 1st Sched., Art. 29.

[14]*Ibid.*, s. 4 and 1st Sched., Art. 22 (1). The sterling equivalent is £6,909.90: Carriage by Air (Sterling Equivalents) Order, S.I. 1968 No. 1316.

[15]*Ibid.*, 1st Sched., Art. 23.

acting within the scope of their employment, of his servants or agents) done either with intent to cause damage or recklessly with knowledge that damage would probably result.[16]

D. CONTRACT

The Law until 1935.—At common law a married woman possessed no contractual capacity whatever and could therefore make a binding agreement neither with her husband nor with any other person.[17] This rule did not apply to a woman whose husband had abjured the realm or been transported,[18] but subject to this exception neither she nor her husband could sue or be sued on any contract made by her (except as his agent), even though she was living apart from him by agreement with separate maintenance[19] or (save by custom in the City of London)[20] engaging in trade on her own account.[1] Moreover the marriage automatically vested in the husband the benefit of all contracts already made by the wife and both spouses were liable during coverture to be sued on them;[2] but if the husband died before the wife and a contract made by her before marriage was still executory, she and not her husband's personal representatives could sue and be sued on it. Any ante-nuptial contract made between the spouses themselves was automatically discharged by the marriage.

Equity did not take the same strict view of a married woman's incapacity as the common law. Hence if a wife had separate property in equity, she could effectively bind this by contract, although she could not render herself *personally* liable on any agreement.[3]

Nineteenth Century Legislation.—The first statutory inroad on this principle was made by the Matrimonial Causes Act 1857, which provided that so long as a decree of judicial separation was in force, a married woman should be considered as a feme sole for the purpose, *inter alia*, of the making and enforcement of contracts.[4] But the first

---

[16]*Ibid.*, 1st Sched., Art. 25. If an action is brought against the carrier's servant or agent, he has the same protection as the carrier if he was acting within the scope of his employment: Art. 25A.

[17]See further Morrison in *A Century of Family Law*, chap. 6. Even if she expressly contracted as a feme sole, she was not estopped from pleading her coverture for capacity cannot be created by estoppel: *Cannam* v. *Farmer* (1849), 3 Exch. 698. But an executed contract seems to have been valid for the purpose of transferring property: *Dalton* v. *Midland Counties Rail. Co.* (1853), 13 C.B. 474.

[18]*Carrol* v. *Blencow* (1801), 4 Esp. 27. Otherwise she would have been wholly unable to provide herself with necessaries, as no tradesman would accept her husband's credit in such circumstances.

[19]*Lean* v. *Schutz* (1778), 2 W. Bl. 1195; *Marshall* v. *Rutton* (1800), 8 Term Rep. 545. An attempt to introduce a contrary rule in *Corbett* v. *Poelnitz* (1785), 1 Term Rep. 5, was apparently abortive. Whether the same rule applied if the husband was a foreigner residing abroad is doubtful: see *De Gaillon* v. *L'Aigle* (1798), 1 B. & P. 357; *Williamson* v. *Dawes* (1832), 9 Bing. 292: *Stretton* v. *Busnach* (1834), 1 Bing. N.C. 139.

[20]See *La Vie* v. *Phillips* (1765), 3 Burr. 1776.

[1]*Clayton* v. *Adams* (1796), 6 Term Rep. 604.

[2]Judgment was entered against both and consequently both became personally liable to satisfy it. Hence before the Debtors Act 1869 the wife could be taken in execution under a *ca. sa.* and held in prison till the debt was paid, although it was the practice to discharge her if she had no separate property: *Edwards* v. *Martyn* (1851), 17 Q.B. 693.

[3]See further Pollock, *Contracts*, 20th Ed., 557-561.

[4]S. 26. Later legislation has made this exception unnecessary.

exception of general application was made by the Married Women's Property Act of 1870, which made the first statutory extension to the equitable concept of separate property by enacting that a married woman's wages and earnings should be regarded as her separate property and giving her a power to maintain an action to recover them in her own name.[5] This Act also abolished the common law rule that a husband should be liable for his wife's ante-nuptial contracts,[6] a provision which worked extreme injustice on her creditors for, since her property continued to a very large extent to vest in her husband on marriage, there was frequently nothing on which they could levy execution. The absurdity of this position which gave the husband the best of both worlds[7] was recognised by the Legislature in the Married Women's Property Act (1870) Amendment Act 1874, which repealed the relevant part of the Act of 1870 but limited the husband's liability for his wife's ante-nuptial contracts to the extent of the value of her property which vested in him *jure mariti*.

The Married Women's Property Act of 1882 extended the principle of statutory separate property by enacting that all property belonging to a woman who married after 1882 should remain her separate property and that any property acquired by a wife after that date (whether she was married before or after the commencement of the Act) should similarly remain her separate property.[8] Furthermore this Act (as amended by the Married Women's Property Act 1893) gave her full contractual capacity and enacted that every contract entered into by her otherwise than as an agent should be deemed to be a contract with respect to her separate property and bind it. But it must be remembered that these Acts did no more than extend the existing principles of equity; hence a married woman's contract bound only her estate and the Act did not make her personally liable. Consequently she could still not be committed under a judgment summons[9] or be made bankrupt if she failed to satisfy a judgment debt.[10]

The Act of 1882 retained the principle of the Act of 1874 by enacting that a husband should be liable for his wife's ante-nuptial debts and contracts only to the extent of property belonging to her which he acquired or to which he became entitled.[11]

The Modern Law.—The modern position is to be found in the Law Reform (Married Women and Tortfeasors) Act of 1935. This Act abolished the concept of the separate estate and enabled a married

---

[5]Ss. 1 and 11. See further *post*, p. 353.

[6]S. 12.

[7]And also had the effect of making it difficult for an engaged woman to obtain credit.

[8]See further *post*, p. 353.

[9]*Scott* v. *Morley* (1887), 20 Q.B.D. 120, C.A. But she was still personally liable on her ante-nuptial contracts: *ibid.*, p. 125.

[10]*Ex parte Jones* (1879), 12 Ch.D. 484, C.A. She was, however, expressly made subject to the bankruptcy laws if she was carrying on a trade separately from her husband: Married Women's Property Act 1882, s. 1 (5). If her separate property was subject to a restraint on anticipation, only income due at the time the contract was made could be seized: Married Women's Property Act 1893, s. 1; *Wood* v. *Lewis*, [1914] 3 K.B. 73, C.A.

[11]S. 14.

woman to hold and dispose of property in all respects as if she were a feme sole.[12] As regards her power to contract, section 1 provides that she shall be capable of rendering herself and being rendered liable in respect of any contract, debt or obligation, and of suing and being sued in contract, and also that she shall be subject to the law relating to bankruptcy and the enforcement of judgments and orders as if she were a feme sole.

It is thus obvious that she now has full power to enter into a contract either with a stranger or with her own husband.[13]   But the law relating to contracts between spouses is subject to one important qualification. Whilst an agreement between them will clearly be enforceable if it represents a business arrangement, the courts are not prepared to interfere in the running of the home by giving legal effect to the sort of arrangements that spouses living together make every day in order to regularise their domestic affairs. The leading case in this field is still that of *Balfour* v. *Balfour*[14] where the Court of Appeal held that an agreement, under which the husband, who was about to go abroad, promised to pay the wife £30 a month in consideration of her not looking to him for further maintenance, was unenforceable because there was no intention to enter into legal relations. If the spouses are cohabiting when they enter into the agreement, there is a presumption that they do not intend to be legally bound.[15] Although public policy obviously demands that the courts should not be compelled to adjudicate on matters of domestic convenience, this principle can work injustice in the situation of which *Balfour* v. *Balfour* itself is typical, where the spouses subsequently separate and the wife takes no steps to obtain a maintenance order in reliance on her husband's promise to make her periodical payments. Consequently the presumption does not operate if the parties have separated or are at arm's length and about to separate: in these circumstances their intention becomes a question of fact to be inferred from all the evidence.[16] In most cases of this sort, where the agreement relates to financial arrangements, it will be almost impossible to conclude that they did not intend to be legally bound by the terms.

The Act of 1935 has entirely abolished the husband's liability for his wife's contracts entered into before marriage, since he now acquires no property out of which he can meet her debts.[17] The only problem that remains is whether marriage automatically discharges executory contracts already entered into between the spouses, since the old common

---

[12]See further *post*, p. 354.

[13]She had power to contract with her husband under the Act of 1882: *Butler* v. *Butler* (1885), 14 Q.B.D. 831 (WILLS, J.); affirmed, 16 Q.B.D. 374, C.A.

[14][1919] 2 K.B. 571, C.A. See also *Spellman* v. *Spellman*, [1961] 2 All E.R. 498, C.A. (agreement as to ownership of car unenforceable).

[15]This appears to be the view of the majority of the Court of Appeal in *Gould* v. *Gould*, [1969] 3 All E.R. 728; [1970] 1 Q.B. 275.

[16]In *Merritt* v. *Merritt*, [1970] 2 All E.R. 760, C.A., LORD DENNING, M.R., was of the opinion that there was a presumption that they intend to be bound; WIDGERY, L.J., went no further than saying that there was no presumption that they did not intend to be bound; KARMINSKI, L.J., regarded the question simply as one of fact.

[17]S. 3.

law rule has never been expressly abolished. In *Butler* v. *Butler*[18] WILLS, J., held that under the Act of 1882 the common law position still obtained. His interpretation of the relevant sections seems to be very narrow, and in any event the unambiguous wording of the 1935 Act suggests that today the spouses may mutually enforce any ante-nuptial contract notwithstanding the marriage.[19] Thus, if a man and woman enter into articles of partnership, it is submitted that the contract will subsist even though they later intermarry. But just as some agreements entered into by the spouses after marriage will be unenforceable because there is no intention to create legal relations, contracts of the same nature entered into beforehand may well be discharged on marriage by a tacit agreement because it cannot be the parties' intention that the obligations created by them should any longer be enforceable by the courts.

The Wife as her Husband's Agent.—At common law a married woman could always act as an agent since the latter does not require to have any contractual capacity. The fact that the agent happens to be the principal's spouse is clearly immaterial if the other party to the contract relies upon an express authorisation or a presumed authority arising from a business relationship or a ratification by the principal of the other's acts.[20] But the relationship of husband and wife presents two particular problems: the wife's presumed agency arising from cohabitation and a particular example of agency by holding out.[1]

Presumption of Agency from Cohabitation.—If a married woman is cohabiting with her husband, there is a presumption that she has his authority to pledge his credit for necessary goods and services which belong to those departments of the household which are normally under her control.[2] Coming within this category are such contracts as those for the purchase of food, clothing for the wife and children, domestic utensils and small articles of furniture, contracts for the hire of domestic servants, contracts for repairs and probably also contracts for the education of children.

This presumption was obviously of much greater importance in times

---

[18]*Ante.* There was no appeal against this part of the decision and the Court of Appeal expressed no opinion on it.

[19]See Chitty, *Contracts*, 23rd Ed., i, 445; Kahn-Freund, 15 M.L.R. 138-140. The Court of Appeal upheld the validity of such a contract in *Re Kendrew*, [1953] 1 All E.R. 551, C.A.; [1953] Ch. 291, but the point was not argued and the contract was made in contemplation of marriage.

[20]As in *West* v. *Wheeler* (1849), 2 Car. & Kir. 714.

[1]Until 1970 the wife also had an agency of necessity: see *post*, pp. 401-402.

[2]*Debenham* v. *Mellon* (1880), 6 App. Cas. 24, H.L.; *Phillipson* v. *Hayter* (1870), L.R. 6 C.P. 38. *Cf. Gregory* v. *Parker* (1808), 1 Camp. 394 (acknowledgment by the wife of a debt incurred by her in purchasing goods deemed to be an acknowledgment by the husband's agent for the purpose of the Statute of Limitations). In *Debenham* v. *Mellon*, where the spouses lived in an hotel as manager and manageress, LORD SELBORNE, L.C., expressed doubts whether there was a sufficient matrimonial establishment to raise the presumption at all (at p. 33). *Sed quaere?* Since the basis of the presumption is the fact of cohabitation, it applies where a man is living with a woman as his wife even though they are not in fact married. But in any case there is no presumption of authority after they have separated and an actual authority must then be proved: *Wallis* v. *Biddick* (1873), 22 W.R. 76.

when a married woman had no contractual capacity than it is today; for as she is the person who normally makes such contracts, tradesmen would have had no remedy at all had she not been acting as her husband's agent. As it was, they had a *prima facie* cause of action against him if the goods supplied were necessaries. Today it may still be necessary to rely on the presumption if the wife has no property and is therefore not worth suing. In other cases the question will be whether the tradesman can properly hold the husband or the wife liable for the price of the goods (or services) supplied, for the husband cannot be made liable if the tradesman has given credit exclusively to the wife and has treated her throughout as the principal.[3] If he has in fact supplied the goods on the husband's credit, he may still rely on the presumption that the wife had her husband's authority to pledge it, and if the husband rebuts this, the wife will then be personally liable on her implied warranty of authority to bind him.[4]

The burden of proving that the goods (or services) supplied were necessaries is on the plaintiff.[5] The term " necessaries " in this context bears the same meaning as it does in other branches of the law of contract, that is, goods (or services) which are suitable to the wife's condition of life and to her actual requirements at the time they are sold and delivered (or rendered).[6] Hence articles of mere luxury can never be necessaries. If the goods (or services) could be classed as necessary but are of an expensive variety, for example an expensive dress, they can be necessaries only if they are not extravagant when tested against the husband's ostensible standard of living and that which he permitted his wife to adopt;[7] and if they were extravagant by this test[8] or if the wife is already adequately supplied with goods of this kind,[9] the action against the husband must fail.

As McCARDIE, J., emphasised in *Miss Gray, Ltd.* v. *Cathcart*,[10] this presumption is rebuttable. In addition to proving that the contract was not one for necessaries or of a sort which one could expect the husband to have given his wife authority to make, the husband may rebut it in any one of three different ways:

(1) By showing that he had already forbidden the plaintiff to give the wife credit.[11]

---

[3] *Miss Gray, Ltd.* v. *Cathcart* (1922), 38 T.L.R. 562; *Callot* v. *Nash* (1923), 39 T.L.R. 292.
[4] For an agent's warranty of authority, see Bowstead, *Agency*, 13th Ed., 397 *et seq.*; Powell, *Agency*, 2nd Ed., 253 *et seq.*; Hanbury, *Agency*, 2nd Ed., 144 *et seq.* The fact that the goods are supplied on the order of a wife cohabiting with her husband raises no presumption of joint liability: *Morel Bros. & Co., Ltd.* v. *Westmorland*, [1904] A.C. 11, H.L. If a tradesman signs judgment against the wife, this amounts to an election to treat her as personally liable: *ibid.*; contrast *C. Christopher (Hove), Ltd.* v. *Williams*, [1936] 3 All E.R. 68, C.A. (obtaining liberty to sign judgment against her not such a conclusive election).
[5] *Callot* v. *Nash*, (*supra*).
[6] *Cf.* the Sale of Goods Act 1893, s. 2, and see Cheshire and Fifoot, *Contract*, 7th Ed., 368-369.
[7] *Morgan* v. *Chetwynd* (1865), 4 F. & F. 451; *Phillipson* v. *Hayter* (1870), L.R. 6 C.P. 38; *Seymour* v. *Kingscote* (1922), 38 T.L.R. 586.
[8] *Miss Gray, Ltd.* v. *Cathcart*, (*infra*).
[9] *Reneaux* v. *Teakle* (1853), 8 Ex. 680; *Miss Gray, Ltd.* v. *Cathcart*, (*infra*).
[10] (1922), 38 T.L.R. 562.
[11] *Miss Gray, Ltd.* v. *Cathcart*, (*supra*).

(2) By proving that he had forbidden his wife to pledge his credit. After considerable judicial controversy it was finally settled by the House of Lords in *Debenham* v. *Mellon*[12] that such a prohibition is effective even though the plaintiff was unaware of it, although of course in such a case the husband may be liable by holding out.[13]

(3) By showing that the wife had an adequate allowance out of which she could herself have paid for the goods or services.[14] In fact the payment of a *fixed* sum (whether it is adequate or not) will usually carry with it an implied prohibition against pledging the husband's credit further and thus defeat the plaintiff.[15] Whether the presumption is raised if the wife has an adequate income of her own, so that she has no need to rely on her husband for money to buy necessaries, is more doubtful; in the absence of an agreement between the spouses that the wife alone shall be liable for necessaries bought by herself (which will of course have the effect of an implied prohibition),[16] the question must be regarded as an open one.[17]

Agency by Estoppel.—If a husband has in the past paid for goods supplied to his wife in such circumstances as to lead the tradesman with whom she has been dealing to conclude that he has given her an authority to buy goods on his credit, he will then be estopped from denying that she had any such authority and will consequently be liable for any further goods sold to her by that particular tradesman.[18] The importance of this rule lies in the fact that the husband's merely forbidding his wife to pledge his credit will not relieve him of liability for debts contracted by her if he has held her out in the past to have such an authority and does not inform those tradesmen with whom she has been dealing that it has been revoked.[19] Consequently his inserting a disclaimer in a newspaper will be insufficient for this purpose unless he can discharge the difficult burden of proving that the plaintiff in fact read the statement: the obvious step to take is to send a private notification to the tradesmen concerned.

What will amount to a sufficient holding out for this purpose must necessarily depend upon the facts of each case. Repeated paying of bills will doubtless create an estoppel, as may taking an active part in

---

[12](1880), 6 App. Cas. 24, H.L., following *Jolly* v. *Rees* (1864), 15 C.B.N.S. 628.

[13]See *infra*.

[14]Even though the plaintiff was unaware of this: *Morel Bros. & Co., Ltd.* v. *Westmorland*, [1904] A.C. 11, H.L.; *Slater* v. *Parker* (1908), 24 T.L.R. 621.

[15]*Remmington* v. *Broadwood* (1902), 18 T.L.R. 270, C.A.; *Miss Gray, Ltd.* v. *Cathcart*, (*supra*). The question whether a mere agreement to pay a fixed allowance would have the same effect was left open in *Remmington* v. *Broadwood*. If the husband opens an account on which he permits the wife to draw, this will not amount to an implied prohibition against pledging his credit if the arrangement is merely for his own convenience: *Goodyear* v. *Part* (1897), 13 T.L.R. 395.

[16]See *Seymour* v. *Kingscote* (1922), 38 T.L.R. 586, at pp. 587-588.

[17]Her income was stated to be immaterial in *Callot* v. *Nash* (1923), 39 T.L.R. 292, 293, and *Seymour* v. *Kingscote*, (*supra*), at p. 587. In *Biberfeld* v. *Berens*, [1952] 2 All E.R. 237, 243, C.A.; [1952] 2 Q.B. 770, 782, these dicta were criticised by DENNING, L.J., but that case was concerned with the wife's agency of necessity (based on the husband's duty to maintain her) where the principle involved was essentially different.

[18]*Drew* v. *Nunn* (1879), 4 Q.B.D. 661, C.A.; *Filmer* v. *Lynn* (1835), 1 Har. & W. 59.

[19]See *Debenham* v. *Mellon* (1880), 6 App. Cas. 24, H.L., at pp. 34, 36-37. Similarly he may be estopped from denying her authority even after they have ceased to live together: *Wallis* v. *Biddick* (1873), 22 W.R. 76, 77.

selecting the goods and directing the performance of the contract.[20]
But a husband does not hold out his wife as having authority to pledge
his credit merely by accompanying her when she shops,[1] or by
giving her a cheque to pay her debts;[2] nor does his having paid for
goods delivered to the matrimonial home in the past make him liable
to pay for those subsequently ordered by the wife to be sent
elsewhere.[3]

Presumably the general law of agency will apply in the case of
contracts made by the wife after the husband's death or bankruptcy,
so that in the former case his personal representatives will not be
estopped from denying the wife's power to render the estate liable,[4]
and in the latter the trustee in bankruptcy will be able to disclaim any
contract made by the wife after the date of the receiving order or of any
available act of bankruptcy[5] of which the tradesman had notice. But
whilst the general rule is that an agency is terminated by the principal's
insanity (whether or not the agent or person dealing with him was
aware of this fact), it was held by the Court of Appeal in *Drew* v.
Nunn[6] that a tradesman who supplied goods to the wife in ignorance
of her husband's insanity could sue him for the value of them after he
had recovered his sanity.

E. TORTS

The fiction of legal unity produced two separate rules in tort:

(1) If a tort was committed by or against a married woman, her
husband had to be joined as a party to the action and failure to do so
could be pleaded in abatement.

(2) No liability in tort could arise between spouses and no action in
tort could be brought by either of them against the other.

We must now consider how far these rules still apply.

Torts committed against the Wife.—At common law the husband
had to be joined as a party to any action brought by the wife in respect
of any tort committed against her, whether before or after the marriage,
on the general principle that he was entitled to reduce her choses in
action into possession. But in one sense the right remained hers rather
than his, for, if she died, the maxim *actio personalis moritur cum*

---

[20]*Jetley* v. *Hill* (1884), Cab. & El. 239 (contract for the supply of furniture and for
the decoration of the matrimonial home).

[1]*Seymour* v. *Kingscote* (1922), 38 T.L.R. 586, 588; *Callott* v. *Nash* (1923), 39 T.L.R.
292, 294.

[2]*Durrant* v. *Holdsworth* (1886), 2 T.L.R. 763.

[3]*Swan & Edgar, Ltd.* v. *Mathieson* (1910), 103 L.T. 832. Similarly a man may be
liable by estoppel for the contracts of a woman with whom he has been living but to
whom he is not married if he has held her out as having his authority: contrast *Ryan*
v. *Sams* (1848), 12 Q.B. 460, with *Gomme* v. *Franklin* (1859), 1 F. & F. 465.

[4]*Cf. Blades* v. *Free* (1829), 9 B. & C. 167.

[5]*I.e.*, any act of bankruptcy committed within the three months preceding the
presentation of the petition for the receiving order: see Bowstead, *Agency*, 13th Ed.,
449 *et seq.*

[6](1879), 4 Q.B.D. 661, C.A. Hanbury, *Agency*, 2nd Ed., 37, submits that this
result, though practically convenient, is inconsistent; Powell, *Agency*, 2nd Ed., 403-404,
doubts the correctness of the case but admits that sometimes it may work justice.

persona applied to prevent him from continuing with the action, but if the husband died, the cause of action survived to the widow. The necessity of joining the husband as a co-plaintiff was abolished by the Married Women's Property Act of 1882 and she may now retain any damages recovered as her own property.[7]

Torts committed by the Wife.—At common law the position where the wife was the tortfeasor was very similar to that where she was the person injured. Her husband had to be joined as a co-defendant in any action brought in respect of a tort committed by her either before or after the marriage;[8] if she died before judgment, the action abated, but if the husband died or the marriage was dissolved, the action survived against her alone.[9] As in the case of contract, the Married Women's Property Acts of 1874 and 1882 limited the husband's liability for her ante-nuptial torts to the extent of her property which he acquired or became entitled to,[10] but, whilst the latter Act made the wife personally liable for all her torts, neither Act affected his liability for torts committed by her during coverture.[11] The retention of the common law rule may have been justified in 1882, because few married women then would have had any property on which a successful plaintiff could execute judgment, but the passage of years rendered absurd the anomaly that the husband could be sued for her torts although he acquired none of her property *jure mariti*.[12] This was eventually removed by the Law Reform (Married Women and Tort-feasors) Act 1935, which has abolished his liability *as husband* for all her torts whenever committed.[13] But he may of course still be vicariously liable on other grounds, for example because he has authorised the commission of the particular act or because his wife was his servant acting in the course of her employment.

Actions between Spouses.—Until 1857 there was no exception at all to the common law rule that neither spouse could sue the other in tort. The Matrimonial Causes Act of that year permitted either to bring an action against the other if a judicial separation was in force,[14] and after the passing of the Married Women's Property Act of 1870 a wife could maintain an action to recover her separate property against

---

[7]See now the Law Reform (Married Women and Tortfeasors) Act 1935, s. 1 (c). A married woman was first given the power to maintain an action in her own name to recover her separate property by the Married Women's Property Act 1870, s. 11.

[8]But the husband was not liable for a tort committed by his wife *during coverture* where the cause of action was substantially contractual: *Liverpool Adelphi Loan Association* v. *Fairhurst* (1854), 9 Ex. 422; *Edwards* v. *Porter*, [1925] A.C. 1 H.L. (obtaining loans by fraud). *Cf.* the law relating to minors' liability in tort.

[9]*Capel* v. *Powell* (1864), 17 C.B.N.S. 743.

[10]See *ante*, p. 119. His liability for ante-nuptial torts was not affected by the Act of 1870 at all.

[11]*Edwards* v. *Porter*, (*supra*).

[12]See the observations of Swift, J., in *Newton* v. *Hardy* (1933), 149 L.T. 165, 168 (an enticement case and therefore more absurd than most).

[13]S. 3.

[14]S. 26. The common law rule was reintroduced (probably unintentionally) by the Law Reform (Married Women and Tortfeasors) Act 1935, which repealed the relevant part of the Supreme Court of Judicature (Consolidation) Act 1925, s. 194, which had replaced the Matrimonial Causes Act 1857, s. 26.

anyone (including her own husband).[15] This principle—that normally
the only action in tort that either spouse could bring against the other
was by the wife for the protection and security of her own property—
produced both anomalies and injustice. It was anomalous that a
husband could not sue his wife for damage to his property, however
maliciously caused, or that, even though the spouses were living at
arm's length, one could slander the other with impunity. It was unjust
that third parties' rights could be affected if the tortfeasor and his
victim happened to be married to each other. For example, if the
driver of a motor car negligently injured his wife, his insurance company
was relieved from its duty to compensate her, for the husband was under
no liability; for the same reason, if the wife was injured as the result
of the combined negligence of her husband and a third person, the latter
had to bear the whole loss and could claim no contribution from the
other.[16]

This situation has been remedied by section 1 of the Law Reform
(Husband and Wife) Act 1962,[17] which provides that each spouse
shall have the same right of action against the other in tort as though
they were not married. This applies equally to an action brought after
the marriage has been dissolved (or presumably annulled) in respect of
a tort committed during matrimony,[18] but in one respect the law here
is different, for if the action is brought during the subsistence of the
marriage, the court has a discretion to stay the action in two cases.
First, it may do so if it appears that no substantial benefit would accrue
to either party from the continuation of the proceedings. This is
designed to prevent trivial actions brought in bitterness to air matrimonial grievances;[19] consequently it is not contemplated that the
power would be exercised if the parties were no longer living together
as an economic unit and the damage was real, or if the spouse was a
purely nominal defendant and the real purpose of the action was to
recover damages from a source outside the family. Such would be the
case, for example, if the driver of a car wished to claim an indemnity
from his insurance company.[20] Secondly, the court may stay the
action if it relates to property and the questions in issue could more
conveniently be disposed of by an application under section 17 of the

---

[15]S. 11. Re-enacted in principle by the Married Women's Property Act 1882,
s. 12, and the Law Reform (Married Women and Tortfeasors) Act 1935, s. 1.
[16]*Drinkwater* v. *Kimber*, [1952] 1 All E.R. 701, C.A.; [1952] 2 Q.B. 281. But a
master was vicariously liable if a servant in the course of employment tortiously injured
his or her spouse: *Broom* v. *Morgan*, [1953] 1 All E.R. 849, C.A.; [1953] 1 Q.B. 597.
[17]Passed as a result of the Ninth Report of the Law Reform Committee, 1961,
Cmnd. 1268. See Stone, 24 M.L.R. 481; Kahn-Freund, 25 M.L.R. 695.
[18]S. 3 (3).
[19]See Cmnd. 1268, paras. 10-13.
[20]For presumably the court would look at all the facts and not stay the action
merely because no substantial benefit would arise from the defendant's satisfying the
judgment. But suppose a third person (*e.g.*, another car driver) were to claim contribution from the husband and the latter were not insured. Could the husband then argue
that an action between the spouses would have been stayed on the ground that no
substantial benefit would accrue to either of them and that consequently he cannot be
made to contribute because he is not a person " who would if sued have been liable for
the damage " for the purpose of the Law Reform (Miscellaneous Provisions) Act 1934,
s. 6 (1)?

Married Women's Property Act 1882. As we shall see,[1] the court has much more extensive powers under that section than it has in a common law action in tort. Consequently if the case raises complex questions of the spouses' rights in matrimonial assets or if a just solution is likely to demand an order for the sale or division of property, it is submitted that it should be dealt with under section 17.[2] On the other hand, if there is no dispute over title and damages or an injunction is the appropriate remedy, the case should proceed as an action in tort.

It must be remembered that, quite apart from the provisions of section 17 of the Married Women's Property Act, other proceedings are also open to a husband or wife in respect of a tortious act committed by the other. In the case of molestation, for example, a criminal prosecution will lie if there is an assault or conduct likely to cause a breach of the peace. If other matrimonial proceedings are being taken in the High Court, either spouse may apply for an injunction to restrain the other from molesting or interfering with the applicant or their children or from intermeddling with property if this is necessary for the applicant's protection.[3]

Some Miscellaneous Rules.—In *Wennhak* v. *Morgan*[4] it was held that the communication by one spouse to the other of a statement defamatory of a third person does not constitute a publication of that statement for the purpose of the law of libel and slander. While this is yet another illustration of the doctrine of unity, it can be more reasonably explained on the ground that any communication between the spouses should be privileged.[5] Upon the latter assumption only can be explained the rule that the publication by the defendant to the plaintiff's spouse of a statement defamatory of the plaintiff is actionable.[6]

Since the doctrine of unity apparently prevents the spouses from being prosecuted alone for a criminal conspiracy,[7] it is doubtful whether they can be sued alone for conspiracy in tort, although of course they could both be sued for conspiring together with a third person.[8]

---

[1]*Post*, pp. 357-359.

[2]See Cmnd. 1268, para. 14. In an action for damages the court may exercise any power that it has under s. 17 or direct that any question should be dealt with under that section: Law Reform (Husband and Wife) Act 1962, s. 1 (2).

[3]The court has no power to make an order if the petition has been dismissed (*Pickering* v. *Pickering* (1959), (unreported), C.A., cited in Rayden, *Divorce*. 11th Ed., 838). It is doubtful whether it still has power to do so after the final decree although an injunction was granted after decree absolute in *Beasley* v. *Beasley*, [1969] 1 W.L.R. 226. An injunction once made can continue in force after the final decree: *Robinson* v. *Robinson*, [1963] 3 All E.R. 813; [1965] P. 39. The court will not grant an injunction if the applicant has it in his own power to avoid the molestation, *e.g.* if the spouses are still living under the same roof and the applicant can afford to move elsewhere: *Freedman* v. *Freedman*, [1967] 2 All E.R. 680.

[4](1888), 20 Q.B.D. 635.

[5]HUDDLESTON, B., and MANISTY, J., both agreed that publication was precluded by the doctrine of unity. MANISTY, J., alone rested his decision on the further ground of public policy.

[6]*Wenman* v. *Ash* (1853), 13 C.B. 836.

[7]See *post*, p. 129

[8]But the doctrine of unity does not apply so as to enable the defendant to plead the wife's contributory negligence in reduction of damages claimed by the husband for loss of consortium: see *ante*, p. 104.

F. CRIMINAL LAW

The doctrine of unity has never applied generally in the criminal law so as to make a husband vicariously liable for his wife's crimes or to prevent either of them from being liable in most cases for a crime committed against the other. But it has made a number of periodical and inconsistent appearances which must be considered *seriatim*.

Marital Coercion.—There was a rule of common law that if a married woman committed certain offences in the presence of her husband, this raised a presumption (which was rebuttable)[9] that she had committed the crime under his coercion and consequently he and not she was *prima facie* liable to be convicted. Both the origin[10] and the extent of this rule are uncertain, but it seems to have applied to all misdemeanours[11] and most felonies, but not to grave felonies such as murder or to treason.[12] It had in any event become anomalous by the twentieth century and it was finally abolished by section 47 of the Criminal Justice Act of 1925 which replaced it by the following statutory defence:

> " On a charge against a wife for any offence other than treason or murder it shall be a good defence to prove that the offence was committed in the presence of, and under the coercion of, the husband."

It will be observed that this section effects two changes in the law. First, the burden of proof is now upon the wife to prove the coercion; secondly, it would seem to apply to all offences, both indictable and summary, except for the two named.[13]

Impeding a Spouse's Arrest.—The generally accepted view is that at common law a wife could not become an accessory after the fact to her husband's felony or a principal to his treason by receiving him, because she was bound in law to do so.[14] The offence of being an accessory after the fact to a felony has now been abolished,[15] but by

---

[9]*R. v. Smith* (1916), 12 Cr. App. Rep. 42, C.C.A.; *R. v. Torpey* (1871), 12 Cox C.C. 45.

[10]Stephen saw in it a method of circumventing the rule that a woman could not plead benefit of clergy: *History of Criminal Law*, ii, 105. Turner thought it more likely that it originated at a time when the wife was considered to have no will of her own and was entirely *sub virga viri sui*: Kenny, *Criminal Law*, 19th Ed. 69. See also Smith and Hogan, *Criminal Law*, 2nd Ed., 145-147.

[11]*R. v. Torpey*, *(supra)*. *R. v. Smith*, *(supra)*, was also a case of a misdemeanour. For the contrary view, see *R. v. Cruse* (1838), 8 C. & P. 541.

[12]Kenny, *op. cit.*, 68.

[13]See further Williams, *Criminal Law: The General Part*, 2nd Ed., s. 249.

[14]But in *R. v. Holley*, [1963] 1 All E.R. 106, C.C.A., the Court of Criminal Appeal were of the opinion that the rule was merely a particular application of the rule of marital coercion and had therefore been abolished by the Criminal Justice Act, 1925, s. 47, *(supra)*, in the absence of actual coercion. *Sed quaere?* In *R. v. Holley* the actual decision was that, if a wife assisted her husband and another together, she might be an accessory after the fact to the *latter's* felony. It was also formerly said that a wife could not be an accessory after the fact by concealing a felon jointly with her husband. Curiously enough, the husband was not bound to shelter his wife and might therefore by so doing become an accessory after the fact to her felony.

[15]By s. 1 of the Criminal Law Act 1967 which abolished the distinction between felonies and misdemeanours and enacted that the law relating to misdemeanours should apply to all indictable offences.

section 4 of the Criminal Law Act 1967 it is now an offence for any
person, knowing or believing that another has committed an arrestable
offence, to do any act with intent to impede his arrest or prosecution
without lawful authority or reasonable excuse. It is arguable that the
old law relating to accessories survives to give a wife a lawful authority
for harbouring her husband or, alternatively, that either spouse must
now have a reasonable excuse for harbouring the other by virtue of
their marital relationship. But even under the old law the courts were
apparently reluctant to permit the wife to raise the defence and they
are probably even less likely to let either spouse do so under the new
statutory provision.[16]

Conspiracy.—It is generally asserted that the doctrine of unity
applies in conspiracy so that a husband and wife may not be convicted
of conspiring together.[17] But this does not prevent them from both
being convicted of conspiring with a third person.

Theft.—Under the doctrine of unity husband and wife were deemed
to have unity of possession so that neither could be guilty of stealing
the other's property. But once the concept of separate property had
been extended by the Married Women's Property Act of 1882, it is
obvious that the fiction once more worked an anomaly. Accordingly
the Act modified the rule by providing, broadly speaking, that either
could be guilty of stealing the other's property if they were not living
together.[18] This effected a compromise between the rule of public
policy which militates against criminal proceedings being instituted by
one spouse against the other and the desirability of protecting interests
in property by the sanctions of the criminal law.

These provisions have been repealed by the Theft Act 1968 which
has produced a different sort of compromise. For the purposes of that
Act a husband and wife are to be regarded as separate persons and each
can now be convicted of theft of the other's property, obtaining it by
deception and so forth.[19] But neither the spouse nor a third person
may institute proceedings against anyone for any offence of stealing or
doing unlawful damage to property which at the time belongs to his or
her spouse, or for any attempt, incitement or conspiracy to commit
such an offence, without the consent of the Director of Public
Prosecutions. There are two exceptions to this rule. The Director's
consent is not required, first, if at the time of the offence the accused
and his or her spouse were not bound to cohabit by virtue of a judicial
decree or order or, secondly, if the accused is charged with committing
the offence jointly with the spouse. It is not immediately obvious what
sort of situation the second exception contemplates. In as much as it
envisages one spouse stealing his or her own property, it would pre-

---

[16]See *R.* v. *Holley*, (*supra*). In any event the offence may be prosecuted only with the
consent of the Director of Public Prosecutions: Criminal Law Act 1967, s. 4 (4).

[17]*Mawji* v. *R.*, [1957] 1 All E.R. 385, P.C.; [1957] A.C. 126. But see Williams,
Legal Unity of Husband and Wife, 10 M.L.R. 20-24. Either spouse may be convicted
of inciting the other to commit a crime.

[18]Married Women's Property Act 1882, s. 12, later replaced by the Larceny Act 1916,
s. 36.

[19]S. 30 (1). Either of them can also be guilty of the theft of property belonging to them
both jointly.

sumably apply, if say, the wife pawned property belonging to her and the spouses then jointly took it back without the pawnbroker's consent.[20]

Institution of Proceedings.—Save in the cases just noticed either spouse now has the same power to institute criminal proceedings against the other as though they were not married.[1]

G. NATIONALITY

Strangely enough, the doctrine of unity had no application at common law with respect to nationality.[2]   A foreign woman did not acquire British nationality by marrying a British subject, and a woman who was a British subject did not lose her status by marrying a foreigner.[3]   This rule was completely reversed by legislation during the nineteenth century,[4] but the swing back of the pendulum can be seen in a series of statutes passed between 1914 and 1933.[5]

The change in status of married women is now reflected in the provisions of the British Nationality Act of 1948, which is peculiar in that it shows a break from the nineteenth century position by reverting to the original common law.   Since 1949 a woman who is not already a citizen of the United Kingdom and Colonies does not become such a citizen by marrying a man who possesses citizenship, nor does a woman who is a citizen of the United Kingdom and Colonies lose her citizenship by marrying an alien.[6]   But a woman who marries a citizen of the United Kingdom and Colonies is entitled to acquire such citizenship by registration,[7] and a woman who becomes a subject of her husband's state on marriage may, like anyone else possessing dual nationality, divest herself of citizenship of the United Kingdom and Colonies by a declaration of renunciation.[8]

---

[20]S. 30 (4). The difficulty inherent in this interpretation to the proviso is that for the purpose of the Theft Act the property would be regarded as belonging to the pawnbroker. See further Smith, *Law of Theft*, paras. 679-684. An offence of theft would include robbery. The sub-section does not prevent the arrest of the thief except by his or her spouse or on an information laid by the spouse.

[1]Theft Act 1968, s. 30 (2).

[2]For a married woman's domicile, see *ante*, pp. 8-9.

[3]Jones, *British Nationality*, 72; Parry, *British Nationality*, 36.   But see Baty, *The Nationality of a Married Woman at Common Law*, 52 L.Q.R. 247.

[4]Aliens Act 1844, s. 16; Naturalization Act 1870, s. 10 (1).

[5]Status of Aliens Act 1914, s. 10; British Nationality and Status of Aliens Act 1918, s. 2 (5); British Nationality and Status of Aliens Act 1933, s. 1 (1). These Acts provided that a British woman marrying a foreigner should not lose her British nationality if she did not acquire that of her husband, that the status of the wife of a man who acquired or lost British nationality after the marriage should not automatically follow that of her husband but that she should be given the option of doing likewise, and that a woman who was a British subject at birth should be entitled to resume British nationality if the state of which her husband was a subject was at war with this country.

[6]Whilst the Act preserved the British nationality of women who had acquired it by marriage before 1949, it revested it in those who had lost it by marriage to an alien under the old law: ss. 12 (5) and 14.

[7]Unless she has formerly renounced or been deprived of citizenship, in which case the registration requires the approval of the Home Secretary: s. 6 (2), (3). Similar provisions apply to a woman who marries a British subject without citizenship: British Nationality Act 1965, ss. 1-3.   For a further case where a woman may rely on her husband's "qualifying connection" with the United Kingdom and Colonies or a protected state, see the British Nationality Act 1964, s. 1.

[8]S. 19. The Home Secretary may withhold the registration of a declaration during wartime.

PART I

HUSBAND AND WIFE

(2) BREAKDOWN OF MARRIAGE

SUMMARY OF CONTENTS

The breakdown of marriage is not synonymous with divorce. A marriage can be said to have broken down when the spouses stop living with each other as husband and wife. This will occur if one deserts the other, if they separate by agreement, if one of them obtains a judicial order releasing him or her from the duty of cohabiting with the other, or if the marriage is brought to an end by a decree of divorce. The significance of this order is that, with each step, the chance of reconciliation becomes more remote.

Desertion will be dealt with in Chapter 7 as one of the grounds on which a spouse may apply for an order under the Matrimonial Proceedings (Magistrates' Courts) Act. The other matters—separation agreements, judicial separation, matrimonial orders made by magistrates' courts and the termination of marriage—will form the subject matter of the four chapters in this second half of Part I.

CHAPTER 5

Separation Agreements

A. INTRODUCTORY

The essence of a separation agreement is that the husband and wife agree to live separate and apart—*i.e.*, each releases the other from his or her duty to cohabit. It is usual for a separation agreement to contain provisions for the maintenance of the wife and children, but this of course is not always true; conversely, it is possible for an agreement to be framed placing the husband under a duty to maintain his wife whilst they are living separately without, however, binding the spouses to live apart.[1] Basically, of course, all such agreements are governed by the general law of contract.

Form.—Provided that each party gives consideration, an agreement will be perfectly valid as a parol contract and consequently may be entered into orally or even by conduct. This is almost invariably the case in the simplest type of separation agreement, and each party gives consideration by foregoing his or her right to the other's consortium.[2] But clearly the agreement will be much more complicated if the spouses wish to agree upon such matters as the maintenance of the wife and children, the custody of the children, and the division and use of the property constituting the matrimonial home. In such a case it will usually be reduced into writing and, by tradition, frequently will be embodied in a deed. Where a deed is intended to be executed, the parties usually enter into a binding preliminary agreement known as " articles of separation ".

Owing to a married woman's inability to contract with her husband at common law, it was formerly necessary to join trustees as parties to a separation deed to enter into covenants on the wife's behalf and thus provide consideration for the husband's covenants. The Married Women's Property Act of 1882, by giving the wife full contractual capacity, has made trustees for this purpose redundant;[3] but they are still occasionally joined and will clearly be necessary where it is proposed that the husband should secure the wife's maintenance by settling property for this purpose.

Legality of Separation Agreements.—Up till the middle of the last century there was considerable doubt whether any separation

---

[1]So that one of them may be in desertion: see *post*, p. 165, n.[15]. If the parties are cohabiting and the maintenance agreement is no more than a domestic arrangement, it will usually not be enforceable: see *ante*, p. 120.

[2]*Cf. Re Weston*, [1900] 2 Ch. 164. See Lush, *Husband and Wife*, 4th Ed., 465-469.

[3]*McGregor* v. *McGregor* (1888), 21 Q.B.D. 424, C.A.; *Sweet* v. *Sweet*, [1895] 1 Q.B. 12.

agreement was valid, on the ground that such agreements tended to undermine the social structure of the state and were therefore contrary to public policy. By adopting this attitude the courts were merely closing their eyes to common practice and refusing to accept the fact that, when a marriage has clearly broken down and there is virtually no immediate possibility of the parties' continuing to live together in amity, it is better for all concerned and for society as a whole that they should be able to settle their differences out of court than that their matrimonial quarrels should be dragged into the open. This view eventually prevailed, and in 1848 the House of Lords held in *Wilson* v. *Wilson*[4] that there was nothing *per se* illegal in an agreement for an *immediate* separation.

In *Wilson* v. *Wilson* the House of Lords was concerned only with the position where the marriage has already broken down. But where spouses who are living together enter into an agreement regulating their legal rights in case they should separate in the future, the agreement is still contrary to public policy and void.[5] To this rule, however, there is one exception. If spouses, who are living apart, negotiate a reconciliation which contains provisions regulating their position if their attempt to live together again should prove to be unsuccessful, it is obvious that they are more likely to resume cohabitation than they would be if their future rights were left entirely in the air. Consequently, since such an agreement tends to promote the spouses' cohabiting rather than the reverse, it was held in *Re Meyrick's Settlement*[6] that it would not be void, even though it envisaged a separation in the future, and consequently would be legally enforceable if they in fact did separate again.

A separation agreement may of course be illegal for other reasons, for example if the parties' purpose is to promote the commission of adultery.[7]

Void and Voidable Agreements.—A separation agreement may be void or voidable for the same reason as any other contract. Thus it may be void on the grounds of mistake. A particular application of this rule to separation agreements is to be seen in *Galloway* v. *Galloway*,[8] where it was held that a separation deed entered into on the assumption that the parties were validly married, when in fact the marriage was (unknown to either party) bigamous, was itself void for mistake.

---

[4] (1848), 1 H.L. Cas. 538, H.L.

[5] *Hindley* v. *Westmeath* (1827), 6 B. & C. 200; *Westmeath* v. *Westmeath* (1830), 1 Dow & Cl. 519, H.L.; distinguished in *Wilson* v. *Wilson*, (*supra*), at p. 573. *A fortiori* an ante-nuptial agreement that the parties will not cohabit after marriage is void: *Brodie* v. *Brodie*, [1917] P. 271.

[6] [1921] 1 Ch. 311; following *MacMahon* v. *MacMahon*, [1913] 1 I.R. 428. Followed in *Lurie* v. *Lurie*, [1938] 3 All E.R. 156.

[7] *Fearon* v. *Aylesford* (1884), 14 Q.B.D. 792, 808, C.A.

[8] (1914), 30 T.L.R. 531; followed in *Law* v. *Harragin* (1917), 33 T.L.R. 381. In *Butcher* v. *Vale* (1891), 8 T.L.R. 93, where the parties were aware of the fact that the wife's first husband might still be alive and that their own marriage might be void but " took their chance ", it was held that the agreement was valid.

Similarly, the agreement may be voidable for fraudulent[9] or innocent misrepresentation or for undue influence.[10]

B. COMMON TERMS IN AGREEMENTS

As has already been stated, separation agreements may vary from simple oral agreements to live apart to somewhat complex deeds. It is therefore impossible to intimate what a standard form of agreement will contain; but the following are some of the terms which will appear in many agreements.

Agreement to live apart.—This is the basic term in all separation agreements by which each spouse is released from the duty of cohabiting with the other.

Non-molestation Clause.—It is frequently a term that neither spouse will " molest, annoy or interfere with the other ". In order to amount to molestation, there must be some act done by the spouse or on his or her authority; the nature of the act was thus described by BRETT, M.R., in *Fearon* v. *Aylesford*[11] (where it was alleged that the wife had failed to observe a covenant not to molest her husband):

> " I am of the opinion that the act done by the wife or by her authority must be an act which is done with intent to annoy, and does in fact annoy; or which is in fact an annoyance; or, to put the latter proposition into another shape, that it must be an act done by her with a knowledge that what she is so doing must of itself without more annoy her husband, or annoy a husband with ordinary and reasonable feeling."

In *Fearon* v. *Aylesford* the spouses entered into a separation agreement in which the wife covenanted not to molest her husband. She later lived in adultery with the Marquis of Blandford and as a result of this adulterous intercourse a child was born which Lord Aylesford alleged was being held out as his son.[12] It was held that the wife's committing adultery could not amount to a molestation of her husband, for that act would be committed, not to annoy him, but to gratify the wife or her paramour; consequently the birth of the child, which was the natural result of the adultery, could no more amount to a molestation than the act which had caused it. On the other hand her holding the child out as the legitimate child of her husband would clearly amount to molestation by this definition; but the action failed on this head too, as there was no evidence that the statements to this effect, which had been made by the wife's servant, had ever been authorised by the wife.

---

[9]*E.g.*, if one party induces the other to enter into the contract without having any intention of fulfilling the terms himself: *Crabb* v. *Crabb* (1868), L.R. 1 P. & D. 601, 604 (*per* LORD PENZANCE).

[10]*Cf. post*, p. 166. In *Evans* v. *Carrington* (1860), 2 De G. F. & J. 481, 491-492, LORD CAMPBELL, L.C., suggested that undisclosed adultery might be a ground for avoiding a separation agreement on the ground that the husband's promise to pay maintenance would be given for no consideration because he would be under no obligation to maintain the wife. *Sed quaere?* It does not seem to be a contract *uberrimae fidei.*

[11](1884), 14 Q.B.D. 792, 801-802, C.A. See also *Besant* v. *Wood* (1879), 12 Ch. D. 605.

[12]See further the *Aylesford Peerage Case* (1885), 11 App. Cas. 1, H.L.

Similarly a spouse's subsequently petitioning for divorce will not amount to a breach of a non-molestation clause if he does so to secure his own release from the marriage, although it clearly will amount to molestation if his purpose is purely to annoy the respondent.[13]

Maintenance of Wife.—The usual form of maintenance clause provides that the husband shall make periodical payments to the wife or to an agent on her behalf. Where it is desired to secure payment, capital will normally be transferred to trustees on trust to pay the wife's maintenance out of the income.

Great care should be taken to define precisely the extent of the husband's liability, for a number of cases have held that the husband's covenant may be construed as independent of the agreement to separate *stricto sensu*. If his obligation is coterminous with the spouses' living apart by consent, then it will clearly cease if they resume cohabitation, live apart under a court order, or if the marriage is annulled, dissolved or terminated by the husband's death.[14] But if the covenant is independent in the sense that it can be construed as a separate undertaking to pay the wife, the obligation may continue notwithstanding the occurrence of any of these events. Little help can be obtained from the cases, for each must depend upon the interpretation of the agreement in question; but it has been held that the liability may continue after the parties have resumed cohabitation,[15] after divorce[16] and after a decree of nullity where the marriage was voidable.[17] The modern tendency is to regard the provision as one to last for the wife's life,[18] and it has been held that such a covenant may be enforced against the husband's executors if he predeceases her.[19]

***Dum Casta* Clause**—The fact that the husband may remain liable on his covenant to maintain the wife whatever may happen in the future means that it is prudent to limit the husband's obligation " so long as the wife shall lead a chaste life ",[20] so that he will no longer remain under any contractual duty to maintain her should she subsequently commit adultery. Although a *dum casta* clause is usually inserted in a formal separation agreement—in fact precisely because it

---

[13]*Hunt* v. *Hunt*, [1897] 2 Q.B. 547, C.A. Similarly if he or she petitions for judicial separation: *Thomas* v. *Everard* (1861), 6 H. & N. 448; or commences proceedings for separation or maintenance in a magistrates' court: *Welch* v. *Welch* (1916), 85 L.J.P. 188, C.A.

[14]As in *Covell* v. *Sweetland*, [1968] 2 All E.R. 1016 (divorce). If this is the true construction of the agreement, the husband's obligation will never arise if the parties never separate at all: *Bindley* v. *Mulloney* (1869), L.R. 7 Eq. 343.

[15]*Negus* v. *Forster* (1882), 46 L.T. 675, C.A.

[16]*May* v. *May*, [1929] 2 K.B. 386, C.A.; *Charlesworth* v. *Holt* (1873), L.R. 9 Exch. 38.

[17]*Adams* v. *Adams*, [1941] 1 All E.R. 334, C.A.; [1941] 1 K.B. 536; *Fowke* v. *Fowke*, [1938] Ch. 774. But this is not necessarily so if the decree is for the annulment of a *void* marriage: see *ante*, p. 135.

[18]*Re Lidington*, [1940] 3 All E.R. 600, 603; [1940] Ch. 927, 934.

[19]*Kirk* v. *Eustace*, [1937] 2 All E.R. 715, H.L.; [1937] A.C. 491; cf. *Re Lidington*, (*supra*). Contrast *Langstone* v. *Hayes*, [1946] 1 All E.R. 114, C.A.; [1946] K.B. 109. For the alteration of maintenance agreements, see *post*, pp. 410-413.

[20]" *Dum casta vixerit.*"

is usually inserted—the Court of Appeal held in *Fearon* v. *Aylesford*[1]
that such a clause will not be implied if it is not expressly included.[2]

Wife's Indemnity and Covenant not to sue for Maintenance.—
If the agreement is in writing, it will usually be a " maintenance
agreement " for the purpose of section 13 of the Matrimonial Proceedings and Property Act 1970 and any clause purporting to restrict either
party's right to apply to any court for an order containing financial
arrangements will be void.[3] This, however, does not avoid any other
financial arrangements contained in the agreement. Some agreements
still include a covenant by the wife to indemnify her husband against
all debts which she may contract after the separation. Such a clause
now seems to have little effect unless the husband is bound by a
contract made by her because he is estopped from denying that she
has his authority to pledge his credit.[4]

Custody and Maintenance of Children.—At common law any
agreement by which a father divested himself of the custody of his
children was considered to be contrary to public policy and therefore
void. So far as separation agreements are concerned, however, the
position is governed by section 2 of the Custody of Infants Act 1873,
which enacts that a separation agreement shall not be invalid merely
by reason of the fact that it provides that the father shall surrender the
custody or control of his children to the mother, but that no court shall
enforce any such provision unless it is for the children's benefit.[5]

If the wife is given custody of the children it is usual to provide that
the husband shall have access to them and also that he shall pay
periodical sums to the wife by way of maintenance for them. In consideration of this, the wife frequently undertakes to be fully liable for
educating and maintaining them. As much care must be taken in
framing the husband's covenant as in framing his covenant to maintain
the wife, as otherwise the husband may find himself liable on his
covenant notwithstanding a subsequent resumption of cohabitation or
even after the children attain their majority.[6]

Agreements relating to Property.—The spouses may obviously
wish to come to an agreement with respect to the property which
formed their matrimonial home or with respect to their interests in
other property. Clauses giving effect to their wishes must necessarily
vary considerably from one agreement to another.

C. EFFECTS OF THE AGREEMENT

The principal effect of a separation agreement, as has already been
pointed out, is to release each spouse from the duty of cohabiting with
the other. This will prevent either side from alleging that the other is

---

[1](1884), 14 Q.B.D. 792, C.A. For the facts, see *ante*, p. 136.
[2]But if it were deliberately omitted in order to give the wife a licence to commit
adultery, the whole agreement might be contrary to public policy and therefore void:
ibid., at p. 808 (*per* COTTON, L.J.). It may be possible to imply a *dum casta* clause from
a recital: *Crouch* v. *Crouch*, [1912] 1 K.B. 378.
[3]Matrimonial Proceedings and Property Act 1970, s. 13 (1). See further *post*, pp. 409-
410.
[4]For agency by estoppel, see *ante*, pp. 123-124.
[5]See *post*, pp. 272-273.
[6]As in *De Crespigny* v. *De Crespigny* (1853), 9 Exch. 192.

in desertion;[7] it may also mean that a husband who has sexual intercourse with his wife without her consent will be guilty of rape, at least if the agreement contains a non-molestation clause.[8] Apart from the general duty placed on both parties to perform and observe their respective covenants, the chief legal effect which the agreement may have is the resulting modification of the wife's right to maintenance.[9]

D. DISCHARGE OF AGREEMENTS

From what has been said about its effects, it will be seen that it may be vital to determine whether an agreement once entered into is still in force. For example, if the agreement is discharged, desertion may commence,[10] the husband may cease to be liable on the contract to maintain his wife and children, and agreements relating to property may similarly be terminated. Basically, of course, the discharge of separation agreements is governed by the law relating to the discharge of contracts generally.

Discharge by Agreement.—The agreement may be effectively discharged in accordance with its terms. Thus, in *Newsome* v. *Newsome*,[11] where the wife promised to be bound only if her husband " remained true to her ", it was held that his subsequently committing adultery terminated the agreement. Similarly, it may be discharged by a later independent agreement between the parties.[12]

Resumption of Cohabitation.—Whether a resumption of cohabitation will amount to a consent to terminate an agreement so as to discharge it automatically is a matter of some doubt. It is submitted, however, that much of the difficulty has been caused by a failure to distinguish between two separate questions. It is obvious that an agreement to separate *stricto sensu* must be discharged on the parties' resuming cohabitation; the problem that has always arisen is whether, if the spouses then separate again, the husband remains liable on the covenant in the original agreement to maintain his wife and children or whether the parties are still bound by terms in that agreement relating to the division and use of their property.[13] Now if those covenants are to remain in force only so long as the spouses are living apart, their resuming cohabitation will have discharged them; on the other hand, if the husband has independently created a trust in favour of the wife and children or covenanted to pay his wife an annuity for the rest of her life, his liability will remain notwithstanding their having

---

[7]See *post*, p. 165.
[8]*Per* LYNSKEY, J., in *R.* v. *Miller*, [1954] 2 All E.R. 529, 533; [1954] 2 Q.B. 282, 290. See further, *ante*, p. 97.
[9]See *post*, pp. 416-417.
[10]See *post*, pp. 166-167.
[11](1871), L.R. 2 P. & D. 306.
[12]But if the deed has created a *trust* in favour of the children, this cannot be discharged by an agreement between the spouses.
[13]As in *Nicol* v. *Nicol* (1886), 31 Ch. D. 524, C.A.

lived together again.[14] The question is therefore one of construction in each individual case and little help can be obtained by applying a decision on the wording of one deed to the entirely different wording of another. LORD ELDON's dictum that there is a presumption that all obligations cease on a resumption of cohabitation[15] has been followed, doubted and criticised, and the whole question has been fully discussed by the Court of Appeal in *Negus* v. *Forster*[16] and *Nicol* v. *Nicol*.[17] But, as BOWEN and FRY, L.JJ., pointed out in the latter case, the question in the end is always that of giving effect to the parties' intention to be inferred from the agreement itself.[18]

Discharge by Breach.—A repudiation of the agreement by one of the spouses will clearly give the other the right to treat it as discharged if he wishes to do so. In this respect these agreements appear to differ from commercial contracts, for, as GREENE, M.R., stated when delivering the judgment of the Court of Appeal in *Pardy* v. *Pardy*,[19] the innocent party is not bound to inform the spouse in breach that he has accepted the repudiation: it is sufficient if there is other evidence that he has not insisted upon the performance of the terms but has treated the agreement as a dead letter.

Whether there has been a repudiation is purely a question of fact. Mere failure on the husband's part to pay maintenance to his wife will not *per se* amount to a repudiation[20] although failure to do so for a long time might well be construed as such,[1] as would non-payment coupled with some other act implying an intention not to be bound by the agreement.[2]

There may also be a breach by failure to perform or observe some other covenant. In order that the other party may lawfully treat himself as discharged, there must be a substantial breach: a trivial breach will clearly not suffice for this purpose.[3] It may in fact be doubted whether a breach of one covenant will ever entitle a party to repudiate liability on another. In *Fearon* v. *Aylesford*[4] BRETT, M.R., stated

---

[14]This distinction was drawn in *Ruffles* v. *Alston* (1875), L.R. 19 Eq. 539, and *Negus* v. *Forster* (1882), 46 L.T. 675, C.A. See also Lush, *Husband and Wife*, 4th Ed., 438-444. In any event resumption of cohabitation will not *per se* destroy a cause of action already vested in the wife, so that she will still be able to sue for arrears of maintenance which had accrued before the reconciliation: *Macan* v. *Macan* (1900), 70 L.J.K.B. 90.
[15]*Bateman* v. *Ross* (1813), 1 Dow 235, 245, H.L.
[16](1882), 46 L.T. 675, C.A.
[17](1886), 31 Ch. D. 524, C.A.
[18]At pp. 529, 530. See also Lush, *loc. cit.*
[19][1939] 3 All E.R. 779, 784-786, C.A.; [1939] P. 288, 305-307.
[20]For it may not be a *wilful* breach: *Clark* v. *Clark* (*No. 2*), [1939] 2 All E.R. 392; [1939] P. 257.
[1]*Pardy* v. *Pardy*, [1939] 3 All E.R. 779, C.A.; [1939] P. 288.
[2]*Waller* v. *Waller* (1910), 26 T.L.R. 223; *Kennedy* v. *Kennedy*, [1907] P. 49; *Balcombe* v. *Balcombe*, [1908] P. 176 (emigration to America).
[3]*Besant* v. *Wood* (1879), 12 Ch. D. 605 (husband's attempt to stop wife from using her married name in contravention of non-molestation clause); *Kunski* v. *Kunski* (1898), 68 L.J.P. 18 (husband's delay in paying maintenance for four days). In neither case was there a sufficiently serious breach to entitle the wife to treat the agreement as discharged. In *Morrall* v. *Morrall* (1881), 6 P.D. 98, it was held that the husband's committing incestuous adultery was such conduct as to entitle the wife to repudiate the deed, but it is not clear what covenant was alleged to have been broken.
[4](1884), 14 Q.B.D. 792, 800, C.A. See further, *ante*, p. 136.

that a husband's covenant to pay maintenance and a wife's covenant not to molest her husband were not interdependent, so that she would still be able to enforce her husband's obligation even if she had failed to observe her own. For this reason a prudent draftsman will make the covenants expressly interdependent.

Subsequent Matrimonial Proceedings.—The problem here, it is submitted, is the same as that presented by a resumption of cohabitation. The agreement to separate *stricto sensu* must necessarily be discharged by a decree of nullity, divorce or judicial separation, for in each case the decree removes the duty to cohabit; it then becomes a question of construction whether such covenants as the husband's covenant to maintain the wife and children remain alive. In *May* v. *May*[5] the Court of Appeal held that divorce does not automatically terminate such an obligation, and in *Adams* v. *Adams*[6] extended this principle to nullity where the marriage is voidable. But, as we have already seen,[7] this rule does not apply to a decree where the marriage is void, for normally the agreement will have been entered into under a mistake as to the subsistence of the marriage. These decisions are less likely to work hardship than might at first be supposed in view of the courts' powers to vary maintenance agreements and post-nuptial settlements.[8]

In *Hyman* v. *Hyman*[9] it was sought to prove that the contract was frustrated by the decree. The spouses entered into a separation agreement in 1919 and after the Matrimonial Causes Act of 1923 came into force the wife obtained a divorce on the ground of her husband's adultery. The latter's argument that the contract was frustrated by the change of law in 1923, which extended the wife's power to petition for divorce, is again of topical interest in view of the recent changes in the law introduced by the Divorce Reform Act of 1969. It was, however, rejected at any rate by LORD ATKIN, who held that since divorce was possible in 1919 the extension of the grounds on which it could be obtained was not so unforeseen as to discharge the agreement automatically.[10] Whilst admittedly LORD BUCKMASTER'S speech seems more in keeping with the view that the contract was frustrated,[11] LORD MERRIMAN, P., has since held that the doctrine of frustration has no application at all where the basis of a separation agreement has been

---

[5][1929] 2 K.B. 386, C.A. The Court followed *Charlesworth* v. *Holt* (1873), L.R. 9 Ex. 38, not so much because they thought it correctly decided as because it had stood unquestioned and acted on for over 50 years. See also *Gandy* v. *Gandy* (1882), 7 P.D. 168, C.A. (judicial separation).

[6][1941] 1 All E.R. 334, C.A.; [1941] 1 K.B. 536. See also *Fowke* v. *Fowke*, [1938] 2 All E.R. 638; [1938] Ch. 774. An attempt to argue that as a result of the doctrine of retroactivity (see *ante*, p. 69) the marriage and therefore the agreement became void *ab initio* failed because (i) the parties knew that the marriage was voidable and consequently there was no mistake, and (ii) at the time the agreement was made the defendant was still bound to maintain his wife and therefore received consideration for his promise to pay her maintenance.

[7]*Ante*, p. 135.

[8]See *post*, pp. 410 (maintenance agreements) and 436 (post-nuptial settlements).

[9][1929] A.C. 601, H.L. See further, *post*, p. 409.

[10]At pp. 627-628.

[11]At pp. 623-624; he did not decide the point directly. No other member of the House considered it.

changed by an alteration in the law.[12] Indeed, if the premise be correct that the question is entirely one of construction, each case must be decided purely upon the wording of the particular agreement.

Husband's Bankruptcy.—As sums payable to the wife in the future under a separation agreement are provable in the husband's bankruptcy, no action will lie against him on the covenant in respect of sums payable afterwards.[13] Consequently, since this effectively terminates his liability and thus destroys the basis of the agreement, the wife is entitled to treat the whole contract as discharged.[14]

E. REMEDIES FOR BREACH OF AGREEMENT

Damages.—Common law damages may always be obtained for breach of the agreement. Whilst this is the obvious remedy for arrears of maintenance, damages may be awarded for failure to perform and observe other covenants as well.[15]

Specific Performance.—Specific performance may be sought in two cases. First, either party refusing to execute a deed of separation may be ordered to do so in accordance with the terms of separation articles to which he is a party,[16] and secondly, if the agreement includes a contract to create a trust, the husband (or other settlor) may be ordered to transfer property or funds to the trustees in accordance with the terms of his promise.[17] In neither case, of course, will an action lie if there is no consideration even though the agreement is under seal.[18]

Injunction.—An injunction may be granted to prevent the breach of a negative covenant, for example the breach of a non-molestation clause.[19] It will similarly be granted to restrain a party from instituting legal proceedings if he has expressly undertaken not to do so.[20]

---

[12]*H——* v. *H——*, [1938] 3 All E.R. 415.

[13]*Victor* v. *Victor*, [1912] 1 K.B. 247, C.A. This is so even though there is a *dum casta* clause or the wife's right is determinable in other circumstances: *Ex parte Neal* (1880), 14 Ch. D. 579, C.A.

[14]*McQuiban* v. *McQuiban*, [1913] P. 208.

[15]*Fearon* v. *Aylesford* (1884), 14 Q.B.D. 792, C.A. (wife's failure to observe non-molestation clause).

[16]*Wilson* v. *Wilson* (1848), 1 H.L. Cas. 538, H.L.; *Hart* v. *Hart* (1881), 18 Ch. D. 670. Specific performance will not be ordered if the articles are in any way contrary to public policy (see *ante*, p. 134): *Vansittart* v. *Vansittart* (1858), 2 De G. & J. 249.

[17]*Lurie* v. *Lurie*, [1938] 3 All E.R. 156.

[18]*Wilson* v. *Wilson*, (*supra*).

[19]*Sanders* v. *Rodway* (1852), 16 Beav. 207.

[20]*Besant* v. *Wood* (1879), 12 Ch. D. 605. But once a High Court action has been commenced, no injunction will lie to restrain its further prosecution: Supreme Court of Judicature (Consolidation) Act 1925, s. 41.

CHAPTER 6

Judicial Separation

The decree of judicial separation is a creature of statute and was first introduced by the Matrimonial Causes Act of 1857 to replace the old ecclesiastical decree of divorce *a mensa et thoro* which that Act abolished. Like the old decree, its prime purpose is to relieve the petitioner from the duty of cohabiting with the respondent. The number of judicial separations granted every year is now very small.[1] These are accounted for principally by petitioners who desire matrimonial relief but for religious or other reasons do not seek divorce but also partly by petitioners who still hope for an ultimate reconciliation but by obtaining a decree of judicial separation obtain an immediate remedy and at the same time leave the way open for divorce on the ground on which the decree has been granted if these hopes are not fulfilled.[2]

Jurisdiction.—The Act of 1857 vested the power of granting decrees of judicial separation in the Divorce Court, from which it was transferred in 1875 to the High Court. Since 1968 divorce county courts have been able to hear *undefended* petitions.[3] The court has jurisdiction if the parties are domiciled in England[4] or are both resident here when the petition is filed.[5] In addition, if the wife is the petitioner, the court has jurisdiction if the husband has deserted her or has been deported, provided that he was domiciled in England immediately before the desertion or deportation.[6]

Grounds for Judicial Separation.—A decree of divorce *a mensa et thoro* could be pronounced on the grounds of the respondent's adultery or cruelty or, if the wife were the petitioner, on the grounds that the husband had committed (or possibly attempted to commit) rape or an unnatural offence. The Matrimonial Causes Act of 1857 preserved all these as grounds for judicial separation, and over the years were added

---

[1]During the years 1965-1969 there were on the average 245 petitions a year and 115 decrees. Over 90% of the petitions were brought by wives.

[2]See *post*, pp. 207-211.

[3]Matrimonial Causes Act 1967, s. 1. See *ante*, p. 4.

[4]*Eustace* v. *Eustace*, [1924] P. 45, C.A.

[5]*Armytage* v. *Armytage*, [1898] P. 178; *Matalon* v. *Matalon*, [1952] 1 All E.R. 1025, C.A.; [1952] P. 233. Residence was the basis of jurisdiction in the ecclesiastical courts. It is in fact sufficient if the respondent alone is resident here, for the petitioner *ipso facto* submits to the jurisdiction of the court by invoking it: *Sim* v. *Sim*, [1944] 2 All E.R. 344; [1944] P. 87. For the meaning of residence in this connection see *Sinclair* v. *Sinclair*, [1967] 3 All E.R. 882, C.A.; [1968] P. 189, (*ante*, p. 85), and *Keserue* v. *Keserue*, [1962] 3 All E.R. 796.

[6]Matrimonial Causes Act 1965, s. 40 (1) (a). Note that three years' residence in this country by the wife will not of itself give the court jurisdiction: this provision applies only to petitions for nullity and divorce: *ibid.*, s. 40 (1) (b).

the respondent's desertion,[7] failure to comply with a decree for restitution of conjugal rights[8] and incurable insanity.[9]

It will be seen that under the old law the main grounds for a judicial separation were the same as the grounds for divorce. Given that the law of divorce was based essentially on the commission of a matrimonial offence by the respondent, this is not surprising. There is, however, another good reason for keeping the grounds the same. For spouses who have a conscientious objection to divorce a decree of judicial separation may mark the *de facto* end of the marriage, and it is arguable that they should be able to obtain a decree only in similar circumstances to those who wish to bring their marriage to a *de jure* end by a decree of divorce. This principle has been adopted by section 8 of the Divorce Reform Act 1969. All the former grounds for a decree of judicial separation were abolished and it is now provided that the five facts on which a petitioner can rely to establish irretrievable breakdown of the marriage as the ground for divorce shall be *grounds* for judicial separation. As these are much more important in connection with divorce, we shall defer a detailed consideration of them until we deal with that subject.[10]

As the decree does not dissolve the marriage bond but can in fact be rescinded, the court is not concerned with whether or not the marriage has irretrievably broken down; if any of the grounds is made out, the court must grant a decree provided that the provisions of section 17 of the Matrimonial Proceedings and Property Act 1970 (relating to the welfare of children) are complied with.[11] Furthermore, sections 4, 5 and 6 of the Divorce Reform Act do not apply to judicial separation:[12] they are all inappropriate because the decree is not irreversible and does not affect the parties' status. On the other hand, the provisions in the Act relating to reconciliation do apply; and the court may adjourn the proceedings, the petitioner's solicitor must provide his certificate, and periods of cohabitation not exceeding six months may be ignored just as in proceedings for divorce.[13]

Unlike a divorce, a petition for judicial separation may be presented within the first three years of the marriage without the consent of the court.

The Decree and its Effects.—Since a decree of judicial separation effects no change of status and may in certain circumstances subsequently be discharged, it is not made in two stages like a decree of divorce or nullity but takes effect immediately it is pronounced.

---

[7] For two years under the Matrimonial Causes Act 1857; for three years under the Matrimonial Causes Act 1937.

[8] Matrimonial Causes Act 1884.

[9] Matrimonial Causes Act 1937.

[10] *Post*, pp. 209-213.

[11] See *post*, p. 288. But if one party petitions for divorce and the other petitions for judicial separation, the court should not grant the latter if it pronounces a decree nisi of divorce: *Lawry* v. *Lawry*, [1967] 2 All E.R. 1131, C.A.

[12] These permit a respondent in certain circumstances to oppose a decree nisi of divorce on the ground of hardship, to have a decree nisi rescinded if his consent was obtained by a misrepresentation, or to delay its being made absolute pending suitable financial provision. *See post*, pp, 212-213 and 215-217.

[13] See *post*, pp. 213-215.

The principal effect of the decree is that it relieves the petitioner from the duty of cohabiting with the respondent.[14] This means that so long as it is in force neither spouse can be in desertion,[15] and also that a husband who has intercourse with his wife against her will may be guilty of rape.[16] In addition the court has power to make a number of orders relating to the custody and welfare of the children of the family and to financial provision.[17] The decree will also affect the devolution of a spouse's property if he or she dies intestate.[18] But it must be remembered that for all other purposes the spouses remain husband and wife; neither of them is at liberty to remarry, for example, and such of the common law disabilities arising from coverture as remain will continue in force.

Discharge of Decrees.—The Matrimonial Causes Act itself provides for the discharge of a decree of judicial separation in two cases. Section 12 (3) enacts:

" The court may, on an application by petition of the spouse against whom a decree for judicial separation has been made and on being satisfied that the allegations in the petition are true, rescind the decree at any time on the ground [i] that it was obtained in the absence of the applicant,[19] or [ii] if desertion was the ground of the decree, that there was reasonable cause for the alleged desertion."

But the respondent's power to appeal to the Court of Appeal has in fact virtually made this section redundant and petitions under it are hardly ever brought. In any case the court's power to reverse the decree is purely discretionary.

The power to discharge the decree is not limited to the cases set out in the section. The ground on which either party is most likely to apply for this to be done is that the spouses have resumed cohabitation. The court clearly has power to order a discharge in such circumstances[20] and there is at least one dictum that the decree will be automatically discharged in such a case.[1] In addition there is probably a residual power to rescind the decree whenever common sense and justice demand it, at least provided both spouses consent.[2]

---

[14]Matrimonial Causes Act 1965, s. 12 (2).

[15]*Post*, pp. 165-166.

[16]*R.* v. *Clarke*, [1949] 2 All E.R. 448. See *ante*, p. 97.

[17]See *post*, pp. 286 (children), and 426 and 474 (financial provision).

[18]See *post*, pp. 504-505.

[19]" Absence " means physical absence: *Wilkinson* v. *Wilkinson*, [1962] 1 All E.R. 922, C.A.; [1963] P. 1. " Where the petitioner has not in fact appeared he may present a petition . . .; in his petition he must state the reasons of his absence, and the grounds on which he asks to be relieved from the results of it; . . . and he must further state circumstances calculated to satisfy the Court that the decree was wrong. The Court . . . in coming to a decision will be at liberty to consider how far the absence of the petitioner was his own fault or was excusable, and whether he has taken reasonably prompt steps for his relief." (*Per* Lord Penzance in *Phillips* v. *Phillips* (1866), L.R. 1 P. & D. 169, 173-174.)

[20]*Oram* v. *Oram* (1923), 129 L.T. 159.

[1]*Per* A. L. Smith, J., in *Haddon* v. *Haddon* (1887), 18 Q.B.D. 778, 782-783. The correctness of this decision is of vital importance if it is alleged that desertion has started to run after a resumption of cohabitation following a decree.

[2]See *Schlesinger* v. *Schlesinger* (1966), *Times*, June 22nd, where a decree was discharged to enable the wife (who was not domiciled in this country) to obtain a divorce in South Africa.

H

Recognition of Foreign Decrees.—The question of the recognition of a foreign decree had to be considered in *Tursi* v. *Tursi*.[3] The husband, who was domiciled in Italy, deserted the wife in 1942. Four years later she obtained a decree of *separazione legale* in Italy on the ground of his desertion and cruelty. This decree relieved the spouses from the duty of cohabiting and was thus similar to the English decree of judicial separation. In 1949 the wife came to England and eventually petitioned for divorce on the ground of her husband's desertion. SACHS, J., held that the existence of the Italian decree prevented the husband from being in desertion after it had been pronounced, but as it was comparable to an English decree of judicial separation, the marriage could be dissolved on the ground that the respondent had been in desertion for a continuous period of three years immediately preceding the institution of the proceedings in Italy.[4]

SACHS, J., based his decision on the ground that, since an English court will recognise a decree of divorce pronounced by the *forum domicilii*, it must *a fortiori* recognise a decree which does no more than regulate the spouses' rights and duties arising from the status of marriage. But *Tursi* v. *Tursi* leaves open a number of questions. In the first place the *separazione legale* was virtually equivalent to our decree of judicial separation; it is extremely doubtful whether English courts would recognise a decree which relieved the spouses of some of the duties of cohabitation but not of them all. Secondly, the decree in that case had been pronounced by the court of the country of the parties' domicile; by analogy with the law of divorce,[5] will an English court recognise a decree granted, for example, by the courts of a country in which the respondent was neither domiciled nor resident but with which the petitioner had a real and substantial connection? Thirdly, in *Tursi* v. *Tursi* the court was concerned merely with the effect of a foreign decree upon subsequent proceedings for divorce; whilst it might well be held that, since a decree is granted to a wife primarily for her protection, a husband could, say, be guilty of rape upon her, SACHS, J., deliberately left open how far such a decree would affect matters like the devolution of her realty situated in England if she died intestate.[6]

---

[3] [1957] 2 All E.R. 828; [1958] P. 54. The court had jurisdiction by virtue of the wife's having resided in England for three years immediately preceding the presentation of the petition: see *ante*, p. 86, and *post*, p. 218.

[4] See the Matrimonial Causes Act 1965, s. 3 (3), *post*, p. 211. (The period of desertion required is now two years.)

[5] See *post*, pp. 220-223.

[6] At pp. 837 and 70, respectively. Some further problems are discussed by Spiro, *Foreign Judicial Separation*, 6 I.C.L.Q. 392. For proposed changes in the law of recognition, see Appendix E, *post*.

CHAPTER 7

Matrimonial Orders made by Magistrates' Courts

A. INTRODUCTORY

Until 1878 no court other than the ecclesiastical courts and their statutory successors, the Divorce Court and the High Court, had had jurisdiction in matrimonial proceedings.[1]　But section 4 of the Matrimonial Causes Act of that year gave a criminal court, before which a married man had been convicted of an aggravated assault upon his wife, power to make an order that she should no longer be bound to cohabit with him if it felt that her future safety was in peril. The court could also order a husband to pay maintenance to a wife in whose favour such a separation order was made and vest in her the legal custody of any children of the marriage under the age of ten years.　In 1886 courts of summary jurisdiction were given a further power to make a maintenance order in favour of a woman whose husband had deserted her and was wilfully refusing or neglecting to maintain her.[2]

These provisions were repealed in 1895 by the Summary Jurisdiction (Married Women) Act which gave magistrates' courts much wider powers to make orders on the application of married women.　The success of that Act was reflected in the way in which its provisions were extended during the next half century in a series of Acts which became collectively known as the Summary Jurisdiction (Separation and Maintenance) Acts 1895 to 1949.[3] Four main lines of development may be observed: the grounds upon which the wife might apply for an order were gradually extended; the maximum sum which the court might order a husband to pay to his wife was increased; an additional power was given to courts to order a married man to pay maintenance in respect of children as well; and finally a more limited power was eventually given to a husband to apply for matrimonial relief.

The Matrimonial Proceedings (Magistrates' Courts) Act 1960.—The Summary Jurisdiction (Separation and Maintenance) Acts were themselves repealed and replaced by the Matrimonial Proceedings (Magistrates' Courts) Act 1960.[4]　The same lines of development

---

[1] Except for magistrates' powers to make an order protecting a deserted wife's money and property under the Matrimonial Causes Act 1857, s. 21.

[2] Married Women (Maintenance in Case of Desertion) Act 1886.

[3] These were: the Summary Jurisdiction (Married Women) Act 1895; the Licensing Act 1902, s. 5; the Married Women (Maintenance) Act 1920; the Summary Jurisdiction (Separation and Maintenance) Act 1925; and the Married Women (Maintenance) Act 1949.

[4] For a critical commentary on the Act see Stone, 24 M.L.R. 144.

noticed above have been further extended: in particular the Act of 1960 has given magistrates a limited power to order a wife to contribute towards her husband's maintenance and the orders that they can make with respect to the custody and maintenance of children have been considerably increased. The main purpose of the Act of 1895 was to afford to women of the working and lower middle classes, who could not afford to take proceedings in the High Court, an opportunity to obtain matrimonial orders cheaply and speedily; and these advantages, together with the comparative informality and privacy of the proceedings, eventually brought to the courts many women in higher income groups. This led to the passing of the Maintenance Orders Act of 1968 which removed the financial limit imposed on magistrates' orders and thus enabled them to make appropriate orders for women whose husbands were relatively well off. Furthermore, magistrates can call upon the services of their probation officers to try to bring about a reconciliation, and their attempts are much more likely to be successful than they would be if the parties had reached the divorce court.[5]

The importance of the matrimonial jurisdiction of magistrates' courts cannot be over-emphasised, for a considerable number of applications for matrimonial relief come before them.[6] In many cases the parties are subsequently divorced and for them magistrates' proceedings have been aptly described as a staging-post on the way to the divorce court; in many others, however, these are the only proceedings that are ever taken between the parties.

Jurisdiction.—Magistrates' jurisdiction is based not upon domicile but upon residence and, being statutory, it cannot be enlarged by agreement or submission.[7] A court may make an order if it has jurisdiction in the place where either spouse normally resides or where the cause of complaint wholly or partly arose.[8] It normally has no jurisdiction at all if the defendant does not reside in England;[9] it may, however, make an order (other than a separation order) against a defendant resident in Scotland or Northern Ireland provided that the complainant resides in England and the parties last ordinarily lived together as man and wife in this country.[10] If the complainant resides in Scotland or Northern Ireland, the court may make an order provided that the defendant resides in England.[11]

---

[5]See the Magistrates' Courts Act 1952, ss. 59 and 62. On the question of privilege attaching to admissions made to a probation officer trying to effect a reconciliation, see *ante*, p. 99.

[6]In 1969, 29,408 applications and 20,045 orders were made under the Matrimonial Proceedings (Magistrates' Courts) Act 1960.

[7]*Forsyth* v. *Forsyth*, [1947] 2 All E.R. 623, 624, C.A.; [1948] P. 125, 132.

[8]Matrimonial Proceedings (Magistrates' Courts) Act 1960, s. 1 (2). In the case of a complaint based on the defendant's conviction of assault or a sexual offence, the cause of complaint arises in the place where the offence or attempt occurred.

[9]*Macrae* v. *Macrae*, [1949] 2 All E.R. 34, C.A.; [1949] P. 397.

[10]Matrimonial Proceedings (Magistrates' Courts) Act 1960, s. 1 (3).

[11]*Ibid.*, s. 1 (3) (b). *Quaere* whether the court has jurisdiction if the complainant resides outside the United Kingdom. There seems to be no objection in principle so long as the defendant resides in England.

B. GROUNDS FOR APPLICATIONS FOR ORDERS

A magistrates' court may not make an order under the Matrimonial Proceedings (Magistrates' Courts) Act 1960 (except for an order relating to children) unless the complainant proves that the defendant is guilty of one of the offences laid down in section 1 (1). Either spouse may apply for an order on any of the first six grounds; there are two further grounds on which the wife alone may apply and one on which the husband alone may apply. In all cases the ground must exist when the summons is taken out and also at the time of adjudication. Hence an order cannot be made if, for example, a deserting husband resumes cohabitation with his wife or the complainant condones the defendant's adultery or cruelty before the case is heard.[12]

I. ADULTERY

Adultery may be defined as sexual intercourse between two persons of whom one or both are married but who are not married to each other.

In order that adultery should constitute a ground for a complaint therefore, the defendant must have had sexual intercourse with someone other than the complainant since the celebration of the marriage.[13]

Nature of the Act.—There need not be full penetration to constitute adultery,[14] but, as the Court of Appeal held in *Dennis* v. *Dennis*,[15] there must be some penetration of the female by the male organ, although, as in the case of rape, any degree of penetration, however slight, will suffice. Hence it seems that a woman who has herself artificially inseminated with another man's seed without her husband's consent does not thereby commit adultery.[16]

Act must be voluntary.—In order to be guilty of adultery, a person must have had sexual intercourse voluntarily.[17] Hence if a married woman is raped, she does not commit adultery.[18] This principle applies equally if a woman's consent is negatived by force, fear or the

---

[12]*Irvin* v. *Irvin*, [1968] 1 All E.R. 271.

[13]Matrimonial Proceedings (Magistrates' Courts) Act 1960, s. 1 (1) (d). A finding of adultery in matrimonial proceedings *in the High Court or a county court* is *prima facie* evidence (which may be rebutted) of its commission in any subsequent civil proceedings: Civil Evidence Act 1968, s. 12. Hence if H obtains a decree of divorce alleging W's adultery with X, X's wife could use this as evidence of X's adultery if she were to bring divorce proceedings or proceedings in a magistrates' court.

[14]*Rutherford* v. *Richardson*, [1923] A.C. 1, H.L.; *Thompson* v. *Thompson*, [1938] 2 All E.R. 727; [1938] P. 162; *Sapsford* v. *Sapsford*, [1954] 2 All E.R. 373; [1954] P. 394.

[15][1955] 2 All E.R. 51, C.A.; [1955] P. 153.

[16]Artificial insemination has been held not to amount to adultery in Scotland: *Maclennan* v. *Maclennan*, 1958 S.L.T. 12. See also Bartholomew, *Legal Implications of Artificial Insemination*, 21 M.L.R. 236, at pp. 251 *et seq.* For the contrary view see Tallin, *Artificial Insemination*, 34 Can. Bar Rev. 1, 166, where a number of problems arising out of this practice are discussed. But she would be guilty of constructive desertion if her husband left her as a result or of cruelty if his health suffered as a consequence.

[17]*Clarkson* v. *Clarkson* (1930), 143 L.T. 775. *Cf. N.* v. *N.* (1963), 107 Sol. Jo. 1025.

[18]*Clarkson* v. *Clarkson*, (*supra*). But since the question whether or not the woman consented is peculiarly within her knowledge, the burden of proving lack of consent is on her: *Redpath* v. *Redpath*, [1950] 1 All E.R. 600, C.A.

influence of drugs; a more difficult problem arises if either party alleges that his act was not voluntary because he was insane at the time that he committed it. The moral turpitude of a person who commits a matrimonial offence resulted in a tendency to regard adultery and cruelty as similar in character to criminal offences and therefore to apply the *M'Naghten* rules to them.[19] Consequently insanity was held to be a defence if the party alleged to have committed adultery was so insane as not to know the nature and quality of his act, or, if he did, that he did not know that what he was doing was wrong in the sense of morally blameworthy or culpable.[20] Although it has now been held that insanity is not necessarily a defence to a charge of cruelty,[1] it is submitted that it should remain so in the case of adultery, at least if its effect was that the party could not be said to have consented to the act at all. The same should also apply to a spouse who has sexual intercourse whilst so drunk as to be unable to give consent provided that this is excusable in all the circumstances.[2]

Standard of Proof.—There has been considerable judicial controversy over the standard of proof required when there is an allegation of adultery. As the proceedings are civil, one would expect it to be sufficient to show that the party was guilty on the balance of probabilities; confusion has arisen because of the tendency (seen above in connection with insanity) to treat adultery as akin to a criminal offence and therefore to require proof beyond reasonable doubt. In *Blyth* v. *Blyth*[3] the House of Lords were divided in their *obiter* views about the correct test. Two years later the Court of Appeal in *Bastable* v. *Bastable*[4] took up an intermediate position and said that the law requires a high standard of proof or " a degree of probability . . . commensurate with the occasion ": a direction which, it is respectfully submitted, is vague and unhelpful. The problem has been further complicated by the rule at common law that the presumption of legitimacy could be rebutted only by evidence putting the matter beyond reasonable doubt; if a husband's evidence of his wife's adultery was the birth of a child of which he alleged he could not be the father, the courts declined to be forced into a position in which they might have to hold that the wife had committed adultery but that the child was legitimate.[5] But now that the Family Law Reform Act 1969 provides that the presumption of legitimacy may be rebutted on the balance of

---

[19]*R.* v. *M'Naghten* (1843), 10 Cl. & F. 200, H.L. See Smith and Hogan, *Criminal Law*, 2nd Ed., 116 *et seq.*

[20]*Yarrow* v. *Yarrow*, [1892] P. 92; *Hanbury* v. *Hanbury* (1892), 8 T.L.R. 559, C.A.; *S.* v. *S.*, [1961] 3 All E.R. 133; [1962] P. 133.

[1]See *post*, pp. 154-155.

[2]But probably not, *e.g.*, if he or she got drunk knowing that sexual intercourse might result: see *Goshawk* v. *Goshawk* (1965), 109 Sol. Jo. 290. In any case, even though force, fraud, insanity, etc., will exculpate one party, the party acting voluntarily will be guilty of adultery: see *Barnett* v. *Barnett*, [1957] 1 All E.R. 388; [1957] P. 78; *S.* v. *S.*, *(supra)*. See further Fridman, *Mental Incompetency*, 80 L.Q.R. 84, pp. 96-98.

[3][1966] 1 All E.R. 524, H.L.; [1966] A.C. 643.

[4][1968] 3 All E.R. 701, 704, C.A.

[5]*F.* v. *F.*, [1968] 1 All E.R. 242; [1968] P. 506, following dicta in *Preston-Jones* v. *Preston-Jones*, [1951] 1 All E.R. 124, H.L.; [1951] A.C. 391, where the same situation had arisen.

probabilities,[6] the courts must surely accept the same standard of proof of adultery: otherwise, in the situation outlined above, they might have to hold that the wife had not committed adultery but that the child was illegitimate—an even more absurd situation than the opposite.

2. PERSISTENT CRUELTY

Either spouse may apply for an order on the ground that the defendant has been guilty of persistent cruelty to the complainant, a minor child of the complainant, or a minor child of the defendant who was at the time a child of the family.[7]

Of all the matrimonial offences cruelty probably presents the most difficulties to the student. The reasons for this are various. In the first place, " legal cruelty " receives a restricted meaning, and not every act or course of conduct which would be called cruel in the popular sense amounts to cruelty in law. On the other hand, judges have deliberately avoided formulating an exhaustive definition of cruelty. Acts of cruelty (like acts of negligence in the law of tort) are infinitely variable, and no list can be drawn up of acts which do—or even may—amount to cruelty and of those which do not. Conduct which is undoubtedly cruel in one case is equally clearly not cruel in another because of the presence of some other fact or circumstance. Consequently, it is dangerous to use one case as a precedent for another presenting similar facts, and all that can be done here is to attempt to extract and formulate from the decided cases the main principles by which the courts will be guided.

Nature of Persistent Cruelty.—Cruelty as a ground for relief in a magistrates' court has the same meaning as it formerly had as a ground for divorce[8] and naturally its latter function has been much more important in the development of the law. Consequently all the reported cases on the subject have been concerned with cruelty to a spouse, but the term presumably has precisely the same meaning in relation to a child. Persistent cruelty is " cruelty continued over a period of time and persisted in ".[9] Clearly the whole course of the defendant's conduct must be looked at: one act can never amount to persistent cruelty,[10] although JEUNE, P., stated obiter that a series of acts on the same day might amount to persistent cruelty.[11] Whether the cruelty was persistent must necessarily be a question of fact in each case.

Underlying Considerations.—Up till 1857 cruelty (or *saevitia*) was a ground for divorce *a mensa et thoro* in ecclesiastical law. Between 1857 and 1923 it was a ground for divorce on the wife's petition if it was coupled with the husband's adultery, but it was still primarily a

---

[6]See *post*, p. 231.
[7]Matrimonial Proceedings (Magistrates' Courts) Act 1960, s. 1 (1) (b). " Child " includes an illegitimate or adopted child: *ibid.*, s. 16 (1). For the meaning of " child of the family ", see *post*, p. 283.
[8]*Barker* v. *Barker*, [1949] 1 All E.R. 247; [1949] P. 219.
[9]*Per* LORD MERRIVALE, P., in *Goodman* v. *Goodman* (1931), 29 L.G.R. 273, 275. Physical cruelty may be coupled with mental cruelty: *Crawford* v. *Crawford*, [1955] 3 All E.R. 592; [1956] P. 195.
[10]*Rigby* v. *Rigby*, [1944] 1 All E.R. 336, C.A.; [1944] P. 33.
[11]*Broad* v. *Broad* (1898), 78 L.T. 687.

ground for judicial separation. Here, of course, the court was concerned with the question whether the petitioner should be relieved of his or her duty to cohabit with the respondent and consequently in these circumstances it was bound to have regard principally to the effect that the latter's conduct was having on the aggrieved spouse.

With the passing of the Matrimonial Causes Act of 1937, however, cruelty became of much greater importance as a ground for divorce. As this Act continued to embody the principle that divorce was to be granted only on the commission of a matrimonial offence, it was inevitable that the courts would now look at the nature of the respondent's conduct rather than at the effect that it was having on the petitioner. The result was that, as in the case of a criminal offence, both *actus reus* and *mens rea* had to be proved before a case of cruelty could be established.

Nevertheless the House of Lords had declared that the Act of 1937 had made no change in the nature of the offence and that cruelty after 1937 meant exactly the same as it had meant before.[12] This was ultimately bound to bring these opposing principles into conflict. Suppose that a husband savagely assaults his wife during a fit of insanity when he is not in control of his actions, or makes his wife mentally ill by ignoring and humiliating her, not out of malice but as a result of selfishly pursuing his own interests to the exclusion of hers. Looked at from the wife's point of view, there can be said to be cruelty in both cases; looked at from the husband's, there is no conscious intention to harm in either. This conflict eventually had to be solved by the House of Lords in two appeals coming before them in 1963—*Gollins* v. *Gollins*[13] and *Williams* v. *Williams*.[14] Both judgments were delivered on the same day and together review almost the whole of the law of cruelty. Broadly speaking, the balance came down in favour of giving relief to the complainant in a situation which has become intolerable. The rule that emerged is that, if the defendant's conduct injures the complainant's health or is likely to do so, it will amount to cruelty if it is grave and weighty and such that the complainant cannot reasonably be expected to tolerate it.[15]

Except for decisions of the House of Lords, any case decided before 1963 must now be regarded with suspicion. Most would probably be decided in the same way[16] but the *rationes decidendi* would almost certainly be different. Whilst these cases may serve as illustrations, care should be taken before using them as precedents.

Injury to Health.—Emphasis in the nineteenth century upon the necessity of protecting the complainant and hence upon the effect of

---

[12]*Jamieson* v. *Jamieson*, [1952] 1 All E.R. 875, H.L., at pp. 883, 887, 888; [1952] A.C. 525, at pp. 544, 550, 551. See also *Williams* v. *Williams*, [1963] 2 All E.R. 994, H.L., at pp. 997, 1007, 1017, 1028; [1964] A.C. 698, at pp. 713, 728, 744, 760.

[13][1963] 2 All E.R. 966, H.L.; [1964] A.C. 644.

[14][1963] 2 All E.R. 994, H.L.; [1964] A.C. 698.

[15]For a full analysis of these two cases and their implications see Brown, *Cruelty without Culpability or Divorce without Fault*, 26 M.L.R. 625.

[16]See LORD REID's view in *Gollins* v. *Gollins*, at pp. 973 and 666 respectively. He regarded *Eastland* v. *Eastland*, [1954] 3 All E.R. 159; [1954] P. 403, alone as definitely incorrectly decided on the facts.

the defendant's conduct led to the decision of the House of Lords in *Russell* v. *Russell*.[17] This established that no conduct can amount to cruelty in law unless it has the effect of producing actual or apprehended injury to the complainant's physical or mental health. In the words of LOPES, L.J., in the same case in the Court of Appeal[18]:

> " there must be danger to life, limb, or health, bodily or mental, or a reasonable apprehension of it, to constitute legal cruelty."

It will be observed that the injury may be to physical or mental health (in the latter case the conduct being frequently referred to as " mental cruelty "). Moreover, there is no need for the injury to be actually suffered: a *reasonable* apprehension that injury will result if the conduct is persisted in will suffice, for the court will not wait for a spouse to be actually injured before affording him relief. But where there is no probability of injury at all, the offence of cruelty has not been made out. Thus, in *Russell* v. *Russell* it was held that a wife who had made unfounded charges that her husband had committed an unnatural offence with another man without belief in their truth was not guilty of cruelty since her conduct, however reprehensible, had not caused any injury or apprehension of injury to her husband's health.

The necessity of proving an injury to the complainant's health raises a difficulty where it is alleged that the defendant's conduct would not have caused any injury to a normal person but that the resulting ill-health is due to hypersensitiveness on the part of the complainant. This state of affairs is obviously more likely to arise in cases of mental cruelty, but the problem may possibly be seen more clearly in the case of physical injury. Thus, if a wife suffers from heart disease to the husband's knowledge and he gives her a sudden shock, his act could amount to cruelty.[19] Similarly, if the wife is pregnant, her health may be more easily affected than at other times, and she is therefore entitled to more considerate treatment from her husband.[20] The question was considered by LORD NORMAND in the House of Lords in *Jamieson* v. *Jamieson*,[1] where he pointed out that each case must depend on the individual circumstances and said:

> " The conduct alleged must be judged *up to a point* by reference to the victim's capacity for endurance, in so far as that capacity is or ought to be known to the other spouse. . . . That leaves it open to find, after evidence, that the [complainant] was the victim of his or her own abnormal hypersensitiveness and not of cruelty inflicted by the [defendant]."

The problem is really one of causation, and whether or not the conduct complained of is to be considered cruel must be judged by reference to its actual effect on the complainant rather than its probable effect on a hypothetical " reasonable spouse ". Thus, the question becomes one of fact, and inconclusive as this test may be, it is doubtful how far a more comprehensive one could be devised to cover such a

---

[17][1897] A.C. 395, H.L.; affirming C.A., [1895] P. 315.
[18][1895] P. at p. 322.
[19]*Per* BUCKNILL, J., in *Barrett* v. *Barrett* (1903), 20 T.L.R. 73.
[20]*Cf. Lauder* v. *Lauder*, [1949] 1 All E.R. 76, C.A.; [1949] P. 277.
[1][1952] 1 All E.R. 875, 877, H.L.; [1952] A.C. 525, 535. See further Allen, *Matrimonial Cruelty*, 73 L.Q.R. 316, at pp. 318-325.

vast class of cases where the court is often faced with the difficult task of striking a fine balance between two spouses neither of whom has been wholly blameless.

Nature of the Defendant's Conduct.—The change in emphasis after the passing of the 1937 Act led the Court of Appeal to formulate the rule that conduct could be cruel only if the defendant intended to hurt the complainant or if his acts were " aimed at " the other. This could clearly work injustice, however, in the case of a defendant whose conduct was not the result of any intention to harm but of pure selfishness or indifference. Consequently the courts were driven back on the presumption that a person may be taken to intend the natural and probable consequences of his acts and thus, for example, granted a decree to a husband whose health was affected when his wife, who was an invalid suffering from physical and mental troubles, made excessive demands upon him to perform various small services, compelled him to read to her throughout the night and prevented him from sleeping.[2]

It was the essential artificiality of this presumption that was attacked by the majority of the House of Lords in *Gollins* v. *Gollins*.[3] In this case the husband was an unsuccessful farmer at the time of the marriage. The wife later discovered that he was heavily in debt and unable to support her. From time to time she lent him money to pay off his debts, and eventually the farm was sold and a house bought which the wife ran as a guesthouse. The husband still did little or nothing to help her except to look after the garden and the poultry but spent his time unsuccessfully trying to invent agricultural machinery whilst his wife was being troubled by his creditors and by bailiffs. In brief he was incorrigibly and inexcusably lazy and just " hung up his hat in the hall ". At no time did he do any physical harm to her, but the strain of his debts finally began to tell on her and she consulted a doctor who diagnosed a moderately severe anxiety state and warned her that her condition might well deteriorate if her domestic situation did not improve. The wife then took proceedings before magistrates who made an order on the ground of the husband's persistent cruelty. The question before the House, therefore, was whether this conduct was capable in law of amounting to cruelty. The majority held that it was. They decisively rejected the view that cruelty necessarily connotes any intention on the defendant's part and held that, if his conduct could fairly be called cruel, it does not matter whether it springs from a desire to hurt or from selfishness or sheer indifference. In other words, what is now important is the defendant's conduct and not the state of his mind.

This approach was pushed even further in *Williams* v. *Williams*.[4] Here the husband, who was mentally ill, began to hear voices telling him that his wife was committing adultery. He repeatedly levelled accusations against her, followed her about the house and sometimes climbed into the loft to look for the men concerned. This injured the

---

[2]*Squire* v. *Squire*, [1948] 2 All E.R. 51, C.A.; [1949] P. 51. For a full discussion, see the 2nd edition of this book, pp. 93-97.
[3][1963] 2 All E.R. 966, H.L.; [1964] A.C. 644.
[4][1963] 2 All E.R. 994, H.L.; [1964] A.C. 698.

wife's health and she petitioned for divorce. The trial judge held that he would have found cruelty proved had he not been bound by authority to apply the *M'Naghten* rules,[5] *viz.* that the defendant will have a good defence to a charge of cruelty (as he would to a criminal charge at common law) if he can prove that, at the time when he committed the acts complained of, he did not know the nature and quality of his acts or, if he did, he did not know that they were wrong. This case clearly came within the second limb and the petition was therefore dismissed. This was upheld by the Court of Appeal but the House of Lords allowed the wife's appeal. Quite apart from the inappropriateness of applying to the law of divorce a set of rules (already discredited as unscientific) designed to define criminal culpability, the majority of the House were of the opinion that, just as selfish stupidity is not necessarily a defence to a charge of cruelty, no more is insanity.[6] As the law then stood, the problem was really that of balancing hardship to the respondent, who might find himself divorced for conduct which he could not control, against hardship to the petitioner, who would otherwise have been unable to obtain a release from marriage with a spouse with whom life was by any standards intolerable. The fact that cruelty is now a ground for relief only in a magistrates' court further emphasises the need to protect the complainant particularly when his or her health and physical safety are imperilled by the defendant's mental disease, for the provisions of the Mental Health Act may not give adequate protection. The majority of the House of Lords were in favour of giving relief in such circumstances even though this may involve stigmatizing the defendant as guilty of a matrimonial offence; as they emphasised, cruelty does not necessarily connote any guilt, culpability or blameworthiness.

Whether or not the defendant has been guilty of cruelty is, therefore, primarily a question of fact. Three members of the House of Lords, LORD MORRIS and LORD HODSON (who delivered the dissenting judgments in both *Gollins* v. *Gollins* and *Williams* v. *Williams*) together with LORD EVERSHED, said that it must be shown that his conduct was cruel in the ordinary sense of that word.[7] LORD PEARCE elaborated this slightly in the following words:[8]

> " It is impossible to give a comprehensive definition of cruelty, but when reprehensible conduct or departure from the normal standards of conjugal kindness causes injury to health or an apprehension of it, it is, I think, cruelty if a reasonable person, after taking due account of the temperament and all the other particular circumstances, would consider that the conduct complained of is such that this spouse should not be called on to endure it."

Similarly LORD REID said that you would be guilty of cruelty " if without just cause or excuse you persist in doing things which you know your wife will probably not tolerate, and which no ordinary woman would tolerate . . . whatever your desire or intention may have been ".[9] But the difficulty arises that one bench's view of the accepted

---

[5] *R.* v. *M'Naghten* (1843), 10 Cl. & Fin. 200, H.L.
[6] At pp. 1003-1004, 1007-1010, 1028-1029, and 721-723, 728-733, 760-762, respectively.
[7] *Gollins* v. *Gollins*, (*supra*), at pp. 976-977, 978, 985, and 671, 674, 684, respectively. See also *Le Brocq* v. *Le Brocq*, [1964] 3 All E.R. 464, C.A., 465, 469, 471.
[8] *Gollins* v. *Gollins*, (*supra*), at pp. 992 and 695, respectively.
[9] *Gollins* v. *Gollins*, (*supra*), at pp. 974 and 666, respectively.

meaning of cruelty may differ radically from another's; magistrates may find cruelty proved on facts which an appellate court feels could not properly be described by that word in its normal sense.[10] Despite this fundamental change, it is submitted that certain principles still apply and the following facts and circumstances must be borne in mind in considering whether a case of cruelty has been made out.

Injury to Health.—This, of course, is still a prerequisite in any case of cruelty. Indeed, in cases of mental cruelty this should be considered first.

Gravity of the Defendant's Conduct.—Magistrates still cannot grant relief on trivial grounds or for mere incompatibility of temperament. Before conduct can be called cruel, it must reach a certain pitch of severity.   This has been variously described as " inexcusable, unpardonable, unforgivable or grossly excessive "[11] and " wilful and unjustifiable acts inflicting pain and misery ",[12] but the commonest description now is " grave and weighty ".[13]   It is for the court to weigh the gravity: the test to be inferred from the parts of LORD PEARCE's and LORD REID's speeches in *Gollins* v. *Gollins* quoted above is that the conduct must be such that no reasonable person would tolerate it or consider that the complainant should be called on to endure it.[14]

The Court of Appeal emphasised the necessity of this in *Le Brocq* v. *Le Brocq.*[15]   The spouses had highly incompatible temperaments: the wife was domineering and the husband suffered from an inferiority complex and submissiveness.   The crux of the wife's case was that the husband ignored and neglected her and failed to take sufficient interest in her and their children and she relied on a mass of trivial incidents in support of her contention.   It was unanimously held that none of these was sufficiently grave and weighty to amount to cruelty in the normal sense of the word.   As SALMON, L.J., pointed out,[16] we have not yet reached the stage where a person can seek relief merely because he or she finds the marriage irritating and exasperating or the other spouse intolerable.

Given that the conduct is grave and weighty, it can take a variety of forms.   On the one hand there are positive acts, such as assaults and other forms of physical violence, sexual perversion and homosexual activities,[17] persistent drunkenness, addiction to gambling, commission of criminal offences (particularly of a sexual character),[18] threats,

---

[10]*Cf. Gollins* v. *Gollins* itself, where five of the ten judges who heard the case at its various stages on appeal held that the husband's conduct, which the magistrates found amounted to cruelty, could not be called cruel in the normal acceptance of that word. See further Brown, *Cruelty without Culpability,* 26 M.L.R. 625.

[11]*Per* LORD NORMAND in *King* v. *King,* [1952] 2 All E.R. 584, 586, H.L.

[12]*Per* BUCKNILL, L.J., in *Horton* v. *Horton,* [1940] 3 All E.R. 380, 384.

[13]*Per* LORD PEARCE in *Gollins* v. *Gollins, (supra),* at pp. 986 and 687, respectively. See also *Noble* v. *Noble (No.* 2), [1964] 1 All E.R. 577, 579; [1964] P. 250, 253; *Griffiths* v. *Griffiths,* [1964] 3 All E.R. 929, 932; *Saunders* v. *Saunders,* [1965] 1 All E.R. 838, 843, 846; [1965] P. 499, 507, 513.

[14]*Cf.* the similar test in desertion and constructive desertion: *post,* pp. 168 and 173.

[15][1964] 3 All E.R. 464, C.A.

[16]At p. 471. *Cf. McEwan* v. *McEwan* (1964), 108 Sol. Jo. 198, C.A.

[17]*Arthur* v. *Arthur* (1964), 108 Sol. Jo. 317, C.A. (husband defendant); *Coffer* v. *Coffer* (1964), 108 Sol. Jo. 465 (wife defendant).

[18]*H.* v. *H.* (1964), 108 Sol. Jo. 544. Contrast *Boushall* v. *Boushall* (1964), *Times,* November 7th.

insults, nagging, humiliation, persistent dishonesty causing embarrass-ment,[19] maliciously taking matrimonial proceedings,[20] and obsessional conduct of various kinds.[1] On the other hand are what may be termed negative acts, such as neglect, indifference, desertion,[2] boorishness, meanness and wilful refusal to provide maintenance.[3] This merely indicates some of the aspects of cruelty; no list could hope to be exhaustive.[4]

The difficulties likely to be caused by *Gollins* v. *Gollins* and *Williams* v. *Williams* are well illustrated by a group of cases decided since 1963 in each of which the basic trouble has been sexual. In the leading case, *Sheldon* v. *Sheldon*,[5] a comparatively young and apparently healthy and virile husband had refused to have sexual intercourse with his wife for about six years although they continued to share the same bed. The wife became depressed and frustrated but the husband refused to change his attitude even when its results were made clear by the wife and her doctor. Eventually she left him and petitioned for divorce on the ground of his cruelty. In the absence of any explanation for his conduct (except for an unproven surmise that he was getting satis-faction with other women) it is not surprising that the Court of Appeal unanimously found that it amounted to cruelty. Both LORD DENNING, M.R., and SALMON, L.J., emphasised that it is necessary to keep this type of case within bounds and stated that a petition could succeed only if, as here, there had been a persistent refusal for a long period and the respondent knew that his or her conduct was causing grave injury to the petitioner's health. LORD DENNING further pointed out that allowances must be made for such excuses as ill health, time of life, age or psycho-logical infirmity.

The difficulty arises from the fact that these two members of the court approved four earlier decisions. In two of these[6] the wife had been found guilty of cruelty by refusing to have intercourse even though in one of them her refusal was due entirely to an invincible fear of con-ception and childbirth. In the other two[7] the husband (apparently undersexed and innately disinclined to have intercourse) had been found not guilty of cruelty even though this resulted in intercourse at rare intervals and in one case in total abstinence for 15 years. The inference to be drawn is that the courts are demanding different standards of sexual participation from husbands and wives. The wife is expected to submit to her husband's demands even though she is inhibited by invincible fears; a husband on the other hand cannot be expected to conquer his innate disinclination and engage in what

[19]*Stanwick* v. *Stanwick*, [1970] 3 All E.R. 983, C.A.
[20]*Buxton* v. *Buxton*, [1965] 3 All E.R. 150; [1967] P. 48.
[1]*Williams* v. *Williams*, (*ante*, p. 154); *Howell* v. *Howell* (1964), *Times*, June 10th (obsessional cleaning of house all night); *Crump* v. *Crump*, [1965] 2 All E.R. 980 (ritual wiping of everything to kill " cancer germs ").
[2]*Stanwick* v. *Stanwick*, (*supra*).
[3]*Gollins* v. *Gollins*, (*ante*, p. 154).
[4]For other examples, see Rayden, *Divorce*, 11th Ed., 1112 *et seq.*; Rosen, *Matri-monial Offences*, 2nd Ed., 186-215.
[5][1966] 2 All E.R. 257, C.A.; [1966] P. 62.
[6]*P.* (*D.*) v. *P.* (*J.*), [1965] 2 All E.R. 456; *Evans* v. *Evans*, [1965] 2 All E.R. 789.
[7]*B.* (*L.*) v. *B.* (*R.*), [1965] 3 All E.R. 263, C.A.; *P.* v. *P.*, [1964] 3 All E.R. 919.

JUDGE HAROLD BROWN described as " a kind of disciplined act to keep a wife happy and in good health ".[8] This distinction seems as crude as it is out of keeping with modern views of the spouses' roles in the sexual side of their marriage. DAVIES, L.J., whilst expressly refraining from deciding the point, suggested that the result of *Gollins* v. *Gollins* and *Williams* v. *Williams* might well be that abstinence from intercourse causing injury to the other spouse's health could amount to cruelty even though it resulted from physical or mental affliction. This view is directly contrary to the earlier decision of the Court of Appeal in *B. (L.)* v. *B. (R.)*,[9] to the opinion of SALMON, L.J., in *Sheldon* v. *Sheldon*, and to the later decision of ORMROD, J., in *Walker* v. *Walker*,[10] but it logically follows from the principle that culpability is no longer an ingredient of cruelty.[11]

The Complainant's Conduct.—Although the defendant's conduct must be grave and weighty, it must be remembered that the question before the court is whether *this* conduct by *this* man to *this* woman, or vice versa, is cruelty.[12] This is not to be measured objectively against any artificial standards laid down by a hypothetical reasonable man. Thus acts which amount to cruelty in one case may not do so in another because of a difference in the circumstances or in the parties' physical and psychological make-up. It is imperative to look at the whole history of the marriage including the parties' conduct after they have stopped living together;[13] in some cases (for example, nagging) a course of conduct may on the whole be cruel although each individual act taken separately will not be.[14] This was stressed by the House of Lords in *Jamieson* v. *Jamieson*,[15] where it was pointed out that every act must be judged in relation to its surrounding circumstances and, one might add, in relation to the spouses' temperaments. Acts which appear on the face to be unpardonable may in the particular circumstances be, if not justified, at least excused by the complainant's own conduct and the amount of provocation he has offered to the defendant. This particular problem was discussed by the House of Lords in *King* v. *King*,[16] where LORD ASQUITH OF BISHOPSTONE pointed out that such questions are always questions of degree and that the court must bear in mind the intensity and degree of the defendant's conduct whilst making allowances for the intensity and degree of provocation

---

[8] *P.* v. *P.*, (*supra*), at p. 920.
[9] [1965] 3 All E.R. 263, C.A.
[10] (1967), 111 Sol. Jo. 436.
[11] See also Michaels, 29 M.L.R. 196.
[12] *Gollins* v. *Gollins*, [1963] 2 All E.R. 966, H.L., 970, 977, 992; [1964] A.C. 644, 660, 672, 695.
[13] *Waters* v. *Waters*, [1967] 3 All E.R. 417; [1968] P. 401. The cruelty must have occurred during the subsistence of the marriage; hence pre-marital acts cannot amount to cruelty: *cf. Carpenter* v. *Carpenter*, [1955] 2 All E.R. 449.
[14] As HENN COLLINS, J., put it: " Dropping water wears the stone." (*Atkins* v. *Atkins*, [1942] 2 All E.R. 637, 638.)
[15] [1952] 1 All E.R. 875, H.L.; [1952] A.C. 525. See particularly LORD TUCKER at pp. 887 and 550, respectively. See also *King* v. *King*, [1952] 2 All E.R. 584, 592, H.L.; [1953] A.C. 124, 138 (*per* LORD REID).
[16] [1952] 2 All E.R. 584, H.L.; [1953] A.C. 124.

offered by the complainant and for all other relevant facts.[17]

The Defendant's Knowledge, Belief, Motive and Intention.—In most cases of physical cruelty these facts will be irrelevant. If a husband makes a savage assault on his wife, his motive is immaterial. But even here knowledge of the probable consequences of the defendant's acts could be decisive. If he buys a cat as a pet, for example, this will not normally constitute cruelty, but it could do if he knows that his wife is made physically ill by cats and *a fortiori* if he introduces it into the house with the intention of injuring her health. Again, if serious injury to the complainant was caused by mishap, this could not fairly be described as cruelty even though the same injury inflicted intentionally would be.[18] In cases of mental cruelty, on the other hand, these matters will usually be important, particularly if the complainant is alleging neglect, and in doubtful cases will be decisive. In the words of LORD PEARCE:[19]

" Whereas a blow speaks for itself, insults, humiliations, meannesses, impositions, deprivations, and the like may need the interpretation of underlying intention for an assessment of their fullest significance."

One may take the illustration that he draws in his speech in *Gollins* v. *Gollins*,[20] where he contrasts the situation of two wives taken seriously ill abroad and left there by their husbands who return to England. The first is a woman who is timorous, unable to speak the language, left without adequate nursing arrangements or money and the reason for the husband's return is that he wishes to watch a football match; the second wife has a more robust and independent nature, a knowledge of the language, a less severe illness and more adequate nursing arrangements and her husband has a more cogent reason for returning. The first case is clearly one of cruelty; the second *prima facie* is not but would be if the husband deliberately intended to hurt. Indeed such an intention must always make conduct cruel if it is sufficiently grave and weighty and has the desired effect.

The State of the Defendant's Mind.—Although the House of Lords laid down the rule in *Williams* v. *Williams*[1] that the defendant's insanity was not necessarily a defence to a charge of cruelty, it is equally clear that his mental state is not to be entirely ignored. It is one of the matters to be taken into account along with the parties' temperaments and other circumstances.[2] If the defendant's acts could amount to cruelty only if he intended to injure the complainant and he is incapable of forming the intent, then there cannot be cruelty in that particular case; conversely, if they would amount to cruelty in any

---

[17]At pp. 597 and 148-149, respectively. Hence if one spouse treats the other with cruelty but then gets back more than he can be said to have asked for, both may be guilty of cruelty: *Kelly* v. *Kelly*, [1968] 1 W.L.R. 152.
[18]But what if the injury was caused by the defendant's negligence?
[19]*Gollins* v. *Gollins*, [1963] 2 All E.R. 966, 989, H.L.; [1964] A.C. 644, 690.
[20][1963] 2 All E.R. 966, 990-991, H.L.; [1964] A.C. 644, 693. See also *Buxton* v. *Buxton*, [1965] 3 All E.R. 150; [1967] P. 48 (husband claiming custody of son aged eight knowing that this was causing distress to the wife and showing a callous indifference to her held to be guilty of cruelty).
[1][1963] 2 All E.R. 994, H.L.; [1964] A.C. 698. For the facts, see *ante*, p. 154.
[2]*Williams* v. *Williams*, (*supra*), at pp. 1009, 1029 and 731, 762, respectively.

event, his insanity is irrelevant.[3] One is at first sight inclined to be more sympathetic towards a defendant who cannot be regarded as wholly responsible for his actions; on the other hand, however, the complainant's need for protection will often be greater in such a case. More latitude will doubtless be allowed to a spouse who does not know what he is doing at all for then, in one sense, these are not his acts. This is particularly true when his mental state is temporary and due to physical causes (for example, a man who strikes his wife a blow while delirious), but obviously a man who attacks his wife with a chopper during an insane fit can be guilty of cruelty. A similar view has been taken in the case of a defendant who knows what he is doing but cannot control his actions and in *Crump* v. *Crump*[4] a decree was granted to a husband whose health was injured by his wife's ritual cleaning of everything to kill " cancer germs " owing to an obsessional psychoneurosis over which she had no control. At the other end of the spectrum, however, is the spouse who subsides into a passive state of withdrawal and in *Priday* v. *Priday*[5] CUMMING-BRUCE, J., held that such a person could no more be regarded as cruel than one who was physically paralysed by a stroke, even though the complainant was worn down as a result. If this case is correctly decided, the question in every such case must be whether the defendant's conduct can be regarded as sufficiently positive to give rise to a charge of cruelty.

Acquiescence by the Complainant.—If the complainant has acquiesced in the defendant's conduct, he or she cannot subsequently turn round and complain of it and obtain matrimonial relief on the ground of cruelty.[6] But the submission to the acts must be voluntary before it can be called acquiescence, and if the complainant has virtually no option but to submit, he will not be precluded from basing a complaint upon these acts.[7] Similarly, in *Meacher* v. *Meacher*,[8] where the husband had repeatedly assaulted his wife for visiting her sister contrary to his wishes, it was held by the Court of Appeal that she was not prevented from relying on these acts as cruelty merely because she could have avoided them by giving in to her husband's unreasonable demands.

Probability of Recurrence of Cruelty in the Future.—So long as cruelty was solely or primarily a ground for judicial separation, it was natural that a decree should be refused unless there was a probability of recurrence of cruelty, for otherwise there would be no danger from which the petitioner should be protected. In legal terms this rule could be explained in one of two ways. It could be argued that, if there was no probability of recurrence, the offence had not been established—in other words, probability of recurrence is one of the constituent elements

---

[3]*Ibid.*, at pp. 1029 and 762, respectively.
[4][1965] 2 All E.R. 980.
[5][1970] 3 All E.R. 554.
[6]*Bravery* v. *Bravery*, [1954] 3 All E.R. 59, C.A.
[7]*Per* EVERSHED, L.J., in *Squire* v. *Squire*, [1948] 2 All E.R. 51, 57, C.A.; [1949] P. 51, 65. *Cf. T.* v. *T.*, [1963] 2 All E.R. 746, C.A.; [1964] P. 85 (submission to sodomy).
[8][1946] 2 All E.R. 307, C.A.; [1946] P. 216.

of cruelty. Alternatively, it could be said that, before granting a decree of judicial separation, the court had to be satisfied of two things, cruelty and the probability of its recurrence—in other words that the latter is an additional requirement and not a constituent element. The correct formulation of the rule became important when cruelty was made a ground of divorce because the Act provided that the court should grant a decree if the respondent *had treated* the petitioner with cruelty,[9] so that the probability of recurrence was relevant only if it was necessary to establish it in order to prove the commission of the offence. In *Meacher* v. *Meacher*[10] the Court of Appeal held that the probability of recurrence was not an essential constituent of cruelty, but this decision has been the subject of forceful criticism in the House of Lords[11] although it was later supported obiter in the Court of Appeal.[12]

The question is still relevant because the Act of 1960 requires the complainant to show that the defendant *has been* guilty of persistent cruelty. If *Meacher* v. *Meacher* is correctly decided, the ground is made out even though there is no probability of recurrence—a situation which might occur, for example, if the defendant's conduct was due to mental illness which has now been cured. Although a separation order should not normally be made in such circumstances,[13] magistrates would be justified in making an order for maintenance and the complainant would be entitled to refuse to resume cohabitation on the ground that he is not bound to condone the other's cruelty. This result is wholly undesirable: no spouse ought to be allowed to rely on the other's past conduct as a justification for living apart in these circumstances. Now that cruelty is no longer a ground for divorce, it is to be hoped that *Meacher* v. *Meacher* will not be followed: an opinion that is fortified by the return to the view, expressed in *Gollins* v. *Gollins* and *Williams* v. *Williams*, that the protection of the complainant is the prime consideration.

3. DESERTION

Either spouse may apply for an order on the ground that the defendant is in desertion.[14] The desertion must be continuing but no minimum period is necessary.

Desertion consists of the unjustifiable withdrawal from cohabitation without the consent of the other spouse and with the intention of remaining separated permanently. It therefore follows that four elements must be present before desertion can be proved:

(a) The *de facto* separation of the spouses;

(b) The *animus deserendi*—i.e., the intention on the part of the spouse in desertion to remain separated permanently;

---

[9]Matrimonial Causes Act 1937, s. 2. Later consolidating Acts used the same form of words.

[10][1946] 2 All E.R. 307, C.A.; [1946] P. 216.

[11]*Per* LORD MERRIMAN and LORD TUCKER in *Jamieson* v. *Jamieson*, [1952] 1 All E.R. 875, H.L., at pp. 882-884 and 888; [1952] A.C. 525, at pp. 546-547 and 551.

[12]*Per* HODSON, L.J., in *Swan* v. *Swan*, [1953] 2 All E.R. 854, 859, C.A.; [1953] P. 258, 267.

[13]See *post*, pp. 198-199.

[14]Matrimonial Proceedings (Magistrates' Courts) Act 1960, s. 1 (1) (a).

(c) The absence of consent on the part of the deserted spouse; and

(d) The absence of any reasonable cause for withdrawing from cohabitation on the part of the deserting spouse.

These four conditions will shortly be considered in turn.

It must not be thought that it is the party who takes the physical step of leaving the matrimonial home or otherwise withdrawing from cohabitation who is necessarily the deserting spouse. In cases of simple desertion this is so, but where one spouse virtually drives the other from the home or behaves in such a way that the latter can no longer reasonably be expected to live with him or her, then it may be the spouse remaining in the matrimonial home and not the spouse who departs from it who is in desertion. Such a case is known as " constructive desertion " and will have to be considered separately.

Separation.—There can be no desertion unless there is a *de facto* separation between the spouses. It is not sufficient for this purpose that one of the spouses has abandoned some of the obligations of matrimony or refused to perform isolated duties (*e.g.*, refused to have sexual intercourse);[15] there must be a rejection of all the obligations of marriage,[16] in other words, there must be a complete cessation of cohabitation.

This state of affairs, of course, is normally brought about by one spouse's leaving the matrimonial home, so that they are no longer living under the same roof. In such a case, there is clearly a sufficient separation. But it may be impossible for the spouse wishing to leave to find accommodation elsewhere, and the situation may arise where the spouses continue to live under the same roof but where one shuts himself off from the other, so that they are living as two units rather than one. Although there is a presumption that in such a case there is no *de facto* separation sufficient to constitute desertion,[17] this is rebuttable, for, in the oft cited words of LORD MERRIVALE, P., " desertion is not the withdrawal from a place, but from a state of things ".[18] Hence, if there has been a total cessation of cohabitation, there can be desertion just as effectively as if the husband and wife were living in two separate houses.

The correct test to be applied in such a case is: Are the spouses living as two households or as one?[19] This must be very strictly construed: cohabitation must have entirely ceased and therefore there cannot be desertion if any matrimonial services are performed even though these are isolated and intermittent.[20] Each case must turn upon its own facts, and the line separating the two types of cases is a fine one as

---

[15]*Weatherley* v. *Weatherley*, [1947] 1 All E.R. 563, H.L.; [1947] A.C. 628.

[16]Per EVERSHED, M.R., in *Perry* v. *Perry*, [1952] 1 All E.R. 1076, 1082, C.A.; [1952] P. 203, 215.

[17]*Bull* v. *Bull*, [1953] 2 All E.R. 601, C.A., at pp. 602, 603; [1953] P. 224, at pp. 226, 228.

[18]*Pulford* v. *Pulford*, [1923] P. 18, 21.

[19]*Hopes* v. *Hopes*, [1948] 2 All E.R. 920, C.A., at pp. 922, 925; [1949] P. 227, at pp. 231, 236; *Bull* v. *Bull*, (*supra*), at pp. 602, 604, and 226, 230, respectively; *Walker* v. *Walker*, [1952] 2 All E.R. 138, C.A.; *Baker* v. *Baker*, [1952] 2 All E.R. 248, C.A.

[20]But the mere fact that the husband pays his wife maintenance will not prevent there being a *de facto* separation: *Smith* v. *Smith*, [1939] 4 All E.R. 533; [1940] P. 49.

can be seen by contrasting two leading cases. In *Naylor* v. *Naylor*[1] the husband returned home after cross-petitions for divorce had both been dismissed. A quarrel took place during which the wife indicated that she had no further intention of being a wife to him by removing her wedding ring, which she never wore again. From that time on the wife performed no marital duties, the husband stopped giving her housekeeping money and, although they continued to reside under the same roof, they lived separately without any communal or family life. The Divisional Court held that in the circumstances there was a sufficient separation to sustain a finding by magistrates that the wife was in desertion. In *Hopes* v. *Hopes*[2] sexual intercourse had ceased and the husband had withdrawn to a separate bedroom because the nature of his work necessitated his getting up (and therefore going to bed) early and he objected to his wife's going to bed at a normal time after he had retired. After this their relationship deteriorated. The wife objected to her husband's going out at night and abused his friends; quarrels were frequent and the husband often retired to his bedroom for the sake of peace. The wife did no mending or washing for him and never cooked separate meals for him, but he had most meals in common with the rest of the family in their dining-room, and when he was not in his bedroom he shared the rest of the house with his wife and daughters. The Court of Appeal held that here there was not sufficient separation to amount to desertion. In this case the husband had for the most part shared a common table and to some extent a common life with the rest of the family so that to an outsider the situation would not have appeared abnormal. To call this desertion would, as BUCKNILL, L.J., pointed out, give that term a very artificial meaning. It will be seen, therefore, that all matrimonial services and any form of common life must entirely cease.

Since all that must be proved is the *factum* of separation, it is irrelevant for this purpose that the spouses are forced to live apart and therefore could not live together even had they wished to do so.[3] Thus, in *Beeken* v. *Beeken*[4] the husband and wife, who were resident in China, were taken prisoners by the Japanese and interned in a camp where they shared a room. The wife formed an attachment to another man and refused to permit her husband to have sexual intercourse or to perform any wifely services for him, and eventually in December, 1942, said that she would do no more for him unless he promised to commence divorce proceedings on his release—an undertaking which the husband refused to give. In the following June they moved to separate camps, and in March, 1944, the wife visited the husband and reaffirmed her intention of marrying the other man. After their release the wife refused to return to her husband, who presented a petition for divorce on the ground of her desertion in July, 1947. It was held by

---

[1] [1961] 2 All E.R. 129; [1962] P. 253, where the earlier cases are fully examined.
[2] [1948] 2 All E.R. 920, C.A.; [1949] P. 227. *Cf. Littlewood* v. *Littlewood*, [1942] All E.R. 515; [1943] P. 11; *Le Brocq* v. *Le Brocq*, [1964] 3 All E.R. 464, C.A.
[3] As to the *animus deserendi*, see *post*, p. 164.
[4] [1948] P. 302, C.A.

the Court of Appeal that desertion had commenced in March, 1944, at the latest, even though at that time the wife could not have rejoined her husband had she wanted to do so.

The converse question was also raised in *Beeken* v. *Beeken, viz.* whether there can be desertion if the parties are forced to live together but where they would have lived apart had they been free to do so. Since the statutory triennium commenced in July, 1944, after they had moved to different camps, the problem did not have to be answered; but BUCKNILL, L.J., seems to have been of the opinion that there could be desertion in such circumstances; LORD MERRIMAN, P., implied that there might be desertion if the wife had taken all possible steps to obtain other accommodation; whilst HODSON, L.J., was content to say that there was no evidence to justify a finding that they were living apart.[5]

Whilst the unusual facts of *Beeken* v. *Beeken* are unlikely to recur, the same problem may arise where a family is living in one or two rooms and owing to financial or other circumstances neither spouse can go and live elsewhere. Again, one must apply the test of whether they are living as two households, and if it is possible for a husband and wife to live as two households in such circumstances, the fact that they are obliged to share living accommodation to a certain extent should not prove fatal.[6]

The *Animus Deserendi.*—Even though there is a *de facto* separation, there will be no desertion unless the guilty spouse has the intention of remaining permanently separated from the other. Clearly there will be no question of desertion if one spouse is temporarily absent on holiday or for reasons of business or health;[7] nor *prima facie* will there be desertion if the absence is involuntary, for example owing to service in the armed forces or imprisonment. But in these cases there will be desertion if the intention can be specifically proved; thus, in *Beeken* v. *Beeken*[8] the wife's *animus* was shown by her statement that she wished to marry another man and to have nothing more to do with her husband.

Normally the *animus deserendi* will be present when one spouse leaves the other, so that the desertion will commence immediately there is a *de facto* separation. But if, when the original separation took place, the parties intended to return to each other, and one of them later resolves not to resume cohabitation, desertion begins as soon as the *animus* is formed.[9]

---

[5]At pp. 311, 307, 312 respectively.

[6]*Cf.* LORD MERRIMAN, P., in *Everitt* v. *Everitt*, [1949] 1 All E.R. 908, 917-918, C.A.; (1949] P. 374, 387-388.

[7]See G. v. G., [1964] 1 All E.R. 129; [1964] P. 133. For the facts, see *post*, p. 169.

[8]*Ante*, p. 163. *Cf. Drew* v. *Drew* (1888), 13 P.D. 97 (husband in desertion although serving a sentence of penal servitude). Contrast *Townsend* v. *Townsend* (1873), L.R. 3 P. & D. 129 (husband in prison—no *animus deserendi*).

[9]*Pulford* v. *Pulford*, [1923] P. 18; *Pardy* v. *Pardy*, [1930] 3 All E.R. 779, C.A.; [1939] P. 288. There can be desertion even though the parties have never cohabited at all: *De Laubenque* v. *De Laubenque*, [1899] P. 42; *Shaw* v. *Shaw*, [1939] 2 All E.R. 381; [1939] P. 269.

If the party alleged to be in desertion is insane, it is a question of fact whether he is capable of forming the necessary *animus*. In *Perry* v. *Perry*[10] the wife left her husband because she suffered from the insane delusion (quite unfounded in reason) that he was trying to murder her. LLOYD-JONES, J., held that her conduct must be judged as though her belief was true and in these circumstances it was clear that there could be no desertion because she believed that she had good cause for leaving her husband.[11] Again, if a party already in desertion becomes insane, the desertion will continue only if he retains the *animus deserendi*. There is a presumption that he does not and the intention to remain in desertion must therefore be specifically proved.[12]

Lack of Consent.—Desertion is a matrimonial offence; consequently if one spouse agrees to the other's departing, he cannot then complain of it: there can be no desertion if the separation is by consent.[13] But "consent" in this context must be construed strictly. In the words of BUCKLEY, L.J., in *Harriman* v. *Harriman*:[14]

> " Desertion does not necessarily involve that the wife desires her husband to remain with her. She may be thankful that he has gone, but he may nevertheless have deserted her."

There must be many cases of deserted spouses who have been thankful to see the other go. The real test is whether the separation is really due to the conduct of the deserting spouse (in which case there can be desertion even though the other is glad to see the back of him) or to the other's consent to a permanent separation.

Whether or not consent to the separation in this sense has been given is, of course, a question of fact. It may be expressly given as a simple licence to go or be embodied in a separation agreement;[15] alternatively, it may be implied by the party's conduct. Thus, as the majority of the Court of Appeal held in *Harriman* v. *Harriman*,[16] if the deserted spouse

---

[10][1963] 3 All E.R. 766. Contrast *Kaczmarz* v. *Kaczmarz*, [1967] 1 All E.R. 416 (wife, who believed husband to be guilty of grave sin—apparently by having sexual intercourse with her—not amounting to a matrimonial offence, held to be in desertion when she refused to cohabit with him as a consequence).

[11]For good cause for separation, see *post*, pp. 168 *et seq.*

[12]*Crowther* v. *Crowther*, [1951] 1 All E.R. 1131, H.L.; [1951] A.C. 723.

[13]*Pardy* v. *Pardy*, [1939] 3 All E.R. 779, C.A.; [1939] P. 288.

[14][1909] P. 123, 148, C.A. See also *Kinnane* v. *Kinnane*, [1953] 2 All E.R. 1144; [1954] P. 41, and *cf. Beigan* v. *Beigan*, [1956] 2 All E.R. 630, C.A.; [1956] P. 313; *Pizey* v. *Pizey*, [1961] 2 All E.R. 658, C.A.; [1961] P. 101.

[15]Where it is alleged that the consent has been embodied in a separation agreement, it is a question of construction whether the agreement binds the parties to live apart. Thus, in *Crabtree* v. *Crabtree*, [1953] 2 All E.R. 56, C.A., it was held that a husband's promise to pay his wife £2 a week " if they shall so long live separate and apart from each other " did not amount to a consent by the wife to his leaving her, for the words merely defined the duration of the husband's financial liability; a similar conclusion was reached in *Bosley* v. *Bosley*, [1958] 2 All E.R. 167, C.A. See further Blom-Cooper, *Separation Agreements and Grounds for Divorce*, 19 M.L.R. 638, where Australian and New Zealand cases are also discussed.

[16][1909] P. 123, C.A.; *Robinson* v. *Robinson*, [1919] P. 352. This is so even though the non-cohabitation clause was inserted in the order by a magistrates' court without the applicant's consent: *Mackenzie* v. *Mackenzie*, [1940] 1 All E.R. 256, C.A.; [1940] P. 81. If a separation order was never made at all but the non-cohabitation clause was left on the printed form inadvertently, this will not prevent desertion from running, at least if the order has never been relied on, for it is a nullity: *Cohen* v. *Cohen*, [1947] 2 All E.R. 69, C.A.; [1947] P. 147.

obtains a judicial separation or a separation order in a magistrates' court, he cannot then allege that the other is still in desertion because the decree clearly shows a desire on the petitioner's part not to have the respondent back and, by relieving the former from the duty of cohabiting with the latter, effectively puts it out of the power of the deserting spouse to return. Similarly, in *Joseph* v. *Joseph*[17] the wife obtained a *get* which by Jewish law effects a divorce; although this would not dissolve the marriage by English law, nevertheless it was held by the Court of Appeal that the wife had thereby shown her consent to living apart from her husband and could therefore no longer assert that he was in desertion.

But in any event, of course, the consent, to be effective, must have been freely given, and what at first sight appears to be a clear consent may, in all the circumstances of the case, prove to be nothing of the sort. Thus, it has been held that a wife, who had been virtually forced by her husband to sign a separation agreement, with no legal advice and under great mental stress because she thought that this would be the only means of obtaining maintenance from him, had not genuinely consented to living apart from him.[18]

If the consent to the separation is withdrawn, desertion will automatically begin provided that the other conditions are all satisfied.[19] It is necessary, however, to draw a distinction between different types of consensual separation. In the first place, the parties might intend originally that it should be purely temporary. This could be for a given period of time (for example, a fortnight's holiday or a business trip); alternatively, it could depend on the happening of some future event or the fulfilment of a condition (for example, the husband's obtaining a suitable job near the matrimonial home). The consent will cease to be effective at the end of the period or on the satisfaction of the condition, and if the other spouse then unjustifiably refuses to resume cohabitation, he will be in desertion.[20] If in the meantime one spouse decides not to return to the other at all, desertion will begin to run as soon as the latter becomes aware of the *animus deserendi*; if he is unaware of it, there can be no desertion because the separation will still be with his consent.[1]

A separation which is not intended to be purely temporary may be of one of two kinds: it can be either for the parties' joint lives or until one of them asks the other to resume cohabitation. If it is not clear into which category a particular agreement falls, the court must try to infer the parties' intention from the terms of the agreement and the circumstances of their parting. In recent years the courts have leaned

---

[17][1953] 2 All E.R. 710, C.A. Distinguished on the facts in *Corbett* v. *Corbett*, [1957] 1 All E.R. 621.

[18]*Holroyd* v. *Holroyd* (1920), 36 T.L.R. 479.

[19]*Pardy* v. *Pardy*, [1939] 3 All E.R. 779, 783, C.A.; [1939] P. 288, 303. The burden of proof is on the spouse alleging that the other is in desertion: *Pizey* v. *Pizey*, [1961] 2 All E.R. 658, 664, C.A.; [1961] P. 101, 110.

[20]*Shaw* v. *Shaw*, [1939] 2 All E.R. 381; [1939] P. 269 (separation until the husband was earning enough to set up a home for himself and his wife).

[1]*Nutley* v. *Nutley*, [1970] 1 All E.R. 410, C.A.

against finding that the parties intended to separate for their joint lives. In the words of PEARCE, L.J., in *Bosley* v. *Bosley*:[2]

> " Often in the rather haphazard parting of husband and wife, the fact of a mutual agreement to separate has to be deduced from things done and things said in emotion and temper. The court should, I think, be slow to decide that there is imported a term that the separation shall be for ever and that there shall be no opportunity for any unilateral change of mind, no right ever to ask the other party to return to cohabitation."

If the separation is for an indefinite period and not for the parties' lives, either of them can resile and if the other unjustifiably rejects an offer to resume cohabitation, he will be in desertion. But there must be a genuine offer and not merely an exploratory approach or preliminary enquiry. If the party making the offer has been guilty of conduct in the past which would have justified the other in leaving, he must also give a credible assurance that it will not be repeated in the future; and in any event there must be no unreasonable conditions attached.[3] But the spouse to whom it is addressed is bound to consider the offer, and as the Court of Appeal held in *Gallagher* v. *Gallagher*,[4] if he fails to do so and rejects it out of hand, he will be in desertion whether it is reasonable or not.

If the agreement is intended to last for ever, it will normally be terminated (like any other contract) only by the consent of both spouses or by a breach by one accepted by the other as terminating his own obligations. In *Pardy* v. *Pardy*[5] the parties had entered into such an agreement under which the husband had covenanted to pay the wife 25/- a week. He paid these sums for twelve weeks and thereafter paid small sums from time to time. For more than three years before the wife presented her petition the husband had paid her nothing at all. The wife never made any attempt to enforce the deed. It was held that in the circumstances the parties had regarded the agreement as a dead letter for over three years and it was therefore incorrect to say that they were any longer living apart by consent. As in the case of commercial contracts, the repudiation of one term may be a repudiation of the whole agreement if the term is fundamental and goes to the root of the contract; but (unlike the case of a commercial contract) there is no need for the other party to inform the party in breach that he elects to treat himself as discharged: it is sufficient if he makes no attempt to insist upon performance and is in fact willing to resume cohabitation.[6]

Similarly, desertion can begin to run if a decree of judicial separation or a magistrates' separation order is discharged.[7]

---

[2][1958] 2 All E.R. 167, 173, C.A.; followed in *Hall* v. *Hall*, [1960] 1 All E.R. 91.

[3]*Fraser* v. *Fraser*, [1969] 3 All E.R. 654. *Cf.* the position when a spouse in desertion asks the other to resume cohabitation, *post*, pp. 179-180.

[4][1965] 2 All E.R. 967, C.A.

[5][1939] 3 All E.R. 779, C.A.; [1939] P. 288. *Cf. Papadopoulos* v. *Papadopoulos*, [1936] P. 108.

[6]But if the party not in breach enforces the agreement and so refuses to accept the repudiation, desertion will not begin: *Clark* v. *Clark* (*No. 2*), [1939] 2 All E.R. 392; [1939] P. 257 (wife's suing on husband's covenant to pay maintenance). See further *ante*, p. 140.

[7]But not automatically: see *Gatward* v. *Gatward*, [1942] 1 All E.R. 477, 478; [1942] P. 97, 99.

Want of Reasonable Cause.—If one spouse has a reasonable cause or excuse for leaving the other, then there will be no unjustifiable separation and consequently he will not be in desertion. Whether a particular excuse is sufficient in law is often a question of great difficulty, but it should be noted at the outset that it may be due either to the other spouse's misconduct or to circumstances (for example, illness) connected with the spouse who would otherwise be in desertion.[8]

The Complainant's Misconduct.—It is obvious that if this amounts to a matrimonial offence (that is, adultery or cruelty) or other ground for applying for a separation order in a magistrates' court, it must necessarily justify the other spouse in breaking off cohabitation unless the latter has put it out of his own power to complain of it by having conduced to it, connived at it or condoned it.[9] Over and above this, the field is so vast and the type of conduct so variable that it is neither profitable nor, indeed, possible to make an analysis of all the cases: each one must ultimately turn upon its own facts. But a number of tests have been propounded and consistently applied. The best known and most frequently cited is that of LORD PENZANCE who said that the conduct must be "grave and weighty";[10] a test modified by BARNARD, J., to " conduct so grave and weighty as to make married life quite impossible ".[11]

It will be recalled that this same test of " grave and weighty conduct " is also applied in cruelty,[12] and recent cases indicate that the two tests are precisely the same. The duty to cohabit is not lightly to be abandoned and by English law mere unhappiness or incompatibility of temperament can no more justify separation than amount to cruelty.[13] The difference between the two offences is that, whereas in cruelty the conduct must cause injury to the other spouse's health, it need not do so to raise a defence to desertion. In *Young* v. *Young*[14] SIMON, P., said:

---

[8]See Irvine, *" Reasonable Cause " and " Reasonable Excuse " as Justification for Separation*, 30 M.L.R. 659.

[9]*Hartnell* v. *Hartnell*, [1951] W.N. 555 (cruelty to children); *Callister* v. *Callister*, [1947] W.N. 221, C.A. (conduct conducing to adultery); *Wells* v. *Wells*, [1954] 3 All E.R. 491, C.A. (condoned adultery).

[10]*Yeatman* v. *Yeatman* (1868), L.R. 1 P. & D. 489, 494.

[11]*Dyson* v. *Dyson*, [1953] 2 All E.R. 1511, 1514; [1954] P. 198, 206. See also *Oldroyd* v. *Oldroyd*, [1896] P. 175, 184 (" practically impossible for the spouses to live properly together "); *Buchler* v. *Buchler*, [1947] 1 All E.R. 319, 326, C.A.; [1947] P. 25, 45-46 (" the ordinary wear and tear of conjugal life does not in itself suffice ").

[12]See *ante*, p. 156.

[13]*Buchler* v. *Buchler*, (*supra*), at pp. 320, 326-327 and 29, 47, respectively.

[14][1962] 3 All E.R. 120, 124; [1964] P. 152, 158, following *Pike* v. *Pike*, [1953] 1 All E.R. 232, C.A.; [1954] P. 81, and *Timmins* v. *Timmins*, [1953] 2 All E.R. 187, C.A. In these cases it was also said that the spouse's motive or intention is relevant in cruelty but not in desertion. But this must now be read in the light of the decision of the House of Lords in *Gollins* v. *Gollins*, (*ante*, p. 154). Hence, if the complainant fails on a charge of cruelty because the conduct complained of was not sufficiently grave and weighty, it will not be open to him to justify any further separation by pleading the same facts: see *Thoday* v. *Thoday*, [1964] 1 All E.R. 341, C.A.; [1964] P. 181, and the cases there cited.

" Where the gravity of the conduct itself is in question, irrespective of . . . its effect, the standard is the same both for good cause for separation and for cruelty: in both cases it must amount to such a grave and weighty matter as renders the continuance of the matrimonial cohabitation virtually impossible. It therefore follows that if the conduct is not of sufficient gravity to justify a charge of cruelty, it is not of sufficient gravity to excuse withdrawal from cohabitation."

Hence the same matters must be borne in mind as in the case of cruelty including the parties' temperaments, the circumstances surrounding the conduct complained of, and the whole history of the marriage. Thus it has been held that, although the separation cannot be justified by want of attention or affection alone,[15] it may be by the fact that the other spouse is overbearing and domineering and always insists on having his own way.[16] Unfounded allegations of adultery may well justify one spouse in leaving the other,[17] as will charges of homosexuality.[18] Similarly, a wife's prodigality has been held to be a good cause for her husband's refusing to take her back when it reached such a pitch that his business partners warned him that he would have to leave the firm if she rejoined him.[19]

One spouse's conduct may entitle the other to withdraw from cohabitation even though it is not culpable. For example, physical or mental illness will justify separation if it is likely to jeopardize the other's health or safety. An extension of the same principle is to be seen in *G.* v. *G.*[20] where the husband developed a mental illness which led him to frighten his children. It was held that the wife was entitled to remain apart from him so long as was necessary for the children's sake. The older cases indicate that, where no blame can be imputed to either spouse, the only justification for the separation that can be raised is the protection of the spouse leaving or of their children. Thus, to take one example, a wilful and inexcusable refusal to have sexual intercourse or insistence on *coitus interruptus* has been held to be a good cause for separation;[1] on the other hand, where a wife's refusal to permit her husband to have intercourse was due to invincible repugnance beyond her control, it was held that her husband was in desertion when he left her.[2] It is arguable, however, that this rule has been changed by the decisions of the House of Lords in *Gollins* v. *Gollins* and *Williams* v. *Williams*[3] that cruelty does not necessarily connote culpability on the part of the respondent or require any

---

[15]*Buchler* v. *Buchler*, (*supra*). Similarly, if a wife tells her husband that she has fallen in love with another man and begs the husband to help her, he should do so and, in the absence of adultery, he will have no defence to a charge of desertion if he leaves her: *Forbes* v. *Forbes*, [1954] 3 All E.R. 461, 467-468.
[16]*Timmins* v. *Timmins*, [1953] 2 All E.R. 187, C.A.
[17]*Marsden* v. *Marsden*, [1967] 1 All E.R. 967; [1968] P. 544.
[18]*Russell* v. *Russell*, [1895] P. 315, C.A.
[19]*G.* v. *G.*, [1930] P. 72. For further examples, see Rosen, *Matrimonial Offences*, 2nd Ed., 81 *et seq.*
[20][1964] 1 All E.R. 129; [1964] P. 133.
[1]*Slon* v. *Slon*, [1969] 1 All E.R. 759, C.A.; [1969] P. 122; *Hutchinson* v. *Hutchinson*, [1963] 1 All E.R. 1; *Rice* v. *Raynold-Spring-Rice*, [1948] 1 All E.R. 188.
[2]*Beevor* v. *Beevor*, [1945] 2 All E.R. 200. *Cf. Chapper* v. *Chapper* (1966), *Times*, May 25th (husband aged 60 held to be in desertion when he left wife aged 57 because her desire for sexual intercourse had " faded with the years ").
[3]See *ante*, pp. 154-155.

intention to injure the petitioner. Applying this principle it has since been held that refusal of sexual intercourse due to an invincible repugnance on the part of the wife could amount to cruelty when it affected the husband's health.[4] If the argument advanced above is correct, it follows that the wife's conduct will now be regarded as sufficiently grave and weighty to justify her husband's leaving her even though there is no threat to his health and notwithstanding that no blame can be attached to her. The only way to reconcile this apparent conflict would be to say that, in addition to being grave and weighty, acts or omissions must either contain an element of misconduct or jeopardize the health or safety of the other spouse or the children of the family if they are to justify a separation and prevent desertion from running. It remains to be seen whether the courts will insist upon this further requirement.

It must be stressed, however, that no conduct can be regarded as a good cause for separation unless it in fact led to it. Hence, if a wife leaves her husband after he has committed adultery, she will none the less be in desertion if she did not know of his offence or was indifferent to it and intended to leave anyway.[5] Furthermore, as in the case of constructive desertion,[6] the other spouse's conduct presumably cannot be a good cause for separation unless it occurred during the marriage. If this is so, discovery after marriage of the other spouse's pre-marital activities can never be a defence to desertion.

The Defendant's Circumstances.—The most obvious example of his own circumstances on which a spouse might rely to justify a separation is an enforced absence due to illness or business. In such cases it will almost always be temporary and for this reason could not amount to desertion. If he is advised to remain away from the other for good medical reason, it would seem on principle that he ought to be able to defeat a charge of desertion on the further ground that he has good cause for remaining apart, even though the separation may be for ever. This reasoning, however, does not seem to have commended itself to the Court of Appeal in *Lilley* v. *Lilley*.[7] Owing to mental illness the wife developed an invincible and apparently incurable repugnance to her husband. After being discharged from a mental hospital, she refused to return to him and made it clear that she never would do so. This was a rational decision in the sense that she was capable of forming an *animus deserendi* and the Court of Appeal accordingly held that she was in desertion. But this entirely overlooks the possible adverse effect of a return upon her mental health. Furthermore, had her illness been curable, her present intention never to return would presumably not have put her in desertion because she would have lost the *animus* on recovering her health; why, then, should the incurable nature of the

---

[4]*P. (D.)* v. *P.J.*, [1965] 2 All E.R. 456. See *ante*, pp. 157-158.
[5]*Herod* v. *Herod*, [1938] 3 All E.R. 722; [1939] P. 11; *Day* v. *Day*, [1957] 1 All E.R. 848; [1957] P. 202. But there is a presumption that the offence has induced the defendant to leave the complainant, so that the burden of proving ignorance or indifference is on the latter: *Earnshaw* v. *Earnshaw*, [1939] 2 All E.R. 698, C.A.
[6]See *post*, p. 174.
[7][1959] 3 All E.R. 283, C.A.; [1960] P. 169.

disease make any difference? The injustice of branding such a spouse as a deserter is manifest, and the case was applied with obvious reluctance in *Tickle* v. *Tickle*,[8] where a Divisional Court was compelled to hold a mentally ill husband to be in desertion in similar circumstances even though the medical evidence indicated that a return to his wife would almost certainly result in his having to go back to hospital.

Reasonable Belief in Grounds for Separation.—It has been held in a series of cases going back to *Ousey* v. *Ousey*[9] in 1874 that if one spouse has a reasonable belief that he has good cause for leaving the other based upon the other's own conduct, then he is entitled to break off cohabitation and will not be in desertion even though the belief is a mistaken one. In *Ousey* v. *Ousey* the husband was held not to be in desertion when he left his wife whom he thought either unable or unwilling to consummate the marriage. In *Glenister* v. *Glenister*[10] the same principle was applied where the husband, who was in the Forces and who believed himself to have been infected with gonorrhea by his wife on a previous occasion, returned home on leave at night to find three men in the house with his wife (one of whom, in fact, was in her bedroom) and was refused admission to the house till the following morning, although he had no positive proof of adultery.

But, as in these two cases, the belief must be based upon the other spouse's conduct and not upon circumstantial evidence: in other words the cause of separation must still be the other spouse's own acts. These cases illustrate an exception to the general rule that an unlawful act cannot be justified by a mistaken belief, however reasonably held, and it would clearly be unjust to the deserted spouse if the exception were extended to cases where that spouse had in no way contributed to the mistake. Thus in *Elliott* v. *Elliott*[11] it was held that a husband had no good cause for living apart from his wife when he had been told by his mother that the wife had committed adultery. Similarly he will not be justified in living apart if the conduct on which the belief in adultery is based was originally brought about or procured by himself any more than he could justify the separation by proof of the commission of adultery at which he had connived.[12]

The belief must be entertained reasonably and in good faith, and whether or not it is reasonable is to be determined objectively.[13] A spouse entertaining a mere suspicion, not based on evidence pointing

---

[8][1968] 2 All E.R. 154.
[9](1874), L.R. 3 P. & D. 223. See Bevan, *Belief in the other Spouse's Adultery*, 73 L.Q.R. 225.
[10][1945] 1 All E.R. 513; [1945] P. 30. Cf. *Pizey* v. *Pizey*, [1961] 3 All E.R. 658, C.A.; [1961] P. 101 (wife, who left husband after confessing to him that she had committed adultery, held to be desertion).
[11][1956] 1 All E.R. 122, C.A.; [1956] P. 160. See also *Wood* v. *Wood*, [1947] 2 All E.R. 95; [1947] P. 103; *Beer* v. *Beer*, [1947] 2 All E.R. 711; [1948] P. 10.
[12]*Hartley* v. *Hartley*, [1955] 1 All E.R. 625.
[13]*Cox* v. *Cox*, [1958] 1 All E.R. 569. In this case the court doubted whether a mistaken belief in anything other than the commission of adultery would justify a separation (at p. 573). This overlooks the facts of *Ousey* v. *Ousey*, (*supra*). The belief may also be a good defence even though it is based on insane delusions: see *ante*, p. 165.

to adultery, must give the other an opportunity of giving an explanation and, if he withdraws from cohabitation before doing so, he will himself be in desertion.[14] *A fortiori* one spouse will have no grounds for leaving the other if the latter produces a reasonable and innocent explanation of his or her conduct;[15] and if the spouse who has left ceases to have reasonable cause for believing that the other has committed an offence, he must resume cohabitation and will himself be in desertion if he fails to do so.[16] Hence he may not set up a reasonable belief in the commission of a matrimonial offence after he has unsuccessfully sought matrimonial relief based upon that very offence. In *Allen* v. *Allen*[17] the husband left the wife because he believed that she had committed adultery. He subsequently petitioned for divorce on this ground and his petition was dismissed. It was held by the Court of Appeal that, although he was not in desertion before the termination of the divorce proceedings, it was no longer open to him to plead that he had good reason for living apart from his wife even though his suspicions had not in fact been allayed.

Constructive Desertion.—As has already been stated, it is not necessarily the spouse who takes the physical step of leaving the matrimonial home who will be in desertion. At least as early as 1864 it was recognised that where one spouse behaves in such a way that the other is virtually compelled to leave, the former may be in law the deserter.[18] In such a case the spouse who intends to bring cohabitation to an end or whose conduct causes the separation is said to be in constructive desertion.

The most obvious example of constructive desertion (although, in fact, the least frequent) is that of the husband who physically evicts his wife or bars the doors of the matrimonial home against her. Similarly, a spouse who virtually orders the other to leave will be in desertion if the circumstances reasonably lead the other to believe that the command was meant and he acts upon it.[19] In these cases it will be observed that the same four elements are present as in simple desertion: there is a *de facto* separation, the eviction shows an *animus deserendi*, the facts negative any consent on the part of the spouse evicted, and there will be no desertion if the evictor had good cause for barring the other from the matrimonial home.

---

[14]*Marsden* v. *Marsden*, [1967] 1 All E.R. 967; [1968] P. 544.
[15]*Beer* v. *Beer*, (*supra*), at pp. 713 and 14, respectively.
[16]*Forbes* v. *Forbes*, [1954] 3 All E.R. 461, where DAVIES, J., pointed out (at p. 466) that failure to bring proceedings based on adultery may raise doubts whether the belief is reasonably held.
[17][1951] 1 All E.R. 724, C.A.; followed in *Bright* v. *Bright*, [1953] 2 All E.R. 939; [1954] P. 270; *West* v. *West*, [1954] 2 All E.R. 505, C.A.; [1954] P. 444.
[18]*Graves* v. *Graves* (1864), 3 Sw. & Tr. 350.
[19]*Dunn* v. *Dunn*, [1965] 1 All E.R. 1043; [1967] P. 217. The complaining spouse must have left in consequence of the order and not of his or her own free will: *Charter* v. *Charter* (1901), 84 L.T. 272. *Cf. Buchler* v. *Buchler*, [1947] 1 All E.R. 319, C.A.; [1947] P. 25, and see *Irvine*, 29 M.L.R. 438. In *Jones* v. *Jones*, [1952] 2 T.L.R. 225, C.A., it was held that the wife was in constructive desertion when the justices who had heard her complaint told the husband that he would have to leave the matrimonial home (which was the wife's property) within seven days, since in so doing they were acting not judicially but at the wife's instigation.

It is not necessary, however, for there to be an actual eviction or order to leave. Other conduct, which need not in itself amount to a matrimonial offence, can be sufficient to justify one spouse in leaving, thus putting the other in constructive desertion. If a domineering and bullying husband treats his wife in such a way that married life with him becomes impossible and she leaves, he has just as effectively brought cohabitation to an end as if he had physically evicted her. Similarly, if the wife refuses to let the husband into the matrimonial home because of his cruel conduct, he will be the deserter.[20] Again it will be observed that this shares with simple desertion the requirements of a *de facto* separation against the complainant's will; whereas in the case of simple desertion the defendant must have left without good cause and with the intention of remaining permanently apart, in constructive desertion his conduct must have been such as to justify the complainant in leaving the matrimonial home, thus bringing cohabitation to an end.

The Defendant's Conduct.—The first question to be asked is what conduct on the part of the defendant will entitle the complainant to depart, thus making the defendant the deserter. There are some kinds of conduct that will clearly justify this just as, at the other end of the scale, there is conduct that will clearly not do so. In between there is a vast " no-man's-land " where the issue is one of fact: was *this* person's conduct to *this* spouse of such a nature that the latter could not reasonably be expected to endure it?[1] Other phrases that have been used are " grave and weighty matters ", " conduct equivalent to driving the other spouse away " and something more than " the ordinary wear and tear of conjugal life ".[2] It will be recalled that the same tests are applied in simple desertion and it now seems beyond doubt that the standard of conduct is the same in each case. Thus, the principle of *Ousey* v. *Ousey* and *Glenister* v. *Glenister*[3] has been applied to constructive desertion, so that if one spouse leaves the other because he reasonably believes from the latter's conduct that he has good cause for doing so, the latter will be in constructive desertion.[4] It must also follow from what has been said in the case of simple desertion[5] that, leaving aside physical eviction and expulsive words, only conduct which is sufficiently grave and weighty to support a charge of cruelty can justify a separation and put the guilty spouse in constructive desertion. It has been repeatedly said—most recently by the Court of Appeal in *Ogden* v. *Ogden*[6]—that a case of cruelty which fails because the conduct was not sufficiently grave and weighty cannot be redressed and succeed as a case of constructive desertion, and findings by

---

[20] *W.* v. *W. (No. 2),* [1961] 2 All E.R. 626; [1962] P. 49.
    [1] *Buchler* v. *Buchler,* (*supra*), at pp. 326 and 46, respectively; *Hall* v. *Hall,* [1962] 3 All E.R. 518, 524, C.A.; *Saunders* v. *Saunders,* [1965] 1 All E.R. 838; [1965] P. 499. See further Rosen, *Matrimonial Offences,* 2nd Ed., 81 *et seq.*
    [2] *Buchler* v. *Buchler,* (*supra*); *Hall* v. *Hall,* (*supra*); *Saunders* v. *Saunders,* (*supra*).
    [3] *Ante,* pp. 171-172.
    [4] *Baker* v. *Baker,* [1953] 2 All E.R. 1199; [1954] P. 33; *Forbes* v. *Forbes,* [1954] 3 All E.R. 461. See further Bevan in 73 L.Q.R. 249 *et seq.*
    [5] *Ante,* pp. 168-170.
    [6] [1969] 3 All E.R. 1055, C.A. See also *Griffiths* v. *Griffiths,* [1964] 3 All E.R. 929; *Slon* v. *Slon,* [1969] 1 All E.R. 759, C.A.; [1969] P. 122; and *ante,* p. 168, n.[14].

magistrates that a defendant is not guilty of cruelty for this reason but
is nevertheless guilty of constructive desertion cannot stand as they
are on the face of them inconsistent.[7] Consequently the whole history
of the marriage must be looked at, and the complainant's own conduct
is as relevant in one case as it is in the other.

If the conduct does not of itself justify one spouse in leaving the
other, the former cannot put the latter in constructive desertion by
presenting him with an ultimatum.[8] The complainant must also have
left as the result of the defendant's conduct: if he intended to leave
anyway, he cannot seize on the other's conduct as an excuse and thus
make him the deserter.[9] Furthermore the conduct complained of must
have taken place during the marriage. In *Sullivan* v. *Sullivan*[10] a
husband left his wife immediately after discovering that she was
pregnant *per alium* at the time of the marriage but failed to take any
steps to have the marriage annulled. He later petitioned for divorce on
the ground of his wife's desertion. The Court of Appeal held that he
must fail because he was in fact complaining of her physical state at
the time of the marriage: the conduct which had given rise to it had
occurred beforehand. This decision is regrettable because it implies
that a husband who leaves his wife in such circumstances is in desertion
himself and he has no immediate remedy if he does not discover the
facts within a year (as might happen if he thought he was the father
himself). A more desirable solution would have been to hold that
pre-marital conduct can give rise to constructive desertion if (as in this
case) it is bound to have an effect on the parties' relationship after
marriage.

The Defendant's Intention.—Just as the *animus deserendi* is an
essential element in simple desertion, earlier cases on constructive
desertion emphasised the necessity of the complainant's proving that
the defendant intended to bring cohabitation permanently to an end.
This meant that the complainant was almost invariably thrown back
on the rule that the defendant may be presumed to intend the natural
and probable consequences of his acts. It seems that this presumption
has never been irrebuttable,[11] but as the Privy Council pointed out in
Lang v. *Lang*,[12] it can be rebutted only by proof of a contrary intention and not by proof of a subjective hope or desire. Thus a man may

---

[7]There would be no inconsistency, of course, if the charge of cruelty had been dismissed
solely on the ground that the defendant's conduct had not injured the complainant's
health.

[8]*Buchler* v. *Buchler*, (*supra*), at pp. 325 and 44-55, respectively; *Bartholomew* v.
Bartholomew, [1952] 2 All E.R. 1035, C.A.

[9]*Cf. Saunders* v. *Saunders*, (*supra*).

[10][1970] 2 All E.R. 168, C.A.

[11]In *Hosegood* v. *Hosegood* (1950), 66 T.L.R. (pt. 1) 735, 738-739, C.A., DENNING,
L.J., expressed the view that there were two schools of thought about this, one which
held that the presumption was rebuttable and one which held the converse. It seems,
however, that the adherents to the latter belief never went so far as to say that it was
an irrebuttable presumption of law, and in any case it is a presumption that *may*—
not must—be drawn from the evidence: *Simpson* v. *Simpson*, [1951] 1 All E.R. 955,
960, 961; [1951] P. 320, 330, 333.

[12][1954] 3 All E.R. 571, P.C.; [1955] A.C. 402. See also *Waters* v. *Waters*, [1956]
1 All E.R. 432, 440; [1956] P. 344, 359-361; *Ingram* v. *Ingram*, [1956] 1 All E.R. 785,
798; [1956] P. 390, 412; Allen, *Matrimonial Cruelty*, 73 L.Q.R. 512 *et seq.*

wish his wife to remain with him, but if he brutally ill-treats her in such a way that, as a reasonable person, he must know that she will leave him as a result, the inference is that he must intend her to leave. Here the *animus* may be inferred because there is no rebutting evidence of his intention as distinct from his desire.

On such a view the real question is what evidence is necessary to rebut the presumption in any given case. The more heinous the defendant's acts have been, the more difficult will it be for him to prove that he did not intend the complainaint to go, and in practice the presumption becomes virtually irrebuttable. It is as artificial in this context as it is in the case of cruelty for most spouses in this position will be too occupied with their own selfish desires to formulate any real intention about the complainant at all. Just as intention to injure is no longer essential in cruelty, LORD REID maintained in *Gollins* v. *Gollins*[13] that the effect of *Lang* v. *Lang* has been to remove the necessity of intention from constructive desertion as well. He said:

" So the decision was that if without just cause or excuse you persist in doing things which you know your wife will probably not tolerate, and which no ordinary woman would tolerate, and then she leaves, you have wilfully deserted her, whatever your desire or intention may have been."

This statement was obviously *obiter*. It is, however, in keeping with the opinion of DIPLOCK, L.J., in *Hall* v. *Hall*,[14] where he said that there would be sufficient *animus* if " *this* husband must have known that *this* wife would in all probability not continue to endure his conduct if he persisted in it ". A fuller analysis is to be found in the following extract from SIMON, P.'s judgment in *Saunders* v. *Saunders*:[15]

" The generally accepted test of what conduct amounts to constructive desertion is this: Has the defendant been guilty of such grave and weighty misconduct that the only sensible inference is that he knew that the complainant would in all probability withdraw permanently from cohabitation with him, if she acted like any reasonable person in her position. So stated *factum* and *animus* and, indeed, absence of consensuality are intimately bound up. Unless the conduct is so grave and weighty as to make matrimonial cohabitation virtually impossible, the defendant cannot know that his wife will *reasonably* withdraw from cohabitation. Unless the conduct is of such a nature as to overbear the complainant's willingness to remain in cohabitation, her withdrawal will have an element of consensuality."

It will be seen that the general rule as stated has two limitations imposed upon it. First, as LORD REID says, the defendant's acts must be persisted in without just cause or excuse. This implies a measure of volition on his part and suggests that conduct over which he has no control (such as a refusal of sexual intercourse due to invincible repugnance) cannot found a charge of constructive desertion. Secondly, all three judges stress the importance of the defendant's knowing that the complainant would probably not endure his conduct. In the vast

---

[13][1963] 2 All E.R. 966, 974, H.L.; [1964] A.C. 644, 666. See further *ante*, p. 154.
[14][1962] 3 All E.R. 518, 527, C.A. (husband's persistent drunkenness held capable of amounting to constructive desertion).
[15][1965] 1 All E.R. 838, 841; [1965] P. 499, 504 (constructive desertion by husband who failed to give wife proper help in their shop). *Cf. Marsden* v. *Marsden*, [1967] 1 All E.R. 967, 972; [1968] P. 544, 555 (husband unreasonably accusing wife of adultery held to be in desertion); *Burton* v. *Burton* (1969), 113 Sol. Jo. 852.

majority of cases this will present no problem for knowledge will of necessity be imputed to him, but it would seem that this leaves it open to the court to find as a question of fact that a particular defendant did not know what the probable effect of his conduct would be either as a result of mental illness or from any other cause.[16]

It is still too early to say whether this approach will be followed in the future. It is to be preferred because it has the advantage of being straightforward and divorced from artificial fictions which are to be welcomed even less in those branches of the law dealing with matrimonial relationships than in others.

Relationship between Simple and Constructive Desertion.—We have already seen that two conditions must be satisfied before a spouse can succeed on either ground: there must be a *de facto* separation and the complainant must not have consented to it. The other connecting factor is the reason for the separation. If, say, a wife leaves her husband because of his treatment of her, she will have a good defence to a charge of simple desertion if his conduct is " grave and weighty " and he will normally be in constructive desertion; if it is not grave and weighty, however, it is she and not he who will be the deserter. This means that simple and constructive desertion are usually complementary in the sense that, if the spouses are living apart otherwise than by agreement, one must be in desertion.

It has already been suggested in the last section that this may not be true if the conduct causing the separation is something over which the party in question has no control, for he may not be in constructive desertion even though the other in law is justified in leaving. Another type of case where neither may be in desertion arises when one spouse is obliged to go away for reasons of business or health and the other cannot or will not go too. If both have good reasons for their conduct, then it may be impossible to allege that either is in desertion. This happened in *Walter* v. *Walter*,[17] where the husband and wife were both working in different parts of London. The husband moved to be nearer his place of work and the wife remained in the former matrimonial home to be near hers. Neither consented to the separation. It was held by WILLMER, J., that in such circumstances neither of them could succeed on petitions based upon desertion because neither could prove that the separation was due to the other's fault.

This decision has been criticised by LORD DENNING who has expressed the obiter view that in such a case both spouses are in desertion.[18] But this opinion can itself be attacked on two grounds. It has been suggested that each spouse has a duty to compromise in such circumstances:[19] in that case, if either rejects a genuine and reasonable

---

[16]*Cf. ante,* p. 159. See also Rosen, *Matrimonial Offences,* 2nd Ed., 47-54; Bates, *Animus Deserendi in Constructive Desertion,* 33 M.L.R. 144; Eekelaar, *Crisis in Divorce Law,* 15 I.C.L.Q. 875, at pp. 893-895.

[17](1949), 65 T.L.R. 680. For choice of the matrimonial home, see *ante,* pp. 95-96.

[18]*Hosegood* v. *Hosegood* (1950), 66 T.L.R. (pt. 1) 735, 740. C.A.; *Beigan* v. *Beigan,* [1956] 2 All E.R. 630, 632, C.A.; [1956] P. 313, 320.

[19]Irvine, *Mutual Desertion,* 30 M.L.R. 46.

compromise put forward by the other, he will be in desertion. But if neither will even propose a compromise or no reasonable compromise is possible in the circumstances, it seems contrary to principle to permit either to allege that the other is in desertion, because neither could show that the other has brought about the separation. Secondly, it has been doubted whether mutual desertion is legally possible.[20] It is submitted, however, that there is no logical basis for this view, even if the facts which could give rise to it are not likely to occur very often. Suppose that a husband, whilst in hospital, decides not to return to his wife and, on his discharge, does not go back to the matrimonial home. His wife in the meantime has decided to leave him and, unbeknown to him, has already gone to live elsewhere. There is a *de facto* separation, each has the *animus deserendi*, each has acted in ignorance of the other's decision and therefore cannot have consented to his or her withdrawal from separation; consequently if neither has any justification for his action, both have satisfied all the conditions for simple desertion.[1] If both have a reasonable cause for leaving (in other words, each drives the other away), there could apparently be mutual constructive desertion in the sort of situation outlined above (although this is likely to occur even more rarely). It remains to be seen, however, whether the courts will accept this argument.

Termination of Desertion.—Desertion is a continuing offence. If it is alleged as a ground for complaint in a magistrates' court, it must still be running at the time of the adjudication. If it is relied on as a fact evidencing the breakdown of marriage in divorce proceedings or as a ground for judicial separation, the petitioner must show that it has been continuous for a period of two years.[2] Consequently its termination is of the same importance as its commencement. All four conditions must be present in order to constitute the offence, so that desertion will terminate if any one or more of these conditions cease to be satisfied.

Resumption of Cohabitation.—If the spouses resume cohabitation, there will then be no *de facto* separation and therefore no desertion.

---

[20]*Simpson* v. *Simpson*, [1951] 1 All E.R. 955, 960; [1951] P. 320, 330 (*per* LORD MERRIMAN, P.); *Lang* v. *Lang* (1953), *Times*, July 7 (*per* JENKINS and HODSON, L.JJ.); *Crossley* v. *Crossley* (1962), 106 Sol. Jo. 223 (*per* SIMON, P.). In *Price* v. *Price*, [1970] 2 All E.R. 497, C.A., DAVIES, L.J., left the question open (at p. 498) and SACHS, L.J., was inclined to follow the dicta in *Lang* v. *Lang* (at p. 501).

[1]See DENNING, L.J., in *Beigan* v. *Beigan*, (*supra*); Irvine, *loc. cit.* On similar facts to these WRANGHAM, J., found both spouses in desertion in *Price* v. *Price*, [1968] 3 All E.R. 543, but this was reversed by the Court of Appeal (*supra*) on the further ground that the wife, having discovered that her husband had gone elsewhere, never put her plan into effect and consequently the husband alone was in desertion. This seems to lay undue weight on the question of which of them took the technical step of leaving the home and, insofar as the wife would have left herself if the husband had come back, makes desertion turn on a question of luck (which it ought not to do). If, as PHILLIMORE, L.J., stated at p. 502, it is necessary for a party, having formed the intention to desert, to leave the other *in pursuance of it*, the case is inconsistent with the earlier decision of the Court of Appeal in *Pardy* v. *Pardy*, *ante*, p. 167. See Irvine, 34 M.L.R. 194.

[2]See *post*, p. 211.

I

Just as desertion is "the withdrawal from a state of things", so, in the words of LORD MERRIMAN, P., in *Mummery* v. *Mummery*:[3]

> "A resumption of cohabitation must mean resuming a state of things, that is to say, setting up a matrimonial home together, and that involves a bilateral intention on the part of both spouses so to do."

A number of points emerge from this.

Normally cohabitation will be resumed by the spouses' living together again in the matrimonial home, but where owing to force of circumstances there is no home, cohabitation may be resumed elsewhere provided that the intention is there. Thus, in *Abercrombie* v. *Abercrombie*[4] the husband was a doctor who had held a number of appointments as a *locum tenens* and, before the spouses separated, they had no settled home. They eventually spent a weekend together in a hotel on what they hoped would be their second honeymoon, but again separated on discovering that they probably could not live happily together again. It was held that since they had spent the weekend together with the intention of starting life together again, there was in the circumstances a resumption of cohabitation.

Conversely, whilst there will be a presumption that cohabitation has been resumed if the spouses start residing under the same roof again,[5] this can be rebutted if it can be shown that there was no intention to live together as husband and wife. In *Bartram* v. *Bartram*[6] the husband went to live with his mother for business reasons and his wife refused to join him because she wanted nothing more to do with him and thus put herself in desertion. Later the husband sold the matrimonial home in the hope of forcing his wife to return to him. She eventually did go to his mother's house because she had nowhere else to live, but she refused to sleep with him, performed no wifely duties for him and generally treated him like a lodger whom she disliked, although she was obliged to share the common meals with him. In these circumstances it was held by the Court of Appeal that there was no true reconciliation and no bilateral intention to set up home again together and therefore she remained in desertion.

Although sexual intercourse between the parties may be evidence of their intending to resume cohabitation and, if they have no home in which they can live together, may in fact amount to resumption of cohabitation,[7] it will not bring desertion to an end if there is no bilateral intention of starting life together again, even though it takes place on a number of occasions.[8] In *Mummery* v. *Mummery*[9] the spouses had separated in consequence of the husband's introducing another woman into the matrimonial home. On his return from

---

[3][1942] 1 All E.R. 553, 555; [1942] P. 107, 110.
[4][1943] 2 All E.R. 465. See also *Lowry* v. *Lowry*, [1952] 2 All E.R. 61; [1952] P. 252.
[5]*Watson* v. *Tuckwell* (1947), 63 T.L.R. 634; *Bull* v. *Bull*, [1953] 2 All E.R. 601, C.A.; [1953] P. 224.
[6][1949] 2 All E.R. 270, C.A.; [1950] P. 1; *Watson* v. *Tuckwell*, (*supra*). Contrast *Bull* v. *Bull*, (*supra*).
[7]*Eaves* v. *Eaves*, [1939] 2 All E.R. 789; [1939] P. 361.
[8]*Perry* v. *Perry*, [1952] 1 All E.R. 1076, C.A.; [1952] P. 203 (where a child was born as the result of the intercourse); *Lynch* v. *Lynch*, [1966] N.I. 41. But there may be intercourse so regular and frequent as to compel a finding of resumption of cohabitation: *Marczuk* v. *Marczuk*, [1955] 3 All E.R. 758, 768; [1956] P. 217, 236.
[9][1942] 1 All E.R. 553; [1942] P. 107.

Dunkirk in 1940, he called upon the wife and spent the night with her, having sexual intercourse. The wife consented to his doing so in the hope of effecting a reconciliation. The husband left her again on the following day and it then became clear that he had never intended to resume cohabitation with her. It was held that the intention on the wife's part alone was not enough to bring the husband's desertion to an end.

Loss of Animus Deserendi.—Desertion will similarly come to an end if the party in desertion loses the *animus deserendi*. But it is not sufficient in this case for him mentally to resolve to return to the other spouse; he must communicate his intention by offering to return.[10] In the case of simple desertion all that is necessary is for the guilty spouse to make the offer. His motive for doing so is irrelevant: the fact that the offeror may formerly have brought unsuccessful divorce proceedings or admittedly hates the offeree and wishes to return merely to obtain maintenance or a roof over her head may be evidence that the offer is not genuine, but, if it is, the other is bound to accept it.[11] If he fails to do so, he himself will be in desertion and " the tables are turned ".[12]

But if the deserting spouse has been guilty of behaviour which entitles the other to stay away, a simple offer to return need not necessarily be accepted. If he has been guilty of adultery, the innocent spouse is never bound to take him back, for to do so would force a condonation of the offence;[13] in other cases the offending spouse must give the other a credible assurance that the conduct complained of will not be repeated in the future. The amends that the guilty spouse must make is a question of degree; obviously the more reprehensible his conduct has been in the past, the stronger must his assurances be for the future, and some conduct may be so gross that the innocent spouse is not bound to accept the offer at all.[14]

In either case the offer must be genuine in the sense that the spouse making it must be prepared to implement it if it is accepted. Where there is real doubt about this, the correct way of resolving it may be

---

[10]*Williams* v. *Williams*, [1939] 3 All E.R. 825-828, C.A.; [1939] P. 365, 369.

[11]*Dyson* v. *Dyson*, [1953] 2 All E.R. 1511; [1954] P. 198; *Price* v. *Price*, [1951] 2 All E.R. 580 n.; [1951] P. 413; *Irvin* v. *Irvin*, [1968] 1 All E.R. 271.

[12]*Pratt* v. *Pratt*, [1939] 3 All E.R. 437, H.L.; [1939] A.C. 417; *Thomas* v. *Thomas*, [1946] 1 All E.R. 170; *Everitt* v. *Everitt*, [1949] 1 All E.R. 908, C.A.; [1949] P. 374.

[13]*Everitt* v. *Everitt*, (*supra*), at pp. 913-916 and 381-386, respectively. This applies equally if the innocent spouse has reasonable grounds for believing that the other has committed adultery even though he has not in fact done so: *Everitt* v. *Everitt*, at pp. 911-913 and 379-381, respectively. It presumably applies also to cruelty.

[14]*Edwards* v. *Edwards*, [1948] 1 All E.R. 157, 160; [1948] P. 268, 272. See also *Thomas* v. *Thomas*, [1924] P. 194, C.A.; *Theobald* v. *Theobald*, [1962] 2 All E.R. 863. Tiley, *Desertion and the Bona Fide Offer to Return*, 83 L.Q.R. 89, argues forcefully that, even though the innocent spouse can never be bound to accept an offer to resume cohabitation made by a spouse who has committed adultery, this will nevertheless terminate the offeror's desertion if it is made in good faith. The logic of this is unassailable if one assumes that the *animus deserendi* must alway be present in the subjective sense. But the cases all indicate that the criterion for the *continuation* of desertion is whether the deserted spouse is justified in refusing to resume cohabitation: see Irvine, 83 L.Q.R. 338; 29 M.L.R. 331.

by accepting the offer,[15] but this is not necessary if the evidence clearly points to the contrary. Thus in *Dunn* v. *Dunn*[16] it was held that a husband was entitled to reject an offer made by his wife (who had previously ordered him to leave the matrimonial home) in view of the fact that she had ordered him out before, had refused to let him have a key to the house, was bringing unjustified charges of cruelty against him, and had sent the invitation, couched in affectionate terms, by registered post. Moreover, a spouse is bound only to accept an offer to resume cohabitation in the full sense of the word and not, for example, on condition that the parties no longer have sexual intercourse.[17] Similarly, an offer with unreasonable conditions attached need not be accepted. In *Barrett* v. *Barrett*[18] the wife deserted her husband in 1941, taking with her the three daughters of the marriage (whose ages ranged from 17 to 19), and went to live in another part of London. The husband asked her to return but refused to have the daughters back. The wife declined to go back without them. On the husband's petition for divorce on the grounds of his wife's desertion, it was held that the wife was entitled to remain apart from him, for there had been nothing in his daughters' conduct to justify him in refusing to have them back, and it was not unreasonable of the mother to decline to leave them to fend for themselves in view of their ages and the conditions obtaining in London during the air raids of 1941.[19]

Supervening Consent.—If the deserted spouse subsequently consents to living apart, the desertion will automatically come to an end.[20] Whether or not he has done so is purely a question of fact: clearly a spouse can no longer allege that the other is in desertion if he obtains a judicial separation or separation order or enters into a separation agreement.

Good Cause for Separation Supervening.—If the deserted spouse commits some act which would justify the other in refusing to live with him any longer, the desertion will come to an end unless it can be shown that this act did not alter the other's intention to live apart. *Prima facie*, therefore, the desertion will cease, and the burden is upon the spouse originally deserted to prove that his conduct did not affect the other's mind.[1] Thus, in *Richards* v. *Richards*[2] the wife committed

---

[15]*Dunn* v. *Dunn*, [1965] 1 All E.R. 1043, at pp. 1048, 1049; [1967] P. 217, at pp. 226, 228-229.

[16][1965] 1 All E.R. 1043; [1967] P. 217. See also *Thomas* v. *Thomas*, [1924] P. 194, C.A.; *W.* v. *W.* (*No. 2*), [1954] 2 All E.R. 829, C.A.; [1954] P. 486.

[17]*Hutchinson* v. *Hutchinson*, [1963] 1 All E.R. 1.

[18][1948] P. 277, C.A. *Cf. Fletcher* v. *Fletcher*, [1945] 1 All E.R. 582, where it was held that a wife was not bound to accept her husband's invitation to join him in a community devoted to service in retreat and believing in the communal ownership of property

[19]Except where the spouse alleged to be in desertion becomes insane (see *ante*, p. 165), he is presumed to retain the *animus*, so that the burden is upon him to prove that desertion has come to an end: *Bowron* v. *Bowron*, [1925] P. 187, 195, C.A.; *W.* v. *W.* (*No. 2*), (*supra*), at pp. 832-833 and 502, respectively; *Coulter* v. *Coulter*, [1962] N.I. 145.

[20]Desertion is presumed to continue, so that the petitioner does not have to show that he was at all times ready and willing to take the respondent back: *Sifton* v. *Sifton*, [1939] 1 All E.R. 109; [1939] P. 221.

[1]*Herod* v. *Herod*, [1938] 3 All E.R. 722; [1939] P. 11. Obviously it cannot affect the other's intention if he is unaware of the commission of the act: *cf. ante*, p. 170.

[2][1952] 1 All E.R. 1384, C.A.; [1952] P. 307.

adultery two years after her husband had deserted her, and it was held that this brought the existing desertion to an end, because she failed to show that her act had not impeded any possible reconciliation. Conversely, as in *Brewer* v. *Brewer*,[3] even if the deserted spouse communicates to the other the clear intention of not having him or her back, this will not bring the desertion to an end if the evidence shows that this did not effectively prevent the deserter from taking steps to bring about a reconciliation.

Condonation.—Although condonation cannot terminate simple desertion unless it is accompanied by a resumption of cohabitation,[4] it may nevertheless bring constructive desertion to an end. If, say, a wife, who has left her husband as a consequence of his adultery or cruelty, condones the offence, she can no longer complain of it and consequently he ceases to be in desertion. As the Divisional Court held in *Howard* v. *Howard*,[5] the same result must follow if the conduct which justified her in leaving did not amount to either of these offences, for otherwise she would be in a better position if her husband's grave and weighty conduct did not injure her health. If the husband then asks her to return to him, she will be in desertion herself if she fails to do so; if neither of them takes any steps to resume cohabitation, neither will be in desertion and the continued separation will be regarded as consensual.[6]

4. ASSAULTS AND SEXUAL OFFENCES

Either spouse may apply for an order if the other has been found guilty of one of the following offences[7]:

(a) *On indictment* of any offence involving an assault upon the complainant;

(b) *By a magistrates' court* of one of the following statutory assaults upon the complainant:

Wounding or inflicting grievous bodily harm,

Aggravated assault (if the wife is the complainant),

Assault occasioning actual bodily harm;[8]

(c) *By a magistrates' court* of a common assault upon the complainant *and* has been sentenced to not less than one month's imprisonment or other form of detention;

---

[3][1961] 3 All E.R. 957, C.A.; [1962] P. 69. See also *Bevan* v. *Bevan*, [1955] 3 All E.R. 332; *Church* v. *Church*, [1952] 2 All E.R. 441; [1952] P. 313 (subsequent adultery); *Pardy* v. *Pardy*, [1939] 3 All E.R. 779, C.A.; [1939] P. 288 (subsequent adultery of which the respondent was unaware). But if the deserted spouse communicates his or her intention of not taking the other back at or near the beginning of the separation, this may be evidence of consensual separation and thus negative desertion: *per* HOLROYD PEARCE, L.J., in *Brewer* v. *Brewer* at pp. 967 and 89, respectively.

[4]*Perry* v. *Perry*, [1952] 1 All E.R. 1076, C.A.; [1952] P. 203. For the meaning of condonation, see *post*, pp. 189 *et seq*.

[5][1962] 2 All E.R. 539; [1965] P. 65, followed in *France* v. *France*, [1969] 2 All E.R. 870, C.A.; [1969] P. 46. See Brown, 26 M.L.R. 699.

[6]*Pizey* v. *Pizey*, [1961] 2 All E.R. 658, C.A.; [1961] P. 101.

[7]Matrimonial Proceedings (Magistrates' Courts) Act 1960, s. 1 (1) (c). For details of the crimes in question, see books on criminal law.

[8]Under the Offences against the Person Act 1861, ss. 20, 43, 47, respectively.

(d) *In any court* of the commission of, or of an attempt to commit, a sexual offence against a minor child of the complainant or against a minor child of the defendant who was at the time a child of the family[9] or an offence under section 1 of the Indecency with Children Act 1960[10] against any such child under the age of 14 years.

It is the conviction that gives the court the power to make the order. If the husband wishes to appeal against the conviction, he must do so under the provisions relating to appeals in criminal matters and he may not question the merits of it in proceedings under the Matrimonial Proceedings (Magistrates' Courts) Act.[11]

5. VENEREAL DISEASE

The complainant may apply for an order on the ground that the defendant, whilst knowing that he or she was suffering from a venereal disease, has insisted on sexual intercourse or permitted intercourse when the complainant was unaware of the presence of the disease.[12]

6. HABITUAL DRUNKENNESS OR ADDICTION TO DRUGS

An order may be made on the ground that the defendant is an habitual drunkard or drug addict.[13] This means

" a person (not being a mentally disordered person within the meaning of the Mental Health Act 1959) who, by reason of habitual intemperate drinking of intoxicating liquor (or by reason of the habitual taking or using, otherwise than upon medical advice, of any drug to which any of the provisions of the Dangerous Drugs Acts for the time being apply)—
(a) is at times dangerous to himself or to others, or incapable of managing himself or his affairs; or
(b) so conducts himself that it would not be reasonable to expect a spouse of ordinary sensibilities to continue to cohabit with him. "[14]

7. COMPULSORY SUBMISSION TO PROSTITUTION

The wife may apply for an order if her husband has compelled her to submit herself to prostitution or has been guilty of conduct which was likely to result in her doing so and has had that effect.[15]

---

[9]Under the Sexual Offences Act 1956, ss. 1-29. For the meaning of " child of the family ", see *post*, p. 283.
[10]*I.e.*, committing an act of gross indecency with the child or inciting the child to commit such an act with him.
[11]*Bryant* v. *Bryant*, [1914] P. 277; *Squires* v. *Squires* (1946), 62 T.L.R. 631. Hence if the defendant was put on probation or given an absolute or conditional discharge, no order can be made as the Criminal Justice Act 1948, s. 12 (1), absolves him from the legal consequences that would otherwise flow from the conviction: *Cassidy* v. *Cassidy*, [1959] 3 All E R. 187.
[12]Matrimonial Proceedings (Magistrates' Courts) Act 1960, s. 1 (1) (e). " Insists " in this context has never been defined; it means something less than physical compulsion (*Rigby* v. *Rigby*, [1944] 1 All E.R. 336, 337, C.A.; [1944] P. 33, 36) and mere mental coercion would probably suffice.
[13]*Ibid.*, s. 1 (1) (f).
[14]*Ibid.*, s. 16 (1). For the meaning of " mental disorder ", see the Mental Health Act 1959, s. 4; for the provisions of the Dangerous Drugs Acts, see 21 Halsbury's Statutes (3rd Ed.), 952 *et seq.*
[15]*Ibid.*, s. 1 (1) (g).

8. HUSBAND'S WILFUL NEGLECT TO PROVIDE REASONABLE MAINTENANCE

The court may make an order on the wife's application if the husband has wilfully neglected to provide reasonable maintenance for her or for any child of the family who is a dependant.[16] The nature of this offence will be considered in detail in the chapter dealing with financial provision on the breakdown of marriage.[17]

9. WIFE'S WILFUL NEGLECT TO PROVIDE REASONABLE MAINTENANCE

This ground is new and was introduced by the Act of 1960. It is complementary to the last in that it permits a husband to apply for an order on the ground of his wife's wilful neglect to maintain him or the dependent children of the family but the circumstances in which an application can be made are much narrower.[18] This too will be dealt with in detail later.[19]

C. DEFENCES

I. LIMITATION OF TIME

In common with other matters of summary jurisdiction, a complaint must normally be made under the Matrimonial Proceedings (Magistrates' Courts) Act within six months of the occurrence of the act complained of.[20] As desertion, wilful neglect to maintain and habitual drunkenness and addiction to drugs are all continuing offences, this limitation will not bar the complainant even though the offence in question had been committed for more than six months before the proceedings were commenced,[1] and in the case of persistent cruelty it is sufficient if one act of cruelty has been committed within this period.[2] The strict application of the six months rule sometimes worked hardship in the case of adultery, for the complainant might not discover that the offence had been committed until the period had run out; consequently it is now provided that a complaint based on this ground may be made within six months of its first becoming known to the complainant.[3]

---

[16]*Ibid.*, s. 1 (1) (h).
[17]See *post*, p. 414.
[18]See the Matrimonial Proceedings (Magistrates' Courts) Act 1960, s. 1 (1) (i).
[19]See *post*, p. 417.
[20]Magistrates' Courts Act 1952, s. 104.
[1]*Bowron* v. *Bowron*, [1925] P. 187, C.A.
[2]*Buxton* v. *Buxton*, [1965] 3 All E.R. 150; [1967] P. 48. If condoned cruelty is revived by conduct which is not itself a ground for complaint, time apparently runs from the original act and not from the revival: see *Dunn* v. *Dunn*, [1962] 3 All E.R. 587. If the complaint is based upon the defendant's conviction of assault or a sexual offence (or an attempt to commit such an offence), the six months' period presumably begins to run from the date of the conviction and not from the commission of the offence or attempt.
[3]Matrimonial Proceedings (Magistrates' Courts) Act 1960, s. 12. If the complainant was serving outside the United Kingdom in H.M. Forces or on board a British ship (or a ship chartered by the Crown) at any time during the six months following the discovery of the commission of the adultery, he or she may apply for an order after that period of six months has expired provided that he or she has not been in the United Kingdom for a continuous period of three months since his or her return: *ibid.*

2. CONNIVANCE AND WILFUL NEGLECT AND MISCONDUCT CONDUCING TO ADULTERY

If the complaint is based upon the defendant's adultery, the court may not make a separation order or an order for the complainant's maintenance if the defendant has connived at it or conduced to it by his wilful neglect or misconduct.[4] This resembles two other established principles of English law: the common law doctrine of *volenti non fit injuria* and the maxim that he who comes to equity must come with clean hands. Common sense demands that a person should not obtain relief on the ground of an offence which he or she has helped to bring about. It will be observed, however, that this does not prevent the court from making an order with respect to the children of the family for the spouses' conduct must not be permitted to prejudice the children's position.

Connivance and conduct conducing are also important for a second and related reason. As we have seen,[5] if one spouse withdraws from cohabitation as a result of the other's adultery, it will normally be the latter who will be in constructive desertion. But the former could not justify the separation if he himself had connived at the adultery or conduced to it, and he himself would be in desertion if he left the other in such circumstances.

The line dividing connivance from conduct conducing is a very fine one. The difference between them used to be of great importance because under the old divorce law connivance was an absolute bar to a petition based on adultery whilst conduct conducing was only a discretionary bar. Now that the bars to divorce have all been abolished, the distinction is no longer vital. In each case the complainant must have contributed in some way to the commission of the offence: what distinguishes them is that in connivance there must be a " corrupt intention ".[6] The complainant must have consented to the adultery or wilfully promoted it in some way. In the words of LORD WENSLEYDALE:[7]

> " To prove connivance it is necessary to show not only that the complainant acted in such a manner as that adultery might result; but also it must be proved that it was his intention that *adultery should result.*"

A foolhardy spouse may be guilty of wilful neglect conducing to adultery, but he cannot be guilty of connivance if this intention is missing.

The Act requires the court to be satisfied that the complainant has not connived at or conduced to the adultery. But there is an initial presumption of innocence in his favour and it is only if the evidence

---

[4] *Ibid.*, s. 2 (3) (a).
[5] *Ante*, p. 168.
[6] *Gipps* v. *Gipps* (1864), 11 H.L. Cas. 1, 25 H.L.; *Churchman* v. *Churchman*, [1945] 2 All E.R. 190, 195, C.A.; [1945] P. 44, 52; *Godfrey* v. *Godfrey*, [1946] 3 All E.R. 154, 164, H.L.; [1965] A.C. 444, 467. For a criticism of the word " corrupt ", see KARMINSKI, J., in *Gorst* v. *Gorst*, [1952] P. 94, 100-101.
[7] *Gipps* v. *Gipps*, (*supra*), at p. 25.

raises a reasonable suspicion of either that the burden shifts on him to show that he has not been guilty of the conduct charged.[8]

Causation.—Generally speaking, the complainant cannot be said to have connived at or conduced to the adultery unless his neglect or misconduct has led to its commission.[9] But a complainant who acquiesces in the continuation of adultery may find himself precluded from complaining of earlier acts. In *Rumbelow* v. *Rumbelow*[10] the wife began an adulterous association with the co-respondent in 1957 of which the husband did not become aware until 1960 when the co-respondent came to live in the house. All three resided together until 1963, when the husband left and petitioned for divorce on the grounds of the adultery committed before 1960. The Court of Appeal held that, as he had connived at the adultery for the last three years, he could not be said to have come to the court with clean hands and consequently it was too late for him to rely on the earlier acts. The members of the court emphasised that the husband had been prepared to acquiesce in the wife's adultery for some years, and as the complainant in a magistrates' court must rely on adultery committed within six months of his becoming aware of it, the case may have little application to proceedings there.

Connivance by Express Consent.—A spouse who expressly consents to the other's adultery must obviously be held to have connived at it. A blatant example of this occurs if two married couples agree to exchange spouses;[11] similarly the husband's entering into a separation agreement may amount to connivance if he thereby gives the wife a virtual licence to commit adultery by consenting to her living wheresoever and with whomsoever she wishes,[12] as may his compromising matrimonial proceedings in the knowledge that she would live in adultery as a result.[13] Once having bargained away his rights in this manner, he cannot later complain of the act to which he has consented.

The consent, however, must be given freely. This does not mean that consent regretfully given cannot amount to connivance: in *Gorst* v. *Gorst*[14] a wife who reluctantly consented to her husband's having sexual intercourse with another woman in the hope that his sexual inhibitions with respect to herself might thereby be cured was held to have connived at it. But if the spouse was, for example, affected by fear or mental illness, so that his apparent consent was in fact no consent at all, there will be no connivance. The whole of the party's conduct

---

[8]*Churchman* v. *Churchman*, (*supra*); *Brown* v. *Brown*, [1956] 2 All E.R. 1; [1956] P. 438. He must satisfy the court on the balance of probability: *cf. Blyth* v. *Blyth*, [1966] 1 All E.R. 524, H.L.; [1966] A.C. 643 (condonation).
[9]*Churchman* v. *Churchman*, (*supra*), at pp. 194 and 50, respectively; *St. Paul* v. *St. Paul* (1869), L.R. 1 P. & D. 739.
[10][1965] 2 All E.R. 767, C.A.; [1965] P. 207. The decision is highly questionable: see Tiley in 28 M.L.R. 712.
[11]As in *Richmond* v. *Richmond*, [1952] 1 All E.R. 838.
[12]*King* v. *King* (1929), 142 L.T. 162 (where, however, the presence of other factors negatived the apparent connivance: see *infra*, n.[15]
[13]*Greenwood* v. *Greenwood*, [1937] 3 All E.R. 63; [1937] P. 157.
[14][1951] 2 All E.R. 956; [1952] P. 94.

must be looked at and words or acts which, torn from their context, seem to amount to connivance, may on examination prove to be no such thing. In *Woodbury* v. *Woodbury*[15] the wife became highly hysterical and scarcely responsible for her actions on discovering that her husband had been committing adultery with their son's governess. In her attempts to preserve the marriage and to keep the child out of the matrimonial dispute, she told both the husband and the governess that their relationship might continue provided that the latter did not come in contact with the son. She subsequently petitioned for divorce. The Court of Appeal held that, although there was *prima facie* evidence of connivance, the context showed that the wife wanted her husband back and her actions could be accounted for by the great mental strain that she was under. She was therefore entitled to a decree.

Connivance by Acquiescence.—A spouse may connive at adultery otherwise than by giving express consent; he may do so equally effectively by standing by and permitting the act to take place. But the necessity for the " corrupt intention " must not be overlooked here. There must be " something more than mere negligence, inattention, overconfidence, dullness of apprehension or indifference ";[16] the complainant must have promoted the adultery by *wilfully* refraining from taking steps to prevent it and thereby lulled the defendant into a false sense of security or shown that he was prepared to suffer the commission of the offence. Hence his knowledge and belief are both very relevant. If he knows or has good reason to believe that the defendant is about to commit adultery and, shutting his eyes to the obvious, wilfully refrains from intervening, he will be presumed to intend the probable consequences of his own act and will therefore *prima facie* be guilty of connivance.[17] Conversely, if he has no knowledge that the defendant is likely to form an adulterous association (even though a more alert spouse would have realised what was going on), his placing opportunities in the way of the other's committing adultery will not amount to connivance.

Great difficulty may arise if one spouse, suspecting that the other is committing adultery, sets a trap to see whether his suspicions are justified. In *Douglas* v. *Douglas*[18] the husband, who was the licensee of an hotel, became suspicious of his wife's relations with a man who regularly took his meals there. He instructed enquiry agents to keep a watch on her. One night he gave her an untrue reason for absenting himself and detectives saw her committing adultery with the man in question. In the subsequent divorce proceedings the question arose

---

[15][1948] 2 All E.R. 684, C.A.; [1949] P. 154. See also *King* v. *King*, (*supra*) (husband forced to enter into a separation deed because of his terror of the co-respondent); *Peters* v. *Peters*, [1963] 3 All E.R. 67 (wife unable to make independent decision owing to her mental condition). Apparent consent may also be negatived by a mistake: *Clayton* v. *Clayton*, [1932] P. 45.

[16]*Per* Sir J. NICHOLL in *Rogers* v. *Rogers* (1830), 3 Hag. Ecc. 57, 59.

[17]*Douglas* v. *Douglas*, [1950] 2 All E.R. 748, 755, C.A.; [1951] P. 85, 100. Hence a greater degree of care is called for if the complainant knows the defendant to have been unchaste in the past: *Lloyd* v. *Lloyd*, [1938] 2 All E.R. 480, 484; [1938] 174, 177.

[18][1950] 2 All E.R. 748, C.A.; [1951] P. 85.

whether the husband had connived at the adultery by promoting it. The proper approach to the problem was formulated by DENNING, L.J., in the following words:[19]

> " The question is, which is the greater evil? To allow the adultery to continue undetected and unproved? or to allow the husband to obtain his proof by creating an opportunity for it? My answer is that, if a husband honestly believes that adultery has already taken place, it is very necessary that his suspicions should either be confirmed or disproved . . . It is better that he should be able to get their adultery proved or disproved, even by creating an opportunity for it, rather than that the suspicion of it should continue to ruin his peace of mind and his home. It is, of course, altogether different if he throws them together before he believes that adultery has taken place."

It was held that Douglas had not connived at the adultery because he had reasonable grounds for his belief that the adulterous association had already begun. Furthermore, his distress when his suspicions were confirmed showed that he had hoped that they were groundless and that he lacked the corrupt intention. If, however, there had been no evidence of a guilty relationship beforehand, the inference of connivance would probably have been irresistible.[20]

Connivance by the Complainant's Agent.—The complainant's seeking to establish proof of an existing adulterous relationship raises a further problem. It is common for a spouse in such circumstances to employ a private detective or other agent to watch the defendant. If the agent connives at the latter's adultery, will that bar the complainant? Applying the general principles of the law of agency, one would think that, if the agent were employed to discover whether or not adultery had already been committed, any act by him tending to promote the inception of a new adulterous relationship would lie outside the scope of his authority and would not therefore be imputed to his principal. In only one old case does this distinction between authorised and unauthorised acts appear to have been clearly drawn,[1] and the later cases (which are, admittedly, all at first instance) indicate that the agent's act will always bar the complainant by a blanket application of the maxim *qui facit per alium facit per se.*[2] Other considerations may make it desirable to hold a person liable for torts committed by his agent and contracts entered into by him even though the acts were unauthorised, but to apply this principle to connivance seems unwarranted in principle and calculated to work injustice in practice.

Connivance Spent.—It was formerly thought that if the complainant once connived at an act of adultery, he was barred for all time from complaining of any further adultery committed by the defendant. Hence if H connived at W's adultery with X on one occasion, he could

---

[10]At pp. 754 and 98, respectively. See also *Mudge* v. *Mudge*, [1950] 1 All E.R. 607, 609; [1950] P. 173, 177.
[20]*Cf. Manning* v. *Manning*, [1950] 1 All E.R. 602, C.A., where the husband had in fact gone out of his way to throw the wife and co-respondent together.
[1]*Sugg* v. *Sugg* (1861), 31 L.J.P.M. & A. 41.
[2]See, for example, *Gower* v. *Gower* (1872), L.R. 2 P. & D. 428; *Poulden* v. *Poulden*, [1938] 1 All E.R. 508; [1938] P. 63. *Cf.* also *Mudge* v. *Mudge*, [1950] 1 All E.R. 607; [1950] P. 173.

not complain if W resumed the relationship years later or if, instead of committing adultery with X, she committed it with Y. He was not allowed to say: " *Non omnibus dormio.*" But, as the House of Lords laid down in *Godfrey* v. *Godfrey*,[3] there is no such absolute rule in English law; the question in such a case always is: is there any causal connection between the initial connivance and the acts of adultery complained of? In that case the husband, who was a little drunk, returned home one evening to find his wife and the co-respondent in each other's arms. He then said: " If you two want to go to bed together, why the hell don't you?" and flung down a glove by way of challenge. He spent the night in his son's bedroom and the following morning found his wife and the co-respondent in bed together. He turned the co-respondent out of the house and unsuccessfully sought a reconciliation with his wife. A month later they parted and the wife continued to meet the co-respondent and to commit adultery with him. Further efforts by the husband to effect a reconciliation were fruitless and eventually, some six months after the original incident, the wife and co-respondent started to live together. The husband then petitioned for divorce and sought to establish that, although he had connived at the original act of adultery, his obviously genuine repentance and attempts to get the wife to resume cohabitation had effectively obliterated it at least by the time that the wife had gone to live with the co-respondent. It was held, however, that the adulterous association had been a continuing one and that the later acts of adultery could not be severed from the earlier. The husband had not discharged the burden of proving that there was no causal connection between his connivance and the adultery complained of and consequently his petition must fail.

Although it may seem hard that a spouse in the position of the husband in *Godfrey* v. *Godfrey* cannot complain of the adultery despite his attempts to get his wife to return to him, it must be remembered that he has only himself to blame if his wife discovers that she prefers the adulterous association which he has encouraged to a continuation of married life. The question is purely one of fact: connivance can only be regarded as spent if the complainant can prove that there is no causal connection between it and the adultery on which his complaint is based. Clearly if there has been a complete reconciliation before the defendant commits adultery again, this in itself will show that the chain of causation is broken,[4] but reconciliation is not necessary. Mere lapse of time may be sufficient,[5] but the burden of proof on the complainant will not be lightly discharged.[6]

---

[3][1964] 3 All E.R. 154, H.L.; [1965] A.C. 444. See Tiley, 28 M.L.R. 712.
[4]As in *Gorst* v. *Gorst*, [1951] 2 All E.R. 956; [1952] P. 94.
[5]As in the Scottish case of *Gallacher* v. *Gallacher*, 1934 S.C. 339 (five years).
[6]LORD REID and LORD MORTON were both of the opinion in *Godfrey* v. *Godfrey* that the complainant also had to show that he had genuinely repented and done all in his power to repair the damage that he had caused (at pp. 157, 159 and 454, 458, respectively), but this view was not expressed by the other three members of the House and is inconsistent with *Gallacher* v. *Gallacher*, (*supra*), which they followed.

Wilful Neglect and Misconduct.—There is a dearth of modern authority on the meaning of this phrase. The earlier cases were reviewed by the Divisional Court in *Brown* v. *Brown*,[7] and it is clear that it is difficult to reconcile them. If the complainant's conduct is a direct cause of the defendant's adultery, it is largely a question of degree whether it can fairly be said to have contributed to it. But in any case two conditions must be satisfied: the conduct must have taken place during the marriage and not before it,[8] and it must be neglect or misconduct by the complainant in his marital capacity—in other words it must be neglect of, or misconduct towards, the defendant.[9] Hence if, say, the husband is sent to prison for theft and the wife forms an adulterous association in his absence, he will not be regarded as having conduced to her adultery, because the theft was not misconduct towards her.[10]

The conduct complained of must also have been *wilful*. Wilful refusal of sexual intercourse,[11] the complainant's own adultery, and an improper association stopping short of adultery but carried on in the face of the defendant's objections[12] have all been held to amount to misconduct conducing to the defendant's adultery. The element of wilfulness becomes more important when the complainant is alleged to have conduced to the defendant's adultery by his neglect. Mere carelessness will not be sufficient: the complainant must have realised from the circumstances that there was a danger that the adultery would result and have been reckless as to the consequences.[13] Hence his knowledge and belief again assume considerable importance. To take one example, desertion (whether simple or constructive) will not of itself amount to conduct conducing as the Divisional Court pointed out in *Jenkins* v. *Jenkins*,[14] but it could, for example, if a deserting husband knew that the immediate consequence of his action would be that his wife would go to live with another man.[15]

3. CONDONATION

As in the case of connivance and conduct conducing, the Matrimonial Proceedings (Magistrates' Courts) Act 1960 expressly provides that no separation order or order for maintenance for the complainant is to be made on the ground of the defendant's adultery if the complainant has condoned it.[16] The same result must follow in the case of cruelty,

---

[7][1956] 2 All E.R. 1; [1956] P. 438. See also *Postlethwaite* v. *Postlethwaite*, [1957] 1 All E.R. 909; [1957] P. 193.

[8]*Allen* v. *Allen* (1859), 28 L.J.P.M. & A. 81. *Cf.* conduct justifying separation: *ante*, p. 170.

[9]*Cunnington* v. *Cunnington* (1859), 1 Sw. & Tr. 745, at 477, 481.

[10]*Cf. Cunnington* v. *Cunnington*, *(supra)* (transportation for theft).

[11]*Callister* v. *Callister*, [1947] W.N. 221, C.A.

[12]*Cox* v. *Cox* (1893), 70 L.T. 200, C.A.

[13]*Dering* v. *Dering* (1868), L.R. 1 P. & D. 531, 536.

[14][1956] 2 All E.R. 596; [1956] P. 458, following *Richards* v. *Richards*, [1952] 1 All E.R. 1384, C.A.; [1952] P. 307, and *Brown* v. *Brown*, *(supra)*.

[15]*Haynes* v. *Haynes*, [1960] 2 All E.R. 401.

[16]S. 2 (3) (a). Note that, like connivance and conduct conducing, condonation does not affect the court's power to make orders with respect to children.

for a spouse who condones the offence is no longer justified in staying away from the other.[17]

The two defences are also similar in two other respects. First, although the court must be satisfied that there was no condonation, there is an initial presumption in the complainant's favour. The onus of proof will become vital, therefore, only if there is *prima facie* evidence of condonation which the complainant cannot rebut on the balance of probability.[18] Secondly, a spouse who condones the other's adultery can no longer rely on it to justify living apart.[19]

Various definitions of condonation have been suggested.[20] One of the latest and fullest is that of SIMON, P., in *Inglis* v. *Inglis*,[1] where he said:

> "Condonation is the reinstatement of a spouse who has committed a matrimonial offence in his or her former matrimonial position in knowledge of all the material facts of that offence with the intention of remitting it, that is to say, with the intention of not enforcing the rights which accrue to the wronged spouse in consequence of the offence."

It will be seen that there are two essential points: first, the innocent spouse must intend to forgive the other or to remit the matrimonial offence and, secondly, he must set the seal upon his forgiveness by reinstating the offending spouse to her matrimonial position. This is a particular application of the general principle running through English law that a person may not approbate and reprobate. If one spouse's misconduct entitles the other to treat himself as discharged from further performance of his marital obligations, he may do so, but he cannot be permitted to enjoy the benefit of the guilty spouse's performance of her obligations and then resile from the relationship.[2] This suggests that there must be mutuality to effect condonation, and there is at least one case at first instance which has held that, whatever the acts and intention of the innocent spouse, condonation cannot be found if the other does not want to be forgiven.[3]

Forgiveness.—Whilst it is usually said that condonation involves a forgiveness of the offence, it must not be thought that forgiveness has the same meaning here as it has, say, in the theological sense of an absolute remission. It means rather a waiver of the right to take matrimonial proceedings and indicates that the innocent spouse overlooks the offence and is prepared to restore the other notwithstanding its commission.[4] But the mental element is important in that the injured spouse will not be bound by his actions if, at the time, he was not in possession of all the material facts, that is, those facts which

---

[17] See *Dunn* v. *Dunn*, [1962] 3 All E.R. 587. For the effect of condonation on desertion, see *ante*, p. 181.

[18] *Blyth* v. *Blyth*, [1966] 1 All E.R. 524, H.L.; [1966] A.C. 643.

[19] See *ante*, p. 168.

[20] See *Keats* v. *Keats* (1859), 1 Sw. & Tr. 334, 346; *Bernstein* v. *Bernstein*, [1893] P. 292, 303, C.A.; *Henderson* v. *Henderson*, [1944] 1 All E.R. 44, 45, H.L.; [1944] A.C. 49, 52; *Swan* v. *Swan* [1953] 2 All E.R. 854, 862, C.A.; [1953] P. 258, 271.

[1] [1967] 2 All E.R. 71, 79-80; [1968] P. 639, 651.

[2] *Hearn* v. *Hearn*, [1969] 3 All E.R. 417, 425. See also *Tynan* v. *Tynan*, [1969] 3 All E.R. 1472.

[3] *Ford* v. *Ford*, [1970] 3 All E.R. 188, 193.

[4] *Hearn* v. *Hearn*, (*supra*), at p. 422.

would reasonably have affected his decision to take the other back. Thus if H reinstates his wife, W, after she has told him that she committed adultery with X on two occasions during H's temporary absence, this would not amount to condonation of her undisclosed adultery with X on previous occasions[5] or of her adultery with another man[6] if H was unaware of these further acts and would not have reinstated her had he known of them. Similarly, if H condoned W's adultery on the assumption that her association with the other man was over, the fact that it was still continuing unknown to the husband would negative the condonation even though no further adultery was committed.[7]

The complainant's knowledge in such circumstances is, of course, a question of fact. But mere belief or suspicion is not enough. The problem was discussed by SACHS, J., in *Burch* v. *Burch*,[8] where he said:

> " . . . It seems to me that a conclusion based on intuition, delusion, jealous obsession, or any other method than reasonable deduction from ascertained facts, does not constitute knowledge. Ingrained suspicion does not become knowledge merely because the man who holds it becomes convinced of its truth without proper supporting evidence."

Conversely, if he had information from which a reasonable man would conclude that the defendant must have been guilty, knowledge of the offence will be imputed to him unless he can show that he did not believe the information and therefore did not possess the necessary *animus*.[9] But he cannot complain of unconfessed adultery if, after the guilty spouse has admitted to some acts, he makes it plain that he wishes to hear no more.[10] Similarly, if he suspects the other of misconduct in the past but is prepared to take her back whether guilty or not, he clearly waives the right to complain of any adultery actually committed.[11] But even here there will be no condonation if the complainant acted in ignorance of a material fact, and in *Burch* v. *Burch* it was implied that if a husband, suspecting that his wife has committed adultery with A, nevertheless takes her back, this will not amount to condonation if she has in fact committed adultery with B and the husband would not have forgiven his wife had he known of the true state of affairs.

Reinstatement.—On the other hand, mere verbal forgiveness will never by itself amount to condonation: there must in addition be a reinstatement of the guilty party to the position of the other's spouse, and until the innocent party has done this, he will not be precluded from bringing proceedings on the ground of the commission of the

---

[5]*Inglis* v. *Inglis*, (*supra*). Contrast *Wells* v. *Wells*, [1954] 3 All E.R. 491, C.A.
[6]*Bernstein* v. *Bernstein*, [1893] P. 292, C.A.
[7]Per DENNING, L.J., in *Tilley* v. *Tilley*, [1948] 2 All E.R. 1113, 1125, C.A.; [1949] P. 240, 262-263.
[8][1958] 1 All E.R. 848, 853. SACHS, J., left open the question whether it must be shown that the petitioner had evidence fit to be laid before a court (p. 854).
[9]*Keats* v. *Keats* (1859), 1 Sw. & Tr. 334, 347.
[10]*Inglis* v. *Inglis*, (*supra*), at pp. 81 and 653, respectively.
[11]*Keats* v. *Keats*, (*supra*), at p. 346; *Cramp* v. *Cramp*, [1920] P. 158, 163-164.

offence forgiven. This is well illustrated by the case of *Fearn* v. *Fearn*.[12]
Whilst the petitioner was serving in the army in Italy during the last
war, his wife wrote to him confessing that she had committed adultery
and was pregnant as a result. He sent her a letter of forgiveness in which
he promised to treat the child as his own, and to the husband's knowledge
the wife obtained a pre-natal allowance and continued to draw her
separation allowance. Subsequently, however, his attitude towards her
changed; he took the necessary steps to have her wife's and child's
allowances stopped and, on returning to England, he did not resume
cohabitation with her but commenced divorce proceedings. It was held
by the Court of Appeal that mere words of forgiveness did not constitute
condonation and that, as the husband had done nothing to reinstate the
respondent as his wife, there was still no bar to his pleading her
adultery.

In most cases reinstatement has taken the form of a continuation[13]
or resumption of cohabitation, which involves of course a bilateral
intention to live together as husband and wife.[14] This need not be
" with all the circumstances which surrounded the spouses' former
life ", and in *Hearn* v. *Hearn*[15] it was held that adultery was condoned
after ten years' cohabitation even though the parties never had sexual
intercourse. On the other hand, a wife clearly does not condone
her husband's adultery by returning to him as his paid housekeeper.[16]
Furthermore, once cohabitation is established, this in itself may give
rise to a presumption of condonation. If one spouse *continues* to cohabit
with the other knowing that the latter has been guilty of adultery or
cruelty, it is a question of fact whether forgiveness is to be inferred. In
Burch v. *Burch*[17] SACHS, J., held that the guilty spouse is notionally
deposed from his or her matrimonial position forthwith and that the
other has a period in which to review the position. If the innocent
spouse reinstates the other by explicit words or conduct or lets things
run on so long that a reinstatement is to be inferred, then there will be
condonation. The inference is not to be so easily drawn if it is the
husband who is the guilty party, for the wife may have nowhere to go
and may not have the means to live apart from her husband.[18] A
resumption of cohabitation by a spouse who knows that the other has

---

[12][1948] 1 All E.R. 459, C.A.; [1948] P. 241; following *Keats* v. *Keats* (1859),
1 Sw. & Tr. 334; *Crocker* v. *Crocker*, [1921] P. 25, C.A.
[13]*Lawrence* v. *Lawrence*, [1946] W.N. 126; *Wilmot* v. *Wilmot*, [1948] 2 All E.R. 123.
[14]See *ante*, p. 178. This is, of course, distinct from a final mutual reconciliation:
Ives v. *Ives*, [1967] 3 All E.R. 79; [1968] P. 375. See the Matrimonial Causes Act 1965,
s. 42 (2) (*post*, p. 193).
[15][1969] 3 All E.R. 417.
[16]*Cook* v. *Cook*, [1949] 1 All E.R. 384.
[17][1958] 1 All E.R. 848. *Cf. Ford* v. *Ford*, [1970] 3 All E.R. 188 (condonation not
inferred after continuation of cohabitation for 14 months because husband unable to see
his way out of difficulties because of weakness of will).
[18]*Mackrell* v. *Mackrell*, [1948] 2 All E.R. 858, C.A., at pp. 860, 861. Thus it has been
held that there was no condonation in the following cases: *Mackrell* v. *Mackrell* (wife
remaining in house for three weeks without sexual intercourse); *Hall* v. *Hall* (1891), 60
L.J.P. 73, C.A. (husband permitting wife to share his bed without intercourse because
she had nowhere else to go).

committed adultery or cruelty must necessarily lead to a much stronger presumption of condonation, but this is also rebuttable as is illustrated by *Swan* v. *Swan*.[19] The husband had treated his wife with cruelty before entering a sanatorium. He was discharged suddenly from the sanatorium and arrived home unexpectedly. His wife took him in because he was ill and he remained in the same house with her for a month before going into a mental hospital. The spouses did not have intercourse during that period. It was held by the Court of Appeal that the wife merely did what in common humanity it was natural and reasonable for her to do in the circumstances, and that there was no condonation because the element of forgiveness was completely absent.

It is obvious that, whereas public policy should encourage attempts at reconciliation between spouses whose marriage may still be saved, these legal rules are more likely to produce the opposite result. Suppose that a wife, whose husband has committed adultery, returns to him in order to try to save the marriage but that the attempt fails and she leaves him again. She is now in a worse position than she was before, for she has put herself in desertion and thus lost her right to maintenance too. She might be well advised therefore not to make the attempt at all. To get round this difficulty, section 42 (2) of the Matrimonial Causes Act 1965 now provides that adultery or cruelty shall not be deemed to be condoned by the continuation or resumption of cohabitation for any one period not exceeding three months with a view to effecting a reconciliation.[20] The three limitations imposed by the statute should be noted: it applies to only *one* period of cohabitation (of however short a duration), it must last for not more than three months, and it must be *with a view to effecting* a reconciliation. It is not necessary that the spouses should agree that cohabitation is being resumed or continued with this object or that there should be a joint intention to treat the cohabitation as a trial period. But the innocent spouse is not entitled to rely on a mental reservation; consequently if he wishes to take advantage of the provisions of this sub-section, it is essential that the other should know that this is his intention.[1] Moreover, as the Court of Appeal held in *Herridge* v. *Herridge*,[2] if the parties are first reconciled and then continue or resume cohabitation as a consequence of their reconciliation, the section has no application and the offence will be condoned.

Even though the spouses did not resume cohabitation, a series of cases[3] laid down the rule that, if a husband had sexual intercourse with his wife knowing that she had been guilty of adultery or cruelty,

---

[19][1953] 2 All E.R. 854, C.A.; [1953] P. 258. In *Hearn* v. *Hearn*, (*supra*), it was said (at p. 423) that the spouses' motive for resuming cohabitation is irrelevant. But this overlooks its significance when considering the question of the presumption.

[20]Re-enacting s. 2 (1) of the Matrimonial Causes Act 1963.

[1]*Quinn* v. *Quinn*, [1969] 3 All E.R. 1212, C.A.

[2][1966] 1 All E.R. 93 C.A., following *Brown* v. *Brown*, [1964] 2 All E.R. 828. In many cases it may well be difficult in practice to establish whether the cohabitation preceded the reconciliation or *vice versa*: the burden of proving the former is on the complainant. See Irvine, *The Concept of " Reconciliation " and the Matrimonial Causes Act 1963*, 82 L.Q.R. 525; Hall, [1965] C.L.J. 51; Michaels, 28 M.L.R. 101.

[3]Culminating in *Henderson* v. *Henderson*, [1944] 1 All E.R. 44, H.L.; [1944] A.C. 49.

that act in itself would raise an irrebuttable presumption of condonation. The reason given for this view was that it would be immoral to
permit him to exercise his marital rights and then seek to have the
marriage dissolved, or, alternatively, that the wife's position might be
prejudiced if she conceived as a result. Consequently the same rule
did not apply if the husband was the guilty party. The fact that the
wife had sexual intercourse with him would not amount to condonation
if " she was not her own mistress, or had not the option of going away,
or had no place to go, or no person to receive her, or no funds to
support her ";[4] in other cases condonation would be presumed
against her only if at the time she had forgiven her husband.[5]
However true this distinction may have been in the nineteenth century,
it had become something of an anomaly by the middle of the twentieth.
Both spouses have now been put on the same footing and section 42 (1)
of the Matrimonial Causes Act 1965, provides:[6]

> " Any presumption of condonation which arises from the continuance or
> resumption of marital intercourse may be rebutted by evidence sufficient to
> negative the necessary intent."

The effect of this ill drafted provision seems to be this: if either spouse
has sexual intercourse with the other knowing that the other has committed adultery or cruelty, this in itself raises a presumption of condonation which can be rebutted, however, by showing that the innocent
spouse had no intention of forgiving and reinstating the guilty one.
This means that the decision (given before the 1963 Act) in *Morley* v.
Morley[7] would now apply *mutatis mutandis* if the wife had been
the guilty spouse. In that case both spouses were engaged in the fair-
ground industry. The wife left her husband and took proceedings
before magistrates to obtain maintenance on the ground of his persistent cruelty. The case was adjourned to enable them to discuss the
possibility of a reconciliation and the wife then agreed to return to her
husband on condition that he did not hit her again and also in the
future travelled in the south of England instead of in the north in order
to get away from his parents who she alleged were the real cause of the
trouble. She then went to join him in his caravan in Newcastle with
the intention that they should both go south, but on the next day he
told her that he had changed his mind and proposed to remain in the
north. The wife did not immediately accept this repudiation of the
agreement and stayed with her husband for two days in an attempt to
persuade him to adhere to his promise and during this time sexual
intercourse, to which the wife was a consenting party, took place
between them on two occasions. She then left him and proceedings in
the magistrates' court were resumed. The husband then sought to
prove that the cruelty complained of had been condoned by the intercourse. The Divisional Court refused to upset the finding that there

---

[4]*Per* HODSON, L.J., in *Baguley* v. *Baguley* (1957), reported [1961] 2 All E.R. 635,
640, C.A.
   [5]*Morley* v. *Morley*, [1961] 1 All E.R. 428, distinguishing *Baguley* v. *Baguley*,
(*supra*); *W.* v. *W.* (*No.* 2), [1961] 2 All E.R. 626; [1962] P. 49.
   [6]Re-enacting the Matrimonial Causes Act 1963, s. 1.
   [7][1961] 1 All E.R. 428. See also *W.* v. *W.* (*No. 2*), (*supra*); *Blyth* v. *Blyth*, [1966] 1 All
E.R. 524, H.L.; [1966] A.C. 643.

had been no condonation. Any inference to the contrary was rebutted by the fact that, as the wife's offer to return to her husband was subject to a condition which he later repudiated, there was no final agreement for a reconciliation, or, alternatively, the forgiveness was subject to a condition precedent which had failed.

If there has been neither a full resumption of cohabitation nor sexual intercourse between the parties, it is extremely doubtful whether any other act can amount to a reinstatement so as to effect a condonation. In *Fearn* v. *Fearn*[8] TUCKER, L.J., expressly left the question open, although he voiced grave doubts whether a husband in the position of the petitioner in that case could finally condone his wife's adultery until he had returned home.

Condonation Procured by Fraud.—It now seems clear that if the alleged condonation is procured by a fraudulent misrepresentation on the defendant's part, it will not bar the complainant. Hence it has been held that a husband can succeed if he has forgiven his wife as the result of her falsely telling him that she was seduced whilst drugged[9] or that she was not pregnant by the co-respondent.[10] But the representation must be of fact. In *Henderson* v. *Henderson*[11] a husband forgave his wife and had sexual intercourse with her on her promising to break off an adulterous association. The next morning she told him that she did not see why she should stop seeing the co-respondent, whereupon the husband left her. It was held that he had condoned her adultery and that it was not open to him to argue that he would not have had intercourse if the wife had not given her promise, for this amounted to no more than a representation as to her future conduct. On the other hand, if he had been able to prove that her statement was fraudulent in the sense that she did not at the time have any intention of breaking with the co-respondent, it is submitted that he would have succeeded on the ground that his forgiveness was procured by fraud.[12]

Conditional Condonation and the Doctrine of Revival.—*Henderson* v. *Henderson*[13] illustrates yet another rule, that, just as there cannot be a resumption of cohabitation subject to a condition subsequent, there cannot be a conditional condonation. In *Henderson* v. *Henderson* it was argued that the husband's condonation was inoperative as it had been given on the condition that the wife should cease to see the co-respondent and she had not fulfilled that condition; it was held, however, that this contention must fail because condonation, having been effected, was absolute and barred the petitioner

[8][1948] 1 All E.R. 459, 464-465, C.A.; [1948] P. 241, 255. For the facts, see *ante*, p. 192.

[9]See the unreported case cited by PILCHER, J., in *Higgins* v. *Higgins*, [1943] 2 All E.R. 86, 87; [1943] P. 58, 59.

[10]*Roberts* v. *Roberts* (1917), 117 L.T. 157.

[11][1944] 1 All E.R. 44, H.L.; [1944] A.C. 49.

[12]For the distinction between a mere statement of intention and a fraudulent misrepresentation of fact, see Cheshire and Fifoot, *Contract*, 7th Ed., 235-236. If the misrepresentation did not induce the complainant's act at all, it will not affect the condonation: *Sneyd* v. *Sneyd*, [1926] P. 27.

[13]*Supra*. See also *Higgins* v. *Higgins*. [1943] 2 All E.R. 86; [1943] P. 58.

completely. It be will observed that in this case the House of Lords was concerned only with the effect of a condition subsequent: it is still an open question whether condonation can be subject to a condition precedent other than that provided for in section 42 (2) of the Matrimonial Causes Act 1965.[14]

But to this rule an exception has been recognised since at least 1730,[15] *viz.* that condonation is conditional upon the guilty spouse's committing no further matrimonial offence. So if a husband is guilty of cruelty, which the wife condones, and he then commits a further matrimonial offence, she may bring proceedings in a magistrates' court on the ground of the cruelty and would also be entitled to rely on it to justify withdrawing from cohabitation. This doctrine of revival is now subject to an important statutory qualification for section 42 (3) of the Matrimonial Causes Act 1965 enacts that *adultery* which has been condoned shall no longer be capable of being revived.[16]

The term " matrimonial offence " in this context is difficult to define. To limit it to its technical meaning of adultery, cruelty and desertion would rob the concept of revival of any significance, for all three are grounds for an application to a magistrates' court and the first two will justify a withdrawal from cohabitation. In *Beard* v. *Beard*[17] SCOTT, L.J., considered that a condoned offence would be revived by any conduct

> " which in the eye of [the Divorce Court] is wrong, whether it does or does not reach the duration, or gravity, or completeness which is necessary to permit of a decree, provided always that it be sufficiently serious for the court to regard it as a substantial breach of duty."

Later, in *Richardson* v. *Richardson*,[18] DENNING, L.J., spoke of "harshness or neglect of a real and substantial kind which is such as to be likely to inflict misery on the innocent party and does indeed lead to a breakdown of the marriage ", whilst BUCKNILL, L.J., referred to conduct which " makes decent married life together impossible ". The longer the time that has elapsed since the offence was condoned, the more serious will be the conduct required to revive it.[19] In *Cundy* v. *Cundy*[20] it was stated that this will depend upon the circumstances of the offence, the time which has elapsed since it was committed, the behaviour of the spouses in the meantime, the seriousness of the

---

[14] The decision in *Morley* v. *Morley*, [1961] 1 All E.R. 428 (*ante*, p. 194) rests on the assumption that condonation may be subject to a condition precedent.

[15] *Worsley* v. *Worsley* (1730), 2 Lee 572.

[16] Re-enacting the Matrimonial Causes Act 1963, s. 3. Although it may be undesirable to enable one spouse to resuscitate adultery condoned a considerable time before, it is submitted that this is a regrettable piece of legislation because it may effectively impede reconciliation. Adultery causing injury to the complainant's health could also amount to cruelty and *this* could be revived: *cf. Chalcroft* v. *Chalcroft*, [1969] 3 All E.R. 1172. The fact that a condoned association short of adultery can be revived may give rise to difficulties in practice: *Hind* v. *Hind*, [1969] 1 All E.R. 1083, 1088.

[17] [1945] 2 All E.R. 306, C.A., at p. 315; [1946] P. 8, at p. 22.

[18] [1949] 2 All E.R. 330, C.A., at pp. 333 and 332; [1950] P. 16, at pp. 23 and 21, respectively. *Cf. Kemp* v. *Kemp*, [1953] 2 All E.R. 553; *Cundy* v. *Cundy*, [1956] 1 All E.R. 245; *Jelley* v. *Jelley*, [1964] 2 All E.R. 866, C.A. Some of the problems presented by the doctrine of revival are discussed by Cross, *The Revival of a Matrimonial Offence by Subsequent Misconduct*, 8 M.L.R. 149 (written before *Beard* v. *Beard*), and by Mitchell, *Revival of Condoned Matrimonial Offences*, 9 M.L.R. 137.

[19] *Jelley* v. *Jelley*, [1964] 2 All E.R. 866, C.A.

[20] [1956] 1 All E.R. 245.

conduct alleged to have revived the offence " and its circumstances, including the manners and customs of the grade of society to which the parties belong ". There may indeed come a time when the offence is completely obliterated so that no future misconduct of any sort will revive it.[21]

In any event, as in the case of desertion, the conduct must in fact have broken up the marriage or prevented the continuance of co-habitation. This is illustrated by *Benton* v. *Benton*.[22] The husband, who had left the wife, petitioned for divorce on the ground of her cruelty. He continued to pay her occasional visits and condoned her offence by an isolated act of intercourse. The wife then filed her answer to the petition, alleging condonation and cross-charging the husband with cruelty by committing and attempting to commit sodomy on her. The husband nevertheless continued to see her from time to time without making any complaint against her charges. It was held by the Court of Appeal that, although cruelty could be revived by such charges if they were false to the wife's knowledge, they did not revive the condoned offence here as there was no evidence that they had had any effect on the husband at all. *A fortiori* the condoned offence will not be revived if the subsequent break up of the marriage is due not to the defendant's acts but to the complainant's.[23]

4. COMPLAINANT'S ADULTERY

The court may not make a separation order or an order for the main-tenance of either spouse if the complainant has committed adultery unless the defendant has condoned it, connived at it or been guilty of wilful neglect or misconduct conducing to it. The complainant's adultery does not affect the court's power to make orders with respect to children.[1]

5. CASES MORE FIT FOR THE HIGH COURT

A magistrates' court may refuse to deal with a case if it considers that it would be more conveniently dealt with by the High Court.[2] This power may be exercised only if the High Court could itself assume jurisdiction;[3] in other cases justices have an absolute discretion, but they rarely refuse to hear a case, nor indeed should they do so, for

---

[21]See *Beale* v. *Beale*, [1950] 2 All E.R. 539 n., 540, C.A.; [1951] P. 48, 49 (not followed by the High Court of Australia: *Schumann* v. *Schumann* (1961), 106 C.L.R. 566).

[22][1957] 3 All E.R. 544, C.A. See also *Jelley* v. *Jelley*, (*ante*).

[23]*Richardson* v. *Richardson*, (*ante*).

[1]Matrimonial Proceedings (Magistrate's Courts) Act 1960, s. 2 (3) (b). It is anomalous that maintenance may be awarded to a wife guilty of adultery in the case of divorce or judicial separation but that magistrates have no power at all.

[2]*Ibid.*, s. 5. No appeal lies from the justices' decision, but the High Court may remit any subsequent proceedings to a magistrates' court: *ibid*. The Act has not been amended to take account of the fact that all other matrimonial proceedings must now be commenced in a divorce county court. This presumably does not affect the practice, although a county court does not have power to remit the case.

[3]Consequently, a magistrates' court should not refuse to deal with an application to vary or discharge an existing order, for the High Court has no jurisdiction to do so: *Smyth* v. *Smyth*, [1956] 2 All E.R. 476; [1956] P. 247. See also *Davies* v. *Davies*, [1957] 2 All E.R. 444; [1957] P. 357.

otherwise the whole purpose of providing a summary procedure would be lost. But there is one class of case where a magistrates' court should make an order only in exceptional circumstances, *viz.* if the High Court or a county court is already seised of substantially the same matter and there is an actual or potential conflict of jurisdiction. If a husband is petitioning for divorce or other matrimonial relief and a magistrates' court entertains an application from the wife, there is a danger that the two courts might well find themselves embarrassed by diametrically opposed orders relating to substantially the same issue.[4] For the same reason a magistrates' court normally ought not to make an order if one of the spouses is about to commence proceedings in a divorce county court.[5] There is, of course, a danger that an unscrupulous husband might try to frustrate the wife's attempts to obtain a magistrates' order by the simple expedient of commencing proceedings in a county court. This led the Divisional Court to hold in *Lanitis* v. *Lanitis*[6] that the wife's need to obtain an order quickly and her anxiety about her children (whom the husband had taken away) could—and on the particular facts did—amount to exceptional circumstances entitling the magistrates to make maintenance and custody orders in her favour.

D. ORDERS THAT MAY BE MADE

If the complainant establishes a ground for complaint, the court may make an order containing any one or more of the following provisions.[7]

Non-Cohabitation Clause.—This relieves the complainant of his or her obligation to cohabit with the defendant and, except in relation to intestate succession,[8] has the effect in all respects of a decree of judicial separation.[9] Whilst no order may be made unless the complainant asks for it,[10] it does not follow that, if that spouse does want it, he or she is entitled to it merely because grounds for applying for it have been made out. The question was considered by the Divisional Court in *Corton* v. *Corton*[11] and *Jolliffe* v. *Jolliffe,*[12] where they pointed out the question is one for the justices' discretion. They should ask themselves specifically whether the order is necessary for the protection of the complainant, whether the case is more serious than usual and, perhaps

---

[4]*Kaye* v. *Kaye,* [1964] 1 All E.R. 620; [1965] P. 100. But there is no reason why magistrates should not make an order if the wife has made it clear that she does not propose to apply for maintenance in the divorce court: *Cooper* v. *Cooper,* [1952] 2 All E.R. 857; [1953] P. 26.

[5]See *Sanders* v. *Sanders,* [1952] 2 All E.R. 767, at pp. 770, 771.

[6][1970] 1 All E.R. 466. An alternative way of dealing with the situation would be to make an interim order and then give the husband the choice of letting the court go into the merits: *ibid.,* p. 472.

[7]It may also make an order for costs: Magistrates' Courts Act 1952, s. 55.

[8]See *post,* p. 505.

[9]Matrimonial Proceedings (Magistrates' Courts) Act 1960, s. 2 (1) (a). For the effect of a decree of judicial separation, see *ante,* p. 145. There is no power to make an order that the defendant be not bound to cohabit with the complainant: *Wall* v. *Wall,* [1967] 3 All E.R. 408.

[10]*Jones* v. *Jones* (1929), 142 L.T. 167.

[11][1962] 3 All E.R. 1025; [1965] P. 1.

[12][1963] 3 All E.R. 295; [1965] P. 6. *Cf.* LORD HODSON in *Gollins* v. *Gollins,* [1963] 2 All E.R. 966, 983-984, H.L.; [1964] A.C. 644, 681-682.

most important, whether a reconciliation is reasonably likely. Consequently a non-cohabitation clause is usually wholly inappropriate in cases of simple desertion and wilful neglect to maintain; on the other hand the mere fact that the husband has been guilty of persistent cruelty is not conclusive. In *Corton* v. *Corton*, for example, the court allowed an appeal against the inclusion of a non-cohabitation clause where the ground of the complaint had been the husband's persistent cruelty, because there was a high chance of a reconciliation.[13]

Maintenance for the other Spouse.—On a complaint by the wife (on whatever ground) the court may order the husband to pay such weekly sum for her maintenance as it considers reasonable in all the circumstances. In certain more limited circumstances it may order the wife to pay maintenance for the husband. These powers will be considered more fully when we deal with financial provision on the breakdown of marriage.[14]

Custody and Maintenance of Children.—The court has wide powers to make orders for the custody, access, supervision and maintenance of any child of the family. These provisions will be discussed in detail later.[15]

Interim Orders.—An interim order is the counterpart in a magistrates' court of an order for maintenance pending suit in the divorce court. An interim order may be made if the court adjourns the hearing for more than a week or refuses to make an order on the ground that the case would be more conveniently dealt with by the High Court. If in the latter case or on appeal from a final order the High Court remits the case to a magistrates' court, an interim order may be made by the High Court, in which case it is deemed to have been made by a magistrates' court for the purposes of enforcement, revocation, revival and variation.[16]

In an interim order the court has the same power to make an order for maintenance for the other spouse and children as it has in a final order. In exceptional cases it may also make an order for the custody and access of any child of the family under the age of 16.[17] The court may put a limit on the time for which the order is to remain in force, and it will cease to have effect when a final order is made, if the court subsequently dismisses the complaint or, in any case, after three months from the first making of any interim order.[18]

[13] In *Squires* v. *Squires* (1946), 62 T.L.R. 631, 632, JONES, J., expressed the opinion that it did not follow that a separation order should be made even though the husband had been convicted of an aggravated assault on his wife. In practice many magistrates' courts are not following the Divisional Court's direction: see Gibson, *The Separation Order: A Study in Textbook Law and Court Practice*, 33 M.L.R. 63.

[14] See *post*, pp. 414 *et seq.*

[15] See *post*, pp. 283-286 and 472-474.

[16] Matrimonial Proceedings (Magistrates' Courts) Act 1960, s. 6 (1), (4). There is an obvious gap because there is no power to make an interim order in favour of a party appealing from the *dismissal* of a summons.

[17] *Ibid.*, s. 6 (2). See further *post*, pp. 420, 473, n.[10], and 286.

[18] *Ibid.*, s. 6. (3).

E. SUSPENSION, CESSATION, REVOCATION, REVIVAL AND VARIATION OF ORDERS

Cohabitation.—It is obviously possible that, however anxious the complainant is to leave the defendant, she (or he) may not be able to do so before obtaining a maintenance order because she may have nowhere else to go and may lack the means of paying for food and accommodation. Consequently, the Act permits a court to make an order notwithstanding that the parties are cohabiting; but neither a final nor an interim order may take effect so long as they continue to cohabit, and if cohabitation continues for three months after the making of a final order, it entirely ceases to have effect, so that it cannot come into force even if they subsequently separate. As we shall see later, however, the court may order a child to be committed to the legal custody of someone other than the parties or to be placed under care or supervision; the continued cohabitation of the spouses is clearly irrelevant in such circumstances, and consequently any part of an order containing such provisions or requiring either or both of the spouses to pay maintenance *to a third person or authority* in respect of a child shall take effect and remain in force notwithstanding the spouses' continued cohabitation unless the court directs otherwise.[19]

If the spouses resume cohabitation after an interim or final order has come into force, it will automatically cease to have effect except for such provisions relating to children as were mentioned in the last paragraph.[20] If in any subsequent proceedings to vary, revive or discharge an order it is proved that the parties have resumed cohabitation, the court is bound to revoke the order except in so far as it contains such provisions.[1]

It will be appreciated that the spouses must cohabit in order to bring these provisions of the Act into operation The mere fact that they are both residing under the same roof will not prevent the order from taking effect (or discharge it if it has already taken effect) if the parties are no longer living as one household—in other words, if they are living in such circumstances as would entitle the court to hold that there is sufficient separation to justify a finding of desertion.[2]

Complainant's Adultery.—The defendant may apply to have a final order revoked on the ground that the complainant has committed adultery during the subsistence of the marriage unless the defendant himself or herself has condoned it, connived at it or been guilty of wilful neglect or misconduct conducing to it.[3] Although adultery committed before the making of the order may be relied on, it would seem that the defendant may not raise the adultery if he has had an

---

[19] *Ibid.*, s. 7 (1).
[20] *Ibid.*, s. 7 (2).
[1] *Ibid.*, s. 8 (2).
[2] See *ante*, pp. 162-164; *Naylor* v. *Naylor*, [1961] 2 All E.R. 129. If the spouses are subsequently divorced and then live together as man and wife, there is no resumption of cohabitation, because they must be married in order to cohabit: *Prest* v. *Prest*, [1949] 2 All E R. 790; [1950] P. 63.
[3] Matrimonial Proceedings (Magistrates' Courts) Act 1960, s. 8 (2). Hence if the spouses are divorced after an order has been made and the complainant subsequently commits adultery with a married person, this is no ground for revoking the order.

opportunity of doing so in previous proceedings but failed to avail himself of it.[4] Unlike resumption of cohabitation, adultery never automatically discharges the order, but if the defendant applies for revocation on this ground, the court is bound to revoke a separation order or an order for maintenance for the complainant, although it need not revoke any provision relating to the custody and maintenance of any child, for otherwise the position of the child might be prejudiced by the party's adultery.[5]

Revocation, Revival and Variation of Orders.—In addition to the cases already considered, the court has a general power to revoke any order, to revive an order previously revoked, and to vary an order by the addition, deletion and alteration of provisions.[6] Unlike the position where the application to revoke the order is based upon adultery, the court in other cases has a discretion (which must of course be judicially exercised) to refuse to entertain the application. Although " fresh evidence " is no longer required before the court can make any alteration to the original order,[7] the party making the application will probably not be permitted to adduce any evidence which he could have adduced in earlier proceedings.[8]

Death, Divorce and Nullity.—The death of either spouse automatically discharges any order made under the Matrimonial Proceedings (Magistrates' Courts) Act.[9] A decree of divorce or nullity must also discharge a non-cohabitation clause.[10]

F. ENFORCEMENT OF ORDERS

The enforcement of maintenance orders will be dealt with when we discuss financial provision on the breakdown of marriage.[11] If a person fails to comply with any other order (for example, by refusing to hand over a child to the spouse to whom custody has been given), he (or she) may be ordered to pay a sum not exceeding £1 for every day that he is in default up to a maximum of £20 or committed to prison until he has complied with the order or for a period of two months, whichever is the shorter.[12]

---

[4]*Brammer* v. *Brammer*, [1954] 1 All E.R. 649. The six months' limitation period does not apply to adultery as a ground for having the order discharged: *Natborny* v. *Natborny*, [1933] P. 1, C.A.

[5]Note that this relates to *any* order in respect of a child and not merely to the orders mentioned in the last section.

[6]Matrimonial Proceedings (Magistrates' Courts) Act 1960, s. 8 (1); Magistrates' Courts Act 1952, s. 53; Maintenance Orders Act 1968, s. 2. These proceedings may be treated as domestic proceedings: Matrimonial Proceedings (Magistrates' Courts) Act 1960, s. 8 (3). For the position where one of the spouses resides outside England, see *ibid.*, s. 9.

[7]As it was under the Summary Jurisdiction (Married Women) Act 1895, s. 7.

[8]*Cf. Brammer* v. *Brammer*, (*supra*), and variation, etc. in the divorce court (*post*, p. 451).

[9]*Re Bidie*, [1948] 1 All E.R. 885; [1948] Ch. 697; affirmed, [1948] 2 All E.R. 995, C.A.; [1949] Ch. 121.

[10]For the effect of these decrees on a maintenance order, see *post*, p. 421.

[11]See *post*, pp. 422-426.

[12]Magistrates' Courts Act 1952, s. 54.

CHAPTER 8

The Termination of Marriage

In English law a marriage may be terminated only by the death of one of the parties or by a decree of dissolution or divorce pronounced by a court of competent jurisdiction. In a sense a decree of nullity terminates a voidable marriage, but death and divorce differ from nullity in that they have no retrospective effect and that afterwards the parties are still regarded in law as having been husband and wife up to the moment of the termination of the marriage.

A. DEATH AND PRESUMPTION OF DEATH

The death of either party *ipso facto* brings the marriage to an end. Before 1938 the disappearance of one of the spouses presented an insurmountable difficulty. If H's wife, W, disappeared in such circumstances as to lead to the reasonable inference that she was dead (although her death could not be proved), H could remarry without committing the felony of bigamy and his second marriage would be *presumptively* valid. But if it were later proved that W was in fact alive when H remarried, then, of course, the second marriage would be *conclusively* void with all the legal consequences that that entailed. In order to meet this situation, the Matrimonial Causes Act of 1937 (in provisions which are now substantially re-enacted in section 14 of the Matrimonial Causes Act 1965) permits the High Court to make a decree of presumption of death and of dissolution of the marriage if it is satisfied that there are reasonable grounds for supposing that the petitioner's spouse is dead.[1] The general presumption of death which may be raised by seven years' absence is specifically applied to these proceedings by the provision that

> ". . . the fact that for a period of seven years or more the other party to the marriage has been continually absent from the petitioner and the petitioner has no reason to believe that the other party has been living within that time shall be evidence that the other party is dead until the contrary is proved."[2]

This has been construed as meaning that nothing must have happened

---

[1] The power is permissive and therefore will not be exercised if there is some probability that the other spouse is still alive, *e.g.*, if the other were an explorer who had gone on an expedition expected to last many years: *Thompson* v. *Thompson*, [1956] 1 All E.R. 603, 608; [1956] P. 414, 424-425.

[2] Matrimonial Causes Act 1965, s. 14 (3). The burden of proving that he has no reason to believe that the other spouse is still alive is on the petitioner and he must therefore give evidence: *Parkinson* v. *Parkinson*, [1939] 3 All E.R. 108; [1939] P. 346. It was also held in this case that the fact that the spouses parted under a separation agreement is no bar to the proceedings.

during that time from which the petitioner, as a reasonable person, would conclude that the other spouse was still alive.[3]

It should be noticed that the petitioner is not bound to rely on this period of absence. The court may accept any satisfactory evidence from which it may be presumed that the spouse is dead:[4] the inference to be drawn from the seven years' absence is of particular importance when there is no evidence at all of what has happened since.

If the proceedings are brought by the husband, he must be domiciled in England; if they are brought by the wife, she must either be domiciled in this country or have been ordinarily resident here for a continuous period of at least three years immediately preceding the commencement of the proceedings.[5] But in order to determine the wife's domicile, the husband is deemed to have died immediately after the last occasion on which she had reason to believe him to be living, so that *for the purpose of these proceedings* the wife may acquire a separate domicile in England if her husband was not domiciled here.[6]

B. DIVORCE

I. HISTORICAL INTRODUCTION

We have already seen that the doctrine of the indissolubility of marriage was accepted by the English ecclesiastical courts after the Reformation, so that these courts had no power to pronounce a decree of divorce *a vinculo matrimonii* which would permit the parties to remarry.[7] In addition to decrees of nullity and jactitation of marriage, they could pronounce decrees of restitution of conjugal rights and divorce *a mensa et thoro*. The former called on a deserting spouse to resume cohabitation with the petitioner, and the latter (which was granted on the grounds of adultery, cruelty or the commission of an unnatural offence) relieved the petitioner from the duty of cohabiting with the respondent without severing the marriage tie.[8] The only way in which an aggrieved party could obtain a divorce *a vinculo matrimonii* was by Act of Parliament, the expense of which was sufficient to put relief beyond the hope of most.[9] In addition, by the end of the eighteenth century, the practice of the House of Lords was to give a reading to a bill introduced on behalf of the husband only on the grounds of adultery and then only after he had obtained a divorce

---

[3]*Thompson* v. *Thompson*, (*ante*). A mere speculation will not be enough to rebut the presumption. *Quaere* whether the petitioner is bound to make all reasonable enquiries: *ibid.*, at pp. 605 and 421, respectively. *Cf. ante*, pp. 53-55.

[4]*E.g.*, the otherwise inexplicable disappearance of an explorer.

[5]Matrimonial Causes Act 1965, s. 14 (2).

[6] *Ibid.*, s. 14 (5).

[7]*Ante*, p. 59. See generally, Jackson, *Formation and Annulment of Marriage*, 2nd Ed., c. 2.

[8]Readers unfamiliar with ecclesiastical reports before 1858 are warned of the confusing terminology. The word " divorce " *simpliciter* always means divorce *a mensa et thoro;* occasionally " divorce *a vinculo matrimonii* " is used, in which case it always means nullity.

[9]There were on the average less than two divorces by statute a year.

a mensa et thoro in an ecclesiastical court and had successfully sued the
adulterer for damages in the old common law action of criminal conversation. Adultery alone would not suffice in the case of a bill presented
on behalf of the wife, who had to show that the adultery was aggravated
(for example, bigamous or incestuous) or that her husband had
committed an unnatural offence.[10]

Matrimonial Causes Act 1857.—This Act was passed to give
effect to the report of a royal commission which had been appointed in
1850 to enquire into the law relating to matrimonial offences. In addition to vesting the existing jurisdiction of the ecclesiastical courts in
a new statutory Divorce Court (from which it was transferred to the
High Court in 1875)[11] the Act for the first time in English law permitted divorce *a vinculo matrimonii* by judicial process. The term
" divorce " was henceforth confined to this decree, whilst that of divorce
a mensa et thoro was renamed " judicial separation ". But the distinction between the position of the husband and that of the wife was
retained, for a husband could petition for divorce on the ground of
adultery alone (provided that he joined the alleged adulterer as a
co-respondent instead of suing him at common law in criminal conversation), whilst a wife had to prove either adultery coupled with
incest, bigamy, cruelty or two years' desertion, or, alternatively, rape
or an unnatural offence.[12]

Extension of the Grounds for Divorce.—The law remained in
this state until 1923, when the Matrimonial Causes Act of that year put
the husband and wife in the same position by permitting the latter to
petition on the grounds of adultery *simpliciter*.[13] A. P. Herbert's
Matrimonial Causes Act of 1937 further extended the grounds for
divorce by permitting either spouse to base his or her petition on the
other's cruelty, desertion for three years, or (subject to certain other
conditions) supervening incurable insanity.[14] This last provision
shows an important departure from the principles underlying the law
of divorce, for whereas before 1938 it had always been necessary for
the petitioner to show that the respondent had committed a matrimonial offence, a petition based upon the respondent's insanity
disclosed a state of affairs in no way due to his fault which nevertheless
made it socially undesirable that the petitioner should still be tied to
the respondent by marriage.

The law was consolidated in the Matrimonial Causes Act 1950, which
was itself extensively amended, in particular by the Matrimonial
Causes Act 1963. These statutes were themselves repealed and the
whole law again consolidated in the Matrimonial Causes Act 1965.

---

[10]There are only four reported cases of parliamentary divorce on a wife's petition.
[11]By the Judicature Acts of 1873 and 1875.
[12]Matrimonial Causes Act 1857, s. 27.
[13]Matrimonial Causes Act 1923, s. 1. It did not strictly equate the spouses' rights
for the wife could still petition on the grounds of the husband's rape or unnatural
offence, while there was no corresponding basis for the husband's petition.
[14]Matrimonial Causes Act 1937, ss. 2 and 3. This Act very largely gave effect to
the recommendations of the majority of the members of a Royal Commission appointed
in 1909 (the Gorell Commission, Cd. 6478). For a lively account of the history of the
passage of this bill through Parliament, see Sir Alan Herbert's *The Ayes have it* (1937).

The Movement for Reform.—The enormous social changes follow-ing the Second World War not only produced a vast increase in the number of divorces but led to much public discussion of the whole basis of the law. The idea that the purpose of divorce was to provide a remedy available only to the " innocent " spouse for a matrimonial wrong committed by the other seemed to many to be a singularly outdated concept. In many cases both spouses were guilty, and cross-petitions were launched purely to give the parties an advantage when it came to the question of financial provision. The social purpose of a decree of divorce is to enable the former spouses to remarry, and so, it was argued, it should be available to either spouse when the marriage has irretrievably broken down. To insist that divorce should be available only if a matrimonial offence has been committed lays stress upon the symptoms of breakdown rather than on the breakdown itself. The essential merits of the two views about divorce can be summed up quite succinctly. The traditional theory (based upon the matrimonial offence) implies that an innocent spouse should not be divorced against his or her will, particularly bearing in mind that many spouses have a conscientious objection to divorce and that a wife in particular may suffer serious financial hardship as a consequence of the decree. The more radical view (based upon the breakdown of the marriage) reduces the number of illicit unions where there is no foreseeable chance of the parties being able to marry or of their children being legitimated because the partner of one of them refuses to release the other on account of conscientious scruple, financial advantage or vindictiveness.

In 1951 a Royal Commission (the Morton Commission) was appointed to enquire into the law of England and Scotland concerning marriage and divorce. Its report was published in 1956.[15] Of the nineteen members only one was in favour of totally scrapping the matrimonial offence as the basis of our divorce law, but nine of the rest would have introduced the breakdown of the marriage as evidenced by separation for seven years as an alternative ground. But apart from one un-successful attempt to change the law in a private member's bill in the House of Commons,[16] little was done until two major publications appeared in 1966. In the first, *Putting Asunder*, a group appointed by the Archbishop of Canterbury to consider the law of divorce in con-temporary society came down in favour of the breakdown theory. Logically they argued that this must be the sole ground of divorce and that possible abuse must be guarded against by a judicial inquest in each case. *Putting Asunder* was referred to the Law Commission who in turn reported in *Reform of the Ground of Divorce: the Field of Choice*.[17] They concluded that the Archbishop's group's proposals were impracticable and put forward a number of possible alternatives based on the fundamental assumption that the aims of a good divorce law are " to buttress, rather than undermine, the stability of marriage, and when, regrettably, a marriage has irretrievably broken down, to

---

[15]Cmd. 9678.
[16]Introduced by Mr. LEO ABSE, M.P. By withdrawing the controversial clauses, he enabled the rest of the bill to get on the statute book as the Matrimonial Causes Act of 1963.
[17]Cmnd. 3123. See further MacKenna, *Divorce by Consent and Divorce for Breakdown of Marriage*, 30 M.L.R. 121; Kahn-Freund, 30 M.L.R. 180.

enable the empty legal shell to be destroyed with the maximum fairness and the minimum bitterness, distress and humiliation ".

The Divorce Reform Act.—The consequence of these two reports was the passing of the Divorce Reform Act 1969. Its essential principle is the abolition of all the old grounds for divorce and their replacement by one ground: that the marriage has irretrievably broken down. This, however, may be established only by proof of one or more of five facts set out in the Act. The old bars to divorce, both absolute (like condonation) and discretionary (like the petitioner's own adultery), are abolished, but various safeguards are to be found to protect the spouse whose conduct has not, on the face of it, brought about the breakdown. Because of the fears expressed that parties (particularly wives) divorced against their will could well suffer financial hardship, the Act did not come into force until 1st January, 1971. This enabled Parliament to pass the Matrimonial Proceedings and Property Act of 1970, which has reformed the whole law of maintenance and other ancillary relief in the High Court and divorce county courts. Apart from a few sections which came into operation on 1st August, 1970, this Act also came into force on 1st January, 1971.[18]

2. PETITIONS AND DECREES

Petitions.—All proceedings must now be begun in a divorce county court. County courts have jurisdiction to try *undefended* petitions.[19]

Petitions during the first three years of Marriage.— When the grounds for divorce were extended in 1937, a counterbalancing restriction was placed upon the presentation of a petition during the first three years of the marriage.[20] No petition may be presented during this period, partly to prevent persons from rushing into marriage and partly to prevent them from rushing out of it again without at least having some time to try to make a success of it. But in case an arbitrary application of this rule should work injustice to some petitioners, the court has power to give leave to present a petition before the expiration of the period if " the case is one of exceptional hardship suffered by the petitioner or of exceptional depravity on the part of the respondent ".[1] The courts have declined to fetter their discretion by

---

[18]For a critical examination of the provisions of the Divorce Reform Act 1969, see Passingham, *The Divorce Reform Act 1969;* Levin, 33 M.L.R. 632. For comparison with other legislation in the Commonwealth, see Selby, *The Development of Divorce Law in Australia,* 29 M.L.R. 473; Holden, *Divorce in the Commonwealth,* 20 I.C.L.Q. 58.

[19]Matrimonial Causes Act 1967, s. 1. See *ante,* p. 4.

[20]See now the Matrimonial Causes Act 1965, s. 2. But a petitioner may always base a petition upon any matter that occurred during the first three years of the marriage: s. 2 (3).

[1]*Ibid.,* s. 2 (2). The case cannot be tried twice. Hence the court must decide whether the allegations, *if true,* amount to exceptional hardship or depravity; it may also take into account the facts disclosed in the petition and any other evidence available at this stage: *W.* v. *W.,* [1966] 2 All E.R. 889; [1967] P. 291; *C.* v. *C.,* [1967] 1 All E.R. 928; [1967] P. 298. If leave is given but it appears to the court at the hearing that it was obtained by the petitioner's misrepresentation or concealment of the nature of the case, the court may either dismiss the petition or grant a decree nisi on condition that it is not made absolute until three years from the date of the marriage: Matrimonial Causes Act 1965, s. 5 (5); *Stroud* v. *Stroud,* [1963] 3 All E.R. 539.

laying down any general rules for its exercise,[2] but it should be noticed that the hardship or depravity must be exceptional, so the mere fact that the respondent has behaved in such a way that the petitioner cannot reasonably be expected to live with him (which the Act itself envisages) cannot *per se* be a ground for giving leave.[3] In particular the court must have regard to the interests of the children of the family[4] and the probability of a reconciliation between the spouses if leave is not given.[5]

There may be exceptional hardship even though the petitioner has brought about the situation himself or herself. Thus in *W.* v. *W.*[6] it was held that the fact that the wife was pregnant by another man whom she wished to marry was relevant but in the circumstances was not sufficient to entitle her to petition immediately because the child could be legitimated after its birth: the position might well have been different, however, if worrying about the situation had brought the wife to the verge of a nervous breakdown.

Divorce after previous Proceedings.—One of the provisions of the Matrimonial Causes Act of 1937 was designed to help the possibility of reconciliation without slamming the door to divorce if the attempt failed. If a husband, say, commits adultery or deserts his wife, she may wish for some form of matrimonial relief less than divorce in the hope of a reconciliation; on the other hand, there would be a danger that, if this hope were not fulfilled, she might later be unable to obtain a divorce because of the difficulty of proving the alleged offence or, in the case of desertion, because she had consented to the separation by obtaining a judicial separation or separation order. Consequently, it is now provided that on a petition for divorce the court *may* treat any previous decree of judicial separation or any order made under the Matrimonial Proceedings (Magistrates' Courts) Act 1960 as sufficient evidence of the ground on which it was granted provided that the petitioner gives evidence in the later divorce proceedings.[7]

---

[2] See *Fisher* v. *Fisher*, [1948] P. 263, C.A.

[3] *Brewer* v. *Brewer*, [1964] 1 All E.R. 539, C.A., where the court was divided on the question whether it should consider the probability of hardship likely to be suffered in the future if leave were not given. See also *Hillier* v. *Hillier*, [1958] 2 All E.R. 261, C.A.; [1958] P. 186. Some examples of cases in which the court has exercised its discretion in the past are given by DENNING, L.J., in *Bowman* v. *Bowman*, [1949] 2 All E.R. 127, 128-129, C.A.; [1949] P. 353, 356-357.

[4] Matrimonial Proceedings and Property Act 1970, s. 35. For the meaning of " child of the family ", see *post*, p. 287.

[5] Matrimonial Causes Act 1965, s. 2 (2); *C.* v. *C.* (*supra*). The court can refer suitable cases to the court welfare officer: see *Practice Direction*, [1971] 1 All E.R. 894; *S.* v. *S.*, [1967] 3 All E.R. 139, 141; [1968] P. 185, 188-189.

[6] [1966] 2 All E.R. 889; [1967] P. 291.

[7] See now Matrimonial Causes Act 1965, s. 3 (1), (2), as amended by the Divorce Reform Act 1969, Sched. 1. But the court is not bound to treat the previous finding as conclusive. If previous proceedings have been brought in the High Court, the parties are generally bound by any findings of facts in issue *provided that they have been the subject of investigation and adjudication.* This applies in any subsequent proceedings in the High Court or in an inferior court, but proceedings in a magistrates' court will apparently not estop a party from alleging or denying the same facts later in the High Court. A divorce county court is now presumably in the same position as the High Court. Nor does an estoppel bind the court, which is under a statutory duty to investigate the facts alleged by each party. See *ante*, pp. 68-69, and *Thoday* v. *Thoday*, [1964] 1 All E.R. 341, C.A.; [1964] P. 181, and the cases there cited.

The special application of these provisions when the petition is based upon desertion will be considered below.[8]

The Decree and its Effects.—The decree is made in two stages: the decree nisi, followed by the decree absolute. Subject to the provisions of section 17 of the Matrimonial Proceedings and Property Act 1970, when the welfare of children is involved,[9] the petitioner may apply for the decree to be made absolute at any time after the expiration of three months from the granting of the decree nisi unless the court fixes a shorter time in the particular case; if the petitioner fails to apply for a decree absolute, the respondent may make the application at any time after the expiration of three months from the earliest date on the which the petitioner could have applied.[10] The purpose of the delay is to enable the Queen's Proctor[11] or anyone else to intervene to show cause why the decree should not be made absolute.

Whether the decree is one of divorce or presumption of death and dissolution, the marriage ceases as soon as the decree is made absolute[12] and either spouse is then free to remarry.[13] The decree nisi does not have this effect, and if either party remarries before that decree is made absolute, the second marriage will be void. If the decree absolute is void (as it will be if no order relating to the children of the family has been made under section 17 of the Matrimonial Proceedings and Property Act[14]) or is rescinded (which it may be if it is obtained contrary to the rules of substantial justice or of the requirements of the Act[15]), the second marriage will thereby automatically become void *ab initio*.[16]

---

[8]*Post*, p. 211.

[9]See *post*, pp. 288-289.

[10]Matrimonial Causes Act 1965, ss. 5 (7) and 7 (2); Matrimonial Causes (Decree Absolute) General Order 1957.

[11]This much maligned officer is not (as is sometimes supposed) a sort of official snooper. This popular misconception of his functions arises from the fact that, under the old law, if he received information that there might be some bar to the divorce which had not been disclosed (for example, the petitioner's own adultery), it might be his duty to investigate and, if necessary, intervene and place the facts before the court. His assistance may be invoked by the court itself, *e.g.* if an undefended suit presents a difficult point of law which counsel for the Queen's Proctor can then argue. See the Matrimonial Causes Act 1965, s. 6, as amended by the Divorce Reform Act 1969, s. 9 (2) and Sched. 2, and the Report of the Morton Commission, Cmd. 9678, paras. 947-968.

[12]The decree dissolves the marriage *status* and not the marriage *ceremony: Thynne* v. *Thynne*, [1955] 3 All E.R. 129, C.A.; [1955] P. 272. In this case the parties, who had already been married secretly, went through a second form of marriage which was therefore a nullity. In the wife's petition for divorce and the decrees made thereon the particulars of the *second* ceremony were inserted. It was held that the decree nisi and the decree absolute could be amended so as to make it clear that the parties' marriage had been dissolved.

[13]This is the combined effect of the Matrimonial Causes Act 1965, ss. 8 (1) and 14 (4), and the Judicature (Consolidation) Act 1925, s. 31 (1) (e). A decree nisi must not be made absolute if an appeal is pending: *Lloyd-Davies* v. *Lloyd-Davies*, [1947] 1 All E.R. 161, C.A.; [1947] P. 53. No clergyman of the Church of England or of the Church in Wales can be compelled to marry any divorced person during the lifetime of his or her former spouse or to permit his church or chapel to be used for the solemnization of such a marriage: Matrimonial Causes Act 1965, s. 8 (2).

[14]See *post*, p. 289.

[15]See Tolstoy, *Divorce*, 7th Ed., 286.

[16]*Rogers* v. *Rogers*, [1962] C.L.Y. 1045.

3. THE GROUND FOR DIVORCE

By section 1 of the Divorce Reform Act 1969, there has been only one ground for divorce since 1st January, 1971: that the marriage has broken down irretrievably. Irretrievable breakdown, however, may be established only by proving one or more of the five facts set out in section 2 (1). If any of these facts is proved, the court must pronounce a decree nisi (subject to certain exceptions mentioned below) unless it is satisfied that the marriage has not irretrievably broken down.[17] In other words, proof of any of these facts raises a presumption of breakdown; the court must enquire into all the facts, but in practical terms the burden on the petitioner is solely to prove one of the facts whilst that on the respondent in a defended suit is to show that the marriage has not broken down irretrievably.

We must now examine the five facts set out in the statute.

Respondent's Adultery.—The first fact on which the petitioner may rely is that the respondent has committed adultery *and* that the petitioner finds it intolerable to live with the respondent.[18]

The meaning of adultery has already been considered.[19] It will be seen that the Act has accepted the fact that adultery may be a symptom of breakdown rather than a cause of it and that an isolated act may not even be a symptom. Whether or not the petitioner finds life with the respondent intolerable is clearly a question of fact and the test appears to be subjective: did this petitioner find it intolerable to live with this respondent? If the court is satisfied of this fact, it seems quite irrelevant that the petitioner's attitude is wholly unreasonable.[20] Although the respondent may be able to bring evidence in rebuttal, in practice it may prove very difficult to go behind the petitioner's own statement in the witness box.

Two matters are not clear. First, must there be a causal connection between the two limbs of this condition? In other words, must the petitioner find it intolerable to live with the respondent because of his adultery, or is it sufficient, as was held in *Goodrich* v. *Goodrich*,[21] that the petitioner finds it intolerable to live with him anyway, for example because of his unpleasant personal habits? One suspects that the legislature meant the former and the courts may therefore interpret the section in that way, but this would certainly involve departing from the literal construction of the words.[1] Secondly, although the former bars to divorce have all been abolished, one doubts whether the courts will be prepared to let a petitioner rely on an act of adultery at which he has connived. If they hold that there must be a connection between

---

[17]S. 2 (3).

[18]S. 2 (1) (a).

[19]*Ante*, pp. 149-150. Unless the court otherwise orders, any person still alive with whom it is alleged that the respondent (whether wife or husband) has committed adultery must be joined as a party to the proceedings: Matrimonial Causes Act 1965, ss. 4 and 44; Matrimonial Causes Rules 1968, r. 13.

[20]Contrast the wording of s. 2 (1) (b), *infra*, and see Passingham, *The Divorce Reform Act 1969*, 8; Levin, 33 M.L.R. 632, 634; Barton, *Questions on the Divorce Reform Act 1969*, 86 L.Q.R. 348.

[21](1971), 115 Sol. Jo. 303 (adultery and rejection of offer of reconciliation).

[1]Passingham and Levin, *supra*. *Cf.* the provisions of s. 3 (3), *post*, p. 214, n.[3]

K

the adultery and the petitioner's attitude towards the respondent, the problem will presumably not arise, because they are hardly likely to take the view that a spouse can be heard to say that he finds life with the other intolerable as a consequence of adultery which he himself has brought about. If, on the other hand, they hold that there need be no such connection, they might still fall back on the general principle of *Volenti non fit injuria* and refuse to let him base a petition on acts which he has brought about himself.

Respondent's Behaviour.—The petitioner may establish that the marriage has irretrievably broken down by showing that the respondent has behaved in such a way that the petitioner cannot reasonably be expected to live wih him.[2]

It will be seen that this fact is different from the last in that the court must be satisfied that the petitioner cannot *reasonably* be expected to live with the respondent: the test is therefore objective. Obviously, however, a large number of personal factors will have to be taken into account. For example, if two husbands behave in identical ways, it might be unreasonable for a young, healthy woman to withdraw from cohabitation if she has offered provocation to her husband, but perfectly reasonable for an older, sick and relatively blameless woman to do so. Again, the state of the respondent's mind and his knowledge, belief, motive and intention all become relevant. If this approach is correct, the similarity with cruelty and desertion immediately becomes apparent, and the view generally held is that the respondent's behaviour will have to have the grave and weighty quality necessary to found a charge of cruelty or constructive desertion or to be a defence to a charge of simple desertion.[3] It is not necessary, however, to prove the injury to health essential to cruelty or the separation essential to constructive desertion.

Even if this view is accepted, some doubts remain. Presumably, as in the case of desertion,[4] the petitioner may not complain of the respondent's behaviour before marriage, even though he does not discover it until after the marriage. This would mean, for example, that a husband could not get a divorce on discovering that his wife was pregnant *per alium* at the time of the marriage. It is less clear whether it will be sufficient for the petitioner to establish conduct which could give rise to constructive desertion but could not amount to cruelty. Suppose, for example, that a husband expels his wife from the matrimonial home or leads her to conclude, mistakenly but reasonably, that he has been guilty of adultery. It is arguable that in neither case would it be reasonable for the wife to continue to cohabit with him in such circumstances: on the other hand it would be highly anomalous if suspicion of adultery were sufficient to give the court jurisdiction to grant a divorce whilst proof of its commission by itself is not.[5] Similarly,

---

[2]Divorce Reform Act 1969, s. 2 (1) (b).
[3]Passingham, *The Divorce Reform Act 1969*, 9-10; Levin, 33 M.L.R. 632, 635. See *ante*, pp. 156, 158 and 173, and *cf. Monk* v. *Monk* (1971), *Times*, April 6th.
[4]See *ante*, p. 174.
[5]Or is the respondent's adultery itself such behaviour that the petitioner can no longer reasonably be expected to live with him? If this is so, s. 2 (1) (a) appears to be redundant. See also Barton, *loc. cit.*

there is little justification for holding that, if a husband tells his wife to pack her bags and she goes, she can petition for divorce forthwith, whereas if she stands firm and lets him leave her, she must wait for two years. In some cases the court might hold that it is not satisfied that the marriage has broken down irretrievably; consistency and justice might be better served if the courts hold that, to satisfy this fact, the behaviour must be such that, had it injured the petitioner's health, it would have amounted to cruelty.

Respondent's Desertion.—The petitioner may show that the marriage has irretrievably broken down by proving that the respondent has deserted the petitioner for a continuous period of two years immediately preceding the presentation of the petition.[6]

Desertion has the same meaning as it has in the Matrimonial Proceedings (Magistrates' Courts) Act.[7] But to establish irretrievable breakdown as the ground for divorce, it must have lasted for a continuous period of at least two years. Subject to a statutory exception which will be mentioned later,[8] two or more periods cannot be added together so as to give a period of two years in the aggregate; consequently if, say, a husband deserts his wife for a year, resumes cohabitation for a period of eight months and then deserts her again, the two years' period must be calculated from the date on which he left her for the second time. Moreover, the period must immediately precede the presentation of the petition: in other words, it must still be running when the proceedings are commenced. To this, however, there is one exception, for if the petitioner has already obtained a judicial separation or a magistrates' order *containing a non-cohabitation clause* and the respondent had been in desertion for a continuous period of two years preceding the institution of the earlier proceedings, the petitioner may rely on that period of desertion to establish irretrievable breakdown provided that the decree or order has been in force continuously and the parties have not resumed cohabitation since it was granted.[9] This provision is necessary because the decree or order prevents desertion from continuing[10] and a petitioner contemplating obtaining a decree or order in the hope of a reconciliation in the future might be tempted to petition for divorce immediately rather than run the risk of finishing up with no ground for divorce at all.

The requirement of a minimum continuous period has resulted in another difference in the law from that applicable in a magistrates' court. If a respondent already in desertion becomes so insane as not to be able to retain the *animus deserendi*, his desertion must come to an end and the petitioner's power to obtain a divorce alleging this fact would go. This might work hardship if the evidence indicates that the respondent would have remained in desertion had he not become insane.

---

[6]Divorce Reform Act 1969, s. 2 (1) (c).

[7]See *ante*, pp. 161 *et seq.*

[8]*Post*, p. 215.

[9]Matrimonial Causes Act 1965, s. 3 (3). *Cf.* the provisions of s. 3 (2), *ante*, p. 207. Note that s. 3 (3) refers to a magistrates' order containing a non-cohabitation clause, whilst s. 3 (2) refers to any order made by a magistrates' court. Other orders would not, of course, prevent desertion from continuing.

[10]See *ante*, pp. 165-166.

Hence it is expressly provided that *for the purpose of divorce and judicial separation* the court may treat the desertion as continuing in such circumstances.[11]

Two Years' Separation.—The petitioner may establish that the marriage has broken down irretrievably by showing that the spouses have lived apart for a continuous period of two years immediately preceding the presentation of the petition *and* that the respondent consents to the decree being granted.[12] This is one of the most controversial provisions of the whole Act because it introduced, albeit to a limited extent, divorce by consent.

" Living apart " in this context means living in two separate households and is therefore identical with the concept of separation necessary to constitute desertion.[13] Two years' separation as a fact establishing irretrievable breakdown also resembles two years' desertion for this purpose in that, save for the statutory exception to be mentioned,[14] the period must be continuous and the separation must be continuing when the petition is presented. But in the case of two years' separation it is immaterial how the separation came about: it could be as the result of an agreement or the petitioner's own desertion or it could be involuntary, for example as the result of one spouse's serving a long term of imprisonment. It could also begin as a temporary separation (for example, until the husband found a suitable matrimonial home) and later turn into a permanent one[15].

It will be observed that the respondent's consent to the decree must be proved: it is not sufficient that he does not oppose the making of the decree.[16] It follows that this fact cannot be alleged if the respondent cannot be found or cannot consent because of mental illness. Steps must be taken to inform the respondent of the consequences of his consenting.[17] He may withdraw his consent at any time until a decree nisi is made, and if he does so (or refuses to give his consent in the first place) and two years' separation is the only fact alleged by the petitioner, the proceedings must be stayed.[18]

After a decree nisi has been made, the respondent has only a qualified power to withdraw his consent and prevent the decree from being made absolute. If the court has found that two years' separation was the only fact on which the petitioner was entitled to rely, the respondent may apply to have the decree nisi rescinded on the ground that the petitioner misled him (whether intentionally or unintentionally) about

---

[11]Divorce Reform Act 1969, s. 2 (4). *Cf. ante*, p. 165.

[12]*Ibid.*, s. 2 (1) (d).   [13]*Ibid.* s. 2 (5).

[14]*Post*, p. 215.

[15]Rayden, *Divorce*, 11th Ed., 273, and Tolstoy, *Divorce*, 7th Ed., 98-100, argue that as cohabitation can continue even though the spouses are no longer living under the same roof (*ante*, p. 94), one or both spouses must also have decided to break off cohabitation. But see Cretney, *When does " Living Apart " start?* 115 Sol. Jo. 295.

[16]The usual way of proving consent is by producing the completed acknowledgment of service on which the respondent is expressly asked whether he consents to the decree if the petitioner relies on two years' separation: Matrimonial Causes Rules 1968, Form 4 (as amended by the Matrimonial Causes (Amendment No. 3) Rules 1970).

[17]Divorce Reform Act 1969, s. 2 (6). The consequences are printed on the Notice of Proceedings served on the respondent: Matrimonial Causes Rules 1968, Form 3 (as amended).

[18]Matrimonial Causes Rules 1968, r. 15A (as amended).

any matter which he took into account in deciding to give his consent.[19] A change of mind after the decree has been made absolute will, of course, be too late.

Five Years' Separation.—The last fact on which a petitioner may rely is that the spouses have lived apart for a continuous period of five years immediately preceding the presentation of the petition.[20] This provision is even more controversial than the last because it enables the marriage to be dissolved against the will of a spouse who has committed no matrimonial offence and who has not been responsible for the breakdown of the marriage. On the one hand it has been hailed as a measure that will bring relief to hundreds of couples who are now living in stable illicit unions but are unable to marry because one or both of them cannot secure release from another union; on the other hand it has been castigated as a " Cassanova's charter ".

This fact is identical with the last except that the period of separation is five years and the respondent's consent is not required. It will thus be seen that a decree could be granted even though the respondent is hopelessly insane.

These provisions represent an unhappy compromise between the matrimonial offence theory and the irretrievable breakdown theory which is unlikely to commend itself to the supporters of either. One of the advantages of adopting the irretrievable breakdown theory is that the decree merely recites a state of affairs without attributing blame or passing any sort of moral judgment, and one would hope that the bitterness might be taken out of some of the proceedings if one party were not to be labelled as technically innocent and the other as technically guilty when in many cases the conduct of both has contributed to the collapse of their marriage. But this is precisely what the court will still have to do if any of the first three facts is alleged. Furthermore, in the other two cases it is arguable that the separation either indicates that the marriage has broken down or it does not and the respondent's consent should not therefore affect the length of time it has to run.

4. RECONCILIATION

The emphasis of the whole of the Divorce Reform Act is on irretrievable breakdown and thus on the possibility of reconciliation. A number of provisions in section 3 of the Act are designed to promote this.

Adjournment of Proceedings.—If at any stage it appears that there is a reasonable possibility of a reconciliation between the spouses, the court may adjourn the proceedings for such period as it thinks fit to enable attempts at reconciliation to be made.[21]

---

[19]Divorce Reform Act 1969, s. 5. The matters on which a respondent is most likely to be misled are those relating to financial provisions.
[20]*Ibid.*, s. 2 (1) (e).
[21]*Ibid.*, s. 3. (2). The case is to be referred to the court welfare officer: *Practice Direction*, [1971] 1 All E.R. 894.

Solicitor's Certificate.—If the petitioner instructs a solicitor to act for him (as he normally will), the latter is required to certify whether or not he has discussed with the petitioner the possibility of a reconciliation and given him the names and addresses of persons qualified to help effect a reconciliation between estranged spouses.[1] There is no indication of the consequences of a failure to have such a discussion: one possibility is that in some cases the court may feel bound to exercise its power to adjourn the proceedings to see whether a reconciliation can be effected.

It is doubtful whether this provision will achieve very much. Most solicitors will presumably discuss the prospects of reconciliation with their clients before launching divorce proceedings anyway; others will turn this into a formality unlikely to lead to any real attempt to resume married life. In most cases the estrangement will probably be too deep by the time either spouse seeks legal advice for there to be any real chance of their coming together again.

Cohabitation.—Certain provisions of the Matrimonial Causes Act of 1963 were designed to enable the spouses to try to effect a reconciliation by resuming cohabitation for a limited period without prejudicing their rights to petition for divorce if the attempts failed. Insofar as they altered the law relating to condonation, they still apply to proceedings brought in magistrates' courts.[2] In proceedings for divorce and judicial separation the principle has been considerably extended by three further provisions contained in section 3 of the Divorce Reform Act.

Adultery.—If the parties live with each other in the same household for any period or periods not exceeding six months in all after the petitioner discovered that the respondent had committed adultery, their living together for this time is to be disregarded in determining whether the petitioner finds it intolerable to live with the respondent. But if they live with each other for more than six months, the petitioner cannot rely on the adultery at all.[3] The similarity with the law of condonation applied in magistrates' courts is obvious, but three important differences will be noticed. More than one period is permitted, the total period must not exceed *six* months, and the resumption of cohabitation does not have to be expressly with a view to effecting a reconciliation.

Respondent's Behaviour.—A similar rule applies if the petitioner relies on the respondent's behaviour. If the parties have lived with each other in the same household for a period or periods not exceeding six months in all after the date of the final incident relied on by the petitioner, this is to be disregarded in determining whether he can reasonably be expected to live with the respondent.[4] But in this case

---

[1] *Ibid.*, s. 3 (1). See *Practice Direction*, [1971] 1 All E.R. 63.
[2] See now the Matrimonial Causes Act 1965, s. 42 (2), *ante*, p. 193.
[3] Divorce Reform Act 1969, s. 3 (3), (6). This seems to be a further indication of the need to show a causal connection between the respondent's adultery and the petitioner's attitude: see *ante*, p. 209.
[4] *Ibid.*, s. 3 (4), (6).

the Act does not expressly state what the position is to be if they cohabit for more than six months. This is obviously strong evidence that the petitioner can be expected to live with the other spouse, but the deliberate omission of any express enactment (as appears in the case of adultery) implies that it is not to be conclusive evidence. It may well be difficult for the court to resist the inference that the petitioner can be expected to live with the respondent or even that the marriage has not irretrievably broken down, but it may do so if the petitioner can show some other reason for his or her actions, for example if he or she cohabited for the protection of the children or because there was nowhere else to live.[5]

Desertion and Separation.—In determining whether there has been two years' desertion or two or five years' separation immediately preceding the presentation of the petition, the court must similarly disregard any period or periods not exceeding six months in which the parties have lived together in the same household. In these cases, however, the periods of cohabitation must be ignored in calculating the length of time the parties have been apart.[6] Hence if the husband deserts his wife, they then live together for four months, and he then deserts her again, she will not be able to petition for divorce alleging his desertion until two years and four months have elapsed from his first deserting her. This is the only exception to the rule that two or more periods of desertion or separation cannot be added together to give a period of two or five years in the aggregate.

5. HARDSHIP, FINANCIAL PROTECTION AND PROTECTION OF CHILDREN

Two provisions of the Divorce Reform Act, contained in sections 4 and 6, are designed to give protection to the respondent when the petitioner relies on two or five years' separation—in other words when the petition does not disclose that there has been any fault on the respondent's part.

Hardship to the Respondent.—If the petitioner relies on *five years'* separation, by section 4 of the Act the respondent may oppose the grant of the decree nisi on the ground that the dissolution of the marriage will result in grave financial or other hardship to him and that it would be wrong in all the circumstances to dissolve the marriage. If the court holds that this is the only fact on which the petitioner is entitled to rely, it must dismiss the petition if it is satisfied that the respondent's allegations are true.

The use of the word " wrong " in this context is obscure and ambiguous and probably does no more than give the court a discretion.

---

[5]*Cf.* the inference of condonation from cohabitation, *ante*, p. 192. See also Levin, 33 M.L.R. 632, 640-641, where the writer argues that, if the respondent has committed adultery and the spouses have cohabitated for more than six months since the petitioner discovered it, the latter might still succeed in establishing irretrievable breakdown by showing that the adultery amounted to such behaviour that the petitioner cannot reasonably be expected to live with the respondent.

[6]Divorce Reform Act 1969, s. 3 (5), (6).

It is unfortunate that the legislature did not give a clearer indication of how it is to be exercised: perhaps the most reasonable test to be applied is the balance of hardship which each party is likely to suffer according to whether the decree is granted or withheld. The type of hardship most likely to be suffered by the respondent divorced against his or her will is obviously financial, but the use of the words " financial *or other* hardship " suggests that such matters as conscientious objection to divorce, injury to feelings and the claims of justice should all be taken into account,[7] although they are likely to be given less weight. Some evidence in support of this view is given by the wording of the section itself which requires the court to consider all the circumstances including specifically the spouses' conduct and the interests of the spouses, any children and any other person concerned. It will thus be seen that the court must consider, for example, the position of a person whom the petitioner wishes to marry and of any children who will be legitimated by their marriage.

One of the difficulties facing a wife divorced against her will is the potential loss of the right to claim a pension as her husband's widow and of national insurance benefits by virtue of his contributions. That this is at least one of the points that Parliament had in mind is shown by the fact that " hardship " for the purpose of this section is defined as including the loss of the chance of acquiring any benefit which the respondent might acquire if the marriage were not dissolved.

Financial Protection for the Respondent.—By section 6 of the Act, if the court pronouncing a decree nisi holds that the only fact on which the petitioner was entitled to rely was *two or five years'* separation, the respondent may apply for the decree not to be made absolute unless the court is satisfied (a) that the petitioner should not be required to make financial provision for the respondent *or* (b) that the financial provision made by the petitioner for the respondent is reasonable and fair or the best that can be made in the circumstances.

This section is designed to afford further protection to the respondent by giving him another weapon that can be used against the petitioner. The threat to delay the latter's remarriage by holding up the decree absolute may be perfectly proper if the petitioner is deliberately evading his financial responsibilities, but obviously it can be abused. Consequently, even though the court finds that the petitioner has not made such financial provision as he should have made, it may nevertheless make the decree absolute if it appears that there are circumstances making it desirable that this should not be delayed *and* the court has obtained a satisfactory undertaking from the petitioner that he will make such financial provision for the respondent as the court may approve.

In deciding what financial provision (if any) the respondent ought to make for the petitioner, the court is bound to consider all the circumstances including specifically the age, health, conduct, earning capacity, financial resources and financial obligations of each of the spouses, and

---

[7] Barton, *loc. cit.*

also the probable financial position of the respondent if the marriage is dissolved and the petitioner dies first.

A comparison of the provisions of sections 4 and 6 shows three important differences between them. First, section 4 applies only to five years' separation, whilst section 6 applies to two or five years' separation. In practice, however, it is unlikely that a respondent will invoke section 6 in the case of two years' separation because he (or she) will consent to the divorce only if he is satisfied of the matters mentioned in the Act and, if he has been misled, he can apply to have the decree nisi rescinded under section 5.[8] Secondly, section 4 applies if there is grave financial or other hardship whilst section 6 refers at the highest to reasonable and fair financial provision. Finally, and reflecting the second point of difference, section 4 enables the respondent to oppose the making of the decree nisi *in limine*, whilst section 6 merely enables him to delay the decree absolute.

Protection of Children.—As we shall see,[9] the court may not pronounce a decree absolute unless it has made an order with reference to the arrangements for the welfare of the children of the family. This provision differs from section 6 of the Divorce Reform Act in that it applies in all cases, whereas section 6 applies only if the respondent invokes it, and a decree absolute will be void if the court fails to make the order with respect to children.

6. THE WORKING OF THE DIVORCE REFORM ACT

It is far too soon to see how the new law is going to work in practice, but one or two guesses as to its probable operation may be justified.

Over 90% of petitions under the old law were undefended. In many other cases cross-petitions were filed: in other words, both spouses were anxious to have the marriage dissolved but each wished the other to appear as the guilty party on the record. The usual reason for this was that a guilty wife was in a worse position than a technically innocent one when it came to the question of the award of maintenance. Now that the cause of the breakdown of the marriage, rather than the technical innocence or guilt of the spouses, is to be taken into consideration when the court hears an application for financial provision, there is less incentive to oppose the making of the decree and it is therefore reasonable to assume that many more petitions will be undefended. This means that the two vital issues between the spouses will usually be those of the welfare of the children and financial provision, and every attempt should be made by the parties and their advisers to come to an acceptable arrangement out of court. To help them, a procedure exists by which the parties (or either of them) may refer to the court any agreement or arrangement made or proposed between them relating to

---

[8]Passingham, *The Divorce Reform Act 1969*, 27-28. For rescission under s. 5, see *ante*, pp. 212-213.

[9]*Post*, p. 288.

the proceedings, so as to obtain the judge's views as to its reasonableness.[10] This procedure can be used even before the petition is presented in order that the parties may have a ruling at a preliminary stage. This is obviously of particular importance if the petitioner proposes to rely on two years' separation because presumably the respondent will wish to be assured that acceptable arrangements will be made for her own financial provision and for the welfare of the children before consenting to the decree.

If the parties cannot agree on terms, the conduct of each and the responsibility of each for the breakdown of the marriage will become of considerable importance before the judge or registrar hearing an application for custody and access of the children or for financial provision.[11] It is in chambers, therefore, rather than in court, that counter-allegations and recrimination may well be heard in future.[12]

C. DIVORCE AND THE CONFLICT OF LAWS

Jurisdiction of English Courts.—An English court has jurisdiction to dissolve a marriage if the husband (and therefore the wife) is domiciled in England when the petition is presented.[13] In addition it also has jurisdiction now in the two cases set out in section 40 (1) of the Matrimonial Causes Act 1965.[14] The criticism of these extensions made before[15]—namely, that the decree may not be recognised by the parties' *lex domicilii* and thus that a limping marriage may result—applies equally in the case of divorce.

In all the above cases the substantive law to be applied is English.[16]

Recognition of Foreign Decrees.—Since the basis of jurisdiction in English law is domicile, English courts will always recognise a divorce which is recognised by the parties' *lex domicilii*. This will normally be by a decree of a competent court of the domicile,[17] but the process may be extra-judicial, for example by legislation, by a unilateral act of

---

[10]Divorce Reform Act 1969, s. 7; Matrimonial Causes Rules 1968, r. 6 (as amended). Under the old law of collusion (when arrangements could be referred to the court) whenever possible the same judge heard the application relating to the agreement and tried the suit to avoid the trial judge's holding that an agreement, which had already been accepted as reasonable, was improper. For the same reason, the same judge now ought to hear the application relating to the agreement and any other application for ancillary relief.

[11]See *post*, pp. 279 and 448.

[12]For a criticism of this position, see Cretney, *The Maintenance Quagmire*, 33 M.L.R. 662, at pp. 666 *et seq*.

[13]*Le Mesurier* v. *Le Mesurier*, [1895] A.C. 517, P.C.; *Leon* v. *Leon*, [1966] 3 All E.R. 820; [1967] P. 275. See North, 30 M.L.R. 333.

[14]See *ante*, p. 86.

[15]*Ante*, p. 86. For an example of the difficulties arising under s. 40, see *Sealey* v. *Callan*, [1953] 1 All E.R. 942; [1953] P. 135; and *cf*. Cheshire, *The International Validity of Divorces*, 61 L.Q.R. 352. See generally the Law Commission Working Paper No. 28.

[16]Either as the *lex domicilii* or under the provisions of the Matrimonial Causes Act 1965, s. 40 (2).

[17]*Harvey* v. *Farnie* (1882), 8 App. Cas. 43, H.L. The husband must be domiciled there at the commencement of the proceedings: *Mansell* v. *Mansell*, [1966] 2 All E.R. 391; [1967] P. 306; North, *loc. cit.*

one of the parties, or even by agreement.[18] Similarly, if the husband is domiciled in state X and obtains a divorce in the courts of state Y, it was held in *Armitage* v. *A.-G.*[19] that English courts will recognise the validity of this decree if it would be recognised by the courts of X. It is of course irrelevant by this test whether the grounds upon which the divorce is granted would be recognised by English municipal law.[20]

Subject to any statutory provisions to the contrary,[1] it is doubtful whether English courts would have recognised any exception to this rule before 1953: certainly they would not have done so if the husband's domicile was English.[2] But an inroad into the principle was made by the decision of the Court of Appeal in *Travers* v. *Holley* in that year.[3] In 1938 the husband and wife (both of whom were up till then domiciled in England) went to Australia. They lived in New South Wales until 1941 when the husband joined the Australian forces. He later transferred to the British forces and in 1944 the wife obtained a divorce in the New South Wales court on the grounds of his desertion. The court based its jurisdiction on his former domicile by virtue of a statute which corresponded with the provisions of section 40 (1) (a) of the English Matrimonial Causes Act 1965.[4] Both parties subsequently remarried, but the husband's second marriage was not a success and he then put the validity of this marriage in issue by petitioning for divorce from his first wife in England (whither he had returned) on the ground of her adultery with the man with whom she had later gone through a form of marriage. He alleged that the New South Wales decree was invalid as he was not domiciled there at the time it was made. The majority of the court were of the opinion that he had acquired a domicile of choice in New South Wales when he deserted his wife, and they all agreed that, even had he lost it after the desertion commenced, the decree would nevertheless be recognised in this country.

The principle underlying this decision is that, if English courts assume jurisdiction on a particular ground, they must recognise a jurisdiction claimed by a foreign court which is substantially the same. This was later approved by the majority of the House of Lords in *Indyka* v. *Indyka*.[5] In 1938 the husband, H, who was then domiciled in Czechoslovakia and was also apparently a Czech national, married W, a Czech citizen, in Czechoslovakia. They lived there until the German invasion of that country in 1939. H then escaped to Poland and ultimately came to England where he acquired a domicile. W stayed in Czechoslovakia and refused to join H thus (as the trial judge

[18]*Har-Shefi* v. *Har-Shefi*, [1953] 2 All E.R. 373; [1953] P. 220 (service of a Jewish bill of divorcement); *Russ* v. *Russ*, [1962] 3 All E.R. 193, C.A.; [1964] P. 315 (*talak*); *Qureshi* v. *Qureshi*, [1971] 3 All E.R. 325 (*talak*); *Lee* v. *Lau*, [1964] 2 All E.R. 248 (written agreement). See Graveson, *Divorce in the Conflict of Laws*, 17 M.L.R. 501.
[19][1906] P. 135, approved by LORD REID, LORD PEARCE and LORD WILBERFORCE in *Indyka* v. *Indyka*, [1967] 2 All E.R. 689, H.L.; [1969] 1 A.C. 33. See further Morris, *Recognition of Divorces granted without the Domicile*, 24 Can. Bar Rev. 73; Tuck, *Recognition of Foreign Divorces*, 25 Can. Bar Rev. 226.
[20]*Bater* v. *Bater*, [1906] P. 209, C.A.
[1]*E.g.*, the Colonial and Other Territories (Divorce Jurisdiction) Acts 1926-1950.
[2]*Shaw* v. *Gould* (1868), L.R. 3 H.L. 55, H.L.
[3][1953] 2 All E.R. 794, C.A.; [1953] P. 246.
[4]See *ante*, p. 86.
[5][1967] 2 All E.R. 689, H.L.; [1969] 1 A.C. 33.

found) putting herself in desertion. In 1949 W obtained a divorce in Czechoslovakia on the ground of deep disruption of marital relations. This decree took effect some ten months before the coming into force of the Law Reform (Miscellaneous Provisions) Act 1949, which for the first time gave the English courts jurisdiction to grant divorce on the ground of the wife's residence in this country for three years.[6] Ten years later H married R in England. R later petitioned for divorce, whereupon H alleged that this marriage was void by English law because English courts would not recognise the Czech decree of 1949. It was this question of recognition that came before the House of Lords.

LORD MORRIS, LORD PEARCE and LORD PEARSON all accepted that the principle of *Travers* v. *Holley* was right. But one difficulty was glossed over. At the time when the Czech decree was granted English courts had no jurisdiction to grant a decree on the basis of the wife's residence. The members of the House in effect took the view that, as the question before them was whether H was capable of marrying R in 1959, they should consider what jurisdiction English courts had then and not what jurisdiction they had had ten years earlier. But if the basis of jurisdiction is reciprocity, it is difficult to see how a change in the law of jurisdiction can retrospectively affect the law of recognition. As RUSSELL, L.J., asked in his dissenting judgment in the Court of Appeal,[7] would this change have retrospectively validated a second marriage if H had married before the Act of 1949 came into force or would it have retrospectively altered the law of succession if he had died intestate during this period? In truth the Lords' decision was dictated not by logic but by a desire to limit the number of limping marriages.

The principle of *Travers* v. *Holley* has been extended to cases where a foreign court has assumed jurisdiction on a ground technically different from our own, provided that the facts disclose a situation which would have given an English court jurisdiction *mutatis mutandis*. This occurred in *Robinson-Scott* v. *Robinson-Scott*,[8] where a court in Zurich had assumed jurisdiction by virtue of the fact that the petitioning wife had, by local law, a domicile in that canton. The decree was recognised because the wife had been resident in Zurich for three years immediately before she brought the proceedings and consequently the position was exactly comparable to that giving an English court jurisdiction under section 40 (1) (b) of the Matrimonial Causes Act 1965.

The real importance of *Indyka* v. *Indyka* lies in the fact that the House of Lords considered the whole question of the recognition of foreign divorces and seized the opportunity of restating the law on the

---

[6]See now s. 40 (1) (b) of the Matrimonial Causes Act 1965, *ante*, p. 86.

[7][1966] 3 All E.R. 583, 591, C.A.; [1967] P. 233, 263. It was for this reason that LATEY, J., refused to recognise the decree at first instance: [1966] 1 All E.R. 781; [1967] P. 233.

[8][1957] 3 All E.R. 473; [1958] P. 71, followed in *Brown* v. *Brown*, [1968] 2 All E.R. 11; [1968] P. 518. See also *Arnold* v. *Arnold*, [1957] 1 All E.R. 570; [1957] P. 237; *Manning* v. *Manning*, [1958] 1 All E.R. 291; [1958] P. 112.

subject.[9] All five members of the House were prepared to adopt a much wider basis for recognition than the classes of decrees already accepted, namely those recognised by the husband's *lex domicilii* and under the principle of *Travers* v. *Holley*. LORD REID felt that we should recognise decrees granted by the courts of the state in which the parties had their matrimonial home or with which they were most closely connected, whilst LORD PEARCE spoke of the " predominant country " with respect to them. LORD MORRIS, LORD PEARSON and LORD WILBERFORCE all emphasised that there must be a real and substantial connection between the petitioner and the country in question, and it seems to be this test which is the most likely to be adopted in the future. Obviously the parties' nationality and residence and the situation of the matrimonial home are all relevant in determining whether there is a real and substantial connection between them and the country in question, but none of these is conclusive. In *Indyka* v. *Indyka* Czechoslovakia was the country of the wife's residence, nationality and pre-marital domicile, and the only matrimonial home the parties had ever shared had been situated there. In three later cases English courts have recognised decrees obtained by the wife in the country of which she was a national, where she had had her pre-marital residence and domicile, and where she had returned after leaving her husband.[10] In another it was held that a wife domiciled in England had been validly divorced in Washington D.C. after $2\frac{1}{2}$ years' residence on the ground that, as she intended to make her home there, she had a real and substantial connection with the District.[11] On the other hand, the fact that the divorce was pronounced in the country where the parties had lived and where the marriage had been celebrated is not sufficient if they left it 16 years earlier and then acquired an English domicile and British nationality and the only other connection with the country in question was a few days' residence by the wife.[12]

Although in all the above cases the courts have been concerned with the connection between the party obtaining the decree (who happens to have been the wife) and the country in question, it is apparent that they will not concern themselves solely with the position of the petitioning wife. In *Tijanic* v. *Tijanic*[13] the parties, who were then Jugoslav nationals, had been married in Jugoslavia where they were domiciled. The husband later came to England where he acquired a domicile of choice and became a naturalised British subject. The wife stayed in Jugoslavia, where the husband ultimately obtained a divorce. The wife consented to his petition and the decree was technically

[9]See further North, *Recognition of Foreign Divorce Decrees*, 31 M.L.R. 257; Latey, *Recognition of Foreign Decrees of Divorce*, 16 I.C.L.Q. 982; Webb, *Travers* v. *Holley Reinterpreted, ibid.*, 997; Mann, 84 L.Q.R. 18; Lipstein, [1967] C.L.J. 182; Wade, 32 M.L.R. 441; Cretney, 119 New L.J. 1121.
[10]*Angelo* v. *Angelo*, [1967] 3 All E.R. 314; *Brown* v. *Brown*, [1968] 2 All E.R. 11; [1968] P. 518; *Hornett* v. *Hornett*, [1971] 1 All E.R. 98.
[11]*Welsby* v. *Welsby*, [1970] 2 All E.R. 467.
[12]*Peters* v. *Peters*, [1967] 3 All E.R. 318; [1968] P. 275. *Cf.* the words of LORD PEARCE in *Indyka* v. *Indyka*, [1967] 2 All E.R. 689, 716, H.L.; [1969] 1 A.C. 33, 88: " It is clear that [the] court is simply purveying divorce to foreigners who wish to buy it; and that does not accord with our notions of genuine divorce "
[13][1967] 3 All E.R. 976; [1968] P. 181.

granted to both parties. In these circumstances SIMON, P., held that, as the decree had been granted to the wife, albeit on the husband's petition, it should be recognised following *Travers* v. *Holley* and the wider principle enunciated in *Indyka* v. *Indyka*. CUMMING-BRUCE, J., went rather further in *Blair* v. *Blair*.[14] The husband, whose domicile of origin was English, decided to remain permanently in Norway on marrying a Norwegian woman and he thus acquired a domicile of choice in that country. The parties later came to England for a temporary period, but the wife became unhappy and returned to Norway where she and the husband then jointly obtained a decree of judicial separation. Had the wife waited, she could have obtained a decree of divorce based on the separation, but in order to expedite matters she asked the husband to petition on the ground of her adultery. Shortly before he did so, he decided to abandon his Norwegian home and career and thus lost his Norwegian domicile. It was held that the situation of the matrimonial home in Norway and the husband's recent Norwegian domicile established a real and substantial connection with Norway with the result that the decree would be recognised—a decision reinforced by the fact that, had the parties waited, they could have joined together in obtaining a divorce and thus brought themselves within *Tijanic* v. *Tijanic*. Finally, in *Mayfield* v. *Mayfield*[15] SIMON, P., extended the principle of *Indyka* v. *Indyka* to the case where the *respondent* wife had a real and substantial connection with the country in question. The wife, who was a German national, returned to Germany where her husband, a British subject domiciled in England, obtained a decree of divorce. As SIMON, P., pointed out, the decree operated on the status of the wife and consequently it was irrelevant that it was her husband, and not she, who had been the petitioner.

Two attempts to extend the principles underlying *Travers* v. *Holley* and *Indyka* v. *Indyka* have produced conflicting decisions.[16] In the first, *Mountbatten* v. *Mountbatten*,[17] the wife, who had been resident in New York for more than three years, had obtained a divorce in Mexico. The courts of the latter state had jurisdiction based on the *de facto* presence of the wife in the country and also on an express submission to the jurisdiction by both spouses. The Mexican decree was recognised by the courts of New York. The husband, who was at all times domiciled in England, then petitioned in this country for a declaration that his marriage had been validly dissolved by the Mexican decree, arguing that, since English courts would always recognise the validity of a decree recognised by the husband's *lex domicilii*, they must now recognise a decree which would be recognised by the courts of the state in which the wife had been resident for three years preceding the

---

[14][1968] 3 All E.R. 639.
[15][1969] 2 All E.R. 219; [1969] P. 119.
[16]*Quaere* whether there was not also an unjustifiable extension of the principle in *Munt* v. *Munt*, [1970] 2 All E.R. 516 (divorce granted to a husband by a court in Virginia after twelve months' residence recognised in this country on the ground that he proposed to stay in that state although there was an express finding that he was still domiciled in England).
[17][1959] 1 All E.R. 99; [1959] P. 43.

petition. DAVIES, J., however, rejected this argument, holding that *Armitage* v. *A.-G.*[18] turned upon the English view that the parties' *lex domicilii* should control their status and that the principle stated there could not be amalgamated with the principle of reciprocity laid down in *Travers* v. *Holley* so as to produce the result desired by the husband. In the later case of *Mather* v. *Mahoney*,[19] however, *Armitage* v. *A.-G.* was successfully amalgamated with *Indyka* v. *Indyka*. The parties were domiciled in England, but the wife was an American citizen resident in Pennsylvania. She obtained a divorce in Nevada which was recognised in Pennsylvania. It was held that, since she had a real and substantial connection with Pennsylvania, we must now recognise the Nevada decree. But for the reasons stated by DAVIES, J., in *Mountbatten* v. *Mountbatten* (which does not appear to have been cited to the court in *Mather* v. *Mahoney*) this is a wholly illegitimate extension of the principle and the earlier case is to be preferred.[20]

If the court pronouncing the divorce is regarded as having jurisdiction, it is immaterial that the grounds on which it was granted would not be grounds for a divorce in England. In *Indyka* v. *Indyka*, for example, the divorce was granted for " deep disruption of marital relations "

There is one aspect of the question of recognition which was not discussed by the House of Lords in *Indyka* v. *Indyka* but which will need consideration at some time in the future. In that case—as in all the other cases involving the same principle that have come before the English courts—the parties were domiciled in England. A consistent application of our own principle, illustrated by *Armitage* v. *A.-G.*, demands that other courts must recognise a decree dissolving the marriage of persons domiciled in England if it is regarded as valid by English courts. By English law, therefore, the widening of the law of recognition in this sort of case can reduce the number of limping marriages but cannot increase it. But suppose that the parties are not domiciled in this country and their own *lex domicilii* will not recognise the decree. A limping marriage must result whatever decision we reach, but it seems to follow from the reasoning of all the members of the House of Lords in *Indyka* v. *Indyka* that we should reject the *lex domicilii* and recognise the divorce provided that there was a real and substantial connection with the country where it was obtained. But this must be regarded as an open point.[1]

In any case an English court will not recognise a foreign decree if the parties have fraudulently misrepresented facts (*e.g.*, their domicile) in

---

[18]See *ante*, p. 219.

[19][1968] 3 All E.R. 223.

[20]*Mather* v. *Mahoney* has since been doubted in *Davidson* v. *Davidson* (1969), 113 Sol. Jo. 813.

[1]The question will frequently be relevant in determining whether one of the parties has capacity to remarry and this must be referred to the *lex domicilii*: see *Padolecchia* v. *Padolecchia*, [1967] 3 All E.R. 863; [1968] P. 314 (*ante*, p. 17. Hence if a couple domiciled in state A obtain a divorce in state B which is recognised here but not in A, we must regard them as single persons with no capacity to remarry. For the draft Hague Convention on the Recognition of Divorces and Legal Separation, see 18 I.C.L.Q. 620 and 658. A Bill was introduced in the House of Lords early in 1971 to implement its provisions: see Appendix E, *post*.

order to lead the court to believe that it had jurisdiction, or if the decree was granted in circumstances which amount to a denial of substantial justice.[2] We might also decline to do so if the parties have themselves ignored it and lived together, so that recognition would work injustice on the parties or their children.[3]

---

[2]As it might be, *e.g.*, if one spouse took divorce proceedings under duress (*Meyer* v. *Meyer*, [1971] 1 All E.R. 378, or if the divorce was by a unilateral act of one spouse of which the other was ignorant (see the grounds on which *R.* v. *Hammersmith Superintendent Registrar of Marriages, ex parte Mir-Anwaruddin*, [1917] 1 K.B. 634, C.A., was distinguished in *Russ* v. *Russ*, [1962] 3 All E.R. 193, C.A.; [1964] P. 315). See further *Middleton* v. *Middleton*, [1966] 1 All E.R. 168; [1967] P. 62, and the cases there cited.

[3]*Hornett* v. *Hornett*, [1971] 1 All E.R. 98, 102-103. On the question of the recognition of *ex parte* divorces, see Cowen, *Divorce and the Domicile*, 68 L.Q.R. 88, and for problems presented by the whole question of recognition, see Kennedy, *Recognition of Foreign Divorce and Nullity Decrees*, 35 Can. Bar Rev. 628; Webb, *Recognition in England of Non-domiciliary Divorce Decrees*, 6 I.C.L.Q. 608; Unger, 29 M.L.R. 327; Mann, 21 M.L.R. 1.

PART II

PARENT AND
CHILD

SUMMARY OF CONTENTS

CHAPTER 9

Legitimacy

Despite recent legislation which has tended in many respects to assimilate the legal position of an illegitimate person to that of a legitimate one, the legal relationship between a child and his parents still depends to a large extent upon whether or not he is legitimate. Consequently, the discussion of that part of family law dealing with the relationship of parent and child must necessarily begin with a discussion of the meaning of legitimacy.

It seems impossible to define legitimacy as an abstract concept without reference to a particular legal system. Nevertheless most, if not all, systems of jurisprudence have drawn a distinction between the legal position of a child born of a legally recognised union and that of a child born of an illicit union or as the result of a casual act of intercourse.[1] Common law, like Roman law and the modern systems based upon it,[2] adhered rigidly to the rule that no child could be legitimate unless it was either born or conceived in wedlock. But it has, of course, always been possible for the legislature to legitimate a person illegitimate at common law. Occasionally, a special Act has been passed for that purpose, although there have been no instances of an Act of this sort in modern times. There are, however, three statutory provisions in force today of general application, which modify the common law rules. First, by the Legitimacy Act 1959 the children of a void marriage may be legitimate in certain circumstances notwithstanding that their parents have not been married at all. Secondly, section 11 of the Matrimonial Causes Act 1965 preserves the legitimacy of the children of parties to a voidable marriage which is subsequently annulled, despite the rule that, once a voidable marriage has been annulled, it is deemed in law never to have been contracted at all. Thirdly, by the Legitimacy Acts of 1926 and 1959 a person born illegitimate may nevertheless be legitimated if his parents subsequently intermarry. We must, therefore, consider first

---

[1]Thus Soviet law, which in 1918 abolished the distinction between legitimate and illegitimate children, nevertheless found it necessary for certain purposes in 1944 to draw a distinction between those born to parents who had registered their marriage and others. Hence, as one writer has observed, " children born outside a registered marriage after July 8, 1944, are comparable to illegitimate children in other countries, even if such terminology is not used ": Gsovski, *Soviet Civil Law*, vol. I, pp. 111, 121-2.

[2]But this is not the only criterion accepted in Western Europe. See further, Wolff, *Private International Law*, 2nd Ed., 385, and the *American Restatement of the Conflict of Laws*, s. 137 and Comment, where it is pointed out that in some legal systems a person may be the legitimate child of one parent but not of the other.

the position at common law and then the effect of these three statutory provisions.

A. LEGITIMACY AT COMMON LAW

A child is legitimate at common law if his parents were married at the time of his conception or at the time of his birth.[3] Although in most cases he will be both conceived and born in wedlock, this need not necessarily be true.

(1) He will be legitimate if his parents were married at the time of his conception, even though the marriage was terminated before his birth. Consequently, a posthumous child will be legitimate, as will be one whose parents' marriage was terminated by divorce between the time of his conception and his birth.[4]

(2) He will be legitimate if his parents were married when he was born even though he must have been conceived before their marriage.[5]

(3) Although there is no authority on this point, there may be one case where he will be legitimate although his parents were married neither when he was conceived nor when he was born. If he is conceived as the result of pre-marital intercourse and his parents then marry but his father dies before his birth, he will presumably be legitimate. Had the father survived, the child would certainly have been legitimate, and, as we have seen, the common law does not bastardise a child merely because he is born posthumously.

It is thus obvious that legitimacy is basically a question of fact. Whether or not a person is legitimate can only be determined by reference to the following questions:

(1) Who was his mother? Normally, this question presents no difficulties, because the fact of birth and identity can be established by the evidence of the doctor or other persons present at the birth. On the other hand, there have been cases where parents have attempted to pass off a supposititious child as their own, usually in order to defraud others who would be entitled to property in default of children of the marriage.[6]

(2) Who was his father? This can never be established by direct evidence: paternity can normally be inferred only from the fact that the alleged father had sexual intercourse with the mother about the time when the child must have been conceived. Consequently, if two men had intercourse with her during the relevant period, it may be impos-

---

[3]Blackstone's *Commentaries*, i, 446, 454-7. For a full account of the common law relating to legitimacy and a detailed examination of the cases before 1836, see Nicolas, *Adulterine Bastardy*. On the question of the legitimacy of a child conceived as a result of A.I.D., see the Report of the Departmental Committee on Human Artificial Insemination: Cmnd. 1105, paras. 160-171.

[4]*Knowles* v. *Knowles*, [1962] 1 All E.R. 659; [1962] P. 161.

[5]Co. Litt. 244a; Blackstone's *Commentaries*, i, 454. See also Nicolas, *op. cit.*, and the cases cited *post*, p. 229.

[6]*E.g.*, *Slingsby* v. *A.-G.* (1916), 33 T.L.R. 120, H.L., where the wife deceived her own husband. *Cf.* the popular belief, current at the time, that the son born to James II's consort was smuggled into the queen's room in a warming-pan in order to prevent the descent of the Crown to James's Protestant daughters.

sible to prove affirmatively which is the father.[7] Moreover, the fact that intercourse took place can in most cases be proved only by the evidence of the parties themselves or circumstantially from their conduct and the opportunities which were presented to them.

(3) Were the father and mother legally married at the relevant time? The problems presented here have already been considered.[8]

Presumption of Legitimacy.—The impossibility of proving affirmatively the paternity of a child led at least as early as the twelfth century to the adoption of the civil law maxim ' *Pater est quem nuptiae demonstrant* ', that is, the presumption that, if a child is born to a married woman, her husband is to be deemed to be its father until the contrary is proved.[9] This means that if it is alleged that it is not legitimate, the burden of rebutting the presumption is immediately cast upon the party alleging the illegitimacy. This presumption will still apply even though the child is born so soon after the marriage that it must have been conceived beforehand, for, in the words of LORD CAIRNS, L.C., in *Gardner* v. *Gardner*[10] (adopting the judgment of LORD GIFFORD in the same case in the Court of Session):

> " Where a man marries a woman who is in a state of pregnancy, the presumption of paternity from that mere fact is very strong. . . . Still further where the pregnancy is far advanced, obvious to the eye, or actually confessed or announced . . . to the intended husband, a presumption is reared up which, according to universal feeling, and giving due weight to what may be called the ordinary instincts of humanity, it will be very difficult indeed to overcome."

But if the husband was ignorant of the wife's pregnancy when he married her, the presumption may be rebutted by other evidence. Thus, in the *Poulett Peerage Case*[11] the wife was three months pregnant at the time of the marriage. Two months later the husband separated from her on the ground that she was pregnant by another man. He had deposed that he had not had sexual intercourse with her before the marriage and that he had never acknowledged the child as his. Evidence was also given that the wife had told a friend that another man was the father of the child. It was held that the presumption of the child's legitimacy was rebutted.

The presumption applies equally in the case of a posthumous child if it is born within the normal period of gestation after the husband's death.[12] Difficulty arises, however, if the birth takes place an abnormally long time afterwards. In *Preston-Jones* v. *Preston-Jones*[13]

---

[7]The significance of this will be seen more clearly when we consider the rebuttal of the common law presumption of legitimacy (*post*, pp. 233-237) and the establishment of the paternity of an illegitimate child where the mother is seeking an affiliation order (*post*, p. 483).

[8]*Ante*, chapter 2.

[9]Glanvil, book 7, ch. 12. See also Bracton, fol. 6; Co. Litt. 373; Blackstone's *Commentaries*, i, 457; Nicolas, *op. cit.*

[10](1877), 2 App. Cas. 723, 729, H.L. See also *R.* v. *Luffe* (1807), 8 East 193; *Anon.* v. *Anon.* (1856), 23 Beav. 273; *Turnock* v. *Turnock* (1867), 36 L.J.P. & M. 85.

[11][1903] A.C. 395, H.L.

[12]*Re Heath*, [1945] Ch. 417, 421-422, *per* COHEN, J.

[13][1951] 1 All E.R. 124, H.L.; [1951] A.C. 391. See further, *post*, p. 232.

the House of Lords were agreed that the court could take judicial notice of the fact that there is a normal period of gestation (although the period is variously given as 270 to 280 days or as nine months),[14] but LORD MACDERMOTT added that judicial notice must also be taken of the fact that the normal period is not always followed and that the actual period in a given case may be considerably longer or shorter. It would seem, however, that the longer the period deviates from the normal, the more easily will the presumption be rebutted, until there comes a time when it is not raised at all, although it is extremely difficult to say where the line is to be drawn.[15]

It seems that the presumption applies equally in the case of a child born after a decree of divorce. In *Knowles* v. *Knowles*[16] the facts were such that the child could have been conceived before or after the decree absolute. WRANGHAM, J., held that the presumption of legitimacy operated in favour of presuming that conception took place whilst the marriage was still subsisting and that the husband was the father although, as he pointed out, in such circumstances it may be rebutted much more easily.

If the child must have been conceived during the subsistence of a marriage, which has since been terminated by the first husband's death or divorce, and the mother has remarried before its birth, two conflicting presumptions arise. But in the absence of evidence to the contrary, it is submitted that it ought to be presumed that the mother has not committed adultery, so that there should still be a presumption that the child is the legitimate issue of the first husband.[17]

There is one case where it is presumed that a child born to a married woman is illegitimate. This occurs when the child must have been conceived at a time when the husband and wife were living apart under a decree of judicial separation or a separation order, for in such circumstances it is presumed that they have obeyed the order and have not had intercourse.[18] But this reasoning has no application if they had separated voluntarily, and consequently a child conceived in such circumstances will be presumptively legitimate even though the husband and wife had entered into a separation agreement.[19]

Former proceedings may also raise an estoppel as to paternity. For example, if the legitimacy of a child has been in issue during divorce proceedings, the finding will bind the spouses *as between themselves*, but

---

[14]*Per* LORD SIMONDS at pp. 127 and 401, LORD MORTON at pp. 136 and 413, LORD MACDERMOTT at pp. 139-140 and 419, respectively.
[15]See *ibid.*, pp. 128, 129, 130, 132, 135-136 and 402, 403, 407, 413-414, respectively.
[16][1962] 1 All E.R. 659; [1962] P. 161. *Cf. Re Leman's Will Trusts* (1945), 115 L.J.Ch. 89. It is submitted that the dictum to the contrary in *Re Bromage*, [1935] Ch. 605, 609, cannot be supported.
[17]See *Re Overbury*, [1954] 3 All E.R. 308; [1955] Ch. 122, where HARMAN, J., found in favour of the first husband's paternity on the facts.
[18]*Hetherington* v. *Hetherington* (1887), 12 P.D. 112; *Ettenfield* v. *Ettenfield*, [1940] 1 All E.R. 293, 301, C.A.; [1940] P. 96, 110. The reason is hardly satisfactory because the decree or order relieves the petitioner from the duty of cohabiting with the respondent; it does not forbid cohabitation, let alone sexual intercourse. The presumption of legitimacy will not be displaced if there is in force a maintenance order but no separation order: *Bowen* v. *Norman*, [1938] 2 All E.R. 776; [1938] 1 K.B. 689.
[19]*Ettenfield* v. *Ettenfield*, (*supra*). But the presumption may be rebutted more easily: *Knowles* v. *Knowles*, [1962] 1 All E.R. 659, 661; [1962] P. 161, 168.

it cannot bind either of them as against a third person nor can it bind the child or any other person who was not a party to the proceedings.[20] One statutory provision should also be noted. If a man has been adjudged to be the putative father of a child *in affiliation proceedings*, this is to be accepted as proof of his paternity in any other *civil* proceedings, whether or not he is a party to them, until the contrary is shown.[1]

Rebutting the Presumption.—The presumption of legitimacy is strictly twofold:
(1) that the husband and wife had sexual intercourse; and
(2) that the child is the issue of that intercourse.
It therefore follows that it may be rebutted either by showing that the spouses could not or did not have intercourse or by establishing by medical or other evidence that, in any event, the husband could not be the father of the child in question.

Standard of Proof.—At common law the generally accepted view was that the presumption could be rebutted only by evidence indicating beyond reasonable doubt that the child was illegitimate. This was due to the serious legal incapacities and social disadvantages attached to bastardy. Now that the position of the illegitimate child has been so much improved both legally and socially, it would be anomalous to retain the common law rule as an exception to the general standard of proof in civil cases. Consequently section 26 of the Family Law Reform Act 1969 now enacts that any presumption of legitimacy or illegitimacy may be rebutted by evidence which indicates the contrary on the balance of probabilities.[2]

Rebutting the Presumption of Access.—That the former presumption can be rebutted has been accepted since at least the thirteenth century.[3] The classic statement of the law is to be found in the opinion of the judges given to the House of Lords in the *Banbury Peerage Case* in 1811,[4] where they stated in substance that the presumption of legitimacy can be rebutted only by proof of the husband's impotence or of the fact that intercourse did not take place between the husband and wife at such time that the child could be the issue of it.[5]

If it can be shown that, at the time when the child must have been conceived, the husband was either permanently impotent (at least

---

[20]*Lindsay* v. *Lindsay*, [1934] P. 162; *B.* v. *A.-G.*, [1965] 1 All E.R. 62; [1965] P. 278; *G.* (*S.D.*) v. *G.* (*H.H.*), [1970] 3 All E.R. 844.
[1]Civil Evidence Act 1968, s. 12.
[2]This implements the recommendations of the Law Commission: see Law Com. No. 16, *Blood Tests and the Proof of Paternity in Civil Proceedings*, para. 15.
[3]Bracton, fol. 6 and fol. 63. See also Co. Litt. 244a; Nicolas, *Adulterine Bastardy*, 249 *et seq.*
[4]1 Sim. & St. 153, H.L. For a full account of the case, see Nicolas, *op. cit.*, 291 *et seq.*
[5]For some exceptional rules of evidence applicable to issues of legitimacy, see textbooks on the law of evidence. The common law rule that neither spouse could give evidence of non-access which would tend to bastardise the wife's children (the so-called rule in *Russell* v. *Russell*, [1924] A.C. 687, H.L.) was abrogated by the Law Reform (Miscellaneous Provisions) Act 1949, s. 7, now repealed and re-enacted in the Matrimonial Causes Act 1965, s. 43 (1), as amended by the Civil Evidence Act 1968, s. 16 (4).

quoad the wife) or temporarily impotent (whether from illness or any other cause), this will generally suffice to prove that he cannot be the child's father.[6] But it must be remembered that, even though the husband could not have had intercourse, the wife might nevertheless have become pregnant as a result of fecundation *ab extra*[7] or of artificial insemination with her husband's seed.[8] Although this problem has not yet been considered by any English court, it is tentatively suggested that once it has been established that the wife could not have conceived as a result of intercourse in the usual way, this would be sufficient to shift on to the party seeking to establish the child's legitimacy the burden of showing that in the special circumstances the husband could in fact be the father.

The presumption of legitimacy can also be rebutted by showing that the husband could not have had intercourse with his wife because of his absence at the relevant time. This will be easy to prove if, for example, he was abroad for the whole period during which the child must have been conceived; in other cases the court must decide on the balance of probability whether the spouses met in such circumstances as to afford them the opportunity of having sexual intercourse. In practice more difficult problems arise when the husband has been absent for a relatively short time and it is sought to establish the child's illegitimacy by showing that it must have been conceived during that period. It will be seen that the problem is basically the same as that which occurs when a child is born to a widow an abnormally long time after her husband's death, and the conclusions to be drawn from *Preston-Jones* v. *Preston-Jones*[9] apply equally to the present problem. In that case the husband did not have access to his wife for a period of 360 days to 186 days before the child's birth, and it was held that the evidence adduced was sufficient to rebut the presumption that he was the father.

Even though sexual intercourse was not impossible owing to the husband's absence, the presumption of legitimacy can still be rebutted if it can be shown that intercourse was so unlikely that it can be concluded on the balance of probability that it did not take place. If the spouses shared the same bed, it would seem to be almost impossible to prove that they did not have intercourse unless the husband is impotent.[10] If they were together in the same house, it will still be very difficult to rebut the presumption, unless it can be shown by other persons present that they were never alone together or that their relationship was such that it is improbable that they had intercourse in the circumstances.[11] If the husband and wife merely continue to live in the same town or district, the presumption can obviously be

---

[6]*Banbury Peerage, (ante).*
[7]As in *Clarke* v. *Clarke*, [1943] 2 All E.R. 540.
[8]As in *L.* v. *L.*, [1949] 1 All E.R. 141; *sub nom. R.E.L.* v. *E.L.*, [1949] P. 211.
[9][1951] 1 All E.R. 124, H.L.; [1951] A.C 391. See *ante*, pp. 229-230.
[10]See *Cotton* v. *Cotton*, [1954] 2 All E.R. 105, C.A.; [1954] P. 305. But the presumption was rebutted in such circumstances in *Smith* v. *May* (1969), 113 Sol. Jo. 1000.
[11]See, *e.g.*, the *Aylesford Peerage Case* (1885), 11 App. Cas. 1, H.L.

rebutted more easily than if they have in fact met in the same house.[12]

Despite some doubts expressed in earlier cases,[13] it has been clear since the decision of the House of Lords in *Morris* v. *Davies*[14] in 1837 that, in order to rebut the presumption that intercourse took place, evidence may be given not only of circumstances existing at the time of the conception and birth but also of relevant facts both preceding and following these. Clearly, the conduct of the spouses towards each other as well as statements made by them are highly relevant if they point to their not having had intercourse for some time.[15] Similarly, the wife's concealing her pregnancy from her husband and his relations or the family doctor, and *a fortiori* concealment of the birth, indicate not only that the wife does not believe that the child is her husband's but also that she knows that he will inevitably draw the same conclusion.[16] The parties' conduct towards the child after its birth is equally relevant; and if the putative father recognises the child as his, either directly[17] or inferentially, for example by permitting his name to be registered as that of the father, by having the child brought up by his own parents,[18] or by paying for medical attention at the birth and for nursing and education afterwards,[19] that is strong evidence that there is no doubt that the husband could not have been the father.

Rebutting the Second Presumption.—It will be seen that the *Banbury Peerage Case* and all the other cases cited above have dealt only with the rebuttal of the first presumption, *viz.* that the husband and wife did not in fact have sexual intercourse. It now remains to consider in what circumstances, if intercourse did take place or must be presumed to have taken place, it is possible to rebut the second presumption, *viz.* that the child must be the issue of that intercourse. The problem is this: if at the time when a child, C, must have been conceived, his mother, M, was having intercourse with her husband, H, and with another man, X, what evidence can be led to show that it is more probable that X is C's father than H?

The fact that the wife committed adultery cannot *per se* rebut the presumption, because this merely shows that either H or X could be the father.[20] But if H is shown to be sterile, this must be conclusive.

---

[12]See *Sibbet* v. *Ainsley* (1860), 3 L.T. 583. The fact that the spouses never met openly is strong evidence of their not having met secretly either: *Atchley* v. *Sprigg* (1864), 33 L.J.Ch. 345.

[13]*E.g.*, by LORD ELDON, L.C., in *Head* v. *Head* (1823), Turn. & R. 138, 141.

[14](1837), 5 Cl. & F. 163, H.L.

[15]Per LORD LANGDALE, M.R., in *Hargrave* v. *Hargrave* (1846), 9 Beav. 552, 555-556.

[16]*Morris* v. *Davies*, (*supra*); *Bosvile* v. *A.-G.* (1887), 12 P.D. 177; *Burnaby* v. *Baillie* (1889), 42 Ch.D. 282.

[17]*Atchley* v. *Sprigg*, (*supra*); *Hawes* v. *Draeger* (1883), 23 Ch.D. 173.

[18]*Morris* v. *Davies*, (*supra*); *Re Bromage*, [1935] Ch. 605; *Re Heath*, [1945] Ch. 417.

[19]*Aylesford Peerage Case* (1885), 11 App. Cas. 1, H.L.; *Burnaby* v. *Baillie*, (*supra*); *Re Heath*, (*supra*).

[20]It was formerly held that this was so even though the husband invariably used a contraceptive (*Francis* v. *Francis*, [1959] 3 All E.R. 206; [1960] P. 17) but this might now rebut the presumption on the balance of probability if the other man did not use one. Similarly, if the presumption is raised by the wife's pregnancy at the time of the marriage, it cannot be rebutted merely by showing that she had intercourse with another man before her marriage: *Gardner* v. *Gardner* (1877). 2 App. Cas. 723. H.L.

In the past the courts have been slow to admit evidence suggesting that C has inherited some physical characteristic from X and must therefore be his child. Evidence of facial resemblance has been held to be too vague,[1] but this is obviously a matter of degree and, with the changed standard of proof, ought now to be admitted in some cases as putting the matter well beyond the balance of probabilities. Other evidence—for example that of race—is much more cogent. If M and H are both white, X is a negro, and C is coloured, it cannot be doubted that C must be X's child.[2]

Much more reliable evidence is produced by blood tests. At the moment most cases fall into one of two categories: first, where the husband is relying on the birth of the child to prove the wife's adultery and he wants the blood test as evidence on which he can obtain a divorce, and, secondly, where the question is whether the child is a child of the family for the purpose of orders relating to custody, financial provision, etc. In the latter type of case the husband is usually trying to prove that he is under no obligation to support the child, but if it is clear that either the husband or a particular individual must be the father, each is sometimes prepared to assume parental obligations if his paternity can be established. In the near future, however, they are also likely to be used extensively in affiliation proceedings, where the question is whether the defendant is the father of the complainant's illegitimate child.[3]   Consequently we shall discuss the question separately.

Blood Tests.—Certain characteristics of a person's blood are inherited. It therefore follows that, if the mother's blood does not possess a characteristic possessed by the child's, he must have inherited it from his father. If the blood of both men who might be the father possesses this characteristic, a blood test cannot establish from which of them the child inherited it, but if the blood of one of them does not possess it, he must be the child of the other. From this it will be seen that, although blood tests cannot be used to prove affirmatively that a particular man must be the child's father,[4] they may establish conclusively that he cannot be. Obviously tests must be carried out on both the child's and the alleged father's blood; in most cases these will be inconclusive unless the mother's blood is tested as well.[5]

This presents a grave difficulty. If all the adult parties and the person with the custody of the child (if it is still of tender years) agree, there is

---

[1]*Slingsby* v. *A.-G.* (1916), 33 T.L.R. 120, H.L., at pp. 122, 123; *Plowes* v. *Bossey* (1862), 31 L.J.Ch. 681, 683.

[2]Such evidence was apparently admissible even before the standard of proof was changed; *Slingsby* v. *A.G.*, (*supra*), at p. 122.

[3]*I.e.*, when Part III of the Family Law Reform Act 1969 is brought into force. See *infra.*

[4]But in some cases the statistical chance of another man possessing the same characteristics may be so slight as to establish paternity on the balance of probabilities.

[5]See Taylor, *Medical Jurisprudence*, 12th Ed., vol. 2, pp. 46-50; Gradwohl, *Legal Medicine*, 2nd Ed., chap. 13; Race and Sanger, *Blood Groups in Man*, 5th Ed., particularly chap. 22; Law Com. No. 16, *Blood Tests and the Proof of Paternity in Civil Proceedings.* For the problems raised by artificial insemination, see Tallin, *Artificial Insemination*, 34 Can. Bar Rev. 166 *et seq.*

no problem. But as the tests can only prove that a given man could not be the father, a wife might well object to submitting herself and the child to them. This is understandable: why should she provide a piece of evidence which might establish her adultery and leave the child unsupported, when it could never affirmatively help her case? Moreover, if a paternity issue is ordered to be tried or the child is made a ward of court, he will usually be separately represented, and his guardian *ad litem* might well object to a blood test for the same reason.[6]

The common law position was eventually settled by the House of Lords in *S.* v. *S.; W.* v. *Official Solicitor.*[7] There is no power to order a blood test of an adult against his will, for this is a battery which, however trivial, no court may authorise.[8] For the same reason, as the power to consent to a surgical operation on a young child lies in the parent with care and control, the court probably cannot order a child's blood to be tested without the consent of the parent or of the child himself if he is old enough to understand the nature of the operation.[9] But if the parent (or child) consents to the test, the court will override any objection on the part of the guardian *ad litem*, the other spouse or any other interested person, unless it can be shown that the test would be against the child's interest.

Defects in the law were pointed out by the Law Commission in their Report on Blood Tests and the Proof of Paternity in Civil Proceedings[10] and their recommendations have been implemented by Part III of the Family Law Reform Act 1969 (which will not be brought into force until the necessary administrative arrangements have been made). By section 20 (1) any court may direct blood tests to be used in any civil proceedings in which the paternity of any person is in issue. The purpose of the test must be to ascertain whether *a party to the proceedings* is or is not excluded from being the father of the person in question and consequently no order could be made, for example, in administration proceedings if the question was whether a claimant was the child of a deceased person, information about whose blood happened to be available. The court may direct that blood samples shall be taken from the person whose legitimacy is in issue, his mother and any *party* alleged to be his father. " Party " in this context presumably means a party to the proceedings; this means that if it is agreed that either the mother's husband or a given man, X, must be the child's father and it is desired to have X's blood tested to see whether he can be excluded, a direction to this effect could be given only if X were joined as a party. In divorce proceedings he will normally be a co-respondent,

---

[6]The position of the Official Solicitor as guardian *ad litem* in a matrimonial cause was considerably strengthened by a *Practice Direction*, [1968] 3 All E.R. 607, which forbids anyone from having the child medically examined with a view to providing evidence without giving the Official Solicitor notice, so that he can consider whether to oppose a blood test. But if the child's blood is tested in defiance of this ban, the evidence is probably admissible, whatever penalties the party might incur: *S.* v. *S.*, [1970] 3 All E.R. 107, 112, H.L.

[7][1970] 3 All E.R. 107, H.L.

[8]*W.* v. *W.* (*No. 4*), [1963] 2 All E.R. 841, C.A.; [1964] P. 67. See also *S.* v. *S.*, (*supra*), at pp. 111 (*per* LORD REID) and 123 (*per* LORD HODSON).

[9]*S.* v. *S.*, (*supra*), at p. 112 (*per* LORD REID).

[10]1968, Law Com. No. 16.

but there is no power to bring him in as a party to, say, proceedings brought under the Guardianship of Minors Act or the Matrimonial Proceedings (Magistrates' Courts) Act 1960.

There is no compulsion attached to the direction. Except in the case of a person suffering from mental disorder, blood samples may not be taken without the consent of the person himself if he is over the age of 16 or of the person having care and control of him if he is under that age.[11] But the court may draw such inferences as appear proper from a person's failure to give consent or to take steps to give effect to the direction, and if he is a party claiming relief in reliance on the presumption of legitimacy, the court may dismiss his claim even though there is no evidence to rebut the presumption.[12] The last provision would apply, for example, to a wife claiming maintenance for a child which she alleges is her husband's who refuses to have herself and the child tested, or to a former ward of court claiming maintenance for himself who refuses to be tested when it is alleged that he is illegitimate. To bar the claimant from relief in such circumstances appears on the face of it to be reasonable: the difficulty is that an adverse inference drawn against an adult party might also be adverse to the child. It is questionable whether the Act was right to give a court power to refuse to make an order for maintenance because the mother declines to submit to a blood test when it could have made submission compulsory; what one must guard against is drawing the wholly illogical and unjustified conclusion that the child must be illegitimate.

A written report of the result of the tests is admissible.[13] It must state whether the party is excluded from being the father and, if not, the value of the results in determining whether he is the father.[14]

It will be seen that these provisions in no way inhibit the giving of evidence: if all the parties agree, they do not have to obtain the court's consent before having a test carried out. What the Act does is to give the court a discretion to direct a test if they do not agree. In *S. v. S.* the House of Lords indicated that the discretion will have to be judicially exercised, but they refused to lay down any guidelines. So far as blood tests of children are concerned, it is submitted that the courts should continue to follow *S. v. S.* itself. All the members of the House were of the opinion that a test should usually be ordered; but the court has a duty to protect a child and the general rule would be displaced if the test " would be against the child's interest ",[15] if " having regard to the facts and circumstances of a particular case, an infant's interests are such that their protection necessitates the withholding from a court of evidence which may be very material "[16] or if " it would be unjust to order a test for a collateral reason to assist a litigant in his or her claim ".[17] Neither the social stigma or the legal disabilities attached to illegitimacy are as great as they used to be, and

---

[11]S. 21. For persons suffering from mental disorder, see s. 21 (4).

[12]S. 23.

[13]S. 20 (2). One hopes that it will rarely be necessary to call persons conducting tests to give oral evidence. For evidence and the procedure to be adopted generally, see ss. 20 and 22.

[14]*I.e.*, presumably, the statistical chances of his being the father.

[15]*Per* LORD REID, [1970] 3 All E.R. at p. 113.

[16]*Per* LORD MORRIS, at p. 120   [17]*Per* LORD HODSON, at p. 124.

the House of Lords refused to accept that the mere fact that a test could establish conclusively that the child was illegitimate was sufficiently against its interest to withhold consent even though, as in *W. v. Official Solicitor*, this would leave it with no known father at all. This danger is far outweighed by the demands of public policy that all relevant evidence should be made available.   Furthermore the suppression of evidence would not encourage the mother's husband, whose suspicions would be unallayed, to accept the child as his, whereas he might be prepared to do so if a test did not exclude his paternity; and the child itself in later life might resent the fact that a full investigation was not conducted at the time. It will usually be in the child's interest—as well as in the public interest—that the truth should out.[18]   There is little doubt that a court would refuse to direct a test if the husband sought it solely in the hope of acquiring evidence of his wife's adultery (a matter which is of diminished importance now the Divorce Reform Act has come into force). What is less clear is how the courts will exercise their discretion in the sort of situation exemplified by *B. v. B. and E.*[19] The mother did not suggest that the child was illegitimate until, three years after its birth, she left her husband to live with the co-respondent who she then alleged was the father. The husband, who wished to retain custody of the child, refused to submit to a blood test and insisted on standing on the presumption of legitimacy. It was held that in the circumstances he was acting reasonably and no adverse conclusions could be drawn from his refusal; that being so, no order would be made with respect to the child. But this overlooks the vital point that, if the evidence of blood groups was neutral, the presumption of legitimacy would prevail; if it proved that the co-respondent and not the husband must be the father, why should the latter be able to take advantage of a legal presumption designed to protect a child in the days when this sort of evidence was unheard of?[20]

B. LEGITIMACY OF CHILDREN OF VOID MARRIAGES

Since a void marriage is not a marriage either in fact or in law, the children of such a marriage were necessarily illegitimate at common law. Many legal systems recognise the legitimacy of children of putative marriages, that is, those void marriages to which one or both parties were unaware of the invalidity. This avoids working an injustice on the children and the Morton Commission on Marriage and Divorce recommended the adoption in England of a rule that has always been a part of the common law of Scotland.[21] Effect has been given to this recommendation in section 2 of the Legitimacy Act of 1959, which provides:

" . . . The child of a void marriage, whether born before or after the commencement of this Act, shall be treated as the legitimate child of his

---

[18]S. v. S., *(supra)*, at p. 113 *(per* LORD REID), p. 122 *(per* LORD MORRIS), p. 124 *(per* LORD HODSON).　　　　[19][1969] 3 All E.R. 1106, C.A.
[20]For further discussion on the problems presented by blood tests, see Hayes, *The Use of Blood Tests in the Pursuit of Truth*, 87 L.Q.R. 86; Hall, [1971] C.L.J. 34.
[21]Cmd. 9678, paras. 1184-1186.

parents if at the time of the act of intercourse resulting in the birth (or at the time of the celebration of the marriage if later) both or either of the parties reasonably believed that the marriage was valid.''

As this provision determines status, it is expressly enacted that it shall apply only if the child's father was domiciled in England at the time of the child's birth or, if he died before the birth, immediately before his death.[1] The Act seems to lay the burden of proof upon the person asserting the legitimacy, a burden which it may well be extremely difficult to discharge. Bearing in mind that the question may arise in relation to the devolution of property upon death, it is easy to see that one or both parties to the marriage may already be dead and the evidence that can be adduced may well be purely circumstantial. If the marriage preceded the conception, the precise time at which it is necessary to prove that the belief was held may also be uncertain. Furthermore, it is not clear what *reasonable* belief means in this context. Presumably the test is an objective one; in other words, the belief must be one that a reasonable man would have held in the circumstances[2] and it is arguable that a mistake of law cannot be reasonably held in this sense so as to create a putative marriage which is void, say, because the parties were ignorant of the law relating to the prohibited degrees of consanguinity or affinity.[3]

The new Act does not affect any vested titles, for it is expressly enacted that, insofar as it affects the succession to any dignity or title of honour or of any property settled so as to devolve therewith, section 2 shall not apply to children born before the commencement of the Act (29th October, 1959) and that it shall not in any event affect any rights under the intestacy of a person dying before the commencement of the Act or the operation or construction of any disposition coming into operation before that date. " Disposition " for this purpose has the same meaning as it has in the case of *legitimatio per subsequens matrimonium*.[4]

C. LEGITIMACY OF CHILDREN OF VOIDABLE MARRIAGES

At common law a decree of nullity, where the marriage was voidable, had retrospective effect and automatically bastardised the issue of the marriage.[5] When the grounds for nullity were extended by the Matrimonial Causes Act 1937, it was appreciated that this rule might work hardship in those cases where the marriage was annulled because the respondent was of unsound mind or epileptic or was suffering from a venereal disease in a communicable form, since the wife might conceive before the petitioner discovered the existence of the impediment. Consequently, this Act expressly provided that in these two cases any child born of the marriage should be legitimate notwithstanding the annulment of the marriage.[6] Where the respondent was pregnant by

---

[1]Section 2 (2). *Cf.* the provisions in the Legitimacy Act 1926 relating to *legitimatio per subsequens matrimonium, post*, p. 240.
[2]*Hawkins* v. *A.-G.*, [1966] 1 All E.R. 392, 397. See Samuels, 29 M.L.R. 559.
[3]This appears to be the law in Scotland: see Walton, *Husband and Wife*, 3rd Ed., 233-4.
[4]Section 2 (3), (4), (5); see *post*, p. 463. It is expressly provided that nothing in the Act shall affect the succession to the throne: s. 6 (4).
[5]See *ante*, p. 69.   [6]S. 7 (2).

a man other than the petitioner, the question of the legitimacy of the child did not arise, and apparently the legislature did not foresee that any child would be born if the marriage had not been consummated. This proved to be untrue, however, for children were born as a result of pre-marital intercourse,[7] of fecundation *ab extra*[8] and of artificial insemination.[9]

This anomaly was removed by section 4 (1) of the Law Reform (Miscellaneous Provisions) Act 1949, which has now been repealed and is substantially re-enacted in section 11 of the Matrimonial Causes Act 1965. This provides:

" Where a decree of nullity is granted in respect of a voidable marriage, any child who would have been the legitimate child of the parties to the marriage if at the date of the decree it had been dissolved instead of being annulled shall be deemed to be their legitimate child."

Normally the child will have been born or conceived between the date of the marriage and the date of the decree, but the Act must also apply if it was legitimated by the parties' marriage or born after the decree. On the other hand, however, if it never was legitimate (for example, because the husband was not the father), it will certainly not acquire the status of legitimacy under the Act.[10]

The Law Reform Act of 1949 did not have retrospective effect. Consequently, except in those cases provided for in section 7 (2) of the Matrimonial Causes Act 1937, the children of voidable marriages annulled before 16th December, 1949, remain illegitimate.[11]

D. LEGITIMATION

Canon law adopted the Roman law rule that a bastard would become legitimate if his parents subsequently intermarried, provided that they had been free to marry each other at the time of the child's birth. But the importance of establishing the identity of the heir at law, to whom descended the valuable private rights and important public duties of the ownership of an inheritable estate of freehold land in the Middle Ages, led the common law to reject this doctrine of *legitimatio per subsequens matrimonium,* and an attempt to introduce it by the Statute of Merton in 1235 was successfully resisted by the temporal peers.[12]

---

[7] As in *Dredge* v. *Dredge,* [1947] 1 All E.R. 29.

[8] As in *Clarke* v. *Clarke,* [1943] 2 All E.R. 540.

[9] As in *L.* v. *L.,* [1949] 1 All E.R. 141; *sub nom. R.E.L.* v. *E.L.,* [1949] P. 211.

[10] *Re Adams,* [1951] 1 All E.R. 1037; [1951] Ch. 716. *Quaere* whether the section operates if the parties are not domiciled in England and the decree bastardises the child by the *lex domicilii.* The wording suggests that it will continue to be regarded as legitimate in this country.

[11] *Re Adams, (supra).*

[12] But under the curious doctrine of *bastard eigne* and *mulier puisne,* if the parents of an illegitimate child (the *bastard eigne*) married and had a legitimate child (the *mulier puisne*) and the bastard entered on the father's freehold land after his death and himself died seised so that it descended to his (the bastard's) issue, this gave the bastard's heirs an indefeasible right to the land and the rights of the *mulier puisne* and all other heirs were completely barred: Jackson, *Formation and Annulment of Marriage,* 2nd Ed., 46-48, and the authorities there cited.

Consequently, no form of legitimation was recognised by English municipal law until the passing of the Legitimacy Act in 1926, by which time the property legislation of 1925 had rendered it almost wholly unnecessary to establish the identity of the heir save in the case of the descent of an unbarred entailed interest.

Conditions under which an Illegitimate Person will be Legitimated.—Section 1 (1) of the Legitimacy Act 1926 provides:

">. . . where the parents of an illegitimate person marry or have married one another, whether before or after the commencement of this Act, the marriage shall, if the father of the illegitimate person was or is at the date of the marriage domiciled in England or Wales, render that person, if living, legitimate from the commencement of this Act, or from the date of the marriage, whichever last happens."

It will be observed that a person will be legitimated by the operation of this section only if his *father* was domiciled in England or Wales *at the time of the marriage.* The reason for this provision is that a legitimate child's status is determined by the law of his father's domicile: hence the mother's domicile is quite irrelevant for this purpose. Moreover, since it is the marriage that legitimates him, it is the father's English domicile at this time that is important.

Whether or not the child is the issue of the husband is of course a question of fact. That the parties married at all in the circumstances affords some slight evidence that the husband is the father of the wife's illegitimate child,[13] but normally the only evidence available will be the husband's recognition of his paternity, whether before or after the marriage. In the words of JAMES, L.J., delivering the opinion of the Judicial Committee of the Privy Council in *La Cloche* v. *La Cloche*:[14]

" The principle . . . is, that where a man marries a woman who has had an illegitimate child, whether that child is thenceforth to be considered the legitimate child of the man must depend on the only evidence which can generally be given of it; that is to say the man's recognition of his paternity— if that is sufficiently and abundantly proved, it does not signify in what particular manner that recognition is effected."

In this case ample evidence of such recognition was to be found in the husband's declarations at the time of the marriage, in letters to the child in which he called him " son ", and in a deed executed by the husband in which he referred to the child's son as his own grandson.

The Act of 1926 adopted the Canon Law rule that a child could be legitimated by the subsequent marriage of his parents only if neither of them was married to any other person at the time of his birth.[15] This did not necessarily prevent the legitimation of an adulterine bastard, for even though he was conceived whilst one of his parents

---

[13]See *Battle* v. *A.-G.*, [1949] P. 358. The existence of an affiliation order against the husband is *prima facie* evidence of his paternity: Civil Evidence Act 1968, s. 12 (*ante*, p. 231).

[14](1872), L.R. 4 P.C. 325, 333, P.C. See also *Battle* v. *A.-G.*, (*supra*).

[15]Section 1 (2). For the position where the first marriage is voidable and is subsequently annulled, see *ante*, pp. 69-71.

was married, he could still be legitimated if this marriage was terminated before his birth, and in many cases decrees of divorce were expedited in order to permit the parents to marry before he was born. Consequently, section 1 of the Legitimacy Act of 1959 extended the provisions of the earlier Act to those cases where either or both of the parents were married when the child was born. In such a case, therefore, the child is legitimated by virtue of the Act of 1959; in all other cases he is legitimated by virtue of the Act of 1926.

It should further be observed that legitimation does not have retrospective effect under either Act, so that no person can be legitimated unless he is still alive when his parents marry (or when the Act by virtue of which he is legitimated came into force).[16] The Act of 1926 came into operation on 1st January, 1927, and the Act of 1959 on 29th October, 1959. Consequently, if the parents were married before the relevant date, the child was legitimated on the day that the Act came into force; if they marry after that date, he is legitimated on the day of the marriage.

Effects of Legitimation.—It is expressly provided that a legitimated person shall have the same rights and obligations in respect of the maintenance and support of himself and other persons as if he had been born legitimate, and any legal claim for damages, compensation, allowances, etc., that could be made by or in respect of a legitimate person, can now be made by or in respect of one legitimated.[17] Similarly, for the purpose of determining whether he is a citizen of the United Kingdom and Colonies, he is to be treated as being born legitimate on the date of his parents' marriage.[18] Subject to what will be said later with respect to rights in property[19] a legitimated person is, after his legitimation, in exactly the same position as if he had been born legitimate. In the words of ROMER, J.:[20]

" Legitimacy is a question of status. . . . This status of legitimacy can be obtained by being born legitimate or by being legitimated by virtue of the provisions of the Act. The plaintiff had attained that status, and it is an irrelevant consideration whether she attained it in one way or the other."

E. LEGITIMACY AND LEGITIMATION BY FOREIGN LAW

Legitimacy at Birth.—Although very real doubts on the question are still entertained, the most widely held view today is that, if a child is the legitimate child of his parents by the law of their domicile at his birth, English law will recognise that status for all purposes save that

---

[16]Legitimacy Act 1926, s. 1 (1); Legitimacy Act 1959, s. 1 (2). But if the parents had married before the relevant Act came into force, the children could be legitimated on that date, even though one or both *parents* had already died: *Re Lowe*, [1929] 2 Ch. 210.

[17]Legitimacy Act 1926, s. 6 (1).

[18]British Nationality Act 1948, s. 23.

[19]See *post*, pp. 462-464 and 507.

[20]*Re Lowe*, [1929] 2 Ch. 210, 212-3. See also *C.* v. *C.*, [1947] 2 All E.R. 50; [1948] P. 19.

L

of succession to an unbarred entail.[1] Thus in *Re Bischoffsheim*,[2]
where the question was whether a child born of parents domiciled in
New York could take an interest in a legacy in favour of his mother's
children contained in an English will, it was held that for the purpose
of construing the will the term "children" must mean legitimate
children as a rule of English law but to determine whether or not the
claimant was legitimate reference must be made to the law of New
York. In the words of ROMER, J.:[3]

> Where the succession to personal property depends on the legitimacy of
> the claimant, the status of legitimacy conferred on him by his domicile of
> origin (*i.e.*, the domicile of his parents at his birth) will be recognised by
> our courts; and if that legitimacy be established, the validity of his parents'
> marriage should not be entertained as a relevant subject for investigation."

These last words are apparently in conflict with the decision of the
House of Lords in *Shaw* v. *Gould*,[4] but ROMER, J., distinguished this
case on the ground that it dealt with the exceptional question of the
heir. If this view is correct, it follows that the question of legitimacy
is to be determined solely by reference to the parties' domicile. If they
both have the same domicile, the answer can be easily ascertained; but
if they have different domiciles, a further problem arises. If the child
is legitimate, its domicile of origin is that of its father; but if it is
illegitimate, its domicile is that of its mother.[5] Consequently, in
order to determine the child's domicile, it is apparently first necessary
to determine its legitimacy, which in turn depends on the domicile.
There are two possible solutions to this problem. One is to concede
that a child will be legitimate only if it has this status by the law of the
domiciles of both parents;[6] the other is to hold that, if there is a conflict,
he will be legitimate if he is legitimate by his father's *lex domicilii*.[7]

---

[1]For a discussion of this topic generally and the difficulties arising, see Dicey and
Morris, *Conflict of Laws*, 8th Ed., 418 *et seq.*; Cheshire, *Private International Law*, 8th Ed.,
426 *et seq.*; Graveson, *Conflict of Laws*, 6th Ed., 378 *et seq.*; Falconbridge, *Legitimacy
or Legitimation in the Conflict of Laws*, 27 Can. Bar Rev. 1963; Inglis, *Adoption and
Succession in Private International Law*, 6 I.C.L.Q. 202.

[2][1947] 2 All E.R. 830; Ch. 79, following *Re Goodman's Trusts* (1881), 17 Ch.D. 266,
C.A. See also *Bamgbose* v. *Daniel*, [1954] 3 All E.R. 263, P.C.; [1955] A.C. 107.

[3]At pp. 836 and 92, respectively.

[4](1868), L.R. 3 H.L. 55, H.L. In this case the child's father, who was domiciled
in Scotland, had married the mother after she had obtained a divorce from
her first husband, who was domiciled in England, in a Scottish court. As the court
had no jurisdiction, the House of Lords, on appeal from an English court, took
the view that the mother was still married to her first husband and that the child
was *therefore* illegitimate.

[5]See *ante*, p. 7.

[6]Supported by Dicey and Morris, *Conflict of Laws*, 8th Ed., 418. *Shaw* v. *Gould*, (*supra*),
could be further distinguished on the ground that by English law the mother was still
married to her first husband and therefore still domiciled in England, by the law of
which country the child must necessarily be illegitimate. A further argument that, where
the child is claiming under an English deed or will, he must as a matter of construction
be legitimate according to the rules of English law (see LORD CHELMSFORD in *Shaw* v.
Gould, (*supra*), at p. 80, and BENNETT, J., in *Re Paine*, [1940] Ch. 46) was demolished by
ROMER, J., in *Re Bischoffsheim* at pp. 833-834 and 86-87, respectively, where he pointed
out that the sole question of construction was that by English law children meant
legitimate children and that it did not follow that this meant children legitimate according to the narrow test of English law.

[7]Supported by Cheshire, *Private International Law*, 8th Ed., 434, and Graveson,
Conflict of Laws, 6th Ed., 380.

The former has the advantage of not leaving the matter in doubt; the latter would bring the recognition of legitimacy into line with the recognition of legitimation (where English law has always concentrated solely on the effect of a subsequent marriage in the father's *lex domicilii*) and also with our own law relating to the legitimacy of children of void marriages.[8] At present the question must be regarded as an open one.

But there is one exceptional case where English law will not necessarily recognise the status of legitimacy conferred by the *lex domicilii*. We have already seen that the rigid rules relating to legitimacy grew out of the necessity in the Middle Ages of establishing the identity of the heir at law; this has also resulted in the judges' laying down the rule that, whatever the claimant's domicile may be, in order to succeed to an entailed interest *as heir*, he must show that he is legitimate by the common law test—that is, conceived or born in wedlock.[9]

Legitimation *per subsequens Matrimonium*.—The common law would recognise legitimation *per subsequens matrimonium* by foreign law only if the father was domiciled in a country recognising legitimation both at the time of the child's birth and at the time of the marriage.[10] Consequently, if the father had no such domicile when the child was born, English law would not recognise the legitimation, whatever the father's domicile was when he married. Now, however, section 8 of the Legitimacy Act 1926 has provided that a person shall be regarded as legitimated for the purpose of English law if the father was domiciled in a country recognising legitimation *per subsequens matrimonium* at the time of the marriage, even though his *lex domicilii* at the time of the birth did not recognise the doctrine.

But in certain cases it is still necessary to bear the common law rule in mind. In order to establish a claim to property, it may be necessary to prove that a child was legitimated before 1927 (or 29th October, 1959), and, as in the case of legitimation under section 1, a person will be recognised as legitimated under section 8 on the marriage of his parents or on the day on which the relevant Act came into force, whichever is the later. Furthermore, his rights to property at common law may be wider than they would be under the Act, as we shall see when we deal with a legitimated person's right to claim as his parents' child.[11]

---

[8]See *ante*, p. 238.

[9]*Birtwhistle* v. *Vardill* (1826), 5 B. & C. 438, K.B.; (1835), 2 Cl. & F. 571, H.L.; (1840), 7 Cl. & F. 895, H.L. This does not apply to a devise to the claimant's father's child, for in such a case he claims as purchaser and not as heir: *Re Grey's Trusts*, [1892] 3 Ch. 88. For the position where the alleged heir's parents' marriage is polygamous, see *ante*, p. 49.

[10]*Re Grove* (1888), 40 Ch.D. 216, C.A. See further, Dicey and Morris, *op. cit.*, 434 *et seq.*; Cheshire, *op. cit.*, 436 *et seq.*; Graveson, *op. cit.*, 387 *et seq.*; Mann, *Legitimation and Adoption in Private International Law*, 57 L.Q.R. 112; Falconbridge, *loc. cit.*

[11]See *post*, p. 464. If either parent was married at the time of the child's birth, his legitimation would not be recognised under s. 8 before the commencement of the Legitimacy Act 1959.

Legitimation otherwise than by subsequent Marriage.—Where the legitimation is by some other act (for example, the parents' recognition), the Legitimacy Act has no application at all. Hence it will be recognised here only if the common law rules are satisfied—that is, the father must be domiciled in a country, the law of which accepts the validity of the legitimation, both at the time of the child's birth and at the time of the performance of the act effecting the legitimation.[12]

F. DECLARATIONS OF LEGITIMACY

As may have already been gathered from what has been said above, the question of a person's legitimacy may be put in issue in a number of ways. This will occur, for example, if he claims an interest in property or if in divorce proceedings the husband relies upon the fact of his birth as evidence of his mother's adultery. Normally, however, any judicial decision will be a judgment *in personam* and consequently will bind only the parties to it and their privies, that is, persons claiming through them.[13] The desirability of some sort of procedure to enable a disputed question of legitimacy to be settled once for all led to the passing in 1858 of the Legitimacy Declaration Act, now repealed and substantially re-enacted in section 39 of the Matrimonial Causes Act 1965. Under the provisions of this section, any person may petition for a decree that he is legitimate or that he or his parents or grandparents are or were validly married. But no petition will lie unless:

(a) the petitioner is a British subject or his right to be deemed a British subject depends wholly or in part on his legitimacy or the validity of any marriage; *and*

(b) *either* he is domiciled in England or Northern Ireland *or* he claims any real or personal estate situate in England.[14]

No provisions exist to enable a petitioner to obtain a declaration of legitimacy of anyone other than himself,[15] nor is there any power to declare anyone illegitimate.[16]

It will be inferred from condition (a) set out above that one of the objects of this piece of legislation is to enable a person to establish not only his legitimacy but also his right to be treated as a British subject. It is accordingly expressly provided that any person who satisfies condition (b) may petition for a decree to this effect even though his legitimacy is not in issue.[17]

---

[12]*Re Luck's Settlement Trusts*, [1940] 3 All E.R. 307, C.A.; [1940] Ch. 864 (criticised by Mann, *loc. cit.*, at pp. 118 *et seq.*). *Quaere* whether the father's *lex domicilii* must permit legitimation *by the particular means*. *E.g.*, if the father is domiciled in England at the child's birth and then, following a change of domicile, legitimates him by recognition, would we now recognise the legitimation?

[13]For the distinction between judgments *in rem* and judgments *in personam* and the doctrine of *res judicata*, see Cross, *Evidence*, 3rd Ed., 271-281.

[14]S. 39 (1). It will be observed that neither domicile nor the situation of property in Scotland will entitle a person to petition; domicile in Northern Ireland will give the court jurisdiction, but the situation of property there will not. The proceedings must be brought in the High Court.

[15]*Aldrich* v. *A.-G.*, [1968] 1 All E.R. 345; [1968] P. 281.

[16]*B.* v. *A.-G.*, [1966] 2 All E.R. 145.

[17]S. 39 (4).

The possibility of a person's legitimation coming into question has been provided for in section 39 (2), which enacts that, where any person claims that he or his parents or any remoter ancestor[18] has been legitimated by virtue of the Legitimacy Acts or that his legitimation has been recognised under section 8 of the Act of 1926, he may petition for a decree to this effect.[19]

The Attorney-General must be joined as a respondent to any petition.[20] A declaration made on a petition brought under this section binds all persons given notice of the proceedings or made parties (including the Crown) and anyone claiming through them, unless the decree was obtained by fraud or collusion.[1] In order to ensure that the petitioner's legitimacy cannot be questioned in any other proceedings, it is clearly imperative to join as a party anyone who, as a result of possible claims to property, might attempt to dispute it later.[2]

---

[18]*I.e.*, lineal ancestor. The expression does not therefore include an uncle: *Knowles* v. *A.-G.*, [1950] 2 All E.R. 6; [1951] P. 54.

[19]Proceedings under this subsection may be brought in the High Court or in a county court: s. 39 (2), (3).

[20]S. 39 (6).

[1]S. 39 (5).

[2]The court may order interested persons to be given notice of the proceedings and they may then become parties and oppose the application: s. 39 (7).

CHAPTER 10

Adoption

A. INTRODUCTORY

In common parlance the term " adoption " is frequently used in a sense much wider than its strict legal one. If a child's parents die or abandon it and it is brought up by someone else, the latter is often said to have adopted the child, particularly if he is a stranger in blood. This relationship is described as foster parenthood in this book, and its legal results will be discussed later.[1] One of the disadvantages of mere *de facto* control is that, since the relationship is one which is strictly not recognised by the law at all, the legal position of the person assuming control is precarious. One of the gravest threats is that the child's parents or legally appointed guardians may try at any time to assert their legal powers, and although their claim may well be defeated on the grounds that it will not be in the interests of the child to be torn away from those who have brought it up,[2] the latter may nevertheless live in real fear of losing the child. It would, of course, always be possible for people in this position to have themselves appointed guardians of the child and thus give legal authority to an existing situation. But the relationship of the parties in cases such as these often resembles that of parent and child rather than that of guardian and ward, and there were no means either at common law or in equity of creating a legal relationship in any way equivalent to that of parent and legitimate child. The view taken by English law that a parent's rights over his child were inalienable meant that it could recognise no change of status comparable to the *adoptio* or *adrogatio* of Roman law. Consequently, spouses who were probably childless and anxious to bring up another's child as their own hesitated to do so, and the child was in turn deprived of the opportunity of a normal home life and remained in the orphanage or some other institution.

The result was a demand for reform which led eventually to the passing of the Adoption of Children Act in 1926. The provisions of this Act were revolutionary, for, subject to certain limitations, it permitted anyone wishing to bring up somebody else's child as his own to apply for an adoption order from a court of competent jurisdiction, the effect of which, if it was granted, was to break entirely the legal relationship between the child and its natural parents and to replace it by a similar

---

[1]*Post*, pp. 319-321.
[2]See also the provisions of the Custody of Children Act 1891, *post*, p. 270.

relationship between the child and its adopters. The result, in brief, is that the adopters for almost all legal purposes step into the shoes of the child's natural parents; by its " parents " in other words are now meant not its natural parents but its adoptive parents.

The relationship between the parties is thus distinguishable from that of parent and legitimate child, parent and illegitimate child, and guardian and ward. It resembles most closely the first, for, although there need be no blood relationship between the parties, the legal consequences are almost the same. It differs most markedly from the second for the law still in some ways gives no effect to the natural rights and duties which the blood relationship creates: adoption in fact creates virtually the converse situation. It resembles the third in that the adoptive parents, like guardians, stand *in loco parentis* to the child to whom they are not necessarily related in blood, but differs from it in that the relationship of guardian and ward does not make the latter a member of the former's family for the purposes, for example, of the devolution and acquisition of property. The relationship might best be summed up in the word " quasi-legitimate ".

The Act of 1926 was extensively amended in the light of subsequent experience and criticisms; all earlier legislation has now been repealed and the law consolidated in the Adoption Act of 1958. In addition to giving a power to make adoption orders, this Act places considerable power to supervise arrangements for adoption' and to secure the well-being of children awaiting adoption in the hands of local authorities, that is, county, county borough and London borough councils.[3] The fact that the number of people wishing to adopt children always far exceeds the number of children to be adopted has led to the possibility of commercial trafficking in adoption; this the Act seeks to prevent by making it illegal for any body of persons to make arrangements for an adoption unless it is a registered adoption society (which must be a charitable association)[4] or a local authority and by forbidding the giving or receiving of any payment or reward in consideration of an adoption or the arrangement of an adoption.[5] Any advertisement is prohibited which indicates that a parent or guardian wishes to have a child adopted or that a person wishes to adopt a child or that anyone except an adoption society or local authority is willing to make arrangements for its adoption.[6] Furthermore, except under the authority of a provisional adoption order, it is forbidden to take or send a minor who is a British subject to any place outside the United Kingdom, Channel Islands or the

---

[3]Local Authority Social Services Act 1970, s. 1. See *post*, pp. 254-255.

[4]S. 29. An adoption society must be registered by the local authority in whose area its administrative centre is situated. An appeal from a refusal to register or the cancellation of a registration lies to Quarter Sessions: ss. 30 and 31. For regulations relating to adoption societies and the inspection of their books, etc., see ss. 32 and 33.

[5]S. 50. But an adoption society or local authority may be paid reasonable expenses and the court to which an application for an adoption order is made may authorise payments or rewards: s. 50 (3).

[6]S. 51.

Isle of Man with a view to his adoption by any person who is not his parent, guardian or relative.[7]

B. THE MAKING OF ADOPTION ORDERS UNDER THE ADOPTION ACT 1958

The vast majority of adoption orders are made in respect of illegitimate children who are placed for adoption very shortly after their birth.[8] Arrangements are usually made by an adoption society or the local authority. There is nothing to stop parents from making arrangements with the proposed adopters personally or through a private individual (for example, a doctor or minister of religion) but this is to be discouraged for two reasons. In the first place adoption societies and local authorities have experienced case workers who can do much more than an inexperienced individual to ensure that the adoption is likely to be a success. They will interview the applicants and form a reliable judgment of their suitability to act as adoptive parents and will also try to match the child and the adopters, for example by placing a child of highly intelligent parents with equally intelligent people. Secondly, provided that the natural parents are prepared to consent to the procedure (which in practice they normally will), the identity of the applicants can be withheld from them. This will prevent any attempt by the parents to get in touch with the child later, which might destroy the security which adoption is designed to give to the child and adopters alike. Any person giving consent to an adoption in ignorance of the applicants' identity may attach conditions stipulating the religion in which the child is to be brought up.[9]

Who may be adopted.—An adoption order may be made only in respect of a person who (i) is under the age of 18, (ii) has never been married, and (iii) except in the case mentioned in the next paragraph, resides in England.[10]

Who may apply for an Adoption Order.—In the first place, the applicant must be domiciled in England or Scotland and resident in England (Scottish courts having jurisdiction if the applicant is resident in Scotland).[11] This limitation on residence produced hardship in

---

[7]S. 52. A British subject includes a citizen of the Republic of Ireland: s. 57 (3). For the meaning of " relative ", see *infra*, n.[15]; for provisional adoption orders, see *post*, p. 257. A provisional adoption order is not required in the case of a child emigrating under the authority of the Home Secretary (see *post*, p. 297, n.[1]: Children and Young Persons Act 1963, s. 55. For criticisms of the existing law and suggestions for reform, see the Working Paper published by the Departmental Committee on the Adoption of Children, 1970.

[8]In 1968, 19,348 out of the 24,831 orders registered were with respect to illegitimate children, 4,479 of whom were adopted by a parent. 4,038 of the 5,483 legitimate children were adopted by a parent.

[9]Adoption Act 1958, s. 4 (2).

[10]Adoption Act 1958, ss. 1 (1), (5) and 57 (1); Family Law Reform Act 1969, s. 1 (3) and Sched. 1. The child's domicile does not affect jurisdiction: *Re B.*, [1967] 3 All E.R. 629; [1968] Ch. 204. But see *post*, p. 255, n.[6].

[11]*Ibid.*, s. 1 (1), (5). For the meaning of " residence ", see *Re Adoption Application 52/1951*, [1951] 2 All E.R. 931; [1952] Ch. 16, criticised as too narrow by McClean, *The Meaning of Residence*, 11 I.C.L.Q. 1153.

the case of applicants domiciled in a part of Great Britain but resident abroad[12] and consequently an application may now be made by persons domiciled in England or Scotland even though they are not normally resident in Great Britain. In such a case the court has jurisdiction even though the infant does not reside in England.[13]

Secondly, an adoption order may not be made unless the applicant satisfies one of the following conditions. He or she must (i) be the mother or father[14] of the child, *or* (ii) have attained the age of 21 and be a relative[15] of the child, *or* (iii) have attained the age of 25 years.[16]

Thirdly, since the effect of an adoption order is to create the legal relationship of parent and legitimate child between the adopter and adopted child, an adoption order may not be made upon the application of more than one person unless the applicants are married to each other, in which case they may apply jointly for an order.[17] In addition *either* (i) one of the applicants must be a parent of the child *or* (ii) one of the applicants must be able to satisfy one of the other two conditions set out above and the other must be at least 21 years old.[18] If a married person is the sole applicant, no order may be made without the consent of his or her spouse: it would be absurd if, say, a wife could create this legal relationship without her husband's approval. But clearly it would be equally absurd if this consent were to be required where the husband and wife had ceased to live together as such, and so it may be dispensed with if the other spouse cannot be found or is incapable of giving consent or if the spouses have separated and are living apart and the separation is likely to be permanent.[19]

Fourthly, an adoption order may not be made in respect of a female child on the sole application of a man unless there are special circumstances which will justify this as an exceptional measure.[20] One of the reasons for this provision is presumably to prevent possible sexual corruption of the child, and whether the court is justified in making an order in any given case must obviously depend upon the facts.[1]

Consents required to the Making of an Order.—Since the effect of an adoption order is to destroy the legal relationship existing between the child and its natural parents, the Act provides that no order may be made except with the consent of every person or body who is a

---

[12]See *Re Adoption Application* 52/1951, (*supra*).

[13]Adoption Act 1958, s. 12; *Re R.*, [1962] 3 All E.R. 238, C.A.

[14]Including the natural father of an illegitimate child: *ibid.*, s. 57 (1).

[15]*I.e.*, grandparent, brother, sister, uncle or aunt, whether of the full blood, of the half blood or by affinity, and includes, in the case of a child who has previously been adopted, any person who would be a relative within this definition if it were the legitimate child of the former adopter, and, in the case of an illegitimate child, its natural father and any person who would be a relative if it were the legitimate child of its father and mother: *ibid.*, s. 57 (1).

[16]*Ibid.*, s. 2 (1).

[17]*Ibid.*, s. 1 (2).

[18]*Ibid.*, s. 2 (2).

[19]*Ibid.*, ss. 4 (1) (b), 5 (4).

[20]*Ibid.*, s. 2 (3).

[1]In *Re R.M.* (1941), 193 L.T.Jo. 7, C.A., it was held that the fact that the child was the applicant's illegitimate daughter did not justify the making of an order. *Quaere* whether this would still be followed.

parent or guardian of the child.[2]   In the case of a child who has been adopted previously, its " parents " are its adoptive parents under the first order.[3] In the case of an illegitimate child the mother's consent will be required[4] but not that of the father for, as he has no rights which the adoption order will extinguish, there is nothing in the Act to rebut the presumption that the term " parent " does not include the father of a bastard.[5] He is entitled to be heard, however, if he is contributing to the child's maintenance under any order or agreement;[6] in other cases the court may permit him to be heard and will normally do so if he is showing parental concern about the child's future. If, contrary to the mother's wishes, he does not want the child to be adopted, he may try to strengthen his hand by applying for custody.[7] In such a case the real question is whether the court should award custody to him or make the adoption order, and in order to arrive at a proper conclusion and enable all parties to be heard, the court should hear both applications at the same time and not give judgment on one until it has heard the other.[8] As in other cases involving custody, the problem must be resolved by reference to what is best for the child's welfare. In such circumstances the tie of blood cannot, of course, be ignored, and in *Re C. (M.A.)*[9] the Court of Appeal upheld a decision in which custody had been given to the father (who was married and could offer the child a good home) even though the applicants for an adoption order had had care and possession of it for 15 months. Two members of the court went so far as to say that adoption is a second best step which should not be taken when a real parent wants the child and can make suitable arrangements for it, but these dicta are in direct conflict with the earlier decisions of the Court of Appeal in *Re Adoption Application 41/61*[10] and *Re O.*[11] and cannot be regarded as a correct statement of the law. The true position, as was emphasised in the two earlier cases, is that the father is entitled to special consideration but no more, and if the welfare of the child demands it, an adoption order will be made.[12]

As the purpose of requiring parents' and guardians' consents is to ensure that their rights are not arbitrarily destroyed, it follows that

---

[2]Adoption Act 1958, s. 4 (1) (a). In the case of a ward of court the consent of the court must also be obtained.

[3]*Ibid.*, s. 1 (4); Adoption Act 1968, s. 10 (3).

[4]*Cf. Re M.*, [1955] 2 All E.R. 911, C.A.; [1955] 2 Q.B. 479; *Watson* v, *Nikolaisen*, [1955] 2 All E.R. 427; [1955] 2 Q.B. 286.

[5]*Re M., (supra).*

[6]Adoption (High Court) Rules 1959, rr. 16 and 17; Adoption (County Court) Rules 1959, r. 10; Adoption (Juvenile Court) Rules 1959, r. 12.

[7]Under the Guardianship of Minors Act 1971, ss. 9 (1) and 14 (1) (see *post*, p. 282). Even if the father is awarded custody, his consent is still not required, for the order does not make him the child's guardian: *Re Adoption Application 41/61*, [1962] 3 All E.R. 553, C.A.; [1963] Ch. 315; *Re O.*, [1964] 1 All E.R. 786, C.A.; [1965] Ch. 23.

[8]*Re O., (supra).* Steps should be taken to prevent the putative father from discovering the adopters' identity if necessary: *Re O., (supra)*; *Re Adoption Application 41/61 (No. 2)*, [1963] 2 All E.R. 1082; [1964] Ch. 48.

[9][1966] 1 All E.R. 838, C.A.

[10][1962] 3 All E.R. 553, C.A.; [1963] Ch. 315.

[11][1964] 1 All E.R. 786, C.A.; [1965] Ch. 23.

[12]As in *Re Adoption Application 41/61 (No. 2), (supra)*, and *Re O., (supra).*

consent is not required if the person concerned has not performed his natural or legal duties or is incapable of giving his consent or is acting unreasonably. Consequently, the court may dispense with the consent if the parent or guardian has abandoned, neglected[13] or persistently ill-treated the child, or has persistently failed without reasonable cause to discharge the obligations of a parent or guardian of the child,[14] or in any case, cannot be found[15] or is incapable of giving his consent[16] or his consent is unreasonably withheld.[17]

Whether or not consent is unreasonably withheld is a question of fact in each case. Although some earlier cases stressed that, before a parent could be deprived of his rights, the court must be satisfied that he had in some way been culpable, this approach was firmly rejected by the House of Lords in *Re W*.[18] All members of the House agreed that the test is objective: would a reasonable parent, placed in the situation of the particular parent, withhold consent? *Prima facie* it must always be reasonable to do so in view of the consequences of the making of an order; consequently it will be exceptional for a court to hold that consent is unreasonably withheld unless the parent has been guilty of culpable conduct.[19] In many cases it will be easy to say whether, looked at objectively, the parent is acting reasonably or not, but in others one parent, acting reasonably, might withhold his consent whilst another, acting reasonably, might not do so. In the latter type of case the court must respect the particular parent's decision to refuse consent and must not substitute its own view. As LORD HAILSHAM, L.C., said:[20]

" The question in any given case is whether a parental veto comes within the band of possible reasonable decisions and not whether it is right or mistaken. Not every reasonable exercise of judgment is right, and not every mistaken exercise or judgment is unreasonable."

All the facts must be looked at, but obviously the reasonable parent will give greatest weight to the child's welfare. This is not the sole consideration; conversely, it is not necessary to show a prognosis of lasting damage to the child before consent can be said to be unreasonably withheld.[21] A reasonable parent must clearly take account of

---

[13] " Abandoned " and " neglected " connote conduct which would render the parent or guardian liable to criminal proceedings under the Children and Young Persons Act 1933, s. 1 (*post*, pp. 306-307). *Watson* v. *Nikolaisen*, (*supra*); *Re W.* (unreported), cited in *Re P.*, [1962] 3 All E.R. 789, 793.

[14] These include the natural and moral duty to show affection, care and interest for the child as well as the legal duty to maintain: *Re P.*, (*supra*); *Re B.*, [1967] 3 All E.R. 629; [1968] Ch. 204.

[15] *I.e.*, cannot be found by taking all reasonable and proper steps: *Re F. (R.)*, [1969] 3 All E.R. 1101, C.A.; [1970] 1 Q.B. 385.

[16] This expression and the last cover the case of a person whose whereabouts is known but with whom it is impossible to communicate: *Re R.*, [1966] 3 All E.R. 613 (impossible to communicate with parents in a country under totalitarian government for political reasons).

[17] Adoption Act 1958, s. 5 (1), (2). This is permissive and the court must consider whether or not to exercise its discretion in any given case: *Re C.S.C.*, [1960] 1 All E.R. 711, 714.

[18] [1971] 2 All E.R. 49, H.L.

[19] *Per* LORD HAILSHAM, L.C., at pp. 55-56, LORD HODSON at p. 72.

[20] At p. 56.

[21] See LORD HAILSHAM, L.C., at pp. 55-56, LORD HODSON at p. 73, LORD DONOVAN at pp. 78-79.

financial and educational prospects, but of much greater importance, of course, is the child's future happiness and the stability of its home life.[1] Although little weight should be given to the parent's vacillation under stress or to the pain that the loss of the child will inevitably cause the applicants,[2] it must be appreciated that to tear the child away from those whom it has come to regard as its parents may have disastrous consequences. This in itself may force the reasonable parent to give his consent to the adoption; and the longer the child has been with the applicants, the greater the danger to be guarded against. In *Re W.* the child, who was illegitimate, had been with the applicants for 18 months and had settled down well with them. The mother (who later withdrew her consent) already had two other illegitimate children; there was a grave risk of more (which would reduce her prospects of marriage); there was no man in the household; and it was doubtful whether she had the capacity to bring up three children. In these circumstances the House of Lords held that there was ample evidence to support the county court judge's finding that the mother was unreasonably withholding her consent.[3]

Consent to the making of an adoption order may be given before or at the time of the hearing; in the former event, documentary evidence of the giving of consent is admissible, except that, if the person giving the consent is the child's mother, the document cannot be admitted unless the child was at least six weeks old when it was executed and it is also attested by a justice of the peace, a county court officer empowered to take affidavits or a magistrates' clerk.[4] The consent must be operative when the order is made, however, and consequently any consent previously given may be withdrawn at any time before that.[5] But if a person, who has given consent to the making of an order without knowing who the applicant is, subsequently withdraws it *solely* on the ground that the applicant's identity is unknown, it is to be deemed unreasonably withheld.[6]

Procedure for the Making of Adoption Orders.—Before a court can make an adoption order, a number of preliminary conditions must be satisfied.

Care and Possession of the Child.—In order to ensure as far as possible that the adopters are suitable people to bring the child up, he must have been continuously in their care and possession for at least three consecutive months preceding the making of the order and after he reached the age of six weeks.[7] In *Re C.S.C.*[8] ROXBURGH, J., held

---

[1]*Cf. Re F.*, [1970] 1 All E.R. 344, C.A., at pp. 347 and 349, where it was stated obiter that the court could dispense with the consent of a father who had strangled the child's mother even though he was found guilty of manslaughter on the ground of diminished responsibility. (See further *post*, p. 325-326).
[2]*Per* LORD HAILSHAM, L.C., at pp. 56-57.
[3]See further Michaels, *The Dangers of a Change of Parentage in Custody and Adoption Cases*, 83 L.Q.R. 547, particularly at pp. 560 *et seq.*; Blom-Cooper, *Adoption Applications and Parental Responsibility*, 20 M.L.R. 473.
[4]Adoption Act 1958, s. 6. The last condition is clearly designed to prevent the mother from being persuaded to give her consent before she has recovered from the child's birth, which is particularly likely to happen if she is the young mother of an illegitimate child.
[5]*Re F.*, [1957] 1 All E.R. 819; *Re K.*, [1952] 2 All E.R. 877, C.A.; [1953] 1 Q.B. 117.
[6]Adoption Act 1958, s. 5 (3).   [7]Adoption Act 1958, s. 3 (1).   [8][1960] 1 All E.R. 711.

that this condition was not satisfied where the applicants had voluntarily parted with the child for one night. Although this decision may have been correct on the facts because it was the mother who had had the possession of the child for the period in question, his approach seems to have been unnecessarily restrictive: the inference is that the period would have to begin to run all over again if, for example, the applicants were compelled to go away for a night and leave the child with a friend or relation. The better view, it is submitted, is that of BUCKLEY, J., in *Re B.*[9] where he applied the test: was the applicant throughout the period in effective control of the child's life and was that control of a kind and exercised in a way which was quasi-parental? In that case the applicant was a nurse who wished to adopt her own illegitimate son aged two years. She was employed in a hospital and because of night duties she left the boy with neighbours with whom he spent on the average four days and five nights a week. As they acted in accordance with the mother's wishes and directions and were really in a similar position to the child's nurse, BUCKLEY, J., concluded that care and control were exercised on the applicant's behalf and therefore vicariously by her, and he held that he had jurisdiction to make the order. Scottish cases have gone even further and it has been held that there is continuous care and possession notwithstanding that the child was in hospital for a part of the time,[10] or that she was a probationer nurse in a hospital and returned to the applicants' home only at the weekends and on holiday.[11] An extreme application would clearly defeat the purpose of the Act; if, for example, the child spent the whole of the time in hospital or at a boarding school, there would be no opportunity of seeing whether he was likely to settle down in his new home. In the absence of any other evidence, the court could refuse to make an order in such a case on the ground that it was not satisfied that it would be for the child's welfare.

If the applicants are normally resident in England, the care and possession will usually be in this country, but it is submitted that this does not prevent them from taking the child out of the jurisdiction, say, for a holiday or for reasons of health.[12] If they are not normally resident in England or Scotland, however, the position is more complicated. If there is only one applicant, the above provisions must be complied with. If the spouses apply jointly, they satisfy the statutory conditions if they both have care and possession for three months although, if the child is above school age (in which case no notice has

---

[9] [1963] 3 All E.R. 125, 129; [1964] Ch. 1, 7. *Cf. Re A.*, [1963] 1 All E.R. 531, 535, where CROSS, J., speaking of a case where the child was aged 20, said that it was artificial to talk of care and possession in such circumstances but stressed that the applicants must be *in loco parentis* to him.

[10] *Re G., Petitioner*, 1955 S.L.T. (Sh. Ct.) 27.

[11] *Re A., Petitioners*, 1953 S.L.T. (Sh. Ct.) 45. In *Re A., Petitioners*, 1958 S.L.T. (Sh. Ct.) 61, it was held "with difficulty and hesitation" that the child was in the care and possession of both applicants when he lived with the wife, and the husband, a soldier, was away on service. A child in the armed forces cannot be in the care and possession of the applicants: *Re M., Petitioner*, 1953 S.C. 227. See Webb and Bevan, *Source Book of Family Law*, 531-532.

[12] In *Re W.*, [1962] 2 All E.R. 875; [1962] Ch. 918, 925, WILBERFORCE, J., said *obiter* that there *must* be care and possession in England or Scotland. *Sed quaere?* See Josling, *Adoption of Children*, 30-34.

to be given to the local authority),[13] this need not be in Great Britain at all.[14] This might be impossible, however, if one of them has to return to their normal place of residence; consequently the Act specifically provides as an alternative that it is sufficient if the child has been in the care and possession of one of them during the previous three months provided that the applicants have lived together in Great Britain for at least one of those months.[15]

Once an application for an order has been made, no parent or guardian who has consented to the adoption nor any adoption society or local authority who has arranged it can demand the return of the child from the applicant without the leave of the court.[16]

Notice to Local Authority.—If the child is below the upper limit of the compulsory school age, no adoption order may be made unless the applicant has given to the local authority within whose area he is then resident three months' notice in writing of his intention to apply for the order. This provision does not apply if the applicant (or one of the applicants) is the child's parent.[17] If he is not normally resident in Great Britain, he must give notice to the local authority in whose area he is then living.[18]

The purpose of the notice is to ensure the proper supervision of children placed for adoption. As soon as the notice is given, the child becomes a " protected child " for the purpose of Part IV of the Adoption Act—a term which also covers most children below the upper limit of the compulsory school age placed for adoption in the care and possession of anyone who is not a parent, guardian or relative by virtue of an arrangement made by someone other than a parent or guardian.[19] The authority's chief duty is to see that the child is visited from time to time, to satisfy themselves as to its well-being, and to give any advice about its care and maintenance.[20] They may prohibit a person from taking the care and possession of a protected child if this would appear to be detrimental to the child unless an adoption society or local authority took part in the arrangements,[1] and a juvenile court can order the removal of a protected child from unsuitable surroundings.[2]

---

[13]See *infra*.
[14]*Re W.*, (*supra*). Presumably this would also apply if the applicant was the child's parent as no notice has to be given in that case either.
[15]Adoption Act 1958, s. 12 (3); *Re W.*, (*supra*). " Living together " has the usual wide meaning given to consortium (see *ante*, p. 94) and the spouses need not have resided in the same house continuously for a month: *Re M.*, [1964] 2 All E.R. 1017; [1965] Ch. 203. In *Re W.* WILBERFORCE, J., stated that the care and possession must be exercised in Great Britain. *Sed quaere?* See Josling, *op. cit.*
[16]*Ibid.*, ss. 34 and 35 (1) (b), (2).
[17]*Ibid.*, s. 3 (2).
[18]*Ibid.*, s. 12 (1), (3). In the case of a joint application, it is sufficient if notice is given by either applicant.
[19]*Ibid.*, s. 37, as amended by the Children and Young Persons Act 1969, s. 52 (4), *q.v.* for the exceptions. Any person or body (other than a parent or guardian) taking part in the arrangements must give notice to the local authority: s. 40 (1)-(3).
[20]*Ibid.*, ss. 38 and 39. The Home Secretary may also authorise an inspection: Children and Young Persons Act 1969, ss. 58 and 59.
[1]*Ibid.*, s. 41. An appeal lies to a juvenile court: s. 42.
[2]*Ibid.*, s. 43. A single justice may act in an emergency. The local authority may receive such a child into their care under s. 1 of the Children Act 1948 (see *post*, p. 296).

Guardian ad litem.—The court must appoint a guardian *ad litem* to safeguard the child's interests.[3]   His duties are extensive and are laid down in the Adoption Rules; they may be broadly classified under four heads. First, he must interview the applicants and get from them all relevant information about their home conditions, means and health. They are bound to provide a medical certificate that they are physically, mentally and emotionally suitable to adopt a child; unless one of the applicants is a parent or relative of the child, they must also name a referee whom the guardian *ad litem* must also interview. Secondly, he must find out all relevant information about the child. A medical report must be submitted, and the guardian *ad litem* must interview the natural parents and anyone who has taken part in arranging the adoption and must obtain a report from the local authority and adoption society. If the child is old enough to understand the nature of an adoption order, he must also find out whether the child wishes to be adopted.   Thirdly, he must make sure that all consents given to the making of the order have been freely given. Finally, he must make a confidential report to the court. This report may not be seen by any party to the proceedings except with the leave of the court: this procedure is objectionable in that an unsuccessful applicant cannot controvert any statement of fact, but on the other hand the guardian *ad litem* might well be inhibited and the value of his report correspondingly reduced if he knew that others might read it. ´

Functions of the Court.—An adoption order may be made by the High Court, a county court or (except where the applicants are not normally resident in Great Britain) a magistrates' court sitting as a juvenile court.[4]

The court must be satisfied of three things: that all those whose consent is required have given it and understand the nature and effects of an adoption order; that no unauthorised payments or rewards for the adoption have been made or agreed upon; and that the order, if made, will be for the child's welfare.[5]   It will obviously have to rely very heavily (although by no means exclusively) on the report of the guardian *ad litem*.

The main benefit that the child is likely to receive is the substitution of statutory parents, who can show real care and affection, for those who are unable or unwilling to perform their parental duties. But "welfare" is a sufficiently wide term to include material benefit as well,[6] and consequently the court may properly make an order for a

---

[3]*Ibid.*, s. 9 (7). The guardian *ad litem* is usually the Official Solicitor (in the High Court) or the Director of Social Services of the local authority or a probation officer (in other courts). No one who has taken part in the arrangements for the adoption or who represents a society or authority which has done so may be the guardian *ad litem*.

[4]*Ibid.*, ss. 9 (1), 12 (2); Adoption (Juvenile Court) Rules 1959, r. 1. About two-thirds of all orders are made by county courts and one-third by juvenile courts; the number made by the High Court is very small (39 out of 24,859 in 1968).

[5]*Ibid.*, s. 7 (1), (2).

[6]*Re A.*, [1963] 1 All E.R. 531, 534. If the child has a substantial connection with a foreign country (for example, if he is domiciled there or is a foreign national), one of the matters to be taken into account in deciding whether the order will be for his benefit is whether it will be recognised in that country: *Re B.*, [1967] 3 All E.R. 629; [1968] Ch. 204.

mother to adopt her own illegitimate child as this will go a long way to remove the social stigma and remaining legal disabilities of illegitimacy.[7] On the other hand, there must be a genuine intention that the applicants should stand *in loco parentis* to the child and in *Re A*.[8] Cross, J., refused to make an order for what he described as an accommodation adoption of a French boy aged 20, which was sought purely in order to give him the advantage of British nationality.

The court may impose any terms and conditions it thinks fit in the order—for example as to religious education or placing the adopters under a duty to tell the child that it has been adopted[9]—and in particular may require the adopter to make financial provision for the child.[10]

Registration of Adoptions.—The Registrar General keeps a separate register of adoptions. Records are also kept at Somerset House enabling connections between entries in this register and the register of births to be traced, but these records may be searched only with the leave of the court.[11]

Interim Orders.—Instead of making the order applied for, the court may make an interim order to last for not more than two years, the effect of which is to give the custody of the child to the applicant subject to any conditions imposed by the court as regards its maintenance, education and the supervision of its welfare.[12] The purpose of an interim order is to enable the adopters to act for a probationary period, and it is thus a useful compromise when the court is genuinely unable to make up its mind upon the advisability of making a permanent order. A court has jurisdiction to make an interim order only if it has jurisdiction to make an adoption order.

Refusal to make an Order.—If the court refuses to make any order at all (or if at any stage the application is withdrawn) and the child was placed for adoption by an adoption society or local authority, it must be returned to that body within seven days.[13] There is no

---

[7] Adoption Act 1958, s. 1 (3); *Re D.*, [1958] 3 All E.R. 716, C.A.; [1959] 1 Q.B. 229.

[8] [1963] 1 All E.R. 531. Distinguished in *Re R.*, [1966] 3 All E.R. 613, where the child was also aged 20 and desired to acquire British nationality, on the ground that there was also a genuine desire that he should become a member of the applicant's family. (Until 1969 an adoption order could be made if the child was under 21.)

[9] But there is no requirement that the child should be brought up in the same faith as its parents unless consent to the adoption has only been given on this condition: see *Re G.*, [1962] 2 All E.R. 173, C.A.; [1962] 2 Q.B. 141.

[10] Adoption Act 1958, s. 7 (3). But it is questionable what effective sanctions exist if the conditions imposed are not observed: *Re G. (T.J.)*, [1963] 1 All E.R. 20, C.A., at pp. 23 and 32; [1963] 2 Q.B. 73, at pp. 88 and 102.

[11] *Ibid.*, ss. 20, 21 and 24. The court for this purpose means the court making the adoption order, the High Court or the Westminster County Court. A search might be ordered, for example, if the child was entitled to a gift under a disposition taking effect before the adoption order but not vesting until after it had been made.

[12] *Ibid.*, s. 8. The period laid down in the original order may be extended provided that the total period is not greater than two years.

[13] *Ibid.*, s. 35. This also applies if an interim order expires without a full order being made. There appears to be no means of ordering a stay in the event of an appeal, although presumably the applicants could invoke the inherent jurisdiction of the High Court by making the child a ward of court.

statutory obligation to return the child in other cases.[14] The reason for the difference is this: in the first case the body concerned must obviously try to find other suitable applicants, whereas in the second there may be good reasons for permitting the applicants to retain care and control even though an adoption order has not been made. This might occur, for example, if the court had to refuse to make the order because the child's mother withdrew her consent; if she wishes to recover care and control it is for her to bring the necessary proceedings, the outcome of which must depend primarily on what is in the child's best interests.[15]

If the application is refused *on its merits*, the applicants may make a further application only if there has been a substantial change in the circumstances since the first one.[16]

Provisional Orders.—Since 1959 the High Court and county courts now have a power that they did not possess before, that of making a provisional adoption order.[17] The purpose of such an order is to enable a person who is not domiciled in England or Scotland (and in whose favour therefore a full adoption order cannot be made) to remove a minor out of Great Britain to obtain an adoption order under his *lex domicilii*. The court has jurisdiction to make such an order only if it would have had jurisdiction to make a full order had the applicant been domiciled in England or Scotland.[18] A provisional order authorises the applicant to remove the child out of the country for the purpose of his adoption elsewhere and in the meantime gives the custody of it to the applicant pending the adoption. Such an order has all the effects of a full order save that it will not affect any devolution of property and will not affect the child's citizenship.

Revocation of Adoption Orders.—It is specifically provided that an adoption order may be revoked if an illegitimate person, who has been adopted by his mother or father alone, is subsequently legitimated by his parents' marriage so that he may have the advantage of being treated as the legitimate child of both parents.[19] In other cases it

---

[14]Unless the child is in the care of a local authority and the authority demands its return: *ibid.*, s. 36.

[15]See *post*, pp. 276 *et seq.*

[16]Adoption (High Court) Rules 1959, r. 6; Adoption (County Court) Rules 1959, r. 6; Adoption (Juvenile Court) Rules 1959, r. 6.

[17]Adoption Act 1958, s. 53. Formerly a magistrate's licence had to be obtained.

[18]But the child must have been in the care and possession of the applicant continuously for *six* months since the former was six weeks old and before the date of the order and *six* months' notice must have been given to the local authority: s. 53 (5). In the case of joint applicants not resident in Great Britain, it is sufficient if the child has been in the care and possession of one of them for six months provided that the applicants have lived together for at least one of the previous *three* months: *Re M.*, [1964] 2 All E.R. 1017; [1965] Ch. 203.

[19]Adoption Act 1958, s. 26. The order may be revoked by the court that made it on the application of any of the parties concerned. An order may also be revoked if a child previously adopted by both parents was legitimated by the Legitimacy Act 1959 (*ante*, p. 241): Adoption Act 1960, s. 1. No revocation will affect the devolution of property in the case of an intestacy occurring or a disposition made beforehand: Adoption Act 1960, s. 1 (2).

is probable that an order once made cannot be revoked at all although an appeal will, of course, lie from the making of an order (as it will from a refusal to make one).[20] No other provision is made for the revocation of an order in the Act, and this omission may be deliberate on the grounds that it might well do more harm to go back on the making of the order than to leave it in effect even though the court would not have made it in the first place had it been in possession of all the facts.[1]

C. THE MAKING OF ADOPTION ORDERS UNDER THE ADOPTION ACT 1968

Whereas the basis of jurisdiction to make adoptions under the Adoption Act of 1958 is the applicants' English (or Scottish) domicile, in many foreign systems the basis of jurisdiction is the parties' nationality. This has naturally caused difficulties in cases with a foreign element and the desire to produce a uniform law of jurisdiction and recognition led to the Hague Convention on the adoption of children in 1965.[2] The terms of the convention have been embodied in the Adoption Act of 1968 and, as it will be seen, the essential connecting links are the nationality and residence of the parties.

The Act will not come into force until a date (not yet specified) to be appointed by the Secretary of State. *It must be emphasised that the jurisdiction it confers is additional to that conferred by the Act of 1958 which is in no way cut down; consequently those who are competent to do so should continue to apply for an order under the earlier Act.*

Only the High Court has power to make adoption orders under the Act of 1968.[3] Subject to what is said below, the procedure to be followed under the 1968 Act is the same as that under the 1958 Act (including, for example, the need for the applicants to have care and possession of the child for three months and the giving of notice to the local authority) and interim orders may be made. The effect of an order made under the 1968 Act is also the same as that of an order made under the 1958 Act.[4]

It will be convenient at the outset to define some of the technical terms used in the Act. A *convention country* is any country designated by the Secretary of State as a country in which the Convention is in force. A *specified country* means Northern Ireland, the Channel Islands, the Isle of Man and any colony designated for this purpose by the

---

[20]In the case of an appeal from a magistrates' court, to a single judge of the High Court (Adoption Act 1958, s. 10); in other cases to the Court of Appeal. An order made by a county court or by a magistrates' court may be quashed by *certiorari*.

[1]This view was put forward as a possible explanation by LORD GREENE, M.R., and SOMERVELL, L.J., in *Skinner* v. *Carter*, [1948] 1 All E.R. 917, C.A., at pp. 920 and 921; [1948] Ch. 387, at pp. 389, 395 and 397, where it was held that an adoption order, which had been made on the joint application of a husband and wife, remained in force notwithstanding that their marriage was void and that the " wife " could obtain an order against her " husband " under the Guardianship of Infants Act (*i.e.*, the child was still in law in the position of their legitimate child).

[2]Cmnd. 2613.

[3]Ss. 1 (1) and 11 (1).

[4]See generally s. 2.

Secretary of State. A *United Kingdom national* is a citizen of the United Kingdom and Colonies satisfying such conditions as the Secretary of State may specify.[5] If a United Kingdom national is also a national of another state, he is to be regarded as a United Kingdom national only; in other cases of dual nationality, the person in question is to be treated as a national of the country with which he is most closely connected unless one only of the countries is a convention country, in which case he is to be treated as a national of that country. A stateless person is to be regarded as a national of the country in which he habitually resides.[6]

Who may be adopted.—An adoption order may be made only in respect of a person who (i) is under the age of 18; (ii) has not been married; (iii) is a national of the United Kingdom or a convention country; and (iv) habitually resides in Great Britain, a specified country or a convention country.[7]

Who may apply for an Order.—An applicant must either (a) habitually reside in Great Britain *and* be a national of the United Kingdom or a convention country, or (b) habitually reside in a convention country or a specified country *and* be a United Kingdom national. A joint application may be made by a husband and wife, in which case both must satisfy either condition (a) or condition (b). No order may be made on the sole application of a married person unless his or her spouse consents or the consent is dispensed with under the provisions of the 1958 Act.[8]

Consents and Consultations.—No order may be made unless the provisions relating to " consents and consultations " of the internal law of the country of which the *child* is a national are complied with. This does not, however, apply to consents by members of the applicant's family or to consultations between them and the applicant. Hence if the child were a United Kingdom national, the consent of parents and guardians would have to be obtained as laid down in the Act of 1958. If consent may be dispensed with under the relevant law, the body empowered to do this is the High Court in the case of any application made in England, whatever the child's nationality.[9]

Restrictions on the making of Orders.—In two cases the court has no power to make an order under the 1968 Act at all:

(1) If the applicant or applicants are not United Kingdom nationals and the order is prohibited by the internal law of the country of which they are nationals.[10] Such a prohibition might relate, for example, to

---

[5] S. 11 (1).
[6] S. 9.
[7] Ss. 1 and 11 (1). The child must also be physically present in England.
[8] Ss. 1 (1), 3 (3) (b), (5), (6) and 11. The applicants (or one of them) must be physically present in England. If they are not normally resident here, the same rules relating to care and possession of the child apply as under the 1958 Act.
[9] Ss. 2 (4), 3 (3) (a), (4) and 10 (1).
[10] Ss. 3 (1) and 10 (1).

the relative ages of the child and the applicants or their blood relationship.

(2) If the applicant or applicants and the child are all United Kingdom nationals *and* all reside in Great Britain or a specified country.[11] The purpose here is clearly to restrict the operation of the 1968 Act to adoptions with a foreign element; in other cases the application will have to be made under the 1958 Act. It will be seen that there is a gap, however, for if the above conditions are satisfied and the applicants are not domiciled in England or Scotland, there is no jurisdiction to make an order under either Act.

D. THE LEGAL CONSEQUENCES OF THE MAKING OF AN ADOPTION ORDER

Rights and Duties with respect to the Child's Person.—As has already been pointed out, the effect of an adoption order is to establish the legal relationship of parent and legitimate child between the adopter and adopted child. This has two aspects. First, the legal rights and duties flowing from the relationship between the child and his natural parents or guardians automatically cease. Section 13 (1) of the Act of 1958 provides that:

> Upon an adoption order being made, all rights, duties, obligations and liabilities of the parents or guardians of the infant in relation to the future custody, maintenance and education of the infant, including all rights to appoint a guardian and . . . to consent or give notice of dissent to marriage, shall be extinguished. . . .

Thus any existing custody or maintenance order with respect to the child is automatically determined without being discharged by the court.[12] Similarly, a care order under the Children and Young Persons Act 1969 or a resolution made under section 2 of the Children Act 1948 will cease to have effect.[13] An affiliation order or an agreement by the father of an illegitimate child to make payments for its benefit is likewise discharged, unless the child is adopted by its mother who is a single woman at the time of the adoption, and no affiliation order may be made after the adoption order unless the child is adopted by its mother alone.[14]

Secondly, these rights and duties then vest in the adopter or adopters as if the child had been born to him or them in lawful wedlock.[15] For this reason, the court should exercise particular care in considering an application from a blood relation of the child who is not its parent; thus, if the maternal grandparents of a child were to adopt it, it would then in law become the brother of its own mother, and it is not difficult

---

[11]Ss. 3 (2) and 10 (1). For the difficulties arising under this Act and its relationship with the Act of 1958, see McClean and Patchett, *English Jurisdiction in Adoption*, 19 I.C.L.Q. 1.

[12]*Crossley* v. *Crossley*, [1953] 1 All E.R. 891; [1953] P. 97.

[13]Adoption Act 1958, s. 15 (3), (4), as amended by the Children and Young Persons Act 1969, Scheds. 5 and 6. See *post*, pp. 294 and 296-297.

[14]*Ibid.*, s. 15 (1), (2). " Single woman " presumably has the same meaning as it has in the Affiliation Proceedings Act 1957 (*post*, pp. 480-481).

[15]Adoption Act 1958, s. 13 (1), (2); *Crossley* v. *Crossley*, (*supra*).

to imagine that this might well lead to strain, disturbance and un-happiness all round.[16] If the child is adopted jointly by two spouses, orders may be made with respect to its custody and education as if it were their legitimate child.[17] So far as marriage is concerned, an adopted child and its adoptive parent are deemed to come within the prohibited degrees of consanguinity, so that they may not intermarry.[18] This, however, does not appear to prevent a marriage between the child and, say, its adoptive parents' own child; conversely since the modern law bears some relation to genetics, the child clearly cannot marry any person to whom it is related in blood and who would have come within the prohibited degrees if no adoption order had been made.

The wording of the Adoption Act is so wide that an adopted child would come within the definition of the word " child " in many other statutes even though it were not expressly included therein. Thus, the Ministry of Social Security Act does not contain any reference to adopted children, but the combined effect of the two Acts clearly places adopters under an obligation to maintain their adopted children.[19] The Fatal Accidents Acts, the Family Allowances Act, the National Insurance Act and the National Insurance (Industrial Injuries) Act have all been amended or phrased so as to include adopted children.[20] Similarly a child who is not a citizen of the United Kingdom and Colonies will acquire such citizenship on adoption if his adoptive parent possesses it.[1]

Rights with Respect to Property.—An adopted child's right to claim property under any disposition or on an intestacy will be dealt with when we consider children's rights to claim property generally.[2]

E. FOREIGN ADOPTION ORDERS

Since 1950 children adopted in Scotland have been in precisely the same position as those adopted in England for the purposes of English law. Under the Adoption Act of 1964, this is now true of children adopted in Northern Ireland, the Isle of Man and the Channel Islands.[3]

A much wider extension has been made by the Adoption Act of 1968. When this Act comes into force, the Secretary for State will be able to specify by order that any class or classes of adoption made outside Great Britain (whether or not in a convention country) shall have the

---

[16]See *Re A.B.*, [1949] 1 All E.R. 709; [1949] Ch. 320, where, however, an order was made on facts similar to these.

[17]Adoption Act 1958, s. 13 (2).

[18]*Ibid.*, s. 13 (3). This remains true even though a subsequent adoption order is made, and the child may not then marry either of the adopters.

[19]See *post*, p. 472.

[20]Fatal Accidents Act 1959, s. 1 (2) (a); Family Allowances Act 1965, s. 17 (4); National Insurance Act 1965, s. 114 (2) (a); National Insurance (Industrial Injuries) Act 1965, s. 86 (2) (a). For the effect of adoption on policies of insurance, see the Adoption Act 1958, s. 14.

[1]Adoption Act 1958, s. 19. In the case of a joint adoption, the child will acquire citizenship of the United Kingdom and Colonies if the male adopter possesses such citizenship.

[2]See *post*, pp. 466-467 and 507.

[3]S. 1. This applies only to acts done and events occurring after the Act came into force (16th July, 1964) and in the two cases mentioned in s. 1 (2) it applies only to orders made after that date. A child adopted in the Isle of Man or the Channel Islands will acquire citizenship of the U.K. on the date of the commencement of the Act or the date of adoption, whichever is later: s. 1 (3).

same effect as an English order for certain specified purposes. The most important consequence is that the child is to be treated as the child of the adopters for the purpose of any statutory provision.[4] English courts will normally have to recognise any decision of the appropriate authority in a convention country or specified country making, confirming or terminating an adoption regulated by the Convention,[5] but in certain cases English courts may annul such an adoption or declare it invalid. Provided that either the adopters or the child adopted resides in Great Britain, the High Court may annul or revoke an order if (i) the adoption was prohibited by the internal law of the country of which the adopters were nationals; (ii) it contravened provisions relating to consents of the internal law of the country of which the child was a national; (iii) it could have been impugned on any other ground under the law of the country where the adoption was made; *or* (iv) the child was adopted by his father or mother alone and has subsequently been legitimated by his parents' marriage. Irrespective of the parties' residence, the High Court may also order that *any* adoption made overseas shall cease to be valid in this country on the ground that it is contrary to public policy or that the authority making it lacked jurisdiction; and *any* court may decide on either of the last two grounds that the adoption shall be treated as invalid for the purpose of the proceedings before it. This means that if, for example, a claim under the Inheritance (Family Provision) Act were brought in a county court on behalf of a child adopted overseas, the court could declare the adoption invalid on the ground that the authority making it had lacked jurisdiction, but this decision would not affect the outcome of any other proceedings which depended on the child's adoption.[6]

The Act does not affect the recognition of foreign adoptions at common law.[7] Even when the Act comes into force, it will still be necessary to decide how far the courts will accord recognition to an order if it does not come within a class covered by an order made by the Secretary for State. The problem is likely to arise in three situations: in claims for custody, in claims to property (either by way of succession or as the adopter's " child " for the purpose of the instrument in question), and in other cases of statutory interpretation.[8] It cannot be doubted that the courts will take a foreign order into account on a custody application, just as they take into account a foreign custody or guardianship order, although the outcome of the proceedings will depend on the welfare of the child. Most statutes in fact specifically define the term " adopted child " for their own purpose.[9] All the reported cases have concerned claims to property and as these present particular problems they will be dealt with later when we consider claims to property by children generally.[10]

---

[4]S. 4. Other matters include citizenship and the effect on affiliation orders.

[5]Ss. 5 and 6 (5). For the meaning of " Convention ", " convention country " " specified country " and other technical terms, see *ante*, pp. 258-259.

[6]Ss. 6, 7 and 9 (3), (5).

[7]S. 10 (2).

[8]*E.g.*, whether the child can be a dependant for the purpose of the Fatal Accidents Acts.

[9]*E.g.*, Matrimonial Proceedings and Property Act 1970, s. 27 (1); Fatal Accidents Act 1959, s. 1 (3). In the absence of such a definition it is submitted that the courts will apply the same principles as they have applied in the cases relating to property.

[10]See *post*, pp. 467-469.

CHAPTER 11

Parental Rights and Duties

A. THE SCOPE OF PARENTAL RIGHTS AND DUTIES

Common Law.—Common law recognised the natural duties of protecting and maintaining one's legitimate minor children, and although the machinery for enforcing these duties was almost wholly ineffectual, nevertheless they could properly be regarded as unenforceable legal obligations. Moreover, it is obvious that, at any rate in early law, these duties could be performed only if the parent actually had the custody of the child, and in many cases the father would be the only member of the family who would be physically capable of carrying them out. Consequently it is not surprising to discover that his duty to protect carried with it the correlative right to the custody of all minor children and that this right was absolute even against the mother except in the rare cases where the father's conduct was such as gravely to imperil the children's life, health or morals. 'Admittedly, on the father's death the mother became entitled to the custody of her children until they came of age, but under the Tenures Abolition Act of 1660 the father could defeat this right too by appointing a testamentary guardian.

Custody carried with it many rights in addition to care and control. A father was entitled to the services of his children in his custody and to correct them by administering reasonable corporal punishment. He alone might determine the form of their religious and secular education. Whilst his powers were never as wide as those of the *paterfamilias* in Roman law, the same fundamental approach is apparent. Physical control represented the kernel of his rights; without it the others could not be enforced, and the procedural machinery of the common law was such that only this right could be specifically enforced by the writ of habeas corpus.

Equity.—The jurisdiction of equity to intervene between parent and child is derived from the prerogative power of the Crown as *parens patriae* to interfere to protect any person within the jurisdiction not fully *sui juris*. This power was naturally exercised by the Lord Chancellor, and although it fell into abeyance when the Court of Wards was set up in 1540, successive Chancellors began to use their powers more and more extensively when this court was abolished in 1660.[1] From the Court of Chancery the jurisdiction passed to the High Court under the Judicature Acts of 1873 and 1875.

---

[1] Holdsworth, *History of English Law*, vi, 648. The Court of Wards was set up by 32 Hen. 8, c. 46, and abolished by the Tenures Abolition Act 1660.

Whilst equity left untouched the common law duties of parents, its attitude towards the exercise of their rights was fundamentally different. At common law a father could always enforce his right to custody save in the most exceptional circumstances; in equity, on the other hand, the welfare of the child has always been regarded as the first and paramount consideration. This did not mean that the court would act solely on its own view of what was best for the child and totally disregard the father's rights—they were in fact *prima facie* to be enforced —but where to give effect to them would be clearly contrary to the best interests of his child, equity would not hesitate to deprive him of them. The necessity of giving effect to the father's rights was thus judicially explained by COTTON, L.J., in *Re Agar-Ellis*:[2]

> " This Court holds this principle—that when, by birth, a child is subject to a father, it is for the general interest of families, and for the general interest of children, and really for the interest of the particular infant, that the Court should not, except in very extreme cases, interfere with the discretion of the father, but leave to him the responsibility of exercising that power which nature has given him by the birth of the child."

One of the best judicial descriptions of the grounds on which the court would interfere is probably to be found in the judgment of LORD ESHER, M.R., in *R. v. Gyngall*:[3]

> " The Court is placed in a position by reason of the prerogative of the Crown to act as supreme parent of the child, and must exercise that jurisdiction in the manner in which a wise, affectionate, and careful parent would act for the welfare of the child. The natural parent in the particular case may be affectionate, and may be intending to act for the child's good, but may be unwise, and may not be doing what a wise, affectionate, and careful parent would do. The Court may say in such a case that, although they can find no misconduct on the part of the parent, they will not permit that to be done with the child which a wise, affectionate, and careful parent would not do. The court must, of course, be very cautious in regard to the circumstances under which they will interfere with the parental right. . . . The Court must exercise this jurisdiction with great care, and can only act when it is shown that either the conduct of the parent, or the description of person he is, or the position in which he is placed, is such as to render it not merely better, but—I will not say ' essential ', but—clearly right for the welfare of the child in some very serious and important respect that the parent's rights should be suspended or superseded; but . . . where it is so shown, the Court will exercise its jurisdiction accordingly."

A further advantage that equity had over the common law was that its procedure was much better adapted to deal with disputes concerning children. Common law, limited as it was to the issue of a writ of habeas corpus, could only enforce the right to physical control; equity, on the other hand, acts *in personam*, so that it could not only make orders concerning, for example, the child's education, but also effectively ensure that they were carried out. Moreover, the Court of Chancery could appoint a guardian to whom the custody of a child could be assigned even during the father's life, so that the child could be removed from the latter's custody when that was in its interest. A further step that could be taken was to have the child made a ward of court. This

---

[2] (1883), 24 Ch.D. 317, 334, C.A.
[3] [1893] 2 Q.B. 232, 241-242, C.A.   See also *Re O'Hara*, [1900] 2 I.R. 232; *Official Solicitor* v. *K.*, [1963] 3 All E.R. 191, H.L.; [1965] A.C. 201.

procedure had a number of advantages. Not only could the guardian appointed in such a case always turn to the court for advice, but also both guardian and ward remained under the permanent control of the court during the ward's infancy, so that any dereliction of duty on the part of the guardian and any interference with either the guardian or the ward were punishable as a contempt of court. Furthermore, the court could give care and control of the child to its own parent, which meant that the child would remain in the latter's possession whilst the court could ensure that the parental powers were exercised in its best interests.

As in other fields, equity ensured that where its own rules were in conflict with those of common law, the former should prevail. It would not only grant an injunction to restrain a person from applying for a writ of habeas corpus to obtain the custody of a child[4] but would also prevent a person who had already obtained the writ from interfering with the child if this was not in its interests.[5] As in the case of other conflicts between law and equity, the Judicature Act of 1873 expressly provided that the rules of equity relating to the custody and education of minors should prevail over those of common law.[6]

Illegitimate Children.—Up to now we have been considering the legal position of legitimate children and their parents. The position of illegitimate children was quite different, for at common law a bastard was *filius nullius* and consequently none of the legal rights and duties which flowed from the relationship of parent and legitimate child was accorded to him or his parents.[7] During the past century, however, there has been a considerable reduction in the legal disabilities attached to bastardy, reflecting a similar change in the illegitimate child's position in society generally. The judges have tended more and more to give legal effect to the natural rights and duties which the relationship creates—a tendency which can also be seen in recent legislation—so that today the sins of the parents are no longer so rigorously visited upon their illegitimate children and the legal position of the latter has been greatly assimilated to that of their legitimate brothers. This is more noticeable in the case of proprietary rights;[8] so far as the personal rights of a parent are concerned, these are vested for the most part in the mother of an illegitimate child to the exclusion of the father, even though the latter's paternity is not in dispute, so that she alone can exercise *vis a vis* her illegitimate children those rights which in the case of legitimate children are vested today in both parents.

Statutes.—In addition to those statutes which have given the Divorce Court power to make orders relating to the custody, education and maintenance of the children of the marriage in matrimonial causes, a mass of legislation has been passed during the past 100 years affecting parental rights and duties. At least six distinct principles can be seen.

[4]*Per* LINDLEY, L.J., in *R.* v. *Barnado, Jones's Case,* [1891] 1 Q.B. 194, 210, C.A.
[5]*Andrews* v. *Salt* (1873), 8 Ch. App. 622.
[6]See now the Supreme Court of Judicature (Consolidation) Act 1925, s. 44.
[7]Blackstone, *Commentaries,* i, 458-459.
[8]See *post,* pp. 465 and 507.

(1) Statutory effect has now been given to the rule of equity that in every case involving the custody or upbringing of a child " the court shall regard the welfare of the minor as the first and paramount consideration ".[9]

(2) Not only were the common law duties of a parent to protect and maintain his children wholly inadequate to ensure that they grew up fit to take their place as members of the complex industrial society which evolved in the nineteenth century, but the unenforceable nature of these duties led to scandalous cruelty, abandonment and depravity. A number of statutes have been passed, therefore, to prevent physical cruelty and neglect and to provide for children's moral and mental welfare as well. For example, an obligation is now laid on parents to ensure that their children receive adequate secular education, and a parent may in certain circumstances be deprived of the custody of a child which is in need of care, protection or control.

(3) The same development that can be seen in all other branches of family law—the evolution of the wife from a subordinate member of her husband's household to the joint, co-equal head of the family—is most noticeable here. Whereas at common law her husband could deprive her of the care even of her young baby and could completely disregard all her wishes, her rights are now in almost every respect the same as his.

(4) Whilst a century ago disputes concerning the custody and maintenance of children could be resolved only in the Court of Chancery or in one of the superior courts of common law, jurisdiction has now been given to county courts and (subject to certain limitations) to magistrates' courts.

(5) Local authorities—that is to say, county, county borough and London borough councils—have been made increasingly responsible for the welfare of children who may be in special need of protection. In particular they are bound to care for those whose parents or guardians are dead or unable or unwilling to look after them, and to supervise the arrangements made for foster-children and children placed for adoption.

(6) At common law a person attained his majority at the age of 21. Now, under section 1 of the Family Law Reform Act 1969, he attains it on his eighteenth birthday. Consequently all parental rights and powers over him cease when he reaches that age and all orders in relation to him (except with respect to financial provision) come to an end.

So far as the exercise of parental rights is concerned, the key-note of the modern law is to be found in section 1 of the Guardianship of Minors Act 1971 which provides:

---

[0]Guardianship of Minors Act 1971, s. 1. *Cf.* the Children and Young Persons Act 1933.
[9]. 44 (1), *post*, p 291.

" Where in any proceedings before any court . . .

    (a) the custody or upbringing of a minor; or

    (b) the administration of any property belonging to or held on trust for a minor, or the application of the income thereof,

is in question, the court, in deciding that question, shall regard the welfare of the minor as the first and paramount consideration, and shall not take into consideration whether from any other point of view the claim of the father, or any right at common law possessed by the father, in respect of such custody, upbringing, administration or application is superior to that of the mother, or the claim of the mother is superior to that of the father."

One of the parental rights, that of refusing to give consent to an infant child's marriage, has already been considered.[10] Another, that of appointing a testamentary guardian, will be considered in the next chapter. We shall now consider in turn the remaining rights and duties.

B. CUSTODY, AND CARE AND CONTROL

I. INTRODUCTORY

Meaning of Custody.—Because of the way in which the law has evolved, custody has developed two meanings. As we have already seen, in the earlier law only a person with *de facto* care and control of a child could exercise the other rights which were attached *de jure* to custody. As a result there was a tendency to confuse custody with control so that the former term is now sometimes used to mean the latter. In *Hewer* v *Bryant*[11] SACHS, L.J., emphasised this dual aspect of the meaning of custody in the following words:

" In its wider meaning the word ' custody ' is used as if it were almost the equivalent of ' guardianship ' in the fullest sense. . . . Adapting the convenient phraseology of counsel, such guardianship embraces a ' bundle of rights ' or to be more exact a ' bundle of powers ', which continue until a male attains [18] or a female infant marries. These include the power to control education, the choice of religion, and the administration of the infant's property. They include entitlement to veto the issue of a passport and to withhold consent to marriage. They include also both the personal power physically to control the infant until the years of discretion and the right . . . to apply to the courts to exercise the powers of the Crown as *parens patriae*. It is thus clear that somewhat confusingly one of the powers conferred by custody in its wide meaning is custody in its limited meaning, namely such personal power of physical control as a parent or guardian may have."

Similarly, as KARMINSKI, L.J., pointed out in the same case,[12] " physical possession is only one aspect of custody ". In LORD DENNING, M.R.'s words (as usual vivid and realistic),[13]

" [custody] is a dwindling right which the courts will hesitate to enforce against the wishes of the child, and the more so the older he is. It starts with a right of control and ends with little more than advice."

To avoid confusion, in this book the word " custody " will be used

[10]*Ante*, pp. 31-33.
[11][1969] 3 All E.R. 578, 585, C.A.; [1970] 1 Q.B. 357, 373.
[12]At pp. 588 and 376, respectively.
[13]At pp. 582 and 369, respectively.

in its wide sense to connote the whole bundle of rights and powers vested in a parent or guardian. The narrow sense of the term will be denoted by the words " care and control " or " possession ".

As custody is a separable concept, the rights inherent in it may be split. In particular this means, as the Court of Appeal held in *Re W.* (*J.C.*),[14] that in a proper case the court may make a " split order " giving custody to one parent and care and control to the other. Whilst such an order is in force, the latter has the physical care of the child but the former retains all the residuary rights of supervising its education and upbringing generally. The court may even award care and control to one parent and make no order with respect to custody at all, thus leaving both parents to exercise such other rights as they have.[15] Similarly, if a child is made a ward of court, care and control must necessarily be given to an individual but the other rights of custody will remain in the court.

Special Meanings of Custody.—It should also be appreciated that, if the term " custody " is used in a statute, it may have a special meaning for that purpose. This problem arose in *Todd* v. *Davison*,[16] where the House of Lords was concerned with the interpretation of the Law Reform (Limitation of Actions, &c.) Act 1954. This provides that an action for damages for personal injuries shall be statute barred three years after the cause of action accrues, but if the plaintiff was under a disability at the time (that is, if he was a minor or a mental defective), time will begin to run against him only if he was in the custody of a parent, grandparent or step-parent.[17] It is obvious that, as this applies to mental defectives as well as to minors and envisages the plaintiff's being in the custody of someone other than a parent, the word " custody " must have a special meaning for the purpose of the Act. The members of the House were agreed that the question is one of fact: was the plaintiff in the care of someone who was looking after him and who could therefore be expected to take all necessary steps to protect his rights?[18] If so, it is immaterial that the particular parent failed to take action because of his own ineffectiveness or lack of intelligence.

Common Law.—At common law the father was entitled to the custody of his legitimate children until they reached the age of 21.[19] His rights might be lost, however, if to enforce them would probably lead to the physical or moral harm of the child[20] or if his claim was not made *bona fide*.[1] After his death, the mother was entitled to the

---

[14][1963] 3 All E.R. 459, C.A.; [1964] Ch. 202.
[15]*Re M.*, [1967] 3 All E.R. 1071, C.A.
[16][1971] 1 All E.R. 994, H.L. See also *Hewer* v. *Bryant*, (*ante*).
[17]S. 2 (2). If he was not in custody, the three years' period begins to run when he ceased to be under any disability. In actions other than for personal injuries, the period is **six** years and begins to run after disability ceases: custody is therefore immaterial.
[18]At pp. 997 (*per* LORD MORRIS), 1001 (*per* LORD DILHORNE), 1006 (*per* LORD PEARSON).
[19]*Thomasset* v. *Thomasset*, [1894] P. 295, C.A.; *Re Agar-Ellis* (1883), 24 Ch.D. 317, C.A.
[20]*E.g.* apprehension of cruelty or grossly immoral or profligate conduct: *Re Andrews* (1873), L.R. 8 Q.B. 153, 158.
[1]*E.g.*, if his purpose was to hand the child over to another: *cf. Re Turner* (1872), 41 L.J.Q.B. 142.

custody of her minor children for nurture,[2] but even this right was superseded after 1660 if the father appointed a testamentary guardian under the provisions of the Tenures Abolition Act.[3] Common law accorded no other right to the mother as such, and so absolute against her were the father's rights that he could lawfully claim from her the possession even of a child at the breast.[4]

Equity.—As the passages cited from *Re Agar-Ellis* and *R. v. Gyngall* will already have shown,[5] equity *prima facie* gave effect to the father's right to the custody of his children, but would deprive him of it if their welfare so demanded. Although originally equity interfered with the father's rights hardly less readily than the common law, by the end of the nineteenth century it would do so if there was any threat of physical or moral harm to the child; and if a father once abandoned or abdicated his right, he would not be allowed to reassert it arbitrarily if this would be contrary to the child's interests.[6]

Even before the Judicature Acts of 1873 and 1875 the common law courts recognised the superiority of the jurisdiction of the Court of Chancery to this extent, that, if proceedings were pending in the latter court, an application for habeas corpus would be stayed until the decision of Chancery was known.[7] Since the rules of equity are now bound to prevail, the circumstances in which common law would refuse a father custody are now of historical interest only.

Statutory Provisions relating to Claims for Custody.—Since the middle of the nineteenth century Parliament has intervened in a series of statutes, the effect of which has been to whittle down the father's rights further and also to give the mother positive rights to custody which even equity did not accord to her. The history of this change in attitude can best be seen by a brief examination of the principal provisions of each statute.

Talfourd's Act 1839.—This Act,[8] although now repealed, marks a decisive point in the history of family law, for it empowered the Court of Chancery to give the mother custody of her children until they reached the age of seven and access to them until they came of age. But the Act specifically provided that no order was to be made if the mother had been guilty of adultery.

Custody of Infants Act 1873.—This extended the principle of Talfourd's Act by empowering the court to give the mother custody until the child reached the age of 16. It did not, however, repeat the proviso relating to her adultery. Section 2, which is still in force, introduced a further reform, which had long been overdue, by enacting that agreements as to custody or control in separation deeds (which had

---

[2]*R. v. Clarke* (1857), 7 E. & B. 186, 200.
[3]See *post*, p. 323.
[4]*R. v. De Manneville* (1804), 5 East 221.
[5]*Ante*, p. 264.
[6]See *Re O'Hara*, [1900] 2 I.R. 232, 240-241; *Re Fynn* (1848), 2 De G. & Sm. 457, 474-475.
[7]*Wellesley* v. *Duke of Beaufort* (1827), 2 Russ. 1, 25-26; *R. v. Isley* (1836), 5 Ad. & El. 441.
[8]2 & 3 Vict., c. 54.

formerly been void as contrary to public policy) should be enforceable so long as they were for the child's benefit.[9]

Guardianship of Infants Act 1886.—This further extended the provisions of the earlier Acts by empowering the court to give the mother custody of her children until they reached the age of 21. Furthermore the father was now stopped from defeating the mother's rights after his death by appointing a testamentary guardian, for it was enacted that the mother was to act jointly with any guardian so appointed, and for the first time she herself was given limited powers to appoint testamentary guardians.

Custody of Children Act 1891.—This Act was passed as the direct result of a number of cases in which parents had succeeded in recovering from Dr. Barnardo children whom they had placed in his now famous " homes " or whom they had abandoned and he had taken in. It provides that if a parent has abandoned or deserted his (or her) child, the burden shall shift to him to prove that he is fit to have custody of the child claimed[10] and that the court may refuse to give him possession of the child altogether.[11]   Moreover, if at the time of the parent's application for custody the child is being brought up by another person, the court may now, upon awarding custody to the parent, order him to pay the whole or part of the costs incurred in bringing it up. [12]

Guardianship of Infants Act 1925.—This Act gave statutory effect to the rule that in any dispute relating to a child the court must regard its welfare as the first and paramount consideration. It also completed the process of assimilation of the parents' rights by enacting that neither the father nor the mother should from any other point of view be regarded as having a claim superior to the other[13] and by giving to the mother the same right to appoint testamentary guardians as the father.[14]   Jurisdiction to make orders relating to custody, etc., which had formerly been exercisable only by the High Court and (since 1886) by county courts was extended (subject to certain limitations) to magistrates' courts.[15]

Guardianship of Minors Act 1971.—This Act repealed the Guardianship of Infants Acts 1886 and 1925 and consolidated their provisions into one Act. It made no changes to the substantive law.

It will be seen that, in the absence of an order vesting custody in the mother, none of these Acts has affected the common law rule that custody is vested exclusively in the father. This is usually only of academic interest because legal entitlement to custody normally becomes important only when the marriage breaks down and custody

---

[9]See further, *post*, p. 273.
[10]See further, *post*, p. 274.
[11]S. 1.
[12]S. 2. The same applies if the application is made by any other person entitled to the custody of the child or legally liable to maintain it: s. 5. Such an order should not be made if it will prejudice the child by reducing the parent's ability to provide for it: *Re O'Hara*, [1900] 2 I.R. 232, 244-245.
[13]For the wording of s. 1 (now s. 1 of the Guardianship of Minors Act 1971), see *ante*, p. 267.
[14]See *post*, p. 323.   [15]See *post*, p. 282.

along with financial provision will become the subject of an order. In any case the parent's last resort will be to the court which will be bound by section 1 of the Guardianship of Minors Act 1971. But occasionally the old rule has a surprising habit of obtruding itself. Until recently, for example, the Foreign Office refused to issue a passport to a minor without his father's authority unless the mother had obtained an order for custody.[16]

Illegitimate Children.—Up to now we have been considering the position with respect to legitimate children (including, of course, legitimated and adopted children). It cannot now be doubted that *prima facie* custody of an illegitimate child is vested in the mother. In *R. v. Nash*[17] in 1883 JESSEL, M.R., formulated the rule that the law will give effect to the natural rights created by the relationship, and eight years later in the leading case of *Barnardo* v. *McHugh*[18] the same view was expressed in the Court of Appeal and the House of Lords. This represents a complete departure from the original rule and provides an outstanding example of the ability of the common law to adapt itself to meet changing social views.

Loss of Custody.—A parent's right to custody can be terminated or suspended in at least four ways.

First, custody has always automatically ceased when the child attained his majority. At common law this occurred at the age of 21, but by statute a child now comes of age on his eighteenth birthday and any existing order relating to custody will cease to have effect when he reaches that age.[19]

Secondly, there are a number of dicta that the right to custody of a minor daughter ceases if she marries.[1] This is apparently equally true of a son.[2]

Thirdly, the right is suspended whilst the child is serving in the armed forces, although it will automatically revive when the service ceases.[3] Although the point has never been decided, it is suggested that the right to custody will also be suspended if the child is engaged on a similar form of service, for example, in the Merchant Navy.

Finally, as the outline of the relevant statutory provisions will have indicated,[4] a parent may lose custody as the result of a court order. Similarly, if a child is made a ward of court, all the rights of custody vest in the court. In certain circumstances a local authority may

---

[16]Similarly some voluntary bodies with whom a child has been left by the mother apparently take the view that they are bound to return it to the father if he demands it even though they do not believe this to be in the child's interest.

[17]10 Q.B.D. 454, C.A.

[18][1891] A.C. 388, H.L.; *sub nom. R.* v. *Barnardo, Jones's Case*, [1891] 1 Q.B. 194, Q.B.D. and C.A.

[19]Family Law Reform Act 1969, ss. 1 (1) and 9 and Sched. 3, para. 3.

[1]See, *e.g.*, the judgment of SACHS, L.J., in *Hewer* v. *Bryant*, cited *ante*, p. 267.

[2]See *R.* v. *Wilmington* (1822), 5 B. & Ald. 525, 526: *Lough* v. *Ward*, [1945] 2 All E.R. 338, 348.

[3]*R.* v. *Rotherfield Greys* (1823), 1 B. & C. 345, 349-350.

[4]See *ante*, pp. 269-270.

assume parental rights[5] and a parent is effectively deprived of custody if a care order[6] or an order under the Mental Health Act 1959 is made in respect of a child.

Custody on the Death of either Parent.—The growth of the concept of equality of parents' rights and powers with respect to their children is reflected in the provisions of section 3 of the Guardianship of Minors Act 1971, which enacts that on the death of either parent the survivor shall be guardian of their legitimate minor children together with any guardian appointed by the other. If the deceased parent has appointed no guardian, or if the guardian or guardians so appointed refuse to act, the court may, if it thinks fit, appoint one to act with the survivor,[7] but this power should be exercised only if the court thinks it will be for the benefit of the infant to have both persons acting jointly and not purely in order to secure some collateral purpose, for example to enable the person appointed to obtain custody.[8] It is very rarely exercised in practice, so that on the death of one parent the other will become solely entitled to custody if the deceased appointed no testamentary guardian.

The father of an illegitimate child can claim its custody as of right after the mother's death only if an order in his favour under the Guardianship of Minors Act is in force. If it is, he will continue to be entitled to the child's custody along with any guardian appointed by the mother.[9] If an affiliation order is in force under which payments are to be made to the mother and she dies (or becomes of unsound mind or is sent to prison), magistrates may appoint some other person to have the custody of the child and receive payments under the order.[10]

Agreements as to Custody.—As in the case of all agreements which tend to curtail a parent's rights or to destroy the unity of the family, any agreement by which a parent purports to assign the custody of his minor child to another is contrary to public policy at common law and therefore void.[11] In one respect this rule proved to be unsatisfactory, for if a husband and wife agree to separate they will naturally usually wish to come to some arrangement about the custody and care of their children and their inability to do so might well lead

---

[5]See *post*, p. 296.

[6]See *post*, p. 294.

[7]Guardianship of Minors Act 1971, s. 3. This power is exercisable by the High Court, a county court, or, if the child is under the age of 16 or over that age and physically or mentally incapable of self support, by a magistrates' court: *ibid.*, s. 15. The power to act jointly with guardians appointed by the father was first conferred on the mother by s. 2 of the Guardianship of Infants Act 1886.

[8]*Re H.*, [1959] 3 All E.R. 746. The proper procedure to obtain custody (or any other order) in such a case is to apply to have the child made a ward of court.

[9]Guardianship of Minors Act 1971, s. 14 (3). For custody orders, see *post*, p. 282.

[10]Affiliation Proceedings Act 1957, s. 5 (4). For penalties for misconduct by such a guardian, see *ibid.*, s. 11. The order may be subsequently revoked and another guardian appointed.

[11]*Vansittart* v. *Vansittart* (1858), 2 De G. & J. 249; *Walrond* v. *Walrond* (1858), John. 18; *Humphrys* v. *Polak*, [1901] 2 K.B. 385, C.A. (illegitimate child).

to unnecessary litigation. This defect has been cured by section 2 of the Custody of Infants Act 1873, which provides:

> " No agreement contained in any separation deed made between the father and mother of an infant or infants shall be held to be invalid by reason only of its providing that the father of such infant or infants shall give up the custody or control thereof to the mother: provided always, that no Court shall enforce any such agreement if the Court shall be of the opinion that it will not be for the benefit of the infant or infants to give effect thereto."

Although the Act specifically refers to separation *deeds*, the better opinion is that such an agreement will be equally valid if it is contained in a parol contract, for either party could then obtain a decree of specific performance to have a deed executed.[12] The proviso that the agreement is not to be enforced if it is not for the child's benefit is no new concept in English law, as we have already seen, and since the passing of the Guardianship of Infants Act of 1925 it would clearly be implied in any event.

The Act does not affect agreements between parents and strangers, which will still be void. But such an agreement might be evidence of the parent's having abandoned his parental rights and thus preclude him from setting them up again.[13]

Access.—Whenever care and control is given to one parent, the other will be given access to the child if he wants it save in exceptional circumstances. Similarly if care and control is given to a third person, access will usually be given to both parents. This may allow periodical visits at specified times—for example between stated hours each Saturday or Sunday—or holidays for longer periods (sometimes referred to as " staying access "). Obviously the court will not grant access if this would be detrimental to the child; in some cases it may impose a condition for the child's protection—for example that it should not be brought into contact with a person with whom the parent given access is committing adultery.

2. DISPUTES OVER CUSTODY AND CARE AND CONTROL

General Principles.—A dispute over custody may take one of two forms: it may be a dispute between the father and the mother, or it may be a dispute between one parent and a stranger, for example a testamentary guardian appointed by the other parent or a person who has obtained *de facto* control of the child either with the parent's consent or as a result of his having abandoned it.

As the House of Lords held in *J. v. C.*,[14] the principle laid down in section 1 of the Guardianship of Minors Act 1971, that the welfare of the child is to be regarded as the first and paramount consideration, applies equally whether the dispute is between the parents or between

---

[12]See Lush, *Husband and Wife*, 4th Ed., 481; Fry, *Specific Performance*, 6th Ed., 718.

[13]See *post*, p. 279.

[14][1969] 1 All E.R. 788, H.L.; [1970] A.C. 668, at pp. 809 and 697 (*per* LORD GUEST), 820 and 709-710 (*per* LORD MACDERMOTT), 832 and 724 (*per* LORD UPJOHN), 835 and 727 (*per* LORD DONOVAN).

M

one or both parents and a stranger.   In the latter case, however, the
wishes of an unimpeachable parent stand high among the remaining
considerations: to give effect to the blood tie will itself normally be
for the child's benefit and usually he should be with his natural parents.
But there is no presumption that the natural parents should have
custody; in the words of LORD MACDERMOTT:[15]

> " . . . when all the relevant facts, relationships, claims and wishes of parents,
> risks, choices and other circumstances are taken into account and weighed,
> the course to be followed will be that which is most in the interests of the
> child's welfare as that term has now to be understood "

If all other considerations are equal, however, the court will give effect
to this relationship and grant custody to a parent rather than to a
stranger.[16]   This was not the case in *J. v. C.* The parents of the child
were Spanish nationals resident in Spain, but the child, who was then
aged ten years, had spent the whole of his life except for eighteen
months with foster parents in England. He had been brought up as an
English boy, spoke little Spanish and scarcely knew his natural parents.
The House of Lords refused to interfere with the order of the trial
judge who left custody, care and control with the foster parents and
refused to give it to the natural parents on the ground that they
" would be quite unable to cope with the problems of adjustment or
with consequential maladjustment and suffering and that the father's
character would inflame the difficulties " if the boy were to go to live
with them in Spain.

The one statutory exception to this rule is to be found in section 3
of the Custody of Children Act 1891. This provides that where a parent
has abandoned or deserted his child or allowed it to be brought up by,
and at the expense of, another person, school, institution or local
authority, in such circumstances as to show that he was unmindful of
his parental duties, no order is to be made giving him the custody of
the child unless he proves that he is a fit person to have it.   But in
order to bring this section into play, the parent's conduct must show
some degree of moral turpitude: if he relinquishes control temporarily
because this is the best that he can do for the child in the circumstances,
the court ought not on this ground alone to deprive him of custody.[17]
In practice this section is rarely invoked.

Power of Appellate Courts.—It will be seen that the court must
always be guided by the interests of the child and, as the House of
Lords emphasised in *J. v. C.*,[18] a court of first instance has a discretion
with which no appellate court will interfere unless it is satisfied that the
lower court has clearly acted on the wrong principles.   Thus an appeal
will lie if the court of trial acted under a misapprehension of fact, or
gave weight to irrelevant or unproved matters, or failed to take
relevant matters into account.[19]   On the other hand, an appellate court

---

[15]*Ibid.*, at pp. 821 and 710-711, respectively. See also pp. 823, 824, 832 and 714, 715,
724, respectively.

[16]As in *Re Thain*, [1926] Ch. 676, C.A.

[17]See *Re O'Hara*, [1900] 2 I.R. 232, at pp. 238, 243, 251; *Re Carroll*, [1931] 1 K.B. 317.
360-363, C.A.; *R. v. Bolton Union* (1892), 36 Sol. Jo. 255.

[18][1969] 1 All E.R. 788, H.L.; [1970] A.C. 668.

[19]*B. (B.) v. B. (M.)*, [1969] 1 All E.R 891, 901; [1969] P. 103, 115.

is not entitled to allow an appeal and substitute its own discretion merely because it would have come to a different conclusion on the evidence.[20] Difficulty arises because in some cases appellate courts are so convinced that the lower court exercised its discretion wrongly that they will reverse the decision even though the latter purported to apply the right principles in reaching it.[21] On hearing an appeal, a court is apparently entitled to consider the relative weight which the lower court attached to the various facts which it had to take into account and to conclude that the court acted on the wrong principles if it disagrees with the weighting.[1]

Nature of the Proceedings.—The fact that the inherent jurisdiction of the High Court is derived from the Crown's prerogative powers as *parens patriae* invests the proceedings with a somewhat unusual character. Inasmuch as there is a justiciable issue between the parties, the court is clearly exercising a judicial function, but as its first duty is to protect the child irrespective of the parents' wishes, its jurisdiction is also administrative. The House of Lords concluded in *Official Solicitor* v. *K.*[2] that this entitled it to depart from the normal rules of evidence if this is necessary in the child's interest. It has always been accepted that the judge is entitled to see the child and each of the parents in private: in *Official Solicitor* v. *K.* it was held that he may receive a confidential report from the child's guardian *ad litem* without disclosing it to the parties if he considers that disclosure would be detrimental to the child. This is an extreme step which should be taken only in the most exceptional circumstances for, once evidence is withheld, justice is not seen to be done, the losing party will leave the court with a sense of grievance, and the proper preparation of an appeal becomes impossible. The last point (and to a less extent the other two) can be met by showing the evidence to the parties' legal advisers if they are prepared not to divulge it to the parties themselves.

Official Solicitor v. *K.* was concerned with the High Court's exercise of its inherent jurisdiction. It is submitted that the same principle should apply to all proceedings relating to custody in the High Court: it would be regrettable if the court's power to receive or withhold evidence should turn upon the technical nature of the proceedings, and it should be able to exercise an inherent power even though the particular jurisdiction is statutory.[3] But as no other courts can claim the prerogative powers of the Crown, it is very doubtful whether they can receive evidence which is not available to all the parties unless they agree.[4]

A further consequence of the administrative nature of the proceedings is that, if the court is of the opinion that the nature of the case is such

[20]*Secus* if evidence is available to the appellate court which was not before the lower court: *Re B. (T.A.)*, [1970] 3 All E.R. 705, 709; [1971] Ch. 270, 275.

[21]*Re O.*, [1971] 2 W.L.R. 784, C.A.

[1]*Cf. Re O.*, [1962] 2 All E.R. 10, C.A.

[2][1963] 3 All E.R. 191, H.L.; [1965] A.C. 201.

[3]It is submitted that *Fowler* v. *Fowler*, [1963] 1 All E.R. 119, C.A.; [1963] P. 311, to the contrary is no longer of authority on this point as it followed the decision of the Court of Appeal reversed by the House of Lords in *Official Solicitor* v. *K.*

[4]This might be a ground on which a divorce county court should be asked to transfer an application for custody to the High Court.

that the child ought to be separately represented, it can of its own motion appoint the Official Solicitor (or any other suitable person prepared to act) as the child's guardian *ad litem*. This power is limited to the High Court and divorce county courts.[5] One situation in which it may be highly desirable to appoint a guardian *ad litem* should be noted. The reception of medical evidence—and particularly of psychiatric evidence—is becoming much more common and there is a danger that a doctor who is consulted and called by one side only may be, at least subconsciously, biased in favour of that party. It is highly desirable, therefore, that a pediatrician or psychiatrist should be consulted jointly by both parents or, if they cannot agree to do so, that a guardian *ad litem* should be appointed so that he can take the necessary steps.[6]

3. FACTS TO BE TAKEN INTO ACCOUNT IN RESOLVING QUESTIONS OF CUSTODY AND CARE AND CONTROL

As we have already seen, the welfare of the child is the first and paramount consideration in determining any question of its custody and upbringing.[7] But it is not the sole consideration. Two other questions must also be borne in mind: the conduct of the parents and the existence of any other order made by a court outside England. Although these are subordinate to the child's welfare, they must not be ignored and may be vital if other facts are evenly balanced.[8]

Welfare of the Child.—In deciding what order will be in the best interests of the child, a number of facts must be borne in mind. In any given case some of these are bound to weigh more heavily in favour of one parent or claimant and others will weigh more heavily in favour of the other. The court must then reach the best decision it can on all the evidence; as MEGARRY, J., pointed out in *Re F.*,[9] one cannot solve the problem arithmetically or quantitatively by using some sort of " points system ".

Personality and Character of the Claimants.—Obviously these are amongst the most important matters to be taken into consideration. To take an extreme case, the court must avoid making an order which is likely to lead to physical ill-treatment of the child. Similarly, although there is a dearth of modern authority, the child must not be exposed to the danger of moral corruption by example or encouragement.[10] Even if there is no suggestion of harm from either parent, the court must always consider which of them is likely to be the better parent and, if they are divorced and propose to remarry, which of their partners will probably make the better parent substitute.[11]

---

[5]Under the inherent jurisdiction and Matrimonial Causes Rules 1968, r. 108.

[6]*B. (M.)* v. *B. (R.)*, [1968] 3 All E.R. 170, C.A.

[7]Guardianship of Minors Act 1971, s. 1, *ante*, p. 267.

[8]See generally Ross Martyn, *Principles and Practice in Infancy Cases*, 120 New L.J. 868, 895; James, *The Legal Guardianship of Infants*, 82 L.Q.R. 323.

[9][1969] 2 All E.R. 766, 768; [1969] 2 Ch. 238, 241.

[10]See *Wellesley* v. *Duke of Beaufort* (1827), 2 Russ. 1 (drunkenness, profligacy and the use of obscene and profane language); *Re Besant* (1879), 11 Ch.D. 508, C.A. (publication of obscene libel).

[11]*Re F., (supra)*.

Whenever there is a contest over care and control, particularly of a young child, the court should see the parents to assess what effect each is likely to have on the child if awarded possession of it.[12]

Medical Evidence.—Medical evidence may be of vital importance in estimating the effect which living with a particular parent may have on the child. Much more is now known about the effects of a change of care and control on the child's development and future mental and physical health; whereas Victorian judges dismissed a child's grief at being parted from a person with whom he had been living as transitory, the result may well be highly detrimental if not disastrous. When there is a grave danger of this sort, the court must try at all costs to avoid a change.[13] Although medical evidence is rarely accepted as decisive, the courts are undoubtedly paying much more attention to it.[14]

Sex and Age of Children.—Common sense dictates that normally the mother should have the care and control of young[15] or sickly children (particularly little girls)[16] or those who for some other reason especially need a mother's care. In recent years courts have tended to take the view that, other things being equal, it may be better for an older boy to have the influence of his father.[17]

Against this, it should be borne in mind that it is generally desirable to keep brothers and sisters together and not to split the family up more than is necessary. But this will not usually be decisive, particularly if staying access to both parents will mean that the children will meet frequently during the holidays.[18] In *Re O.*[19] an Englishwoman who had married a Sudanese brought the son and daugher of the marriage back to this country. It was held that the boy, who was aged six or seven, should go back to the Sudan with his father where he would eventually succeed to his business, whilst the girl, who was a year or so younger, should stay in this country with her mother apparently on the ground that the future prospects of a girl of mixed parentage was better here.

Education.—The problem of care and control may go hand in hand with that of education, particularly of religious education. It is hardly likely that a parent will be refused custody today on the ground of atheism, as Shelley was,[20] and in the case of a very young child (or

---

[12]*H.* v. *H. and C.*, [1969] 1 All E.R. 262, C.A. The resolution of issues of custody purely on affidavit evidence was also deprecated in *W.* v. *W.* (1971), 115 Sol. Jo. 367, C.A.

[13]*Cf.* the observations of Cross, J., in *Re W.*, [1965] 3 All E.R. 231, 249.

[14]See Michaels, *The Dangers of a Change of Parentage in Custody and Adoption Cases*, 83 L.Q.R. 547.

[15]See *Re B.*, [1962] 1 All E.R. 872, C.A. Contrast *H.* v. *H. and C.*, [1969] 1 All E.R. 262, C.A., where custody and care and control of a child aged three were refused to the mother who had left the child with her husband and had not seen him for 20 months.

[16]*Re F.*, [1969] 2 All E.R. 766, 769; [1969] 2 Ch. 238, 243.

[17]But there is no principle to this effect: *Re C. (A.)*, [1970] 1 All E.R. 309, C.A.

[18]*Re P.*, [1967] 2 All E.R. 229 (where separation was described on the facts as the least bad course); *Re B.* (1966), *Times*, April 5, C.A.

[19][1962] 2 All E.R. 10, C.A.

[20]*Shelley* v. *Westbrooke* (1817), Jac. 266 n.

probably with any child of no fixed religious beliefs) the question of religious upbringing will probably have little bearing on the issue of care and control.[1] But if the child has already had religious instruction, the continuation of his education will be of vital importance if a break in it would produce emotional disturbance.[2]

During the nineteenth century, when religious passions tended to run higher than they do now, the courts were loth to give custody to a person whose beliefs differed from those of the child on the ground that this might drive a wedge between parent and child or, alternatively, because of the fear of proselytism.[3] Today it is not uncommon to give custody or care and control to a person who does not share the child's beliefs on his undertaking that his religious education will be continued. In *Re E.*[4] a Roman Catholic mother had placed her illegitimate son for adoption after formally abdicating her right to choose the boy's religious education. She later changed her mind and the application for an adoption order failed as the court held that her consent had not been unreasonably withheld. The applicants, who were Jewish but practised no religion, then took proceedings to have the child made a ward of court and themselves made guardians. The mother opposed this, not because she wanted to have custody herself but because she wished to hand the boy over to a religious society for adoption. This would have been extremely difficult to effect in view of the child's age and the fact that he was of mixed English, Cuban and Chinese blood. In these exceptional circumstances the court declined to restore him to his mother but appointed the applicants guardians on their undertaking to have him brought up in the Roman Catholic faith.

Accommodation and Material Advantages.—The fact that one claimant to custody or care and control is in a position to give the child a better start in life than another does not give him a prior claim. It is the happiness of the child, not its material prospects, with which the court is concerned, and any other rule would automatically put a poor parent at a disadvantage. On the other hand, a party's financial position is clearly relevant in an extreme case; for example, if apparent is so poor that he cannot even provide a home for his children, this might be enough to refuse him care and control.[5] Similarly, other things being equal, a parent who can offer the child good accommodation must have the edge over one who cannot.[6]

The Child's Wishes.—If the child is old enough to express its own wishes, the court will interview it, not so that it can give effect to those wishes but to be the better able to judge what is for its welfare. But it

---

[1] *Cf. Re C. (M.A.)*, [1966] 1 All E.R. 838, C.A. at pp. 856 and 864-865.
[2] This certainly influenced WILLMER, L.J., considerably in *Re M.*, [1967] 3 All E.R. 1071, 1074, C.A.
[3] See the pithy comment of LORD ESHER, M.R., in *R. v. Barnardo, Jones's Case*, [1891] 1 Q.B. 194, 205, C.A., where referring to habeas corpus proceedings, he said, " It is a dispute not over the body, but over the soul of the child."
[4] [1963] 3 All E.R. 874.
[5] *Re Story*, [1916] 2 I.R. 328, 345-346.
[6] *Re F.*, [1969] 2 All E.R. 766; [1969] 2 Ch. 238.

must be remembered that the child may have been coached by one parent and that sometimes the child's own wishes are so contrary to its long-term interests that the court may feel justified in disregarding them altogether.[7]

The Parties' Conduct.—During the nineteenth century it was the practice of the Divorce Court not to give care and control to a mother who had been guilty of adultery[8] and it was not until the turn of the century that the courts were prepared to concede that this should not automatically deprive her of her rights.[9] The current view is that expressed by the Court of Appeal in *Willoughby* v. *Willoughby*,[10] where they held that a mother who had committed adultery should have the custody of her daughter, aged two years, in the absence of any evidence that she was promiscuous, a bad housekeeper or a bad mother. But the fact that one spouse alone has been responsible for the breakdown of the marriage must be taken into consideration. If a wife deserts her husband to live with another man, one cannot ignore the fact that, had she not done so, the family would still be living together and there would be no contest over custody at all. In *Re L.*[11] the Court of Appeal gave care and control to the father of two girls aged six and four years in such circumstances; in the words of LORD DENNING, M.R.:[12] " Whilst the welfare of the children is the first and paramount consideration, the claims of justice cannot be overlooked."

The fact that a parent has abandoned or deserted the child will normally in itself indicate that he is unfit to have care and control and should be refused it for this reason.[13] Similarly, a parent who permits another to bring up his child cannot be allowed arbitrarily to put an end to this arrangement if to do so would be injurious to the child.[14]

The court will obviously not accede to a claim for possession of a child if it is not made *bona fide*—for example, if the claimant's purpose is to deliver the child to another. Nor at one time would it normally give care and control to a person who was likely to take the child permanently out of the country (and thus out of the jurisdiction of the court), particularly if this would deprive a parent of access. But today the latter's interests must be subordinated to the child's and emigration will be permitted if this is for the latter's welfare. The problem caused considerable anxiety to the Court of Appeal in *P. (L.M.)* v. *P. (G.E.)*.[15] Custody of the child of the marriage, aged two years,

---

[7]*Re S.*, [1967] 1 All E.R. 202, 210.
[8]See, e.g., *Clout* v. *Clout* (1861), 2 Sw. & Tr. 391. *Cf.* the provisions of Talfourd's Act, *ante*, p. 269. But custody was not refused to an adulterous father in the absence of some further factor likely to lead to the child's corruption.
[9]*Re A. and B.*, [1897] 1 Ch. 786, C.A.
[10][1951] P. 184, C.A., following *Allen* v. *Allen*, [1948] 2 All E.R. 413, C.A.
[11][1962] 3 All E.R. 1, C.A. In *H.* v. *H. and C.*, [1969] 1 All E.R. 262, 263, C.A., SALMON, L.J., said that it was of no consequence which parent was responsible for the breakdown of the marriage. But it is submitted that, as this dictum is directly in conflict with the *ratio decidendi* of *Re L.*, it should be ignored: see *Re F.*, (*supra*), at pp. 768 and 241, respectively.
[12]At p. 4.
[13]*Cf.* the Custody of Children Act 1891, s. 1.
[14]*Re Mathieson* (1918), 87 L.J. Ch. 445, C.A.
[15][1970] 3 All E.R. 659, C.A.

had been given to the mother when her marriage was dissolved. She later remarried and she and her second husband now wished to emigrate to New Zealand provided that they could take the boy with them. The court was of the opinion that, on balance, the welfare of the child would be better served by permitting the family to go abroad than by remaining in contact with his father in this country; at the same time, however, they imposed a condition that the stepfather should deposit a sum of money with a solicitor to enable the child to be flown back to England if the court subsequently ordered this or to enable the father to fly to New Zealand to see his son.

Foreign Orders.—Since the jurisdiction of equity in suits involving children is based upon the Crown's prerogative as *parens patriae*, all minors within the jurisdiction are entitled to the same protection even **though they are neither domiciled in this country nor even British subjects. In all cases the welfare of the infant must be the court's first** consideration, and consequently, although an English court must take an order for custody made by a foreign court into consideration, it is not bound to give effect to it if this would not be for the child's benefit. This is clear from the decision of the Privy Council in *McKee* v. *McKee*[16] following the earlier English case of *Re B's Settlement*.[17] The husband and wife, who were both United States citizens, had been divorced in 1942, and a Californian court, which had jurisdiction, ultimately gave the mother the custody of the child of the marriage, a boy born in 1940. At the same time the court affirmed an agreement previously entered into between the parties that neither of them should remove the child from the United States without the written permisson of the other. In contravention of this order, the father took the boy to Canada in 1946. The mother then instituted habeas corpus proceedings in Ontario and the trial judge awarded custody to the father. On appeal the Privy Council affirmed this order. Two years had elapsed between the making of the two orders and in this time the child had developed rapidly and the father's circumstances had undergone a considerable change. Taking all things into consideration, there was no reason for interfering with the trial judge's exercise of discretion.

4. METHODS BY WHICH DISPUTES OVER CUSTODY AND CARE AND CONTROL MAY BE RESOLVED

Preliminary Observations.—It was always a rule of common law that the parent's right to custody would not be enforced against the child's will once the latter had reached the so-called age of discretion. This was fixed at 14 in the case of a boy and 16 in the case of a girl and, because of the difficulties which might otherwise ensue, the same age applied in all cases and no allowance was made for the precocity of the

---

[16][1951] 1 All E.R. 942, P.C.; [1951] A.C. 352.
[17][1940] Ch. 54. See also *Re Kernot*, [1964] 3 All E.R. 339; [1965] Ch. 217. For criticisms of the present state of the law relating to possible conflict of orders made by different courts in the United Kingdom, see the Report of the Committee on Conflicts of Jurisdiction affecting Children (1959, Cmnd. 842).

individual child.[18] This rule has since been adopted by equity and in the Divorce Court.[19] It must not be supposed, however, that it would be applied arbitrarily today in exceptional cases, for example if the child in question were mentally retarded.[20]

Writ of Habeas Corpus.—The writ of habeas corpus, which may be used by anyone to regain his liberty if he is unlawfully detained against his will, may also be used by anyone claiming the custody of a child who has not yet reached the age of discretion. Before that age the child cannot in law exercise any choice in the matter, for to permit him to do so " would only expose him to danger and seductions ",[1] and consequently he is deemed to be at liberty when he is in the custody of the person with the right to it.[2] It is therefore extremely doubtful whether this remedy is available at all once the child has reached the age of discretion, although CASSELS, J., in *Lough* v. *Ward*[3] expressed the opinion that it would be, at any rate in exceptional circumstances.

Wardship of Court.—If a parent wishes to invoke the jurisdiction of the Family Division of the High Court without taking other matrimonial proceedings, the simplest procedure is to make an application under the Guardianship of Minors Act.[4] If a stranger, who is not the child's guardian, wishes to obtain care and control, he should start proceedings to have the child made a ward of court. Any interested person may do this but he naturally runs the risk of having to pay costs if he is unsuccessful.[5] An application may also be made by a parent to have the child made a ward of court, a procedure which has the advantage that either parent may be given care and control whilst the exercise of his parental rights will remain under the supervision of the court.[6]

Injunctions.—An injunction may also be obtained to restrain the defendant from interfering with the plaintiff's right to custody. This was granted in *Lough* v. *Ward*[7] where the plaintiff's daughter was

---

[18]*R.* v. *Howes* [1860], 3 E. & E. 332; *Ex parte Barford* (1860), 8 Cox C.C. 405. In the case of a daughter this age was apparently fixed by reference to the statute 4 & 5 Ph. & M., c. 8, s. 3 (which has now been repealed and re-enacted in the Sexual Offences Act 1956, s. 20, *post,* p. 312); in the case of a boy the age of 14 was presumably taken as being the age at which guardianship for nurture ceased at common law.

[19]*Re Agar-Ellis* (1883), 24 Ch.D. 317, C.A.; *Thomasset* v. *Thomasset,* [1894] P. 295, C.A.; *Hall* v. *Hall* (1945), 175 L.T. 355, C.A.

[20]*Cf. Thomasset* v. *Thomasset,* (*supra*); *Stark* v. *Stark,* [1910] P. 190, C.A.; *Hall* v. *Hall,* (*supra*).

[1]*Per* LORD DENMAN, C.J., in *R.* v. *Greenhill* (1836), 4 Ad. & El. 624, 640.

[2]*R.* v. *Greenhill,* (*supra*); *R.* v. *Clarke* (1857), 7 E. & B. 186, 193-194; *Barnardo* v. *McHugh,* [1891] A.C. 388, H.L. (illegitimate child). The writ will lie only against the person with actual control of the child at the time and not against one who once had it but has now lost it: *Barnardo* v. *Ford, Gossage's Case,* [1892] A.C. 326, H.L. Unlike cases where the writ is sought to obtain release from an unlawful detention, *either* party may appeal from an order granting or refusing it: *Barnardo* v. *McHugh.*

[3][1945] 2 All E.R. 338, 348 (although this may be due to a misreading of the judgments in *Re Egar-Ellis, supra*). But see also *R.* v. *Lewis* (1893), 9 T.L.R. 226, 227.

[4]*Infra.*

[5]*Re McGrath,* [1893] 1 Ch. 143, 146-147, C.A.

[6]See further, *post,* pp. 332 *et seq.*

[7][1945] 2 All E.R. 338. The application for the injunction was coupled with an action for damages for enticement. Although enticement is no longer a tort (see *post,* p. 314), an injunction can clearly still be granted to protect the parent's right to custody.

over the age of 16. It will thus be seen that the court may grant an injunction even though it would not positively enforce the right to custody by ordering the child to return to its parents.

Guardianship of Minors Act.—Either parent (including the mother or father of an illegitimate child) may apply for an order for the custody of a minor or access to it under the Guardianship of Minors Act.[8] Such an order may be made by the High Court, a county court or a magistrates' court.[9] In the last case, however, there is an important limitation upon the court's jurisdiction, for no magistrates' court may make an order with respect to a child over the age of 16 unless he is physically or mentally incapable of self support, although an order once made may remain in force until the child reaches the age of 18 and an *existing* order may be varied or discharged at any time during the child's minority.[10] If the court awards custody to the mother, it may also order the father to pay her maintenance in respect of a *legitimate* child only.[11] The court also has power to award custody to one parent and care and control to the other.[12]

An order may be made even though the parents are residing together —a provision which is designed to ensure that, if the children are living with one of them at the time of the application, the other may remain with them till the determination of the case. But the order is unenforceable so long as the spouses reside together at any time and it will cease to have effect entirely if they reside together continuously for any period of three months.[13]

Any order may be subsequently varied or discharged on the application of either parent.[14] On hearing such an application, the court has greater latitude in admitting evidence which could have been

---

[8]Guardianship of Minors Act 1971, ss. 9 (1) and 14 (1). The editors of Clarke Hall and Morrison, *Children*, consider that the Acts deal only with disputes between parents and that as against a stranger a parent should enforce his right by habeas corpus (7th Ed., 794). *Sed quaere?*

[9]A county court has jurisdiction only if the parties are resident in England or a summons can be served on the respondent in England. A magistrates' court has jurisdiction if all the parties reside in England, or if the defendant resides here and the applicant resides in Scotland or Northern Ireland, or if the mother and child reside in England and the defendant father resides in any other part of the United Kingdom: *ibid.*, s. 15.

[10]*Ibid*, s. 15 (2). A magistrates' court may refuse to make an order if it considers the matter would be more conveniently dealt with by the High Court and no appeal will lie from such a refusal: *ibid.*, s. 16 (4).

[11]*Ibid.*, ss. 9 (2) and 14 (2).

[12]*Re W.* (*J.C.*) (*an Infant*), [1963] 3 All E.R. 459, C.A.; [1964] Ch. 202. But see *post*, p. 285, n. [12]. Although there is no express statutory power, the court may presumably also make an order for access in favour of a parent who does not have *de facto* care and control.

[13]Guardianship of Minors Act 1971, s. 9 (3). "Residing with" was formerly regarded as meaning something different from "cohabiting with" and was interpreted as "living under the same roof as" (*Evans* v. *Evans*, [1947] 2 All E.R. 656; [1948] 1 K.B. 175; *Wheatley* v. *Wheatley*, [1949] 2 All E.R. 428; [1950] 1 K.B. 39). but in *Naylor* v. *Naylor*, [1961] 2 All E.R. 129; [1962] P. 253, a Divorce Divisional Court held that it was contradictory to say that, if one spouse was in desertion, he could be said to be residing with the other and thus stated *obiter* that "residing with" must mean the same as "cohabiting with". See further, *ante*, pp. 162-164.

[14]*Ibid.*, s. 9 (4).

adduced when the original order was made, for in custody disputes no relevant fact should be excluded.[15]

Failure to comply with an order for custody made in the High Court or a county court is punishable with committal until the child is handed over to the parent to whom custody has been granted.[16] If the order is made in a magistrates' court, the party refusing to carry it out may be ordered to pay a sum not exceeding £1 for every day that he is in default up to a maximum of £20 or committed to prison until he has complied with the order or for a period of two months whichever be the shorter.[17]

Matrimonial Proceedings (Magistrates' Courts) Act.—One of the most radical changes introduced by the Matrimonial Proceedings (Magistrates' Courts) Act 1960 was the considerable extension of magistrates' powers to make orders relating to children when proceedings are instituted under this Act by either wife or husband. Whereas up till 1960 an order could be made only in respect of a child of the marriage and in favour of the complainant, the category of children, the type of order and the circumstances in which it can be made have all been widened appreciably.

Children of the Family.—So far as custody, care and access are concerned, a magistrates' court acting under this Act may make an order with respect to any child of the family under the age of 16. A child of the family *for the purpose of this Act* is defined as a child of both spouses or a child of one of them who has been accepted as a member of the family by the other, and in either case the child may be legitimate, illegitimate or adopted.[18] It thus includes the biological child of both of them and a child adopted by them jointly; provided that the other has accepted it as a member of the family, it also includes a child of one of them by a previous marriage, the illegitimate child of one of them, and a child adopted by one of them only.

Whether or not one spouse has accepted the other's child as a member of the family is a question of fact.[19] It is not enough that a man should marry a woman knowing that she has children: it must be clear that he intends to treat them as his own.[20] Indeed, the court should be cautious before inferring an acceptance for fear that a prudent husband, foreseeing the possibility of being saddled with the maintenance of another man's children, might be led expressly to reject them—the very opposite situation to that which the Act intended to bring about.[1] But in any event, one spouse cannot accept the other's child as a member of the family against the parent's will. There must be " a mutual arrangement between the spouses . . . that the child shall be treated

---

[15]*Per* JENKINS, J., in *Re Wakeman*, [1947] 2 All E.R. 74, 78; [1947] Ch. 607, 613-614; *B. (B.)* v. *B. (M.)*, [1969] 1 All E.R. 891, 900; [1970] P. 103, 114.

[16]R.S.C., O. 45, r. 5; County Court Rules, O. 25, r. 67.

[17]Guardianship of Minors Act 1971, s. 13 (1); Magistrates' Courts Act 1952, s. 54.

[18]Matrimonial Proceedings (Magistrates' Courts) Act 1960, s. 16 (1).

[19]*Bowlas* v. *Bowlas*, [1965] 3 All E.R. 40, C.A.; [1965] P. 450. A child who has been held to be a child of one family in divorce proceedings can become the child of another family as the result of a parent's remarriage: *Newman* v. *Newman*, [1970] 3 All E.R. 529; [1971] P. 43.

[20]*Bowlas* v. *Bowlas*, (*supra*).

[1]*Per* ORMROD, J., in *H.* v. *H.*, [1966] 1 All E.R. 356, 357.

both by its natural parent and by the natural parent's spouse as if it were the child of both ",[2] and in the absence of an explicit arrangement the inference from their conduct must be clear and unequivocal.[3] Undue possessiveness on the part of the natural parent or a failure to ask the other to make any substantial contribution to the child's maintenance does not necessarily imply that there has been no such arrangement, but determination on the parent's part that the other shall have no control over the children at all precludes the possibility of any agreement that the latter shall accept them as his and consequently they cannot be children of the family.[4]

In *R. v. R.*[5] it was said that the parent's spouse can accept a child as a member of the family only if he has full knowledge of the relevant facts at the time. In that case the wife had a daughter who the husband assumed was his. Five years later he discovered that another man was the father and immediately rejected the child. In those circumstances it was held that he had never accepted her. Despite the wide way in which the principle has been worded, it is very doubtful whether it applies at all if the mistake relates to anything other than paternity. The Divisional Court has certainly refused to extend it to the case where the husband believed the wife's children to be the children of a previous marriage whereas they were in fact illegitimate.[6]

Clearly there must be a family into which the child can be accepted. In *B. v. B. and F.*[7] the wife left her husband taking her six children with her. She then told him that he was not the father of the two youngest. STIRLING, J., found as a fact that she had never agreed that the husband should treat them as his own, but, following *R. v. R.*, he added that acceptance was impossible in the circumstances. The husband was not in possession of the facts until the wife and children had left him and by this time the family had broken up so that the children could not be accepted into it.[8] But, given that there is a family in existence, can the spouse accept the other's child as a member of it at any time? In *Bowlas v. Bowlas*[9] (where the question was whether the husband had accepted the wife's children by a previous marriage) SALMON, L.J., said the test to be applied was: " Did this man, immediately before or at the time of the marriage (and I stress these words) accept the children as members of the family and marry the [wife] on that basis?" The principle was pushed to somewhat surprising lengths in *Caller v. Caller.*[10] The husband married the wife knowing that she was pregnant by another man. It was agreed that he should treat the child as his own and he even went so far as to tell his friends

---

[2]*Per* WRANGHAM, J., in *Dixon* v. *Dixon*, [1967] 3 All E.R. 659, 662.

[3]*Per* ORMROD, J., in *H.* v. *H.*, (*supra*), at p. 357. See also *B.* v. *B. and F.*, [1968] 3 All E.R. 232; [1969] P. 37.

[4]*P.* (*R.*) v. *P.* (*P.*), [1969] 3 All E.R. 777.

[5][1968] 2 All E.R. 608; [1968] P. 414; approved by LORD DENNING, M.R., in *Re L.*, [1968] 1 All E.R. 20, 25-26, C.A.; [1968] P. 119, 158, and by STIRLING, J., in *B.* v. *B. and F.*, (*supra*).

[6]*Kirkwood* v. *Kirkwood*, [1970] 2 All E.R. 161.

[7][1968] 3 All E.R. 232; [1969] P. 37. See Hall, [1969] C.L.J. 37.

[8]*Quaere* whether he could still have accepted them as members of his family if the wife had left them with him when she told him that he was not the father.

[9][1965] 3 All E.R. 40, 46, C.A.; [1965] P. 450, 461; followed in *Dixon* v. *Dixon*, (*supra*).

[10][1966] 2 All E.R. 754; [1968] P. 39.

that he was the father. He deserted the wife before the child's birth, but the Divisional Court held that, as he had married on the understanding that he should treat the child as his own, he had accepted it as a member of the family even though it was *en ventre sa mere*. But SALMON, L.J.'s test is obviously too narrow in the sense that it would preclude a child from ever being accepted as a member of the family if it was conceived after the marriage. In such a case the question must be: did the spouses agree that the husband should accept the child as a member of the family after discovering that it was not his, whether or not the child had yet been born? Furthermore, since the object of the Act is to widen the category of children with respect to whom orders can be made, there seems to be no objection to the parties' changing their minds and subsequently agreeing to *accept* the child.

Orders that can be made.—The court may order the legal custody of any child of the family under the age of 16 to be committed to either spouse or to a third person. It may also make an order for access in favour of either spouse or, if the child is not the child of both of them, of the child's other parent. If a custody order is made, the court may further order the child to be placed under the supervision of a probation officer or the local authority if there are exceptional circumstances making this desirable. If it is impracticable or undesirable to entrust the child to any individual, the court may commit the care of it to the local authority.[11] But it should be noted that it was held in *W.(C.)* v. *W.(R.)*[12] that the court has no power under the Matrimonial Proceedings (Magistrates' Courts) Act to make a "split order" giving custody to one spouse and care and control to the other. The reason is that to hold otherwise would make nonsense of the provision that only the spouse with custody can obtain an order for maintenance and that access can be ordered only in favour of a person who does not have custody. Hence if custody were given to the husband and care and control to the wife, she could not get maintenance and he could not get access.

An order committing a child to the care of a local authority remains in force until he reaches the age of 18 notwithstanding any claim by a parent or guardian.[13] A supervision order remains in force until the child's sixteenth birthday.[14]

---

[11]Matrimonial Proceedings (Magistrates' Courts) Act 1960, ss. 2 (1) (d)-(g) and 3 (1). The court has no power to make an order with respect to a child over the age of 16 even though he is incapable of self-support. The local authority is the county, county borough or London borough in which the child is resident. Notice of the proceedings must be given to a parent who is not a spouse (except the father of an illegitimate child against whom no affiliation order has been made) and the parent (including the father of an illegitimate child in any case) is entitled to appear and be represented: s. 4 (6).

[12][1968] 3 All E.R. 608; [1969] P. 33. The first part of the argument also applies to the Guardianship of Minors Act, which enables a mother to obtain maintenance from the father only if she is awarded custody (see p. 478, *post*). Nevertheless the court can make a split order under these Acts (see *ante*, p. 282). The court's attention was apparently not drawn to this point in *W. (C.)* v. *W. (R.)* and the decisions are clearly partially inconsistent.

[13]Matrimonial Proceedings (Magistrates' Courts) Act 1960, s. 3 (2)-(5). See further, *post*, pp. 297-298.

[14]*Ibid.*, s. 3 (9).

An interim order may contain a provision committing the child to the custody of either spouse or of a third person and a provision for access.[15]

It will be seen that the court's powers under this Act are very wide. It is bound to consider what orders (if any) it should make in relation to children irrespective of the spouses' own wishes and it may call upon a probation officer or the director of social services of the local authority to make such reports as it considers necessary.[16]   In order to protect the child and to avoid further proceedings, it may make an order even though the complaint is dismissed.[17]   Again, the court is not precluded from making any order with respect to children by reason of the fact that the complainant is in desertion or has been guilty of adultery or, where the ground of complaint is the defendant's adultery, that the complainant has condoned it, connived at it or conduced to it by his own wilful neglect or misconduct;[18] nor is it bound to discharge such an order if the complainant later commits adultery.[19]   Similarly an order relating to children (other than an order committing their custody to either spouse) may take effect immediately even though the spouses are cohabitating and will not be discharged if they continue to cohabit for three months or subsequently resume cohabitation.[20]   But the court's powers are to a certain extent limited, for it may make no order at all if there is already in force any other order made by an English court and may not commit the child to the care of a local authority or make an order relating to supervision or access if the child is already in the care of a local authority.[1]

Orders relating to custody, care, supervision and access may be varied and revoked.   The rules relating to the admissibility of evidence which was available at the time of the making of the original order under the Guardianship of Minors Act[2] probably apply also to applications to vary and revoke orders made under the Matrimonial Proceedings (Magistrates' Courts) Act.

Custody of Children in Matrimonial Causes.—The court[3] may make an order for the custody of any child of the family under the age of 18 in proceedings for divorce, nullity and judicial separation and also in proceedings brought under section 6 of the Matrimonial Proceedings and Property Act 1970 on the ground of wilful neglect to provide reasonable maintenance.[4]

---

[15]*Ibid.*, s. 6 (2) (b). But this applies only where " by reason of special circumstances the court thinks it proper ". For interim orders, see *ante*, p. 199.

[16]*Ibid.*, s. 4 (2)-(5), (8).

[17]*Ibid.*, s. 4 (1). This also applies on any application to revoke an order containing provisions relating to custody, care or supervision, or to vary an order by adding or altering provisions relating to custody.

[18]See *ibid.*, s. 2 (3); *Vaughan* v. *Vaughan*, [1963] 2 All E.R. 742; [1965] P. 15.

[19]*Ibid.*, s. 8 (2) (b).   [20]*Ibid.*, ss. 7 (1), (2) and 8 (2).

[1]*Ibid.*, s. 2 (4).

[2]*Ante*, pp. 282-283.

[3]*I.e.* the court (High Court or county court) in which the matrimonial cause is proceeding. A county court judge may transfer an application for custody to the High Court if this seems desirable: Matrimonial Causes Act 1967, s. 2; Matrimonial Causes Rules 1968, rr. 80, 80A and 97 (as amended by the Matrimonial Causes (Amendment No. 3) Rules 1970).

[4]For proceedings under section 6, see *post*, p. 427.

Children of the Family.—A child of the family *for the purpose of this Act* is defined as a child of both spouses (including a child adopted by both of them) or any other child who has been treated by both of them as a child of their family, provided that it has not been boarded out with them by a local authority or voluntary organisation.[5]

It will be seen that this definition is wider than the definition of a child of the family for the purposes of the Matrimonial Proceedings (Magistrates' Courts) Act. The child need not be a child of either spouse and it is sufficient if it was treated (as distinct from accepted) as a member of the family. Again, the question must be one of fact. Apparently there need be no consent to the child's being treated as a member of the family and the fact that the husband mistakenly believed the child to be his own will not prevent the child from being a child of the family if he has treated it as such.[6] Common sense clearly excludes some children, for example young lodgers, au pair girls, and relations who are being looked after during their parents' temporary absence. In other cases the payment of maintenance by the child's natural parents may indicate that it has not become a member of the foster parents' family, but this is clearly not decisive.[7]

Orders that may be made.—In the case of divorce, nullity and judicial separation, the court may make an order for the custody and education of any child of the family under the age of 18 before, by or after the final decree. Alternatively, it may direct the child to be made a ward of court. The court may also make an order if the petition is dismissed.[8] In the case of proceedings under section 6, the court may make an order for custody only if it makes an order for financial provision and the custody order will remain in force only so long as the order for financial provision is in force and the child is under the age of 18.[9] In either case the court is not limited to giving custody or care and control to one of the spouses and may order the child to be committed to a third person. It may make a " split order " giving custody to one person and care and control to another[10] and may make an order for access in favour of a person who does not have *de facto* possession.

As in the case of proceedings under the Matrimonial Proceedings (Magistrates' Courts) Act, the court may order the child to be placed under the supervision of a welfare officer or the local authority if there are exceptional circumstances making this desirable.[11] Similarly, if it is impracticable or undesirable to entrust a child under the age of 17 to any individual, the court may commit it to the care of a local

---

[5]Matrimonial Proceedings and Property Act 1970, s. 27 (1).

[6]Because in deciding what order for financial provision to make the court must have regard to whether the husband knew the child was not his: *ibid.*, s. 5 (3) (b), *post*, p. 476.

[7]See Law Com. No. 25, paras. 23-32.

[8]Matrimonial Proceedings and Property Act 1970, s. 18 (1). In the case of an order made on the dismissal of the petition, it must be made forthwith or within a reasonable time after the dismissal. The court may make an order with respect to a child born after the final decree: *Knowles* v. *Knowles*, [1962] 1 All E.R. 659; [1962] P. 161.

[9]*Ibid.*, s. 19 (1).

[10]See *Wakeham* v. *Wakeham*, [1954] 1 All E.R. 434, C.A.

[11]Matrimonial Causes Act 1965, s. 37.

authority.[12] Both orders remain in force until the child reaches the age of 18.[13]

The parents and guardians of children of the family who are not the children of both spouses are protected by the provision that no order is to affect the rights over a child of any person (other than a party to the marriage) unless the child is the child of one of the parties (or a child adopted by one of them) and the person concerned has been made a party to the proceedings.[14]

Variation and Discharge of Orders.—All orders relating to custody, care, access, and supervision are made " from time to time " and may be varied, suspended, revived and discharged.[15] They all automatically come to an end on the child's eighteenth birthday.

Withholding of Decrees.—It is a notorious and lamentable fact that the persons most likely to suffer when a marriage breaks down are the children. As a means of ensuring that proper arrangements have been made for them, the court must withhold a decree unless the provisions of section 17 of the Matrimonial Proceedings and Property Act are complied with. These apply to any child of the family who is (i) under the age of 16, or (ii) under the age of 18 and in receipt of instruction at an educational establishment or undergoing training for a trade, profession or vocation (whether or not he is also in gainful employment), or (iii) any other child of the family if the court so directs on the ground that special circumstances make this desirable in the child's interests. The last limb enables the court to ensure that provision is made for, say, a mentally or physically handicapped child over 16 or a child over 18 who is still receiving education or training.

The court may not pronounce a decree absolute of divorce or nullity or a decree of judicial separation unless it has by order declared that it is satisfied:

(a) that there are no such children ; *or*

(b) that the only children to whom the section applies are those named in the order and that
   (i) arrangements for their welfare are satisfactory or the best that can be devised in the circumstances ; *or*
   (ii) it is impracticable for the party or parties appearing before the court to make any such arrangements ; *or*

(c) that there are circumstances making it desirable that the decree should be made absolute (or made) without delay notwithstanding that there are or may be children of the family to whom the section applies and the court cannot make a declaration in accordance with (b) above.

---

[12]*Ibid.*, s. 36. Again, the circumstances must be exceptional.

[13]Presumably a care order made in proceedings under s. 6 will continue in force even though the order for financial provision is discharged. It is, however, arguable that the order is made in pursuance of a power given by s. 19 of the Matrimonial Proceedings and Property Act and therefore ceases when financial provision ceases.

[14]Matrimonial Proceedings and Property Act 1970, ss. 18 (2) and 19 (2). *Quaere* whether evidence which could have been adduced at the trial may be given to controvert express findings; the point was left open by SALMON and FENTON ATKINSON, L.JJ., in *F. v. F.*, [1968] 2 All E.R. 946, 950, C.A. Evidence may be adduced if it has become available only since the trial or if it relates to matters not then in issue: *cf. post*, p. 449.

[15]*Ibid.*, ss. 18 (5), (6) and 19 (2); Matrimonial Causes Act 1965, ss. 36 (7) and 37 (6).

In the case of (c) the court must not make the declaration unless it obtains a satisfactory undertaking from either or both of the parties to bring the question of the arrangements before the court within a specified time. " Welfare " includes custody, education and financial provision.[16]

Any decree absolute of divorce or nullity or decree of judicial separation made in the absence of such a declaration will be void. Consequently if a party remarries on the faith of such a decree absolute of divorce, the second marriage will itself be void. But if the declaration is made, no one may challenge the validity of the decree on the ground that the conditions prescribed were not fulfilled.

Declaration of Unfitness.—The court may include in a decree absolute of divorce or a decree of judicial separation a declaration that either party is unfit to have the custody of the children of the family. This means that, if he (or she) is a parent of any child of the family, he is not entitled as of right to the custody or guardianship of it on the death of the other parent.[1] If he then seeks custody, the burden is on him to prove that his conduct has so changed that he is now a fit and proper person to have it.[2] Consequently the court will not cast such a stigma upon a parent unless a very strong case is made out against him.[3] It has been made where the husband has been guilty of ill-treating his children[4] and where he has forced his wife to submit to grossly depraved and perverted sexual practices;[5] on the other hand it has been refused where the grounds upon which it was sought were that he had committed adultery and failed to support his children for ten years.[6]

Concurrent Orders —It is obvious that the various proceedings open to parents may produce a clash in jurisdiction. One spouse may be taking proceedings in one court whilst the other is taking proceedings in another, or an application may be made in one court whilst an order in respect of the same child is still in force in another.[7]

When a conflict arises between the jurisdiction of the High Court and an inferior court, the latter must give way. If the former is already seised of the matter, the accepted view is that no other court should interfere.[8] The converse case, where proceedings are brought in the High Court when another order is already in force, was considered in

---

[16]The proposed arrangements must be reasonably permanent and the court should not accept arrangements which are intended to last for only a short period: *McKernan* v. *McKernan* (1970), 114 Sol. Jo. 284. For a study of custody in matrimonial proceedings and the operation of s. 33 of the Matrimonial Causes Act 1965 (which s. 17 of the Matrimonial Proceedings and Property Act has replaced), see the Law Commission's Working Paper No. 15 (written by J. C. Hall).
[1]Matrimonial Proceedings and Property Act 1970, s. 18 (3), (4).
[2]*Webley* v. *Webley* (1891), 64 L.T. 839; *S.* v. *S.*, [1949] 1 All E.R. 285 n.; [1949] P. 269.
[3]*Per* JEUNE, J., in *Woolnoth* v. *Woolnoth* (1902), 86 L.T. 598, 599.
[4]*Webley* v. *Webley*, (*supra*).
[5]*S.* v. *S.*, (*supra*). See also *Hitchings* v. *Hitchings* (1892), 67 L.T. 530.
[6]*Woolnoth* v. *Woolnoth*, (*supra*).
[7]Before the creation of the Family Division there could also be a conflict of jurisdiction between the Chancery and Probate Divisions of the High Court (*e.g.*, if one of the parents of a ward of court took divorce proceedings).
[8]*R.* v. *Middlesex Justices; ex parte Bond*, [1933] 2 K.B. 1, C.A.

Re P.,[9] where the mother brought wardship proceedings in the High Court after the father had obtained custody in a magistrates' court. STAMP, J., held that, although he undoubtedly had jurisdiction to hear the case, he should exercise it only in exceptional circumstances. This could be done if, for example, the case showed special complexity,[10] if the jurisdiction of the High Court were more extensive, efficacious or convenient, or if it were necessary to supplement the magistrates' jurisdiction by giving relief which they had no power to give. Thus in *Re H.(G.J.)*[11] the same judge continued the wardship of a child and issued an injunction prohibiting the father from taking it out of the jurisdiction as a means of giving effect to a magistrates' order awarding custody to the mother. In other cases the correct procedure is to apply to the magistrates for a variation or discharge of their order or to appeal against it.

In which court a parent chooses to seek an order is a question of practical expediency. If proceedings are pending in the divorce court or in a magistrates' court under the Matrimonial Proceedings (Magistrates' Courts) Act, it is clearly best that all matters relating to the family should be dealt with together in the same court. If no other proceedings are pending, it will be necessary to have the child made a ward of court if the parent wishes to obtain a comprehensive order containing directions as to the child's religious or secular education or to invoke the High Court's power to make supplementary orders (for example, restraining a parent with custody from removing the child from the jurisdiction).[12] In other cases the applicant (if he is a parent) will generally choose the relatively cheap and speedy procedure offered in the county court or a magistrates' court under the Guardianship of Minors Act (although it must be remembered that the jurisdiction of a magistrates' court is limited if the child is over the age of 16).[13]

5. CHILDREN IN THE CARE OF LOCAL AUTHORITIES

For the past quarter of a century the policy of successive administrations has been to increase the responsibility of local authorities for the provision of welfare services. For this purpose local authorities are counties, county boroughs and London boroughs[14] and the Local Authority Social Services Act of 1970 now compels them to consolidate their welfare work by establishing a single social services committee which will be responsible for all the services. The day to day running of the authority's social services is under the control of the Director of Social Services.[15]

So far as children are concerned, the authority's first duty is to give advice, guidance and assistance in order to prevent a child having to be received into care or brought before a juvenile court. In addition to

---

[9][1967] 2 All E.R. 229.
[10]See *Re P. (A.J.)*, [1968] 1 W.L.R. 1976.
[11][1966] 1 All E.R. 952.
[12]*Cf. T.* v. *T.*, [1968] 3 All E.R. 321.
[13]See *ante*, p. 282.
[14]Local Authority Social Services Act 1970, s. 1.
[15]*Ibid.*, s. 6.

working with voluntary organisations, the authority may give assistance in kind and, in exceptional cases, in cash.[16]

Its second function—that with which we are primarily concerned in this chapter—is to look after children in its care. Other duties include the supervision of the welfare of foster-children under Part I of the Children Act 1958,[17] children placed for adoption[18] and children who are the subject of supervision orders.[19]

Children may come into the care of a local authority as the result of a court order. There is power to make an order under the Matrimonial Proceedings and Property Act[20] and the Matrimonial Proceedings (Magistrates' Courts) Act,[1] in wardship proceedings,[2] in care proceedings and in criminal proceedings. The first three are dealt with elsewhere in this book; we must now consider the last two. We must then discuss the reception of children into care under the provisions of the Children Act 1948 and finally consider the duties and powers of an authority with respect to children in their care.

Care Proceedings.—Early legislation dealt with three distinct types of children: juvenile offenders, children in need of care and protection, and children beyond parental control. It is obvious that the last two categories overlap, and it has long been recognised that juvenile delinquency may well be the result of home surroundings.[3] The law relating to all three has therefore gradually been assimilated. Essentially it is to be found in the Children and Young Persons Acts 1933 to 1969:[4] the basic principle underlying their provisions is thus stated in section 44 (1) of the Act of 1933:

> " Every court in dealing with a child or young person who is brought before it . . . shall have regard to the welfare of the child or young person and shall in a proper case take steps for removing him from undesirable surroundings, and for securing that proper provision is made for his education and training."

The relevant law was radically altered by the provisions of the Children and Young Persons Act 1969, the main purpose of which was to give effect to the White Paper " Children in Trouble ".[5] It was

---

[16]Children and Young Persons Act 1963, s. 1. The authority has similar powers with respect to a person under the age of 21 formerly in their care: *ibid.*, s. 58. *Cf.* their duty of after-care under the Children Act 1948, s. 34. Voluntary organisations would include such bodies as a Family Service Unit, the Family Welfare Association and the W.R.V.S.

[17]See *post*, pp. 320-321.

[18]See *ante*, p. 254.

[19]See *ante*, pp. 285 and 287, and *post*, pp. 293 and 338.

[20]See *ante*, pp. 287-288.

[1]See *ante*, p. 285.

[2]See *post*, p. 338.

[3]*Cf.* the Infant Felons Act of 1840 which enabled the court to assign the custody of an infant convicted of felony to anyone willing to take charge of him if this would be for his benefit.

[4]Children and Young Persons Act 1933; Children and Young Persons (Amendment) Act 1952; Children and Young Persons Act 1963; Children and Young Persons Act 1969. For the sake of brevity, these will be referred to as the 1933 Act, etc.

[5]1968, Cmnd. 3601. For a critical review of the provisions of the Act, see Stone, *Children without a Satisfactory Home*, 33 M.L.R. 649.

obvious that it would be some time before the necessary administrative arrangements could be made and consequently the Home Secretary was empowered to introduce the new scheme piecemeal. Most of the provisions considered here came into force at the beginning of 1971; the rest are expected to come into operation shortly and the following account anticipates this.[6]

Under the 1969 Act care proceedings have replaced proceedings for bringing a child under the age of 17[7] before the court as being in need of care, protection or control, and they will eventually partly replace criminal proceedings as well. A local authority is under a duty to investigate if they believe that there are grounds for bringing care proceedings and to bring them if necessary;[8] care proceedings may also be brought by a constable or other authorised person or by an officer of an authorised society (such as the N.S.P.C.C.), who must first give notice to the local authority.[9] In some cases the child's parent or guardian may himself want proceedings to be taken (for example if the child is beyond control). He may ask the local authority to take them, and if the authority refuses to do so or takes no action within 28 days, the parent or guardian may then apply to the juvenile court which, after investigating the facts, may order the authority to bring the child before it.[10]

A juvenile court before which the child is brought may make an order only provided that at least one of six specified conditions is satisfied and also that, in any case, the child is in need of care or control which he is unlikely to receive unless an order is made.[11] The six conditions are:

(a) The child's proper development is being avoidably prevented or neglected or his health is being avoidably impaired or neglected or he is being ill-treated.

(b) Condition (a) will probably be satisfied having regard to the fact that it has been satisfied in the case of another child who is or was a member of the same household.

(c) The child is exposed to moral danger. Problems may arise in the case of immigrants and foreigners resident in this country, for the principle was laid down in *Mohamed* v. *Knott*[12] that account must be taken of their background and customs in deciding whether a child is exposed to moral danger. In that case it was held that a Nigerian girl aged 13 was not exposed to moral danger merely because she was having sexual intercourse with a man aged 26 to whom she was validly married by Nigerian law. The difficulty facing the courts now is to decide what

---

[6]Fit person orders made under the 1933 Act committing a child to the care of someone other than a local authority remain in force. Orders committing a child to a local authority as a fit person have become care orders: 1969 Act, 4th Sched., paras. 8 and 9.

[7]The Children and Young Persons Acts differentiate between a child under the age of 14 and a young person between 14 and 17. The word "child" is used in the text to include both.

[8]1969 Act, s. 2 (1), (2).

[9]*Ibid.*, ss. 1 (1), (6) and 2 (3).

[10]1963 Act, s. 3, as amended by the 1969 Act, Sched. 5. This procedure is designed to avoid parent and child confronting each other in the same proceedings.

[11]1969 Act, s. 1 (2).

[12][1968] 2 All E.R. 563; [1969] 1 Q.B. 1. See Karsten, 32 M.L.R. 212.

standards of morality they are to apply if they depart from those traditionally adopted in this country. Would the decision in *Mohamed* v. *Knott* have been the same, for example, if the girl had been aged 10 or if the union had been incestuous? Sooner or later the courts will have to determine at what point an immigrant community must be compelled to abandon family laws and customs which are not only different from English ones but which *mutatis mutandis* would be regarded in this country as contrary to public policy or even criminal.

(d) He is beyond the control of his parent or guardian.

(e) He is of compulsory school age and is not receiving efficient full-time education suitable to his age, ability and aptitude.[13]

(f) He is guilty of an offence other than homicide. The proceedings may be brought only by a local authority or a constable and the court can make an order only if it would have found the child guilty had he been prosecuted. This means that this condition can never be satisfied if the child is under the age of ten.[14] Furthermore the child is entitled, for example, to plead autrefois acquit or convict (including the fact that the same offence has been considered in previous care proceedings) or that the six months' limitation period has expired in the case of a summary offence.[15]

The court has no jurisdiction to entertain care proceedings if the child is over the age of 16 and is or has been married.[16] If he is under the age of five, the court may permit proceedings to be taken even though he is not in court, provided that his parent or guardian has been given notice of the proceedings or is in court.[17]

Orders that may be made.—If the court finds that the above conditions are satisfied, it may make one of the following orders.[18]

(a) An order requiring the child's parent or guardian to enter into a recognisance to take proper care of him and exercise proper control over him.[19]

(b) A *supervision order* placing the child under the supervision of the local authority or, at the request of the authority, of a probation officer who has already worked with the family.[20] This replaces the court's former power to place the child on probation or under the supervision of a probation officer. There are elaborate provisions in the 1969 Act laying down the directions that a supervision order may contain relating to residence, medical treatment for mental illness (including treatment

---

[13]In this case proceedings may be brought only by the local education authority: 1969 Act, s. 2 (8). See further *post*, p. 300.
[14]Because he is legally incapable of committing a crime: 1933 Act, s. 50, as amended by the 1963 Act, s. 16 (1).
[15]1969 Act, s. 3.
[16]*Ibid.*, s. 1 (5) (c).
[17]*Ibid.*, s. 2 (9).
[18]*Ibid.*, s. 1 (3). If a child is found guilty of an indictable offence, the court may also order the payment of compensation for loss of property or damage to it: *ibid.*, s. 3 (6). See further *post*, p. 311.
[19]An order may be made only with the parent's or guardian's consent and must not be for an amount exceeding £50 or for a period of more than three years or extending beyond the child's eighteenth birthday (whichever is the shorter): *ibid.*, s. 2 (13).
[20]*Ibid.*, ss. 11 and 13 (2).

as an in-patient), and what the White Paper termed "intermediate treatment" such as residence away from home for not more than 90 days and participation in specified activities. Supervision orders and their directions may be varied, replaced by care orders (provided that the supervised person is under the age of 18), or discharged, and the court may punish a supervised person over the age of 18 for failing to comply with the order. No order may last for more than three years (or any shorter period specified in the individual order); an order made in care proceedings or on the discharge of a care order must terminate on the supervised person's eighteenth birthday if this occurs earlier.[1]

(c) A *care order* committing the child to the care of a local authority. Unless the order is varied, it remains in force until the age of 18 or, if he has already reached the age of 16 when it is made, the age of 19. There are powers to extend orders to the age of 19 if this is in the child's interest or the public interest in view of his mental condition or behaviour, and if he is over the age of 15, the local authority may apply to a juvenile court to have him sent to a borstal institution if his behaviour is detrimental to other persons accommodated in a community home. Either the authority or the child may apply to have the order discharged, in which case the court has a discretion to replace it by a supervision order. Interim orders may also be made for a period not exceeding 28 days.[2]

The authority is bound to keep the child in their care so long as the order is in force notwithstanding any claim by the parent or guardian[3] and by section 24 (2) of the Act of 1969

> " A local authority shall . . . have the same powers and duties with respect to a person in their care by virtue of a care order . . . as his parent or guardian would have apart from the order . . . and may . . . restrict his liberty to such extent as the authority consider appropriate."

The authority must not cause him to be brought up in any religious creed other than that in which he would have been brought up apart from the order, and in certain circumstances it must appoint a visitor for him if he is not visited by his parent or guardian or communication with them is infrequent.[4]

(d) A *hospital order* under the Mental Health Act 1959 directing him to be detained in a mental hospital if he is found to be suffering from certain types of mental disease.

(e) A *guardianship order* under the Mental Health Act 1959 placing him under the guardianship of a local health authority or other approved person in similar circumstances.[5]

The court may make a care order and a hospital order simultaneously, but apart from this not more than one order may be made.[6] If the court is not in a position to decide what order to make, it may make

---

[1]See generally *ibid.*, ss. 11-19. Variations and discharge are dealt with in ss. 15 and 16.
[2]See generally *ibid.*, ss. 20-24 and 31.
[3]*Ibid.*, s. 24 (1).
[4]*Ibid.*, s. 24 (3), (5).
[5]For the circumstances in which hospital and guardianship orders can be made and the effects of such orders, see the Mental Health Act 1959, ss. 60 and 63.
[6]1969 Act, s. 1 (4).

an interim care order.[7] If care proceedings are brought in respect of a child *over the age of 14 found guilty of an offence*, the court may, if he consents, order him to enter into a recognisance to keep the peace or to be of good behaviour instead of making any of the above orders.[8]

Detention in a Place of Safety.—In cases of urgency there is a more peremptory power to take children out of their parents' or guardians' control. This can be exercised only in certain specified circumstances: for example, if he is being assaulted, ill-treated or neglected, if certain offences have been committed in respect of him, or if any of conditions (a) to (e) set out above in relation to care proceedings is satisfied. In such a case a court or magistrate may authorise or order a child under the age of 17 to be taken to a place of safety, and in certain circumstances a constable may take a child there without any previous authorisation.[9] The authorisation or order must state a period of time not exceeding 28 days in which care proceedings must be brought unless the child has been previously released or received into the care of a local authority; if he is taken to a place of safety otherwise than on such an authorisation or order or if he has taken refuge there himself, the period is eight days.[10]

Criminal Proceedings.—A child under the age of ten cannot be guilty of a criminal offence at all.[11] Under the 1969 Act the Home Secretary has power to make an order providing that a person who has reached that age but has not reached the age stated in the order (which must not exceed 14) shall not be *charged* with a criminal offence.[12] The Act also imposes restrictions on bringing criminal proceedings against a child aged between 14 and 17, but the present Government does not intend to bring the relevant section into operation.[13]

It follows that, unless and until these provisions become operative, there are two ways of proceeding against a child between the ages of ten and 17 who has committed a criminal offence: either (as before) he may be charged in a juvenile court or care proceedings may be brought in respect of him. If criminal proceedings are taken and he is found guilty, various orders can be made; in particular a care order may be made if the offence is punishable with imprisonment if committed by an adult.[14]

---

[7] *Ibid.*, ss. 2 (10) and 20 (1).

[8] *Ibid.*, s. 3 (7). The recognisance must not be for an amount exceeding £25 or for a period of more than a year.

[9] See 1933 Act, s. 40; 1969 Act, s. 28; Children Act 1958, s. 7; Adoption Act 1958, s. 43. A "place of safety" means a community home, police station, hospital, surgery, or other suitable place the occupier of which is willing to receive a child temporarily: 1933 Act, s. 107 (1), as amended by the 1969 Act, Sched. 5.

[10] 1963 Act, s. 23; 1969 Act, s. 28 and Scheds. 5 and 6.

[11] 1933 Act, s. 50, as amended by the 1963 Act, s. 16 (1). But the fact that he has committed the offence may be evidence that some other condition has been fulfilled enabling care proceedings to be taken in respect of him.

[12] 1969 Act, ss. 4 and 34. The consent of both Houses of Parliament is needed to raise the age above 12: s. 34 (7).

[13] See 1969 Act, s. 5.

[14] 1969 Act, ss. 7 (7) and 34 (1) (c).

Reception of Children into Care.—By section 1 of the Children Act 1948, a local authority is under a duty to receive a child under the age of 17 into care if it appears

" (a) that he has neither parent nor guardian, or has been and remains abandoned by his parents or guardian, or is lost; *or*

(b) that his parents or guardian are, for the time being or permanently, prevented by reason of mental or bodily disease or infirmity or other incapacity or any other circumstances from providing for his proper accommodation, maintenance and upbringing; *and*

(c) in either case, that the intervention of the local authority is necessary in the interests of the welfare of the child."

If necessary, they may keep the child in their care until he reaches the age of 18.[15]

This section envisages a purely temporary arrangement made in an emergency. In addition to the circumstances specifically mentioned in the section, one can imagine other cases where parents find themselves unable for financial or other reasons to take care of their children for the time being. Once the position has changed, they will wish to regain custody, and consequently the authority has no power *under this section* to retain the child against the parent's or guardian's will if the latter wishes to take over the care of him. But this places the authority under no absolute duty to return the child,[16] and if the parent or guardian takes proceedings to recover care of it, the authority can still raise any other defence to the action, for example that this would not be for the child's welfare. In any case they must endeavour to secure that care is taken of him by a parent, guardian, relative or friend provided that this is consistent with his welfare.[17]

Assumption of Parental Rights.—Obviously these provisions are going to be inadequate if the circumstances which led to the child's being received into care are likely to remain permanent or if it is not in the child's interests that his parents or guardian should be permitted to regain custody of him. Consequently section 2 of the Children Act 1948[18] provides machinery whereby the authority may assume parental rights over a child received into their care under section 1 even against the parents' or guardian's will. This may be done only if at least one of the following seven conditions is satisfied:

(a) The child's parents are dead and he has no guardian;

(b) His parent or guardian has abandoned him;

(c) The parent's or guardian's whereabouts have remained unknown for at least twelve months;

(d) The parent or guardian suffers from some permanent disability rendering him incapable of caring for the child;

---

[15]Children Act 1948, s. 1 (2).

[16]*Krishnan* v. *Sutton London B.C.*, [1969] 3 All E.R. 1367, C.A.; [1970] Ch. 181.

[17]Children Act 1948, s. 1 (3). The parent or guardian may apparently take over the care of the child by ensuring that he is accommodated and maintained by someone else: *Re A.B.*, [1954] 2 All E.R. 287; [1954] 2 Q.B. 385.

[18]As amended by the Mental Health Act 1959, 7th Sched., and extended by the Children and Young Persons Act 1963, s. 48.

(e) The parent or guardian suffers from a mental disorder rendering him unfit to have the care of the child;

(f) The parent or guardian is of such habits or mode of life as to be unfit to have the care of the child;

(g) The parent or guardian has so persistently failed without reasonable cause to discharge his obligations as to be unfit to have the care of the child.

To assume parental rights and powers, the authority must pass a resolution to this effect, whereupon they vest in them. If the child has a parent or guardian alive whose whereabouts are known, the authority must immediately give him notice of the resolution unless he has consented in writing to its being passed. He then has a month in which he may object to it; if he does so, the resolution will lapse 14 days after the service of notice of objection unless the authority in the meantime makes a complaint to a juvenile court. If the court is satisfied that the parent or guardian has abandoned the child or is unfit to have custody of him, it may order that the resolution shall not lapse.[19]

The resolution may remain in force until the child reaches the age of 18; but the local authority may rescind it at any time if this would be for his benefit, and a juvenile court may also determine it at any time on the application of his parent or guardian.[20]

Powers and Duties of Local Authorities.—By whatever means a child has come into care, the duty of the authority is the same: to further his best interests, to afford him opportunity for the proper development of his character and abilities, and to provide accommodation and maintenance for him either by boarding him out with foster parents or by maintaining him in a community home or a voluntary home. They may also permit him to be under the charge and control of a parent, guardian, relative or friend.[1] In the case of children committed to their care by the High Court or a county court in matrimonial proceedings or by the High Court in wardship proceedings, however, the exercise of the authority's powers is subject to the overriding control of the court making the order.[2]

Community homes, which are planned by local authorities on a regional basis, have not only replaced approved schools, remand homes and probation homes and hostels but have also superseded children's homes and hostels. This means that a number of different types of community home must be provided and, in the case of children in respect of whom a care order has been made, the local authority, and not the court, has become the classifying authority to determine what

---

[19]Children Act 1948, ss. 2 and 3 (1), (2).   [20]*Ibid.*, s.4.

[1]Children Act 1948, ss. 12 and 13 (as substituted by the Children and Young Persons Act 1969, s. 49). For the powers of the Home Secretary to authorise the emigration of a child received into care under the Children Act or under a care order, see *ibid.*, s. 17. The child must consent if he is of an age to be able to do so and, whenever possible, his parents or guardian must be consulted.

[2]Matrimonial Causes Act 1965, s. 36 (5). Family Law Reform Act 1969, s. 7 (2), (3). The power to authorise the child's emigration cannot be exercised in either of these cases or if the child is committed to the care of a local authority by magistrates acting under the Matrimonial Proceedings (Magistrates' Courts) Act: *ibid.*, s. 3 (2) (a).

type of home an individual child is to be sent to.[3]

If the child is in care by virtue of a care order (other than an interim order made under the Children and Young Persons Act 1969) or has been received into care under section 1 of the Children Act 1948, his father and mother are under a duty to contribute to his maintenance until he reaches the age of 16. Once the child has reached this age, he is liable to contribute to his own maintenance if he is engaged in remunerative full-time work.[4] The amount of contribution is to be fixed by agreement between the parent and the authority or, if they cannot agree, by the court in proceedings for a contribution order.[5] If no contribution order is in force, the authority may apply for an arrears order requiring the contributory to pay such weekly sums as the court thinks fit which must not, in the aggregate, exceed what he should have paid for the child's maintenance during the previous three months.[6]

Disputes over Care and Control.—If the child is in care by virtue of a court order, he continues in care notwithstanding any claim by a parent or any other person.[7] But in the past attempts have been made to invoke the prerogative jurisdiction of the court, particularly after the child has been received into care under the Children Act. Three distinct bodies may have an interest in his custody, care and control: his parents or guardian, the authority itself, and the foster-parents with whom he is boarded out. The authority may wish to terminate the arrangement with foster-parents who are unwilling to return the child, or his natural parents or guardian may wish to resume care and control which the authority or foster-parents (or both) are anxious to retain.

As between the authority and foster-parents the latter are usually bound to return the child whenever the former demands it and the authority may recover custody by habeas corpus.[8] In *Re M.*,[9] where the child was in care under section 2 of the Children Act, and in *Re T. (A.J.J.)*,[10] where he was in care by virtue of a fit person order, the

---

[3]See the Children and Young Persons Act 1969, ss. 35-48. For the arrest of absconders and the prosecution of those aiding and abetting them, see *ibid.*, s. 32.

[4]But no contribution is payable so long as the child is permitted to be under the control of a parent, guardian, relative, friend or applicant for an adoption order. Contribution orders may be varied, suspended, revived and discharged, and are enforceable in the same way as an affiliation order (see *post*, p. 422). See the Children and Young Persons Act 1933, ss. 86 and 87, as amended by the Children Act 1948, ss. 23 and 24; Magistrates' Courts Act 1952, s. 53; Adoption Act 1958, s. 36 (2); Criminal Justice Act 1961, Sched. 5; Children and Young Persons Act 1969, s. 62 and Scheds. 5 and 6. A child over 16 in care by virtue of an order made under the Matrimonial Proceedings (Magistrates' Courts) Act 1960 is also liable to contribute to his own maintenance: *ibid.*, s. 3 (2) (b).

[5]Children and Young Persons Act 1969, s. 62. The amount proposed by the local authority or ordered by the court must not exceed the amount which the authority would normally be prepared to pay if the child were boarded out.

[6]Children and Young Persons Act 1963, s. 30. Arrears orders are treated as contribution orders and are enforceable in the same way.

[7]Matrimonial Proceedings (Magistrates' Courts) Act 1960, s. 3 (3); Matrimonial Causes Act 1965, s. 36 (3); Children and Young Persons Act 1969, s. 24 (1).

[8]*Re A.B.*, [1954] 2 All E.R. 287; [1954] 2 Q.B. 385. The agreement which foster parents are required to sign under the Boarding-out of Children Regulations 1955 includes an undertaking to permit the authority to remove the child.

[9][1961] 1 All E.R. 788, C.A.; [1961] Ch. 328. Followed in *Re Baker*, [1961] 3 All E.R. 276, C.A.; [1962] Ch. 201.

[10][1970] 2 All E.R. 865, C.A.; [1970] Ch. 688.

foster-parents tried to tie the authority's hands by making the child a ward of court. In both cases the Court of Appeal held that the court's prerogative jurisdiction is not entirely superseded by the statute so that wardship proceedings may still be brought even though the child is in the care of a local authority. It will not exercise control over those matters in respect of which the Act has given the authority a discretion, however, unless the latter has acted with impropriety or in breach or disregard of its statutory duties.[11] As the sole question in each case related to the child's care and control which lay exclusively within the authority's discretion and no attack had been made on the propriety of its actions, the court ordered that the child should cease to be a ward of court thus leaving the authority free to regain the child from the foster-parents.

On the other hand the assistance of the court can be invoked to supplement the authority's statutory duties.[12] This is particularly important if the child has been taken into care under section 1 of the Children Act and his parent or guardian demands his return. If any of the conditions laid down in section 2 is satisfied, they can assume parental rights against the claimant's will,[13] but this will not always be the case. In these circumstances the authority can itself apply to have the child made a ward of court, for the parent's request exhausts the statutory powers and therefore revives the court's jurisdiction in full.[14] In *Re S.*[15] the Court of Appeal went even further. A local authority wished to return a boy, whom they had received into care under section 1 of the Act, to his mother and therefore demanded his return from the foster-parent with whom he had been boarded out. The foster-parents, believing that the boy's welfare demanded that he should remain with them, made him a ward of court. The authority contended that they were bound to return the child and that the court should therefore make no order as in *Re M.* It was held, however, that the court must consider the question of care and control on its merits. *Re M.* (which was a case under section 2) was distinguished on the ground that, when a child is in care under section 1, the authority's interest is purely transient and consequently the court must have jurisdiction because otherwise an arbitrary re-assumption of control by the parent might imperil the child's well-being.[16] In any case it is submitted that if the contest is solely between the authority and the foster-parents,

---

[11]*E.g.*, if those responsible for the resolution recalling the child have been motivated by malice or personal hostility towards the foster-parents. A flagrant disregard of the child's welfare would be a disregard of the authority's duty, but where it is a matter of discretion, the court will not substitute its own for the authority's: *Re C. (A.)*, [1966] 1 All E.R. 560.

[12]*Re G.*, [1963] 3 All E.R. 370.

[13]Although as PEARSON, L.J., pointed out in *Re S.*, [1965] 1 All E.R. 865, 871, C.A., it is arguable that once the parent expresses a wish to resume care of the child, the authority's powers under s. 1 cease and consequently they no longer have a power to pass a resolution under s. 2. But is the child still not in their care under s. 1 even though they are not authorised to keep it any longer? PEARSON, L.J's dictum was doubted by GOFF, J., in *Krishnan* v. *Sutton London Borough Council*, [1970] Ch. 181, 186.

[14]*Re R. (K.)*, [1963] 3 All E.R. 337; [1964] Ch. 455.

[15][1965] 1 All E.R. 865, C.A.

[16]The distinction between the local authority's position under ss. 1 and 2 was also emphasised in *Re T. (A.J.J.)*, (*supra*).

the principles laid down in *Re M.* and *Re T.* (*A.J.J.*) will apply and the court will not normally interfere; where, however, the problem has arisen because of the parent's desire to resume care and control, the court's jurisdiction may be invoked by anyone, including the foster-parents, even though the authority does not support them.[17]

C. SECULAR AND RELIGIOUS EDUCATION

1. PARENTS' DUTY TO SECURE THE EDUCATION OF THEIR CHILDREN

Although common law and equity both recognised the parents' moral and social duty to give their children an education suitable to their station, neither system provided the legal means for enforcing it.[18] It was not till 1870 that Parliament took steps to see that a sufficient number of public elementary schools should be built, and finally, in the Elementary Education Act of 1876, placed all parents under a duty to ensure that their children should receive " efficient elementary instruction in reading, writing and arithmetic ". Now, under the Education Act of 1944, the parent of every child between the ages of five and fifteen[19] must ensure that he receives " efficient full-time education suitable to his age, ability and aptitude either by regular attendance at school or otherwise ".[20] Parents who fail to perform this duty or whose children fail to attend school regularly are liable to be prosecuted and the local education authority can take care proceedings with respect to the child.[1]

Parents have never been under any legal duty to provide their children with religious education. In the past courts have put pressure on them indirectly to do so (for example, by refusing custody to an atheistic parent), but in view of the attitude towards the absence of religious belief which society takes today, it is doubtful whether this policy is now pursued.

2. PARENTS' RIGHT TO DETERMINE THEIR CHILDREN'S RELIGIOUS AND SECULAR EDUCATION

Problems of secular and religious education almost invariably go together. Disputes over religious education usually arise out of " mixed " marriages or, more rarely, out of one parent's changing his

---

[17]See further Lasok, *Custody—Judicial or Administrative Decision*, 120 New L.J. 817; Cretney, 33 M.L.R. 696.

[18]*Hodges* v. *Hodges* (1796), Peake, Add. Cas. 79.

[19]If the child's fifteenth birthday falls between 1st September and 31st January, inclusive, he remains of compulsory school age until the end of the spring term; in other cases until the end of the summer term: Education Act 1962, s. 9.

[20]Education Act 1944, ss. 35 and 36. If the child is living with both parents, the statutory duty is cast on both of them: *Plunkett* v. *Alker*, [1954] 1 All E.R. 396; [1954] 1 Q.B. 420. There is a power under the Act of 1944 to raise the compulsory school age to 16 as soon as it is practicable to do so: s. 35. For children at special schools for those requiring special educational treatment (*e.g.*, physically or mentally handicapped children) the upper limit of the compulsory school age is already 16: s. 38. See generally Dutchman-Smith, *Parental Duty to Educate*, 114 Sol. Jo. 921.

[1]*Ibid.*, ss. 37, 39, 40 and 40A, as amended by the Education (Miscellaneous Provisions) Acts 1948 and 1953 and the Children and Young Persons Acts 1963 and 1969. For care proceedings, see *ante*, pp. 291-295.

religious belief after the marriage. Disputes over secular education reflect the same problem because they usually arise out of one parent's desire to have the child educated at a school under the direction of a particular religious sect or order, and there are few reported cases in which the dispute has been over two types of secular education *simpliciter*. The following discussion will therefore be confined to the determination of religious education; but it should be remembered that disputes over secular education will be resolved according to the same principles and that in all cases the court's first consideration must be for the welfare of the child.

Subject to certain exceptions, both at common law and in equity the father had the absolute right to determine the form of his legitimate minor children's education and his wishes had to be respected after his death.[2] After the passing of the Guardianship of Infants Act in 1886, however, the courts began to pay more attention to the welfare of the child than to the father's wishes,[3] and the Guardianship of Infants Act of 1925 went further by making it obligatory for the court to put the child's welfare first and by giving the mother powers equal to those of the father in this respect.[4] In strict legal theory a minor cannot choose his own religion and certainly cannot determine what form of education he is to have,[5] and the court must give effect to the parents' wishes unless they clearly run contrary to the child's welfare.

Since the decision of the Court of Appeal in *Re Carroll*,[6] there seems no doubt that the right to select the type of education that an illegitimate child should have and the religious belief in which it should be brought up is vested *prima facie* in the mother.

Even if the court refuses to enforce a parent's right to the custody or care and control of a child, it has power to make an order to secure that his wishes with respect to its religious upbringing shall be observed.[7] Similarly a local authority is not to cause a child who is in their care under a care order or over whom they have assumed parental rights to be brought up in any religious creed other than that in which he would otherwise have been brought up.[8]

Disputes over Religious Education.—The change of emphasis from the almost absolute enforcement of the parent's right to choose his children's religion (which was forfeited in far fewer circumstances than his right to custody) to the paramount consideration of the child's welfare has been so much more marked than in the case of his right to custody that many cases decided before 1925 are no longer of any real authority. Nevertheless some are still of help in illustrating the principles which the court will bear in mind in solving disputes of this kind.

---

[2]*Andrews* v. *Salt* (1873), 8 Ch. App. 622.
[3]See the remarks of VISCOUNT CAVE in *Ward* v. *Laverty*, [1925] A.C. 101, 108, H.L.
[4]*Re Collins*, [1950] 1 All E.R. 1057, C.A.; [1950] Ch. 498.
[5]*Re Carroll*, [1931] 1 K.B. 317, 336, C.A. *Cf. Re May*, [1917] 2 Ch. 126.
[6][1931] 1 K.B. 317, C.A. See also *Re E.*, [1963] 3 All E.R. 874.
[7]Custody of Children Act 1891, s. 4. This does not apply if the parent has for any reason lost the right to determine the child's religious education (*vide infra*). In any case the making of the order is permissive not obligatory.
[8]Children and Young Persons Act 1969, s. 24 (3); Children Act 1948, s. 3 (7).

No Bias in Favour of any one Faith.—The courts will never attempt to adjudicate between the merits of different faiths, whether they be different sects of the Christian church or non-Christian religions.[9] On the other hand it may still be true to say that they favour some form of religious instruction to none at all.

Child with Fixed Beliefs.—If the child is old enough to have developed fixed religious convictions of its own, the court will never attempt to disturb them. This is illustrated by *Stourton* v. *Stourton*.[10] A boy aged ten (who appears to have been unusually precocious) had been brought up for the previous five or six years as a member of the Church of England. His father had been a Roman Catholic and the boy himself had been baptised according to the rites of that Church. Proceedings were then taken to have him made a ward of court and directions were sought with respect to his religious education. The Court of Appeal in Chancery was of the opinion that it was now too late to change his Anglican beliefs. In the words of KNIGHT BRUCE, L.J.:[11]

> " He spoke . . . in a manner convincing me that the Protestant seed sown in his mind has taken such hold, that if we are to suppose it to contain tares, they cannot be gathered up without great danger of rooting up also the wheat with them. Upon much consideration, I am of the opinion that the child's tranquillity and health, his temporal happiness and, if that can exist apart from his spiritual welfare, his spiritual welfare also, are too likely now to suffer importantly from an endeavour at effacing his Protestant impressions, not to render any such attempt unsafe and improper."

But the principle of *Stourton* v. *Stourton* will be applied only when a change of religious education is fraught with such consequences. When there is no such danger, the court will not let the child determine its own education against the express wishes of those who have a right to determine it themselves, and no encouragement to begin proselytising will be given to those who have the custody of a child of tender years. In *Hawksworth* v. *Hawksworth*[12] the Court of Appeal in Chancery issued a warning against extending *Stourton* v. *Stourton* and ordered that a girl aged eight, who was being brought up as a Protestant, should be brought up as a Roman Catholic in accordance with her father's wishes, as she had not yet formed such definite opinions that to change them would work to her prejudice.

As in the case of disputed custody, the court will interview the child in suitable cases, not in order to give effect to its wishes but to discover whether its opinions are so set as to make a change of education dangerous.[13]

Religion and Custody.—It has already been pointed out that problems of care and control and religious upbringing may go hand in hand.[14]

[9]*Re Carroll*, [1931] 1 K.B. 317, C.A., at pp. 323, 336, 347, 353. This view has been expressed in many other cases.
[10](1857), 8 De G. M. & G. 760. See also *Ward* v. *Laverty*, [1925] A.C. 101, H.L.; *Re Newton*, [1896] 1 Ch. 740, C.A.; *Re Meades* (1871), I.R. 5 Eq. 98.
[11]At pp. 767-768. The fact that it is *per se* irrelevant that the child has already been baptised or otherwise initiated in a different religion is further illustrated by *D'Alton* v. *D'Alton* (1878), 4 P.D. 87.
[12](1871), 6 Ch. App. 539. See also *Davis* v. *Davis* (1862), 10 W.R. 245.
[13]*Stourton* v. *Stourton*, (ante), at p. 772.
[14]*Ante*, pp. 277-278.

In cases of this sort, if the child is too young to have developed any fixed religious convictions, the court will generally consider the question of custody first and let that solve the question of religious education. It will also try to secure that all the children are brought up in the same religion in order to avoid creating a division of faiths in the same family.[15]

Parents' Acquiescence in a Particular Education.—Before 1926 there were many cases in which the father's acquiescence in his children's being brought up in a different religion from his own was treated as an " abdication " of his right so as to disentitle him from later insisting on their being educated in his own faith. In most of these cases the court would have refused to enforce his right on the further ground that the child had already acquired fixed ideas of its own, but this was not always so, as is shown by *Hill* v. *Hill*.[16] A Roman Catholic father had agreed that his daughters should be brought up as Protestants, had permitted his wife (who was a Protestant) to have them both baptised as Protestants and to appoint a Protestant governess for them, and had himself attempted to give them no religious instruction at all. In his will he nevertheless appointed a Roman Catholic to act with his wife as guardian and directed that the children should be brought up in the Roman Catholic faith. Although the elder girl was aged only seven at the time of the suit, the court held that the father had waived his right to determine their religious education and directed that they should be brought up as Protestants.

Today one parent's acquiescence in the other's bringing a child up in a different religion may still be important in resolving a question of religious education when the child is too young to have fixed opinions of its own and no dispute over custody arises. The observation of LINDLEY, L.J., in *Re McGrath*[17] that, where the father is indifferent and his children are in fact being brought up in a particular religion, it is not in their interest to change it, is no less true now than it was in 1893.

Agreements relating to Education and Religion.—Like agreements relating to custody, agreements as to religious and secular education are contrary to public policy and therefore void. The parent is given the right to determine his children's education for their benefit and not his own, and consequently he cannot divest himself of it.[18] This is particularly important because of the practice of some churches of insisting in the case of " mixed " marriages that the parents should give an undertaking to have all the children brought up in that particular faith. Such a promise might be evidence of the promisor's having abdicated his right to choose his children's religion[19] and consequently the court might give effect to the marital agreement on this ground.

---

[15]*Re Clarke* (1882), 21 Ch.D. 817; *Re Newton*, [1896] 1 Ch. 740, C.A.; *Ward* v. *Laverty*, [1925] A.C. 101, H.L. For a case in which this was not done, see *Re W.*, [1907] 2 Ch. 557, C.A.

[16](1862), 31 L.J.Ch. 505.

[17][1893] 1 Ch. 143, 151, C.A.

[18]*Andrews* v. *Salt* (1873), 8 Ch. App. 622, 636-637; *Re Agar-Ellis* (1878), 10 Ch. D. 49, C.A., at pp. 60, 71.

[19]*Per* MELLISH, L.J., in *Andrews* v. *Salt*, (*supra*), at p. 637.

As in the case of agreements to custody, an agreement relating to secular or religious education contained in a separation deed may be enforced provided it is for the child's benefit. In *Condon* v. *Vollum*[20] it was held that the words " custody or control " in section 2 of the Custody of Infants Act 1873 are sufficiently wide to include agreements of this kind.

Means of determining Disputes.—As a parent with custody has the power to determine a child's education, any court with jurisdiction to do so may effectively direct what education the child shall have by making a custody order. It is more usual, however, for directions for education to be made by the Family Division under its inherent jurisdiction if the child is made a ward of court. On divorce, nullity and judicial separation, the court is expressly empowered to make orders with respect to the education of a child of the family,[1] but there is no power to make such an order in proceedings under section 6 of the Matrimonial Proceedings and Property Act.

D. MISCELLANEOUS PARENTAL RIGHTS

Right to punish a Child.—A parent has the right to inflict moderate and reasonable corporal punishment for the purpose of correcting a child or punishing an offence.[2]   Whether or not the punishment is reasonable must depend upon all the facts of the case, and in particular the age and strength of the child and the nature and degree of the punishment. If it goes beyond what is reasonable, it is unlawful and would therefore render the parent criminally liable for assault.[3]

When a parent sends a child to school, he delegates to the school authorities the power to administer corporal punishment for breaches of the school regulations.[4] But only a parent or person *in loco parentis* has this right and it has been held to be unlawful for an elder brother to administer corporal punishment where both sons were living with their father and consequently the elder could not be considered as being *in loco parentis* to the younger.[5]

Right to a Child's Services.—The father, and, at any rate where the father is dead or the parents are living apart, the mother, are entitled to the domestic services of their children under the age of 18 actually living with them as part of their family. The legal enforcement

---

[20](1887), 57 L.T. 154.   For the Custody of Infants Act 1873, s. 2, see *ante*, p. 273.

[1]Matrimonial Proceedings and Property Act 1970, s. 18 (1).   Such orders may always be varied from time to time: s. 18 (6).

[2]*R.* v. *Hopley* (1860), 2 F. & F. 202; *R.* v. *Woods* (1921), 85 J.P. 272.

[3]Or, if the child died, for manslaughter or even murder: see *post*, p. 306

[4]*R.* v. *Newport (Salop) Justices, ex p. Wright*, [1929] 2 K.B. 416, where it was held that a headmaster could lawfully cane a boy for breaking a school rule by smoking in the street out of school hours.   But it is arguable that, at any rate in the case of a school administered by a local authority under the Education Act 1944, the school authorities have an *independent* power to administer corporal punishment. Consequently, as it is not delegated, the parent could not lawfully forbid the school to administer it. See Street, *Torts*, 4th Ed., 87.

[5]*R.* v. *Woods*, (*supra*).

of this right is of course impossible; its significance lies in the fact that it provides the parent with his only common law remedy against a stranger for interference with parental rights.[6]

Child's Name.—A legitimate child takes his father's surname. A child's surname can apparently be changed during infancy by both parents acting in agreement or, probably, by the father alone or, if he is dead, by the child's guardian. But if the father refuses to consent, he may obtain an injunction to restrain anyone else from changing the child's name unless this would be in the child's interest.[7]

An illegitimate child normally takes its mother's surname. The father's name may be entered on the registration of its birth only at the joint request of both parents or at the request of the mother alone provided that she produces a statutory declaration made by the man acknowledging himself to be the father.[8]

E. PROTECTION

I. PHYSICAL PROTECTION

The common law duty to afford physical protection to a child is partly a reflection of the obvious natural duty, but it is also an example of the general proposition that if anyone willingly undertakes to look after another who is incapable of looking after himself, there is a duty to perform that task properly. Consequently the duty does not necessarily last till the child comes of age: it would be absurd, for example, to say that a crippled mother is under any duty to protect a healthy son aged 17. Thus in *R. v. Shepherd*,[9] where a girl aged 18, who normally lived away in service but returned home from time to time, died there in childbirth, it was held that her mother was under no duty to send for a midwife because the girl was beyond the age of childhood and was entirely emancipated. Conversely the duty to afford physical protection may continue after the child comes of age if it is unable to look after itself owing to some physical or mental disability.[10] Moreover, since the obligation arises out of the assumption of responsibility for protection, a similar duty may be owed to a step-child or foster child.[11] Whether or not the duty exists in any given case, therefore, is a question of fact depending upon the necessity of protection and the assumption of responsibility.

---

[6] See *post*, pp. 313 *et seq.*

[7] *Re T.*, [1962] 3 All E.R. 970; [1963] Ch. 238 (injunction granted to prevent mother, who was divorced from first husband and had custody of their daughter aged 10, from changing child's name to that of her second husband). The court might refuse an injunction *e.g.*, if the name had notorious associations owing to the father's conduct. In the case of a change of name by deed poll, the application must show that the change will be for the child's benefit. His consent is required if he is over the age of 16: Enrolment of Deeds (Change of Name) Regulations 1949, r. 8, as amended by the Enrolment of Deeds (Change of Name) (Amendment) Regulations 1969.

[8] Births and Deaths Registration Act 1953, s. 10; Family Law Reform Act 1969, s. 27.

[9] (1862), Le. & Ca. 147. (The age of majority was then 21.)

[10] *R. v. Chattaway* (1922), 17 Cr. App. Rep. 7, C.C.A. (starvation of a helpless daughter aged 25).

[11] *R. v. Bubb* (1850), 4 Cox C.C. 455; *R. v. Gibbins and Proctor* (1918), 13 Cr App. Rep. 134, C.C.A.

N

Death of the Child.—In accordance with the general principles of the law relating to homicide, if a child's death is caused or accelerated by a breach of this duty to protect, the parent (or any other person owing the duty) will at the least be guilty of manslaughter.[12] This may be the result of some positive act (for example by beating a child so severely that it dies[13]) or by some omission, as where a parent abandons the child so that it dies of exposure,[14] or neglects to give it food so that it starves to death,[15] or fails to give it medical aid or call in medical advice.[16] If the parent's act or omission is intended to cause the child's death (for example by intentional starvation) then he or she will be guilty of murder, and the same is true if the conduct is so intrinsically likely to do so that a jury can infer that the death must have been contemplated.[17]

Where Death does not ensue.—A parent will be criminally liable for assault if he inflicts physical injury on a child or puts it in fear that he will do so. The Offences against the Person Act 1861 has also created the specific statutory offence of an aggravated assault upon a boy under the age of 14 or upon any female, as well as the more serious offence of unlawfully and maliciously wounding or inflicting grievous bodily harm.[18]

But where the breach of parental duty takes the form of neglect, abandonment or some other omission, the common law criminal sanctions are wholly inadequate to ensure the child's protection. In *R*. v. *Friend*[19] the judges gave it as their opinion that it is an indictable misdemeanour at common law for a person under a duty to provide for an infant of tender years to neglect to do so and thereby injure its health. Few indictments appear to have been preferred, and in any case no offence was committed unless the child's health actually suffered as a result. It was not till 1889 that the Legislature eventually intervened and passed the first Prevention of Cruelty to, and Protection of, Children Act. The principles underlying this Act were considerably extended by later statutes, and the modern law is largely contained in the Children and Young Persons Acts 1933 to 1969.[20]

By far the most important provision is to be found in section 1 of the Children and Young Persons Act of 1933, which enacts:

---

[12]*R*. v. *Middleship* (1850), 5 Cox C.C. 275.

[13]*R*. v. *Griffin* (1869), 11 Cox C.C. 402.

[14]*R*. v. *Walters* (1841), Car. & M. 164.

[15]*R*. v. *Bubb*, (*supra*); *R*. v. *Mabbett* (1851), 5 Cox C.C. 339; *R*. v. *Gibbins and Proctor*, (*supra*).

[16]Whether this amounts to manslaughter *at common law* is doubtful. The point is now academic as there is a statutory duty to provide medical treatment (see *infra*): *R*. v. *Downes* (1875), 1 Q.B.D. 25; *R*. v. *Senior*, [1899] 1 Q.B. 283.

[17]*R*. v. *Walters*, (*ante*); *R*. v. *Bubb*, (*ante*); *R*. v. *Handley* (1874), 13 Cox C.C. 79; *R*. v. *Gibbins and Proctor*, (*ante*).

[18]Ss. 20 and 43. For criminal assault generally, see Smith and Hogan, *Criminal Law*, 2nd Ed., 249 *et seq.*

[19](1802), Russ. & Ry. 20. See also *R*. v. *Hogan* (1851), 2 Den. 277.

[20]Children and Young Persons Act 1933; Children and Young Persons (Amendment) Act 1952; Children and Young Persons Act 1963; Children and Young Persons Act 1969.

" If any person who has attained the age of sixteen years and has the custody, charge, or care of any child or young person under that age, wilfully assaults, ill-treats, neglects, abandons, or exposes him,[1] or causes him to be assaulted, ill-treated, neglected, abandoned, or exposed, in a manner likely to cause him unnecessary suffering or injury to health (including injury to or loss of sight, or hearing, or limb, or organ of the body, and any mental derangement), that person shall be guilty of [an offence] . . .''[2]

By section 17 of the Act the following are liable under section 1 :[3]

The parent[4] or legal guardian of the child;
Any person legally liable to maintain him;
Any person to whose charge the child is committed by any of the above;
Any person having actual possession or control of him.

This wording is extremely wide and would cover, for example, a school teacher and anyone over the age of 16 years acting as a baby sitter.

It will be seen that the object of the Act is to make criminal any deliberate course of conduct foreseeably likely to cause physical or mental injury to the child. The Act itself specifies failure to provide adequate food, clothing, medical aid[5] or lodging or, if the parent or guardian is unable to provide any of them, failing to take steps to procure them through the Department of Health and Social Security.[6] But clearly many other types of cruelty and neglect are covered, such as beating a child, locking it up alone, leaving it in an otherwise deserted house or shutting it out in inclement weather, if such acts are likely to cause the child concerned suffering or ill-health.

Parents (and others having the care or custody of children) may also be criminally liable for causing the death of a child under the age of three by overlying it in bed whilst drunk,[7] for allowing a child under the age of 12 to be in a room containing an unguarded fire or other heating appliance with the result that the child is killed or seriously injured,[8] or for permitting children under the age of 16 (subject to certain exceptions) to take part in or train for dangerous performances.[9]

---

[1]These terms are not mutually exclusive. Hence conduct may amount to ill-treatment even though it also constitutes an assault or neglect: *R.* v. *Hayles*, [1969] 1 All E.R. 34, C.A.; [1969] 1 Q.B. 364.
[2]The phrase " in a manner likely to cause . . . injury to health " governs the whole of the preceding phrase " wilfully assaults . . . abandoned, or exposed ": *R.* v. *Hatton*, [1925] 2 K.B. 322, C.C.A. This section has virtually superseded the Offences against the Person Act 1861, s. 27, which relates to the abandonment and exposure of children under two years of age. The maximum punishment is a fine of £100 and two years' imprisonment.
[3]The Act says " presumed to be liable ", but the presumption is apparently irrebuttable: *Brooks* v. *Blount*, [1923] 1 K.B. 257.
[4]This does not include the father of an illegitimate child who has not obtained an order for custody. He will not be liable, therefore, unless he is legally liable to maintain the child or has actual possession or control of it: *Butler* v. *Gregory* (1902), 18 T.L.R. 370; *Liverpool S.P.C.C.* v. *Jones*, [1914] 3 K.B. 813.
[5]Unreasonable refusal to permit a surgical operation may amount to wilful neglect: *Oakey* v. *Jackson*, [1914] 1 K.B. 216.
[6]Children and Young Persons Act 1933, s. 1 (2) (a).
[7]*Ibid.*, s. 1 (2) (b).
[8]*Ibid.*, s. 11, as amended by the Children and Young Persons (Amendment) Act 1952, s. 8.
[9]*Ibid.*, ss. 23 and 24; Children and Young Persons Act 1963, s. 41 and Scheds. 3 and 5. The punishments vary for each offence: the maximum is five years' imprisonment or a fine of £200.

Defence of Children.—Just as a person may use reasonable force to protect himself against attack, he is entitled to use such reasonable force as is necessary to defend his children. He may even lawfully kill an assailant if he believes that his act is absolutely necessary to preserve the child's life. A child may take similar steps to defend his parent.[10]

2. MORAL PROTECTION

Although a parent might be refused the custody of his child on the ground that he was not taking adequate steps to secure its moral welfare, there was no positive method of ensuring that he did so either at common law or in equity. But just as the Legislature has intervened to enforce the parent's duty to afford physical protection to his child, it has cast on him the obligation to afford moral protection as well. An attempt has been made to prevent the acquisition of sexually depraved habits by making it an offence for a parent to cause or encourage the seduction or prostitution of his daughter under the age of 16, or to permit a child between the ages of four and 16 to be in a brothel.[11] Similarly it is an offence to allow a child under the age of 16 to beg,[12] and penalties are imposed upon parents who permit children to take part in entertainments or to go abroad for the purpose of performing for profit except under stringent conditions.[13]

3. CIVIL LIABILITY

Up to now only the criminal sanctions for a breach of the duty to protect have been discussed. These are clearly the more important because, quite apart from the unlikelihood of litigation between parent and child, cruelty and neglect are on the whole more rife amongst poorer families. It remains to consider, however, whether any civil action will lie. The liability of a parent may be relevant if he is insured (as in the case of a car driver), and it is conceivable that a child might sue his own parent if the natural ties which would normally prevent his doing so have been severed by the breaking up of the family as a whole.

It seems clear that the only possible action (apart from assault) is a common law action for damages for negligence. The child must therefore prove that he has been injured as a result of his parent's breach of duty to take care to avoid such acts or omissions as are foreseeably likely to injure him.

Independent Duty of Care.—Where a duty of care exists independently so that, had the injured person been a stranger, he could have recovered from the tortfeasor, the relationship of parent and child should not *ipso facto* bar the action. An obvious example would occur if a child, who is a passenger in his father's car, is injured as a result of

---

[10]*Anon. (circa* 1695), 3 Salk. 46; *R.* v. *Rose* (1884), 15 Cox C.C. 540.
[11]Sexual Offences Act 1956, s. 28; Children and Young Persons Act 1933, s. 3. These provisions also apply to anyone having the custody, charge or care of the child.
[12]Children and Young Persons Act 1933, s. 4.
[13]*Ibid.*, s. 25; Children and Young Persons Act 1963, ss. 37-40 and 42.

the latter's negligent driving. The only possible defence—that it is contrary to public policy to permit a child to sue its own parent— does not seem to have been raised in the past.[14]

No independent Duty.—Where there is no independent duty, so that the child has to rely solely on the common law duty to protect owed to him by his parent or other person having charge of him, the position is less clear. Suppose a parent negligently lets a young child run on to a road with the result that he is injured by a passing vehicle; can the child recover damages for his injury from the parent? It is submitted that he can and the existence of such liability was recognised by the New Zealand Court of Appeal in *McCallion* v. *Dodd*.[15] In that case parents alighted from a bus at night with their two children and started to walk along the road in the dark. The mother, who was deaf and, as the father knew, was not wearing her hearing aid, took the plaintiff, aged four, by the hand and the father carried the baby in his arms. A car driven by the defendant hit the mother and the plaintiff, killing the mother and severely injuring the boy. The plaintiff sued the defendant in negligence and the defendant claimed contribution from the father on the ground that he had also broken a duty of care owed to the plaintiff. The jury found that the defendant had been negligent and also found that the father had been negligent in permitting the boy to walk in the road on the wrong side and in the path of oncoming traffic. They assessed the father's contribution at 20% and this was upheld by the Court of Appeal. All three members of the court took the view that, even though the boy was under the immediate control of his mother, the father continued to be under a special duty because of her deafness. It should be noticed, however, that they did not agree on the extent of the duty. TURNER and McCARTHY, JJ., were both of the opinion that no duty of care was set up purely by the relationship of parent and child but that it arose from the fact that the father had taken the boy on to the road,[16] although admittedly the relationship is evidence of the fact that the parent has undertaken the duty to supervise and control the child's conduct.[17] NORTH, P., however, took the view that, although a stranger would be liable in negligence only if he had assumed or accepted the care of the child, parents " at all times *while present* are under a legal duty to exercise reasonable care to protect their children from foreseeable dangers " and that duty cannot be shed by a parent who is present.[18] In most cases it will make little difference which view is correct but the wider rule formulated by NORTH, P., is to be preferred. Indeed, it is submitted that it should be even more broadly based. If a parent leaves a child in the care of one known to be unreliable and the child comes to harm as the result of the

---

[14]*Ash* v. *Ash* (1698), Comb. 357 (daughter's suing mother for assault). Such an action will lie in Scotland (*Young* v. *Rankin*, 1934 S.C. 499), Canada, Australia and New Zealand: see the cases cited in *McCallion* v. *Dodd*, [1966] N.Z.L.R. 710, 728.

[15][1966] N.Z.L.R. 710. See Mathieson, 30 M.L.R. 96.

[16]At pp. 725 and 728.

[17]*Per* McCARTHY, J., at p. 729.

[18]At p. 721. (Italics supplied.)

latter's irresponsibility, analogy with criminal liability at common law[19] suggests that the parent should be civilly liable as well.

All the members of the court in *McCallion* v. *Dodd* were agreed that the doctrine of identification could not apply and that there was no question of the plaintiff's damages being reduced as the result of the father's negligence.   Here they followed *Oliver* v. *Birmingham and Midland Omnibus Co., Ltd.*[20] The plaintiff, aged four, was crossing a road with his grandfather, who was holding his hand, when an omnibus bore down on them.   The grandfather let go of the plaintiff's hand and jumped to safety; the plaintiff was struck by the omnibus owing to the driver's negligence and was injured.   It was held that his action for damages against the omnibus company was not affected by his grandfather's contributory negligence.

F. PARENTS' LIABILITY FOR CHILDREN'S ACTS

Contracts.—A parent will never be liable as such for any contract made by his child.[1] But he may of course be liable on the ordinary principles of agency if he has authorised the child to make the contract or, in the case of unauthorised contracts, by estoppel or ratification.[2]

Torts.—As in the case of contracts, a parent will not be liable as such for his child's torts.   But he may be liable on some other ground, for example if he has authorised the commission of the tort or if the child is for this purpose his servant.   If the child commits a tort whilst running an errand for his parent, the latter may be liable as the master *quoad hoc*.[3]

A parent may also be personally liable if he himself has been negligent in affording the child an opportunity of injuring another.   This is a particular application of the tort of negligence, and the test is therefore: did the parent by his act or omission cause or permit his child to do an act which was foreseeably likely to harm the person injured and against which a reasonably prudent parent would have guarded?   If so, he will be liable.   This is illustrated by *Newton* v. *Edgerley*.[4] The defendant, a farmer, permitted his twelve year old son to have possession of a shotgun.   He instructed the boy in the use of it but forbade him to take it off the farm or to use it when other children were near and therefore did not instruct him how to handle it when others were present.   Ultimately the boy disobeyed his father and took the gun to a wood with other boys (including the plaintiff).   Whilst they were walking in single file the gun, which was loaded and cocked, went off as the result of interference by another boy and the plaintiff was injured.   It was held that the defendant was personally liable in negligence for he ought to have foreseen that his son would succumb

---

[19]*Ante*, p. 306.
[20][1933] 1 K.B. 35.
[1]*Mortimore* v. *Wright* (1840), 6 M. & W. 482.
[2]See generally works on the law of contract and on agency.
[3]For liability for servants' torts generally, see works on the law of tort.
[4][1959] 3 All E.R. 337.   See also *Bebee* v. *Sales* (1916), 32 T.L.R. 413.

to temptation and consequently should either have forbidden him to use the gun at all or have instructed him how to handle it in the presence of others.

But the parent will not be liable if he could not reasonably have foreseen that the child's act would injure the plaintiff or if he took all precautions that a reasonably prudent parent would have taken. In *Donaldson* v. *McNiven*[5] the defendant had let his son aged 13 buy an airgun. He forbade him to fire it outside the house and the boy gave his word that he would not do so. He always fired it in a cellar under the house until one day he took it outside, fired it and in so doing put out the plaintiff's eye. It was held that the father was not liable, for he had taken all reasonable precautions to ensure that the gun was fired in a safe place and no damage would have resulted but for the son's disobedience, unfaithfulness and folly which the defendant could not reasonably have foreseen.

Although these cases both deal with a parent's liability for permitting his child to have a dangerous toy or weapon, there is no reason why it should be restricted to this field. Thus if a parent (or other adult) in charge of a young child on a busy road negligently lets it run out into the traffic with the result that the driver of a car, in swerving to avoid the child, injures himself or another, the parent must on principle be liable for the damage.[6]

Crimes.—At common law a parent was not liable for his child's crimes unless he himself was guilty of aiding and abetting. But the fact that a child's criminal propensities may be due to bad home influences or a lack of parental supervision has now been recognised by statute. If a court imposes a fine, damages or costs or orders compensation for the commission of an offence by a child under the age of 17, it may, and if the child is under the age of 14 it must, order that these be paid by the child's parent or guardian unless the latter cannot be found or the court is satisfied that he has not conduced to the commission of the offence by neglecting to exercise due care or control of the child.[7]

G. LIABILITY FOR INTERFERENCE WITH PARENTS' AND CHILDREN'S RIGHTS

I. CRIMINAL LIABILITY

Kidnapping, that is, stealing a child under the age of 21 against its parents' will, is a common law misdemeanour.[8] A number of statutory

---

[5][1952] 2 All E.R. 691, C.A. See also *Gorely* v. *Codd*, [1966] 3 All E.R. 891.
[6]*Cf. Carmarthenshire County Council* v. *Lewis*, [1955] 1 All E R. 565, H.L.; [1955] A.C. 549, where a school authority was liable in similar circumstances for negligently letting a child run out of the school premises on to a road with the result that a lorry driver was killed. See further Waller, *Visiting the Sins of the Children*, 4 Melbourne U.L.R. 17.
[7]Children and Young Persons Act 1933, s. 55; Criminal Justice Act 1961, s. 8 (4); Children and Young Persons Act 1969, s. 3 (6) and Scheds. 5 and 6; Administration of Justice Act 1970, Sched. 11. For the court's power to require a parent to enter into recognisances to exercise care and control of the child, see *ante*, p. 293.
[8]1 East, *Pleas of the Crown*, 429-430.

offences have also been created and prosecutions today are invariably brought under one of these enactments. They are now principally contained in section 56 of the Offences against the Person Act 1861 and sections 19 to 21 of the Sexual Offences Act 1956 (which repealed and consolidated earlier legislation on the subject).[9] Three distinct cases must be considered.

Children under the age of 14 years.—It is an offence by force or fraud to lead, take away, decoy, entice away, or detain any child under the age of 14 with intent to deprive its parent, guardian, or other person having lawful care or charge of it, of its possession, or to harbour a child knowing it to have been obtained in this way.[10] The offence may be committed in respect of a child of either sex, and there need be no intention to deprive the parent or other person of custody permanently.[11] Either force or fraud[12] must be used, and therefore it will not be an offence to *persuade* a boy under the age of 14 to leave his parents. The statute specifically provides that neither the mother nor any person claiming a right to possession of the child can be prosecuted for this offence.

Girls under the age of 16 years.—It is an offence for a person acting without lawful authority or excuse to take an unmarried girl under the age of 16 out of the possession of her parent or other person having the lawful care or charge of her against his will.[13] Unlike the offence just considered, this can be committed only in respect of a girl and neither force nor fraud is necessary:[14] mere persuasion to leave home is sufficient. If she leaves without any persuasion or force on the part of the accused, no offence is committed, even though he subsequently acquiesces in her suggestion that they should stay together and takes no steps to send her home; but if he takes the active step of suggesting that she should leave her parents, he will be liable.[15] Since the object of the section is to protect the parents' rights, the consent of the girl is irrelevant.[16]

---

[9]See also the Children Act 1948, s. 3 (8) (as amended by the Children and Young Persons Act 1963, Sched. 3) and the Children and Young Persons Act 1969, s. 32 (3) which make it an offence knowingly to compel, persuade, incite or assist a child in the care of a local authority to become or continue to be absent.

[10]Offences against the Person Act 1861, s. 56. (Maximum punishment: 7 years imprisonment.)

[11]*R. v: Powell* (1914), 24 Cox C.C. 229.

[12]The fraud may be perpetrated on the child, parent or, apparently, anyone else: *R. v. Bellis* (1893), 17 Cox C.C. 660.

[13]Sexual Offences Act 1956, s. 20. (Maximum punishment: 2 years' imprisonment.) The importance of this provision has been considerably lessened since the Criminal Law Amendment Act 1885 made it an offence to have unlawful sexual intercourse with a girl under the age of 16.

[14]But taking a girl by either of these means will of course amount to the commission of the offence: *R. v. Hopkins* (1842), Car. & M. 254, where the accused fraudulently induced the parent to let him take the girl away.

[15]*R. v. Jarvis* (1903), 20 Cox C.C. 249; *R. v. Olifier* (1866), 10 Cox C.C. 402. But it is to be inferred from the earlier cases that if the accused and the girl leave her house together, he will be liable whoever made the suggestion: *R. v. Robins* (1844), 1 Car. & Kir. 456; *R. v. Biswell* (1847), 2 Cox C.C. 279.

[16]*R. v. Robins, (supra)*; *R. v. Manktelow* (1853), 6 Cox C.C. 143. The parent's having previously permitted the girl to lead an immoral life may be evidence that her leaving was not against his will: *R. v. Primelt* (1858), 1 F. & F. 50; *R. v Frazer and Norman* (1861), 8 Cox C.C. 446.

As in the case of children under the age of 14, a person may be guilty even though he did not intend to deprive the parent of custody permanently. The offence is committed once the accused puts the girl in a situation which is inconsistent with her parents' custody of her. In *R.* v. *Timmins*[17] it was held that there was a sufficient taking where the accused took a girl to London for three days for the purpose of sleeping with her and at the end of that time told her to return to her father. On the other hand, a mere temporary absence will not suffice if it is not inconsistent with the relationship of parent and daughter.

The accused will have a good defence if he neither knew nor ought to have known that the girl was in anyone's custody, for then there will be no *mens rea* at all.[18] But if he knows that he is interfering with parental rights, it will be no defence that he thought that the girl was over the age of 16.[19] Similarly it will be a good defence that the accused honestly believed that he had a right to the girl's custody;[20] but no other motives, for example religious or philanthropic, will excuse his conduct.[1]

Girls under the age of 18 years and Defective Girls.—It is an offence to abduct any unmarried girl under the age of 18 years or a girl or woman of any age who is a defective with the intention in either case that she should have unlawful sexual intercourse.[2] The offence is the same as in the case of a girl under the age of 16 except that the prosecution must also prove the accused's intent.[3] It is also a defence that the accused had reasonable cause to believe that the girl was over the age of 18 or that he had no reason to suspect her of being a defective as the case may be.

2. DAMAGES FOR LOSS OF SERVICES

At common law one could obtain damages for the abduction of one's heir. But the action did not extend to the abduction of other children,[4] and although it has never been formally abolished, it is now completely obsolete.[5] This meant that there was no civil remedy for interference with parental rights—a gap which the common law judges filled at the latest in 1653 by adapting the existing action which a master had for the loss of his servant's services and permitting a

---

[17](1860), 8 Cox C.C. 401.
[18]*R.* v. *Hibbert* (1869), L.R. 1 C.C.R. 184. But the number of cases today where the accused would not have constructive knowledge must be negligible.
[19]*R.* v. *Prince* (1875), L.R. 2 C.C.R. 154.
[20]*R.* v. *Tinkler* (1859), 1 F. & F. 513.
[1]*R.* v. *Booth* (1872), 12 Cox C.C. 231.
[2]Sexual Offences Act 1956, ss. 19 and 21. (The maximum punishment in either case is 2 years' imprisonment.) " Unlawful " sexual intercourse means intercourse outside the marriage bond: *R.* v. *Chapman*, [1958] 3 All E.R. 143, C.C.A.; [1959] 1 Q.B. 100. Hence no offence will be committed if the accused takes the girl away from her parents with the honest and *bona fide* intention of marrying her.
[3]*R.* v. *Henkers* (1886), 16 Cox C.C. 257.
[4]*Barham* v. *Dennis* (1600), Cro. Eliz. 770
[5]HOLROYD, J., thought it was still extant in 1825: *Hall* v. *Hollander* (1825), 4 B. & C. 660, 662, but there seems to have been no attempt to bring such an action for over 300 years.

parent to sue alleging as special damage the loss of his child's services.[6] It thus became an actionable tort to do any act which wrongfully deprives a parent of his child's services. This is an independent cause of action vested in the parent. If the loss was due to a tort committed against the child, he too would have a cause of action, but in the commoner examples of loss of services—enticement (where the child went voluntarily with the defendant) or seduction (where the loss was due to a daughter's pregnancy and childbirth as a consequence of sexual intercourse with the defendant)—the child clearly could not sue at all.

Actions were rare and it was coming to be considered an anomaly that the child's voluntary act could give rise to an action by the parent. Consequently section 5 of the Law Reform (Miscellaneous Provisions) Act 1970 now provides that no action shall lie for loss of services due to rape, seduction, enticement or harbouring.[7] This limits the action to loss of services resulting from the commission of a tort against the child, and even this will not lie if the tort consisted of battery involving rape. One sees the connection between rape and seduction but it is anomalous that a parent may sue a man who negligently knocks his daughter down but not one who deliberately rapes her.[8]

Loss of Services.—Although the real cause of action is interference with parental rights, its theoretical basis is still loss of services, and accordingly the plaintiff must show that the child performed some service for him.[9] This may of course be a contractual service (although it rarely will be); in almost every case the parent will rely on domestic services rendered at home which may be real but may be purely nominal such as making tea.[10] If the child is over the age of 18, the burden is on the plaintiff to prove that some sort of service was in fact performed, but if the child is still a minor, the mere fact that he is living in the parent's family is sufficient to raise a presumption of service which need not therefore be specifically proved.[11]

But the necessity of showing loss of services means that there will be two cases where the parent cannot sue at all. First, no action will lie if the child is too young to render any services, as happened in *Hall* v. *Hollander*,[12] where it was held that no action for loss of services could be brought by the father of a boy aged two whom the defendant had injured by running him down with his carriage. Secondly, no loss of service can be proved if the child owes a contractual service to another

---

[6]*Norton* v. *Jason* (1653), Sty. 398. See Holdsworth, *History of English Law*, viii, 427–429; Pollock, *Torts*, 15th Ed., 167 *et seq.*; Winfield, *Tort*, 8th Ed., 528.

[7]Following the recommendations of the Law Commission (Working Paper No. 19).

[8]But he can presumably sue if he can prove that the loss of services was due to another tort committed at the same time as the rape, *e.g.* a blow knocking the girl unconscious beforehand.

[9]See the cases cited in the following footnotes, and in particular *Hall* v. *Hollander*, (*ante*); *Grinnell* v. *Wells* (1844), 7 Man. & G. 1033; *Evans* v. *Walton* (1867), L.R. 2 C.P. 615.

[10]*Per* ABBOTT, C.J., in *Carr* v. *Clarke* (1818), 2 Chit. 260, 261.

[11]*Peters* v. *Jones*, [1914] 2 K.B. 781, 784.

[12](1825), 4 B. & C. 660.

and as a result is no longer living with the parent.[13] The law on the latter point is not entirely clear but is now of little practical importance because the difficulties almost always arose when a daughter was living with another family as a domestic servant: a situation which now rarely arises.

Illogicality was caused by the courts' having caught at straws to give the parent a remedy where perhaps in strict legal theory he should have none. A further example of the same kind is seen in the development of the concept of constructive service. In *Terry* v. *Hutchinson*[14] the plaintiff's daughter had been employed by a milliner in Deal who dismissed her. On her way home to Canterbury she was seduced by the defendant in a railway carriage. The Court of Queen's Bench held that the father could recover damages for the seduction for, since the girl was a minor, his right to her services revived as soon as she left the milliner's service with the intention of returning home, and there was an immediate constructive service even though he had not yet exercised his right. This decision might still be relevant if the child in question were living away from home in lodgings or a flat of its own. There will clearly be no *de facto* service and so no action will lie if the child is over the age of 18. But if the child is still a minor, it could be argued by analogy with *Terry* v. *Hutchinson* that there is a constructive service because the child is serving no other master at the time, and in view of the court's evident desire to give the parent a remedy whenever possible the argument might well succeed.

It was held as recently as 1937 that, if the parents are living together, a legitimate child's services are owed exclusively to the father as head of the family and consequently the mother has no cause of action for loss of them.[15] But it is doubtful whether this is still good law in view of the courts' changing attitude in other fields to the wife's position in the family. The English cases are both at first instance and the Court of Appeal may now hold that they are no longer to be regarded as binding. An illegitimate child's services will normally be owed to the mother but apparently these too are owed to the father if he is living with the mother.[16]

As in the case of a husband's action for the loss of his wife's consortium or services,[17] no damages may be claimed for the loss of services caused by the child's death as a result of the defendant's tortious act.[18] But again this rule will not apply where the parent sues for breach of contract. Hence we once more have the anomalous

---

[13]For the problems arising when the child is at home during holidays or free time, see *Hedges* v. *Tagg* (1872), L.R. 7 Exch. 283; *Dent* v. *Maguire*, [1917] 2 I.R. 59. A parent can sue with respect to a child *living at home* even though he is contractually employed by another during working hours: *Ogden* v. *Lancashire* (1866), 15 W.R. 158. Nor does a temporary absence from home prevent the action from lying: *Griffiths* v. *Teetgen* (1854), 15 C.B. 344.

[14](1868), L.R. 3 Q.B. 599.

[15]*Beetham* v. *James*, [1937] 1 All E.R. 580; [1937] 1 K.B. 527; following *Hamilton* v. *Long*, [1903] 2 I.R. 407, affirmed, [1905] 2 I.R. 552, and *Peters* v. *Jones*, [1914] 2 K.B. 781.

[16]*Beetham* v. *James*, (*supra*), at pp. 584 and 532-533, respectively.

[17]See *ante*, p. 106.

[18]*Clark* v. *London General Omnibus Co., Ltd.*, [1906] 2 K.B. 648, C.A.; following *Osborn* v. *Gillett* (1873), L.R. 8 Exch. 88.

rule that if, say, the child is killed whilst riding on an omnibus owing
to the driver's negligence, the father could recover for loss of services
if he had bought the tickets for them both, but he could not do so if
the child were travelling alone and contracted on its own behalf. Where
the defendant's tort results in death, the parent's remedy (if he has
one at all) will exist under the Fatal Accidents Acts.[19]

Acts depriving a Parent of Services.—The act depriving the
parent of the child's services must now consist of a tort committed
against the child (other than a battery involving rape).[20]

It has never been decided how far the defendant may raise against
the parent any defence that he could raise in an action brought against
him by the child. Since the parent's cause of action is independent, it
would seem on principle that the defences ought to be independent too.
Hospitals certainly take this view; although a child over the age of 16
now has a statutory power to consent to any medical, surgical or dental
treatment without his parent's concurrence,[1] medical authorities still
insist on obtaining the parent's consent to an operation on a child
under that age.[2] On the other hand it is absurd to suppose that a
participant in a boxing match could be liable to his opponent's parent
for an injury caused to his child on the ground that, unknown to the
first person, the parent had forbidden the other to take part in it, if a
claim brought by the child himself would be defeated by the application
of the maxim *Volenti non fit injuria*. A child's contributory negligence
should not affect the parent's claim,[3] but if the court were to hold that
this was the sole cause of the damage so that the child could recover
nothing, it would seem that the parent's claim should be dismissed as
well on the ground that the contributory negligence has made the
damage too remote.

This branch of the law is sadly in need of reform. The complications
and anomalies arise from the fact that English law has never recognised
an action for loss of parental rights as such but has had to adapt
another action which has filled the gap imperfectly. Whilst it is founded
upon a fiction, the trouble is that " for that fiction there must be some
foundation, however slender, in fact ".[4] Consequently the Law Reform
Committee has recommended that the actions for loss of services
should be abolished and that instead a father or mother should be able
to recover expenses reasonably incurred as the result of a tortious
injury inflicted on a dependent child. This would include medical and
nursing expenses, the cost of visiting the child in hospital or elsewhere,

---

[19]See *ante*, pp. 108-118.
[20]See *ante*, p. 314.
[1]Family Law Reform Act 1969, s. 8. For some problems arising under this section,
see Foulkes, *Consent to Medical Treatment*, 120 New L.J. 194.
[2]But they do not usually obtain the infant's consent. Yet would the parent's
consent be a good defence to an action brought by an infant old enough to exercise a
discretion in the matter who had expressed his unwillingness to undergo the operation?
[3]*Cf.* a husband's claim for loss of his wife's consortium and services, *ante*, p. 104.
[4]*Per* KELLY, C.B., in *Hedges* v. *Tagg* (1872), L.R. 7 Exch. 283, 285. For early
calls for reform, see notes to the reports of *Speight* v. *Oliviera* (1819), 2 Stark. 493, 496,
and *Grinnell* v. *Wells* (1844), 7 Man. & G. 1033, 1044.

and any consequential loss of earnings. The age of the child and the existence of any services should be immaterial.[5]

3. THE FATAL ACCIDENTS ACTS

We have already seen that parents and children come within the category of dependants for the purposes of the Fatal Accidents Acts, so that either may sue any person who has unlawfully caused the death of the other for compensation for pecuniary loss resulting from the death.[6]

H. NATIONALITY

As citizenship of the United Kingdom and Colonies is acquired almost wholly by operation of law, it cannot strictly be considered a question of parental rights and duties. But since in certain circumstances a person may be a citizen of the United Kingdom and Colonies solely by virtue of his father's possessing such citizenship, the subject will be dealt with here for the sake of completeness.

At common law British nationality was acquired at birth by those born within British territory and only in very limited circumstances (for example in the case of children of a British ambassador) by those born outside it.[7] Legislation during the eighteenth century conferred the status of a British subject on anyone born abroad whose father or paternal grandfather was a natural-born British subject.[8] The Naturalization Act of 1870 extended British nationality to the children of naturalized subjects provided that they resided in this country during their minority,[9] and the same Act also provided that, if his parents lost British nationality by naturalization in a foreign country, a minor residing in that country would also lose his British nationality.[10] These rules were considerably modified by the British Nationality and Status of Aliens Acts 1914 to 1943 and again underwent complete revision in the British Nationality Act of 1948 which created the new status of citizen of the United Kingdom and Colonies.

This Act retains the common law rule by enacting that almost all children born within the United Kingdom and Colonies shall be citizens thereof.[11] In addition, anyone born outside the United Kingdom and

---

[5]Eleventh Report of the Law Reform Committee (Loss of Services, etc.), 1963, Cmnd. 2017, paras. 20-23. Presumably any claim by the parent would be reduced in proportion to the child's contributory negligence: see *ante*, p. 108, n. ²

[6]See *ante*, pp. 108 *et seq.*

[7]Jones, *British Nationality*, (1947 Ed.), 34 *et seq.*

[8]Foreign Protestants (Naturalization) Act 1708; British Nationality Acts 1730 and 1772. See Jones, *op. cit.*, 69-72. Another remarkable example of nationality by descent is to be found in the provisions of 4 Anne, c. 16, 1705 (now repealed), under which all the issue of Princess Sophia, the mother of King George I, other than Roman Catholics, who were born before 1949, are British subjects: *A.-G.* v. *Prince Ernest Augustus of Hanover*, [1957] 1 All E.R. 49, H.L.; [1957] A.C. 436.

[9]S. 10 (5). See Jones, *op. cit.*, 101-103.

[10]S. 10 (3).

[11]For the exceptions, see the British Nationality Act 1948, s. 4; Parry, *British Nationality*, 121-128; Jones, *British Nationality Law*, Revised Ed., 154-156.

Colonies will be a citizen thereof by descent, if at the time of his birth[12] his father is a citizen of the United Kingdom and Colonies otherwise than by descent or, alternatively, if his father is a citizen by descent and one of the following conditions is also satisfied:

(a) the child or his father was born in a place where the Crown lawfully had jurisdiction over British subjects; or

(b) the birth is registered within a year at a United Kingdom consulate; or

(c) the father at the time of the birth is in Crown service under the United Kingdom government; or

(d) the child is born in a Commonwealth country but does not become a citizen of that country at birth.[13]

It will thus be seen that, unless one of these conditions is satisfied, citizenship will be conferred only on the first generation born abroad and not on two generations as it was under the earlier Acts.

Naturalization of a parent no longer *ipso facto* confers citizenship on his minor children if they reside in this country (as happened under the Act of 1870) or if their names are included in his certificate of naturalization (as was the position under the Act of 1914). But the Home Secretary has a discretionary power on their parents' application to register any such children as citizens of the United Kingdom and Colonies.[14]

---

[12]Or, in the case of a posthumous child, at the time of the father's death: British Nationality Act 1948, s. 24.

[13]*Ibid.*, s. 5. See Parry, *op. cit.*, 129-140; Jones, *op. cit.*, Revised Ed., 156-160. For the somewhat wider application of these provisions to a person who would otherwise be stateless, see the British Nationality (No. 2) Act 1964, ss. 1-3, and the British Nationality Act 1965, s. 4.

[14]Under the provisions of s. 7 (1). If a person has dual nationality, he may renounce citizenship of the United Kingdom and Colonies by declaration after he comes of age: s. 19. A minor who lost British nationality by reason of his parents' naturalization in a foreign country before 1949 may obtain citizenship of the United Kingdom and Colonies by making a declaration to that effect within twelve months of coming of age (or such longer period of time as the Home Secretary shall allow): s. 16. See also the British Nationality Act 1964, s. 1 (resumption of citizenship after renunciation).

CHAPTER 12

Guardianship

A. INTRODUCTORY

Strictly speaking, the term " guardian " is sufficiently wide to include a parent, for parents are regarded at common law as the natural guardians of their children and now by statute after the death of one parent the survivor is the guardian of their minor children either alone or jointly with any testamentary guardian appointed by the other.[1] But in common parlance the concepts of parent and guardian are quite distinct, for the rights and duties of the former arise automatically and naturally on the birth of the child, whilst the latter voluntarily places himself *in loco parentis* to his ward and his rights and duties flow immediately from this act. It is in this latter sense—that of the person who places himself *in loco parentis* to his ward, as distinct from the natural parent—that the word will be used in this chapter.

Foster Parents.—A guardian must be also distinguished from a foster parent, who has *de facto* control and custody of a child without being its legal guardian. If a parent is dead or is unfit to exercise his parental rights and duties, it is clearly essential that they should be exercisable by somebody else standing *in loco parentis* to a child; but by English law they will not vest in a guardian unless he has been appointed in one of a number of recognised ways, for example by a court order or by the will of a deceased parent. In a large number of cases, of course, this never happens; and if both parents die, a child's grandparents or other near relations will assume *de facto* control of the child without taking steps to have themselves appointed legal guardians at all. The position of such people, like all those who assume legal rights and powers without a good title, is precarious. Both at common law and under the Children and Young Persons Act 1933 there will be a duty to afford protection.[2] Although there is no common law duty to maintain the child, the person with control will be criminally liable under the Children and Young Persons Act 1933 if he wilfully fails to provide it with adequate food, clothing, medical aid or lodging.[3] Similarly, the Education Act 1944 places him under a duty to see that the child receives full-time education.[4] So long as no one else claims the care and control of the

---

[1]Guardianship of Minors Act 1971, s. 3. *Ante*, p. 272
[2]*Ante*, pp. 305 *et seq.*
[3]Ss. 1 (2) (a) and 17. See *ante*, pp. 306-307.
[4]Ss. 36 and 114. See *ante*, p. 300.

child, the person who actually has it will be clearly entitled to retain it; if this is disputed, the court must be guided by the child's welfare in determining in whose favour to make an order.[5] It seems that a person standing *in loco parentis* to a child may sue for damages for loss of services provided that actual services were being rendered to him by the child;[6] but whether he can recover possession itself by habeas corpus proceedings is much more doubtful. The point appears never to have been decided, and it would clearly be safer for him to take steps to have himself appointed guardian by the court and then to pursue the remedies open to a guardian to recover the custody of his ward.[7]

Anyone (other than a relative[8] or guardian) who undertakes the care and maintenance of a child (whether for reward or not) is now subject to the provisions of Part I of the Children Act 1958,[9] the purpose of which is to ensure that the child is visited periodically by officers of the Social Services Department of the local county, county borough or London borough council who must satisfy themselves of his well-being and give any necessary advice to the foster parent.[10] These provisions apply only to children below the upper limit of compulsory school age,[11] but if they apply to a child when he reaches that age they will continue to apply until he attains the age of 18 provided that he continues to reside with the same foster parent.[12] The Act does not apply if he resides in the same premises as a parent, guardian or adult relative, or, broadly speaking, whilst he is in the care of a local authority, or in a school in which he is receiving full-time education,[13] hospital, nursing home or other institution maintained by a local or public authority, or whilst he is in the care of anyone by virtue of a supervision order, for in all these cases proper supervision will be effected by the body or authorities concerned.[14] Nor is it intended to control purely temporary arrangements frequently entered into during parents' absence, and consequently the Act does not apply if the person in question does not intend to undertake the child's care and maintenance for more than 27 days (six days if he is a " regular foster parent ") and does not in fact do so.[15] As these provisions are complementary to those relating to protected children under the Adoption Act, they do not apply to such children either.[16]

---

[5]Guardianship of Minors Act 1971, s. 1.

[6]*Irwin* v. *Dearman* (1809), 11 East 23; *Peters* v. *Jones*, [1914] 2 K.B. 781.

[7]But it is submitted that he ought to be able to recover possession by habeas corpus even though he does not first have himself appointed guardian. No objection on this point was raised in *Re Kerr* (1889), 24 L.R. Ir. 59.

[8]" Relative " has the same meaning as it has in the Adoption Act 1958; see *ante*, p. 249, n. [15].

[9]These provisions have been extensively amended by the Children and Young Persons Act 1969 and will be referred to " (as amended) " Ss. 1-6 and 14 (as amended) are set out in Sched. 7 of the Act of 1969.

[10]S. 1 (as amended); Local Authority Social Services Act 1970, ss. 1 and 2 and Sched. 1. *Cf.* the provisions of the Nurseries and Child-Minders Regulation Act 1948, which places local authorities under a duty to control certain nurseries and arrangements for looking after children under five years of age for reward.

[11]See *ante*, p. 300.

[12]Ss. 2 (1) and 13 (as amended).

[13]Except for certain schools during school holidays: s. 12 (as amended).

[14]For details, see s. 2 (as amended).

[15]S. 2 (3A) (as amended), *q.v.* for the definition of regular foster parent.

[16]S. 2 (4A) (as amended). For protected children, see *ante*, p. 254.

Anyone proposing to maintain a foster child must give notice to the local authority.[17] The authority may empower its officers to inspect premises in which foster children are being kept and may also impose conditions *inter alia* upon the number, age and sex of the children that may reside there and the accommodation, equipment and medical arrangements to be provided for them. It may completely forbid a person to keep foster children (or a particular child) or to use premises for that purpose.[18] An appeal from the authority's ruling may be made to a juvenile court, which may also order the removal of any foster children if the foster parent is unfit to have the care of them or has failed to comply with requirements laid down by the authority.[19] Certain persons, whose previous history or connections indicate that they are not fit to have the care of foster children, are forbidden to maintain foster children unless they first obtain the local authority's permission.[20]

Guardians.—Once a guardian is lawfully appointed, most of the rights and duties which a parent has with respect to his legitimate children vest in him. The close similarity between the position of a parent and a guardian naturally gave the Crown as *parens patriae* the power to intervene, if necessary, to protect the ward, and after the abolition of the Court of Wards in 1660 the Court of Chancery assumed a general supervisory jurisdiction over guardians.[1] From 1875 this jurisdiction was exercised by the Chancery Division of the High Court, from which it has now been transferred to the Family Division. In addition, jurisdiction was given to county courts in guardianship matters by the Guardianship of Infants Act of 1886, and to magistrates' courts by the Guardianship of Infants Act of 1925. As in the case of disputes between parents, however, magistrates' courts have no power to entertain any application (other than the variation or discharge of an existing order) relating to a child who has attained the age of 16 unless he is physically or mentally incapable of self-support, or to entertain any application involving the administration or application of any property belonging to or held in trust for a minor or the income thereof.[2]

In view of the intervention of equity, it is hardly surprising to see a marked similarity between the office of guardian and that of trustee. As regards the ward's property, the guardian is a trustee in every respect, with precisely the same powers and duties as the trustee has over any other trust property; and as a trustee he is bound to account to his beneficiary, the ward, when his guardianship comes to an end. But whereas a trustee has no personal rights and duties with respect to his beneficiary, these are today the guardian's chief responsibility. But the similarity between the two offices can be seen here too. As in

---

[17]S. 3 (as amended).
[18]S. 4 (as amended). The Home Secretary also has power to authorise an inspection: Children and Young Persons Act 1969, ss. 58 and 59.
[19]Ss. 5 and 7. A further appeal lies to Quarter Sessions: s. 11.
[20]For details, see s. 6 (as amended). Failure to comply with the requirements of the Act renders the foster parent liable to six months' imprisonment and a fine of £100: s. 14.
[1]Holdsworth, *History of English Law*, v, 315; vi, 648-650.
[2]Guardianship of Minors Act 1971, s. 15 (2).

the case of a trustee, no one may be appointed a guardian against his will, but once he has accepted the office he cannot resign it by his unilateral act.   The nature of the office was thus described by ROMILLY, M.R.:[3]

> " The relation of guardian and ward is strictly that of trustee and *cestui que trust*. I look on it as a peculiar relation of trusteeship. . . . A guardian is not only trustee of the property, as in an ordinary case of trustee, but he is also the guardian of the person of the infant, with many duties to perform such as to see to his education and maintenance. . . . Of all the property which he gets into his possession in the character of guardian, he is trustee for the benefit of the infant ward."

These two different duties of guardians—the protection of the person and the protection of the property of the ward—may in fact be vested in two entirely different sets of people: guardians of the person, with no right to control the ward's property, and guardians of the estate, with no right to control the ward's person.[4]   The property legislation of 1925 has virtually rendered the latter type of guardianship obsolete, for now in almost every case property, in which an infant has an interest, will be vested in trustees; and although the guardians may be appointed the trustees for this purpose, it will be in the latter capacity and not in the former that they will control the property.

B. APPOINTMENT OF GUARDIANS

At common law the feudal overlord automatically became the guardian of an infant tenant by knight service or grand serjeanty, and since the guardian was entitled to the profits of the ward's estate, this right was extremely valuable to the Crown and the mesne lords. Wardship was never an incident of tenure by petit serjeanty or socage, and consequently, after the abolition of knight service and the incidents of tenure by grand serjeanty in 1660, guardianship assumed its modern characteristic of an office of trust and responsibility rather than that of a valuable piece of property.[5]   Accordingly, the Tenures Abolition Act for the first time gave a parent the right to appoint a testamentary guardian for his infant children—a right which has since been extended by the Guardianship of Infants Acts of 1886 and 1925.

Once equity had established its right to supervise guardians and wards, it followed as a corollary that the Court of Chancery had the power to appoint guardians.   In addition, there still exist some customary rights to guardianship, *e.g.*, that of the City of London over orphans of deceased freemen;[6] and an infant apparently has a power to appoint a guardian for himself, although the powers of such a guardian never seem to have been defined.[7]   In practice, guardians are

---

[3] *Mathew* v. *Brise* (1851), 14 Beav. 341, 345.
[4] *Rimington* v. *Hartley* (1880), 14 Ch. D. 630, 632.
[5] See Holdsworth, *History of English Law*, iii, 512-3; Simpson, *Introduction to the History of the Land Law*, 17-19.
[6] Comyns' *Digest*, Gardian (G). See also Simpson, *Infants*, 4th Ed., p. 162.
[7] *Re Brown's Will* (1881), 18 Ch.D. 61, C.A., at pp. 65, 67, 72.

always appointed either by a parent or by the court, and it is with these two modes of appointment that we shall now deal in greater detail.[8]

Testamentary Guardians.—Section 8 of the Tenures Abolition Act 1660 empowered a father by deed or will to appoint a guardian or guardians of his legitimate children, who were under the age of 21 and unmarried on the father's death, until they respectively reached their majority or for any less time. As the mother had no right as such to the custody of her children at common law, it is hardly surprising that no power of appointing testamentary guardians was given to her. Section 3 of the Guardianship of Infants Act of 1886 gave her a limited power to do so, but her nominees could only act after the death of both parents (when they would act jointly with any guardians appointed by the father) or, if the father survived her, jointly with him if the court considered that he was unfit to be the sole guardian. It was not until 1925 that the mother was given equal rights with the father in this respect. Now both the father and the mother may by deed or will appoint one or more guardians for their legitimate children.[9]

The Tenures Abolition Act gave the father no power to appoint a testamentary guardian for his illegitimate children,[10] but in *Re A.*[11] BENNETT, J., held that the Guardianship of Infants Act of 1925 had given such a power to the mother. The Schedule to that Act[12] provided that after the death of the mother of an illegitimate minor, the guardian appointed by her must consent to the child's marriage and thus impliedly gave her the power to appoint a testamentary guardian. A more limited power was given to the father by the Legitimacy Act 1959; now he may appoint a testamentary guardian provided that a custody order made under the Guardianship of Minors Act in his favour is in force at the time of his death.[13]

The reduction in the age of majority means that no guardian may now be appointed for any child (legitimate or illegitimate) over the age of 18.[14]

Although a deed is usually irrevocable, a deed appointing a guardian is a " testamentary instrument in the form of a deed ",[15] and consequently an appointment by deed is revoked by a subsequent appointment by will.[16] Although the point has never been decided, an appointment by deed may presumably be similarly revoked by a later deed;

---

[8]For a full list of the various types of guardian, see Simpson, *op. cit.*, pp. 149 *et seq.*
[9]Guardianship of Minors Act 1971, s. 4. The Act states that they may appoint " any person to be guardian ", but s. 3 assumes that there may be more than one so appointed. If the court appoints another to act as guardian with the surviving parent under s. 3 (see *ante*, p. 272), that person shall continue to act after the death of the surviving parent together with any testamentary guardians appointed by the latter: s. 4 (6).
[10]*Sleeman* v. *Wilson* (1871), L.R. 13 Eq. 36.
[11](1940), 164 L.T. 230.
[12]Now repealed and re-enacted in the Marriage Act 1949, Sched. 2 (see Appendix C, *post*).
[13]See now the Guardianship of Minors Act 1971, s. 14 (3). For custody orders, see *ante*, p. 282.
[14]Family Law Reform Act 1969, s. 1.
[15]Per LORD ELDON, L.C., in *Ex parte Ilchester* (1803), 7 Ves. 348, 367.
[16]*Shaftsbury* v. *Hannam* (1677), Cas. *temp.* Finch 323.

but in view of the wording of section 20 of the Wills Act 1837, it would appear that an appointment by will cannot be revoked by a subsequent appointment by deed.[17] Since a minor has no power to make a will unless he is a soldier or airman on active service or a sailor at sea,[18] it will be seen that the only way in which a minor, who does not come within this category, can appoint a guardian for his own children is by deed.

Whether the appointment will be effective if the child, in respect of whom it is made, is married when the testator dies is doubtful. Section 8 of the Tenures Abolition Act (now repealed) expressly excluded this case, but the Guardianship of Infants Act imposes no such limitation. On the other hand, it is rare for a guardian to be appointed by the court for a married infant, and, even assuming the power to make a testamentary appointment in such a case, the court might well remove a testamentary guardian who attempted to interfere with a married ward.

Presumably the parents' power is no less than the father's power was under the Tenures Abolition Act. Under that Act the appointment could be during the child's minority or for any less period, and could take effect immediately or in the future. Hence an appointment "of X till the child reaches the age of 16 and then of Y " ought still to be valid. Moreover, it was held in *In the Goods of Parnell*[19] that under the earlier Act a father could give another the power to appoint a guardian. A testator appointed X and Y to be the guardians of his daughter and on the death of either of them he gave the survivor power to appoint another in the place of the deceased. X subsequently died and Y by deed appointed Z to be joint guardian with himself. It was held by LORD PENZANCE that Z's appointment was valid.

If they accept the office, testamentary guardians act jointly with the surviving parent unless the latter objects.[20] In the event of such an objection, or if the guardian considers the parent unfit to have the custody of the child, the guardian may apply to the court[1] which must then decide whether either the parent or guardian is to act to the exclusion of the other or whether they are to act jointly. The child's welfare must of course be the court's chief concern, and it is hardly likely that it will be in his best interest to have them acting together in such circumstances. If the court orders that the testamentary guardian is to be the sole guardian, it may make such order as it

---

[17]Unless it is made in contemplation of marriage, a will is revoked by the subsequent marriage of the testator (Wills Act 1837, s. 18; Law of Property Act 1925, s. 177). But this probably does not apply to the appointment of a guardian by *deed*, in which case the appointment will include the guardianship of the children of a subsequent marriage as well: *Ex parte Ilchester*, (*supra*).

[18]Wills Act 1837, s. 11; Wills (Soldiers and Sailors) Act 1918, ss. 4, 5 (2); Family Law Reform Act 1969, s. 3 (1). For the persons included in this exception, see Jarman, *Wills*, 8th Ed., pp. 122-4.

[19](1872), L.R. 2 P. & D. 379. But in the absence of any express power a testamentary guardian may not assign his office: *Mellish* v. *De Costa* (1737), 2 Atk. 14

[20]Guardianship of Minors Act 1971, s. 4 (3).

[1]*I.e.*, the High Court, a county court or (subject to the limitations upon its jurisdiction) a magistrates' court.

thinks fit as to the custody of the child and the right of access of the surviving parent.[2]

If both parents appoint testamentary guardians, all the guardians so appointed, who are willing to act, do so jointly after the death of the surviving parent.[3]

Guardians appointed by the Court.—The High Court now has the inherent jurisdiction formerly possessed by the Court of Chancery to appoint guardians.[4] In addition a statutory power to appoint guardians is conferred in two cases on the High Court, county courts and (subject to the limitations on their jurisdiction) magistrates' courts by the Guardianship of Minors Act. If a deceased parent has appointed no testementary guardian, or if the guardian or guardians so appointed refuse to act, the court may, if it thinks fit, appoint one to act with the survivor.[5] A similar power exists if the child has no parent, guardian or other person exercising parental rights over him.[6] Again, if the court gives custody of a child of the marriage to a third person under the Matrimonial Proceedings and Property Act or the Matrimonial Proceedings (Magistrates' Courts) Act,[7] that person in effect becomes the child's guardian. A guardian can probably be appointed even though the child is married but there is no precedent for such an appointment and the court would probably be slow to act in such a case.

In determining whom to appoint as guardians

" the Court, according to its ordinary practice, gives a preference to the nearest blood relations, and does not appoint strangers when fit persons are to be found among the relations " .[8]

But this preference may be displaced by a number of other factors. Personal unfitness will certainly exclude anybody, the ward's religious education will be taken into account whenever it is relevant,[9] and due attention will be paid to a deceased parent's wishes even though the latter has not availed himself of the power of appointing a testamentary guardian.[10] But both the parent's and the nearest relative's wishes will be ignored if this is necessary in the interests of the child. In *Re F.*[11] the father of a girl only a few months old had strangled his wife,

---

[2]Guardianship of Minors Act 1971, s. 10. Such an order may be varied or discharged at any time.

[3]*Ibid.*, s. 4 (5).

[4]*Quaere* whether this can be exercised only if the child is made a ward of court. See *post*, p. 337.

[5]Guardianship of Minors Act 1971, s. 3. See *ante* 272.

[6]*Ibid.*, s. 5 (1). The court may exercise this power even though a local authority has assumed parental rights by resolution under s. 2 of the Children Act 1948 (see *ante*, p. 296), in which case the resolution will cease to have effect: s. 5 (2). In practice there are few applications under this sub-section, for a near relative usually takes *de facto* control of the child without troubling to obtain an order. For the duties of local authorities when there is no one to take care of a child, see *ante*, p. 296.

[7]See *ante*, pp. 285 and 287.

[8]*Per* CHITTY, J., in *Re Nevin*, [1891] 2 Ch. 299, 303. An appellate court will not interfere with the discretion of the judge at first instance except for very strong reasons: *Re Kaye* (1866), 1 Ch. App. 387.

[9]See *ante*, pp. 277-278.

[10]*Re Kaye*, (*supra*).

[11][1970] 1 All E.R. 344, C.A.

the girl's mother, and had been convicted of manslaughter on the ground of diminished responsibility. He wanted the girl to be brought up by his brother and sister-in-law (who lived in the same neighbourhood) and obviously had some hope of making contact with her again in the future. The child was then made a ward of court. The Court of Appeal had no doubt that it was highly desirable that her connection with her father (and therefore his family) and the neighbourhood should be completely severed and therefore gave care and control to the mother's cousin and her husband who had taken care of the child, were prepared to move away and hoped to adopt her.

Foreign Guardians.—Although in *Johnstone* v. *Beattie*[12] and *Stuart* v. *Bute*[13] the House of Lords laid down the rule that, even if a guardian has been validly appointed by a foreign court, the High Court is not precluded from appointing another guardian in this country, subsequent cases have shown that a foreign guardian's rights may be enforced here provided, at any rate, that they do not conflict with our ideas of public policy. It is clearly desirable that a child should not have one set of guardians in one country and another elsewhere, and guardianship being a question of status, the proper law to apply is obviously that of the child's domicile:[14] it is only where the protection of the child requires the courts of this country to interfere that the rights of a guardian validly appointed in another country should not be recognised here. Clearly, if a foreign guardian comes within the jurisdiction, he can apply to be appointed guardian here; and even if he does not do so his rights over the ward's person and property may be enforced. Thus, in *Nugent* v. *Vetzera*[15] the defendant had been appointed guardian of five minor children by an Austrian court. He had sent them to England for their education where they had been in the control of their elder sister, the plaintiff. On the defendant's demanding that they should be restored to him, the plaintiff commenced proceedings to have them made wards of court. PAGE WOOD, V.C., exercised his power to appoint guardians in this country but ordered that this appointment was to be without prejudice to the defendant's rights under Austrian law and that Vetzera was to have the exclusive right to their custody and control with liberty to apply to remove them from the jurisdiction. He added:

> " I have no right to deprive the guardian appointed by the foreign court over them of the control which he has lawfully and properly acquired, has never relinquished and never abandoned, and under which authority alone they have remained here, and been maintained and supported here "[16].

There is similar authority for the proposition that a foreign guardian can give a valid receipt for income out of a trust fund in which the ward

---

[12](1843), 10 Cl. & F. 42, H.L.

[13](1861), 9 H.L. Cas. 440, H.L.

[14]Although in *Re P. (G.E.)*, [1964] 3 All E.R. 977, C.A.; [1965] Ch. 568, the Court of Appeal preferred the test of ordinary residence as more realistic.

[15](1866), L.R. 2 Eq. 704. See also *Monaco* v. *Monaco* (1937), 157 L.T. 231.

[16]At 715. For the circumstances in which the court will order the child to be returned to another country without considering the merits of the application, see *post*, p. 335.

has a beneficial interest, although the court again has a discretion in the matter and may, for example, withhold payment until it is satisfied that the sums paid will be used for the ward's benefit.[17]

C. GUARDIANS' RIGHTS AND DUTIES WITH RESPECT TO THE PERSON OF THE WARD

A guardian has custody of his ward and therefore, broadly speaking, has the same rights and duties with respect to his person as a parent has with respect to his legitimate child. These may therefore be considered very briefly and the chief differences between the two noted.

Physical and Moral Protection.—A duty to protect the ward at common law will clearly arise once the guardian assumes responsibility for doing so.[18] The Children and Young Persons Act 1933 specifically renders a guardian criminally liable for breach of the various duties imposed by the Act to ensure the physical and moral protection of children.[19]

Maintenance.—As we have already seen, a guardian will be criminally liable under section 1 of the Children and Young Persons Act 1933 if he wilfully fails to provide his ward with adequate food, clothing, medical aid or lodging.[20]

If the guardian is acting jointly with the surviving parent or an order has been made that he shall act to the exclusion of the surviving parent, the latter may be ordered to pay such periodical sums to the guardian for the ward's maintenance (including education) as is reasonable having regard to the parent's means.[1] The parties to the marriage may also be ordered to pay maintenance to anyone to whom custody of the child has been given under the Matrimonial Proceedings (Magistrates' Courts) Act or the Matrimonial Proceedings and Property Act.[2] Moreover, if the ward is a beneficiary under a trust, the settlor may have authorised the trustees to pay the guardian income or capital for the maintenance or advancement of the ward. Even if he has not done so, the High Court may order income and, in certain circumstances, capital to be used for these purposes, and the Trustee Act 1925 has given trustees wide powers of the same nature.[3] But a guardian may not otherwise recoup himself out of the ward's property.[4]

---

[17]*Re Chatard's Settlement*, [1899] 1 Ch. 712. See also *Re Brown's Trust* (1865), 12 L.T. 488; *Mackie* v. *Darling* (1871), L.R. 12 Eq. 319.

[18]See *ante*, p. 305.   [19]S. 17. See *ante*, p. 307.   [20]*Ante*, p. 307.

[1]Guardianship of Minors Act 1971, ss. 10 (1) (b), (2), 11 (b), (c), and 20 (2). " Parent " includes the father of an illegitimate child who has obtained a custody order: s. 14 (3). These powers are exercisable by the High Court, county courts and (subject to the limitations upon their jurisdiction) magistrates' courts. The order may remain in force until the ward reaches the age of 21 and, if he is over 18, the court may direct that payments should be made to him personally: s. 12 (1).

[2]See *post*, p. 473. (Matrimonial Proceedings (Magistrates' Courts) Act) and 474 (Matrimonial Proceedings and Property Act).

[3]Ss. 31-33 and 53. See Lewin, *Trusts*, 16th Ed., cc. 17 and 18; Snell, *Equity*, 26th Ed., 285 *et seq*. The guardian may also be entitled to a guardian's allowance of £2.45 a week if one of the ward's parents was insured under the National Insurance Act: National Insurance Act 1965, ss. 29 and 42 and Sched. 3, as amended by the National Insurance Act 1969, s. 2.

[4]*Cf. Walker* v. *Wetherell* (1801), 6 Ves. 473.

Care and Control.—Where there is only one guardian, he will *prima facie* have the right to the care and control of his ward, a right which he may enforce by habeas corpus[5] or alternatively by proceedings in the Chancery Division, in which case the child may have to be made a ward of court.[6] Where there are more guardians than one, however, this *prima facie* rule cannot operate: in fact when a guardian is acting with a surviving parent, it will obviously usually be the latter who will be entitled to care and control.[7] Moreover, a parent appointing a guardian may direct that someone other than the guardian should have care and control, in which case, although the person nominated will clearly have no absolute right to have the testator's wishes carried out, the court will give effect to them unless it is contrary to the ward's welfare, whilst leaving the guardian with a general control and superintendence.[8]

But, of course, as in the case of a claim by a parent, the court's first concern must be for the ward's welfare. The same facts must be borne in mind in each case: the ward's religion, family ties, and, if he is old enough to exercise a choice, his own wishes, are clearly as important in one type of dispute as in the other.

Education.—A guardian is under the same statutory duty to ensure that his ward receives an efficient full-time education as a parent.[9] But so far as the choice of secular and religious education is concerned, the guardian's position is radically different from the parent's, for his duty is to see that the ward has a secular education befitting his position and expectations and is brought up in the faith in which he would have been brought up had his parents still been alive. Formerly, of course, this meant that, if the child was legitimate, the father's wishes had to be implemented, but, as the Court of Appeal pointed out in *Re Collins*,[10] the guardian must today observe the mother's wishes as much as the father's. These may be deduced either directly or inferentially from the parents' own acts, for example, by express directions, by their having children brought up in a particular faith during their lifetime, or by the appointment of testamentary guardians professing a particular creed;[11] if there is no other guide, then it is presumed that parents wish to have their children brought up in the same religion as they themselves practised.[12]

---

[5] *R.* v. *Isley* (1836), 5 Ad. & El. 441.
[6] Since the application would have to be made under the inherent jurisdiction of the court and not under any statutory power: see *post*, p. 337. The court may award custody to a guardian living abroad if this would be for the child's benefit: *Ex parte Nickells* (1891), 7 T.L.R. 498.
[7] The court has power to make orders regarding custody and the access of the parent in such a case: Guardianship of Minors Act 1971, s. 11 (a).
[8] *Knott* v. *Cottee* (1847), 2 Ph. 192.
[9] Education Act 1944, ss. 36, 114.
[10] [1950] 1 All E.R. 1057, C.A.; [1950] Ch. 498.
[11] See *Re Nevin*, [1891] 2 Ch. 299, C.A.; *Hill* v. *Hill* (1862), 31 L.J.Ch. 505; *Andrews* v. *Salt* (1873), 8 Ch. App. 622; *Re McGrath*, [1893] 1 Ch. 143, C.A.
[12] *Re McGrath*, (*supra*), at p. 148; *Hawksworth* v. *Hawksworth* (1871), 6 Ch. App. 539; *Re Scanlon* (1888), 40 Ch.D. 200, 213; *F.* v. *F.*, [1902] 1 Ch. 688, 689. Would the court now implement a direction by the parent that the child should be brought up as an atheist?

But, as in the case of disputes between parents over the religious upbringing of their children, the final choice of a ward's religious education must depend upon what is best for its own welfare and the same factors must be borne in mind in each case. If the father's and mother's wishes were not the same, the same test must be applied as is applied during their lifetime, and the court will not order a ward to be educated in its parents' religion if it has already developed firm convictions of its own and has reached an age when it would be dangerous to attempt to effect a change.[13] Moreover, less attention will be paid to a parent's wishes after his death than during his life, because he could not possibly have foreseen all the circumstances which might subsequently arise.[14]

Ward's Marriage.—The guardian's consent is required for the marriage of a ward over the age of 16.[15]

Guardian's Liability for his Ward's Acts.—A guardian's liability for his ward's acts are precisely the same as a parent's, for in both cases he will be liable if he has authorised or ratified the act and he will also be liable for a tort if it has been occasioned by his own negligence in failing to avert its commission.[16] The provisions empowering a court to order a parent to pay any fine, damages, compensation or costs imposed in respect of an offence committed by a child under the age of 17 apply equally to guardians.[17]

Liability for interfering with Guardian's Rights.—Criminal liability will be incurred for taking a ward under the age of 14 or a female ward over that age out of the custody of his or her guardian in the same circumstances as it will for taking a child out of the custody of its parents.[18] As regards civil liability, no action will lie at the suit of a guardian as such[19] under the Fatal Accidents Acts; but it would seem that, as a person with *de facto* control of a child can apparently sue for loss of its services,[20] *a fortiori* a guardian can do so provided the ward was in fact rendering services to him. There is no authority on the question of a guardian's ability to sue in reliance upon a constructive service: whether the courts would be prepared to extend the parent's right to a guardian is highly doubtful.

Disputes between Guardians.—In *Gilbert* v. *Schwenck*[21] PLATT, B., delivering the judgment of the Court of Exchequer, laid down the rule that one of two joint guardians cannot act in defiance of the other

---

[13]*Stourton* v. *Stourton* (1857), 8 De G. M. & G. 760; *Re W.*, [1907] 2 Ch. 557, C.A.; *Ward* v. *Laverty*, [1925] A.C. 101, H.L.

[14]*Re Meades* (1871), I.R. 5 Eq. 98, 112.

[15]Marriage Act 1949, Sched. 2 (see Appendix C *post*, p. 528). The Act has not been amended to require the consent of a guardian appointed by the father of an illegitimate child. For the position if the guardian's consent cannot be obtained or is refused, see *ante*, pp. 31-33.

[16]See *ante*, pp. 310-311.

[17]See *ante*, p. 311.

[18]See *ante*, pp. 312-313.

[19]But he might be able to sue, *e.g.*, as a grandparent or other relation. For the Fatal Accidents Acts, see *ante*, pp. 108-117.

[20]*Ante*, p. 320.

[21](1845), 14 M. & W. 488, 493.

and that each has an equal power. Machinery for solving disputes is provided by section 7 of the Guardianship of Minors Act 1971, which gives any of them the power to apply to the High Court, county court or (subject to the limitations upon its jurisdiction) a magistrates' court, which may then make such order as it thinks proper.[1]

D. GUARDIANS' RIGHTS AND DUTIES WITH RESPECT TO THE PROPERTY OF THE WARD

We have already seen that a guardian will become a trustee of any of his ward's property of which he possesses himself, but that modern legislation has greatly reduced the importance of guardianship of the estate by virtually ensuring that almost all a minor's property will be held by trustees. If trustees pay the income to the guardian for the maintenance of the ward under any express or statutory powers, they will be discharged by the guardian's receipt.[2]

On the termination of the guardianship the guardian must account to the ward for all property that has come into his hands.[3] As a result of the doctrine of undue influence, however, the court may order the account to be re-opened if it is accepted and the guardian released by the former ward immediately after the latter comes of age.[4]

Undue Influence.—The office of a guardian is so confidential and the opportunities that he has to influence his ward so great that equity will assume that, in any transaction between the parties from which the guardian reaps an advantage, he has exercised undue influence over the other. The attitude of the courts was thus summarised by LORD BROUGHAM, L.C., in *Hunter* v. *Atkins*:[5]

" There are certain relations known to the law, as attorney, guardian, trustee; if a person standing in these relations to client, ward, or *cestui que trust*, takes a gift or makes a bargain, the proof lies upon him, that he has dealt with the other party . . . exactly as a stranger would have done, taking no advantage of his influence or knowledge, putting the other party on his guard, bringing everything to his knowledge which he himself knew. In short, the rule rightly considered is, that the person standing in such relation must, before he can take a gift, or even enter into a transaction, place himself in exactly the same position as a stranger would have been in, so that he may gain no advantage whatever from his relation to the other party, beyond what may be the natural and unavoidable consequence of kindness arising out of that relation."

It will, of course, be difficult for the guardian to prove that he exercised no influence over his ward; virtually the only way of doing so is to show that the latter received genuinely independent advice. If the guardian fails to discharge the burden cast upon him, the ward may

---

[1] If one of the guardians is the child's surviving parent, the court may grant him or her access: Guardianship of Minors Act 1971, s. 11 (a).

[2] *Re Long,* [1901] W.N. 166. But one guardian is not discharged by payment to a co-guardian: *Re Evans* (1884), 26 Ch. D. 58, C.A.

[3] It will be presumed that money paid to a guardian for maintenance has been properly so used unless the contrary is clearly shown, when the guardian will have to account for all sums so received: *Re Evans, (supra)*; *Macrae* v. *Harness* (1910), 103 L.T. 629. On the question of periods of limitation, see *Mathew* v. *Brise* (1851), 14 Beav. 341.

[4] *Steadman* v. *Palling* (1746), 3 Atk. 423.

[5] (1834), 3 My. & K. 113, 135. See also LORD LYNDHURST, L.C., in *Archer* v. *Hudson* (1846), 15 L.J.Ch. 211.

have the gift or contract set aside and demand to be put back in the position he was in before he entered into the transaction, and he may also recover any property passed from anyone into whose hands it has come except a *bona fide* purchaser for value without notice of the way in which the property was originally obtained.

Moreover, it is absurd to consider that any influence which the guardian may have over his ward will automatically come to an end as soon as the relationship of guardian and ward ceases, and consequently the doctrine will also apply for some time after the ward comes of age. It is, of course, impossible to draw any hard and fast line at any point of time, and whether the presumption will be raised in any given case must depend upon its particular facts. An illustrative case is *Maitland* v. *Irving*.[6] The defendants agreed to sell their business to Maclean who was unable to raise the money but who told them that he would obtain a guarantee from the plaintiff who had property, who was his niece, and who had been his ward until she had come of age some 18 months previously. He then induced her to draw a cheque for £3,000 in favour of the defendants which he transferred to them. It was held that the plaintiff was not liable to the defendants because she had been induced to act as a result of the influence which Maclean had over her and, since he had told the defendants of the relationship between himself and the plaintiff, they had sufficient notice of her right in equity to have the transaction set aside.

E. TERMINATION OF GUARDIANSHIP

Death, Majority or Marriage of the Ward.—The guardian's duties will clearly cease if the ward dies: they automatically determine when he comes of age. Whether the guardian's powers cease if the ward marries before he or she reaches the age of 18 is doubtful. It seems to have been accepted in the past that they came to an end on the marriage of a girl but not of a boy,[7] but this cannot now be accepted with any certainty. The Tenures Abolition Act gave a parent no power to appoint a guardian for a married child but did not state that the guardianship would terminate if the ward subsequently married, and the Guardianship of Minors Act does not impose any limitations of this sort at all.[8] In any event, as the guardian must consent to the marriage, it is highly unlikely that the court will permit him to interfere with a married ward.

Death of the Guardian.—Although a deceased guardian's personal representatives will have no rights or duties with respect to the person of the ward, the estate will be liable for any breach of trust committed by the guardian in his dealings with the ward's property. In the case

---

[6](1846), 15 Sim. 437. See also *Maitland* v. *Backhouse* (1848), 16 Sim. 58; *Archer* v. *Hudson*, (*ante*). *Cf.* the re-opening of an account presented immediately after the ward comes of age, *ante*, and the presumption of undue influence exercised by a parent over his child, *post*, p. 460.

[7]See the views of LORD HARDWICKE, L.C., in *Mendes* v. *Mendes* (1748), 1 Ves. Sen. 89.

[8]It does not seem to have been suggested in *Eyre* v. *Shaftesbury* (1725), 2 P. Wms. 103, that the guardianship of Eyre, C.B., was determined on his ward's marriage, nor does wardship of court cease on marriage (see *post*, p. 337).

of joint testamentary guardians the survivors continue to act,[9] but
if one guardian appointed by the court dies, the guardianship of all the
others automatically determines as well[10] although they are almost
invariably re-appointed.

Discharge and Removal of a Guardian by the Court.—Like a
trustee, a guardian once having accepted the office cannot resign it at
will,[11] and although in some earlier cases the court did not look
favourably upon a guardian's request to be discharged, the modern
view is that, if he is unwilling to act, it will be in the ward's interest
that he should be replaced.[12]

But the court's jurisdiction is not confined to those cases where the
guardian wishes to be released and the High Court has power to remove
a guardian whenever the welfare of the ward so demands.[13] This may
be due to the actual or threatened misconduct of the guardian (for the
court will attempt to avert a possible danger to the ward rather than
wait for it to happen)[14] to the abandonment of his rights for such a
length of time that it would not be in the ward's interest to permit him
to reassert them,[15] or merely to a change of circumstances which
render it for some reason better for the ward to have a new guardian
and which do not necessarily cast any reflection on the existing
guardian's integrity at all.[16]

F. WARDS OF COURT

Historically the jurisdiction to make a child a ward of court goes
back to the Crown's rights over infant tenants in chief in chivalry and
its prerogative powers as *parens patriae*. Wardship of court differs
from other forms of wardship in one important respect: if a child is
made a ward of court, custody in the sense of the sum of parental
rights and powers will vest in the court. Care and control must of
course be given to an individual but he will be more in the nature of an
agent of the court, responsible solely for the day to day supervision of
the ward. Two consequences flow from the fact that the residuum of
powers remains in the court. First, the person in whose care the child is
must keep the court informed of the progress of the ward and may
always turn to the court for guidance and assistance. All major
decisions, for example those relating to control, access, education and

[9]*Eyre* v. *Shaftsbury*, *(supra)*, at p. 107.
[10]*Bradshaw* v. *Bradshaw* (1826), 1 Russ. 528.
[11]*Spencer* v. *Chesterfield* (1752), Amb. 146.
[12]Contrast the view taken by LORD HARDWICKE, L.C., in *Spencer* v. *Chesterfield*, *(supra)*,
with that of ROMILLY, M.R., in *Kay* v. *Johnston* (1856), 21 Beav. 536, at p. 539.
[13]*Re McGrath*, [1893] 1 Ch. 143, 147-148, C.A.; *Re X.*, [1899] 1 Ch. 526, 531, C.A.;
Guardianship of Minors Act 1971, ss. 6 and 17 (1). In *Smith* v. *Bate* (1784), 2 Dick. 631, a
guardian was removed on the grounds of bankruptcy; whilst this might still be a reason
for removing him if he held a large amount of the ward's property, there seems to be
no reason for removing him from the guardianship of the person if no moral slur is cast
on him.
[14]*Beaufort* v. *Berty* (1721), 1 P. Wms. 703, 704-705; *Re X.*, *(supra)*, at p. 531.
[15]*Andrews* v. *Salt* (1873), 8 Ch. App. 622.
[16]*Re X.*, *(supra)*, at pp. 535-536; *F.* v. *F.*, [1902] 1 Ch. 688, where a guardian who
had become a Roman Catholic was removed although she had made no attempt to
influence her ward, a Protestant.

marriage, must be made by the court itself. Secondly, any interference with the ward or the guardian will amount to a contempt of court even though the person interfering is unaware that the child is a ward of court, although his ignorance may well excuse him in the sense that the court will not punish him.[17] Similarly, the ward himself may be committed for contempt if he wilfully refuses to obey the court's directions.[18]

In practice children are made wards of court in two sorts of situation.[19] First of all there are cases where orders relating to custody are sought in the Family Division but no other matrimonial proceedings are pending so that the court cannot exercise its jurisdiction under the Matrimonial Proceedings and Property Act. This might occur if a comprehensive order was required or if the case raised some particular difficulty (for example, the existence of a foreign order) so that it was inappropriate to take advantage of the statutory jurisdiction under the Guardianship of Minors Act. Alternatively this procedure would have to be used if someone other than a parent wished to invoke the jurisdiction of the court on the ground, for example, that neither parent was fit to have custody. One advantage of making a child a ward of court in these circumstances is that the father or mother may be given care and control of it, whilst the exercise of his or her parental rights will be constantly subject to the supervision of the court. The effect is to give the maximum control over, and protection to, the ward but to leave the minimum discretion to the parent, and consequently this procedure should usually be adopted only when this balance is desirable. In the second type of case the child is made a ward of court solely in order to prevent his or her associating with undesirable companions or contracting a marriage opposed by the parents. This type of ward is almost always a girl nearing the age of majority and, whereas in the first sort of case the parents will usually be opposed to each other, in the " teenage wardship " the parents will be acting together but in open conflict with the child.[20] Consequently the court will consider only the point at issue and will not interfere with other matters, such as education and maintenance, which remain in the parents' hands.

A problem arises if the purpose of making the child a ward of court is to obtain an order relating to some matter, the power to determine which has been vested by statute in some other body. The latter's discretion cannot usually be fettered by warding the child, and consequently the court will not entertain the proceedings unless the body has acted with impropriety or in disregard of its statutory duties, for otherwise the court and the body, both acting in good faith, might reach opposing decisions.[1]

---

[17] *Re H.'s Settlement*, [1909] 2 Ch. 260.
[18] *Re H.'s Settlement*, (*supra*).
[19] For an authoritative description of the working of this jurisdiction by a judge of the Chancery Division, see Cross, *Wardship of Court*, 83 L.Q.R. 201.
[20] See Cross, *loc. cit.*, pp. 209-211.
[1] See *ante*, pp. 298-300. Similarly the discretion vested in an immigration officer to refuse a child admission into the country cannot be called in question by warding the child: *Re A.*, [1968] 2 All E.R. 145, C.A.; [1968] Ch. 643.

Jurisdiction to make a Child a Ward of Court.—Since the jurisdiction is based upon the necessity of protecting the child, any minor actually in England may be warded even though he is neither domiciled here nor a British subject. Thus in *Re D.*[2] a German Jewish refugee who had been brought to this country in 1939 was made a ward of court even though he was not a British subject and had no property within the jurisdiction. But it is clearly only in the most exceptional circumstances that this should be done if the child is here only temporarily, for example for educational purposes or on holiday.[3] Conversely, the court has jurisdiction if the child is a British subject even though he is not resident in England at all, because he continues to be entitled to the protection of the Crown as *parens patriae* wherever he may happen to be.[4] In *Re P. (G. E.)*[5] the Court of Appeal went further and held that there is jurisdiction to make an order in respect of an alien who is ordinarily resident here even though he is not in the country when the application is made. In that case the stateless parents of a child who was almost seven years old when the proceedings were commenced had left Egypt following the Suez crisis and had come to England. They later separated and agreed that the boy should live with his mother but spend every weekend with his father. One Saturday the father, having obtained a British travel document, flew to Israel with the son. On the mother's application to have the boy made a ward of court it was held that the court had jurisdiction to do so as the son's ordinary residence was in England with his mother, and the father, having agreed to this, could not change it without the mother's consent or acquiescence. This conclusion was fortified by the fact that the father still held the travel document, which entitled him to return to England, and had entered Israel on only a temporary visa and also that justice demands that a parent left in this country should have a remedy here when the other has spirited the child out of the jurisdiction by force, deception or fraud.

But it does not follow that the court is bound to continue the wardship even though it has jurisdiction. It will always be slow to do so if the child is not in the country, particularly if proceedings are also being taken elsewhere and the other court is the *forum conveniens*.[6] Nor will it make an order if there are no means of enforcing it and no probability that it will be obeyed or if it would be contrary to the law of the state where the child is.[7]

---

[2] [1943] 2 All E.R. 411; [1943] Ch. 305. See also *Johnstone* v. *Beattie* (1843), 10 Cl. & F. 42, H.L.

[3] *Per* LORD CAMPBELL, L.C., in *Stuart* v. *Bute* (1861), 9 H.L. Cas. 440, 464-465, H.L.; *per* PEARSON, L.J., in *Re P. (G.E.)*, [1964] 3 All E.R. 977, 983-984, C.A.; [1965] Ch. 568, 588.

[4] *Hope* v. *Hope* (1854), 4 De G. M. & G. 328. See also *Re Willoughby* (1885), 30 Ch. D. 324, C.A. In *Re P. (G.E.)*, (*supra*), RUSSELL, L.J., was prepared to extend the jurisdiction to the case of a stateless person travelling abroad on a British travel document or *a fortiori* an alien holding a British passport (at pp. 988 and 595, respectively).

[5] [1964] 3 All E.R. 977, C.A.; [1965] Ch. 568. See Webb in 14 I.C.L.Q. 663.

[6] *Re S. (M.)*, [1971] 1 All E.R. 459, 462 (proceedings pending in Scotland where the child was domiciled and resident).

[7] *Hope* v. *Hope*, (*supra*), at pp. 347-348; *Dawson* v. *Jay* (1854), 3 De G. M. & G. 764, 772.

" *Kidnapping* " *Cases.*—Speedy international transport has recently given rise to a number of " kidnapping " cases in which a parent, who has failed to obtain custody in another country, has brought the child to England in the hope of being successful here. Naturally the court will do its utmost to discourage this practice. Consequently it may order the child to be sent back to the country where the original order was made without considering the merits of the case at all, provided that it is satisfied that this can be done without fear of immediate harm. As CROSS, J., pointed out in *Re H.*,[8] this procedure is consonant with the general principles of comity and is called for if the foreign court is the *forum conveniens*: if the case were delayed for an enquiry as to the merits, the child would begin to acquire roots in this country which it might not be in his interest to sever, with resulting injustice to the wronged parent. In that case a New York court had given the custody of two boys to their mother with liberal access to the father. It had further ordered that the children should not be removed from the jurisdiction without the father's written consent. In breach of this order and in contempt of the New York court the mother brought her sons to England where she intended to settle permanently. The children were then made wards of court. The Court of Appeal affirmed the decision of CROSS, J., that this was a case where the court should do no more than order the children to be sent back to New York where the question of their future custody could be considered on its merits. A number of considerations led them to this conclusion: this was a serious example of " kidnapping "; the father and both children were American citizens so that an American court was the *forum conveniens*; an enquiry on the merits of the parents' claims (which might have resulted in the court's giving custody to the father in the U.S.A.) would have led to great delay during which time the children would have settled down in England; and there was no evidence that sending them back with their father would cause them any harm.

As was said in *Re E. (D.)*,[9] where there is a foreign order the proper course is to send the child back unless there are compelling reasons to the contrary. There were such compelling reasons in that case. The parents of a baby girl were divorced in New Mexico. Custody was originally given to the mother, but this was later varied in favour of the father with whom the girl lived until, nearly four years later, he was killed in a motor accident. The father, who was convinced that his wife was wholly unfit to have custody, had previously indicated that in the event of his death he wished his sister, Mrs. Z who lived in England, to have custody. Immediately after the father's death, the child's paternal grandfather took her from the hospital where she was being treated and handed her over to Mrs. Z with an assurance that there was no legal objection to her being taken to England. In the meantime the mother

---

[8][1965] 3 All E.R. 906; affirmed, [1966] 1 All E.R. 886, C.A. A similar conclusion was reached in *Re G.*, [1969] 2 All E.R. 1135, where the child was ordered to be returned to Scotland.

[9][1967] 1 All E.R. 329, 338; [1967] Ch. 287, 301 (CROSS, J.); [1967] 2 All E.R. 881; [1967] Ch. 761, C.A.

had obtained an injunction from the New Mexico court prohibiting the child from being removed from the U.S.A. and giving her temporary custody, but Mrs. Z and the girl had left the country before the injunction could be served. The mother later came to England and Mrs. Z made the child a ward of court. It was held that she should stay in this country with Mrs. Z. The latter had acted more or less innocently, she had believed the mother was unfit to have custody, she had become a second mother to her niece, who had no other home, and—the critical consideration—the court felt that it would be disastrous for the child to remove her and send her back to the U.S.A.

But this principle has been modified in recent cases. The older the child is and the longer the order has been in force, the weaker becomes the presumption that the child should be sent back.[10] In *Re A*.[11] the Court of Appeal held that the principle does not apply at all if the child was originally brought to this country not by stealth but with the agreement of both parties and *a fortiori* if, as in that case, one parent is normally resident here, the other has the means of coming to this country, the parties are probably domiciled here and matrimonial proceedings are about to be launched here.

Procedure to make a Child a Ward of Court.—Until 1949 a child automatically became a ward of court in a number of cases, for example on a petition to appoint a guardian or on payment into court under the Trustee Act of a fund belonging to him or, in fact, upon any application made to the court on his behalf.[12] But now section 9 of the Law Reform (Miscellaneous Provisions) Act 1949, has enacted that a child shall be made a ward of court only by virtue of an order to that effect made by the court. Immediately an application for an order is made, the child becomes a ward of court; but he ceases to be one unless an appointment to hear the summons is obtained within 21 days or if the court refuses to make the order.[13]

A divorce court may also direct proceedings to be taken to have the children of the marriage made wards of court in any proceedings for divorce, nullity or judicial separation, either before, by or after the final decree.[14] This power is rarely exercised but is useful if the court feels that the continuous supervision that this will produce is necessary for the child's welfare.

The child can always be ordered to be separately represented and the Official Solicitor then acts as guardian *ad litem*. If the dispute is between a " teenage " child and its parents, separate representation is always ordered; but if it is between the parents themselves or others claiming

---

[10]*Re T.*, [1969] 3 All E.R. 998 (principle not applied when boy in question was aged 16 and the order was 12 years old).

[11][1970] 3 All E.R. 184, C.A.; [1970] Ch. 665.

[12]See Simpson, *Infants*, 4th Ed., 165.

[13]Law Reform (Miscellaneous Provisions) Act 1949, s. 9 (2); R.S.C. O. 91, r. 2. The applicant must state his relationship to the child, and if the application appears to be an abuse of process, the summons may be dismissed forthwith: *Practice Direction*, [1967] 1 All E.R. 828 (made following *Re Dunhill* (1967), 111 Sol. Jo. 113, where a night-club owner made a girl a ward of court as a piece of advertisement).

[14]Matrimonial Proceedings and Property Act 1970, s. 18 (1).

custody, this will be done only if the case presents particular difficulty or for some other reason it is desirable for the court to have the benefit of an independent opinion.[15]

The court may at any time order that a child shall cease to be a ward of court.[16] If this is not done, the court's jurisdiction ceases immediately the ward reaches the age of 18, but it does not cease on the ward's marriage.[17]

Exercise of the Inherent Jurisdiction in other Proceedings.—The rule that a child can be made a ward of court only if the procedure laid down by the Law Reform (Miscellaneous Provisions) Act 1949 is followed has led to some doubt whether the court can now exercise its inherent jurisdiction at all if the child is not warded. In *Re E.*[18] ROXBURGH, J., concluded that this procedure must now be followed whenever it is desired to invoke the inherent jurisdiction, but this has since been doubted by STAMP, J., in *Re N.*[19] and by SIMON, P., in *L. v. L.*[20] Difficulty arises in the first place because it is not clear whether the court had such a power before 1949; the dicta conflict but on balance suggest that any summons invoking the inherent jurisdiction automatically made the child a ward of court.[1] If this is so, the Act of 1949 could have had one of two results. On the one hand, as was held in *Re E.*, it prescribes the only way in which the inherent jurisdiction can now be invoked. On the other hand, it may permit an order to be made with respect to the child without its becoming a ward of court if the procedure laid down is not followed. If, as in *L. v. L.*, an injunction is required immediately for the protection of the child, the court should be able to grant it forthwith without warding the child. If this view is correct, the Act does not cut down the court's powers but limits the consequences of their exercise. It is submitted that this is the interpretation to be preferred and that *Re N.* and *L. v. L.* should be followed rather than *Re E.*

Supervision by the Court.—Apart from the fact that discretion will have to be exercised by the court and not by the guardian, the principles to be applied when the ward is under the supervision of a testamentary guardian or guardian appointed by the court are equally applicable when he is a ward of court. Thus the court must make all necessary orders relating to care and control, access and education. Five points call for special comment.

---

[15]See Cross, *loc. cit.*, pp. 207-208. For the desirability of obtaining an independent medical opinion, see *post*, p. 338.
[16]Law Reform (Miscellaneous Provisions) Act 1949, s. 9 (3).
[17]*Cf. Re Elwes* (1958), *Times*, July 30.
[18][1955] 3 All E.R. 174; [1956] Ch. 23.
[19][1967] 1 All E.R. 161, 168-169; [1967] Ch. 512, 529-531.
[20][1969] 1 All E.R. 852, 854; [1969] P. 25, 27.
[1]See *Stuart* v. *Bute* (1861), 9 H.L.C. 440, 446, H.L.; *Brown* v. *Collins* (1883), 25 Ch.D. 56, 61; Simpson, *Infants*, 4th Ed., 165. In *Re McGrath*, [1892] 2 Ch. 496, 511, NORTH, J., held that the court could act even though the children were not warded, but the Court of Appeal limited its power to the appointment and removal of guardians: [1893] 1 Ch. 143, 147.

Care and Supervision.—Section 7 of the Family Law Reform Act 1969 has given two new powers to the court, both of which can be exercised only if there are exceptional circumstances making this desirable. If it is impracticable or undesirable to leave the ward in the care of either parent or a third person, he may be committed to the care of a local authority. Alternatively, he may be placed under the supervision of a welfare officer or a local authority. It will be seen that this brings the powers of the Family Division in wardship proceedings into line with its powers in divorce and other matrimonial proceedings.[2]

Medical Evidence.—If psychiatric evidence is desired, a psychiatrist should not be appointed without the court's approval. If both sides agree on the necessity for an examination and on the name of the psychiatrist, the court will normally follow their wishes. In the event of a disagreement, the Official Solicitor should be appointed guardian *ad litem* (if he has not been appointed already) and he can then decide (subject to the court's direction) whether an examination is necessary. This procedure has the advantage that the psychiatrist will not be the witness of either of the parties in dispute[3] and that the Official Solicitor can obtain a second opinion if necessary.[4]

Maintenance.—Formerly the court could not order maintenance to be paid for a ward of court unless there was some fund out of which sums could be paid for his benefit. Now, however, the court can order either parent of a *legitimate* child who is a ward of court to make periodical payments to the other or to a third person who has care and control of the child.[5]

Marriage of Ward of Court.—The court's consent must be obtained to the marriage of its ward[6] and the consent will be withheld if the court is of the opinion that the proposed match would be unsuitable. It is a contempt for a ward to marry (or even to attempt to marry)[7] without this consent, for which not only the parties but also anyone else who has brought about the marriage or has taken any active part in its celebration[8] may be punished.

Removal of a Ward of Court from the Jurisdiction.—The danger that, if a ward left the jurisdiction, the court might lose complete control of him because it had no means of securing his return, led to the formulation of the rule that a ward of court would never be permitted to leave England. Thus, in 1801, LORD ELDON, L.C., stated that the court would never make an order for taking a ward out of the jurisdiction and he refused the guardian permission to take his ward to his own

[7] See *ante*, pp. 287-288.
[3] See *ante*, p. 276.
[4] See the views of CROSS, J., in *Re S.*, [1967] 1 All E.R. 202, 209, approved and followed in *Re R. (P.M.)*, [1968] 1 All E.R. 691, 693, and *B. (M.) v. B. (R.)*, [1968] 3 All E.R. 170, 174, C.A.
[5] See *post*, p. 479.
[6] *Re H.'s Settlement*, [1909] 2 Ch. 260; Marriage Act 1949, s. 3 (6).
[7] *Warter v. Yorke* (1815), 19 Ves. 451, 453. (In this case the marriage was void but nevertheless was held to be a contempt.)
[8] *E.g.*, the parties' parents or the officiating clergyman: *Warter v. Yorke, (supra)*.

house in Scotland.[9] But by the middle of the last century the courts were coming round to the view that a ward might be taken out, at least temporarily, if sufficient reason were shown, for example for the sake of his health or to rejoin his family, provided that his return could be ensured if the court demanded it.[10] This wider rule was gradually extended and by the end of the century it was accepted that an application should be granted whenever it was shown to be for the ward's benefit.[11] It must now be extremely common for wards to be taken abroad for holidays and only in the most exceptional circumstances would the court refuse to permit a ward to be taken out of the jurisdiction permanently if its welfare so demanded. The person most likely to oppose the application is one of the parents if the proposal is that the child should emigrate with the other; in such circumstances the court must take into account the same facts as it would if this situation arose after a divorce.[12]

---

[9]*Mountstuart* v. *Mountstuart* (1801), 6 Ves. 363.

[10]See *Campbell* v. *Mackay* (1837), 2 My. & Cr. 31, and *Dawson* v. *Jay* (1854), 3 De G. M. & G. 764.

[11]See *Re Callaghan* (1884), 28 Ch.D. 186, 189, C.A.

[12]See *ante*, pp. 279-280. See also *ReBenner*, [1951] W.N. 436; *Re O.*, [1962] 2 All E.R. 10, C.A. The court would usually deward the child if it was going abroad permanently.

PART III

PROPERTY AND FINANCIAL
PROVISION

SUMMARY OF CONTENTS

CHAPTER 13

The Economic Aspects of Family Law

In this Part we shall be concerned with property and maintenance. Broadly speaking these two subjects reflect the difference between capital and income and between them they compose the economic aspects of family law.

The rights in property which we must examine are of course only those which concern members of the family as such and they are essentially of two different sorts. First we must consider ownership and title, in other words the question: to whom does a particular piece of property belong? Secondly we must consider rights of possession, occupation and use, in other words the question: what rights does one member of the family have in property belonging to another? These two problems are particularly relevant in connection with the matrimonial home. Beneficial ownership will not only *prima facie* give the spouse in whom it is vested the right to occupy as owner but will also determine who is entitled to the proceeds if the house is sold; but if, say, the house and furniture belong exclusively to the husband, the further problem arises what rights, if any, the wife has to occupy the house and use the furniture even against his wishes. The same problems can arise, although to a much more limited extent, between parent and child. It will, therefore, be necessary to consider first the rights in property created and affected by the relationship of husband and wife and the spouses' duty to maintain each other and, secondly, the rights in property created and affected by the relationship of parent and child and the former's duty to maintain the latter.

Husband and Wife.—So long as the family is a going concern, rights in property and rights to maintenance are of purely academic interest. If the spouses are living together in the matrimonial home, it is of no practical consequence whether it belongs to one or both of them or, if one is the owner, what legal right the other has to be there. Again, if both spouses have an income, it does not matter at this stage whether the husband accepts the sole responsibility for supporting the family and lets the wife do what she likes with her own money or whether the wife uses her own income to pay the household bills and leaves the husband to use his to pay off the mortgage on the house, plough it back into his business or invest it and save for their future enjoyment or their children's education. The need for precise definition and formulation of these rights normally arises in one of three situations.

The commonest—and that which most frequently gives rise to litigation—occurs when the marriage breaks down during the parties' lifetime. If the husband has deserted his wife and children, it may be a matter of prime importance to her to know whether she can stay in the former matrimonial home; if the house is to be sold, probably for much more than they paid for it, both spouses may lay claim to the proceeds of sale. Maintenance will be of equal or greater importance to most wives in this position because their earning capacity, which may be less than their husband's in any case, will probably be reduced by their having to look after the children. Again some spouses—husbands as well as wives—who are incapable of self-support as a result of age, infirmity or disability may well have been completely dependent on the other. As the breakdown of the marriage usually produces two families instead of one, it almost always involves a reduction in the standard of living of at least one of the spouses; the question that has to be settled is how this reduction is to be borne.

Secondly, these rights may become relevant on the death of one of the spouses. A dispute may arise between the survivor and the other's personal representatives over the ownership of a particular piece of property, or the former may claim that the property in question was beneficially vested in both spouses jointly and so does not form part of the other's estate. Similar disputes may arise between the personal representatives and the Estate Duty Office over the payment of death duties. Alternatively a survivor, left completely unsupported as a result of the other's testamentary dispositions, may wish to claim maintenance from the estate. This is most likely to occur if the marriage broke down before the death and the deceased deliberately cut the other out of his will or left the whole estate to the woman or man with whom he or she was living at death. A similar problem can arise if the deceased has been married twice and leaves the bulk of his estate to the children by his first marriage who, resentful of their stepmother, refuse to make her an adequate allowance. More rarely, an unreasonable or eccentric testator may leave his or her spouse nothing as the result of groundless suspicion or an obsessional interest in the objects of a particular charity.

Finally, the same problems arise if one spouse becomes insolvent. The following are the sort of questions which then become vital. Does a particular piece of property belong to the insolvent spouse (in which case it will now vest in the trustee in bankruptcy) or the solvent one? Does the insolvent spouse's obligation to maintain his family take priority over his trade debts? Can a spouse with a maintenance order claim in the other's bankruptcy? There is, of course, a danger that the spouses might conspire to defeat creditors by vesting all their property in one (usually the wife) and leaving the other to take all the commercial risks which may result in bankruptcy, and consequently, as we shall see,[1] certain transactions which prejudice creditors may be set aside.

---

[1]*Post*, pp. 367-370.

As a general rule a spouse's claim to maintenance is subordinated to the claims of the other's creditors so that, for example, arrears under a maintenance order are not provable in bankruptcy.[2] This is a question of social policy and has been justified on the ground that, marriage being a partnership, neither partner should be permitted to claim against the other until all the partner's debts are paid.[3] This argument unfortunately confuses the social partnership of marriage with a commercial partnership between persons carrying on a business in common with a view to profit and is, to say the least, unconvincing.

Parent and Child.—Spouses' rights become confused because property is frequently bought for their common use: both may have contributed, directly or indirectly, to the price and little or no thought is given to the question of ownership at the time of purchase. These complications do not often occur in the case of parent and child and consequently this relationship rarely affects rights in property.[4] Like the spouses' duty to maintain each other, the parents' duty to maintain their children is normally of no practical importance so long as the whole family is living together. The question of its enforcement will usually arise if the marriage breaks down, and may also arise if a deceased parent's will or the rules of intestate succession leave a child without support (as might happen, for example, if the surviving spouse refuses to accept responsibility for the other's children by a previous marriage). But it should be appreciated that the obligation to maintain can also be relevant in other circumstances. Even though the husband and wife are still cohabiting, their children may be living not with them but with relations or foster parents who may seek a contribution towards their maintenance. Conversely, a woman who is bringing up her illegitimate child may wish to claim maintenance for it from the father even though she has never lived with him and has no right to maintenance for herself.

The Interrelationship of Property and Maintenance.—It is obvious that rights in property and rights to maintenance are inevitably interrelated. For example, a deserted or divorced wife who owns or remains in occupation of the former matrimonial home is in a better financial position than one who does not and who will therefore require a lump sum payment to enable her to buy a house or flat or periodical payments to enable her to lease one. Again, income from investments or a settlement may provide adequate maintenance. Consequently, if a court is to be able to ensure that proper financial provision is made for the members of the family on the breakdown of the marriage, it must have power to deal with capital as well as income —in other words, to order the transfer and settlement of property and the variation of settlements as well as the payment of money.

---

[2] See *post*, pp. 422, n.[1], and 452, and also p. 393 (occupation of the matrimonial home).
[3] Law Com. No. 25, para. 78.
[4] See *post*, pp. 458-459.

It is proposed to consider these subjects in the following order:

Rights in property created and affected by the relationship of husband and wife;

Financial provision for the spouses on the breakdown of the marriage;

Rights in property affected by the relationship of parent and child and financial provision for children;

Property and maintenance on the death of a member of the family.

CHAPTER 14

Rights in Property Created and Affected by the Relationship of Husband and Wife

A. HISTORICAL INTRODUCTION

During the last century legislation has considerably simplified the law of property as it is affected by the relationship of husband and wife. But since this branch of the law shows the development of the status of the wife from a subservient member of the family to the co-equal head of it more clearly than any other (except possibly the parents' rights with respect to their children), we shall start with a brief historical conspectus of the effects of coverture upon rights in property.[1]

I. COMMON LAW

Freeholds.—The highly technical nature of the common law relating to real property is well reflected in the effects which coverture produced.

The Husband's Interest in his Wife's Freeholds.—It was not unnatural that the medieval law should look to the husband rather than to the wife for the performance of the feudal dues which arose from freehold tenure. By marriage a husband gained seisin of all freehold lands which his wife held at the time of the marriage or acquired during coverture and was entitled to the rents and profits of them. If he predeceased the wife, she immediately resumed the right to all her freeholds; if she predeceased him, her estates of inheritance descended to her heir subject to the husband's right to retain seisin as tenant by the curtesy of England. This arose if the husband had issue born alive by the wife which was *capable* of inheriting her freeholds,[2] in which case he was

---

[1]For further details and authorities reference must be made to the editions of standard works on real and personal property and equity published during the nineteenth and early twentieth centuries. The classic exposition of the common law position is to be found in Blackstone's *Commentaries*, vol. ii. See also Dicey, *Law and Opinion*, 2nd Ed., 371-395.

[2]Hence if the wife were tenant in tail female, the birth of a son would not give the husband curtesy. Once the child was born alive, it was immaterial that it did not survive. See further Farrer, *Tenant by the Curtesy of England*, 43 L.Q.R. 87.

entitled as tenant by the curtesy to an estate for his life in all her free-holds of inheritance to which on her death she was entitled in possession otherwise than as a joint tenant.

The wife had no power to dispose of her realty at all during coverture,[3] and the husband alone could not dispose of it for more than his own interest. But together they could dispose of the whole estate. This was done by both spouses' levying a fine, when the court would examine the wife separately in order to ensure that her consent had been freely given. After the Fines and Recoveries Act 1833 the disposition was effected by deed which had to be separately acknow-ledged by the wife before a judge or commissioners who still had to examine her.[4]

The Wife's Interest in her Husband's Freeholds.—During coverture the wife took no interest in her husband's realty at all, but, if she survived him, she became entitled by virtue of her dower to an estate for life in a third of all her husband's freeholds of inheritance of which he had been seised in possession (otherwise than as a joint tenant) *at any time during coverture* provided that she *could* have borne a child capable of inheriting, whether such a child was ever born or not.[5] Since dower created a legal estate, it attached even though the husband alienated the land, and it could be barred only by the wife's levying a fine. The practical inconvenience of this is obvious, so much so that the Statute of Uses enacted that dower could be barred by making a jointure in favour of the wife[6] and conveyancers went to great lengths to ensure that a husband should never be solely seised of an estate of inheritance in possession.[7] These difficulties were eventually obviated by the Dower Act of 1833, which provided that dower should not attach to any land which the husband disposed of during his life-time or by will and that the wife's right to dower out of his estates of inheritance in respect of which he died intestate should be barred if he made a declaration to this effect by deed or will. As a *quid pro quo* the Act gave the wife dower in her husband's equitable freeholds in respect of which he died intestate, if he had not barred her right by declaration.

Tenancy by Entireties.—The doctrine of unity of legal personality produced another striking consequence in the law of property.[8] If

---

[3]But even at common law she could exercise a power of appointment given to her without her husband's concurrence.

[4]The necessity of acknowledgment was abolished by the Law of Property Act 1925, s. 167.

[5]Hence if land were limited to H and the heirs of his body by his wife W, and after W's death H married X, X could not claim dower in the land since no child of hers could ever succeed to the tail special.

[6]If the jointure was settled before marriage, the dower was barred absolutely; if it was settled after marriage, the wife could elect between her jointure and her dower.

[7]The usual way of doing this was to vest a life estate in the husband until forfeiture, with remainder to trustees for the rest of the husband's life, with remainder to the husband's heirs. Although the trustees' estate would rarely vest in possession, it was a vested remainder and therefore prevented the husband's life estate from merging with his fee simple in remainder.

[8]Another consequence was that at common law there could be no conveyance between spouses. After the passing of the Statute of Uses in 1535, this difficulty was overcome by a grant to feoffees to the use of the other spouse.

land were granted to a husband and wife and their heirs, they were said to take by entireties and received an interest which could not be turned into a tenancy in common by severance. Hence, unless they disposed of the estate during coverture, the survivor was bound to take the whole. Similarly, if land were granted in fee simple to a husband, his wife and a third person, the spouses were regarded as one person and consequently they were entitled to only one half of the rents and profits and the third person was entitled to the other half.

Copyholds.—As a general rule the law relating to copyholds was the same as that relating to freeholds. But the husband did not take as tenant by the curtesy unless there was a custom of the manor to that effect, and a widow's interest in her deceased husband's copyhold land was known as her freebench. The exact nature of this varied from place to place and sometimes gave her an interest in the whole of her husband's copyholds and sometimes only in a third. But it usually attached only to that land which he had neither devised nor alienated in his lifetime and consequently did not give rise to the same difficulties as dower. Freebench was unaffected by the Dower Act.

Leaseholds.—The wife's leaseholds belonged to the husband during coverture and he therefore had the absolute power to dispose of them *inter vivos.* If the wife predeceased him, he took the whole of the balance of the term *jure mariti;* but if he predeceased the wife, her leaseholds automatically reverted to her and the husband had no power to dispose of them by will.

Pure Personalty.—All choses in possession belonging to the wife at the time of the marriage or acquired by her during coverture vested absolutely in the husband who therefore had the power to dispose of them *inter vivos* or by will. Even if he died intestate during the wife's life, they did not revert to her. The only exception to this rule applied to the wife's paraphernalia, that is those articles of apparel and personal ornament which were suitable to her rank and degree. Whilst the husband could dispose of these during his lifetime and the wife could alienate them neither *inter vivos* nor by will during coverture, nevertheless the husband could not deprive her of them by bequest and on his death they became her property and did not form a part of his estate.[9]

The wife's choses in action belonged to the husband if he reduced them into possession or obtained judgment in respect of them during coverture. If he died before this was done, the right of action survived to the wife; if she predeceased him, he could sue by taking out letters of administration.[10] It follows that if the chose in action was reversionary, the husband would not be entitled to it if he died before it fell into possession leaving his wife surviving him.

Fraud on the Husband's Marital Rights.—A contract to marry clearly gave the husband an expectant interest in all his wife's property

---

[9] Unless the husband's estate was insolvent, in which case his creditors could take the wife's paraphernalia in satisfaction but not her necessary clothing.
[10] See *ante*, pp. 118 and 124-125.

—an interest in return for which he would of course on marriage be liable to maintain her and would be saddled with the liability for all her ante-nuptial torts and contracts.[11]   Consequently the rule developed that any disposition made by an engaged woman without her fiancé's consent was voidable by him as a fraud on his marital rights.   Since it was voidable only, it could not be set aside against a *bona fide* purchaser for value without notice of the engagement.

2. EQUITY

As a general rule equity followed the law. Thus the husband had the same rights over his wife's equitable freeholds and leaseholds and her equitable interests in pure personalty and the same power to dispose of them (subject to her concurrence in the case of her freeholds) as he had in respect of her legal estates and interests.[12]   In only one case was there a marked difference: whilst the husband was entitled to a life interest in his deceased wife's equitable freeholds as tenant by the curtesy, the wife was not entitled to dower in her deceased husband's equitable freeholds until the passing of the Dower Act in 1833.[13]

The Wife's Equity to a Settlement.—The husband's right to his wife's equitable interests in property was indefeasible once he had got possession of it, as would be the case, for example, if a trustee paid over the trust fund or an executor paid over a legacy. But if the husband was obliged to invoke the aid of Chancery to obtain the property, the court applied the maxim " He who seeks equity must do equity " and, if the property was such that the husband would have an absolute power to dispose of it, it would lend him its assistance only on condition that he settled an adequate part of it on his wife and children for their maintenance.[14]   This " equity to a settlement " was personal to the wife and she could compromise her claim to it, but once the order had been made, it took priority over any assignment made by the husband and the claims of his creditors.   In order to prevent the husband and trustee from acting together so as to defeat the wife's equity, it was eventually held that she might bring an action herself to enforce her right before the fund was paid over.

Assignment of Choses in Action.—In equity the husband alone had the right to assign any chose in action, legal or equitable, vested in the wife, subject to her equity to a settlement. But, as we have already seen, his interest in her reversionary choses in action was contingent, and consequently, since she had no power to assign, it was impossible for the spouses even jointly to make an absolute assignment

---

[11]See *ante*, pp. 118 and 124.

[12]A power of appointment given to a married woman could be exercised without her husband's concurrence.

[13]But then only if he died intestate with respect to them and had not barred her dower: see *ante*, p. 348.

[14]Usually he would be ordered to settle half his interest, but this would clearly depend upon the wife's financial circumstances and on occasion the husband was ordered to settle the whole fund. The husband took the reversionary interest.

of such an interest. This difficulty was removed in 1857 by Malins' Act[15] which enabled her by a deed acknowledged under the Fines and Recoveries Act[16] to concur in any disposition of a future interest in personalty to which she should be entitled under any instrument (other than her marriage settlement) made after 1857 unless it were subject to a restraint upon anticipation. The Act also permitted her in the same way to release and extinguish her equity to a settlement out of personalty in possession.

The Wife's Separate Estate.—But by far the most important contribution of equity to the law relating to a married woman's property was the development of the concept of the separate estate. By the end of the sixteenth century[17] it was established that if property was conveyed to trustees *to the separate use* of a married woman, she retained in equity the same right of holding and disposing of it as if she were a feme sole.[18] This applied whether the interest was in realty or personalty and whether it was in possession or reversion. She could therefore dispose of it *inter vivos* or by will and, like any other beneficiary of full age who was absolutely entitled, she could call upon her trustees to convey the legal estate. Only if she died intestate in respect of her separate estate did the husband obtain the same interest that he would have had in her equitable property had it not been settled to her separate use. Moreover it was finally held that not even the interposition of trustees was necessary, and if property were conveyed, devised or bequeathed to a married woman to her separate use so that the legal estate vested in the husband *jure mariti*, he was deemed in equity to hold it on trust for her and he acquired no greater interest in it than he would have done if it had been conveyed to trustees on similar terms.[19]

The Restraint upon Anticipation.—Whilst separate estate in equity did much to mitigate the harshness of the common law rule, there was still one situation which it did not meet. For there was nothing to prevent a married woman from assigning her beneficial interest to her husband and thus vesting in him the interest which the separate use had sought to keep out of his hands, and the temptation presented to a grasping, spendthrift or insolvent husband was great. To circumvent this, equity developed about 1800 a second concept, complementary to the first, that of the restraint upon anticipation.[20] This could be imposed only if property was conveyed, devised or bequeathed to a woman's separate use, and, once it attached, it prevented her from anticipating and dealing with any income until it actually fell due. A restraint could be and usually was attached to the

---

[15]The Married Women's Reversionary Interests Act 1857.
[16]See *ante*, p. 348.
[17]See Holdsworth, *History of English Law*, v, 310-315.
[18]If property were settled on an unmarried woman to her separate use, it also remained her separate estate after marriage. Hence, if an engaged woman settled her property on herself to her separate use without her fiancé's concurrence, he could have the settlement set aside as a fraud on his marital rights: see *ante*, pp. 349-350.
[19]For the wife's power to bind her separate estate by contract, see *ante*, p. 118.
[20]See Hart, *The Origin of the Restraint upon Anticipation*, 40 L.Q.R. 221.

corpus too, in which case the whole fund became completely inalienable during coverture.

A restraint on anticipation could even be attached to the separate property of an unmarried woman. In this case she could deal with the property as if there were no restraint and could also totally remove the restraint by executing a deed poll to this effect. A woman to whose separate property a restraint had been attached before or during coverture could do the same after the marriage was terminated by her husband's death or by divorce. But in the absence of any such deed, as soon as she married or re-married, the restraint became operative as regards any property not alienated whilst she was a feme sole.

The restraint on anticipation was designed to protect not only the wife but also the members of her family who would be entitled to the property on her death.[1] Whilst it effectively kept the property out of the hands of the husband and his creditors, it had one obvious drawback. There might be a number of occasions on which it might be in the wife's interest to deal with property subject to a restraint, but nothing short of a private Act of Parliament could remove it. It was in order to overcome this difficulty that the Conveyancing Act 1881 gave the court power to bind her interest in such property provided that this was for her benefit.[2] But the court could only render a specific disposition binding and it had no general power to remove the restraint altogether.

3. MODERN LEGISLATION

By the middle of the nineteenth century it was clear that the old rules would have to be reformed. More and more women were earning incomes of their own, either in trade, or on the stage or by writing, and there were a number of scandalous cases of husband's impounding their wive's earnings for the benefit of their own creditors or even mistresses. No relief could be obtained by the woman whose husband deserted her and took all her property with him. The separate use and restraint upon anticipation were clumsy creatures and were in practice unlikely to affect the property of any but the daughters of the rich who would have carefully drawn marriage settlements and would be the beneficiaries under complicated wills. Agitation for reform was discernible in many quarters and eventually produced a series of Acts of ever wider scope.[3]

The Matrimonial Causes Act 1857.—So far as married women's property was concerned, this Act sought to remedy two existing defects in the law only. First, so long as a judicial separation was in force, the wife was now to be deemed to be a feme sole with respect to any property which she should acquire and thus for the first time in the history of English law she had the sole power to dispose of a legal interest either *inter vivos* or by will.[4] If the parties resumed cohabitation, all

---

[1]Kahn-Freund in *Matrimonial Property Law* (ed. Friedmann), 274. For the position in equity generally, see Dicey, *Law and Opinion*, 2nd Ed., 375-382.

[2]S. 39, subsequently replaced by the Conveyancing Act 1911, s. 7, and the Law of Property Act 1925, s. 169.

[3]See Dicey, *op. cit.*, 382-395.

[4]S. 25.

property so acquired was to be held for her separate use. Secondly, if a wife were deserted, she might obtain a protection order which would have the effect of protecting from seizure by her husband and his creditors any property and earnings to which she became entitled after the desertion and of vesting them in her as if she were a feme sole.[5]

The Married Women's Property Act 1870.—As originally conceived, this Act was to anticipate the much wider provisions of the Act of 1882. But the Bill was so cut down in Parliament that in its final form the Act presented no more than a series of exceptions to the common law rule by providing that in a number of specified cases property acquired by the wife (for example, her earnings, deposits in savings banks, stocks and shares, and in very limited circumstances property devolving upon her on an intestacy) should be deemed to be held for her separate use. Moreover certain provisions applied only to women marrying after the passing of the Act. The whole Act was repealed by the Married Women's Property Act of 1882, but it remains of historical importance in that it gave a statutory extension to the existing equitable concept of the separate estate: the device that was later to be used in the Act of 1882.[6]

The Married Women's Property Act 1882.—Historically this Act is the most important of the whole series. It was of universal application, although it did not affect any rights which had vested by marriage before 1883. It provided that any woman marrying after 1882 should be entitled to retain all property owned by her at the time of the marriage as her separate property and that, whenever she was married, any property acquired by a married woman after 1882 should be held by her in the same way.[7] It also enacted that

" A married woman shall . . . be capable of acquiring, holding, and disposing by will or otherwise, of any real or personal property as her separate property, in the same manner as if she were a feme sole, without the intervention of any trustee ".[8]

It further provided that the law relating to restraint upon anticipation should remain unaffected.[9]

The sweeping nature of these changes is obvious. It now became impossible for a married man to acquire any further interest in his wife's property *jure mariti* by operation of law. It immediately rendered obsolete the doctrine of fraud upon a husband's marital rights. Henceforth a widower could claim an interest in his deceased's wife's property acquired after 1882 only if she died intestate with respect to it. The necessity of both spouses' joining in a conveyance of the wife's realty and the provisions of Malins' Act became obsolescent. But in one sense the changes were even more fundamental than these, for whilst the

---

[5] S. 21.
[6] For the effect of the Act of 1870 on spouses' liability in contract and tort and the modification of these provisions by the Married Women's Property Act (1870) Amendment Act 1874, see *ante*, pp. 119 and 125.
[7] Ss. 2 and 5.
[8] S. 1 (1).
[9] S. 19.

statute adapted the equitable concept of separate property,[10] it went further by vesting in the wife the *legal* interest in her property. The detailed provisions of the Act are too complex to be considered here,[11] but subject to the restraint on anticipation a married woman's capacity to hold and dispose of property was very nearly the same as that of a feme sole.

The Married Women's Property Acts 1884, 1893, 1907 and 1908. —These four Acts effected no change of principle but were passed to clear up a number of difficulties and ambiguities in the Act of 1882 and to fill one or two gaps which this Act had left.

The Property Legislation of 1925.—This legislation only incidentally affected rights in property of spouses as such. Its most important effect in this field lay in the changed rules of succession on an intestacy;[12] in particular dower and freebench[13] were abolished and the husband's right to his wife's freeholds as tenant by the curtesy is now limited to the case where she is a tenant in tail and has not barred the entail by deed or will.[14] Tenancy by entireties has also been abolished, so that a grant to a husband, his wife and a third person will now give each of them a third interest in the property.[15]

The Law Reform (Married Women and Tortfeasors) Act 1935.—By 1935 almost all married women's property was owned by them as their separate property. To speak of " separate property " therefore was becoming something of an anomaly, since married women in almost all cases had the same capacity to hold and dispose of it as a man or a feme sole. This was eventually recognised by the Legislature in the Law Reform (Married Women and Tortfeasors) Act of that year which abolished the concept of the separate estate and gave to the wife the same rights and powers as were already possessed by other adults of full capacity. It provided:[16]

" . . . A married woman shall be capable of acquiring, holding, and disposing of, any property . . . in all respects as if she were a feme sole.

" . . . All property which—

(a) immediately before the passing of this Act was the separate property of a married woman or held for her separate use in equity; *or*

---

[10]Hence, for example, a married woman still could not be made bankrupt unless she came within the express provisions of s. 1 (5) by carrying on a trade separately from her husband: see *ante*, p. 119.

[11]Amongst them are spouses' liability in contract (see *ante*, p. 119), tort (*ante*, p. 125) and criminal law (*ante*, p. 129), claims in bankruptcy (*post*, p. 371), policies of insurance in favour of a spouse or children (*post*, pp. 372-373), and disputes over property arising between spouses (*post*, pp. 357-359).

[12]See *post*, pp. 502 *et seq.*

[13]Copyhold tenure was emancipated and converted into freehold tenure by the Law of Property Act 1922.

[14]Administration of Estates Act 1925, s. 45. Although this section does not apply to entailed interests, the Act repealed the Dower Act which gave the wife the right to dower in her husband's equitable freeholds. It thus entirely abolished dower, as a fee tail can now exist only as an equitable interest. There may also be curtesy in certain circumstances of the wife's determinable fee simple: Farrer, *Tenant by the Curtesy of England*, 43 L.Q.R. 87, at pp. 100-102.

[15]Law of Property Act 1925, s. 37. After 1882 the spouses could sever their half share as *between themselves* they took as ordinary joint tenants.

[16]Ss. 1 (a) and 2 (1).

(b) belongs at the time of her marriage to a woman married after the passing of this Act; *or*

(c) after the passing of this Act is acquired by or devolves upon a married woman,

shall belong to her in all respects as if she were a feme sole and may be disposed of accordingly."

The Act did not affect any rights in property which had accrued as the result of a marriage before 1883[17] nor did it touch any existing restraint on anticipation.[18] But it sounded the death knell of the latter, for it rendered void any attempted imposition of a restraint on anticipation in any instrument executed after 1935 and in the will of any person dying after 1945, even though it was executed before 1936.[19]

The Married Women (Restraint upon Anticipation) Act 1949.—Although after 1945 restraint upon anticipation was bound to disappear in the course of time, the Act of 1935 did not affect the validity of restraints already imposed. Whilst in 1882 it was apparently still necessary to protect a married woman's property in this way, the restraint could no longer be justified in the middle of the present century, when it served no further purpose but merely acted as an undue fetter on the wife's powers of alienation. Although the court could sanction individual dispositions if these were for her benefit,[20] the only way in which a restraint could be wholly removed was by a private Act of Parliament. It was the presentation of a bill for this purpose that ultimately led to the passing of the Married Women (Restraint upon Anticipation) Act in 1949, which removed all restraints whenever imposed and thus rendered the property to which they were attached freely alienable.

B. THE MODERN LAW

I. GENERAL PRINCIPLES

The Effect of the Married Women's Property Acts.—By extending the equitable principle of the separate estate, the Married Women's Property Acts replaced the total incapacity of a married woman to hold property at common law by a rigid doctrine of separate property. In the well known words of DICEY,[1] "the rules of equity, framed for the daughters of the rich, have at last been extended to the daughters of the poor". But, as PROFESSOR KAHN-FREUND has shown,[2] the effects of the Acts were much wider than this. Spouses' property may be broadly divided into two types: that intended for common use and consumption in the matrimonial home and that intended for personal use and enjoyment. The latter is often in the

[17]S. 4 (1) (a).
[18]S. 2 (1).
[19]S. 2 (2), (3).
[20]See *ante*, p. 352. If the restraint were attached to land, the woman could sell the land under the provisions of the Settled Land Act, but the restraint continued to attach to the capital.
[1]*Law and Opinion*, 2nd Ed., 395.
[2]In *Matrimonial Property Law* (ed. Friedmann), 267 *et seq*. See also his article, *Recent Legislation on Matrimonial Property*, 33 M.L.R. 601.

form of investments or derived from the interest on investments, and it is obvious that, whilst in a poor family almost the whole of the property will fall into the first category, the richer the spouses the greater fraction of their property will fall into the second. Before 1883 the matrimonial home and its contents would almost invariably be vested in the husband to the exclusion of the wife, and the latter's separate property did little more than protect her investments. But, impelled by a movement which was ultimately to secure the almost complete legal equality of the sexes, Parliament extended the doctrine of separation to property forming the matrimonial home as well—a situation which the equitable concept was never intended to cover and with which it was ill adapted to deal.

This was inevitably bound to produce difficulties. But so long as the husband remained the bread winner, they were not acute, as it could still be argued that he retained the ownership of property bought out of his earnings. But during the Second World War most married women were wage earners as well, and what before 1939 had been something of an exception has now become the usual situation in most families, at least during the early years of married life. To apply the strict doctrine of separate property to matrimonial assets in such circumstances is manifestly absurd. As a result, judges have sought to adapt the principle by regarding both the spouses as having an interest in the matrimonial home in many cases, even though the legal estate is vested solely in the husband. Legislation has also been passed to overcome some difficulties, particularly with respect to the occupation of the matrimonial home.

Doctrines effecting such radical changes are bound to bristle with difficulties. Whilst clear patterns seem to emerge from time to time in decided cases, they are liable to be suddenly obscured by a new case out of line with recent trends. The real trouble is that such legislation as there has been during this century has merely sought to tackle isolated problems and marked differences of opinion amongst the judges have been reflected in confusing and sometimes contradictory decisions. It is clear that only a complete statutory overhaul of the whole field of matrimonial property law can now produce a rational system and the time is ripe for such legislation.[3]

It may be helpful to start by considering the various means of solving the legal problems that may arise.

Issues between the Spouses.—Two questions arise here: in whom are the legal and equitable interests in the property vested and what rights short of ownership may one spouse have in the property of the other? So long as they are living amicably together, these questions

---

[3]The Law Commission is actively considering the question at the time of writing (April, 1971). See also the Report of the Morton Commission, Cmd. 9678, Part IX; Simon, " *With all my Worldly Goods . . .* " (published by the Holdsworth Club of the University of Birmingham). For discussion of some foreign systems, comparison with which is interesting and profitable, see *Matrimonial Property Law* (ed. Friedmann); Milner, *A Homestead Act for England*, 22 M.L.R. 458; Tarlo, *Possession of the Matrimonial Home in Australia*, 22 M.L.R. 479; Górecki, *Matrimonial Property in Poland*, 26 M.L.R. 156; Pedersen, *Matrimonial Property Law in Denmark*, 28 M.L.R. 137; Johnson, *Matrimonial Property in Soviet Law*, 16 I.C.L.Q. 1106.

never have to be answered, and they become vital only if the marriage breaks down. This adds considerably to the difficulty, for the parties rarely contemplate the collapse of the marriage when they acquire property, and their respective rights in it are never discussed, let alone defined. Hence the courts are faced with the problem of having to impute to them an intention which they never possessed at all.[4]

There are three different ways of solving disputes open to the spouses.

Action for Damages in Tort.—As we have already seen,[5] either spouse may now protect his or her interests in property by suing the other in tort, for example in trespass, detinue or conversion. Either may also bring an action against the other for the recovery of land. In this connection it should be remembered that if the spouses are jointly in possession of property or are jointly entitled to possession, one may be liable in trespass if he or she completely ousts the other or in conversion if he or she completely destroys the property.[6]

It will be recalled that the court may stay the action if the questions in issue could be disposed of more conveniently by an application under section 17 of the Married Women's Property Act 1882.[7]

Proceedings for an Injunction.—Either spouse may obtain an injunction to prevent the other from committing a continuing or threatened wrong against the plaintiff's property.[8] In practice this remedy is most frequently sought when the wife is trying to exclude the husband from entering the matrimonial home, and the particular problems that arise here will be dealt with later.[9]

Proceedings under Section 17 of the Married Women's Property Act 1882.—This section[10] provides that " in any question between husband and wife as to the title to or possession of property "[11] either of them may apply for an order to the High Court or a county court and the judge " may make such order with respect to the property in

---

[4]*Cf. Re Rogers' Question,* [1948] 1 All E.R. 328, C.A.; *Cobb* v. *Cobb,* [1955] 2 All E.R. 696, 699, C.A.

[5]*Ante,* p. 126.

[6]Salmond, *Torts,* 15th Ed., 60, 143; Street *Torts,* 4th Ed., 53; Derham, *Conversion by Wrongful Disposal as between Co-owners,* 68 L.Q.R. 507.

[7]*Ante,* pp. 126-127. For proceedings under s. 17, see *infra.*

[8]This may be done either by bringing an action in tort under the Law Reform (Husband and Wife) Act 1962 or by way of ancillary relief in other matrimonial proceedings.

[9]*Post,* pp. 387 *et seq.*

[10]Replacing and extending the Married Women's Property Act 1870, s. 9. The section has been amended by the Law Reform (Husband and Wife) Act 1962, Sched., (repealing s. 23 of the Act of 1882) and the Statute Law (Repeals) Act 1969, Sched. Part III, which have taken away the power of a deceased wife's personal representatives and of banks, companies and other bodies to take proceedings under s. 17.

[11]Including choses in action (*Spellman* v. *Spellman,* [1961] 2 All E.R. 498, 501, C.A.) and property of which the claimant is a bare trustee and in which he has no beneficial interest at all (*Re Knight's Question,* [1958] 1 All E.R. 812; [1959] Ch. 381). If there is no question as to title or possession but one spouse is, *e.g.,* seeking to enforce a trust for sale against the other, proceedings under s. 17 are inappropriate and the same proceedings should be taken as would be taken between strangers: *Rawlings* v. *Rawlings,* [1964] 2 All E.R. 804, C.A.; [1964] P. 398.

dispute . . . as he thinks fit ".[12] These proceedings are of course usually invoked when the marriage has broken down. Disputes over rights in property may still be going on after the marriage has been legally terminated, and consequently section 17 has now been extended to enable former spouses to make an application for a period of three years after a decree absolute of divorce or nullity.[13] Similarly, engaged couples may well buy furniture and start to buy a house in contemplation of their marriage, and this may give them rights in property which are virtually indistinguishable from those acquired by married couples. The abolition of actions for damages for breach of promise of marriage deprived them of the means of recovering the expenses they had lost if the marriage did not take place. Consequently the summary procedure of section 17 has now been made available to the parties to an agreement to marry which has been terminated as well. An application must relate to property in which either or both of them had an interest while the agreement was in force and must be brought within three years of the termination of the agreement.[14]

It will be seen that the court has jurisdiction to determine questions of title and possession. In order that it may do this, it was formerly held that there must be in existence specific property or a specific fund with respect to which the order might be made and that if the property or fund had ceased to exist, there was no power to make what would be in effect an order for damages for trespass, conversion or debt.[15] This clearly worked injustice if the defendant had already disposed of the property or fund in question; this has been remedied by section 7 of the Matrimonial Causes (Property and Maintenance) Act 1958, which has given the court power in such a case either to order the defendant to pay to the plaintiff such sum of money as represents the latter's interest in the property or fund or to make an order with respect to any other property which now represents the whole or part of the original.[16]

For some years there was considerable judicial controversy over the width of the powers which the wording of the section gave to the judges. It was, however, finally settled by the House of Lords in *Pettitt* v. *Pettitt*[17] that the court has no jurisdiction under this section to vary existing titles and no wider power to transfer or create interests in property than it would have in any other type of proceedings. At the most it has, in the words of LORD DIPLOCK, " a wide discretion as to

---

[12]Proceedings in the High Court are now assigned to the Family Division. The county court has jurisdiction whatever the value of the property, but if this exceeds the normal statutory maximum of the court's jurisdiction, the defendant may have the case transferred to the High Court: s. 17.

[13]Matrimonial Proceedings and Property Act 1970, s. 39.

[14]Law Reform (Miscellaneous Provisions) Act 1970, s. 2 (2). For the abolition of actions for breach of promise, see *ante*, p. 13, and also see generally Law Com. No. 26 (Breach of Promise of Marriage).

[15]*Tunstall* v. *Tunstall*, [1953] 2 All E.R. 310, C.A.

[16]But a specific property or fund must have been in existence originally and proceedings cannot be brought under s. 17 for the recovery of a debt: *Crystall* v. *Crystall*, [1963] 2 All E.R. 330, C.A. The Limitation Act has been held not to apply to such proceedings and consequently an order may be made even though the property was disposed of more than six years earlier: *Spoor* v. *Spoor*, [1966] 3 All E.R. 120.

[17][1969] 2 All E.R. 385, H.L.; [1970] A.C. 777.

the enforcement of the proprietary or possessory rights of one spouse in any property against the other ".[18] Furthermore, the fact that the marriage has broken down, the circumstances of the breakdown and the conduct of the parties cannot affect title in the absence of an agreement between the spouses and are therefore all irrelevant to the outcome of proceedings brought under section 17.[19] But there are clearly two types of case in which the court will still have a wide discretion. In the first place, the spouses' rights may not be precisely defined: for example, they may both have contributed to the purchase of the matrimonial home, so that they both have a beneficial interest in it, but there may be no agreement over the size of their shares. In such a case the court can usually ensure that justice is done by ordering the interest to be divided in such proportions as it thinks fit. Secondly, by using its powers to make different types of orders, the court may effectively control the way in which the property is used without departing from the principle that it cannot alter the title. Thus it may order a spouse to give up possession of a house, to deliver up chattels, to transfer shares and other choses in action or to pay over a specific fund, and it may even forbid him to dispossess the other spouse or to deal with the property in any way inconsistent with the other's rights.[20] Similarly the court may order the property to be sold and direct how the proceeds of sale are to be divided.[1]

Issues between one of the Spouses and a Stranger.—The question to be considered here is how far rights in property created or affected by marriage can be enforced by one of the spouses against a third person. The latter may claim in one of a number of capacities, for example as a purchaser for value from the other spouse, as the other's creditor or trustee in bankruptcy, or as a beneficiary entitled to a deceased spouse's estate. It is essential to decide first what rights the claiming spouse has against the other spouse and then how far these rights are enforceable against the third person. This will depend upon the application of general principles of the law of property and in particular the nature of the latter's title. If he is, say, the husband's donee, the wife may enforce against him all those rights (other than purely personal rights) which she would have against her husband; if he is a purchaser for value, then he will take the property subject to the wife's legal rights and will be bound by her equitable interests unless he purchased in good faith and without notice of them.

2. PROPERTY ACQUIRED BY THE SPOUSES

Property owned by the Spouses at the Time of the Marriage.—Presumptively marriage will not affect the ownership of property vested in either of the spouses at the time. This will also be true of property

---

[18]At pp. 411 and 820, respectively.

[19]*Pettitt* v. *Pettitt*, (*supra*).

[20]As in *Lee* v. *Lee*, [1952] 1 All E.R. 1299, C.A.; [1952] 2 Q.B. 489 *n.* In *Re Bettinson's Question*, [1955] 3 All E.R. 296; [1956] Ch. 67, it was held that an order could be made with respect to property which was subject to the doctrine of community of property under the law of the parties' domicile (California).

[1]Matrimonial Causes (Property and Maintenance) Act 1958, s. 7 (7).

which is used by them jointly in the matrimonial home (for example, furniture) in the absence of an express gift of a joint interest in law or in equity.[2]

Income.—The income of either spouse, whether from earnings or from investments, will *prima facie* remain his or her own property.[3] But where the spouses pool their incomes and place them into a common fund, it seems that they both acquire a joint interest in the whole fund.

This occurred in *Jones* v. *Maynard*.[4] In 1941 the husband, who was about to go abroad with the R.A.F., authorised his wife to draw on his bank account, which was thereafter treated as a joint account. Into this account were paid dividends on both the husband's and the wife's investments, the husband's pay and allowances and rent from the matrimonial home which was their joint property and which had been let during the War. The husband's contributions were greater than the wife's; the spouses had never agreed on what their rights in this fund were to be, but they regarded it as their joint savings to be invested from time to time. The husband withdrew money on a number of occasions and invested it in his own name, and finally, after the spouses had separated in 1946, he closed the account altogether. The marriage was later dissolved and the plaintiff sued her former husband for a half share in the account as it stood on the day it was closed and in the investments which he had previously purchased out of it. VAISEY, J., held that the claim must succeed. He said:[5]

> " In my judgment, when there is a joint account between husband and wife, a common pool into which they put all their resources, it is not consistent with that conception that the account should thereafter . . . be picked apart, and divided up proportionately to the respective contributions of husband and wife, the husband being credited with the whole of his earnings and the wife with the whole of her dividends. I do not believe that, when once the joint pool has been formed, it ought to be, and can be, dissected in any such manner. In my view a husband's earnings or salary, when the spouses have a common purse and pool their resources, are earnings made on behalf of both; and the idea that years afterwards the contents of the pool can be dissected by taking an elaborate account as to how much was paid in by the husband or the wife is quite inconsistent with the original fundamental idea of a joint purse or common pool.
> " In my view the money which goes into the pool becomes joint property. The husband, if he wants a suit of clothes, draws a cheque to pay for it. The wife, if she wants any housekeeping money, draws a cheque, and there is no disagreement about it."

---

[2] Since the cases indicate that a joint interest will not be created unless both have contributed in some way to the purchase, in which case they will probably already own the property jointly before marriage: see *post*, p. 378. For the effect of the subsequent acquisition of an English domicile by parties whose original *lex domicilii* imposed on them the doctrine of community of property, see *De Nicols* v. *Curlier*, [1900] A.C. 21, H.L.; for the converse case of the parties' acquiring a foreign domicile after the marriage, see *Re Egerton's Will Trusts*, [1956] 2 All E.R. 817; [1956] Ch. 593. See also Stone, *The Matrimonial Domicile and the Property Relations of Married Persons*, 6 I.C.L.Q. 28; Goldberg, *The Assignment of Property on Marriage*, 19 I.C.L.Q. 557.

[3] *Cf. Dixon* v. *Dixon* (1878), 9 Ch.D. 587 (stock settled to the wife's separate use); *Barrack* v. *M'Culloch* (1856), 3 K. & J. 110 (rents from houses settled to the wife's separate use); *Heseltine* v. *Heseltine*, [1971] 1 All E.R. 952 (income from wife's investments).

[4] [1951] 1 All E.R. 802; [1951] Ch. 572.

[5] At pp. 803 and 575, respectively.

What, then, constitutes a " common purse "? It would seem on principle to be essential that there must be a fund intended for the use of both spouses from which either may withdraw money and this will normally take the form of a joint bank account. Where they both contribute to this fund, as in *Jones* v. *Maynard*, it is submitted that this intention will be imputed to the parties in the absence of any other agreement; where, however, the fund is derived from the income of one spouse alone, it is a question of fact whether this is to remain his or her exclusive property or whether there is an intention to establish a common fund. If the husband is the sole contributor to a joint account, the presumption of advancement will operate so as to give the wife a *prima facie* interest in it;[6] on the other hand the presumption will be rebutted if, for example, it can be shown that the power to draw on the account was given for the husband's convenience by enabling the wife to draw cheques for the payment of housekeeping expenses.[7] Even though the beneficial interest in a joint account is initially vested in one spouse alone, his or her intention may change and it may be converted into a joint interest.[8] The courts will doubtless tend to find a joint beneficial interest today much more readily than they did in the past.

If either spouse withdraws money from the common purse, property bought with it will *prima facie* belong solely to that spouse and not to both jointly. Where the property is for personal use (for example, clothes), this presumption will not normally be rebuttable; in the case of investments it could be rebutted if it were clear that they were still intended to represent the original fund. In *Re Bishop*[9] large sums had been withdrawn by both spouses to purchase investments in their separate names. In many cases blocks of shares were bought and half put in one name and the other half put in the other; other money was spent in taking up shares offered to the husband by virtue of rights which he possessed as an existing shareholder in the companies concerned. In these circumstances STAMP, J., had no difficulty in holding that the presumption could not be rebutted and that the spouse in whose name the shares had been purchased was entitled to the whole beneficial interest in them. He distinguished *Jones* v. *Maynard* where VAISEY, J., had held that the husband was to be regarded as trustee for them both of investments which he had purchased, for in that case they had agreed that when there had been a sufficient accumulation the money should be invested and that that was to be their savings.

Like any other joint interest the balance of the fund will accrue to

---

[6] *Re Figgis*, [1968] 1 All E.R. 999; [1969] 1 Ch. 123. Conversely, if the wife is the sole contributor, she will *prima facie* take the whole beneficial interest; *Heseltine* v. *Heseltine*, (*ante*) (houses purchased by husband out of joint account provided by wife's money held to belong to her absolutely). Although the effect of these presumptions is considerably weaker today than it used to be (see *post*, p. 364), they will still operate in a case like *Re Figgis* where both spouses are dead, and there is virtually no direct evidence of the parties' intentions at all.
[7] *Marshal* v. *Crutwell* (1875), L.R. 20 Eq. 328; *Hoddinott* v. *Hoddinott*, [1949] 2 K.B. 406, 413, C.A.; *Harrods, Ltd.* v. *Tester*, [1937] 2 All E.R. 236, C.A. (where the whole of the balance of a bank account opened by the husband in the wife's name was held to belong to the husband).
[8] *Re Figgis*, (*supra*), at pp. 1011 and 145, respectively.
[9] [1965] 1 All E.R. 249; [1965] Ch. 450.

the survivor on the death of either spouse as it did in *Re Bishop*. It can of course be severed by agreement or assignment in the lifetime of both; in such a case or where, as in *Jones* v. *Maynard*, the marriage breaks down and the court is asked to effect a partition, then, as we have seen from the passage of VAISEY, J.'s judgment quoted above, the spouses will hold the balance of the fund as tenants in common in equal shares.[10]

Allowances for Housekeeping and Maintenance.—This question is obviously closely allied to the last and the same principles were applied. Hence it was consistently held that if a husband supplied his wife with a housekeeping allowance out of his own income, any balance and any property bought with the allowance *prima facie* remained his property.[11] This might well work an injustice for it took no account of the fact that any savings from the housekeeping money were as much due to the wife's skill and economy as a housewife as to her husband's earning capacity.[12] It was to remedy this that the Married Women's Property Act 1964 was passed. Section 1 provides:

> " If any question arises as to the right of a husband or wife to money derived from any allowance made by the husband for the expenses of the matrimonial home or for similar purposes, or to any property acquired out of such money, the money or property shall, in the absence of any agreement between them to the contrary, be treated as belonging to the husband and wife in equal shares."

In the first place it should be noted that the Act applies only if the allowance is provided by the husband; it does not apply to the case (admittedly rare but not entirely unknown) where the wife goes out to work to support an invalid husband who does the housekeeping. In such a case the allowance and any property bought with it presumably remain the wife's.[13] Secondly, it is not clear what the phrase " expenses of the matrimonial home or similar purposes " covers. If, for example, a husband gives his wife money to pay off instalments of the mortgage on the matrimonial home, she may well be regarded as no more than his agent and thus acquire no interest in the house; but if he gives her a housekeeping allowance out of which it is intended that she should pay the instalments, it is arguable that the term " expenses of the matrimonial home " is wide enough to include the purchase of it so that the section gives her a half share in the fraction represented by each payment.[14] If the allowance is made for this purpose, however,

---

[10]*Cf. post*, p. 382.

[11] *Blackwell* v. *Blackwell*, [1943] 2 All E.R. 579, C.A.; *Hoddinott* v. *Hoddinott*, [1949] 2 K.B. 406, C.A.

[12]See the judgments of DENNING, L.J., in *Hoddinott* v. *Hoddinott*, (*supra*), at p. 416, and *Rimmer* v. *Rimmer*, [1952] 2 All E.R. 863, 868-869, C.A.; [1953] 1 Q.B. 63, 74.

[13]Earlier cases indicate that if the wife gives money to her husband for use in the home, she is deemed to give it to him as head of the family and the money therefore becomes his: see, *e.g.*, *Edward* v. *Cheyne* (*No. 2*) (1888), 13 App. Cas. 385, H.L.; *Re Young* (1913), 29 T.L.R. 319 (where the presumption was rebutted on the facts). But it is very doubtful whether the courts would take such a view today. The Morton Commission recommended that the allowance should belong to both spouses equally, whichever of them provided it: Cmd. 9678, para. 701.

[14]See the conflicting views in *Tymoszczuk* v. *Tymoszczuk* (1964), 108 Sol. Jo. 676, and *Re Johns' Assignment Trusts*, [1970] 2 All E.R. 210, 213.

the rule applies not only to the money but also to any property bought with it. Hence, if the wife were to buy furniture with the housekeeping savings, this would presumptively belong to her and her husband equally. This can be rebutted by proof of an express agreement between the spouses; what is not clear is whether the courts will be prepared to spell out an implied agreement when the circumstances demand it. If the wife uses part of the allowance to buy clothes for herself, it seems absurd that a half share of them should belong to the husband; can it be argued that there must be a tacit agreement that the whole should belong to the wife?[15]

Two further weaknesses may be seen in the Act. First, the money or property is to be treated as belonging to the spouses in equal shares. Consequently on the death of one the whole beneficial interest will not automatically pass to the survivor (as it does in the case of the "common purse ")[16] but half will go to the personal representatives of the other. It is highly doubtful whether this is what the spouses will want or expect. In their desire to remedy the injustice caused by earlier cases where the marriage had broken down, the promoters of the Bill apparently overlooked the obvious fact that most marriages survive and that, whilst a joint interest can always be severed by the unilateral act of one party, it requires the conscious act of both to turn a tenancy in common into a joint tenancy. Neither this rule nor its consequences will be known to the vast majority of spouses and it is not inconceivable that a half share of furniture will inadvertently pass under a residuary bequest. Secondly, it is not clear whether the Act is to have retrospective effect. As there is no clear intention to affect vested rights, it is submitted that money and property belonging to the husband when the Act came into force[17] should remain his. Obviously in the course of time it will be forgotten when particular pieces of property were bought and it will become impossible to divide the balance of the fund into that which was provided before the operative date and that which was provided afterwards, so that the courts will probably be forced to hold that the Act does have retrospective effect. This can potentially work as much injustice as it avoids.

Property purchased by one Spouse.—Any property purchased by one spouse with his or her own money will presumptively belong exclusively to the purchaser. Property bought out of money coming from the " common purse" will also presumptively belong to the purchaser except for investments representing joint savings which will remain part of the spouses' joint property.[18]

But this presumption is obviously rebuttable. Thus property bought

---

[15]Perhaps a more difficult case would arise if the wife bought herself an expensive piece of jewellery. In the case of a " common purse " contributed to by both the property would belong to the wife exclusively: see *ante*, p. 361.

[16]See *ante*, pp. 361-362.

[17]25th March, 1964. This view seems to have commended itself to GOFF, J., in *Re Johns' Assignment Trusts*, (*supra*), at p. 213. The opposite view was taken by Master JACOB in *Tymoszczuk* v. *Tymoszczuk*, (*supra*), on the ground that the Act creates a presumption and therefore changes adjective law. For further difficulties that may arise, see Stone, 27 M.L.R. 576.

[18]See *ante*, p. 361.

by one spouse as a gift for the other will become the donee's. Hence if a husband buys clothes for his wife or gives her money to buy them for herself, they become her property,[19] and the same rule will *prima facie* apply in any other case where goods are bought for the other's personal use.[20]

Difficulties can arise if one spouse buys property with his own money and has it conveyed into the other's name or into joint names. The courts used to solve the problem by applying two maxims of equity. If the wife provided the purchase money, there was a resulting trust in her favour and the husband (or the spouses jointly if the legal estate was vested in both) was presumed to hold the property in trust for her absolutely. On the other hand, if the husband provided the purchase money, he was presumed to intend a gift to his wife, and the presumption of advancement operated so as *prima facie* to give her the beneficial interest.[21] These presumptions were always rebuttable by evidence that the wife intended a gift in the first case or that the husband intended to keep the beneficial interest in the second.[1] But as the members of the House of Lords agreed in *Pettitt* v. *Pettitt*,[2] they are much less strong today because some explanation of the parties' conduct will usually be available unless they are both dead. LORD DIPLOCK went so far as to question whether they were still valid at all. As he observed, they are no more than a judicial inference of what the spouses' intention most probably was, drawn in cases relating to the propertied classes of the nineteenth and early twentieth century among whom marriage settlements were common and where the wife rarely contributed to the family income by her earnings. As such, they have little significance today when the parties may be legally aided, the wife is working, and their biggest asset, the matrimonial home, is being purchased by means of a mortgage.[3] The particular application of this problem to the purchase of the matrimonial home will be considered later.[4]

---

[19]*Masson, Templier & Co.* v. *De Fries*, [1909] 2 K.B. 831, C.A. Contrast *Rondeau, Le Grand & Co.* v. *Marks*, [1918] 1 K.B 75, C.A., where it had been agreed that they should remain the husband's property.

[20]*Re Whittaker* (1882), 21 Ch.D. 657 (piano).

[21]*Mercier* v. *Mercier*, [1903] 2 Ch. 98, C.A. (presumption of resulting trust for wife); *Silver* v. *Silver*, [1958] 1 All E.R. 523, C.A. (presumption of advancement). Hence if the husband had property conveyed to both spouses and a stranger, all three would hold on trust for the husband and wife jointly: *Re Eykyn's Trusts* (1877), 6 Ch.D. 115. There is a presumption of advancement even though the marriage is *voidable*: *Dunbar* v. *Dunbar*, [1909] 2 Ch. 639; but not if the husband knows it to be *void*, for then there is to his knowledge no duty to maintain: *Soar* v. *Foster* (1858), 4 K. & J. 152. *Quaere* if he does not know it is void. The presumption of advancement is also raised if a man has property conveyed into his fiancée's name: *Moate* v. *Moate*, [1948] 2 All E.R. 486.

[1]The husband may not rebut the presumption by adducing evidence of his own fraudulent or unlawful intention: *Gascoigne* v. *Gascoigne*, [1918] 1 K.B. 223 (defrauding creditors); *Re Emery's Investment Trusts*, [1959] 1 All E.R. 577; [1959] Ch. 410 (evasion of tax in the U.S.A.); *Tinker* v. *Tinker*, [1970] 1 All E.R. 540, C.A.; [1970] P. 136.

[2][1969] 2 All E.R. 385, H.L.; [1970] A.C. 777, at pp. 389 and 793 (*per* LORD REID); 404 and 811 (*per* LORD HODSON); 406-407 and 814-815 (*per* LORD UPJOHN); 414 and 824 (*per* LORD DIPLOCK).

[3]At pp. 414 and 823-824, respectively. See also LORD DENNING, M.R., in *Falconer* v. *Falconer*, [1970] 3 All E.R. 449, 452, C.A.

[4]*Post*, p. 378.

A recent extension of the general equitable principle is to be seen in *Heseltine* v. *Heseltine*.[5] The wife transferred assets to her husband at his request in order to preserve them for the benefit of the family as a whole. The Court of Appeal had no difficulty in finding that he must be regarded as holding them in trust for her absolutely.

Gifts to Spouses.—Whether a gift belongs to one spouse alone or to both of them is a question of the donor's intention. This rule applies equally to wedding presents, so that if the marriage breaks up, the court, exercising its discretion under section 17 of the Married Women's Property Act, may order the presents either to be given up to the spouse whose relations or friends gave them or to be divided equally between them both.[6]

3. TRANSACTIONS BETWEEN HUSBAND AND WIFE

We must now consider the legal effect of certain transactions between the spouses. It should be noted that there is never a presumption that a husband has exercised undue influence over his wife.[7]

Transactions involving Land.—The relationship of husband and wife would seem to affect such transactions in only one particular. An oral contract for the sale or other disposition of land or any interest in land will usually be wholly unenforceable, for if one spouse goes into or remains in possession of the other's land, this could normally be explained on the ground that he is there with the other's leave as spouse and is therefore not sufficiently unequivocal to amount to an act of part performance.[8]

Transactions involving Chattels Personal.—A sale of goods by one spouse to the other normally creates no difficulty, as property usually passes independently of delivery.[9] But gifts, which will be the usual transactions between spouses, raise more complicated problems.[10] In order to perfect a gift of a chattel there must be an intention on the part of the donor to pass property to the donee and, in addition, either a deed executed by the former or a delivery of the chattel to the latter. Gifts by deed will be rare between spouses but, when they do occur, will again present no difficulties since the intention can be inferred from the execution of the deed. But a spouse who alleges that the other has effected a gift by delivery has to surmount two obstacles. First, since spouses frequently use each other's property, an intention to make a gift cannot readily be inferred from permission

---

[5][1971] 1 All E.R. 952, C.A. The court was clearly influenced by a desire to protect the wife after the breakdown of the marriage. This is irrelevant: see *ante*, p. 359, and Lloyd, *Matrimonial Trusts*, 121 New L.J. 157.

[6]*Samson* v. *Samson*, [1960] 1 All E.R. 653, C.A.; *Kelner* v. *Kelner*, [1939] 3 All E.R. 957; [1939] P. 411 (£1,000 deposited by the wife's father at the time of the marriage in a joint bank account in both spouses' names ordered to be divided equally between them).

[7]*Howes* v. *Bishop*, [1909] 2 K.B. 390, C.A.; *MacKenzie* v. *Royal Bank of Canada*, [1934] A.C. 468, P.C. Contrast *Bank of Montreal* v. *Stuart*, [1911] A.C. 120, P.C., where undue influence was in fact exercised.

[8]Law of Property Act 1925, s. 40 See Anson, *Contract*, 23rd Ed., 77-80; Cheshire and Fifoot, *Contract*, 7th Ed., 184-188; Treitel, *Law of Contract*, 3rd Ed., 146-148.

[9]Sale of Goods Act 1893, ss. 17 and 18.

[10]See Thornely, *Transfer of Choses in Possession between Members of a common Household*, 11 C.L.J. 355; Diamond, 27 M.L.R. 357.

to use the chattel in question, and consequently the burden of proof upon a spouse alleging a gift will probably be higher than upon a stranger.[11] Secondly, it may be wellnigh impossible in many cases to prove delivery. Where the goods are intended for the exclusive use of the donee (for example, clothes or jewellery), delivery will normally take place at the time the gift is made by a physical handing over and taking; but if the goods in question have already been used by both spouses in the home and will continue to be used in this way (for example, articles of furniture), there is not likely to be any apparent change of possession. There may indeed be an effective symbolic delivery of one chattel as representing the whole but spouses are hardly likely to carry out such an artificial act, the significance of which will not occur to them.[12] Where the possession of goods could be in one of two people (as will happen in the case of furniture used by both spouses in the matrimonial home), it is presumed to be in the owner, so that if ownership is changed by a sale or deed of gift, the buyer or donee will be presumed to have taken possession as soon as the transaction is complete;[13] but this presumption cannot apply in the case of a gift by delivery since the delivery must be proved before a change in ownership can be established.[14] English courts have always been slow to infer a delivery of a chattel from one spouse to the other, doubtless because of the danger that they may fraudulently allege a prior gift of the husband's goods to the wife in order to keep them out of the hands of the former's creditors. An example of this reluctance can be seen in *Re Cole*.[15] In this case the husband completely furnished a new house before his wife set foot in it. When she arrived, he put his hands over her eyes, took her into the first room, uncovered her eyes and said " Look ". She then went into all the other rooms and handled various articles; at the end the husband said to her: " It's all yours ". The furniture nevertheless remained insured in his name. He subsequently became bankrupt and the question arose whether the trustee or wife was entitled to the goods in question. It was held that she had failed to establish an effective delivery and consequently the gift to her was never perfected. In the circumstances it would always seem wisest for a gift of goods used by both spouses to be made by means of a deed.[16]

Two statutory provisions should also be noticed. Under section 10 of the Married Women's Property Act 1882, a gift made by a husband to his wife may be avoided by his creditors if the property continues to be " in the order and disposition or reputed ownership of the hus-

---

[11]*Cf. Bashall* v. *Bashall* (1894), 11 T.L.R. 152, C.A .

[12]*Lock* v. *Heath* (1892), 8 T.L.R. 295 (husband held to have given all his furniture to wife by symbolic delivery of chair); Thornely, *loc. cit.*, 357-358. For an effective constructive delivery by a father to his daughter, see *Kilpin* v. *Ratley*, [1892] 1 Q.B. 582.

[13]*Ramsay* v. *Margrett*, [1894] 2 Q.B. 18, C.A.; *French* v. *Gething*, [1922] 1 K.B. 236, C.A.

[14]*Hislop* v. *Hislop*, [1950] W.N. 124, C.A.

[15][1963] 3 All E.R. 433, C.A.; [1964] Ch. 175. Would the court have arrived at the same decision if, say, after the husband's death the question had arisen whether the goods belonged to the wife or to his personal representatives? See also *Bashall* v. *Bashall*, *(supra)*; *Valier* v. *Wright* & *Bull, Ltd.* (1917), 33 T.L.R. 366.

[16]A similar difficulty would arise if one spouse pledged goods with the other. A mortgage would not create this problem, but it would have to comply with the Bills of Sales Acts: see Thornely, *loc. cit.*, 373-374.

band ". The Court of Appeal in *French* v. *Gething*[17] has in effect rendered this section inapplicable to goods in the matrimonial home by holding that the maxim " possession follows title " puts the goods outside the order and disposition or reputed ownership of the husband once the property has changed hands by the execution of a deed or by delivery;[18] but it will presumably apply to goods on, say, the husband's business premises of which the wife is never in apparent possession at all.[19] Secondly, a bill of sale will be void against the transferor's creditors with respect to goods in his possession or apparent possession seven days after the bill is executed, unless the bill is registered or the transferee obtains possession of the goods before the transferor becomes bankrupt or assigns his property for the benefit of his creditors generally or before an execution creditor levies execution.[20] A bill of sale is defined to include a number of documents by which property is transferred in goods capable of transfer by delivery.[1] But with respect to furniture and other goods used by both spouses in the matrimonial home and transferred by one of them to the other, *French* v. *Gething* has made the provisions of the Bills of Sale Act as inapplicable as those of section 10 of the Married Women's Property Act, since the goods will be in the actual possession of the transferee and not in the apparent possession of the transferor.[2]

Voidable Transactions.—It is easy to see how transactions between husband and wife might be used as a means of defrauding creditors. To a man who is on the verge of bankruptcy or who is about to engage in a hazardous business operation there is a great temptation to settle the bulk of his property on trust for his wife and children and thus keep it out of the hands of his creditors and at the same time ensure that his family will be provided for. In a number of statutory provisions the Legislature has sought to protect the creditors of the rogue who incidentally benefits his family whilst not prejudicing the members of the family of a man who settles property in good faith and then runs into financial difficulties.

Section 172 of the Law of Property Act 1925.—This section[3] enacts that every conveyance[4] of property made with intent to defraud creditors shall be voidable at the instance of anyone thereby prejudiced. But this does not apply to disentailing assurances (which are therefore

---

[17][1922] 1 K.B. 236, C.A.
[18]This assumes, of course, that the delivery can be proved.
[19]BANKES, L.J., suggested in *French* v. *Gething*, at p. 244, that the operation of the Act might be limited to cases where the spouses were living on premises where the husband was carrying on business.
[20]Bills of Sale Act 1878, s. 8.
[1]*Ibid.*, s. 4, *q.v.*
[2]For the Act to apply the goods must in effect remain in the transferor's sole possession or apparent sole possession or be in premises solely occupied by him or be solely used or enjoyed by him: *Koppel* v. *Koppel*, [1966] 2 All E.R. 187, C.A. See also *Ramsay* v. *Margrett*, (*ante*), and contrast *Hislop* v. *Hislop*, (*ante*). But the Act would apply in the case of a sale of goods if the property was not to pass immediately and the buyer's title depended on a written contract: Thornely, *loc. cit.*, 371.
[3]Replacing 13 Eliz. 1, c. 5.
[4]This includes any assurance of property or any interest in property by any instrument except a will: Law of Property Act 1925, s. 205 (1) (ii).

valid even though executed to defraud creditors) or any conveyance made in good faith for valuable or good consideration to any person not having notice of the intent to defraud at the time of the conveyance.

It will be observed that only transactions made with intent to defraud are caught by this section. The intent may be inferred from the circumstances in which the disposition was made, for example from the settlor's being about to engage in a hazardous business undertaking[5] or from the fact that this would be the natural and probable consequence of the transaction;[6] but it is a question of fact to be determined in each case and the inference may be rebutted by other evidence.[7]

The conveyance may be set aside by any person prejudiced by it. He must have an enforceable debt at the time when he seeks to have it rescinded;[8] normally he will also have to have been a creditor at the time of the conveyance, but it has been held that, if the settlement is made to defraud possible future creditors, it may be set aside by them even though they had no claim againts the settlor at the time it was executed.[9] Since the transaction is voidable and not void, it may not be set aside as against a *bona fide* purchaser for value from a beneficiary, provided that the purchaser himself had no notice of the intent to defraud.[10]

Section 42 of the Bankruptcy Act 1914.—The provisions of this section are designed to give even wider protection to a settlor's creditors. No intent to defraud them need be proved, but whereas any creditor prejudiced may have a settlement set aside under section 172 of the Law of Property Act, section 42 of the Bankruptcy Act applies only if the settlor has been adjudicated bankrupt.

Under sub-section (1) a settlement of property is voidable by the settlor's trustee in bankruptcy for a period of ten years after the date of the settlement. The two most important transactions excluded from the operation of this sub-section are settlements made before and in consideration of marriage and settlements made in good faith and for valuable consideration;[11] on the other hand, the fact that a settlement or transfer of property was made in order to comply with an order for financial provision on divorce, nullity or judicial separation made under section 4 of the Matrimonial Proceedings and Property Act 1970 will not prevent it from being a voidable settlement for this purpose.[12]

The term " settlement " for the purpose of this sub-section includes any conveyance or transfer of property.[13] Hence the husband's trustee

---

[5]*Mackay* v. *Douglas* (1872), L.R. 14 Eq. 106; *Re Butterworth, Ex p. Russe* l(1882), 19 Ch.D. 588, C.A.

[6]*Freeman* v. *Pope* (1870), 5 Ch. App. 538.

[7]*Re Wise, Ex p. Mercer* (1886), 17 Q.B.D. 290, C.A.

[8]*Re Maddever* (1884), 27 Ch.D. 523, C.A., in which it was held that a specialty creditor could set the conveyance aside ten years after it had been executed and that the doctrine of laches has no application to actions brought under s. 172.

[9]*Mackay* v. *Douglas, (supra).*

[10]*Harrods, Ltd.* v. *Stanton,* [1923] 1 K.B. 516.

[11]Any settlement made on or for the settlor's wife or children of property which has accrued to the settlor after marriage in right of his wife is also excluded, but this is now of little practical importance.

[12]Matrimonial Proceedings and Property Act 1970, s. 23.

[13]Bankruptcy Act 1914, s. 42 (4).

in bankruptcy can recover jewellery which the husband has given to his wife as a present[14] and shares which he has settled for her benefit.[15] But the settlor must intend the property to be preserved and consequently a gift of money to be spent at the time is not a settlement for this purpose.[16] The sub-section " is clearly framed to prevent properties from being put into the hands of relatives to the disadvantage of creditors "[17] and the courts will pay more attention to the substance of a transaction than to its form. In *Re A Debtor*[18] a husband, having contracted to sell the matrimonial home, entered into negotiations for the purchase of another house. In the contract and conveyance the wife was named as purchaser and she, as beneficial owner, then charged the property by way of legal mortgage. The husband, however, provided the deposit and paid the instalments on the mortgage until a short time before he became bankrupt. In these circumstances STAMP, J., had no difficulty in holding that the husband had in effect made a settlement of the house on his wife and, although she had entered into an obligation to pay off the mortgage (which she had to fulfil after her husband became insolvent), this did not make her a purchaser for valuable consideration because the provision must be construed in a commercial sense and the wife's undertaking was not " consideration moving to the debtor which replaced the property extracted from his creditors ".[19] Accordingly the husband's trustee in bankruptcy was entitled to the house as against the wife.

Any transaction which is a settlement for the purpose of section 42 (1) can always be set aside by the trustee in bankruptcy if the settlor becomes bankrupt within a period of two years after its execution. If it was made more than two years but less than ten years before the bankruptcy, the Act strikes a compromise between the competing claims of the beneficiaries and the creditors by providing that the settlement cannot be avoided if the beneficiaries can prove that at the time of making it the settlor was able to pay all his debts without the aid of the property settled and that his interest passed to the trustees of the settlement or to the beneficiaries at the time of its execution.[20] In neither case, however, can the trustee recover property which has come into the hands of a *bona fide* purchaser for value without notice of an act of bankruptcy on the part of the settlor, for until the trustee actually has the transfer set aside the beneficiaries have a voidable title which will be cured by the subsequent sale.[1]

---

[14]*Re Vansittart, Ex parte Brown*, [1893] 1 Q.B. 181.
[15]*Re Ashcroft, Ex parte Todd* (1887), 19 Q.B.D. 186, C.A.
[16]*Re Player, Ex parte Harvey* (1885), 15 Q.B.D. 682.
[17]*Per* STAMP, J., in *Re A Debtor*, [1965] 3 All E.R. 453, 457.
[18][1965] 3 All E.R. 453.
[19]At p. 457. The wife was entitled to a lien on the property for the amount she herself paid under the mortgage.
[20]Bankruptcy Act 1914, s. 42 (1); *Re Lowndes, Ex parte Trustee* (1887), 18 Q.B.D. 677. The bankruptcy relates back and is deemed to commence on the commission of the act of bankruptcy on which the receiving order was made or on the commission of any earlier act of bankruptcy occurring not more than three months before the bankruptcy petition was presented: Bankruptcy Act 1914, s. 37 (1).
[1]*Re Hart, Ex parte Green*, [1912] 3 K.B. 6, C.A. (notwithstanding that the Act states that the transaction shall be *void* against the trustee in bankruptcy).

P

Ante-nuptial settlements and settlements executed in pursuance of an ante-nuptial agreement are dealt with in sub-sections (2) and (3). These apply to

> " any covenant or contract made by [the settlor] in consideration of his or her marriage, either for the future payment of money for the benefit of the settlor's wife or husband, or children, or for the future settlement on or for the settlor's wife or husband or children, of property, wherein the settlor had not at the date of the marriage any estate or interest, whether vested or contingent, in possession or remainder,[2] and not being money or property in right of the settlor's wife or husband."

Two situations must be considered. First, if the covenant has not been executed by the payment of the money or the transfer of the property at the date of the commencement of the bankruptcy, it may be avoided by the trustee in bankruptcy and the sole remedy of the beneficiaries entitled under the covenant or contract is to claim in the settlor's bankruptcy. In that case, however, they will be entitled to nothing until all other creditors for valuable consideration in money or money's worth have been paid in full. Secondly, once the covenant or contract has been executed, any payment of money (other than the payment of premiums on a policy of life assurance) or transfer of property made in pursuance of it may be avoided by the trustee in bankruptcy. The payee or transferee may prove for the sum or value of the property which he has lost but again he will be postponed to all creditors for valuable consideration in money or money's worth. But the trustee's power to avoid an executed payment or transfer is limited in two important respects. First, he will lose his right altogether if the payee or transferee can prove:

> " (a) that the payment or transfer was made more than two years before the date of the commencement of the bankruptcy; *or*
>
> " (b) that at the date of the payment or transfer the settlor was able to pay all his debts without the aid of the money so paid or the property so transferred; *or*
>
> " (c) that the payment or transfer was made in pursuance of a covenant or contract to pay or transfer money or property expected to come to the settlor from or on the death of a particular person named in the covenant or contract and was made within three months after the money or property came into the possession or under the control of the settlor."

It will be seen that this protects the beneficiaries whose interests cannot be upset at an indefinite time after their interest vested and who will take their benefit in full if the settlor was not insolvent at the time of the payment or transfer; it also protects a third person providing money or property to be settled, as this cannot be touched by the creditors provided that the conditions in (c) above are satisfied. Secondly, as under sub-section (1), the trustee may not recover property which has come into the hands of a *bona fide* purchaser for value without notice of an act of bankruptcy on the part of the settlor.

---

[2]The clause " wherein the settlor . . . in possession or remainder " governs only " property " and not " money ": *Re Cumming and West*, [1929] 1 Ch. 534. " Property " in s. 42 does not include property over which the settlor merely has a power of appointment: *Re Mathieson*, [1927] 1 Ch. 283, C.A.

Money lent by one Spouse to the Other.—A loan by one spouse to the other usually raises no presumption of a gift by way of advancement, so that the lender will be able to recover the sum lent in the absence of evidence that a gift was intended.[3] This same principle has been applied to other transactions of a similar nature, for example the guarantee of the other's credit[4] and the fulfilling of the other's legal obligations;[5] in each case the spouse making the payment is *prima facie* entitled to recover it from the other.

But if one spouse becomes bankrupt, the other is a deferred creditor in respect of any money or other estate lent or entrusted to the bankrupt *for the purpose of his or her trade or business* and may not claim for such loans until all other creditors for valuable consideration have been paid in full,[6] which in practice will mean that trade loans of this sort will rarely be repaid if the borrower becomes bankrupt. But the section has been strictly construed. Thus it has been held that a wife who has lent money to a firm in which her husband is a partner may prove against the joint estate as an ordinary creditor[7] and that a wife, who has given security to a bank for advances to her husband for the purpose of his trade and then redeemed her security by paying off the loan, is subrogated to the rights of the lender and may therefore prove in her husband's bankruptcy on the same footing as other creditors.[8] Similarly if the original loan is discharged and replaced by an obligation of a different kind, this is not a loan for the purpose of trade or business and is therefore not caught by the section.[9]

4. CONTRACTS OF INSURANCE

Insurable Interests.—Because of the relationship of husband and wife and their mutual rights and duties, each has an insurable interest in the life of the other. This means that if, say, a husband insures his wife's life up to any amount, he may recover the sum due on her death

---

[3]*Hall* v. *Hall*, [1911] 1 Ch. 487 (mortgage of the wife's property to secure a loan to the husband). Contrast *Paget* v. *Paget*, [1898] 1 Ch. 470, C.A., where the facts indicated that a gift was intended. See further George, *Disputes over the Matrimonial Home*, 16 Conv. 27, 31-3.

[4]*Re Salisbury-Jones*, [1938] 3 All E.R. 459; *Anson* v. *Anson*, [1953] 1 All E.R. 867; [1953] 1 Q.B. 636.

[5]*Outram* v. *Hyde* (1875), 24 W.R. 268 (husband's discharging incumbrance on wife's realty); *Re McKerrell*, [1912] 2 Ch. 648 (wife's paying money due from husband on insurance policy). But if the husband purchases realty in the wife's name (thus raising a presumption of advancement) and raises the purchase money by a mortgage, sums paid on the mortgage will likewise be construed as a gift: *Moate* v. *Moate*, [1948] 2 All E.R. 486; *cf. Silver* v. *Silver*, [1958] 1 All E.R. 523, C.A.

[6]Bankruptcy Act 1914, s. 36 (replacing and extending the Married Women's Property Act 1882, s. 3); *Re Clark*, [1898] 2 Q.B. 330, C.A. Consequently the lender cannot exercise a right of retainer in respect of such a debt as personal representative of the borrower: *Re Patten*, [1936] 2 All E.R. 1119; [1936] Ch. 735. But *quaere* whether *all* such lenders are not in the same position: *Re Meade*, [1951] 2 All E.R 168; [1951] Ch. 774.

[7]*Re Tuff* (1887), 19 Q.B.D. 88.

[8]*Re Cronmire*, [1901] 1 Q.B. 480, C.A.

[9]*Re Slade*, [1921] 1 Ch. 160, where the original loan was replaced by a bond to pay the lender £40 *per annum* for life and it was held that the wife *as annuitant* could prove in competition with other creditors. But the conversion of the original debt into a judgment debt does not substantially change its character and the creditor is therefore still deferred: *Re Lupkovics*, [1954] 2 All E.R. 125.

without proving any financial loss at all.[10] Each may also apparently insure any of the other's property which forms a part of the matrimonial home, as the use which he or she enjoys is sufficient to create an insurable interest.[11]

Life Assurance Policies in favour of the Spouse or Children of the Assured.—By section 11 of the Married Women's Property Act 1882, if either spouse effects a policy of assurance on his or her own life[12] expressed to be for the benefit of the assured's spouse or any or all of his or her own children[13] (or for the benefit of both the spouse and children), this creates a trust in favour of those persons. This has two important results. First, in the absence of privity of contract between the objects and the insurance company, the former would not normally be able to sue on the policy.[14] Secondly, the objects as beneficiaries under a trust are entitled to the whole of the sum assured notwithstanding the bankruptcy of the assured or the insolvency of his estate. In only one case will his or her creditors have any claim on the policy, for the Act specifically provides that if the policy was effected to defraud them, they shall be entitled to receive out of the money payable under the policy a sum equal to the premiums so paid.[15]

If the policy is taken out in favour of a *named* spouse or children, they take an immediate vested interest in equity. Thus in *Cousins* v. *Sun Life Assurance Society*,[16] where the policy was issued for the benefit of Lilian Cousins, the assured's wife, who predeceased the life assured, it was held that the husband held the policy on trust for her personal representatives. But where the beneficiaries are merely designated as the husband, wife or children of the assured without being specifically named, this is construed as referring to those who fall into this category at the moment when the trust falls in, *i.e.*, at the assured's death, and before that time the spouse and existing children have only a contingent interest dependent upon their surviving the assured. In *Re Browne's Policy*[17] H, who was then married to W, took out a policy

---

[10]*Reed* v. *Royal Exchange Assurance Co.* (1795), Peake, Add. Cas. 70; *Griffiths* v. *Fleming*, [1909] 1 K.B. 805, C.A.; Married Women's Property Act 1882, s. 11. Otherwise the policy would be void under the Life Assurance Act 1774. For joint policies taken out on both lives to be paid to the survivor on the death of either, see *Griffiths* v. *Fleming*.

[11]*Goulstone* v. *Royal Insurance Co.* (1858), 1 F. & F. 276.

[12]This includes a policy providing for payment on death or disablement as the result of an accident provided that the sum is in fact paid on death (*Re Gladitz*, [1937] 3 All E.R. 173) and an endowment policy payable on the earlier death of the assured (*Re Ioakimidis' Policy Trusts*, [1925] Ch. 403).

[13]This includes adopted children and, in the case of policies effected after 1969, illegitimate children: Adoption Act 1958, s. 14 (3); Family Law Reform Act 1969, s. 19 (1), (3).

[14]*Cleaver* v. *Mutual Reserve Fund Life Association*, [1892] 1 Q.B. 147, C.A., at pp. 152, 157, 160.

[15]S. 11. This is particularly important in the case of a single premium policy.

[16][1933] Ch. 126, C.A. See also *Re Smith's Estate*, [1937] 3 All E.R. 472; [1937] Ch. 636. If there are more beneficiaries than one, they take a joint interest: *Re Seyton* (1887), 34 Ch.D. 511. But the interest may of course be made expressly conditional upon the beneficiary's surviving the assured, in which case the former will have only a contingent interest during the assured's life: *Re Fleetwood's Policy*, [1926] Ch. 48.

[17][1903] 1 Ch. 188. See also *Re Parker's Policies*, [1906] 1 Ch. 526; *Re Seyton*, (*supra*).

on his own life for the benefit of his wife and children. W predeceased H, who then married X. H was survived by X, five children of his first marriage and one child of his second. It was held that X and the six surviving children took a joint interest in the insurance money. If all the objects fail, there will be a resulting trust in favour of the assured's estate.[18]

Unless other trustees are appointed, the assured holds the policy as trustee, and as such must exercise options and otherwise deal with it in the way most favourable to the beneficiaries.[19] Similarly, after the death of a named object with a vested interest, the assured is presumed to continue to pay premiums to preserve the property for those entitled to the deceased beneficiary's estate and consequently may recover premiums paid after the death from the deceased's personal representatives.[20]

5. INCOME TAX

Husband's Liability to pay Wife's Tax.—If the spouses are living together, the wife's income is deemed to be that of her husband for the purpose of tax and he is therefore assessed in respect of it.[1] For this purpose they are regarded as living together unless they are separated under a court order or a deed of separation or are in fact separated in such circumstances that the separation is likely to be permanent.[2]

A married man's personal allowance is greater than that of a single person but is less than twice that sum;[3] on the other hand if the wife has an earned income, additional personal relief is given.[4] Consequently the spouses' tax position under joint assessment will be better than it would be under independent assessment if the wife has no income at all or only a small income (particularly if it is earned): the details will obviously change with every change in rates of tax and allowances. The larger the wife's income, the worse their position will become; this is particularly true in connection with surtax, for the charge to surtax is calculated on their combined incomes and may thus become payable even though neither spouse's income taken alone would bring him or her within the surtax range.[5]

---

[18]*Re Collier*, [1930] 2 Ch. 37. *Cf. Cleaver* v. *Mutual Reserve Fund Life Association*, (*supra*).

[19]*Re Equitable Life Assurance Society of the United States* (1911), 27 T.L.R. 213.

[20]*Re Smith's Estate*, (*supra*). For a fuller discussion of the operation of the section and criticisms of the existing law, see Finlay, " *Family* " *Life Insurance Problems*, 2 M.L.R. 266.

[1]Income and Corporation Taxes Act 1970, s. 37. For exceptions, see *ibid.*, ss. 226 (8) and 414 (1). But this gives the husband no interest in the wife's income so that he must pay over to her any repayment of tax arising from her financial affairs: *Re Cameron*, [1965] 3 All E.R. 474; [1967] Ch. 1.

[2]*Ibid.*, s. 42 (1). If one spouse is resident in the U.K. and the other is not or is absent, they are also regarded as separated: *ibid.*, s. 42 (2).

[3]At present the allowances are £465 and £325 respectively: *ibid.*, s. 8 (1), as amended by the Finance Act 1970, s. 14 (1) (a).

[4]*Ibid.*, s. 8.

[5]Similarly if each income taken separately is within the surtax range, the combined income may attract a higher rate.

The husband is also liable to pay the whole of the tax on their combined incomes unless separate assessment has been claimed. Should he fail to do so, however, the wife is bound to pay the tax on her own income as though a separate assessment had been made.[6] These rules not only produce the result that " it is cheaper to live in sin than to marry " (which is scarcely socially desirable) but also give considerable advantages to the Crown which seem to rest on suppositions about the husband's right to the wife's income which have not been true since the passing of the Married Women's Property Act of 1870.

During the financial year in which the parties marry the husband is assessed only in respect of that part of his wife's income which accrued after the marriage but he is entitled to a personal allowance as a married man for that part of the year during which he was married.[7] His wife is assessable as though she were unmarried in respect of that part of her income which accrued before the marriage and she may claim a full year's allowances as a single person.[8]

Separate Assessment.—Either spouse may claim to be separately assessed for income tax and surtax. Separate assessment makes no difference to the total amount of tax which the spouses together have to pay but this sum is apportioned between them according to their respective incomes, reliefs and allowances and the wife is solely legally liable for the payment of her own part to the exclusion of her husband.[9]

Effect of Death, Separation, Divorce and Nullity.—If the spouses are living together and the wife dies, the husband remains liable to pay tax in respect of her income up to the date of her death and may claim a full year's allowances as a married man. If the husband dies, his personal representatives are liable to pay tax on both spouses' incomes up to the date of the death and may claim a full year's allowances as for a married man; the widow is liable to pay tax on that part of her own income which has accrued since the death but may claim a full year's allowances as a single woman.[10]

If the spouses separate in the sense in which this word is used in the Income and Corporation Taxes Act,[11] they are thereafter treated as single persons for income tax purposes. They are assessed separately, given the allowances and reliefs appropriate to single persons and are liable for the payment of tax in respect of their own incomes only.[12] For the financial year in which they separate the husband is liable to pay tax on both incomes up to the date of separation and may claim a full year's allowances as a married man; the wife is liable for the payment of tax on her own income after that date but may claim a full year's

---

[6]Income and Corporation Taxes Act 1970, s. 40. For separate assessment, see *infra*.
[7]*Ibid.*, s. 8 (3), as amended by the Finance Act 1970, s. 14 (1) (a) (iv).
[8]As to age relief if the wife is over the age of 65, see *ibid.*, s. 9; for the effect on claims for relief in respect of policies of life assurance, see ss. 19 (7) and 20 (6).
[9]*Ibid.*, ss. 38 and 39.
[10]See *Palmer* v. *Cattermole*, [1937] 2 All E.R. 667; [1937] 2 K.B. 581. For the power of a widower to disclaim liability for his deceased's wife's tax, see the Income and Corporation Taxes Act 1970, s. 41.
[11]See *ante*, p. 373.
[12]Since they do not come within the provisions of the Income and Corporation Taxes Act 1970, s. 37.

allowances as a single person. Divorce and nullity will normally be preceded by a separation for the purposes of the Act; if they are not, however, exactly the same principles apply if the marriage is dissolved or a voidable marriage is annulled as apply in the case of separation.[13] If the marriage is void, the spouses are of course treated as single persons throughout.

If after separation the husband pays maintenance to his wife or former wife in pursuance of an agreement imposing a legal obligation, he is entitled to deduct income tax at the standard rate before payment and then to pay her only the balance.[14] If the wife is not liable to tax or is entitled to reliefs not already given, she may then claim a refund of the whole or part of the tax already paid. It should be borne in mind that if the husband pays the wife maintenance for the children, this becomes her income and will be taxed accordingly unless the agreement constitutes her a trustee for the children.[15]

C. THE MATRIMONIAL HOME

We have already seen that the main problem that still has to be solved in English matrimonial property law is the adaptation to modern conditions of the doctrine of separate estate introduced by the Married Women's Property Act of 1882.[16] It is when the property in question constitutes a " family asset "—that is to say the matrimonial home and its contents—that the problem becomes most acute, for the spouses do not regard the house and furniture as belonging to either of them exclusively but, at least in a loose sense, to both of them together. There are of course two distinct problems—that of ownership and title and that of occupation and use. The first is concerned with the question, in whom are the legal and equitable interests in the property vested? The second is concerned with the question, what rights of occupation and use does one spouse have in property beneficially owned by the other? They will be considered in that order.

An engaged couple may well begin to buy furniture and purchase their proposed matrimonial home before they marry and in this respect their position may be little different from a newly married couple. Consequently, if an agreement to marry is terminated, the principles relating to the rights of husbands and wives to property have now been extended to property in which either or both of the parties to the agreement had a beneficial interest whilst the agreement was in force.[17]

---

[13]For the effect of a decree of nullity where the marriage is voidable, see further *ante*, p. 71, n. 20.

[14]Income and Corporation Taxes Act 1970, ss. 52 and 53. Thus if the husband is paying tax at the standard rate of 38·75% and covenants to pay the wife £1,000 a year, he will first deduct £387.50 and pay her the balance of £612.50.

[15]This will rarely be the case unless the wife is expressly made a trustee. If there is a trust and the husband is the father of the children and they are unmarried and under 18 (or under 21 if they are not working regularly), the income is deemed still to be his: *ibid.*, s. 437. In other cases of a trust the income will be that of the children but will be aggregated with that of the mother in whose actual custody they are if they are under 18, unmarried and not regularly working: ss. 43 and 44. If it exceeds £115 a year in the case of any child, the wife will lose her child relief in respect of that child to the extent of the excess: *ibid.*, s. 10 (5). For the position with regard to maintenance orders, see *post*, p. 432.

[16]See *ante*, p. 356.

[17]Law Reform (Miscellaneous Provisions) Act 1970, s. 2 (1). See further *ante*, p. 14.

I. OWNERSHIP

Earlier cases followed the general rule that property purchased by one spouse with his or her own money presumptively belonged to that spouse to the exclusion of the other. Hence if the house was bought out of the husband's earnings (which would usually be the case) the whole beneficial interest vested in him;[18] if he had it conveyed into his wife's name, the presumption of advancement operated to give the whole interest to her.[19] This rule will still obviously apply to property purchased before the parties became engaged; if, for example, the spouses set up home in a house already owned by the husband, the wife will acquire no interest in it in the absence of any express agreement.[20]

In recent years, however, the whole position has had to be re-examined. The wife is now frequently a wage earner making a contribution to the common expenses of buying and running the home and justice demands that, even though property is purchased in the husband's name, she should be given some credit for her help. The position has been further complicated by the steady increase in the value of most houses during the past 25 years. Suppose, for example, that a house was bought in 1960 for £4,000, to which the wife contributed £1,000, and that it has recently been sold for £8,000. Assuming that her contribution gives the wife some interest in the property, it is vital to determine whether she can merely recover her £1,000, or a quarter of the present value (which will give her £2,000), or some other fraction of the price at which it was sold. A further difficulty has arisen because some judges (notably LORD DENNING) have been prepared to go much further than others in giving credit to the wife for her services in kind as a housekeeper or for the use of her own income or savings in such a way as to enable her husband to use his for the purchase of a house, and this in turn has led to a tendency to divide the proceeds of sale equally between the spouses whenever it can be said that they both contributed to its purchase. Some principles have now been settled by the two recent decisions of the House of Lords in *Pettitt* v. *Pettitt*[1] and *Gissing* v. *Gissing*[2] but many problems still remain unsolved. The truth is that the extent to which the judges can adapt legal rules to meet changed social and economic circumstances is necessarily limited and only Parliament can now make the radical changes which are already overdue in this branch of the law.[3]

Nevertheless two fundamental rules can be stated immediately. It

---

[18]*Re Sims' Question*, [1946] 2 All E.R. 138. Consequently rent received from a lodger was held to belong exclusively to the husband: *Montgomery* v. *Blows*, [1916] 1 K.B. 899, C.A.

[19]*Moate* v. *Moate*, [1948] 2 All E.R. 486; George, *Disputes over the Matrimonial Home*, 16 Conv. 27.

[20]A legal estate would have to be conveyed by deed and an equitable interest in writing: Law of Property Act 1925, ss. 52 (1), 53 (1) (c). Any contract or declaration of trust would have to be evidenced in writing: *ibid.*, ss. 40, 53 (1) (b).

[1][1969] 2 All E.R. 385 H.L.; [1970] A.C. 777.

[2][1970] 2 All E.R. 780, H.L.

[3]See Miller, *Family Assets*, 86 L.Q.R. 98 (written after *Pettitt* v. *Pettitt* but before *Gissing* v. *Gissing*); Tiley, [1969] C.L.J. 191 and [1970] C.L.J. 210; Jones, [1969] C.L.J. 196.

is clear from *Pettitt* v. *Pettitt* that English law knows of no community of property nor of any special rules of law applicable to family assets.[4] Consequently if one spouse buys property for their common use—whether it is a house, furniture or a car—this cannot *per se* give the other any proprietary interest. From this it must follow, as was stated in *Gissing* v. *Gissing*,[5] that if one spouse seeks to establish a beneficial interest in property, the legal title to which is vested in the other, he or she can do so only by proving that the legal owner holds the property on trust for the claimant. If it becomes necessary to determine the spouses' interests on the breakdown of the marriage, the courts are faced with a problem which is logically insoluble, for the ownership of property depends upon the purchaser's intention at the time it is bought and spouses buying a house and furniture will rarely contemplate the termination of the marriage except by death. Hence in many cases the court is bound to attribute to them an intention that they clearly never had. As in other branches of English law where a person's intention is of vital importance, in the absence of direct evidence the court must infer what it was from his conduct at the time. As the majority of the House of Lords held in *Pettitt* v. *Pettitt*,[6] if the spouses did not apply their minds at all to the question of how the beneficial interest in a particular piece of property should be held when it was bought, the court cannot give effect to an agreement which they never entered into even though it is satisfied that they would have made it had they thought about it. In other words, it can impute to them an intention which they probably never had but it cannot impute to them an agreement which they clearly did not make. This nicety reflects ingrained principles of English law, but its application here is unfortunate because the opposite rule would have been much more likely to work justice. The court's function was thus summed by by EVERSHED, M.R., in *Re Rogers' Question*:[7]

> " What the judge must try to do . . . is . . . to conclude what at the time was in the parties' minds and then to make an order which, in the changed conditions, now fairly gives effect in law to what the parties, in the judge's finding, must be taken to have intended at the time of the transaction itself."

It is submitted, therefore, that one must start with the conveyance and *prima facie* give effect to its wording. If this expressly declares in whom not only the legal title but also the beneficial interests are to vest, LORD UPJOHN stated in *Pettitt* v. *Pettitt*[8] that this will be conclusive in the absence of fraud or mistake. This dictum probably goes further than the *ratio* of any case in which the court has had to consider

---

[4]At pp. 395 and 800-801 (*per* LORD MORRIS), 403 and 810 (*per* LORD HODSON), and 409 and 817 (*per* LORD UPJOHN).
[5]At pp. 782 (*per* LORD REID), 785 (*per* LORD DILHORNE), and 789 (*per* LORD DIPLOCK).
[6]At pp. 398 and 804 (*per* LORD MORRIS), 403 and 810 (*per* LORD HODSON), and 408 and 816 (*per* LORD UPJOHN).
[7][1948] 1 All E.R. 328, C.A.
[8][1969] 2 All E.R. 385, 405, H.L.; [1970] A.C. 777, 813.

the effect of such a conveyance,[9] but it is clear that strong evidence will be required before the court will go behind an express declaration of trust. Hence if, as is common, the matrimonial home is conveyed to both spouses on express trust for sale for themselves as joint tenants in equity, it will be very exceptional for either to be able to claim that this gives each anything other than a joint interest in the proceeds of sale or, on severance, an equal half share. If the beneficial interests are not declared, *prima facie* they will follow the legal title; consequently a conveyance to both spouses jointly at law will presumptively give them a joint interest in equity, and a conveyance to the husband alone on the face of it gives the wife no interest at all. But provided at any rate that the equitable interests are not spelled out, this presumption can be rebutted by parol evidence which shows that the spouses had a different common intention, and if this indicates, for example, that when the husband purchased the house in his own name, they intended to take a joint interest, he will hold the legal estate on trust for them both jointly in equity. The problem is therefore: what evidence will suffice to show a contrary intention?

It is clear that proof of an express agreement between the spouses may always be adduced: indeed this is the best possible evidence of their common intention.[10] The alternative method of rebutting the presumption is to show that the party claiming the beneficial interest has made a contribution to the purchase of property conveyed in the other's name. In these circumstances the presumptions of advancement and a resulting trust may come into play if there is no other evidence but, as we have already seen,[11] these are of considerably less importance today than they used to be. LORD UPJOHN has said:[12]

> "In the absence of all evidence, if a husband puts property into his wife's name he intends it to be a gift to her, but if he puts it into joint names then . . . . the presumption is the same as a joint beneficial tenancy. If a wife puts property into her husband's name it may be that in the absence of all other evidence he is a trustee for her, but in practice there will in almost every case be some explanation (however slight) of this (today) rather unusual course. If a wife puts property into their joint names I would myself think that a joint beneficial tenancy was intended, for I can see no other reason for it."[13]

In practice, however, the problem is usually the converse of those discussed here, for one party (in most cases the wife) alleges that both

---

[9]RUSSELL, L. J., seems to have regarded this form of wording as conclusive in *Wilson* v. *Wislon*, [1963] 2 All E.R. 447, C.A., and *Bedson* v. *Bedson*, [1965] 3 All E.R. 307, C.A.; [1965] 2 Q.B. 666. The other members of the court in *Wilson* v. *Wilson* were more hesitant; in *Bedson* v. *Bedson* LORD DENNING, M.R., held that the parties took as joint tenants because they expressly intended to do so and DAVIES, L.J., so held on the ground that there was no evidence that they did not intend to do so. In *Re Johns' Assignment Trusts*, [1970] 2 All E.R. 210, GOFF, J., held that the conveyance accorded with the parties' probable intention and wishes. See further Miller, *Conveyances and Beneficial Interests*, 34 Conv. 156.

[10]But it must be possible to infer the existence of an agreement from the evidence. The court may not impute to the parties an agreement they never made at all: see *ante*, p. 377.

[11]*Ante*, p. 364. See also Earnshaw, *Presumption of Advancement*, 121 New L.J. 96, 120.

[12]*Pettitt* v. *Pettitt*, [1969] 2 All E.R. 385, 407, H.L.; [1970] A.C. 777, 815.

[13]But see *Grzeczkowski* v. *Jedynska* (1971), 115 Sol. Jo. 126, where property purchased with the wife's money but conveyed into joint names to satisfy the building society's requirements was held to belong beneficially to the wife alone.

have contributed but that the conveyance has been taken in the other's name. In a series of cases decided between 1950 and 1969 the Court of Appeal had in effect established the rule that if both spouses had made a contribution to the purchase (whether directly or indirectly), this gave both an interest in the property bought and presumptively they would take equal shares in the proceeds of sale. But this has now been limited by the decisions of the House of Lords in *Pettitt* v. *Pettitt* and, particularly, *Gissing* v. *Gissing*.

There is no doubt that a *direct cash contribution* to the purchase will be regarded as sufficient evidence of the spouses' common intention that the party making it should take a beneficial interest so as to turn the other into a trustee provided, at least, that it is substantial. It may be to the price as a whole (if the house is purchased for cash outright), to the deposit, to mortgage repayments, or even to legal charges. This principle, which had been followed in a number of cases in the Court of Appeal,[14] seems implicit in all the speeches in *Gissing* v. *Gissing* and was spelt out by LORD DILHORNE and LORD DIPLOCK.[15] The position with respect to *indirect contributions* has always been less certain. The problem arises, for example, if both spouses are working and they agree that the easiest way to manage is for the husband to pay the instalments due on the mortgage and for the wife to pay for the food and fuel. Is it then to be said that, because the payment of the price of the house came exclusively from the husband's earnings, he has the sole beneficial interest? It is submitted that such an approach is fundamentally wrong, for the truth of the matter is that both are contributing to the total cost of the home in the way that happens to be most convenient at the time and title to property (which may be of considerable value) ought not to depend on the accident of temporary convenience, particularly when the parties have given no thought to the possible legal consequences of their agreement. This was certainly the view of DENNING, L.J., in *Fribrance* v. *Fribrance*[16] where he said:

" In the present case it so happened that the wife went out to work and used her earnings to help run the household and buy the children's clothes, whilst the husband saved. It might very well have been the other way round . . . The title to the family assets does not depend on the mere chance of which way round it was. It does not depend on how they happened to allocate their earnings and their expenditure. The whole of their resources were expended for their joint benefit . . . and the product should belong to them jointly. It belongs to them in equal shares."

After initial hesitation[17] the Court of Appeal followed LORD DENNING'S lead and held that the wife acquired an interest in the matrimonial home purchased in her husband's name when she augmented the family's income by going out to work,[18] by giving unpaid help in the husband's greengrocery business (and thus saving the wages he would

---

[14]See, *e.g.*, *Rimmer* v. *Rimmer*, [1952] 2 All E.R. 863, C.A.; [1953] 1 Q.B. 63 (deposit and mortgage repayments); *Ulrich* v. *Ulrich*, [1968] 1 All E.R. 67, C.A. (deposit and charges).
[15][1970] 2 All E.R. 780, H.L., at pp. 786 and 791-792, respectively.
[16][1957] 1 All E.R. 357, 360, C.A.
[17]See *Allen* v. *Allen*, [1961] 3 All E.R. 385, C.A.
[18]*Ulrich* v. *Ulrich*, (*supra*); *Chapman* v. *Chapman*, [1969] 3 All E.R. 476, C.A.

have had to pay to an assistant)[19] and by going into partnership with the husband.[20]

Gissing v. *Gissing* has left the law in an uncertain state. LORD REID could see no good reason for the distinction between direct and indirect contributions and thought that in many cases it would be unworkable.[1] On the other hand, LORD DILHORNE said that " proof of expenditure for the benefit of the family by one spouse will not of itself suffice to show any such common intention as to the ownership of the matrimonial home ".[2] LORD PEARSON stated:[3]

> " Contributions are not limited to those made directly in part payment of the price of the property or to those made at the time when the property is conveyed into the name of one of the spouses. For instance there can be a contribution if by arrangement between the spouses one of them by payment of the household expenses enables the other to pay the mortgage instalments."

LORD DIPLOCK was more specific. He pointed out that, if the wife had made an initial contribution to the deposit or legal charges which indicated that she was to take some interest in the property, the court should also take account of her contributions to the mortgage instalments, even though these were indirect, because this would be consistent with both spouses' intention that her payment of other household expenses would release the husband's money to pay off the mortgage and would thus be her contribution to the purchase of the home. But, he added, if the wife has made no initial contribution to the purchase, no direct contribution to the repayment of the mortgage, and " no adjustment to her contribution to other expenses of the household which it can be inferred was referable to the acquisition of the house", she cannot claim an interest in it " merely because she continued to contribute out of her own earnings or private income to other expenses of the household ".[4]

It will be seen that the majority of the House were of the opinion that a wife can claim an interest in the house as a result of indirect contributions in certain circumstances. It seems that she must show that this was referable to the acquisition of the house in the sense that it freed the husband's own money and thus enabled him to use it to pay the deposit, legal charges or mortgage instalments—in other words, without the wife's help the husband could not have bought the property at all. An even narrower interpretation may be put on LORD PEARSON'S and LORD DIPLOCK'S words and it may be necessary for the wife to prove an arrangement that she should continue to work or use her own income for this purpose. It remains to be seen what construction the courts will now put on these conflicting (and in places imprecise) views. In the later case of *Falconer* v. *Falconer*[5] LORD DENNING, M.R., was of the opinion that *Gissing* v. *Gissing* enabled the court to draw the

---

[19]*Nixon* v. *Nixon*, [1969] 3 All E.R. 1133, C.A.
[20]*Muetzel* v. *Muetzel*, [1970] 1 All E.R. 443, C.A.
[1][1970] 2 All E.R. 780, 783, H.L.
[2]At p. 786.
[3]At p. 788.
[4]At pp. 792-793.
[5][1970] 3 All E.R. 449, 452, C.A. The other members of the court did not comment on this point. *Cf. Davis* v. *Vale* (1971), 115 Sol. Jo. 347.

inference of a trust whenever both spouses had made a contribution to the price, even though this was indirect, " as where both go out to work, and one pays the housekeeping and the other the mortgage instalments. It does not matter which way round it is. It does not matter who pays what ". This, it is submitted, is a most desirable principle, but LORD DENNING may be too sanguine in his views that the courts can now apply it broadly.

In any event, the contribution must be a substantial one, and a spouse will not be able to claim any interest in the house by virtue of an insignificant contribution or the purchase of other property, for example furniture. In *Gissing* v. *Gissing* the husband had bought a house for £2,695, partly out of his own savings, partly by a loan and partly by a mortgage. The wife spent £220 on furniture and equipment and on relaying the lawn. The House of Lords had no difficulty in holding on these facts that she had made no substantial contribution, direct or indirect, *to the purchase of the house* and that she took no interest in it.

It should also be appreciated that the contribution may be by labour rather than in cash. In *Smith* v. *Baker*[6] a husband and wife built a bungalow themselves, and the wife gave up a job that brought her in about £10 a week to do so. This was regarded as a contribution in money's worth and it is submitted that the decision is unaffected by *Gissing* v. *Gissing*.

If the purchase money (or part of it) comes from a " common purse " in which the spouses have a joint interest, a house bought as the matrimonial home for their common use will presumably be intended by both of them to represent the original fund. In the absence of any evidence in rebuttal, therefore, this must give them both an interest in the property bought even though the conveyance is taken in the name of one only.[7]

As the parties' rights must be determined by reference to their common intention when the property was purchased, no account must be taken of the responsibility for the breakdown of the marriage.[8] Once this has occurred, however, there can be no further presumption of a gift from one to the other; consequently if, for example, the husband continues to pay instalments on a mortgage of property, half the beneficial interest in which is vested in the wife, she will have to account to him for half the payments made after they separated.[9]

The principle that a trustee must not take advantage of his position to make a personal profit for himself[10] applies equally when one spouse holds the matrimonial home or other property on trust for the other. In *Protheroe* v. *Protheroe*[11] the husband purchased the leasehold of the matrimonial home which he held for himself and his wife in equal

---

[6][1970] 2 All E.R. 826, C.A.
[7]For the " common purse ", see ante, pp. 360-362.
[8]*Hickson* v. *Hickson*, [1953] 1 All E.R. 382, C.A.; [1953] 1 Q.B. 420; *Wilson* v. *Wilson*, [1963] 2 All E.R. 447, 454, C.A.
[9]*Cobb* v. *Cobb*, [1955] 2 All E.R. 696, C.A.; *Wilson* v. *Wilson*, (*supra*).
[10]*I.e.* the rule in *Keech* v. *Sandford* (1726), 2 Eq. Cas. Abr. 741.
[11][1968] 1 All E.R. 1111, C.A. For a criticism of the case, see Cretney, *The Rationale of Keech* v. *Sandford*, 33 Conv. 161.

shares. He later purchased the freehold reversion and it was held that he held this on the same trusts subject to his right to be repaid the price and legal costs incurred.

Division of Proceeds.—Up to now we have been considering the circumstances in which a spouse may take a beneficial interest in the matrimonial home even though the legal estate is vested in the other. Where the beneficial title is vested in one of them only, the position on sale is simple. If, say, the husband holds the legal fee simple on trust for the wife alone, she has the equitable fee simple and after the sale of the house is absolutely entitled to the proceeds. But if it was the spouses' common intention that both should take a beneficial interest, a further question is raised. If the marriage breaks down and the property has to be sold, how are the proceeds to be divided?

If it was the parties' intention that the beneficial interest should be jointly owned, this can always be severed, so as to produce a tenancy in common in equal shares.[12] If it is not severed, on the death of either spouse the whole interest will survive to the other.[13] In other cases where it was the parties' intention that both should take an interest but where there was no clear indication that this should be a tenancy in common in identifiable shares, there has been an increasing tendency in recent years to order a division in equal shares. But this has received a decided check in *Gissing* v. *Gissing*.[14] Both LORD REID and LORD PEARSON were of the opinion that the maxim " Equality is equity " has been applied too widely in this type of case. The approach most likely to be followed in the future is that indicated by LORD REID and LORD DIPLOCK.[15] If each spouse's contribution has been in cash, then in the absence of any agreement between them, the inference is that the proceeds of sale should be divided in proportion to their contributions. This will be easily calculable if there has been one lump sum payment or regular payments (for example of mortgage instalments) over a period of time. But the calculation will become more difficult if the payments have been erratic, so that in many cases the division will have to be a rough and ready one. Eventually one reaches the point where the spouses' financial affairs have become so inextricably entangled that " an equitable knife must be used to sever the Gordian knot " and an equal division will be the only possible solution.[16] Again, if the wife, having made a direct cash contribution, makes further payments, the inference is that the spouses intended that she should take more than the proportion represented by her initial contribution and that the

---

[12]See the judgment of RUSSELL, L.J., in *Bedson* v. *Bedson*, [1965] 3 All E.R. 307, 318, C.A.; [1965] 2 Q.B. 666, 689. LORD DENNING, M.R.'s view that neither can sever without the other's consent (at pp. 311 and 678, respectively) seems wholly without foundation: see RUSSELL, L.J., *ibid.*, at pp. 319 and 690, respectively; *Re Draper's Conveyance*, [1967] 3 All E.R. 853; [1969] 1 Ch. 486; R.E.M. in 82 L.Q.R. 29.

[13]For the nature of joint tenancies and tenancies in common, see works on real property generally.

[14][1970] 2 All E.R. 780, H.L.

[15]At pp. 782-783 and 791-793, respectively.

[16]See LORD UPJOHN in *National Provincial Bank, Ltd.* v. *Ainsworth*, [1965] 2 All E.R. 472, 487, H.L.; [1965] A.C. 1175, 1236; LORD MORRIS in *Pettitt* v. *Pettitt*, [1969] 2 All E.R. 385, 397, H.L.; [1970] A.C. 777, 804; LORD HODSON, *ibid.*, at pp. 403 and 810, respectively.

interest should be quantified when the total amount contributed by each was known. Obviously the problem becomes much more difficult if the contribution has been indirect and an equal division may be the only possible way of dealing fairly with both parties. In many cases (particularly if the house is bought in the early days of the marriage) the wife's earning capacity (and consequently her ability to make direct or indirect contributions to the purchase) will drop if she has children, and in this sort of situation the court may well infer that their intention was that each should contribute what he or she could afford from time to time but that the beneficial interest should be held in equal shares.

Some cases decided by the Court of Appeal before *Gissing* v. *Gissing* would obviously still be decided in the same way today. In one case where the wife had paid £100 in cash towards the price of £1,000 and had made it clear that this was the limit of her contribution, the court divided the proceeds in the ratio of nine to one.[17] In other cases where both contributed directly and indirectly what they conceived to be their share towards the purchase over a number of years, the court ordered an equal division.[18] Again, an adjustment has been made to take account of unequal contributions or other financial advantages.[19] But many other decisions doubtless gave rise to the strictures in *Gissing* v. *Gissing* on the too ready resort to equal division and can no longer be regarded as any sort of precedent at all.

Improvements to the Matrimonial Home.—The value of the matrimonial home may be considerably enhanced after its purchase by extension, improvement or other work done on it. Suppose that the beneficial title is vested in one spouse exclusively but the other contributes to the improvement by cash payments or by doing some of the work himself; will this give him any interest in the property? This is the question that had to be answered in *Pettitt* v. *Pettitt*.[20] The husband alleged that as a result of doing work on the matrimonial home (which had been purchased by the wife out of her own money) he had increased its value by over £1,000. Most of the work had consisted of redecorating the bungalow in question, but he had also made the garden, built a wall and patio, and done other jobs outside. All the members of the House were agreed that he could claim nothing, on the ground that he could acquire no interest by doing work of an ephemeral nature or " do-it-yourself " jobs which any husband could be expected to do in his leisure hours. They were, however, divided on the question whether, in the absence of an agreement, one spouse could acquire an interest in the other's property by doing work of a more substantial nature on it.

---

[17]*Re Rogers' Question*, [1948] 1 All E.R. 328, C.A.
[18]See *Rimmer* v. *Rimmer*, [1952] 2 All E.R. 863, C.A.; [1953] 1 Q.B. 63; *Smith* v. *Baker*, [1970] 2 All E.R. 826, C.A.
[19]See *Nixon* v. *Nixon*, [1969] 3 All E.R. 1133, C.A.; *Muetzel* v. *Muetzel*, [1970] 1 All E.R. 443, C.A. See also *Falconer* v. *Falconer*, [1970] 3 All E.R. 449, C.A. (decided after *Gissing* v. *Gissing*) where the wife recovered the value of the site but the value of the building on it was divided equally between the spouses.
[20][1969] 2 All E.R. 385, H.L.; [1970] A.C. 777.

As a consequence the law was made more certain by section 37 of the Matrimonial Proceedings and Property Act 1970.[1] This provides:

" . . . where a husband or wife contributes in money or money's worth to the improvement of real or personal property in which or in the proceeds of sale of which either or both of them has or have a beneficial interest, the husband or wife so contributing shall . . . be treated as having then acquired by virtue of his or her contribution a share or an enlarged share, as the case may be, in that beneficial interest . . . ."

It will be observed that this section (which refers to any property and is not limited to improvements to the matrimonial home) applies whether the contribution is in money or money's worth: in other words, it does not matter whether the spouse does the job himself or pays a contractor to do it. But it will be seen that there are two limitations on its operation. First, the section will apply only if the contribution is of a substantial nature. Whether any particular improvement is sufficiently substantial to bring it within the ambit of the section is, of course, a question of fact, but it seems clear that the sort of work done by the husband in *Pettitt* v. *Pettitt* will still not give him any interest in the matrimonial home. Secondly, the section applies " subject to any agreement between the spouses to the contrary express or implied ", so that if they agreed that the improvements should confer no interest on the party making them, this will be conclusive.

The operation of section 37 is not confined to cases arising under section 17 of the Married Women's Property Act but applies in any proceedings including, for example, litigation between one spouse and a stranger claiming through the other. If the parties agreed on the size of the interest which the improvements were to confer on the spouse making them, the court must give effect to the agreement; in other cases it has power to make such order as appears just in all the circumstances. Normally, it is submitted, this should reflect the amount by which the value of the property was increased at the time; if, for example, the wife puts the value of the husband's house up from £4,000 to £5,000, she should obtain one-fifth of the price when it is sold. The section also applies if both spouses have a beneficial interest in the property before the improvements are made: hence if in the above example the spouses were tenants in common of the house in equal shares when the wife made the improvements, she should now obtain three-fifths of the price.

Sale of the Property.—If the legal estate is vested in one spouse only but both have a beneficial interest, the equitable joint tenancy or tenancy in common should take effect behind a trust for sale.[2] Consequently the legal owner should appoint another trustee (who would normally be the other spouse) and the trustees must consider the wishes of both beneficial owners before dealing with the property.[3] In many cases this will not be done, however, and a purchaser will take a legal

---

[1] Enacted on the recommendation of the Law Commission: see Law Com. No. 25, paras. 56-58 and pp. 102-105. For difficulties arising under the section, see Oerton, *Matrimonial Home—Spouse's Improvements*, 120 New L.J. 1008.

[2] Law of Property Act 1925, ss. 34 and 36; Settled Land Act 1925, s. 36 (4).

[3] Law of Property Act 1925, ss. 26 (3) and 27 (2); Trustee Act 1925, ss. 14 (2) and 36 (6). See *Waller* v. *Waller*, [1967] 1 All E.R. 305; *Taylor* v. *Taylor*, [1968] 1 All E.R. 843, 846-847, C.A.

estate from one spouse alone. In such circumstances he will probably be protected by the general equitable doctrine that a *bona fide* purchaser of a legal estate for value will take it free of an equitable interest vested in another of which he does not have actual or constructive notice.[4] The mere fact that the wife is residing in the house with her husband will not give the purchaser constructive notice of her rights, for her presence there is consistent with her husband's being the sole beneficial owner: nor does the fact that so many matrimonial homes are bought with money provided by the wife (which will give her a beneficial interest) put a purchaser on enquiry if he finds the legal estate vested in the husband alone.[5]

Death of one of the Spouses.—A further problem arises if the marriage ends not by breakdown during the parties' lifetime but by the death of one of them. If both have a beneficial interest in the house, it may be vital to decide whether they hold as joint tenants or tenants in common, for the whole interest in a joint tenancy will pass to the survivor *jure accrescendi* if it has not been severed during the lifetime of both whilst an undivided share will form a part of the deceased's estate.

There is no reported case in which this problem has had to be faced. If the beneficial interests have been spelled out in the conveyance, effect will obviously be given to them. In the vast majority of the other cases where the court would order an equal division of the proceeds of sale *inter vivos*, the parties would doubtless wish and expect the *jus accrescendi* to operate, and consequently it is urged that there should be at least an initial presumption that the spouses take as joint tenants in equity and not as tenants in common.[6] There are some dicta that suggest that, if the court would order an unequal division *inter vivos*, the spouses hold the property as joint tenants in unequal shares,[7] but it is submitted that this offends against fundamental principles of our land law. The unilateral severance of a joint tenancy has always produced equal undivided shares;[8] conversely in the absence of other evidence equity has always regarded an unequal contribution towards the purchase money as producing a tenancy in common.[9] If we accept the principle that the matrimonial home is governed by the same rules as other property—as we are bound to do since the decision in *Gissing*

---

[4]See Rudden, *The Wife, the Husband and the Conveyancer*, 27 Conv. 51; Garner, *A Single Trustee for Sale*, 33 Conv. 240.

[5]*Caunce* v. *Caunce*, [1969] 1 All E.R. 722. STAMP, J., left open the question what the position would be if the wife was living alone in the house after her husband had left her (at pp. 724-725).

[6]The presumption might be rebutted more easily in the case of the house than the furniture.

[7]*E.g.* by LORD DENNING, M.R., in *Bedson* v. *Bedson*, [1965] 3 All E.R. 307, 314, C.A.; [1965] 2 Q.B. 666, 681-682; *Nixon* v. *Nixon*, [1969] 3 All E.R. 1133, 1137, C.A.; *Muetzel* v. *Muetzel*, [1970] 1 All E.R. 443, 445, C.A.

[8]*Cf.* the judgment of RUSSELL, L.J., in *Bedson* v. *Bedson*, (*supra*), at pp. 318 and 689, respectively; Megarry and Wade, *Law of Real Property*, 3rd Ed., 416.

[9]*Lake* v. *Craddock* (1733), 3 P. Wms. 158.

v. *Gissing*[10]—facts producing an unequal division *inter vivos* must necessarily create a tenancy in common and consequently, however undesirable this may be in many cases, the property will not pass to the survivor by operation of law but will become part of the other's estate.

2. OCCUPATION

We must now consider what rights the spouses have to occupy the matrimonial home and to use the furniture in it. *Prima facie* each has a right to the other's consortium, and as this will be normally enjoyed in the matrimonial home, each will have a right to use the house and its furniture in whichever of them the legal or equitable title is vested.[11] The question of occupation, however, like the question of title, becomes important if the marriage breaks down and the spouses assert adverse claims.

The right to occupy the matrimonial home is now partly statutory and is governed by the Matrimonial Homes Act 1967, which was passed following the decision of the House of Lords in *National Provincial Bank, Ltd.* v. *Ainsworth*,[12] which had the effect of considerably cutting down the rights of a deserted wife. This Act in no way affects any other rights and remedies possessed by the spouses and, as we shall see, the Act does not apply at all if both have a legal title and there may be other situations in which it may be advantageous for a spouse to rely on his or her common law rights. We shall therefore begin with a brief description of the position at common law and then consider the provisions of the Act.

The Position at Common Law.—If the legal and equitable title to the matrimonial home is vested in the husband exclusively, the wife can claim a right to occupy it not only by virtue of her right to her husband's consortium but also by virtue of her right to be maintained by him. Generally speaking, these rights are co-extensive, and the husband's duty to provide his wife with maintenance is primarily discharged by his providing her with a home.[13] Consequently, even though he deserts her and she ceases to enjoy his consortium, she will be entitled to remain in the matrimonial home unless she forfeits her right to maintenance by her own conduct, for example by committing adultery. But her right to her husband's consortium does not entitle her to occupy any other property belonging to him and he may obtain an injunction restraining her from entering it even though he has no justification for his refusal to cohabit.[14]

---

[10][1970] 2 All E.R. 780, H.L. See *ante*, p. 377.

[11]See *National Provincial Bank, Ltd.* v. *Ainsworth*, [1965] 2 All E.R. 472, H.L.; [1965] A.C. 1175.

[12][1965] 2 All E.R. 472, H.L.; [1965] A.C. 1175. See further *post*, p. 391.

[13]See *post*, p. 402. She also has a right, within reason, to invite guests into the home: *Jolliffe* v. *Willmett & Co.*, [1971] 1 All E.R. 478, 483 (no right to authorise entry of enquiry agent seeking evidence of husband's adultery 13 years after wife had left home). *Quaere* whether the husband may forbid her to do so.

[14]*Nanda* v. *Nanda*, [1967] 3 All E.R. 401; [1968] P. 351 (*ante*, p. 94). If the wife remains in possession of the matrimonial home with the husband's consent (and probably in other cases if his obligation to pay her maintenance is *pro tanto* reduced), he retains sufficient beneficial occupation to make him liable for the payment of rates: but not after the relationship of husband and wife is terminated by divorce: *Des Salles d'Epinoix* v. *Royal Borough of Kensington and Chelsea* [1970] 1 All E.R. 18; *Mourton* v. *Hounslow London B.C.*, [1970] 2 All E.R. 564; [1970] 2 Q.B. 362.

If the legal and equitable interests are vested solely in the wife, her duty to cohabit with her husband will normally mean that he will have a right to the use and occupation of the matrimonial home.[15] If he has forfeited the right to her consortium by his own conduct, the position is the same *mutatis mutandis* as when the property is vested solely in the husband.[16]

Whichever spouse is the beneficial owner, the courts will normally be slow to make any order which deprives either of them of the use of the matrimonial home.[17] But they have a discretion under section 17 of the Married Women's Property Act 1882 to control the spouses' right to possession and they will completely exclude one of them if this is necessary for the protection of the other.[18] Thus the wife has obtained an injunction forbidding the husband to enter her house after he had lost the right to consortium when his presence was diminishing the value of the property.[19] Conversely, if the husband unlawfully tries to evict his wife or to deal with his property in any way which might prejudice her right to occupy it (or even declines to give an undertaking not to do so), she may obtain an order forbidding him to perform the threatened act until he provides her with suitable alternative accommodation or at least reasonable financial provision.[20]

If the marriage is dissolved or annulled, the wife's right to her husband's consortium and maintenance go and consequently, as the Court of Appeal held in *Vaughan* v. *Vaughan*,[21] in the absence of any agreement to the contrary, she ceases to have any right at all to remain in the former matrimonial home if this is the husband's property. Similarly, he will no longer be entitled to remain in the wife's house.[1]

If the house is the property of both spouses, each has a right to occupy it arising directly out of beneficial ownership. Hence *prima facie* neither can have a better right than the other[2] and the court must have a much wider discretion under section 17 of the Married Women's Property Act than it has in most cases. It will presumably be slower than ever to make an order forbidding either spouse to enter and use the home, but its power to protect a spouse with a proprietary right cannot be less than its power to protect a spouse who has none. Consequently, where an impasse has been reached, the court's discretion must be exercised against the spouse at fault who may be excluded from the home if this is necessary to protect the

---

[15]*Shipman* v. *Shipman*, [1924] 2 Ch. 140, 146, C.A. This right extends to the husband's visitors as well (*Jolliffe* v. *Willmett & Co.*, *ante*) but not to one entering the house on the husband's authority for the purpose of annoying the wife: *Weldon* v. *De Bathe* (1884), 14 Q.B.D. 339, C.A.

[16]*Shipman* v. *Shipman*, (*supra*).   [17]*Hall* v. *Hall*, [1971] 1 All E.R. 762, C.A.

[18]*Stewart* v. *Stewart*, [1947] 2 All E.R. 813, C.A.; [1948] 1 K.B. 507. Unpleasantness, tension and inconvenience are not enough: *Hall* v. *Hall*, (*supra*).

[19]*Shipman* v. *Shipman*, (*supra*); *Symonds* v. *Hallett* (1883), 24 Ch.D. 346, C.A. *Cf. Wood* v. *Wood* (1871), 19 W.R. 1049. See George, *Disputes over the Matrimonial Home*, 16 Conv. 27.

[20]*Halden* v. *Halden*, [1966] 3 All E.R. 412, C.A., following *Lee* v. *Lee*, [1952] 1 All E.R. 1299; [1952] 2 Q.B. 489 n. *Cf. Pinckney* v. *Pinckney*, [1966] 1 All E.R. 121 (husband ordered to remove mistress whom he had installed in the matrimonial home).

[21][1953] 1 All E.R. 209, C.A.; [1953] 1 Q.B. 762. If the wife is in possession in pursuance of an agreement, the contract might be altered under the provisions of s. 14 of the Matrimonial Proceedings and Property Act 1970: see *post*, p. 410.

[1]*Morris* v. *Tarrant*, [1971] 2 W.L.R. 630.

[2]See *Richman* v. *Richman* (1950), 66 T.L.R. (Pt. 2) 44.

other's person or property or even possibly to permit the innocent spouse to live in peace. This protection may be even more necessary if there are children and the court may in effect restore a spouse who has been compelled to leave by ordering the other out.[3]

Clearly such a situation cannot last indefinitely. Whether the spouses are joint tenants or tenants in common, there will be a statutory trust for sale and either of them may call for an order that the trusts be executed.[4] So long as the marriage is a going concern and the house is being used as the matrimonial home, a sale will not be ordered because this would defeat the purpose of the trust. But once the marriage has irretrievably broken down (whether or not it has been formally brought to an end), the court will normally implement the trust for sale so as to enable both parties to realise their capital.[5] Special circumstances may justify a postponement, for example if one of the spouses needs time to find other accommodation,[6] if other matrimonial proceedings are pending, or perhaps if there is a reasonable chance of a reconciliation. The court will also be less ready to force the wife to leave the house if she has not lost her right to maintenance, but it will still do so if the cost to the husband in locking up his capital is far in excess of any financial provision he would have to make for her.[7] There may be other cases where it would be unjust to order an immediate sale: thus in *Bedson* v. *Bedson*[8] the court refused to do so where the wife was in desertion and the property in question (a draper's shop with a flat over it) had been bought out of the husband's savings and was his sole livelihood.

Where other Matrimonial Proceedings are pending.—If other proceedings (for example, divorce) are pending, the rights in the matrimonial home are usually best dealt with at the same time as other questions of financial provision, and consequently there is a tendency to maintain the *status quo* until the outcome of the petition is known.[9] Earlier cases suggested that the court will protect the wife's rights by excluding

---

[3]*Gurasz* v. *Gurasz*, [1969] 3 All E.R. 822, C.A.; [1970] P. 11. In *Des Salles d'Epinoix* v. *Des Salles d'Epinoix*, [1967] 2 All E.R. 539, 544, C.A., WILLMER, L.J., stated that the court would not grant an injunction restraining the wife from locking the husband out of the matrimonial home of which they were joint lessees because this was not necessary to protect his person or such right of property as he had in the house. *Sed quaere?*

[4]Law of Property Act, 1925, ss. 34-36; *Rawlings* v. *Rawlings*, [1964] 2 All E.R. 804, C.A.; [1964] P. 398; *Waller* v. *Waller*, [1967] 1 All E.R. 305.

[5]*Jones* v. *Challenger*, [1960] 1 All E.R. 785, C.A.; [1961] 1 Q.B. 176. *Jackson* v. *Jackson*, [1970] 3 All E.R. 854.

[6]*Mayes* v. *Mayes* (1969), 210 Estates Gazette 935 (husband temporarily unemployed and therefore finding it difficult to raise mortgage to buy another flat). In *Re Johns' Assignment Trusts*, [1970] 2 All E.R. 210, it was suggested that the spouses, who were trustees for sale, might let the house to the husband who was still living there.

[7]*Jackson* v. *Jackson*, (*supra*). In *Re A Debtor, Ex parte Trustee*, v. *Solomon*, [1966] 3 All E.R. 255; [1967] Ch. 573, the court ordered a sale with vacant possession when the husband, who had deserted the wife, later became bankrupt and it was necessary to realise his assets. For a criticism of this case, see Palley, *Wives, Creditors and the Matrimonial Home*, 20 N.I.L.Q. 132.

[8][1965] 3 All E.R. 307, C.A.; [1965] 2 Q.B. 666. See also Samuels, *Forcing a Sale of the Joint Matrimonial Home*, 110 Sol. Jo. 5.

[9]*Stewart* v. *Stewart*, [1947] 2 All E.R. 813, C.A.; *Boyt* v. *Boyt*, [1948] 2 All E.R. 436, C.A.; *Short* v. *Short*, [1960] 3 All E.R. 6, C.A.

the husband only if this is necessary for her safety,[10] if she would otherwise be left at his mercy,[11] if he is using the threat to return as a means of putting pressure on her[12] or if irreparable harm might be done if the wife were not so protected.[13] In *Jones* v. *Jones*,[14] however, the Court of Appeal held that an injunction could be granted whenever the court considers that the wife is entitled to return to the matrimonial home pending the hearing of the petition and that she will not be able to do so if the husband is there. Presumably *mutatis mutandis* a husband could also obtain an order to keep his wife out. Similarly the problem may be resolved by reference to the interests of the children.[15]

Furniture.—The only reported case dealing solely with the spouses' rights with respect to the furniture—*W.* v. *W.*[16]—indicates that the courts will not protect the wife's right to use it as fully as they will protect her right to remain in the matrimonial home. The furniture (the ownership of which was not in dispute) belonged partly to the husband and partly to the wife. After the husband had left the wife, he claimed his portion of the goods, which included a table and chairs and the matrimonial bed. It was held that the court's discretion under section 17 of the Married Women's Property Act will not necessarily be exercised in the same way with respect to the furniture as it will with respect to the house itself, and that in this case the husband should be entitled to take his own property because the wife could be expected to replace it in the course of time. But DEVLIN, J., stated that he would not have been prepared to make this order if the husband had been acting vindictively or, in any case, if the wife would have been left with nothing but bare boards. If she has not forfeited the right to be maintained, she must be left with the means of subsistence; it then becomes a question of fact in each case where the line is to be drawn.

The Matrimonial Homes Act 1967.—The purpose of this Act is to give greater protection to a spouse who cannot claim any proprietary right to occupy the matrimonial home. Consequently it applies only " where one spouse is entitled to occupy a dwellinghouse by virtue of any estate or interest or contract or by virtue of any enactment giving him or her the right to remain in occupation, and the other spouse is not so entitled ".[17] Hence the Act does not apply if, for example, the spouses are joint legal tenants of the matrimonial home; on the other hand it will apply if the husband is a statutory tenant under the Rent

---

[10]*Richman* v. *Richman* (1950), 66 T.L.R. (Pt. 2), 44, 46.

[11]*Silverstone* v. *Silverstone*, [1953] 1 All E.R. 556; *Cook* v. *Cook*, [1961] 2 All E.R. 791; [1964] P. 220.

[12]*Boyt* v. *Boyt*, (*supra*); *Teakle* v. *Teakle* (1950), 66 T.L.R. (Pt. 2) 588.

[13]*Murcutt* v. *Murcutt*, [1952] 2 All E.R. 427, 428; [1952] P. 266, 270.

[14][1971] 1 W.L.R. 396, C.A. (husband ordered to leave house with his mistress whom he had installed there). But the court will not restrain the husband from bringing proceedings for possession if the wife will ultimately have to surrender possession to him whatever the outcome of the petition: *Murcutt* v. *Murcutt*, (*supra*).

[15]*Boyt* v. *Boyt*, (*supra*); *Pinckney* v. *Pinckney*, [1966] 1 All E.R. 121.

[16][1951] 2 T.L.R. 1135.

[17]S. 1 (1).

Act because he will be entitled to occupy the house by virtue of a statute. This created a difficulty if the house had been conveyed into the husband's name but the wife could claim an interest in equity because she had contributed to the purchase money. This was sufficient to take her right of occupation outside the Act so that it could not be registered; on the other hand, her interest would not appear on the title and consequently she lost the protection she could otherwise have had against a purchaser from the husband. To solve this problem it is now provided that a spouse who has an equitable interest in a dwelling-house or in the proceeds of sale may nevertheless have a statutory right of occupation provided that he or she has no legal estate in the land either solely or jointly.[18]

For the sake of convenience in the following discussion it will be assumed that the beneficial interest in the matrimonial home is vested in the husband to the exclusion of the wife. It must be remembered, however, that exactly the same principles apply *mutatis mutandis* if it is vested in the wife to the exclusion of the husband.

The Act gives the wife a statutory right of occupation. If she is in occupation of the dwellinghouse, she has a right not to be evicted or excluded from any part of it except by a court order; if she is out of occupation, she has a right to apply for an order permitting her to enter and occupy.[19] The term "dwellinghouse" includes any building or part of a building occupied as a dwelling together with any yard, garden, garage or outhouse. The Act does not apply, however, to any house which has never been the spouses' matrimonial home; consequently, although the wife is protected if she has been constructively deserted, she has no right to occupy premises into which the husband has moved after leaving her.[20] Jurisdiction to make orders is vested in the High Court or a county court.[1]

So long as the wife has a right of occupation, either spouse may apply to the court for an order declaring, enforcing, restricting or terminating it. The court may make such order as it thinks just and reasonable and must have regard to all the circumstances including the spouses' conduct towards each other, their needs and resources and the needs of the children. The court may limit the wife's right to occupy the house and in particular may exclude her from any part of it used for the husband's trade, business or profession. Hence, if the husband is a medical practitioner, the wife might be forbidden to enter his surgery or use his garage. The court is also given a general power to regulate either spouse's right to occupy the house: this obviously means that the husband's right may be limited to certain parts of it, but it seems that he cannot be entirely excluded from it indefinitely.[2] The court

---

[18]S. 1 (9), added by the Matrimonial Proceedings and Property Act 1970, s. 38. See further Law Com. No. 25, para. 59.

[19]S. 1 (1).   [20]S. 1 (7) and (8).   [1]S. 1 (6).

[2]In *Maynard* v. *Maynard*, [1969] 1 All E.R. 1; [1969] P. 88, BAKER, J., drew a distinction between the words " terminating " and " regulating " and held that he had no jurisdiction to order the husband out of the house. In *Tarr* v. *Tarr*, [1971] 1 All E.R. 817, the Court of Appeal was of the opinion that he could not be excluded for ever but held that he could be excluded until further order. In the earlier case of *Baynham* v. *Baynham*, [1969] 1 All E.R. 305, C.A., the Court of Appeal upheld an order excluding him without comment.

may also order the wife to pay the husband an occupation rent and may impose on either of them obligations to repair and maintain the house and to pay other outgoings (for example, mortgage repayments). Orders may be for a limited period of time and the court may make an interim order to last, for example, until the hearing of divorce proceedings.[3]

The wife's right of occupation under the Act subsists only during coverture and will come to an end on the husband's death or on the dissolution or annulment of the marriage. But in the event of matrimonial dispute or estrangement the court may order that the right shall continue after the marriage has been terminated (whether by the husband's death or a court order).[4]

The Spouses' Rights against Third Persons.—Up to now we have been considering the spouses' rights *inter se*. A series of cases from 1952 had gone much further by laying down the rule that a deserted wife could enforce her right to remain in the matrimonial home (of which her husband was the beneficial owner) not only against him but also against anyone claiming through him other than a *bona fide* purchaser for value of a legal or equitable estate or interest without notice of her claim. The validity of this so-called " deserted wife's equity " was eventually considered by the House of Lords in *National Provincial Bank, Ltd.* v. *Ainsworth*.[5] The husband had deserted his wife (the respondent) and left her and their children in the matrimonial home. He then conveyed the house to a company in which he had a controlling interest and which in turn charged it to the appellant bank to secure a loan. This was not repaid and the bank, as mortgagee, claimed possession of the property charged. The wife set up her " deserted wife's equity " but it was unanimously held that her defence must fail. The only case in which the wife's equity will avail her is where the sale by the husband is a completely sham transaction designed to enable him to obtain possession. Four of the members of the House of Lords in *Ainsworth's* case[6] considered that the earlier case of *Ferris* v. *Weaven*[7] could still be justified on its special facts. In that case the husband, having deserted his wife and left her in the matrimonial home, sold the house to the plaintiff, his brother-in-law, for the sum of £30 which was never paid. The sole purpose of this conveyance

---

[3]S. 1 (2), (3) and (4); *Baynham* v. *Baynham*, (*supra*).

[4]Ss. 1 (8) and 2 (2). It is not clear what is meant by the expressions " matrimonial dispute or estrangement "; presumably they cover litigation and separation. See further generally Crane, *The Matrimonial Homes Act 1967*, 32 Conv. 85, 33 Conv. 148; Stone, 31 M.L.R. 305; Kahn-Freund, *Recent Legislation on Matrimonial Property*, 33 M.L.R. 601, particularly at pp. 609 *et. seq.*

[5][1965] 2 All E.R. 472, H.L.; [1965] A.C. 1175. For a detailed discussion of this decision, see Crane, *After the Deserted Wife's Licence*, 29 Conv. 254 and 464. See also Bailey in [1965] C.L.J. 216.

[6]LORD HODSON (with whom LORD GUEST concurred) at pp. 479 and 1223; LORD UPJOHN (" it may possibly be justified ") at pp. 489 and 1240; LORD WILBERFORCE at pp. 501 and 1258, respectively.

[7][1952] 2 All E.R. 233 (although the *ratio decidendi* is no longer good law). MEGARRY, J., concluded that the case was correctly decided on its facts in *Miles* v. *Bull*, [1968] 3 All E.R. 632; [1969] 1 Q.B. 258, but as he pointed out (at pp. 636 and 264, respectively) the fact that the price is low or not paid in full does not necessarily mean that the transaction is a sham. See further *Miles* v. *Bull* (*No. 2*), [1969] 3 All E.R. 1585.

was to enable the husband, who could not personally have obtained possession in the circumstances, to do so through the purchaser. It was held that the plaintiff could have no greater right than the husband and his claim must fail. The decision may still be of importance if the wife has not registered her right of occupation under the Matrimonial Homes Act,[8] but in many cases the wife could have the sale set aside as a transaction intended to defeat her claim for financial provision.[9]

The real problem is to balance the claims of the deserted wife against those of the husband's purchaser or (as is usually the case) his creditors either acting through his trustee in bankruptcy or seeking to realise their own security as mortgagees of the house in which the wife is living. Looked at from the conveyancing point of view, there are two fatal objections to the " deserted wife's equity ". In the first place the wife's rights against the purchaser can clearly be no greater than they are against the husband himself. As against him she would lose her right to remain in the house if, for example, she were to commit adultery or the husband were to offer her suitable alternative accommodation. It is therefore transient and determinable and lacks the qualities of being definable, identifiable, permanent and stable which are essential if it is to be regarded as a right in property capable of binding the land in the hands of subsequent purchasers.[10] In the second place it must be possible for the prospective purchaser to discover precisely what rights exist in the land and these are of such a highly personal nature, known only to the spouses themselves, that he would be in an impossible position when he made enquiries.[11]

One of the main objects of the Matrimonial Homes Act was to overcome these difficulties. For the sake of convenience in the following discussion it will again be assumed that the beneficial interest in the matrimonial home is vested in the husband to the exclusion of the wife, but it must be remembered that exactly the same principles apply if it is vested in the wife to the exclusion of the husband. The way the Act seeks to protect both the wife and the purchaser is by providing that her right to occupy the matrimonial home (whether or not a court order has been made) shall be a charge on the husband's estate or interest in the property. The charge takes effect on the husband's acquisition of the property, the date of the marriage, or the commencement of the Act (1st January, 1968) whichever last happens. It terminates on the husband's death or the dissolution or annulment of the marriage unless the court has previously made an order that it shall continue.[12]

As the right of a wife who is out of occupation is limited to enter and occupy the matrimonial home with the leave of the court, it seems that she has no registrable charge until leave has been given.[13]

---

[8]See *infra*.

[9]See *post*, p. 454. Such an attempt failed in *Ainsworth's* case because the bank was a *bona fide* purchaser for value without notice of the husband's intention.

[10]*National Provincial Bank, Ltd.* v. *Ainsworth*, [1965] 2 All E.R. 472, H.L., at pp. 479-480, 485-486, and 494-495; [1965] A.C. 1175, at pp. 1224, 1233-1234, and 1248-1250.

[11]*Ibid.*, pp. 486 and 495-496, and 1234 and 1250, respectively.

[12]S. 2 (1) and (2).

[13]*Rutherford* v. *Rutherford*, [1970] 3 All E.R. 422. The point was left open in *Baynham* v. *Baynham*, [1969] 1 All E.R. 305, C.A.

The charge is registrable as a Class F Land Charge under the Land Charges Act 1925.[14] It will bind any person deriving title under the husband except that it will be void against any subsequent purchaser of the land or any interest in it for value unless it is registered. Whether it has been registered or not, however, it will be void against the husband's trustee in bankruptcy or his creditors' trustees if he assigns the house to them under a deed of arrangement. Even if the court has ordered the right to continue after the husband's death, the charge will also be void if the husband's estate is insolvent.[15] One sees here another example of the principle that the claims of the husband's creditors are to be preferred to those of his wife; one can also see the anxiety of the legislature that the creditors should not be defrauded by the registration of a charge intended to defeat their claim to the property.

The wife is entitled to have only one charge registered under the Act. Consequently, if the spouses have two homes (for example, a town flat and a country cottage), she must make up her mind which occupation right she will register. If, after registering one, she registers another, the first registration must be cancelled.[16] Registration must also be cancelled if the court terminates the wife's right of occupation and when the marriage comes to an end unless the court has ordered that her right shall continue.[17] The wife may release her right in whole or in part in writing and may agree in writing that another charge or interest shall take priority over it. If the charge is registered, the normal conveyancing procedure is for the wife to deliver to the purchaser on completion an application for the cancellation of the registration.[18]

As the cases indicate, in practice the wife has more to fear from a mortgagee than from a purchaser of the whole of the husband's estate. If he tries to sell the matrimonial home, she will be put on her guard by potential buyers' coming to view the premises; but if he mortgages the house to secure his overdraft, she may know nothing about the transaction until the bank tries to enforce its security. *Ex hypothesi* a solicitor will be acting for the husband alone when the matrimonial home is bought so there will be no one to advise her to register her right of occupation and in any event, like the wives in the cases concerned with the ownership of the house, she will not contemplate the necessity of protecting her interest. When the marriage does break down, the property may already be mortgaged and her registration will come too late unless she can protect herself by continuing to pay the mortgage instalments herself.[19] Herein lies the weakness of the Act

---

[14]S. 2 (6). In the case of registered land registration is effected by notice or caution: s. 2 (7).

[15]S. 2 (3)-(5) and Sched.; Land Charges Act 1925, s. 20 (8). For the power to tack mortgages, see s. 2 (8).

[16]S. 3.

[17]S. 5. If the wife has an order continuing her right of occupation after the termination of the marriage, she must renew her registration (or register her charge if it was not registered before).

[18]Ss. 4 and 6.

[19]Any tender or payment in respect of rates, rent, mortgage instalments or other outgoings made by a spouse in occupation shall be as good as if made by the other spouse: s. 1 (5).

which will give effective protection only when an automatic registration of the wife's right of occupation becomes a common practice.[20]

3. THE RENT ACT

In the preceding discussion it has been assumed that the husband owned the matrimonial home in fee simple or for a long term of years. But so many homes are leasehold property (usually on a weekly, monthly or quarterly tenancy) and subject to the Rent Act that we must now consider the position in the light of its provisions.

Rent control is the immediate outcome of the chronic shortage of houses and began in this country in 1915 as the result of the shortage in the First World War. The details of the scheme are extremely complex and are now contained in the Rent Act 1968, which consolidated provisions formerly contained in more than twenty statutes. The purpose of the Act is twofold: to prevent the charging of exorbitant rents and to protect the tenant from arbitrary eviction. The former is achieved by severely limiting the landlord's power to increase the rent; the second is achieved by limiting the landlord's right to obtain possession. It is with the latter that we are principally concerned.

Controlled and Regulated Tenancies.—The Act applies only to a house or part of a house let as a separate dwelling: a definition wide enough to include a flat.[1] Certain tenancies are not protected; of these the more important are premises let at no rent or at a rent which is less than two-thirds of their rateable value, agricultural holdings occupied by the farmer, furnished premises, and premises let by the Crown, Government departments, local authorities, development corporations, housing trusts and (in certain circumstances) housing associations.[2]

Rent control is designed to protect the poorer tenant and consequently it has always been limited to leases of premises of less than specified rateable values. During the 1950's it was felt that the building of new houses had sufficiently eased the position to enable a progressive scheme of decontrol to be introduced. The Housing Repairs and Rents Act of 1954 excluded from the operation of the Acts premises erected after 29th August, 1954, as well as separate and self-contained premises produced by the conversion of other premises after that date. The Rent Act of 1957 went further and provided that the Acts should not apply to premises the rateable value of which exceeded £40 in London and £30 elsewhere in England and Wales or which were let for a period of more than 21 years (thus immediately decontrolling some 800,000 dwellings) and excluded almost all new lettings coming into operation after 5th July, 1957. It will be seen that these provisions contemplated the eventual extinction of rent control as fewer and fewer leases would

---

[20]See further Palley, *Wives, Creditors and the Matrimonial Home*, 20 N.I.L.Q. 132.
[1]See Megarry, *Rent Acts*, 10th Ed., 72 *et seq.*
[2]For the full list, see the Rent Act 1968, ss. 2, 4 and 5; Megarry, *op. cit.*, c. 4. Tenants of furnished premises are given protection by Part VI of the Act and tenants of long tenancies at a low rent by the Landlord and Tenant Act 1954.

be covered by the Rent Acts—a process which could be speeded up by the Minister of Housing and Local Government, who was empowered by the 1957 Act to release other dwellings from control from time to time. This Act also introduced the " rent limit " which enabled land-lords to charge an economic rent based upon the gross rateable value of the property and thus remedied an injustice suffered by many who had to meet their liability to keep in repair premises let at an absurdly low rent.[3]

Within less than a decade, however, it had become apparent that this policy of decontrol would not work. Large scale immigration from other Commonwealth countries caused a further shortage of property (especially of the cheaper type) and this, coupled with some scandalous cases of " racketeering " by property speculators, produced continuing inflation of rents. The result was the passing of the Rent Act of 1965, which extended protection by introducing a slightly different concept, that of the regulated tenancy. A regulated tenancy is a tenancy of a dwelling, the rateable value of which did not exceed £400 in London and £200 elsewhere on the appropriate day[4] and which is not controlled because its rateable value exceeded the maximum laid down in the 1957 Act, or because it was erected or converted after 29th August, 1954, or because the letting came into operation after 5th July, 1957, or because the lease was originally for more than 21 years.[5] The Act of 1965 called a temporary halt to the increase of rents in the case of regulated tenancies and introduced machinery whereby either the landlord or the tenant can have a fair rent fixed by a local rent officer from whom an appeal lies to an area assessment committee.[6] It also empowered the Minister of Housing and Local Government to convert existing con-trolled tenancies into regulated tenancies and entirely release from rent regulation any specified class or classes of dwellings in an area where the demand does not substantially exceed the number of houses available.[7]

Except for the recovery of possession by an owner-occupier and by landlords who have let houses to ministers of religion and agricultural employees[8] the provisions of the Rent Act (including those relating to transmission on the death of a tenant[9]) apply equally to controlled and regulated tenancies.

Statutory Tenants.—So long as a tenant is in occupation under a contractual lease, he is clearly protected from arbitrary eviction by the terms of his contract. The Act goes much further by giving him a wide measure of protection after his lease ends. A contractual lease to which the Act applies (whether it is controlled or regulated) is known as a *protected tenancy;* if a tenant under a protected tenancy remains in

---

[3] See now Part V of the Rent Act 1968.

[4] *I.e.,* 23rd March, 1965, if the dwelling-house had a rateable value shown in the valuation list then in force, and the date on which such a value was first shown in other cases: *ibid.,* s. 6 (3).

[5] *Ibid.,* s. 7 and Sched. 2.

[6] See now *ibid.,* Parts III and IV.

[7] See now *ibid.,* ss. 8 and 100. The functions of the Minister of Housing and Local Government have now been transferred to the Secretary of State for the Environment: S.I. 1970 No. 1681.

[8] See *post,* p. 398. [9] See *post,* pp. 517 *et seq.*

possession after his contractual lease has been determined—for example,
if his term has expired or he has been given notice to quit in accordance
with the provisions of the lease—his tenancy becomes a *statutory
tenancy*.[10]   Furthermore in certain circumstances a member of a
deceased statutory or protected tenant's family also becomes a statutory
tenant.[11]   A statutory tenant is generally speaking bound by all the
terms and conditions in the original lease and entitled to the benefit
of them.[12]

In order to claim the benefit of the Act the statutory tenant must
continue in personal occupation of the premises as his home, for the
policy of the Act is to protect the home and not to give the tenant
any wider privileges. A person may be in occupation of more than one
home for this purpose simultaneously, as where he works in two places
and has a home in each of them which he occupies when he is at that
particular place;[13] and a temporary absence will not suffice to bring
his statutory tenancy to an end.[14] But he must retain both the *corpus*
of possession and an *animus revertendi*. Thus it has been held that a
wife who had gone away because of illness leaving her furniture in the
house, in which her husband occasionally slept and to which she hoped
to return as soon as her health improved, was still in occupation and
was entitled to the protection of the Act.[15] But a mere *animus*
without the *corpus* will not be sufficient, and consequently it has been
held that a man who left his house deserted whilst serving a sentence
of imprisonment ceased to be a statutory tenant.[16] He could have
averted this result only " by coupling and clothing his inward intention
with some formal, outward, and visible sign of it ", for example by
installing a caretaker or relative to preserve the premises for his home-
coming.[17] Conversely, if the tenant leaves the premises with no intention of ever returning there at all, he loses the status of a statutory
tenant even though he leaves his furniture there with a caretaker or
relative.[18]

But to this rule that the occupation must be personal is one important
statutory exception designed to protect the tenant's spouse—particularly the deserted wife. If one spouse is a protected or statutory tenant
but the other is in actual occupation of the premises, this is deemed to

---

[10]Rent Act 1968, ss. 1 and 3; Megarry, *op. cit.*, 178 *et seq.* A husband's permitting
his wife to remain in possession of the matrimonial home as a condition of paying a
reduced sum under a maintenance order does not create the relationship of landlord
and tenant so as to give the wife the protection of the Rent Act: *Bramwell* v. *Bramwell*,
[1942] 1 All E.R. 137, C.A.; [1942] 1 K.B. 370. *Cf. Marcroft Wagons, Ltd.* v. *Smith*,
[1951] 2 All E.R. 271, C.A.; [1951] 2 K.B. 496 (daughter permitted to remain in possession after her mother's death for a short time not protected by the Act).
[11]See *post*, p. 517 *et seq.*
[12]Rent Act 1968, s. 12.
[13]See Megarry, *op. cit.*, 186-188 and the cases there cited.
[14]Megarry, *op. cit.*, 191-195.
[15]*Wigley* v. *Leigh*, [1950] 1 All E.R. 73, C.A.; [1950] 2 K.B. 305.
[16]*Brown* v. *Brash*, [1948] 1 All E.R. 922, C.A.; [1948] 2 K.B. 247.
[17]*Per* ASQUITH, L.J., *ibid.*, at pp. 926 and 254-255, respectively.
[18]*Skinner* v. *Geary*, [1931] 2 K.B. 546, C.A. (sister); *Robson* v. *Headland* (1948),
64 T.L.R. 596, C.A. (divorced wife and son); *Beck* v. *Scholz*, [1953] 1 All E.R. 814, C.A.;
[1953] 1 Q.B. 570 (caretakers).

be the occupation of the tenant himself even though the spouse in occupation has been deserted by the tenant and is there against his will.[19]

It will be recalled that the provisions of the Matrimonial Homes Act will continue to apply notwithstanding that one spouse holds the premises on a protected or statutory tenancy. Consequently the court can make an order permitting the tenant's spouse to enter the home and regulating both parties' right to occupy it.[20]

Recovery of Possession.—If the statutory tenant and his or her spouse both leave the premises, this automatically brings the statutory tenancy to an end, and the landlord may retake possession or, if necessary, recover it by suing any trespasser on the property.[1] But if a protected or statutory tenant or his or her spouse is still in occupation, the landlord may obtain an order for possession only if two conditions are fulfilled.[2] First, the court must be satisfied that, having regard to all the circumstances, it is reasonable to make the order. Secondly, the landlord must prove the existence of one of the following statutory grounds on which the court can make an order:

(a) that rent has not been paid or any other of the tenant's covenants has not been performed or observed;

(b) that the tenant, any person residing with him, or his sub-tenant has been guilty of conduct which is a nuisance or annoyance to adjoining occupiers, or has been convicted of using the premises for an immoral or illegal purpose or permitting such use;

(c) that the tenant has caused or permitted the premises to deteriorate by waste, neglect or default;

(d) that the tenant has given notice to quit and as a consequence the landlord has contracted to sell or let the premises or taken some other step as a result of which he would be seriously prejudiced if he could not obtain possession;

(e) that the tenant has assigned or sub-let the whole of the premises[3] without the landlord's consent;

(f) that, if the dwelling house consists of or includes an off-licence, the tenant has prejudiced the business in one of the ways specified in the Act or a renewal of the licence has been refused;

(g) that, if the premises were let to the tenant in consequence of his being employed by the landlord, that employment has now ceased and the landlord reasonably requires the premises for a person in the whole-time employment of the landlord or one of his tenants;

---

[19]Matrimonial Homes Act 1967, s. 1 (5). No order need have been made under the Act. Before the passing of this Act the wife's occupation was attributed to the husband but not *vice versa*.

[20]See *ante*, pp. 389-391. But once the landlord has obtained an order for possession and this has taken effect, the tenant is no longer entitled to remain in possession by virtue of the Rent Act and consequently the spouse loses the right of occupation under the Matrimonial Homes Act and becomes a trespasser: *Penn* v. *Dunn*, [1970] 2 All E.R. 858, C.A.

[1]*Brown* v. *Draper*, [1944] 1 All E.R. 246, C.A.; [1944] K.B. 309; *Middleton* v. *Baldock*, [1950] 1 All E.R. 708, 710, C.A.; [1950] 1 K.B. 657, 661-662.

[2]Rent Act 1968, s. 10 and Sched. 3. See further Megarry, *op. cit.*, c. 7. See also the Landlord and Tenant Act 1954, s. 12 (1).

[3]Or has sub-let part of the premises, the remainder being already sub-let.

(h) that the landlord reasonably requires the premises for occupation as a residence by himself, a child of his over the age of 18, his father or mother, or (in the case of a regulated tenancy only) his spouse's father or mother, provided that greater hardship would not be caused by granting the order than refusing it;

(i) that the tenant has charged his sub-tenant an excessive rent;

(j) that suitable alternative accommodation is available to the tenant.

In the case of a *regulated* tenancy there is a further ground on which possession may be recovered and which is primarily designed to protect a person who occupies premises as his residence (called in the Act an " owner-occupier ") and wishes to let them during a temporary absence. If an owner-occupier, having let the premises on a regulated tenancy, requires them as a residence for himself or for any member of his family[4] who was residing with him when he last occupied them as a residence, the court must make an order for possession in his favour if he would have been entitled to possession but for the operation of the Rent Acts. In such a case it is not necessary for the claimant to prove that it is reasonable for the court to make the order, but he can rely on this provision only if he gives the tenant notice in writing that possession may be recovered under this section before the commencement of the tenancy.[5] Similar power is given to landlords to recover possession of a dwelling-house let on a regulated tenancy for occupation by a minister of religion as such or by an agricultural employee as such or required by the landlord for an agricultural employee as a consequence of an agricultural amalgamation.

The parties may not contract out of the Rent Act. Hence a contract between the landlord and tenant that the latter shall surrender the premises (and *a fortiori* a notice by the tenant terminating the lease) will not give the landlord the right to recover possession unless the facts come within ground (d) above.[6] Similarly the court has no jurisdiction to make an order if the landlord rests his case on none of these statutory grounds, even though the tenant does not defend the action;[7] but if the landlord alleges that a ground exists and the tenant does not contest this, the court may make an order without enquiring into the truth of the allegation.[8]

It will thus be seen that where the matrimonial home is held on a controlled or regulated tenancy, the spouses have a large measure of security. The significance of this will be appreciated when it is realised that the dwelling house will be subject to the Rent Act in many cases where hardship would otherwise result.

The Position of the Deserted Spouse.—If the wife (or husband) of a tenant holding on a weekly or other periodical tenancy is deserted and continues to pay the rent herself, a number of legal consequences

[4]For the meaning of " member of the family ", see *post*, pp. 519-520.
[5]Or by 7th June, 1966, in the case of a tenancy created before 8th December, 1965.
[6]*Brown* v. *Draper*, (*ante*); *Middleton* v. *Baldock*, (*ante*).
[7]*Middleton* v. *Baldock*, (*ante*).
[8]*Middleton* v. *Baldock*, (*ante*), at pp. 710, 715, and 661, 669, respectively.

follow. If the landlord is unaware of the desertion and assumes that the husband is still in personal occupation of the premises, he will regard the wife merely as an agent and the lease will still be vested in the husband. If the landlord is aware that the husband has left but continues to take the rent from the wife, it is a question of fact whether he is continuing to treat the wife as her husband's agent (in which case the husband will remain the legal tenant) or whether he has accepted her as a new tenant (in which case the wife will become a new contractual tenant). The mere fact that the landlord accepts rent from the wife with full knowledge of the facts is not *per se* evidence of his having granted a new lease to her, for, as we shall see, he cannot evict the wife and consequently has no alternative to taking the rent from her.[9] But if no new tenancy is brought into existence, the original tenant, and not the spouse, continues to hold under the old tenancy. Hence, the members of the spouse's family could not claim a right to remain in possession after her death.[10]

The position of the deserted spouse is the result of his right to occupy the matrimonial home under the Matrimonial Homes Act 1967 and the attribution of occupation to the tenant. If the landlord serves a notice to quit, this will have no other effect than to convert a contractual tenancy into a statutory one and he still cannot obtain possession unless he can prove the existence of one of the statutory grounds.[11] The tenant presumably remains liable for the rent,[12] but as non-payment of rent is one of the grounds on which the landlord may obtain possession, the wife may clearly have to pay it herself to secure her own occupation, in which case she may recover any sums paid from her husband.[13]

It follows from these principles, as well as from the decisions of the Court of Appeal in *Brown* v. *Draper*[14] and *Middleton* v. *Baldock*,[15] that the wife cannot be evicted (except on one of the statutory grounds) even though her husband wishes to terminate the tenancy too. In the latter case the husband had deserted his wife and left her in the matrimonial home. The landlord then served a notice to quit on the husband who acknowledged the landlord's right to the premises and offered to

[9]*Cf. Morrison* v. *Jacobs*, [1945] 2 All E.R. 430, C.A.; [1945] K.B. 577. See also the alternative ground for the decision in *Wabe* v. *Taylor*, [1952] 2 All E.R. 420, C.A.; [1952] 2 Q.B. 735, as explained in *S. L. Dando, Ltd.* v. *Hitchcock*, [1954] 2 All E.R. 335, 337-338, C.A.; [1954] 2 Q.B. 317, 324, and *Cove* v. *Flick*, [1954] 2 All E.R. 441, 442, C.A.; [1954] 2 Q.B. 326 n., 327. Payment of rent by the spouse in occupation is as good as if made by the tenant: Matrimonial Homes Act 1967, s. 1 (5).

[10]See *post*, p. 518.

[11]He must join the husband as a party since he is the statutory tenant: *Brown* v. *Draper*, [1944] 1 All E.R. 246, C.A.; [1944] K.B. 309. Presumably he must also join the wife as the person actually in possession: *cf. post*, p. 400, n. [16].

[12]Assumed " for the moment " by LORD GODDARD, C.J., in *R.* v. *Twickenham Rent Tribunal; ex p. Dunn*, [1953] 2 All E.R. 734, 735; [1953] 2 Q.B. 425, 430, even though the husband were to give notice to the landlord.

[13]On the principle that if A discharges a legal obligation vested in B in order to preserve his (A's) own rights, B is under a quasi-contractual obligation to compensate A: see Cheshire and Fifoot, *Contract*, 7th Ed., 585-589.

[14][1944] 1 All E.R. 246, C.A.; [1944] K.B. 309. In this case the action was bound to fail as the landlord had not joined the husband as statutory tenant as a party to the action.

[15][1950] 1 All E.R. 708, C.A.; [1950] 1 K.B. 657. See also *Old Gate Estates, Ltd.* v. *Alexander*, [1949] 2 All E.R. 822, C.A.; [1950] 1 K.B. 311.

give him immediate possession. The landlord then brought separate actions against the spouses for possession, which the wife alone defended. Judgment was entered for the plaintiff in both actions, but both orders were reversed on the wife's appeal to the Court of Appeal. Since the landlord's claim was based on none of the statutory grounds for obtaining possession, he could succeed only if the premises were vacated; and as the husband could not lawfully evict his wife, his acknowledgment of the landlord's right to enter could have no legal effect whatever. Only if the husband terminates her authority because she has committed a matrimonial offence or otherwise forfeited her right to remain in the husband's house, can she be evicted, and even then an order would have to be obtained terminating her right of occupation under the Matrimonial Homes Act. Thus it will be seen that the deserted wife of, say, a weekly tenant under a controlled or regulated tenancy has greater security than the deserted wife of a husband who holds the matrimonial home in fee simple or for a long term of years, for she can in effect claim the protection of a statutory tenant.[16]

Transfer of Tenancies on Divorce and Nullity.—If the marriage is dissolved or annulled, the tenant's spouse will lose the right to stay in occupation of the premises given by the Matrimonial Homes Act and consequently could be evicted.[17] To meet this difficulty, section 7 of that Act provides that the court pronouncing a decree nisi of divorce or nullity may make an order transferring a protected or statutory tenancy to the spouse from the date of the decree absolute. In the case of a protected tenancy this takes effect as a compulsory assignment, and the transferee takes subject to all the benefits and burdens of the covenants and the transferor ceases to be liable on them. In the case of a statutory tenancy the transferee becomes the statutory tenant in place of the transferor. If the spouses are joint tenants, the court has a similar power to extinguish the interest of one of them and vest the tenancy exclusively in the other.[18]

---

[16]In the case of a statutory tenancy the husband presumably remains under a liability to pay the rent even though he has given notice to the landlord to determine the lease: see *supra*, n.[12]). The possibility of the husband and landlord seeking to defeat the wife's right by collusively agreeing that the landlord shall falsely allege a ground for obtaining possession which the husband will not deny is defeated by the necessity of joining the wife, who can then challenge the landlord herself. See also Crane, *After the Deserted Wife's Licence*, 29 Conv. 254, at pp. 264-265.

[17]The court may make an order that the right of occupation shall continue after the termination of the marriage (see *ante*, p. 391). If the tenant then gives notice of his intention to terminate the tenancy, it is arguable that the landlord can accept the notice and evict the wife because she is no longer a *spouse* entitled to occupy the dwelling-house. But could it be said that the tenant has produced a merger of his tenancy with the reversion by surrender so as to give the wife the protection of s. 2 (4) of the Matrimonial Homes Act?

[18]For the court's power to make orders with respect to liabilities and obligations arising before the decree absolute, see s. 7 (4).

CHAPTER 15

Financial Provision for the Spouses on the Breakdown of Marriage

A. INTRODUCTORY

Maintenance at Common Law.—The common law rules relating to the maintenance of a spouse were the inevitable consequence of the doctrine of unity of legal personality. The wife, lacking the capacity to hold property and to contract, could neither own the bare necessities of life nor enter into a binding contract to buy them. Two principles followed. One of the essential obligations imposed upon a married man was to provide his wife with at least necessaries, and a married woman could in no circumstances be held liable to maintain her husband. The common law rule that neither spouse could sue the other precluded her from enforcing her right by action if her husband failed to fulfil his duty to maintain her; this difficulty was overcome by giving the wife a power to pledge her husband's credit for the purchase of necessaries if he did not supply her with them himself.

The Agency of Necessity.—The power to pledge the husband's credit was termed the wife's agency of necessity. It extended to the purchase of necessaries both for herself and for the spouses' minor children, and the term " necessaries " in this context included not only necessary goods such as food and clothing but also necessary services such as lodging, medical attention and education. Although the wife might divest herself of the right to be maintained by her own conduct, the husband could not revoke the authority by his unilateral act.

The agency of necessity was obviously of great importance so long as the wife was generally incompetent to contract and own property at common law. Both these disabilities were removed by the Married Women's Property Act of 1882, and by the end of the nineteenth century she could obtain maintenance from her husband not only in the High Court but also much more speedily in a magistrates' court. Consequently it became rare for a married woman to use her agency of necessity because tradesmen were naturally reluctant to give credit to a man who had deserted his wife and left her penniless. When it became possible for the wife to obtain immediate assistance from the Department of Health and Social Security and to claim the benefits of the National Health Act and the legal aid and advice scheme, the doctrine became

Q

401

an anachronism and was eventually abolished by the Matrimonial
Proceedings and Property Act 1970.[1]

Scope of the Husband's Duty.—Despite the abolition of the agency
of necessity the precise scope of the husband's liability at common law
is still important because it forms the basis of the modern law. As
LORD HODSON has repeatedly pointed out,[2] the husband's duty to
provide his wife with the necessities of life is *prima facie* complied with
if he provides a home for her. The wife has no right to separate
maintenance in a separate home unless she can justify living apàrt
from her husband. But it must not be forgotten that a man may fail
to maintain his wife even though he is cohabiting with her, and he
must still provide her with necessities, for example food and clothing.
Conversely, as the Court of Appeal held in *Lilley* v. *Lilley*,[3] his obligation
remains if the spouses are obliged to live apart, for example owing to
the illness of one of them, provided that the wife is not in desertion.

The fact of marriage, therefore, raises a presumption at common law
that the husband is bound to maintain his wife. But the wife may lose
her right by her own conduct. Generally speaking her right to maintenance is co-extensive with her right to her husband's consortium,
so that if her conduct releases him from the duty to cohabit with her,
he automatically ceases to be under a duty to maintain her.[4] This
principle is particularly important if the wife has committed adultery
or deserted her husband.

If the wife commits a single act of adultery, she automatically
forfeits her right to maintenance.[5] As in the case of the duty to
cohabit, the husband cannot plead his wife's adultery if he has connived
at it or condoned it or, probably, conduced to it by his own neglect or
misconduct: in those circumstances his obligation to maintain her
continues.[6] But in other cases his own conduct is wholly irrelevant.[7]
Just as a reasonable though mistaken belief that the wife has committed adultery will relieve the husband from the duty of cohabiting
with her provided that the mistake was induced by her own conduct,[8]
it was held in *Chilton* v. *Chilton*[9] that in similar circumstances he is
relieved from the duty of maintaining her. Similarly, however, the duty

---

[1]S. 41. This followed the recommendations of the Law Commission: see Law Com.
No. 25, paras. 108-109 and Appendix II, paras. 41-52 and 108.
[2]*McGowan* v. *McGowan*, [1948] 2 All E.R. 1032, 1034; *Price* v. *Price*, [1951] P. 413,
420-421, C.A.; *W.* v. *W.* (*No. 2*), [1954] 2 All E.R. 829, 840, C.A.; [1954] P. 486, 515-516.
[3][1959] 3 All E.R. 283, C.A.; [1960] P. 169.
[4]*Chilton* v. *Chilton*, [1952] 1 All E.R. 1322, 1325; [1952] P. 196, 202.
[5]*Wright and Webb* v. *Annandale*, [1930] 2 K.B. 8, C.A.
[6]*Wilson* v. *Glossop* (1888), 20 Q.B.D. 354, C.A. (connivance); *Harris* v. *Morris* (1801),
4 Esp. 41 (condonation). A husband whose conduct has conduced to his wife's adultery
certainly has no defence if she seeks to enforce her right by applying for a maintenance
order under the Matrimonial Proceedings (Magistrates' Courts) Act 1960: see *ante*, p. 197.
[7]*Govier* v. *Hancock* (1796), 6 Term Rep. 603 (husband not liable for maintenance of
adulterous wife even though he had committed adultery himself and had treated her
with cruelty); *Stimpson* v. *Wood & Sons* (1888), 57 L.J.Q.B. 484 (husband guilty of
adultery).
[8]See *ante*, p. 171.
[9][1952] 1 All E.R. 1322; [1952] P. 196. See also *West* v. *West*, [1954] 2 All E.R.
505, C.A.; [1954] P. 444. But a mistake of *law* is no defence: *Biggs* v. *Burridge* (1924),
22 L.G.R. 555.

to maintain revives when he ceases to have any reasonable ground for thinking her guilty.[10]

If the wife deserts her husband, she again loses her right to be maintained by him; but whereas adultery terminates the right entirely (unless the husband subsequently condones it), desertion merely suspends it and it will revive immediately the desertion comes to an end. This is illustrated by *Jones* v. *Newtown and Llanidloes Guardians*.[11] The appellant's wife deserted him but later became so insane as to lose the *animus deserendi*. She was then supported by the respondent guardians of the poor law, who were now seeking to recover the sums expended from the appellant. The point in issue was whether he was still under a duty to maintain his wife, and it was held that he was under such a duty since her insanity had terminated the desertion. Precisely the same result must follow if she is in constructive desertion.[12] But it will be appreciated that it is always open to her to take the necessary steps to effect a reconciliation and thus restore her right whether the husband accepts her offer or not.[13]

Conversely, of course, it follows that if the husband is in desertion or constructive desertion, the wife's right to maintenance remains unimpaired.[14]

Bankrupt and Mentally Ill Spouses.—If a spouse becomes bankrupt or mentally ill, the question of maintenance of himself and his family is largely governed by discretionary powers conferred by statute.

Bankruptcy.—The Official Receiver may make an allowance for the support of a bankrupt and his family out of the bankrupt's property which is in his hands, as may a trustee in bankruptcy provided that he has the permission of the committee of inspection.[15] The bankrupt may also keep his personal earnings insofar as they are needed for the same purpose.[16]

Mental Illness.—If a person is incapable of managing and administering his property and affairs as a result of mental disorder, the Court of Protection may make such order with respect to them as is necessary or expedient for the maintenance of the patient or the maintenance or other benefit of any member of his family.[17] The Court may also order a settlement or gift of the patient's property for the same purposes.[18]

---

[10]*Allen* v. *Allen*, [1951] 1 All E.R. 724, C.A. See *ante*, p. 172.

[11][1920] 3 K.B. 381. See also *Price* v. *Price*, [1951] 2 All E.R. 580, n., C.A.; [1951] P. 413; *Dyson* v. *Dyson*, [1953] 2 All E.R. 1511; [1954] P. 198; *Naylor* v. *Naylor*, [1961] 2 All E.R. 129.

[12]*Per* BUCKNILL, L.J., in *Winnan* v. *Winnan*, [1948] 2 All E.R. 862, 865, C.A.; [1949] P. 174, 181; *Rice* v. *Raynold-Spring-Rice*, [1948] 1 All E.R. 188.

[13]*Price* v. *Price*, *(supra)*; *Markovitch* v. *Markovitch* (1934), 151 L.T. 139; *Burrow* v. *Burrow* (1930), 143 L.T. 679, 680.

[14]*Holborn* v. *Holborn*, [1947] 1 All E.R. 32 (constructive desertion). If the parties are living apart, it will be for the wife to establish that she is justified in doing so: *Stirland* v. *Stirland*, [1959] 3 All E.R. 891.

[15]Bankruptcy Rules 1952, r. 313; Bankruptcy Act 1914, s. 58.

[16]*Re Roberts*, [1900] 1 Q.B. 122, C.A.

[17]Mental Health Act 1959, ss. 101 and 102 (1). For the definition of mental disorder, see *ibid.*, s. 4 (1).

[18]*Ibid.*, s. 103 (1) (d). A settlement may be varied if material facts were not disclosed when it was made or if there is a substantial change in the circumstances: s. 103 (4).

The Court is expressly required to have regard to the desirability of making provision for the patient's obligations even though these are not legally enforceable[19] and accordingly it has been held that orders may be made for any person whom the patient might have been expected to benefit had he been capable of doing so.[20]

We must now consider the various ways in which the spouses' rights to maintenance and financial provision generally may be enforced.

Maintenance Agreements.—Once it was accepted that separation agreements were not contrary to public policy, it became possible for a husband to enter into an enforceable contract to pay maintenance to his wife, and now of course either spouse may covenant to pay maintenance to the other. Their rights will, of course, be basically governed by the general principles of the law of contract but, as we shall see, some special rules apply to maintenance agreements.

Maintenance in Divorce Courts.—The ecclesiastical courts were able to give financial protection to a wife by ordering the husband to pay her alimony pending suit (or *pendente lite*) and permanent alimony after granting a decree of divorce *a mensa et thoro*. After 1857 this power was vested in the Divorce Court and subsequently in the High Court and divorce county courts. The Divorce Court set up in 1857 was also empowered on granting a decree of divorce to order the husband to secure maintenance for the wife's life.[1] If the husband had no capital which could be secured, hardship was likely to be caused to the wife; this was cured in 1866, when the court was given the power to order the husband to pay unsecured maintenance to the wife. As this would have to come out of his income, however, the maximum term for which it could be ordered was the spouses' joint lives.[2] In 1907 these powers were extended to nullity.[3] After 1937 a wife petitioning for divorce or judicial separation on the ground of her husband's insanity could be ordered to pay him alimony pending suit and, if the decree was granted, maintenance (secured or unsecured) or permanent alimony.[4] Finally in 1963 the courts were given a power, long overdue, to order the payment of a lump sum in addition to or instead of maintenance or alimony on divorce, nullity and judicial separation.[5] Ancillary orders could also be made by a court granting a decree of restitution of conjugal rights to a wife.[6]

Except in the rare case of divorce or judicial separation on the ground of the husband's insanity, the wife could never be ordered to pay maintenance or alimony to her husband. This gap was partly filled as

---

[19] *Ibid.*, s. 102 (2).
[20] *Re D.M.L.*, [1965] 2 All E.R. 129; [1965] Ch. 1133. *Cf. Re T.B.*, [1966] 3 All E.R. 509; [1967] Ch. 247 (settlement on patient's illegitimate son to exclusion of other relations who had taken no interest in him).
[1] Matrimonial Causes Act 1857, s. 32.
[2] Matrimonial Causes Act 1866, s. 1.
[3] Matrimonial Causes Act 1907, s. 1.
[4] Matrimonial Causes Act 1937, s. 10 (2).
[5] Matrimonial Causes Act 1963, s. 5.
[6] Alimony pending suit, alimony on making the decree on the wife's application, and periodical payments (which could be secured) if the husband failed to comply with the decree: Matrimonial Causes Act 1857, s. 17; Matrimonial Causes Act 1884, s. 2.

early as 1857 by a power to order the settlement of the property of a wife whose husband obtained a divorce or judicial separation on the ground of her adultery—a power that was later extended to the property of wives who were divorced for cruelty or desertion or whose husbands obtained a decree for restitution of conjugal rights.[7] On divorce or nullity, either party could benefit from the exercise of the court's power, going back to 1859,[8] to vary ante-nuptial and post-nuptial settlements.

It will be seen that the court could make these orders only by way of ancillary provision in other matrimonial proceedings. Consequently a wife might be compelled to seek some other form of matrimonial relief in order to obtain maintenance. Restitution of conjugal rights was often the only decree immediately available, and most wives who petitioned for it did so, not in the expectation that it would encourage their husbands to return to them, but to enforce their right to financial support. This absurd procedure was made unnecessary in 1949 when a wife was enabled to petition for maintenance alone on the ground that her husband had wilfully neglected to provide reasonable maintenance for her or their children.[9] The court could order a guilty husband to make periodical payments (which could be secured).

The Matrimonial Proceedings and Property Act 1970.—As often happens, piecemeal modifications of the law spread over more than a century produced confusing anomalies. Whatever reasons there might originally have been for giving the courts different powers according to the nature of the decree, they had largely become obscure by the middle of the present century. Why, for example, could a wife obtain secured maintenance if she petitioned for restitution of conjugal rights but not if she petitioned for judicial separation? Why could the court order maintenance to be secured for the wife's life on divorce or nullity but only for the spouses' joint lives in proceedings for wilful neglect to maintain? It was as difficult for the layman to grasp these subtleties in a branch of the law that was more likely to affect him than most as it was for the lawyer to justify them.

Pressure for immediate reform increased after the passing of the Divorce Reform Act 1969, when the fear was expressed that many innocent wives, divorced against their will, would be left with inadequate provision. The result was the passing of the Matrimonial Proceedings and Property Act 1970, which was based upon the recommendations of the Law Commission[10] and which now governs the award of maintenance in the High Court and divorce county courts. Its provisions will be discussed in detail later in this chapter but five

---

[7]Matrimonial Causes Act 1857, s. 45; Matrimonial Causes Act 1884, s. 3; Matrimonial Causes Act 1937, s. 10 (3).

[8]Matrimonial Causes Act 1859, s. 5.

[9]Law Reform (Miscellaneous Provisions) Act 1949, s. 5, subsequently re-enacted in the Matrimonial Causes Act 1950, s. 23, and the Matrimonial Causes Act 1965, s. 22.

[10]Law Com. No. 25, Report on Financial Provision in Matrimonial Proceedings, 1969. For critical reviews of the provisions of the Act, see Cretney, *The Maintenance Quagmire*, 33 M.L.R. 662; Kahn-Freund, *Recent Legislation on Matrimonial Property*, *ibid.*, 601, particularly at pp. 615 *et seq.*

basic principles, which are radically different from those underlying the old law, should be noted.

(1) The old confusing terminology (alimony, maintenance and periodical payments) is abolished. All are now described as financial provision and may take the form of periodical payments or a lump sum payment.

(2) The court is no longer virtually restricted to ordering maintenance in favour of the wife. It now has equal powers to order either spouse to make financial provision for the other.

(3) There is no distinction between the court's powers to order financial provision for the petitioner and its powers to order financial provision for the respondent. This is an essential consequence of the passing of the Divorce Reform Act, because if the marriage is dissolved after two or five years' separation, the petitioner may well have been responsible for the breakdown.

(4) The court's powers to order financial provision, the transfer and settlement of property, and the variation of ante-nuptial and post-nuptial settlements are the same in divorce, nullity and judicial separation.[11]

(5) The court can now make an order against either spouse in the case of wilful neglect to maintain and has much wider powers to order financial provision on such applications than it had before.

Maintenance in Magistrates' Courts.—Until 1878 only the ecclesiastical courts or their successors, the Divorce Court and the High Court, could make orders for maintenance. That year saw an entirely new departure in the power given by section 4 of the Matrimonial Causes Act to courts of summary jurisdiction to order a husband who had been convicted of an aggravated assault on his wife to pay maintenance to her. Although the scope of the Act was extremely limited, it is of great historical importance because it proved to be the forerunner of the Matrimonial Proceedings (Magistrates' Courts) Act 1960.[12] Under this Act magistrates' courts today have jurisdiction to order a husband to pay maintenance to his wife for herself and the dependent children of the family. There is now no limit on the sums that they can order, and it is to the magistrates' court that the average wife turns today if her husband fails in his duty to maintain her. Since 1960 magistrates have also had a power (admittedly rather more limited) to order a wife to pay maintenance for the husband and children.

Concurrent Orders.—The embarrassment which might result if two courts were seised of the question of maintenance simultaneously has led to the formulation of the rule that two orders should not be in force at the same time. We have already seen that a magistrates' court should refuse to deal with an application when proceedings are

---

[11]The Act abolished decrees for restitution of conjugal rights: see *ante*, p. 102.
[12]See *ante*, p. 147.

pending in a divorce court;[13] for the same reason a rule of practice was evolved that normally a divorce court would not make an order for maintenance so long as a magistrates' order was in force. Consequently, if the wife had previously obtained an order in a magistrates' court and then wished to apply for financial provision in a divorce court (as she might do if she later petitioned for divorce or wished to obtain security), she usually had to have the first order discharged and thus leave the way clear for relief in the divorce court.

This meant of course that she must run the risk of obtaining less than she was already getting and also that there might be a period before any order could be made in the divorce court, when she would be in receipt of nothing at all. The second difficulty has now been removed and in such a case the High Court or a divorce county court may direct that an interim order or a final order containing provisions for the payment by either spouse of maintenance to the other or for a child of the family shall cease to have effect at any time.[14] This presumably means that the court will discharge the first order from the date on which its own order is to come into force, but the wife still runs the risk of finishing up financially worse off than she was before, for the Act has not apparently altered the old rule of practice that she is not permitted to apply for a second order and then enforce the more favourable.[15]

Supplementary Benefits.—Broadly speaking, anyone over the age of 16 whose income falls below the relevant sum laid down by the Ministry of Social Security Act 1966 is entitled to apply to the Department of Health and Social Security for supplementary benefit. As any sum awarded will be payable immediately, a spouse left without support will frequently turn to the Department before taking any other action. If assistance is given to a married person, its value may in an appropriate case be recovered from that person's spouse.

Rights of Wives of Serving Members of the Armed Forces.— The rights of wives of men serving in the regular army[16] are peculiar in two respects. First, if an order for maintenance is in force in respect of a soldier's wife or any child of his or his wife's,[17] the Defence Council may authorise deductions to be made from his pay and appropriated towards payments due under the order.[18] Secondly, similar deductions may be authorised, even though no order is in force, if the Defence Council is satisfied that he is neglecting without reasonable cause to maintain his wife or any child of his under the age of 16.[19] In either

---

[13]*Ante*, p. 198.

[14]Matrimonial Proceedings (Magistrates' Courts) Act 1960, s. 7 (3), as amended by the Matrimonial Proceedings and Property Act 1970, s. 33.

[15]See *Ross* v. *Ross*, [1950] 1 All E.R. 654; [1950] P. 160.

[16]*I.e.*, military forces other than the army reserve, the Territorial Army, the Home Guard and retired officers: Army Act 1955, s. 225 (1).

[17]Including an illegitimate or adopted child.

[18]Army Act 1955, s. 150, as amended by the Army and Air Force Act 1961, s. 29, and the Defence (Transfer of Functions) (No. 1) Order, S.I. 1964 No. 488, Sched. 1.

[19]*Ibid.*, s. 151. In certain circumstances deductions may be made after the child has reached the age of 16. This provision does not extend to illegitimate children.

case the amount which may be deducted depends upon his pay and his rank.[20] There are similar provisions with respect to men serving in the Royal Navy and the Royal Air Force.[1]

Whether wives of men serving in visiting forces (for example from the Commonwealth or the U.S.A.) have similar privileges depends upon the nature or orders made under the Visiting Forces Act of 1952.

As this examination of the ways in which one spouse can obtain maintenance from the other will show, maintenance agreements stand in a class apart. In their case the obligation is purely contractual and we shall consider them first. In all other cases the duty to maintain arises directly out of the parties' status. It is proposed to consider these in the order in which a spouse will normally resort to them: supplementary benefits, maintenance orders made by magistrates, and orders made by the High Court and divorce county courts.

B. MAINTENANCE AGREEMENTS

In order to be legally enforceable, a maintenance agreement must constitute a contract between the parties. Consequently, if it is not under seal, the party seeking to enforce a promise to pay maintenance must show that she (or he) has furnished consideration. This will normally not be difficult because the undertaking will be embodied in a separation agreement in which each party gives consideration by releasing the other from the duty to cohabit or will be part of a much more complicated financial transaction involving the division of property and the compromising of other claims. If there is no consideration at all, however, a promise not given under seal will be void.

Basically the parties' rights and duties are determined by the general law of contract. If the agreement is a maintenance agreement for the purpose of section 13 of the Matrimonial Proceedings and Property Act 1970, however, two peculiar rules apply to it: certain provisions may be void by statute, and in certain circumstances either party may apply to have the agreement altered.

Definition of Maintenance Agreement.—To come within section 13 of the Matrimonial Proceedings and Property Act 1970, an agreement must be *in writing*. It must also be

(a) an agreement containing financial arrangements, whether made during the continuance or after the dissolution or annulment of the marriage; *or*

(b) a separation agreement which contains no financial arrangements in a case where no other agreement *in writing* between the same parties contains such arrangements.

From this it will be seen that an agreement entered into after a decree absolute of divorce or nullity can come within the statute only if it contains financial arrangements. An agreement containing no such arrangements can come within the statute only if it is a separation agreement made whilst the parties are still married to each other.

---

[20] *Ibid.*, s. 152.
[1] Naval Forces (Enforcement of Maintenance Liabilities) Act 1947, s. 1 (extended to reserve forces by the Naval and Marine Reserves Pay Act 1957, s. 1 (2) and Sched.); Air Force Act 1955, ss. 150-152 (as amended). In addition wives of serving men are entitled to marriage allowances subject to certain conditions.

Financial arrangements are defined as

" provisions governing the rights and liabilities towards one another when living separately of the parties to a marriage (including a marriage which has been dissolved or annulled) in respect of the making or securing of payments or the disposition or use of any property, including such rights and liabilities with respect to the maintenance or education of any child, whether or not a child of the family ".[2]

Void Provisions.—It was at one time fairly common in separation agreements for the husband to covenant to make periodical payments to the wife in exchange for her giving an undertaking not to take any other steps to obtain maintenance from him. An application for maintenance in other matrimonial proceedings might also be compromised by the wife's promising to withdraw it in consideration of the husband's paying her maintenance or transferring property to her. It was held by the House of Lords in *Hyman* v. *Hyman*,[3] however, that no arrangement of this sort can preclude her from applying for financial relief in divorce proceedings. The reason for this decision is that the court's power to order the husband to maintain his former wife after divorce is intended to protect not only her but also any person dealing with her and, indirectly, the state in view of the possibility of her having to apply for supplementary benefit. Consequently it would be contrary to public policy to permit the parties to oust the court's jurisdiction by agreement.[4] This reasoning is equally applicable in nullity proceedings and, despite earlier authority to the contrary in the Court of Appeal,[5] it is submitted that the same principle must also be applied in the case of judicial separation. But provided that the wife's undertaking not to claim financial provision is not the sole or main consideration, it does not make the whole agreement illegal, so that she may still elect to sue him on his covenant rather than to apply for maintenance.[6]

Section 13 of the Matrimonial Proceedings and Property Act 1970 provides that any term in a " maintenance agreement " purporting to restrict any right to apply to a court for an order containing financial arrangements shall be void. It also provides that any other financial arrangements in the agreement shall not *thereby* be rendered void or unenforceable but shall be binding on the parties unless void or unenforceable for any other reason.[7] The precise effect of this section

---

[2]Matrimonial Proceedings and Property Act 1970, s. 13 (2).
[3][1929] A.C. 601, H.L.
[4]*Ibid.*, at pp. 608 and 629.
[5]*Gandy* v. *Gandy* (1882), 7 P.D. 168, C.A. *Cf. Gaisberg* v. *Storr*, [1949] 2 All E.R. 411, C.A.; [1950] 1 K.B. 107 (promise not to sue for alimony pending suit on divorce not binding).
[6]*Goodinson* v. *Goodinson*, [1954] 2 All E.R. 255, C.A.; [1954] 2 Q.B. 118, followed in *Williams* v. *Williams*, [1957] 1 All E.R. 305, C.A. But if this is the sole or main consideration for the husband's promise to pay her maintenance, the whole agreement is illegal and unenforceable even if it is under seal: *Bennett* v. *Bennett*, [1952] 1 All E.R. 413, C.A.; [1952] 1 K.B. 249; *Combe* v. *Combe*, [1951] 1 All E.R. 767, C.A.; [1951] 2 K.B. 215; following *Gaisberg* v. *Storr*, (*supra*). But an agreement by which the jurisdiction of a foreign divorce court is ousted is not contrary to English public policy and consequently the husband's covenant may be enforced here: *Addison* v. *Brown*, [1954] 2 All E.R 213.
[7]S. 13 (1), replacing provisions originally contained in the Maintenance Orders Act 1958, s. 1 (2).

is uncertain. Clearly the inclusion of the offensive term no longer makes the whole agreement illegal: consequently even if the wife's undertaking not to apply for an order is the sole or main consideration, the husband can be sued if his covenant to pay her maintenance is given under seal. If it is not under seal, however, it is submitted that the husband's promise is still not actionable if the sole consideration is the wife's undertaking not to institute other proceedings for the further reason that, as her promise is void, his promise is supported by no valuable consideration at all.[8]

Alteration of Agreements.—Although any sum agreed on by the parties by way of maintenance might well have been reasonable at the time the agreement was made, it is obvious that in some cases an adherence to this in the light of subsequent events could work serious hardship. The husband's earning capacity may be reduced, which will make a reduction in the sum he has undertaken to pay the wife reasonable; alternatively, the wife's illness or the constant increase in the cost of living consequent upon chronic inflation may well make the sum absurdly small, particularly if it was agreed on some years ago. In order to overcome difficulties such as these, sections 14 and 15 of the Matrimonial Proceedings and Property Act 1970 empower the court in certain circumstances to alter any agreement which is a maintenance agreement for the purpose of section 13.[9]

Alteration during the Lifetime of both Parties.—Either party may apply to a divorce county court to have the agreement altered if each of them is either domiciled or resident in England.[10] Alternatively, the application may be made to a magistrates' court, in which case both parties must reside in England.[11]

No alteration is possible unless one of two conditions is satisfied: either there must have been a change in the circumstances in the light of which the particular financial arrangements were made (or financial arrangements were omitted) or the agreement must fail to contain proper financial arrangements with respect to any child of the family.[12] It will be observed that in the latter case the party seeking the alteration does not have to prove any change of circumstances; but where such a change has to be shown, the Act places the court and the parties in a dilemma. On the one hand, if they are not held to the terms that they have freely entered into, there is no incentive to settle differences out of court; on the other hand, if the courts are slow to make alterations, legal advisers are bound to recommend their clients not to enter

---

[8]See Dew, 56 Law Soc. Gaz. 365. For the contrary view that the statute has made the husband liable on a promise for which there is no consideration, see Treitel, *Mutuality in Contract*, 77 L.Q.R. 83, at pp. 92-95.
[9]For the definition of a maintenance agreement, see *ante*, p. 408. The power was originally given by the Maintenance Orders Act 1958.
[10]Matrimonial Proceedings and Property Act 1970, s. 14 (1) and Sched. 2, para. 2 (1) (a); Matrimonial Causes Act 1967, s. 2. The county court judge may order the application to be transferred to the High Court if this seems desirable: Matrimonial Causes Rules 1968, rr. 80 and 100, as amended by the Matrimonial Causes (Amendment No. 3) Rules 1970.
[11]Matrimonial Proceedings and Property Act 1970, s. 14 (3).
[12]*Ibid.*, s. 14 (2). For the meaning of " child of the family ", see *ante*, p. 287.

into an agreement but to obtain a court order which can be varied from time to time to take account of changes in their financial circumstances. With this difficulty in mind, the Court of Appeal has established two principles. First, as they held in *Gorman* v. *Gorman*,[13] the circumstances in the light of which the financial arrangements were agreed must *prima facie* be viewed objectively. Although in some cases it might be right to have regard only to those circumstances which the evidence shows did influence the parties, normally the court must look at the circumstances which reasonable people in their position would have taken into account. This at least prevents a party from arguing in most cases that the court cannot make an alteration because he did not have particular circumstances in contemplation even though they would clearly have affected the action of a reasonable person. Secondly, the court must be satisfied that the agreement has become unjust as a result of the change. The Act expressly provides that the court is not to be precluded from making an alteration merely because the change was foreseen;[14] if this were not so, a party could rarely rely on an increase in the cost of living or the covenantor's income or on a deterioration in earning capacity due to advancing age. On the other hand, it is unlikely that he will be able to rely on a change brought about by himself, and in *Ratcliffe* v. *Ratcliffe*[15] the court refused to relieve a husband of his obligations under a covenant to pay his wife £450 a year when he voluntarily threw up a post bringing him in £1,400 a year to become a schoolmaster at £550 a year. Similarly in *Gorman* v. *Gorman* they declined to order the husband to pay anything to his wife in view of the fact that he was voluntarily making her an allowance and permitting her to reside in the matrimonial home, whilst she in turn was receiving weekly payments from national insurance and was living with adult children who could be expected to help her financially.

Powers of the Court.—All courts may alter the agreement by varying or revoking any financial arrangements contained in it or by inserting in it financial arrangements for the benefit of either of the parties or a child of the family. In deciding whether to make an order against a party in favour of a child who is not his biological or adopted child, the court must take into account the same matters as it would in the case of divorce.[16]

The High Court and county courts may alter and insert any provisions so long as they are " financial arrangements " within the meaning of the section. There are, however, two restrictions on their powers. If the court inserts a provision for the making or securing of periodical payments by one party to the other or increases the rate of such payments, the period for which they (or the increase) are to be made must not exceed the parties' joint lives if they are unsecured or the payee's life if they are secured and, in either case, must cease on the payee's

---

[13][1964] 3 All E.R. 739, C.A.
[14]S. 14 (2) (a), reversing the decision in *K.* v. *K.*, [1961] 2 All E.R. 266, C.A.
[15][1962] 3 All E.R. 993, C.A.
[16]Matrimonial Proceedings and Property Act 1970, s. 14 (2). See *post*, p. 476. For the meaning of " financial arrangements ", see *ante*, p. 409.

remarriage.[17]   If it inserts a provision for the making or securing of periodical payments for the maintenance of a child of the family or increases the rate of such payments, they (or the increase) may not last for a period longer than the court could order on divorce.[18]

The powers of magistrates' courts are much more circumscribed and are analogous to their powers to make orders under other statutes. If the agreement contains no provision for the making of periodical payments at all, the court can insert a provision for the payment of *unsecured* maintenance for the benefit of the other party or for any child of the family. If it contains a provision that one of the parties shall make *unsecured* periodical payments, the court may increase or reduce their rate or terminate them altogether. The maximum period for which any such payment (or increase) may be ordered is the same as in other courts.[19] This limitation is unfortunately narrow. It means, for example, that if the husband has undertaken to maintain the children but not the wife, a magistrates' court cannot insert a term in her favour: there seems no justification for compelling her to go to a county court in these circumstances.

If any agreement is altered, it has effect as though the alteration had been made by the parties themselves for valuable consideration, so that any person to whom money is due or property is to be transferred under the amended agreement has the normal remedies for breach of contract.[20] A further valuable power, introduced by the Act of 1970, that he or she has is to apply to have set aside any disposition made by the other party with the intention of defeating a claim for alteration or to restrain him from making such a disposition in the future.[1] The alteration does not affect the powers of any court to make any other order containing financial arrangements or of the parties to apply for such an order.[2]

Alteration after the Death of one of the Parties.—If either party dies domiciled in England and the agreement provides for the continuation of payments, either that party's personal representatives or the survivor may apply for an alteration. In such case only the High Court or a county court has jurisdiction and the application must not be made more than six months after the date when representation was first taken out except with the permission of the court.[3] The court's powers are the same as they are when an application is made during both parties' lifetime, and any alteration takes effect as though the

---

[17]*Ibid.*, s. 14 (4). Remarriage includes a void or voidable marriage: *ibid.*, s. 27 (2). *Cf.* the duration of orders after divorce, etc., *post*, p. 430.

[18]*Ibid.*, s. 14 (5). See *post*, pp. 476-477.

[19]*Ibid.*, s. 14 (3)-(5). The Act speaks of the *making* of payments, but as the rest of the Act distinguishes between the making and securing of payments, this must refer to the making of *unsecured* payments only.

[20]*Ibid.*, s. 14 (2).

[1]*Ibid.*, s. 16. See further *post*, pp. 454-455.

[2]*Ibid.*, s. 14 (6).

[3]*Ibid.*, s. 15. A county court has jurisdiction only if the deceased's net estate does not exceed £5,000 (or such larger sum as may be fixed by order of the Lord Chancellor). If the court permits an application after six months, the personal representatives will not be personally liable but assets may be traced in the hands of beneficiaries.

agreement was varied by the parties themselves for valuable consideration immediately before the death.[4]

C. SUPPLEMENTARY BENEFITS

The old poor law, which dated from Elizabethan times, was swept
away by the National Assistance Act of 1948 which introduced a totally
new system.[5] This was modified in turn by the Ministry of Social
Security Act of 1966. This Act established a new ministry (later
amalgamated with the Ministry of Health into the Department of
Health and Social Security) responsible for many aspects of social
security; it also transferred the powers of the National Assistance
Board, set up under the Act of 1948, to a new Supplementary Benefits
Commission. The basic principle underlying the Act is that, with certain
exceptions, everyone over the age of 16 whose resources fall short of his
requirements, calculated in accordance with the provisions of the Second
Schedule, is entitled to have his resources made up to the minimum by
a supplementary pension or a supplementary allowance payable
through the Post Office.

For the purpose of the Act spouses are under a duty to maintain each
other),[6] and if either of them claims or receives benefit, the Supplementary Benefits Commission may apply to a magistrates' court to
recover contribution from the other. Decisions on the old poor law
legislation had laid it down as a rule of law that a husband could not
be liable to maintain his wife if he was not under an obligation to do so
at common law. This principle was carried forward in early cases under
the Act of 1948 and so it was held in *National Assistance Board* v.
Wilkinson[7] that the Board was not entitled to recover the cost of
assistance given to a wife who was in desertion: a principle which was
clearly going to raise difficulty when an attempt was made to recover
from the wife who was under no common law liability to maintain her
husband at all. But this case must now be read in the light of the later
decision of the Court of Appeal in *National Assistance Board* v. *Parkes*.[8]
In that case the defendant and his wife had entered into a separation
agreement under which the latter had expressly covenanted that she
would not claim maintenance from her husband. She had later obtained
assistance from the National Assistance Board who now sought to
recover the cost of it from the husband. It was held that they were
entitled to do so. Whilst the court approved of the decision in
Wilkinson's case on the facts, they approached the problem from a
rather different angle. It appears that on the true interpretation of the
Act *all* spouses are included and the fact that the wife has committed
adultery or is in desertion does not automatically exclude the husband

---

[4] But there is no power to avoid transactions intended to defeat the claim.

[5] See Aikin, *Social Insurance and the Family*, 8 J.S.P.T.L. 167. In the case of families
with children, further assistance is now given by the Family Income Supplements
Act 1970.

[6] S. 22 (1). If assistance is given to either spouse as a result of the other's persistent
refusal or neglect to maintain him or her, the spouse in default is liable to prosecution:
s. 30.

[7] [1952] 2 All E.R. 255; [1952] 2 Q.B. 648.

[8] [1955] 3 All E.R. 1, C.A.; [1955] 2 Q.B. 506.

from the operation of its provisions. But this is a highly relevant circumstance—in fact it may be a conclusive circumstance—to be taken into account by the court in determining whether to make an order against him, and whilst there may be some other circumstances which may make him liable in a particular case, it seems as a general rule that no order should be made if he has ceased to be under a common law liability to maintain his wife. On the other hand he clearly cannot shift his responsibility on to the community as a whole by entering into a separation agreement which exonerates him from liability to maintain his wife or by which he agrees to pay her no more than a specified sum.[9] The same principles presumably apply *mutatis mutandis* to the wife, so that she will not be under any obligation to repay the Commission if her husband's conduct has been such that, had the position been reversed, he would not have been liable.

The court hearing the application may order the defendant to pay such sum, weekly or otherwise, as it considers appropriate having regard to all the circumstances and, in particular, to the resources of the spouse in default. Its powers are not limited to obliging him to reimburse the Commission for the value of benefit already given; the order may last indefinitely and the sums may be made payable to the Secretary of State (in so far as they are attributable to any benefit paid before or after the order is made) or to the spouse or some other person on his or her behalf. The order is enforceable in the same way as any other order for maintenance made by magistrates and may be varied or revoked.[10] Obviously an order made or varied so as to be payable to the spouse is indistinguishable from a maintenance order in his or her favour.

D. MAINTENANCE ORDERS MADE BY MAGISTRATES' COURTS

I. APPLICATIONS FOR ORDERS

The grounds upon which an application may be made to a magistrates' court and the defences open to the defendant have already been considered,[11] but two grounds must now be discussed in greater detail. It will be recalled that in all cases no order can be made if the complainant has been guilty of adultery which the defendant has not connived at, conduced to, or condoned. It thus follows that a spouse may be better off if she (or he) petitions for divorce or judicial separation—a highly undesirable situation.[12]

Husband's Wilful Neglect to provide Reasonable Maintenance.
—The court may make an order on the wife's application if the husband has wilfully neglected to provide reasonable maintenance for her or for

[9]*Stopher* v. *National Assistance Board*, [1955] 1 All E.R. 700; [1955] 1 Q.B. 486, impliedly accepted as correct in *Parkes's* case at pp. 4, 8 and 517, 523, respectively. See further Brown, *Separation Agreements and National Assistance*, 19 M.L.R. 623.
[10]Ministry of Social Security Act 1966, s. 23.
[11]See *ante*, pp. 149 *et seq.*
[12]See *ante*, p. 197. For a criticism of this anomalous situation, see Cretney, *The Maintenance Quagmire*, 33 M.L.R. 662.

any child of the family who is, or would but for that neglect have been, a dependant.[13] The scope of the husband's duty to maintain dependent children of the family will be considered later;[14] what we must now examine is the concept of wilful neglect to maintain the wife.

Burden of Proof on the Wife.—In order to succeed on the ground of wilful neglect, the wife must prove not only that the husband has failed to provide reasonable maintenance but also that he has wilfully neglected to do so.[15] Whether she is receiving reasonable maintenance is a question of fact depending on all the circumstances of the case.[16] So far as wilful neglect is concerned, it imports some element of misconduct,[17] and consequently, as LORD MERRIVALE, P., said in *Weatherley* v. *Weatherley*:[18]

> " What seems requisite, before a husband can be found guilty of a wilful breach of his duty to maintain his wife, is that there must be a refusal to maintain, which has no explanation reasonable in common sense and good faith."

Hence, if the wife has already obtained an order for maintenance and the husband has complied with it, he cannot be guilty of wilful neglect if there has been no change in her financial circumstances.[19] Similarly, if the husband is no longer under a duty to maintain his wife at all, he will have a good defence to an application based upon his wilful neglect to maintain her, for he cannot be liable for failing to do that which he has no duty to do.[20] It is for this reason that the husband may not be guilty of *wilful* neglect if he has no reason to believe that his wife is not adequately provided for. Thus, in *Stringer* v. *Stringer*,[1] the spouses separated by consent but entered into no agreement about maintenance. Twenty months later the wife issued a summons alleging wilful neglect to maintain but without giving prior warning to the husband. Whilst the absence of any agreement was such as to preclude him from being liable to maintain her anyway,[2] the fact that the wife had never approached her husband and thus left him in ignorance of her financial position certainly negatived any wilful neglect.

Moreover, as was held in *Earnshaw* v. *Earnshaw*,[3] it is obvious that a man cannot be guilty of wilful neglect to maintain his family unless he has the means, actual or potential, of doing so. Whilst he might be guilty if he wilfully abstained from earning sufficient money to keep them, he could not be if he had no income and owing, say, to ill health he was incapable of work.

---

[13]Matrimonial Proceedings (Magistrates' Courts) Act 1960, s. 1 (1) (h).

[14]See *post,* pp. 472-474.

[15]See Brown, *The Offence of Wilful Neglect to Maintain a Wife,* 23 M.L.R. 1.

[16]*Morton* v. *Morton,* [1942] 1 All E.R. 273, 277. Whether it is reasonable must be judged by the husband's standard of living: *Scott* v. *Scott,* [1951] 1 All E.R. 216, 217-218; [1951] P. 245, 248. It must be reasonable *at the time of the application: Tulip* v. *Tulip,* [1951] 2 All E.R. 91, 97, C.A.; [1951] P. 378, 389.

[17]*Morton* v. *Morton, (supra),* at p. 274.

[18](1929), 142 L.T. 163, 165.

[19]*Smith* v. *Smith* (1962) (unreported), C.A., cited in *Baynham* v. *Baynham,* [1969] 1 All E.R. 305, 307, C.A.

[20]*Cooke* v. *Cooke,* [1960] 3 All E.R. 39; [1961] P. 16.

[1][1952] 1 All E.R. 373, 378; [1952] P. 171, 181-182. See also *Jones* v. *Jones,* [1958] 3 All E.R. 410; [1959] P. 38; Brown, *loc. cit.*

[2]See *post,* p. 416.

[3][1896] P. 160. Once failure to maintain has been proved, it is for the husband to show that this was not wilful: *Stirland* v. *Stirland,* [1959] 3 All E.R. 891.

Consensual Separation.—If the spouses separate by consent and the husband in fact pays the wife a sufficient allowance (whether in pursuance of the agreement or independently of it), it is obvious that he cannot be guilty of failing to provide her with reasonable maintenance. Conversely, if the contract is avoided or discharged[4] or if he fails to pay the sum agreed so that she is not receiving adequate maintenance, he can equally clearly be made liable on this ground.[5]

Since the decision of the Court of Appeal in *Tulip* v. *Tulip*[6] it seems to have been settled law that the mere fact that the husband has performed a covenant in the agreement to pay maintenance to his wife will not preclude her from alleging a failure to provide her with reasonable maintenance and thus claiming payment over and above the sum agreed if that sum is inadequate in the circumstances. But the fact that he has faithfully paid his wife and that she has been willing to accept those payments is strong evidence that his neglect has not been wilful. In the words of SINGLETON, L.J., in *Morton* v. *Morton (No. 2)*:[7]

> " I regard it of the utmost importance that the existence of an agreement and its terms should not be overlooked in considering whether an application should be made [for an order on the ground of wilful neglect to maintain]. The courts ought not lightly to be asked to upset, or to go behind, the terms of an agreement freely entered into between the parties, even though . . . the court is clothed with power . . . to make an order in a proper case. . . ."

Hence the agreement may present a formidable obstacle to the wife. It is only if she can prove the kind of hardship that would have been worked had the court taken a contrary view in *Tulip* v. *Tulip* that she is really likely to succeed. In that case the separation agreement had been entered into in 1932 and the husband had covenanted to pay his wife £156 a year free of tax. During the next 18 years his financial position improved appreciably, whilst that of the wife, who had become an invalid suffering from spinal arthritis, had deteriorated. In view of the spouses' changed circumstances and the phenomenal increase in the cost of living between 1932 and 1950 it is hardly surprising that the court held that the husband could be guilty of wilful neglect to maintain.[8]

If the agreement contains no provision for maintenance at all, it now seems settled by the decision of the Court of Appeal in *Northrop* v. *Northrop*[9] that the wife can establish wilful neglect to maintain herself

---

[4]See *ante*, pp. 139-142.

[5]*McCreanney* v. *McCreanney* (1928), **138** L.T. 671.

[6][1951] 2 All E.R. 91, C.A.; [1951] P. 378. See also *Dowell* v. *Dowell*, [1952] 2 All E.R. 141.

[7][1954] 2 All E.R. 248, 254, C.A. See also LORD MERRIMAN, P., in *Morton* v. *Morton*, [1942] 1 All E.R. 273, 276.

[8]But it should be noted that in *Tulip* v. *Tulip*, *(ante)*, the Court of Appeal merely held that the deed was no bar in law to the wife's application. They ordered a fresh trial and expressed no views on the merits of the application. For a case where an agreement was held to be no bar on the facts, see *Dowell* v. *Dowell*, *(supra)*.

[9][1967] 2 All E.R. 961, C.A.; [1968] P. 74. See further Brown, *Maintenance and Esoterism*, 31 M.L.R. 121.

only if she can prove that the separation was on the basis (express or implied) that the husband would continue to maintain her. The question thus becomes one of interpretation; if, for example, she has a child who needs her care to such an extent that she is prevented from supporting herself by her own earnings (as may happen in the case of a very young or sick child), it may well be a necessary implication that the husband will continue to maintain her until she is able to support herself. But where the court can spell out no agreement, the rule is liable to work injustice. The wife may be adequately provided for at the time of the separation but may later become incapable of self-support. Failure to provide for maintenance is probably more likely to occur if the parties do not enter into a written agreement and consequently she will be unable to apply to have it altered under section 14 of the Matrimonial Proceedings and Property Act.[10] An application of the principle underlying *Tulip* v. *Tulip* is obviously desirable and it is regrettable that the Court of Appeal did not seize the opportunity to extend it.

The wife may make an application under the Matrimonial Proceedings (Magistrates' Courts) Act even though the agreement contains an express covenant by her not to take other proceedings to obtain maintenance.[11] Thus normally she will be able to apply either for the agreement to be altered or for an order on the grounds of the husband's wilful neglect to maintain. Other things being equal, she would probably be better advised to have the agreement altered, for if the husband then defaults she has the comparatively simple remedy of suing for breach of contract. But other facts may determine her course of conduct. If the husband was unaware of the change in the wife's circumstances, she might succeed in obtaining an alteration in the agreement although the husband would not be guilty of wilful neglect to maintain; on the other hand, if she seeks to obtain maintenance independently of the agreement, she can presumably be defeated by any other defence available to the husband. For example, if the spouses separated as a result of the wife's uncondoned adultery, she should be able to obtain nothing apart from what her husband has agreed to pay her. To hold otherwise would lead to the absurd conclusion that by making a voluntary payment he had unwittingly revived a discharged obligation.

Wife's Wilful Neglect to provide Reasonable Maintenance.

Under the earlier legislation dealing with the matrimonial jurisdiction of magistrates there was no power at all to order a married woman to pay maintenance to her husband. This is understandable because few married women likely to come before magistrates' courts at the end of the last century would have been in a position to make any financial

---

[10]See *ante*, pp. 408 and 410.

[11]Matrimonial Proceedings and Property Act 1970, s. 13 (applying to written agreements only). In *McCreanney* v. *McCreanney*, (*ante*), LORD MERRIVALE, P., doubted whether the court could order the husband to pay more than the agreed sum, but this dictum is inconsistent with the decision in the later case of *Dowell* v. *Dowell*, (*ante*). These cases are still relevant if the agreement is not in writing. She can also bring proceedings on the ground of wilful neglect even though the agreement has been altered: *ibid.*, s. 14 (6).

provision for their husbands. This, of course, had ceased to be true long before 1960 but it was not until that year that the Matrimonial Proceedings (Magistrates' Courts) Act finally recognised that there may be cases where it is appropriate to cast the obligation on to the wife. The Act limits the power of a magistrates' court, however, to the situation where the husband's earning capacity has been impaired through age, illness or disability of mind or body. In particular he may apply for an order on the ground that his wife

"... has wilfully neglected to provide, or to make a proper contribution towards, reasonable maintenance for the husband or for any child of the family who is, or would but for that neglect have been, a dependant, in a case where, by reason of the impairment of the husband's earning capacity through age, illness, or disability of mind or body, and having regard to any resources of the husband and the wife respectively which are, or should properly be made, available for the purpose, it is reasonable in all the circumstances to expect the wife so to provide or contribute."[12]

It is easy to see the situation that these provisions envisage: that of the husband whose income is reduced by old age, illness or accident and whose wife has an income of her own but refuses to use it (or an adequate part of it) for the maintenance of the family But it is not so easy to predict how they will be applied in detail despite their similarity to the provisions of the Act relating to the husband's wilful neglect to provide reasonable maintenance. The difficulty arises from the fact that in the case of the husband " wilful neglect " imports a breach of duty and that duty exists at common law independently of the statute, whereas there is no general duty laid upon a married woman to support her husband. As we have seen, the husband's adultery may preclude him from obtaining an order for maintenance for himself;[13] in the absence of any authority it is submitted that if the husband is in desertion or the spouses have separated by agreement, the same principles will be applied *mutatis mutandis* as when the wife alleges that the husband has wilfully neglected to maintain her.

2. ORDERS THAT MAY BE MADE

Orders in Favour of the Wife.—On a complaint by the wife (on whatever ground) the court may order the husband to pay her such weekly sum for her maintenance as it considers reasonable in all the circumstances. The husband may also be ordered to pay her maintenance if *he* obtains an order containing a non-cohabitation clause on the ground that she is an habitual drunkard or drug addict.[14]

---

[12]S. 1 (1) (i).
[13]*Ante*, p. 197.
[14]Matrimonial Proceedings (Magistrates' Courts) Act 1960, s. 2 (1) (b) and (2); Maintenance Orders Act 1968, s. 1 and Sched.

Orders in Favour of the Husband.—If the husband is the complainant, the court may order the wife to pay him maintenance only if this appears reasonable in all the circumstances by reason of the impairment of his earning capacity through age, illness, or disability of mind or body.[15] She may also be ordered to pay him maintenance if *she* obtains an order containing a non-cohabitation clause on the ground that he is an habitual drunkard or drug addict.[16]

Assessment and Income Tax.—The same facts must be borne in mind in assessing maintenance in a magistrates' court as in assessing financial provision in the High Court or a county court.[1] Magistrates' courts have the advantage of being able to instruct a probation officer to investigate the parties' means.[2]

Earlier cases indicated that, even though the wife could establish a ground for complaint, an order for maintenance ought not to be made in her favour if her husband was no longer under an obligation to maintain her at common law. But this view has not been tenable since the decision of the Court of Appeal in *Northrop* v. *Northrop*.[3] The spouses had separated consensually and the husband had left with the wife their child aged 13. The magistrates had found him guilty of wilful neglect to maintain the child but had made no specific finding as to whether the separation had been on the understanding that he would continue to maintain his wife. The majority of the court held that the justices had power to make an order in the wife's favour as she had established a ground (wilful neglect to maintain the child) on which an order could be made; it was not necessary for her to prove in addition that the husband was guilty of wilful neglect to maintain her (which she could do only by showing that they had separated on the basis that he would continue to support her). As they pointed out, maintaining the child might involve the wife in expenses over and above that of feeding and clothing it: she might, for example, have to live in more expensive accommodation than she would live in by herself, and looking after the child might severely curtail, if not wholly take away, her capacity to work and so reduce her income—a situation more likely to arise in the case of a young or sickly child. In these circumstances the court could properly order the husband to contribute to the wife's own expenses. The importance of the decision is of course greatly reduced now that there is no limit to the sum which magistrates can order for the child's maintenance, for these additional expenses could be covered by an order with respect to the child itself. If the wife has forfeited her right to maintenance by reason of her own adultery, this will prevent her from obtaining an order in her own favour in any event;[4] if she has been guilty of any other matrimonial offence, the

---

[15]But the order need not have been made on the ground of the wife's wilful neglect to provide reasonable maintenance.

[16]Matrimonial Proceedings (Magistrates' Courts) Act 1960, s. 2 (1) (c) and (2); Maintenance Orders Act 1968, s. 1 and Sched.

[1]See *post*, pp. 443-449.

[2]Magistrates' Courts Act 1952, s. 60.

[3][1967] 2 All E.R. 961, C.A.; [1968] P. 74. See Brown, *Maintenance and Esoterism*, 31 M.L.R. 121; Donaldson, [1967] C.L.J. 177.

[4]See *ante*, p. 197.

court must take this into account in deciding what is a reasonable sum to award.[5] It is submitted that they should not normally make an order if the facts do not establish wilful neglect to maintain the wife. For example, if she deserts her husband who then gives her a ground for complaint by committing adultery without terminating her desertion, it does not seem right that this should entitle her to claim maintenance.

If the order is for a sum not exceeding £7·50 a week for the spouse or any child it will be a " small maintenance order " for the purpose of the Income and Corporation Taxes Act 1970.[6]

Interim Orders.—It will be recalled that there is a power to make interim orders for maintenance. There is no limit to the amount that may be awarded, but the Act lays down the maximum time for which interim orders may remain in force.[7]

Payment of Maintenance.—In order to ensure that payments will be made as promptly as possible (and also to prevent embarrassment) the court must order them to be made to the clerk of a magistrates' court on behalf of the recipient unless the latter shows that for some reason this would be undesirable.[8] Alternatively, the court may order the payments to be made to some other person to the recipient's use.[9]

Maintenance payable under a magistrates' order is inalienable like unsecured periodical payments made under the Matrimonial Proceedings and Property Act.[10]

3. SUSPENSION, CESSATION, REVOCATION, REVIVAL AND VARIATION OF ORDERS

The general law relating to the suspension, cessation, revocation, revival and variation of orders has already been considered.[11] With respect to maintenance orders, however, it should be appreciated that it is not contrary to public policy for the husband to bind himself not to apply to have the order reduced below a certain figure and, if he does so, the court may not order a variation contrary to the agreement.[12] It is also necessary to discuss in rather more detail the effect of a subsequent decree of divorce or nullity.

---

[5]*Northrop* v. *Northrop*, at pp. 976 and 112, respectively.
[6]See *post*, p. 432.
[7]See *ante*, p. 199. No appeal lies from an interim award of maintenance: Matrimonial Proceedings (Magistrates' Courts) Act 1960, s. 6 (2).
[8]Magistrates' Courts Act 1952, s. 52 (1), (2).
[9]Matrimonial Proceedings (Magistrates' Courts) Act 1960, s. 13 (2). The court might wish to use this power if, for example, the recipient was receiving treatment for habitual drunkenness or addiction to drugs.
[10]*Paquine* v. *Snary*, [1909] 1 K.B. 688, C.A. See further *post*, pp. 432-433.
[11]*Ante*, pp. 200-201. Note particularly the effect of cohabitation and the complainant's adultery. The court may not order a variation or revocation to take effect from a date earlier than that on which the complaint for this purpose was made: *Fildes* v. *Simkin*, [1959] 3 All E.R. 697; [1960] P. 70.
[12]*Russell* v. *Russell*, [1956] 1 All E.R. 466, C.A.; [1956] P. 283.

A decree of divorce does not automatically terminate a maintenance order. The problem was considered by the Court of Appeal in *Wood* v. *Wood*,[13] where it was held that it is immaterial whether the decree is pronounced on the husband's petition or the wife's or by an English court or a foreign court: in each case the court should look at all the circumstances and exercise its discretion accordingly. In that case the wife had originally obtained an order in a magistrates' court on the ground of her husband's desertion. He had later acquired a domicile in Nevada and had there obtained a divorce on the ground that he and his wife had not cohabited for over four years; the wife had had no notice of the proceedings as service had been effected by advertisement in a local newspaper. In these circumstances it was held that the magistrates' court had rightly exercised its discretion in not only refusing to discharge the order but also in increasing the amount in view of the husband's improved financial position.

Nullity presents a more difficult problem. On general principle it is submitted that, if the marriage is void, the whole order must be inoperative as it rests on the false assumption that the parties were in fact married. If the marriage is voidable, the order will presumably be discharged automatically if the courts adhere to the doctrine of retroactivity, but it will not be if they regard the decree as resembling a decree of divorce.[14] If the latter view is adopted, the defendant may apply for the order to be discharged or varied and the same principles will apply as in the case of subsequent divorce.

If a maintenance order in favour of either spouse remains in force after the marriage has been dissolved or annulled, it will automatically cease to have effect if that spouse remarries.[15] If the other continues to make payments in the mistaken belief that the order is still subsisting, he (or she) (or his personal representatives, if he has died) may recover them from the payee (or the payee's personal representatives) in an action in a county court.[16] In some cases an order for the repayment of the whole sum might be unjust, for example if the payee had received the sums paid in good faith and had already spent them; accordingly the court has power to order the repayment of such smaller sum as it thinks fit or to dismiss the application altogether. Magistrates' clerks and collecting officers under attachment of earnings orders are

---

[13][1957] 2 All E.R. 14, C.A.; [1957] P. 254. Contrast *Sternberg* v. *Sternberg*, [1963] 3 All E.R. 319, where, after the wife had obtained a maintenance order on the ground of the husband's desertion, he obtained a divorce on the ground of her desertion. The Divisional Court held that, as the findings of the High Court in the divorce proceedings bound the magistrates' court, it must be conclusively presumed that the latter had no jurisdiction to make the order which must therefore be discharged. See further Webb and Bevan, *Source Book of Family Law*, 262-263.

[14]See *ante*, pp. 69-71. An application for an order in a magistrates' court might amount to approbation of the marriage: see *ante*, p. 63.

[15]Matrimonial Proceedings (Magistrates' Courts) Act 1960, s. 7 (4), (5) and (6) (added by the Matrimonial Proceedings and Property Act 1970, s. 30 (1)). It is immaterial that the second marriage is void or voidable, but these provisions do not apply if the re-marriage took place before 1st January, 1971.

[16]Or in the High Court if the order is registered there and proceedings are being brought there for its enforcement.

given statutory protection unless they receive written notice of the remarriage from one of the former spouses (or their personal representatives).[17]

4. ENFORCEMENT OF ORDERS

The Matrimonial Proceedings (Magistrates' Courts) Act provides that maintenance orders shall be enforceable in the same way as affiliation orders.[18] The procedure is now laid down by the Magistrates' Courts Act 1952. If payments are being made to a magistrates' clerk, the clerk himself may take proceedings provided that he has the written consent of the person to whom the money is to be paid.[19] For the purpose of simplicity, it will be assumed in the rest of this section that the wife is seeking to enforce an order made against the husband, but the procedure is precisely the same *mutatis mutandis* if the husband seeks to enforce an order for maintenance against his wife.

The first step in the process is for the wife to apply for a summons in a magistrates' court.[20] The court must first decide whether to enforce the arrears *in toto* or to remit the whole or any part of them;[1] the answer to this question must obviously depend upon the spouses' financial position, their conduct and all the circumstances of the case. The court may then issue a warrant of distress, make an attachment of earnings order or issue a warrant committing the husband to prison.[2]

Distress.—Distress is little used in practice. The warrant directs the police to distrain on the husband's goods and to sell them to raise the sum adjudged to be paid.[3]

Attachment of Earnings.—The Maintenance Orders Act 1958 introduced a wholly new means of enforcing an order for maintenance— that of attaching the husband's earnings. The relevant part of that Act has now been replaced by the Attachment of Earnings Act 1971, which has extended the power to apply for such an order to judgment

---

[17]Matrimonial Proceedings (Magistrates' Courts) Act 1960, s. 13A (added by the Matrimonial Proceedings and Property Act 1970, s. 31). The court may order the repayment to be made by instalments. For similar provisions in the case of orders made under the Matrimonial Proceedings and Property Act 1970, see *post*, p. 453.
[18]S. 13 (1).
[19]Magistrates' Courts Act 1952, s. 52 (3).
[20]*Ibid.*, s. 74 (1), (2).
[1]*Ibid.*, s. 76. The court may also remit arrears on hearing an application to vary, discharge or revive the order. The six months' limitation period does not apply so that arrears up to any amount may be recovered, but normally they should not be enforced if they have been due for more than a year: *Pilcher* v. *Pilcher* (*No. 2*), [1956] 1 All E.R. 463, 465. Because arrears can be remitted, they are not provable in the husband's bankruptcy but continue to be enforceable in the same way as before: *James* v. *James*, [1963] 2 All E.R. 465; [1964] P. 303. *Cf. post*, p. 452, n. [20].
[2]*Ibid.*, s. 64 (1); Attachment of Earnings Act 1971, s. 1 (3) (a).
[3]Magistrates' Courts Rules 1952, r. 43. Clothing and bedding are exempt from distress as are also tools of the husband's trade up to the value of £5. The court may also order the husband to be searched and any money belonging to him and found on him to be applied towards payment of the arrears: Magistrates' Courts Act 1952, s. 68.

debtors generally.[4] The payment of any order for maintenance made under the Matrimonial Proceedings (Magistrates' Courts) Act may be secured in this way.[5]

An attachment of earnings order may be applied for by the person to whom payments are due under the related maintenance order, by a magistrates' clerk if an order is in force directing payments to be made through him, or by the debtor himself.[6] Unless the debtor makes the application, the court may make an order only if it appears that he has failed to make one or more payments owing to his wilful refusal or culpable neglect.[7]

The order must specify two rates: the *normal deduction rate*, which is the amount which the court thinks is reasonable to secure the payment of sums falling due under the order in the future together with the arrears already accrued, and the *protected earnings rate*, that is the rate below which the husband's earnings shall not in any event be reduced by payments deducted under the order.[8] In assessing the latter, the court must take into account the husband's resources and needs and the needs of others for whom he is bound to provide or may reasonably be expected to provide[9] but may consider only his actual earnings from his particular employer at the time and not his potential earnings in some other occupation.[10]

The order is directed to the husband's employer, and when it has been served on him, he is bound to deduct certain sums from the husband's earnings[11] and to pay them over to the collecting officer of the court.[12] In the normal way he will on each " pay day " (which may, of course, be weekly, monthly or quarterly) pay over the normal deduction, but if the husband's " attachable " earnings[13] are less than the aggregate of his protected earnings and the normal deduction, then the employer must pay over only the amount by which the attachable earnings exceed the protected earnings, so that the husband

---

[4]The Act comes into force on such day as the Lord Chancellor shall appoint: s. 29 (4). No order has yet been made bringing it into operation. In the meantime Part II of the Maintenance Orders Act 1958 still governs the making of attachment of earnings orders to enforce maintenance orders.

[5]Attachment of Earnings Act 1971, Sched. 1, para. 4.

[6]*Ibid.*, ss. 3 (1) and 17-21.

[7]*Ibid.*, s. 3 (3), (5). Unless the debtor makes the application, 15 days must have elapsed since the related order was made: s. 3 (2).

[8]*Ibid.*, s. 6 (5), (6).

[9]*Ibid.*, s. 25 (3).

[10]*Pepper* v. *Pepper*, [1960] 1 All E.R. 529, 534-535.

[11]" Earnings " means any salary, wage or pension and includes sums payable by the Crown or out of public revenue in the United Kingdom (except Northern Ireland); it does not include sums payable by any other government, pay or allowances payable to members of H.M. forces, wages payable to seamen (other than seamen of fishing boats), or pensions, allowances or benefit payable under enactments relating to social security or in respect of the debtor's disablement or disability: Attachment of Earnings Act 1971, ss. 22 and 24 and Sched. 4. It also includes payments made at irregular intervals or under discretionary powers: *Edmonds* v. *Edmonds*, [1965] 1 All E.R. 379.

[12]*I.e.*, the clerk of that or another magistrates' court: Attachment of Earnings Act 1971, s. 6 (7).

[13]*I.e.*, his earnings less income tax, National Insurance, Industrial Injuries and National Health Service contributions, and superannuation contributions deductible by the employer: *ibid.*, Sched. 3, para. 3.

takes the latter intact. If on any pay day it is impossible for the employer to pay over the normal deduction, then on any subsequent pay day on which the attachable earnings exceed the sum of the protected earnings and the normal deduction, the employer must deduct and pay over such part of the excess as is necessary to cover the unpaid part of the normal deduction.[14] The collecting officer of the court must then pay the money received to the wife or other person to whom the money due under the order is payable.[15]

Once an attachment of earning order has been made, no committal order may be made as a consequence of proceedings begun beforehand; similarly if a committal order is made or a warrant is issued after an attachment of earnings order has been made, the latter will automatically be discharged.[16] A court before which proceedings for committal or distress are brought may always make an attachment of earnings order instead if it thinks that that would be a more efficacious means of securing payment.[17]

Variation and Discharge.—The court has a general power to order the variation or discharge of an attachment of earnings order and must vary or discharge it when the debtor has paid off the arrears and the sum attachable is greater than that payable under the related maintenance order.[18] If the debtor ceases to be employed by the person to whom the order has been directed, it lapses until the court directs it to a fresh employer,[19] and it ceases to have effect if the related maintenance order is discharged unless arrears are still unpaid and the court directs that the attachment order shall remain alive.[20]

---

[14]Attachment of Earnings Act 1971, s. 6 and Sched. 3, Part I. Suppose the normal deduction rate is £10 a week and the protected earnings rate is £12 a week; the following table shows how the husband's earnings will be dealt with:

	Attachable earnings £	Paid to husband £	Paid to collecting officer £	Normal deductions unpaid £
Week 1	26	16	10	—
Week 2	19	12	7	3
Week 3	21	12	9	4
Week 4	25	12	13	1
Week 5	26	15	11	—
Total	117	67	50	—

If more than one attachment of earnings order is in force, the employer must deal with them in the order laid down in Sched. 3, Part II. For details of the employer's duties generally and penalties for failing to comply with the Act, see ss. 7, 9, 12 and 23; for the powers of the court to obtain statements of earnings and to determine whether particular payments are earnings, see ss. 14 and 16.

[15]*Ibid.*, s. 13 (1). The sums paid must go first in payment of arrears and then in payment of costs: s. 13 (2).

[16]*Ibid.*, s. 8 (1), (3).

[17]*Ibid.*, s. 3 (4).

[18]*Ibid.*, ss. 9 and 10.

[19]*Ibid.*, s. 9 (4). For the duties of the debtor, the old employer and a new employer who knows that the order is in force, see *ibid.*, ss. 7 (2) and 15.

[20]*Ibid.*, s. 11 (1) (c), (3). For the effect of registration of the maintenance order in a magistrates' court on attachment of earnings orders, see *post*, pp. 456-457.

Effectiveness of Orders.—In many cases it may be questioned whether the value of an order to the wife is worth the administrative trouble that it causes. The procedure will be most effective when the husband is in steady employment, but when he is in casual employment, he can escape the order by the simple expedient of changing jobs frequently. Similarly the temptation to an employer to " lay off " a man with an order made against him when labour is redundant is obviously great.[1]

Committal.—A warrant of committal (which may also be issued if the distress is insufficient to satisfy the debt) commits the husband to prison for a period varying from five days to six weeks, the maximum period being graduated according to the sum owed.[2] But since committal proceedings are in effect designed to punish the husband for failing to carry out the order, he may be imprisoned only if the default was due to his wilful refusal or culpable neglect and the court feels that it is inappropriate to make an attachment of earnings order.[3]

Two further powers that the court possesses are those of ordering the payment of arrears by instalments and of postponing the issue of a warrant of committal upon conditions.[4] Used together these powers constitute a valuable weapon, particularly when it is financially impossible for the husband to pay off all the arrears at once. For example, suppose that £50 is due under the order: the court may order the husband to be imprisoned for six weeks but the issue of the warrant of committal to be postponed on condition, say, that he pays the arrears within six months or at at the rate of £2 a week.

If the husband pays the arrears, the order for committal immediately ceases to have effect, and if he pays a part of the sum due, the period of imprisonment is proportionately reduced.[5] But serving the sentence does not wipe off the arrears[6] although no further arrears accrue whilst the husband is in custody unless the court orders otherwise.[7] A husband who is in prison may apply to have the warrant of committal cancelled, in which case the court has power to release him either absolutely or with a postponed warrant of committal

---

[1] See also Brown, *Attachment of Earnings Orders in Practice*, 24 M.L.R. 486.

[2] Magistrates' Courts Act 1952, ss. 64 (2), (3), 74 and 107 (1) and 3rd Sched., as amended by the Maintenance Orders Act 1958, s. 16, and the Criminal Justice Act 1967, s. 93.

[3] Magistrates' Courts Act 1952, s. 74, as amended by the Maintenance Orders Act 1958, s. 16. No order for committal may be made unless the the husband has appeared in court; he may be arrested if he fails to answer the summons.

[4] Magistrates' Courts Act 1952, ss. 63, 65, as amended by the Maintenance Orders Act 1958, s. 18.

[5] Magistrates' Courts Act 1952, s. 67.

[6] *Ibid.*, s. 74, as amended by the Maintenance Orders Act 1958, s. 16. But a husband cannot be imprisoned more than once for failure to pay the same sum: Maintenance Orders Act 1958, s. 17.

[7] Magistrates' Courts Act 1952, s. 75, for the committal will probably deprive the husband of the power of earning his living in the meantime.

for a period not exceeding the balance of the term to be served and may at the same time remit the whole or any part of the sum still unpaid.[8]

E. FINANCIAL PROVISION IN THE HIGH COURT AND DIVORCE COUNTY COURTS

I. ORDERS THAT MAY BE MADE

Divorce, Nullity and Judicial Separation.—A court hearing a petition for divorce, nullity or judicial separation can make an order against *either spouse* with respect to any one or more of the following matters:

 (1) Maintenance pending suit;

 (2) Unsecured periodical payments to the other spouse;

 (3) Secured periodical payments to the other spouse;

 (4) Lump sum payments to the other spouse;

 (5) Unsecured periodical payments for any child of the family;

 (6) Secured periodical payments for any child of the family;

 (7) A lump sum payment for any child of the family;

 (8) Transfer of property to the other spouse or for the benefit of any child of the family;

 (9) Settlement of property for the benefit of the other spouse or any child of the family;

 (10) Variation of any ante-nuptial or post-nuptial settlement.

The court has similar powers in those rare cases where a marriage has been dissolved on the ground that one spouse is presumed to be dead and he or she is later found to be still alive.[9] Orders in favour of children only (that is, (5), (6) and (7) above) will be dealt with in the next chapter when we consider financial provision for children generally. The rest will be dealt with in this part of this chapter.[10]

Except for maintenance pending suit and orders with respect to children, no order may be made unless a decree nisi of divorce or nullity or a decree of judicial separation has been granted and, in the case of divorce and nullity, it may not take effect until the decree is made absolute.[11] An application for financial provision is not a cause of action which survives against the other party's estate so that no order can be

---

[8]Maintenance Orders Act 1958, s. 18 (4), (5), (6). The order cannot be enforced against the husband's personal representatives after his death: *Re Bidie*, [1948] 1 All E.R. 885; [1948] Ch. 697; affirmed, [1948] 2 All E.R. 995, C.A.; [1949] Ch. 121. It is doubtful whether an order can ever be enforced after it has been discharged: *per* AVORY, J., in *Outerbridge* v. *Outerbridge*, [1927] 1 K.B. 368; consequently the wife should resist an order for discharge until all arrears have been paid or remitted.

[9]*Deacock* v. *Deacock*, [1958] 2 All E.R. 633, C.A.; [1958] P. 230.

[10]There are transitional provisions relating to orders made before 1971 in the Matrimonial Proceedings and Property Act 1970, Sched. 1.

[11]*Ibid.*, s. 24. An order may be made at any time after the decree, but the leave of the court may have to be obtained if the application is not made in the petition or the respondent's answer: Matrimonial Causes Rules 1968, r. 68.

made after the death of either of them.[12] It is also a general principle of the new Act that, if a former spouse remarries, she (or he) must look to her new partner for financial provision for herself and not to the old one. Consequently a party who has remarried cannot apply for any order at all except one for periodical payments or a lump sum payment for a child of the family.[13] This rule applies even if the second marriage is void or voidable:[14] the party's remedy lies in seeking financial provision in the nullity proceedings.

Even though the suit is not defended, a county court judge may order the application for financial relief to be transferred to the High Court if this seems desirable.[15]

Wilful Neglect to Maintain.—Either spouse may now apply for an order under section 6 of the Matrimonial Proceedings and Property Act 1970 on the ground of the other's wilful neglect to provide reasonable maintenance. The court has jurisdiction (in the sense in which that term is used in the conflict of laws) in the same circumstances as it has in the case of judicial separation.[16] The proceedings must be commenced in a divorce county court. If the respondent contests the applicant's claim on the ground that he (or she) is not liable to maintain the applicant at all or if he contests the court's jurisdiction, the application *must* be transferred to the High Court; in other cases the county court judge *may* order it to be transferred if this seems desirable.[17]

The wife may apply for an order on the ground that the husband has wilfully neglected (i) to provide reasonable maintenance for her, or (ii) to provide, or to make a proper contribution towards, reasonable maintenance for any child of the family for or towards whose maintenance it is reasonable in all the circumstances to expect him to provide or contribute. A husband may apply for an order on the ground that the wife

"has wilfully neglected to provide, or to make a proper contribution towards, reasonable maintenance—

---

[12]*Dipple* v. *Dipple*, [1942] 1 All E.R. 234; [1942] P. 65. The survivor has only the much more limited rights given by the Inheritance (Family Provision) Act and s. 26 of the Matrimonial Causes Act 1965; see *post*, pp. 508-517.

[13]*Ibid.*, s. 7 (4). The Law Commission, who assumed that this proposal would be highly controversial, found that it received almost unanimous support: Law Com. No. 25, para. 14.

[14]*Ibid.*, s. 27 (2). This means that, if the second husband is a person of no substance at all, the taxpayer may have to support the wife even though her first husband is capable of doing so.

[15]Matrimonial Causes Rules 1968, rr. 80 and 80A, as substituted by the Matrimonial Causes (Amendment No. 3) Rules 1970. For payment of money and transfer of property for the benefit of a party suffering from mental disorder, see the Matrimonial Proceedings and Property Act 1970, s. 26.

[16]*Ibid.*, s. 6 (2); *King* v. *King*, [1953] 2 All E.R. 1029, C.A.; [1954] P. 55. For jurisdiction in judicial separation, see *ante*, p. 143.

[17]Matrimonial Causes Act 1967, s. 2; Matrimonial Proceedings and Property Act 1970, Sched. 2, para. 2 (1) (a); Matrimonial Causes Rules 1968, r. 99 (1), (2) (as substituted). The parties must be married to each other at the time of the order and the court has no power to make an order if the marriage has been dissolved (either in this country or abroad) since the issue of the summons: *Turczak* v. *Turczak*, [1969] 2 All E.R. 317 (criticised by Karsten, 33 M.L.R. 205).

(i) for the applicant in a case where, by reason of the impairment of the applicant's earning capacity through age, illness or disability of mind or body, and having regard to any resources of the applicant and the [wife] respectively which are, or should properly be made, available for the purpose, it is reasonable in all the circumstances to expect the [wife] so to provide or contribute; or

(ii) for any child of the family [for whose maintenance it is reasonable in all the circumstances to expect the wife to provide or towards whose maintenance it is reasonable in all the circumstances to expect the wife to make a proper contribution.] ".[18]

It will be seen that, in each case, the wording of subparagraph (i) is identical with the wording of the comparable provision of the Matrimonial Proceedings (Magistrates' Courts) Act 1960 and the reader is referred to the last section for a discussion of its meaning.[19] The two subparagraphs (ii) will be considered more fully when we discuss financial provision for children generally.[20] But two points should be noticed. First, if the husband alleges that the wife has been guilty of wilful neglect to maintain *a child*, it is not necessary for him under the 1970 Act to show that his earning capacity has been impaired as it is under the 1960 Act. Secondly, as in the case of applications before magistrates, the applicant can establish a ground for an order by proving wilful neglect to maintain either herself (or himself) or a child and the court may therefore make an order in the applicant's favour even though she (or he) only establishes wilful neglect of a child.[1]

Orders that may be made.—If the applicant makes out a ground mentioned above, the court may order *the respondent* to make any one or more of the following payments:[2]

(1) Periodical payments pending suit;

(2) Unsecured periodical payments to the applicant;

(3) Secured periodical payments to the applicant;

(4) A lump sum payment to the applicant;

(5) Unsecured periodical payments for any child to whom the application relates;

(6) Secured periodical payments for such a child;

(7) A lump sum payment for such a child.

Orders for the benefit of children will be dealt with in the next chapter when we consider financial provision for children generally. The rest will be dealt with in this part of this chapter.

2. MAINTENANCE PENDING SUIT

The court may order *either spouse* to make periodical payments to the other pending suit on any petition for divorce, nullity or judicial separation.[3] In the case of an application under section 6 of the

---

[18]Matrimonial Proceedings and Property Act 1970, s. 6 (1) and (3).
[19]See *ante*, pp. 414-418.
[20]See *post*, pp. 474-475.
[1]Cf. *ante*, p. 419.
[2]Matrimonial Proceedings and Property Act 1970, s. 6 (5) and (6).
[3]*Ibid.*, s. 1.

Matrimonial Proceedings and Property Act 1970 on the ground of the respondent's wilful neglect to maintain, the court may order *the respondent* to make periodical payments to the applicant if it appears that the applicant or any child to whom the application relates is in immediate need of financial assistance but it is not yet possible to determine what order (if any) should be made.[4]

The power to order the husband to pay maintenance pending suit (or alimony *pendente lite*, as it was formerly called) goes back to the ecclesiastical courts. It was based on the fact that the wife as such was entitled to be maintained by her husband so long as the marriage was still in existence, and the purpose of interim orders of this sort was to ensure that she and any children of the marriage living with her obtained a sufficient allowance until the outcome of the proceedings. Consequently she was entitled to an order even though she was alleged to have been guilty of adultery or desertion or the marriage was alleged to be void, so long as the issue was *sub judice*.

The new powers are of course considerably wider and can no longer be related to the obligation to maintain at common law. Even under the old law the courts had a wide and unfettered discretion in deciding whether to make an order and in assessing the amount to be paid.[5] The new Act is much more explicit in stating the conditions to be satisfied before an interim order can be made in the case of an application under section 6, but it is submitted that the same facts must be relevant whatever the nature of the proceedings. All the circumstances must be taken into account including the spouses' conduct if this is not in dispute, but the court must obviously pay most attention to their immediate financial position and the needs of the children of the family.[6]

Maintenance pending suit is usually ordered to be paid retrospectively from the service of the petition. Unless the court orders otherwise, it remains payable until the determination of the suit, that is until decree absolute in the case of divorce and nullity, the decree in the case of judicial separation, or the final order in the case of proceedings under section 6, or alternatively until the petition or application is dismissed or the suit abates by reason of the death of either party.[7] In the event of an appeal, the court may order the payment of maintenance pending suit to be continued if it is fair and reasonable to do so in the circumstances.[8]

---

[4]*Ibid.*, s. 6 (5).

[5]*Waller* v. *Waller*, [1956] 2 All E.R. 234, C.A.; [1956] P. 300; *Slater* v. *Slater*, [1960] 3 All E.R. 217, C.A.; [1962] P. 94.

[6]The old practice (long since discontinued) was to bring the wife's income (if any) up to one-fifth of the spouses' joint income. At one time the courts were reluctant to give a wife who had entered into a maintenance agreement more than the husband had covenanted to pay her (see *Birch* v. *Birch*, [1908] W.N. 81, C.A.) but it is highly doubtful whether they would feel themselves so bound today. For the exercise of the court's discretion in favour of a spouse in receipt of a supplementary benefit (when an order will merely reduce the amount of benefit payable), see *Slater* v. *Slater*, (*supra*).

[7]Matrimonial Proceedings and Property Act 1970, ss. 1 and 6 (5); *Scott* v. *Scott*, [1952] 2 All E.R. 890 (husband's death). The old rule that alimony pending suit automatically ceased if the wife was found guilty of adultery had probably become obsolete before 1971, at least if there were extenuating circumstances (see *Gordon* v. *Gordon*, [1969] 3 All E.R. 1254); it must surely be regarded as completely dead now.

[8]*Corbett* v. *Corbett* (*No. 2*), [1970] 2 All E.R. 654, 657.

3. PERIODICAL PAYMENTS

On granting a decree of divorce, nullity or judicial separation, the court may order *either spouse* to make unsecured periodical payments to the other and to secure periodical payments to the other.[9] In proceedings under section 6 of the Matrimonial Proceedings and Property Act 1970 on the ground of wilful neglect to maintain, the court may make a similar order against *the respondent* in favour of the applicant.[10]

As periodical payments are intended for the payee's maintenance, they must in any event terminate on her (or his) death. Unsecured periodical payments will normally come out of the payer's income which will presumably come to an end on his death; consequently an order for their payment cannot extend beyond the joint lives of the parties.[11] There is, however, no reason why secured payments should not continue after the payer's death, as the capital will already have been charged; consequently in this case the order can last for the payee's life. Furthermore, on divorce or nullity (whether the payments are secured or not) the order must also provide for their termination on the payee's marriage; if an order made on judicial separation or under section 6 remains in force notwithstanding the subsequent dissolution or annulment of the marriage, it will automatically come to an end on the payee's remarriage.[12]

If a party is not in need of immediate provision but may need maintenance in the future, the usual procedure is to make a nominal order so that it can be varied and a substantial sum can be ordered when necessary.

Secured Payments.—The very fact of security obviously makes secured payments more attractive to the payee, for there is no problem of enforcement. By tying up the payer's capital, it also prevents him from trying to frustrate the order by disposing of his assets. We have also seen that the payee can continue to benefit from a secured order after the other's death; moreover, although the survivor cannot apply for an order after the other party's death, an order made before his death may be implemented by his personal representatives who may therefore be called upon to carry it out.[13] Because of these advantages, the court may order a smaller sum to be secured than it would have ordered by way of unsecured provision.[14]

Payments are normally secured by ordering the spouse against whom the order is made to transfer specified assets to trustees who will then hold them on trust to pay the sum ordered to the payee and the balance to the payer. Alternatively, the court may order specific

---

[9]Matrimonial Proceedings and Property Act 1970, s. 2 (1) (a), (b).

[10]*Ibid.*, s. 6 (6) (a), (b).

[11]The survivor can then exercise the much more limited rights under the Inheritance (Family Provision) Act and s. 26 of the Matrimonial Causes Act 1965; see *post*, pp. 508-517.

[12]Matrimonial Proceedings and Property Act 1970, s. 7 (1)-(3). It is immaterial that the second marriage is void or voidable: *ibid.*, s. 27 (2).

[13]*Hyde* v. *Hyde*, [1948] 1 All E.R. 362; [1948] P. 198; *Mosey* v. *Mosey*, [1955] 2 All E.R. 391; [1956] P. 26.

[14]*Chichester* v. *Chichester*, [1936] 1 All E.R. 271; [1936] P. 129.

property to be charged with the payment of the sum in question.[15] When the order comes to an end, the capital must be returned to the payer (or his estate, if he has already died) and any charge must be cancelled.

Whether the court will order maintenance to be secured must depend on the capital or secured income which the party has available, and the number of spouses against whom such an order can be made is obviously small. A party cannot normally be expected to use all his property for this purpose, for example to sell up all his furniture.[16] The court may order both secured and unsecured periodical payments, and under the old law it was unusual for more than a third or a half of the total sum to be secured.

If a party is not in need of immediate provision but may require it in the future, a nominal order may be made secured on assets yielding a substantial income. She (or he) can then apply for a suitable variation if necessary; in the meantime the income can be paid over to the other party.[17]

Consent Orders.—There is nothing to prevent the parties themselves from agreeing on the sum to be paid: indeed the whole trend during recent years has been to encourage them to do so. Such an agreement will be carefully scrutinised by the court and, if it is unobjectionable, it may then be embodied in a court order. Difficulty arises, however, if the parties come to an arrangement which is perfectly proper in itself but which is in terms outside the powers conferred by the Matrimonial Proceedings and Property Act—for example, to make periodical payments to the wife for her life even though the husband should predecease her or she should remarry. The inference to be drawn from the judgments of GREENE, M.R., in *Mills* v. *Mills*[18] and of MORRIS, L.J., in *Hinde* v. *Hinde*[19] is that *ultra vires* agreements of this sort should not be embodied in an order and that, even if they are, they are not orders for periodical payments *stricto sensu* and cannot be enforced as such. They could be included in an undertaking to the court (which could be enforced by committal in the event of noncompliance) or the court could dismiss the application conditionally

---

[15]The court may refer the matter to one of the conveyancing counsel of the court to settle a proper instrument to be executed by all necessary parties and has power to defer the grant of the decree in question until the instrument has been duly executed: Matrimonial Proceedings and Property Act 1970, s. 25.

[16]*Barker* v. *Barker*, [1952] 1 All E.R. 1128, 1134, C.A.; [1952] P. 184, 194-195. The security must be on specific assets and not a general charge on all the party's property: *Barker* v. *Barker*. It is doubtful whether reversionary interests should be charged because they cannot be used to secure present payments: *Allison* v. *Allison*, [1927] P. 308; but see *Harrison* v. *Harrison* (1887), 12 P.D. 130. The applicant could apply for a variation of the order when the interest fell in. Capital held on protective trusts should not be secured, for the order will automatically terminate the interest: *cf. Re Richardson's Will Trusts*, [1958] 1 All E.R. 538; [1958] Ch. 504. For a case where the court ordered payments to be secured on a party's sole asset (the former matrimonial home), see *Aggett* v. *Aggett*, [1962] 1 All E.R. 190, C.A.

[17]*Foarde* v. *Foarde*, [1967] 2 All E.R. 660.

[18][1940] 2 All E.R. 254, C.A.; [1940] P. 124.

[19][1953] 1 All E.R. 171, C.A.

upon the parties' entering into the agreement in question.[20] The payee's
remedy would then be an action for breach of contract.[1] If she (or he)
wishes to keep alive the power to apply for further provision later, he
should apply for a nominal order which can be varied later if necessary.[2]

Income Tax.—With income tax at its present high rate, it is of
paramount importance to determine whether the sum ordered is to be
paid before or after the payer has deducted tax. If the order is " free
of tax ", he must pay the net sum ordered; if it is " less tax " or no
mention is made of tax,[3] he is bound to pay only the balance after he
has deducted income tax. An illustration will make this clearer.
Suppose that an order for £1,000 a year is made against a husband who
is paying income tax at the standard rate of 38·75%. If it is free of
tax, £1,633 of his income must be allocated to pay it, of which £633
will go to Inland Revenue and £1,000 to the wife. On the other hand,
if it is less tax, he first deducts from the £1,000 the sum of £387·50
which will go to Inland Revenue and then pays his wife the balance of
£612·50. She may then be entitled to a refund of the whole or part of
the £387·50 depending on her own liability to tax and entitlement to
relief. In view of the frequent fluctuations in the rate of income tax,
orders free of tax should not be made.[4]

This procedure, involving a claim for refund by the payee, is highly
complicated. If the sum is relatively small, the payee will usually be
entitled to a refund of the whole of the tax paid but may well be a
person unused to making official claims and frightened by the idea.
Consequently a simplified procedure has been introduced with respect
to " small maintenance orders ", that is orders in favour of a spouse
(or former spouse) or person under the age of 21 not exceeding £7·50 a
week or £32·50 a month. The payer pays the gross sum ordered and
then deducts it entirely from his income for the purpose of the assessment of his own income tax; the money then becomes a part of the
recipient's income on which her (or his) tax (if any) will be assessed.[5]

Assignment of Periodical Payments.—Unsecured periodical
payments have always been regarded as inalienable.[6] Two reasons are

---

[20]In *Russell* v. *Russell*, [1956] 1 All E.R. 466, C.A.; [1956] P. 283, the Court of Appeal
upheld the validity of an undertaking given by the husband and incorporated in the
decree that he would not apply for a reduction in an existing maintenance order unless
he was out of work.

[1]But an undertaking given neither under seal nor for valuable consideration (and
therefore not a contract) creates an obligation only towards the court. Consequently
it can be enforced, *e.g.*, by attachment but not by an action for arrears by the payee:
Re Hudson, [1966] 1 All E.R. 110; [1966] Ch. 209. This may leave the payee completely
unprotected on the other party's death, as in *Re Hudson*.

[2]For if her application is dismissed, she cannot make a fresh application for financial
provision later: *L.* v. *L.*, [1961] 3 All E.R. 834, C.A.; [1962] P. 101, criticised by Samuels
in 25 M.L.R. 473. Nor apparently could she apply to have the order varied: see *post*,
p. 452.

[3]*Smith* v. *Smith*, [1923] P. 191, C.A.

[4]*Wallis* v. *Wallis*, [1941] 2 All E.R. 291, 295-298; [1941] P. 69, 74-76. Contrast
J. v. *J.*, [1955] 2 All E.R. 85; [1955] P. 215.

[5]Income and Corporation Taxes Act 1970, s. 65. The Treasury may by statutory
instrument increase the maximum sum.

[6]*Re Robinson* (1884), 27 Ch.D. 160, C.A.; *Watkins* v. *Watkins*, [1896] P. 222, C.A.

given for this rule: they are intended as personal provision for the payee and, as they can be varied at any time, no absolute transfer is possible. Consequently any purported assignment of future payments or charge upon them will be completely void and, for the same reason, the payee may not release them by agreement with the other party.[7] Whilst this restriction fetters the fund in the hands of the payee, it also protects her, for a judgment creditor has no power to seize it in satisfaction of his debts.[8]

Secured payments are regarded more in the nature of the payee's property and consequently it has been held that she can assign it and release the other party from further liability in respect of it.[9] One of the reasons formerly advanced for distinguishing secured from unsecured payments was that the court had no power to vary the former;[10] it is therefore arguable that the power, introduced in 1949, to vary orders for secured maintenance has had the incidental effect of making them inalienable.

4. LUMP SUM PAYMENTS

On divorce, nullity and judicial separation the court may order *either party* to pay a lump sum or lump sums to the other.[11] In proceedings under section 6 of the Matrimonial Proceedings and Property Act 1970 on the ground of wilful neglect to provide reasonable maintenance, *the respondent* may be ordered to pay a lump sum to the applicant.[12]

The power to order the payment of a lump sum was first given to the courts in 1963 and has been comparatively little used. The reason is perhaps to be found in a dictum of WILLMER, L.J., in the Court of Appeal in *Davis* v. *Davis*,[13] where he said that it was likely to be used only in relatively rare cases where the party had sufficient assets to justify it; one hopes with the Law Commission[14] that wider use may be made of it in the future. The Act itself provides that a lump sum may be ordered to enable the payee to meet any liabilities or expenses already reasonably incurred in maintaining himself (or herself) or any child of the family.[15] In other cases the power can properly be exercised whenever a capital sum is more valuable to the payee than periodical payments. An obvious example would be the payment to a former wife

---

[7]*Campbell* v. *Campbell*, [1922] P. 187. But an agreement to release payments will be taken into consideration in deciding what arrears are to be enforced against the other party.

[8]*J. Walls, Ltd.* v. *Legge*, [1923] 2 K.B. 240, C.A.

[9]*Harrison* v. *Harrison* (1888), 13 P.D. 180, C.A.; *Maclurcan* v. *Maclurcan* (1897), 77 L.T. 474, C.A.

[10]*Watkins* v. *Watkins*, (*supra*); *Harrison* v. *Harrison*, (*supra*).

[11]Matrimonial Proceedings and Property Act 1970, s. 2 (1) (c).

[12]*Ibid.*, s. 6 (6) (c).

[13][1967] 1 All E.R. 123, 126, C.A.; [1967] P. 185, 192, repeated in *Hakluytt* v. *Hakluytt*, [1968] 2 All E.R. 868, 871, C.A.

[14]Law Com. No. 25, para. 9. See further Miller, *Maintenance and Property*, 87 L.Q.R. 66; Cretney, *Matrimonial Property—Courts' Powers*, 121 News L.J. 218.

[15]Ss. 2 (2) (a) and 6 (7) (a). In the case of proceedings under s. 6, the Act refers to a child of the family to whom the application relates.

R

who wished to purchase a house or the goodwill of a business;[16] similarly lump sums have been awarded against husbands who are largely living on capital and whose income therefore does not fairly represent their standard of living[17] and against a husband who had voluntarily reduced his income by taking part of his naval pension as a lump sum.[18] A lump sum payment may also be ordered to protect the payee against probable default on the other's part, for example if it appears that the party against whom financial provision is being sought is likely to remove his assets out of the jurisdiction,[19] or to enable the payee to take bankruptcy proceedings against a contumacious party.[20]

The court can order the sum to be paid in instalments and may also require the payment of instalments to be secured.[1]

5. TRANSFER AND SETTLEMENT OF PROPERTY

On granting a decree of divorce, nullity or judicial separation, the court may order *either party* to the marriage to transfer such property as may be specified to the other party or to or for the benefit of a child of the family. The court may also order *either party* to settle any property for the benefit of the other party or any child of the family.[2] There is no comparable power in proceedings under section 6 of the Matrimonial Proceedings and Property Act on the ground of wilful neglect to maintain. The reason for this is that such transfers and settlements should represent a final adjustment of rights in property between the parties and consequently should be ordered only when the marriage has broken down permanently. The sole justification for giving the court these powers on judicial separation is that this may be the final severance of the matrimonial bond if the parties have a conscientious objection to divorce.[3]

These provisions are new. The only comparable power that the court had before 1971 was to order a settlement of the wife's property in certain circumstances when she had been responsible for the breakdown of the marriage: in other words it enabled the court to make appropriate provisions notwithstanding that the wife could not be ordered to pay maintenance to the husband. Consequently decisions on the way in which that power was to be exercised appear to be no longer relevant at all. The new power will probably be of importance in three situations: first, as an alternative to the payment of a lump

---

[16]As in *Von Mehren* v. *Von Mehren*, [1970] 1 All E.R. 153, C.A., where the husband, whose capital was worth less than £9,000, was ordered to pay £4,000 to his former wife to enable her to purchase a house which she intended to run as a boarding house. See also *Davis* v. *Davis*, (*supra*) (husband's assets worth £400,000; wife awarded £25,000 on divorce to buy a house and furniture with a balance to use for amenities or in emergency).

[17]*Brett* v. *Brett*, [1969] 1 All E.R. 1007, C.A. (husband's assets worth about £500,000; wife awarded £25,000 on divorce together with a further £5,000 if husband did not obtain a gett which would permit her to remarry by Jewish law).

[18]*Hakluytt* v. *Hakluytt*, (*supra*) (wife given £500 to carry out repairs to her house after judicial separation).

[19]*Brett* v. *Brett*, (*supra*).

[20]*Curtis* v. *Curtis*, [1969] 2 All E.R. 207, C.A. (husband, who had considerable means and was taking delaying tactics, ordered to pay wife £33,600, capitalising an annual sum of £2,400).

[1]Matrimonial Proceedings and Property Act 1970, ss. 2 (2) (b) and 6 (7) (b).

[2]*Ibid.*, s. 4 (a), (b).   [3]Law Com. No. 25, para. 65.

sum when it is more sensible to order one spouse to transfer investments than to compel him to sell them to raise the necessary capital; secondly, to supplement or replace periodical payments when the party in question has a limited interest (for example, a life interest under a family settlement) which can conveniently be used for this purpose; thirdly, to enable the court to make appropriate orders with respect to the matrimonial home and similar assets, for example furniture or the family car. If the husband is beneficially entitled to the home, either solely or jointly with the wife, the most reasonable and just solution to the financial problems created by his bringing about the breakdown of the marriage might well be to transfer the whole of his interest to her so that she can stay there with the children. The wife will not have to look elsewhere for accommodation and the husband will be compensated by not having to give her a lump sum to buy another house or make periodical payments to cover the rent if she leases one.[4]

Property that may be the Subject of an Order.—The Act empowers the court to make an order with respect to any property to which the spouse in question is entitled either in possession or in reversion. This form of words follows that of earlier Acts dealing with settlements of the wife's property, under which it was held that " property " included income as well as capital[5] and " reversionary interests " embraced those to which the wife was contingently entitled as well as those already vested in interest.[6] But it seems that the party must be able to claim the property *as of right;* hence, if he is a beneficiary under a discretionary trust, the court apparently has no power to order the settlement of any income which the trustees *may* in their discretion pay him,[7] nor presumably could it order the settlement of any property which *might* come to him as the result of the exercise of a power of appointment vested in another.

No transfer or settlement will be ordered if the property is outside the jurisdiction and effective control of the court.[8] But the fact that the property is situated abroad will not prevent the order from being made provided that it can be effectively enforced; and so the court might order the settlement of income receivable in this country from capital invested elsewhere. But if such an order might prove to be difficult to enforce, the court will prefer to make an order with respect to property in England.[9]

A series of cases before 1949 laid down the rule that the court could not make an order with respect to property subject to a restraint on

---

[4]*Cf.* the power to transfer a protected a statutory tenancy on divorce or nullity: *ante*, p. 400.

[6]See *Savary* v. *Savary* (1898), 79 L.T. 607, 610, C.A.; *Style* v. *Style*, [1954] 1 All E.R. 442, C.A.; [1954] P. 209.

[6]*Stedall* v. *Stedall* (1902), 86 L.T. 124; *Savary* v. *Savary*, (*supra*).

[7]*Milne* v. *Milne* (1871), L.R. 2 P & D. 295.

[8]*Tallack* v. *Tallack*, [1927] P. 211 (property situated in Holland and Dutch court would disregard any order made by an English court).

[9]See *Style* v. *Style*, (*supra*).

anticipation if the wife was married at the time.[10] The rule is of course no longer of any practical interest now that the restraint on anticipation has been abolished, but the wider rule to be inferred is still of importance, for it implies that the court cannot order a transfer or settlement that the party could not make voluntarily. This will arise in the case of a protected life interest, for this is determinable if any event occurs which will deprive the beneficiary of the right to receive any part of the income.[11] It is submitted that such an interest cannot be settled.[12]

Orders that can be made.—The court can apparently order an absolute transfer of the whole of the party's interest in the property specified or any part of it. It has equally wide powers when ordering a settlement and may either divest the spouse of his whole interest[13] or grant a limited interest to the other spouse or children, leaving the beneficial owner with the reversion.[14] The facts which the court should take into account when deciding what order (if any) to make will be considered later.[15]

6. VARIATION OF ANTE-NUPTIAL AND POST-NUPTIAL SETTLEMENTS

On granting a decree of divorce, nullity or judicial separation the court may make

" an order varying for the benefit of the parties to the marriage and of the children of the family or either or any of them any ante-nuptial or post-nuptial settlement (including such a settlement made by will or codicil)[16] made on the parties to the marriage; ana

an order extinguishing or reducing the interest of either of the parties to the marriage under any such settlement;

and the court may make an order . . . notwithstanding that there are no children of the family"[17]

As in the case of transfer and settlement of property, these are intended to be final orders made only when the marriage has permanently broken down. Consequently there is no power to order the variation of settlements in proceedings under section 6 of the Matrimonial Proceedings and Property Act on the ground of wilful neglect to maintain.[18]

The court's powers are wider than they were before 1971 in two respects: they can be exercised on judicial separation, and the court can

---

[10]See in particular *Loraine* v. *Loraine*, [1912] P. 222, C.A.

[11]See the Trustee Act 1925, s. 33.

[12]The question was left open by LORD PENZANCE in *Milne* v. *Milne*, (*supra*). In *Loraine* v. *Loraine*, (*supra*), COZENS-HARDY, M.R., stated obiter that a settlement would probably not amount to a forfeiture on the construction of the will in question (at p. 230).

[13]As in *Compton* v. *Compton*, [1960] 2 All E.R. 70; [1960] P. 201, where property was settled on children for life with remainder to grandchildren. *Quaere* whether the remainder to the grandchildren was not *ultra vires* as this does not benefit *children of the family*.

[14]*Style* v. *Style*, [1954] 1 All E.R. 442, C.A.; [1954] P. 209 (settlement on husband for life).

[15]See pp. 443-449 (spouse) and 475-476 (children).

[16]The words in parentheses reverse the decision in *Garratt* v. *Garratt*, [1922] P. 230.

[17]Matrimonial Proceedings and Property Act 1970, s. 4 (c), (d).

[18]See *ante*, p. 434.

now extinguish or reduce a party's interest even though neither the other party nor the children are benefited as a result. These powers are complementary to those already discussed and may well be used less in view of the wider powers to order transfers and settlements of property. For example, a conveyance of a house to the husband and wife jointly clearly constitutes a post-nuptial settlement. If it was desired to extinguish the husband's interest on divorce before 1971, this could be done by varying the settlement; now he can be ordered to transfer his interest to the wife. But if there is a settlement in the usual sense of the word, the parties may still wish to invoke the court's powers to effect the fairest possible financial provision in the new situation created by the breakdown of the marriage.

The parties cannot oust the court's jurisdiction by agreement, nor apparently is this jurisdiction in any way fettered by express provisions in the settlement as to how the property is to be held if the marriage is terminated.[19] In nullity proceedings a settlement may be varied even though the marriage is void,[20] but if it is not to take effect until the celebration of the marriage, it would appear not yet to be in existence and therefore to be incapable of variation.

The court has power to vary any settlement in existence at the time of the decree absolute.[1] Although a party who remarries cannot apply for an order against the other,[2] the court's jurisdiction is in no way fettered by the remarriage of the other or the death of either of them.[3]

Transactions to which the Act applies.—The terms " ante-nuptial and post-nuptial settlements " are used in a sense much wider than that usually given to them by conveyancers. The courts' desire to do justice between the parties has led them to extend the section to a very large number of transactions indeed.[4] One of the best known definitions is that of HILL, J., in *Prinsep* v. *Prinsep*:[5]

" Is it [*i.e.*, the settlement] upon the husband in the character of husband or in (*sic*) the wife in the character of wife, or upon both in the character of husband and wife? If it is, it is a settlement on the parties within the meaning of the section. The particular form of it does not matter. It may be a settlement in the strictest sense of the term, it may be a covenant to pay by one spouse to the other, or by a third person to a spouse. What does matter is that it should provide for the financial benefit of one or other or both of the spouses as spouses and with reference to their married state."

---

[19]*Cf. Prinsep* v. *Prinsep*, [1930] P. 35, 49, C.A.; *Woodcock* v. *Woodcock* (1914), 111 L.T. 924, C.A.; DENNING, L.J., in *Egerton* v. *Egerton*, [1949] 2 All E.R. 238, 242, C.A. The decision to the contrary in the early case of *Stone* v. *Stone* (1864), 3 Sw. & Tr. 372, cannot now be regarded as good law.
[20]*Cf. Radziej* v. *Radziej*, [1967] 1 All E.R. 944; affirmed, [1968] 3 All E.R. 624, C.A.
[1]*Dormer* v. *Ward*, [1901] P. 20, C.A.
[2]Matrimonial Proceedings and Property Act 1970, s. 7 (4). See *ante*, p. 427.
[3]*Churchward* v. *Churchward*, [1910] P. 195 (death); *Jacobs* v. *Jacobs*, [1942] 2 All E.R. 471, C.A.; [1943] P. 7 (remarriage). Before 1971 the rule was that a variation would not be granted after a party's death if the sole effect would be to benefit a stranger (*e.g.* the persons entitled to the deceased party's estate): *Thomson* v. *Thomson*, [1896] P. 263, C.A. Although this fact may remain of vital importance in deciding whether to make an order, it is submitted that the express power to extinguish a party's interest now gives the court jurisdiction to do so.
[4]See *Melvill* v. *Melvill*, [1930] P. 159, C.A., at pp. 173, 175.
[5][1929] P. 225, 232.

Denning, J., spoke in similar terms in *Smith* v. *Smith*:[6]

> " The principle, as I understand it, is that where a husband makes a con-
> tinuing provision for the future needs of his wife in her character as a wife,
> which is still continuing when the marriage is dissolved [or annulled], the
> provision is a " settlement " which can be brought before the court to see
> whether the provision should continue now that she has ceased to be a wife.
> The same applies to a provision by a wife for her husband or by each or
> either for both."

The essential therefore is that the benefit must be conferred on either
or both of the spouses *in the character of spouse or spouses*.[7] It is
immaterial whether it comes from one of the spouses or from a third
person, provided that this condition is satisfied.[8] Although this
point has never been directly decided, it is possible that a transaction
may be a settlement for this purpose if it confers a benefit upon the
children of the marriage, even though it confers none upon either
spouse, provided that the beneficiaries take *in the character of children
of the family*.[9] Conversely, a transaction which would otherwise be a
settlement will not cease to be one merely because it makes provision
for any after taken spouse of either of the parties or the children of
such a marriage.[10]

The most obvious types of transaction coming within this provision
are ante-nuptial and post-nuptial settlements in the ordinarily accepted
conveyancing sense of the word. As in *Prinsep* v. *Prinsep* itself, provided that the condition stated above is fulfilled, it is immaterial that
one or both of the spouses are merely the objects of a discretionary trust
and can therefore claim nothing as of right.[11] Further, it is not difficult
to see from the definitions of settlements cited above that a separation
agreement comes within the section,[12] as does a conveyance of property
to the husband and wife as joint tenants or tenants in common as this
will create a statutory trust for sale.[13]

---

[6][1945] 1 All E.R. 584, 586.

[7]See also *Bosworthick* v. *Bosworthick*, [1927] P. 64, 69, C.A.; *Worsley* v. *Worsley*
(1869), L.R. 1 P. & D. 648, 651.

[8]*Prinsep* v. *Prinsep*, (*supra*).

[9]Apparently so held in *Compton* v. *Compton*, [1960] 2 All E.R. 70; [1960] P. 201
(where, however, wife was trustee and had a power of appointment in favour of children).
Cf. Greer, L.J., in *Melvill* v. *Melvill*, (*supra*), at pp. 176, 177. But it is difficult to
see how this could be a " settlement *made on the parties to the marriage* ".

[10]As in *Prinsep* v. *Prinsep*, (*supra*).

[11]See also *Janion* v. *Janion* (1926), [1929] P. 237 *n*. A protected life interest can
also be varied without producing a forfeiture: *General Accident, Fire and Life Assurance
Corporation, Ltd.* v. *Inland Revenue Commissioners*, [1963] 3 All E.R. 259, C.A. In
Howard v. *Howard*, [1945] 1 All E.R. 91, C.A.; [1945] P. 1, MacKinnon, L.J. left open
the question whether a discretionary trust can be a post-nuptial settlement merely
because one of the spouses comes within the class of possible beneficiaries. The court
may vary such a settlement even though it is in a foreign form because the parties were
domiciled elsewhere at the time of the marriage: *Forsyth* v. *Forsyth*, [1891] P. 363.

[12]*Tomkins* v. *Tomkins*, [1948] 1 All E.R. 237, C.A.; [1948] P. 170; *Jeffrey* v. *Jeffrey*
(*No. 2*), [1952] 1 All E.R. 790, C.A.; [1952] P. 122. They may also be varied under
s. 14 of the Matrimonial Proceedings and Property Act (*ante*, p. 410).

[13]*Brown* v. *Brown*, [1959] 2 All E.R. 266, C.A.; [1959] P. 86; *Ulrich* v. *Ulrich*, [1968]
1 All E.R. 67, C.A. In *Cook* v. *Cook*, [1962] 2 All E.R. 811, C.A.; [1962] P. 235, this was

But the tendency in recent years to widen the scope of the concept even further (owing no doubt to a desire to do justice in a large number of cases where the marriage has broken down) has been checked by the Court of Appeal in *Prescott* v. *Fellowes*.[14] In this case immediately before their marriage and allegedly in consideration of it the wife transferred to the husband securities to the value of £15,000 " as an absolute gift ". The deed further provided that if at any time within the next two and a half years the husband qualified for membership of Lloyd's, the wife would provide him with a loan of £20,000. The securities were transferred to the husband but, as he never became a member of Lloyd's, the provision with respect to the loan lapsed. Some time later the marriage was dissolved and the wife sought to have the settlement varied as an ante-nuptial settlement and to recover the value of the securities which the husband had already sold. The court unanimously held that they had no power to make the order sought. The clear rule emerges that, where there has been an absolute and unqualified transfer of property (as there had been of the securities in this case), there is not a settlement for the purposes of the Act, unless *at the time when the court has to enquire into the existence of the settlement* there are periodical payments still to be made. Hence the wife's covenant to lend £20,000 probably made the deed an ante-nuptial settlement at the time that it was executed, but the husband's failure to satisfy the condition precedent and the consequent extinction of the obligation meant that when the case came before the court there was no longer any property settled with respect to which the order could be made. On this ground many of the cases decided before 1958 are easily explicable, for example *Bosworthick* v. *Bosworthick*,[15] in which the Court of Appeal held that a bond executed by a wife in which she undertook to pay her husband £300 a year for life was a settlement, and *Gunner* v. *Gunner*,[16] where WALLINGTON, J., held that a policy of life assurance taken out by a husband for the benefit of his wife came into the same category Although the court in *Prescott* v. *Fellowes* did not expressly overrule a number of cases decided at first instance before 1958,[17] it did doubt

---

extended to a conveyance which had been made to the husband alone but which created a tenancy in common in equity because the wife had contributed to the purchase money: see *ante*, pp. 378-381. The court may vary a joint tenancy which has been severed and turned into a tenancy in common: *Radziej* v. *Radziej*, [1967] 1 All E.R. 944; affirmed, [1968] 3 All E.R. 624, C.A., but not once the parties have exercised the power of sale and divided the proceeds for there is no settlement left in existence: *Sievwright* v. *Sievwright*, [1956] 2 All E.R. 616.

[14][1958] 3 All E.R. 55, C.A.; [1958] P. 260.

[15][1927] P. 64, C.A. *Cf. Parrington* v. *Parrington*, [1951] 2 All E.R. 916.

[16][1948] 2 All E.R. 771; [1949] P. 77, followed in *Bown* v. *Bown*, [1948] 2 All E.R. 778; [1949] P. 91.

[17]*Halpern* v. *Halpern*, [1951] 1 All E.R. 315; [1951] P. 204 (gift of a share of the house which was used as the matrimonial home held to be a " settlement "); *Brown* v. *Brown*, [1936] 2 All E.R. 1616; [1937] P. 7 (purchase of annuity for husband held not to be a " settlement ").

their correctness and it is submitted that they should no longer be followed.

The distinction between settlements and gifts is of course of considerably less importance today because of the court's power to order a transfer of property. Thus in *Prescott* v. *Fellowes* the husband could now be ordered to return the securities if this would be a fair financial adjustment in the circumstances.

The Meaning of " Ante-nuptial " and " Post-nuptial ".—We have up till now been considering what constitutes a " settlement ". We must now examine the meaning of the terms " ante-nuptial " and " post-nuptial ". In each case it is essential that the settlement should have been made on the footing that the particular marriage which is being dissolved or annulled should continue.[18] Thus in *Hargreaves* v. *Hargreaves*[19] a settlor, who was then a bachelor, settled property on himself for life with remainder to his children or remoter issue and reserved a power to appoint an interest in favour of any wife he might marry. Later, on the eve of his marriage to the petitioner, he appointed £500 *per annum* to her during coverture. It was held that this could not be varied so as to give the former wife a life interest in place of an interest during coverture, since the original settlement had not been made in contemplation of the particular marriage—or indeed of any marriage at all.

A case illustrating this principle even more clearly is *Burnett* v. *Burnett*.[20] In 1925 the respondent husband, who was then married to A, settled a fund on trustees on discretionary trusts in favour of himself, *any* wife that he might have and his issue. In 1927 he brought further property into the same trusts and in the following year he settled a part of this fund on the two daughters of his marriage with A. This marriage was later dissolved, and on the eve of his marriage to the petitioner, B, in 1929 the husband appointed £600 on trust for B and subject thereto to any child of the marriage with B. B then divorced the husband and applied to have the settlement varied. It was held that this could not be done. The settlements of 1925, 1927 and 1928 were all post-nuptial settlements with respect to the marriage with A, and BUCKNILL, J., rejected the argument that a settlement could be post-nuptial with respect to one marriage and ante-nuptial with respect to another. Quite apart from the impossibly complicated situation which would arise from a series of variations " which would be limited only by the possible number of wives of the settlor ",[1] it follows from *Hargreaves* v. *Hargreaves* that this could not be an ante-nuptial settlement with respect to a marriage which was not contemplated at the time. Whilst the settlement of 1929 was clearly ante-nuptial with respect to the marriage with B, it was again held that this could not be varied for the court has no power " to vary an appointment in such a way that in the result the principal settlement is also varied although that settlement is not within " the Act.

---

[18] *Young* v. *Young* (*No. 1*), [1961] 3 All E.R. 695, C.A.; [1962] P. 27.
[19] [1926] P. 42.
[20] [1936] P. 1.
[1] At p. 11. See also pp. 15-16.

If, as in *Young* v. *Young (No. 1)*,[2] the agreement was ostensibly entered into on the footing that the marriage would be dissolved or annulled, it cannot be a post-nuptial settlement. Conversely, if a particular transaction is on the face of it clearly an ante-nuptial or post-nuptial settlement, then in accordance with the usual rules of construction other evidence may not be adduced to show that it was not intended to be any such thing. In *Melvill* v. *Melvill*[3] some months after the husband had petitioned for divorce on the ground of the wife's adultery, she assigned certain funds to trustees to hold on trust for herself for life with remainder to her children and she reserved a power to appoint not more than half the fund to any husband for life. In the instrument the settlor was described as " the wife " and the settlement was declared to be made in consideration of her natural love and affection for her two children. In fact the wife's object was to prevent this property from being settled for the benefit of the husband. After the decree absolute the wife executed a deed poll by which she directed that the income under this settlement was to be subject to a restraint on anticipation in the event of her marrying the co-respondent, whom she in fact married five days later. On an application by the husband to have the original trust deed and the deed poll varied as a post-nuptial settlement, it was held that since on the face of them they appeared to be such, evidence could not be admitted to show that the wife's real purpose was to benefit the husband of a future intended marriage.

Variation of Powers of Appointment in favour of future Spouse and Children.—The problem here presented is a common one. Let us suppose an ante-nuptial settlement to have been made by the husband with the following usual limitations: to the husband for life, with remainder to the wife for life if she survives the husband, with remainder to such of the children as the spouses (or the survivor) shall appoint, and in default of appointment to all the children of the marriage in equal shares, with a power, however, in the *surviving* spouse to appoint a certain portion of the fund to any after taken spouse or to the children of such a marriage. Let us further suppose that the husband obtains a divorce and, still a young man, is contemplating a second marriage. It can be assumed that, if the wife was responsible for the breakdown of the marriage, her life interest will be extinguished; if there is only one child of the marriage, that child must take the whole of the fund on the husband's death subject to the exercise of the power of appointment in favour of any future spouse or children. The question then is: can the husband apply to have the settlement varied so that this power may be exercised by him during his former wife's lifetime notwithstanding that he is not (and may never be) the survivor of the two?

---

[2][1961] 3 All E.R. 695, C.A.; [1962] P. 27. Surrounding circumstances may be taken into consideration if they do not contradict the written agreement, although the settlor's motive is *per se* immaterial: *Joss* v. *Joss*, [1943] 1 All E.R. 102; [1943] P. 18; *Parrington* v. *Parrington*, [1951] 2 All E.R. 916, 919; *Prinsep* v. *Prinsep*, [1929] P. 225, 236.

[3][1930] P. 159, C.A.

Under the old law it was not the practice of the courts to accelerate
the exercise of the power of appointment in favour of the guilty spouse
and they sometimes went further and extinguished that spouse's power
to appoint amongst the children of the marriage that had been dissolved.[4] But if the application is made by the spouse who has provided
the fund and who has not been responsible for the breakdown of the
marriage, the problem is different; here the court is faced with the
difficulty that, if it accedes to the application, it is prejudicing the child
(or children) of the former marriage, whose interests it is bound to look
after. In the example given there is a high chance that the one child
will take the whole fund, but if the husband is given a power to appoint
in favour of his second wife and other children, there is a high probability that the existing child's expectancy will be appreciably reduced.
To off-set this, however, it must be borne in mind that there is now no
chance of his interest being reduced by his having to share the reversion
with other children of the first marriage, and that to refuse the request
may well cause the husband and his children by any later marriage to
feel that they have been unjustly treated and thus lead to friction and
ill feeling in the family.[5]

This problem and the leading cases were discussed by CAIRNS, J., in
Purnell v. *Purnell*.[6] It is now clearly established that whatever in-
tangible advantage the children of the first marriage may get out of
permitting their parent to exercise a power to appoint among children
of a second marriage, nothing must be done which on the whole would
be for the disadvantage of the former; consequently the settlement will
not be varied to enable a benefit to be conferred upon a stranger to it
unless at the same time some approximately equivalent financial
benefit is also conferred upon the child or children of the first marriage
as a *quid pro quo*. Whilst the extinction of the guilty spouse's life
interest in remainder gives some advantage to the child insofar as it
may accelerate the vesting of his own remainder, this is so slight that
it cannot now be regarded as sufficient in itself.[7] But the following,
either singly or in combination, have been held to be enough to support
such a variation: giving the child an additional vested annuity,[8] giving
the child a vested interest instead of a contingent interest under the
settlement,[9] increasing the child's share by reducing the portion which
the parent is permitted to settle on the children of a subsequent
marriage,[10] and by making a consent order under which the guilty

---

[4]See, *e.g.*, *Noel* v. *Noel* (1885), 10 P.D. 179; *Hartopp* v. *Hartopp*, [1899] P. 65;
Wadham v. *Wadham*, [1938] 1 All E.R. 206.
[5]*Garforth-Bles* v. *Garforth-Bles*, [1951] 1 All E.R. 308, 310; [1951] P. 218, 222; *Best* v.
Best, [1955] 2 All E.R. 839, 843; [1956] P. 76, 84.
[6][1961] 1 All E.R. 369; [1961] P. 141. In this case, as in *Best* v. *Best*, [1955]
2 All E.R. 839; [1956] P. 76, the situation was unusual because the wife wished to
have the settlement varied so as to be able to exercise the power in favour of a child
whom she and her first husband had adopted.
[7]*Best* v. *Best*, (*supra*); *Tagart* v. *Tagart* (1934), 50 T.L.R. 399.
[8]*Newson* v. *Newson* (1934), 50 T.L.R. 399; *Wadham* v. *Wadham*, (*supra*); *Maxwell* v.
Maxwell, [1950] 2 All E.R. 979; [1951] P. 212.
[9]*Scollick* v. *Scollick*, [1927] P. 205; *Garforth-Bles* v. *Garforth-Bles*, (*supra*); *Purnell* v.
Purnell, (*supra*).
[10]*Wadham* v. *Wadham*, (*supra*); *Hodgson Roberts* v. *Hodgson Roberts*, [1906] P. 142;
Colclough v. *Colclough*, [1933] P. 143. In *Newson* v. *Newson*, (*supra*), as a *quid pro quo*
the mother's power to limit the sum which the child should take under his grandmother's
settlement was extinguished.

spouse settles another fund on the children[11] or a third person covenants to make payments towards the child's maintenance or education.[12]

Destruction of Ultimate Remainders.—If there is no issue of the marriage, a further problem arises, that of the destruction of ultimate remainders. Let us suppose that there is a settlement of the wife's fund on the usual trusts with an ultimate remainder over to the wife's brothers and sisters and their issue if there åre no children of the marriage. If there have been no children, so that this ultimate remainder is now bound to take effect, can the settlement be varied by striking out this remainder with the result that the wife will take an absolute interest in the fund? The answer is apparently "yes", provided that all the persons now alive who have an interest in the fund consent, even though this may have the effect of extinguishing contingent interests of persons as yet unborn.[13] This has even been done where the remainder was in favour of the children of any subsequent marriage of the applicant on the ground that he could be expected to make provision for them himself in any case.[14] But the court will not accede to the proposal if this would extinguish the interest of a living person who does not consent to the order.[15]

Retrospective Variations.—The court apparently has no power to order a retrospective variation. But if the innocent spouse is prejudiced by the delay, the court can compensate for this by giving him or her a temporary or permanent increased benefit.[16]

7. ASSESSMENT OF FINANCIAL PROVISION

The general principles relating to assessment are now laid down in section 5 (1) of the Matrimonial Proceedings and Property Act 1970. In addition to specifying certain matters which must be taken into account (and which will be considered in greater detail shortly), this sub-section provides that the court shall have regard to all the circumstances of the case and so exercise its powers "as to place the parties, so far as it is practicable and, having regard to their conduct, just to do so, in the financial position in which they would have been if the marriage had not broken down and each had properly discharged his or her financial obligations and responsibilities towards the other".

This embodies in statutory form the basic principle underlying the courts' exercise of their discretion before the new Act came into force. So far as possible they will try to restore the parties to the financial

---

[11]*Purnell* v. *Purnell*, (*supra*).

[12]*Newson* v. *Newson*, (*supra*) (covenant by the wife's mother); *Scollick* v. *Scollick*, (*supra*) (covenant by the wife's second husband).

[13]*Morrissey* v. *Morrissey*, [1905] P. 90; *Bowles* v. *Bowles*, [1937] 2 All E.R. 263; [1937] P. 127.

[14]*Meredyth* v. *Meredyth*, [1895] P. 92.

[15]*Webb* v. *Webb*, [1929] P. 159, distinguishing *Wynne* v. *Wynne* (1898), 78 L.T. 796, where the wife could have defeated the remaindermen in any case by exercising a power of appointment by will.

[16]See *Constantinidi* v. *Constantinidi*, [1905] P. 253, 276, C.A.

position they were in before the marriage broke down, but if one party has to suffer as a consequence of the breakdown, it is just and reasonable that this should normally be the party who has brought it about. Whenever possible, the standard of living of the innocent spouse should not be permitted to fall below that of the guilty one.[17] It is to this extent alone that the parties' conduct is relevant: it has been said repeatedly that the courts must not use their power to order financial provision as a means of punishing the spouse who has brought about the breakdown of the marriage.[18] Conversely, as was held in *Sansom* v. *Sansom*,[19] an award to a wife will not be reduced merely because she chooses to petition for judicial separation rather than divorce and thus prevents the other party from remarrying until he is in a position to petition for divorce himself. She may have a number of reasons for her action apart from spite: the Act has given her the right to pursue either remedy and her motive is no concern of the court. This is really an example of a wider principle, *viz.* that financial provision is intended to give protection to the spouse and the children of the family and should not be ordered for some ulterior purpose. In *Wakeford* v. *Wakeford*[20] it was held that a sum which had been fixed disproportionately high in order to force the husband to grant the wife a tenancy of the former matrimonial home should be reduced; conversely in *Wharton* v. *Wharton*[1] the figure was increased where it would not have been unfair to say that it was designed " to starve the wife into a reconciliation ".

Nevertheless in many cases—perhaps in most cases—a party's standard of living will have to suffer even though he or she has been wholly blameless, because there will be two families to support instead of one.[2] If the husband brings about the breakdown of the marriage, his first duty is clearly towards his children and the innocent wife he has repudiated. Consequently, as the Divisional Court held in *Roberts* v. *Roberts*,[3] if another woman lives with him, either as his second wife or his mistress, her rights must, so to speak, be postponed to those of the first wife. But if his income is so low that he cannot support more than one household, he must obviously be allowed to retain sufficient to maintain himself and any dependants living with him. In *Ashley* v.

[17]For statements of general principle under the old law, see *N.* v. *N.* (1928), 44 T.L.R. 324, 328; *J.* v. *J.*, [1955] 2 All E.R. 617, 620, C.A.; [1955] P. 215, 242; *Schlesinger* v. *Schlesinger*, [1960] 1 All E.R. 721, 727-728; [1960] P. 191, 197; *Kershaw* v. *Kershaw*, [1964] 3 All E.R. 635, 636-637; [1966] P. 13, 17; *Attwood* v. *Attwood*, [1968] 3 All E.R. 385; [1968] P. 591. See also *Lorriman* v. *Lorriman*, [1908] P. 282, 289, and *Matheson* v. *Matheson*, [1935] P. 171, 176 (settlement of property); *Prinsep* v. *Prinsep*, [1930] P. 35, C.A., and *Tomkins* v. *Tomkins*, [1948] 1 All E.R. 237, C.A.; [1948] P. 170 (variation of settlements).
[18]See *e.g. Attwood* v. *Attwood*, [1968] 3 All E.R. 385, 388; [1968] P. 591, 595 (periodical payments); *Ulrich* v. *Ulrich*, [1968] 1 All E.R. 67, C.A. (variation of settlement); *Moy* v. *Moy*, [1961] 2 All E.R. 204, 205, C.A. (settlement of wife's property).
[19][1966] 2 All E.R. 396, 399; [1966] P. 52, 55-56.
[20][1953] 2 All E.R. 827. *Cf. Howard* v. *Howard*, [1945] 1 All E.R. 91, C.A.; [1945] P. 1, where it was held that pressure should not be indirectly applied to trustees to increase the income which they were allowing to the husband under discretionary powers.
[1][1952] 2 All E.R. 939.
[2]*Kershaw* v. *Kershaw*, [1964] 3 All E.R. 635, 636-637; [1966] P. 13, 17.
[3][1968] 3 All E.R. 479; [1970] P. 1.

Ashley[4] the husband had deserted his wife leaving her with their two children. As a result she had been compelled to seek national assistance (the forerunner of the present supplementary benefit). It was held that, although anything the wife received from her husband would merely reduce the amount that she received from the National Assistance Board and consequently would benefit the Board and not herself, this was irrelevant in assessing the sum the husband should be ordered to pay: any other decision would merely permit the husband to shift his duty to maintain his wife and children on to the community as a whole. On the other hand, his own income must not be reduced below subsistence level even though, as in *Ashley* v. *Ashley*, this means that the innocent wife must still turn to the Department of Health and Social Security to bring her own resources up to the minimum.

Although under the Act either party can be compelled to make financial provision for the other, an order will of course normally be made against the husband because his earnings will greatly exceed the wife's. His opportunities will frequently be better than hers; most wives are forced to give up work at some stage in order to bring up children and, even if they later return to full-time employment, their prospects of promotion and advancement have usually been greatly reduced as a result.

Reference has already been made to the fact that the Act requires the court to have regard to all the circumstances of the case. The interests of the children of the family must be put first and if, say, they are living with the wife and the court orders the husband to make financial provision for them all, the practical solution is to assess the total sum that the wife needs to keep herself and the children and then to divide this very roughly when deciding how much should be paid for each on the order.[5] Although the matters which section 5 (1) requires the court to take into account are not intended to be exhaustive, with the addition of one further consideration—the parties' conduct—they cover almost all the matters to which the courts have always had regard in the past. Strictly speaking, these provisions apply only to orders made on divorce, nullity and judicial separation, but the same principles are equally important in proceedings under section 6 of the Matrimonial Proceedings and Property Act or when magistrates are deciding what sum to award for the benefit of the other spouse under the Matrimonial Proceedings (Magistrates' Courts) Act. We shall therefore first consider the matters referred to in the Act, grouped in the order in which they are set out in the sub-section, and then discuss the effect of the parties' conduct on the assessment of provision.

(a) *The Parties' Income, Earning Capacity, Property and other Financial Resources.*—The court must take into account not only the

---

[4] [1965] 3 All E.R. 554; [1968] P. 582.
[5] Many husbands who are loth to pay maintenance for their wives will willingly pay it for their children. It may therefore sometimes be wise to allocate a disproportionately large fraction for the children. The wife can apply for a variation in the amount payable to herself when the orders with respect to the children terminate.

resources which each party has at the time of the hearing[6] but also those which they are likely to have in the foreseeable future. It has been held that the court should take into consideration the husband's ability to earn higher wages by working overtime[7] or to raise money by overdrafts.[8] Similarly account must be taken of voluntary allowances which are likely to continue to be made to either party, since they effectively swell his or her gross income.[9] On the same principle allowance must be made for any payment made by one party of which the other is enjoying the benefit, for example the husband's repayment of a mortgage on the matrimonial home or hire-purchase instalments in respect of the furniture if the wife still lives in the house and uses the furniture.[10] Capital assets are of particular importance in the case of a very rich man who may well live largely on capital and capital profits.[11]

In the past the courts were reluctant to force a wife to go out to work if she had not been responsible for the breakdown of the marriage and would not have worked had the marriage continued. This was due partly to their anxiety to retain the economic *status quo ante* and partly to their unwillingness to put the wife in the position where she would feel that her exertions were merely going to relieve her husband of a financial liability which he had himself created.[12] But in many cases today, particularly if the wife is young and childless and the marriage has not lasted for long, it cannot be unreasonable to expect her to work—and this might even prove to be therapeutic. A new note seems to have been struck by the Divisional Court in *Attwood* v. *Attwood*,[13] where they held that justices had been wrong to ignore the wife's wages. In such cases, however, they emphasised that the court should not bring the whole of her earnings into account but should leave her free to enjoy at least a part of the fruits of her own labours.

In all cases, of course, it is the parties' net income which must be brought into account and they are entitled to offset their business and

---

[6]Where a party's income varies from year to year, it is customary to take an average in order to assess future earnings: *Sherwood* v. *Sherwood*, [1929] P. 120, C.A.; and the fact that these fluctuations make it precarious may be a reason for reducing the amount of periodical payments ordered against the party in question: *Dean* v. *Dean*, [1923] P. 172. Increases in the husband's income since the parties ceased to cohabit are equally relevant, for the wife would have reaped the benefit of them had they still been living together: *Le Roy-Lewis* v. *Le Roy-Lewis*, [1954] 3 All E.R. 57; [1955] P. 1. On the question of allowances of men serving in the armed forces, see *Powell* v. *Powell*, [1951] P. 257, C.A.; *Collins* v. *Collins*, [1943] 2 All E.R. 474; [1943] P. 106; *Buttle* v. *Buttle*, [1953] 2 All E.R. 646.
[7]*Klucinski* v. *Klucinski*, [1953] 1 All E.R. 683.
[8]*J.* v. *J.*, [1955] 2 All E.R. 617, C.A.; [1955] P. 215.
[9]*Martin* v. *Martin*, [1919] P. 283, C.A. (allowance to husband); *Nott* v. *Nott*, [1901] P. 241 (allowance to wife). In *Donaldson* v. *Donaldson*, [1958] 2 All E.R. 660, and *Ette* v. *Ette*, [1965] 1 All E.R. 341, account was taken of free board and lodging provided by the husband's business partner who was also his mistress. But see *Sansom* v. *Sansom*, [1966] 2 All E.R. 396; [1966] P. 52, where SIMON, P., left open the question how far the court should take into account increases in income which a party would not have enjoyed had the marriage not broken down.
[10]*Roberts* v. *Roberts*, [1968] 3 All E.R. 479, 487; [1970] P. 1, 10.
[11]*Brett* v. *Brett*, [1969] 1 All E.R. 1007, C.A.
[12]*Rose* v. *Rose*, [1950] 2 All E.R. 311, C.A.; [1951] P. 29; *Le Roy-Lewis* v. *Le Roy-Lewis*, (*supra*).
[13][1968] 3 All E.R. 385; [1968] P. 591.

other liabilities.[14] A further relevant fact on an application to vary a settlement is the sum which each party (or his or her family) contributed in the first place.[15]

(*b*) *The Parties' Financial Needs, Obligations and Responsibilities.*— The most obvious examples of facts to be considered under this head are the parties' need to maintain themselves and their responsibility to provide for their dependants. The maintenance of children must come first; in addition one must take into account the needs of a second spouse, infirm parents, brothers and sisters unable to work, and any other person whom it is reasonable to expect either party to look after in the circumstances. It will be seen that not all these obligations are legally enforceable: in this context a moral obligation and the voluntary assumption of a responsibility (provided that it is reasonable) may be as relevant as a legal obligation. For example, a father's moral duty to make voluntary payments for the upkeep of his illegitimate child is indistinguishable for this purpose from his legal liability to comply with an affiliation order.[16]

As in the case of the parties' resources, the court must have regard to the needs, obligations and liabilities that they are likely to have in the foreseeable future as well as those already incurred at the time of the order.

(*c*) *The Standard of Living enjoyed by the Family before the Breakdown of the Marriage.*—To this might be added the standard of living which the claimant could have been expected to enjoy if the marriage had not broken down as the result of the other's misconduct. If, for example, a husband buys a car immediately after deserting his wife, it is reasonable to suppose that she would have had the benefit of it had the marriage continued. But her standard of living should not be raised above what it otherwise would have been, for this would in effect mean that the order was being used as a means of punishing the husband.[17]

(*d*) *The Age of each Party and the Duration of the Marriage.*—Even before the 1970 Act it was clear that a young wife, whose marriage had lasted only for a short time, would generally get much less favourable provision than an innocent wife who had been deserted after years of married life.[18]

(*e*) *The Physical or Mental Disability of either Party.*

(*f*) *The Contribution made by each of the Parties to the Welfare of the Family.*—It is expressly provided that this is to include any contribution made by looking after the home or caring for the family. This principle, which primarily seeks to give the wife credit for her contribution in kind as a housekeeper, wife and mother, is new. Before 1971

---

[14]*E.g.*, the husband's insurance and superannuation contributions if the wife may reap the benefits of these on his retirement and (possibly) death: *Sansom* v. *Sansom*, [1966] 2 All E.R. 396, 402; [1966] P. 52, 60. *Cf. Schlesinger* v. *Schlesinger*, [1960] 1 All E.R. 721; [1960] P. 191 (liability for tax abroad).

[15]*March* v. *March* (1867), L.R. 1 P. & D. 440, 443.

[16]*Roberts* v. *Roberts*, [1968] 3 All E.R. 479, 484; [1970] P. 1, 7. See also *Williams* v. *Williams*, [1964] 3 All E.R. 526, C.A.; [1965] P. 125, and *P.* (*J.R.*) v. *P.* (*G.L.*), [1966] 1 All E.R. 439 (liability to educate children of a previous marriage).

[17]*Cf. Attwood* v. *Attwood*, [1968] 3 All E.R. 385, 388; [1968] P. 591, 595.

[18]*P.* (*J.R.*) v. *P.* (*G.L.*), (*supra*), at p. 443.

the courts were taking this into account to a limited extent, but their hands were partly tied by their restricted powers to make adjustments to rights in property. The result was that a wife who continued to work and hired domestic help was usually in a better position than the wife who stayed at home and did the job herself. Their positions will be truly equalised only when the whole basis of matrimonial property is altered to take proper account of contributions in kind, but at least this new guideline will go part of the way to remove existing injustice.

(g) *In the Case of Divorce and Nullity, the Value of any Benefit which either Party will lose the Chance of acquiring.*—The obvious example of such a benefit (which the Act in fact names) is a pension which can no longer enure for the benefit of the wife as the husband's widow. Another right which the divorced wife loses is that of claiming National Insurance benefits by virtue of her husband's contributions: a matter which requires the urgent attention of Parliament. These problems were made more acute by the passing of the Divorce Reform Act which permits a husband to divorce his wife even though he has been wholly to blame for the breakdown of the marriage; before 1971 an innocent wife could take these potential losses into account before deciding whether to take proceedings for divorce. It is clearly going to be difficult to assess the value of the benefit lost. Not only are there many imponderables (some of which, like the expectation of life of each spouse, can be actuarially assessed) but in many " top hat " pension schemes the benefits are held on discretionary trusts which the widow could not claim as of right. If the husband is rich, he can be ordered to purchase an annuity for his wife, but it is virtually impossible to give adequate compensation to a woman who would have depended largely on a widow's pension or retirement pension for her support in the event of her husband's death.[19]

The Parties' Conduct.—The point has already been made that the parties' conduct is relevant only to the extent that, if either of them has to suffer financially as a consequence of the breakdown of the marriage, it is just that the loss should be borne by the party responsible for the breakdown. Before 1971 many petitions were defended and cross-petitions brought because the technically " innocent " wife would be in a much stronger position when it came to applying for financial provision. It may be in the future that most petitioners will rely on two or five years' separation as evidence of breakdown, in which case there will be no finding of fault (even by implication) when the decree is granted. If this is so, the real contest will take place and the cross-recriminations made not in court but before the registrar on the application for financial provision, when a full scale investigation into the parties' conduct and the cause of the breakdown of the marriage may still have to be made.

Even under the old law the increasing tendency for petitions not to be defended when the marriage had irretrievably broken down had

---

[19]A wife over 60 when the decree is made absolute may be able to claim retirement benefit by virtue of her husband's contributions: See Munro, *Retirement Pensions after Divorce,* 121 New L.J. 159.

resulted in the courts' laying much less stress on the technical finding of innocence or guilt in the decree. The idea of a " compassionate allowance " for a wife guilty of adultery had become completely out-dated: the courts were much more concerned with the reason for the breakdown of the marriage.[20] It must be remembered, however, that the parties are estopped *per rem judicatam* from contradicting any express findings at the trial. Consequently, if the court grants a decree of divorce on a finding that the respondent husband has deserted the petitioner, he is not permitted in proceedings for financial provision to adduce evidence to show that this finding was wrong.[21] But now that irretrievable breakdown is the sole ground for divorce and, where the marriage has broken down, little purpose will be served in defending the petition, this rule is construed very narrowly and will not be extended to matters which were never in issue at the trial and could not have affected the outcome of the proceedings.[1]

Maintenance after a Decree of Nullity.—There is clearly power to order financial provision after a decree of nullity even though the marriage is void. But it must be appreciated that a claim must be weaker because neither of the parties is losing a right to be maintained either at common law or by statute. Obviously the parties' knowledge and belief at the time of the ceremony will be of particular importance. There is every difference between, say, a woman who unwittingly con-tracts a marriage which, as the man knows, is bigamous and therefore void, and a woman who takes a risk because she does not know what has happened to her former husband. It is highly doubtful whether the court will be prepared to make any order in favour of a party who contracted a marriage knowing that it was void.[2]

8. VARIATION, DISCHARGE, SUSPENSION AND REVIVAL OF ORDERS

Orders that may be varied.—The court has power to vary, discharge or suspend any of the following orders and to revive any term suspended:[3]

Maintenance pending suit and interim orders under section 6 of the Matrimonial Proceedings and Property Act;

Periodical payments (secured and unsecured);

An order relating to instalments in the case of a lump sum payment (but not the amount awarded);

The settlement (but not the transfer) of property on judicial separation;

The variation of ante-nuptial and post-nuptial settlements on judicial separation.

Periodical payments must always be variable because they are intended as maintenance for the payee and, if either party's needs or

---

[20] *Porter* v. *Porter*, [1969] 3 All E.R. 640, C.A. See also *Milliken-Smith* v. *Milliken-Smith*, [1970] 2 All E.R. 560, C.A.

[21] *Duchesne* v. *Duchesne*, [1950] 2 All E.R. 784; [1951] P. 101.

[1] *Tumath* v. *Tumath*, [1970] 1 All E.R. 111, C.A.; [1970] P. 78.

[2] *Cf.* applications under the Inheritance (Family Provision) Act by persons who have *in good faith* entered into a void marriage: *post*, pp. 509-510.

[3] Matrimonial Proceedings and Property Act 1970, s. 9 (1), (2). The court may also order any instrument to be varied, etc.: s. 9 (3).

resources change, justice may demand a corresponding change in the amount payable. On the other hand, once a lump sum has been paid, it cannot be cancelled or varied; it would, therefore, be grossly unfair to the payee if her right to a sum not yet paid could be prejudiced on the ground that the court had softened the blow to the payer by providing that he could pay the sum in question over a period of time. The same objection cannot be raised, however, to a change in the period or manner in which the instalments are paid, and consequently these can be varied by an alteration of their size or frequency. The reason that, generally speaking, orders relating to property cannot be varied is that they are designed to make a final adjustment of the spouses' rights at the time of the decree with the result that the parties' subsequent conduct and any change in their needs and resources are irrelevant. Settlements of property and variations of ante-nuptial and post-nuptial settlements made on judicial separation come into a different category, however, because a further adjustment may have to be made if the marriage is later dissolved, and the spouses themselves may wish to have the order varied if they become reconciled. Consequently variations of these orders may be made only in proceedings for the rescission of the decree or the dissolution of the marriage.[4]

For the same reasons, the court cannot order a lump sum payment, the transfer or settlement of property, or the variation of an ante-nuptial or post-nuptial settlement on an application to vary an order for periodical payments.[5]

If an order for secured periodical payments continues in force after the death of the party against whom it was made, either his personal representatives or the person entitled to the payments may apply for a variation, etc. Except with the leave of the court this may not be done more than six months after representation was first taken out; if leave is given, the personal representatives will not be liable for having failed to anticipate the possibility of such an application but a claim may be made against beneficiaries to whom any part of the estate has been transferred.[6]

Facts to be taken into Consideration.—The Act expressly provides that, on hearing an application for variation, the court shall have regard to all the circumstances of the case including any change in the matters to which it was required to have regard when making the order in the first place. If the application is made after the death of the party against whom the order was originally made, the court must also take into account the changed circumstances resulting from the death.[7]

---

[4]Matrimonial Proceedings and Property Act 1970, s. 9 (4).
[5]*Ibid.*, s. 9 (5). Apparently the court can order a lump sum payment on an application to vary an order relating to property after a judicial separation.
[6]*Ibid.*, s. 9 (6), (8) and (9). For variation generally, see Law Com. No. 25, paras. 85-93.
[7]*Ibid.*, s. 9 (7). Neither party is under any duty to make a voluntary disclosure of any change in his or her means: *Hayfield* v. *Hayfield*, [1957] 1 All E.R. 598.

The original order is taken as the starting point and the court must then take any relevant changes into account. But its discretion is completely unfettered.[8] Thus it has been held that the subsequent adultery of a wife who has obtained an order on the ground of her husband's wilful neglect to provide her with reasonable maintenance does not entitle him to have the order discharged even though, had she committed adultery before the hearing, she would not have been able to obtain an order at all.[9] Sexual misconduct after divorce is no more relevant than any other form of immoral conduct unless the party's financial position is changed as a result.[10] Two judicial limitations have been placed on the court's power, however. First, the parties are still estopped *per rem judicatam* from raising matters inconsistent with a previous decree or order and neither party may adduce evidence which could have been put before the court when the original order was made.[11] Secondly, a party who has led the other to act to his or her detriment on the assumption that he will continue to honour the order may not later apply to have it reduced or discharged. In *B. (M.A.L.) v. B. (N.E.)*[12] the husband and wife had entered into a separation agreement before the wife petitioned for divorce, with the result that she did not immediately seek financial provision. Some years later the husband was adjudicated bankrupt and the wife agreed to consent to his discharge on his undertaking not to oppose an application by her for leave to apply to the court for maintenance. In the maintenance proceedings the husband alleged that the wife had been guilty of adultery but in the event he did not pursue these allegations and submitted to a consent order for periodical payments against himself. He later established that the wife's youngest child was illegitimate and then sought to have the maintenance order discharged on the ground that the wife had obtained it by fraud. It was held that he must fail for two reasons. Having raised the matter of the wife's adultery at a time when he had evidence to prove it and then submitted to judgment by consent, he was estopped from opening the question again: it certainly did not lie in his mouth to say that she had misled the court. Furthermore, having induced the wife to consent to his discharge in bankruptcy by undertaking to maintain her, he could not now argue that he was under no liability to do so.

If the change of circumstances on which the application is based is not likely to be permanent (for example, the husband's temporary unemployment), the order should be suspended rather than discharged, so that it can be revived later if necessary.[13]

Variation of Consent Orders.—The fact that a party has consented to an order being made against him cannot act as an estoppel or give the other party a contractual right to have the order kept in force

---

[8]See EVERSHED, L.J., in *Bellenden v. Satterthwaite*, [1948] 1 All E.R. 343, 345, C.A.
[9]*Spence v. Spence*, [1964] 3 All E.R. 61; [1965] P. 140.
[10]*Stead v. Stead*, [1968] 1 All E.R. 989; [1968] P. 538.
[11]*B. (M.A.L.) v. B. (N.E.)*, [1968] 1 W.L.R. 1109; *Hall v. Hall* (1914), 111 L.T. 403, C.A.
[12][1968] 1 W.L.R. 1109.
[13]*Cf. Mills v. Mills*, [1940] 2 All E.R. 254, C.A.; [1940] P. 124.

indefinitely, and a consent order can generally be varied in the same circumstances as any other order.[14] But it is very doubtful whether the court can vary or discharge an order which it had no power to make in the first place, for example an order for unsecured periodical payments for the payee's life.[15] In any event if either party seeks a variation on the ground that his or her consent was given as the result of a mistake (for example, a mistake about the other's income), this should be ordered only if justice demands it and a substantially different order would be made: otherwise the parties and their solicitors might be deterred from negotiating consent orders altogether.[16]

9. ENFORCEMENT OF ORDERS

Periodical Payments.—If periodical payments are secured, there is of course no question of enforcement. When arrears of unsecured periodical payments accrue, the payee has a number of means of enforcing the order at his or her disposal. But his position is basically different from that of a successful plaintiff in an action for damages for tort or breach of contract for the order is not a final judgment and he does not have the full rights of a judgment creditor.

In the first place, the court has a discretion to determine how much of the arrears is to be paid and may remit them in part or even entirely.[17] In order to prevent large sums from mounting up, arrears which have been due for twelve months or more may not be enforced without the leave of the court: this gives some protection to a party who has stopped paying the full sum ordered and has been mistakenly led to believe by the other's acquiescence that he will not enforce the rest.[18] The court can also give the debtor time to pay and, in particular, may order payment by instalments. Because of this discretion, the arrears do not constitute a legal debt and cannot be sued for as such;[19] nor may the payee institute bankruptcy proceedings as a means of execution or prove in the other party's bankruptcy for arrears.[20] But with these important exceptions he has available all the usual means of execution open to a judgment creditor in the High Court or a county court, as the case may be.[1]

One of the most useful ways of enforcing the payment of arrears is by issuing a judgment summons under the Debtors Act of 1869, when

---

[14]*B. (G.C.) v. B. (B.A.),* [1970] 1 All E.R. 913.

[15]*Cf. Mills* v. *Mills* and *Hinde* v. *Hinde, ante,* p. 431. But they probably can be varied, etc., by consent, and an undertaking given to the court may be discharged: *Russell* v. *Russell,* [1956] 1 All E.R. 466, C.A.; [1956] P. 283.

[16]*B. (G.C.) v. B. (B.A.), (supra),* disapproving *Wilkins* v. *Wilkins,* [1969] 2 All E.R. 463. where it had been held that a consent order could be varied on this ground only if the consent had been procured by fraud.

[17]*MacDonald* v. *MacDonald,* [1963] 2 All E.R. 857, C.A.; [1964] P. 1.

[18]Matrimonial Proceedings and Property Act 1970, s. 10. See further Law Com. No. 25, para. 92.

[19]*Bailey* v. *Bailey* (1884), 13 Q.B.D. 855, C.A.; *Robins* v. *Robins,* [1907] 2 K.B. 13.

[20]Consequently the arrears are not affected by an adjudication in bankruptcy and may be enforced by other methods: *Linton* v. *Linton* (1885), 15 Q.B.D. 239, C.A.; *Re Henderson* (1888), 20 Q.B.D. 509, C.A.

[1]An order made by a divorce county court can be transferred to the High Court if it cannot be conveniently enforced in the county court. It is then enforceable as though it had been made by the High Court: Matrimonial Causes Rules 1968, r. 91.

the court can make an order for the payment by instalments and commit the payer for contempt if he wilfully fails to pay them.[2] Alternatively, the payee may apply for an attachment of earnings order. The detailed provisions are *mutatis mutandis* the same as those relating to attachment orders made in a magistrates' court.[3]

In view of the personal nature of the obligation and the fact that arrears do not constitute a legal debt, there is some doubt whether they can be enforced against the payer's personal representatives after his death.[4]

Recovery of Overpayments.—The court may well feel that, because of some change of circumstances, the payee has been overpaid. To take two examples: the payee may have failed to inform the other party of an unexpected improvement in her financial position, or the payer may not have realised that a decrease in his income entitled him to apply for a variation. In some cases justice may demand that the payee should repay some or all of the money received since the change in circumstances; in others—for example, where the payee was unaware of the change in the payer's circumstances and has already spent the money—justice may demand that the loss should continue to lie where it has fallen. Consequently by section 11 of the Matrimonial Proceedings and Property Act, where there has been a change in the circumstances of either the person entitled to the payments or the person liable to make them (including a change produced by the death of the latter) so that the amount received by the payee since then has exceeded the amount which the other should have been required to pay, the court may order the repayment of the whole or any part of the excess as it thinks just. Alternatively it may decide that nothing should be repaid at all. Section 22 of the Act gives the court precisely the same powers if the payee has remarried and the other party (or his personal representatives) has continued to make payments in the mistaken belief that the order was still subsisting. Both sections apply to periodical payments (secured and unsecured); section 11 also applies to maintenance pending suit and interim payments under section 6. In both cases the action may be brought by and against personal representatives and the court may order any sum to be repaid by instalments.

The High Court or a county court may make an order for repayment in proceedings for variation or discharge or for the enforcement of arrears.[5] Alternatively the payer or his personal representatives may bring an action for repayment in a county court.[6]

---

[2] This procedure is preserved for the non-payment of a maintenance order by the Administration of Justice Act 1970, s. 11.

[3] See *ante*, pp. 422-425. If the order is a High Court order, the collecting officer is the proper officer of the High Court or the registrar of a county court specified in the order; if it is a county court order, he is the registrar of that court: Attachment of Earnings Act 1971, s. 6 (7).

[4] In *Re Stillwell*, [1916] 1 Ch. 365, it was held that arrears could be recovered against a solvent estate, but the decision of the Court of Appeal in *Sugden* v. *Sugden*, [1957] 1 All E.R. 300; [1957] P. 120 suggests the contrary. By analogy with the law of bankruptcy, the payee presumably could not claim in any event if the estate were insolvent.

[5] But a magistrates' court has no power to make an order for repayment in the case of a High Court or county court order registered there.

[6] *Cf.* the recovery of overpayments under a magistrates' order, *ante*, pp. 421-422. Magistrates' clerks and collecting officers have similar protection.

Other Orders.—An order for the payment of a lump sum is more in the nature of a judgment for damages and may be enforced in the same way. This means that, if the party against whom it is made becomes insolvent before he implements it, the other party may prove in his bankruptcy.[7] The payee may also issue a judgment summons or apply for an attachment of earnings order.[8] As in the case of periodical payments, a lump sum payment (or any part payable by instalment) cannot be enforced more than twelve months after it falls due without the leave of the court.[9]

Failure to comply with an order to transfer or settle property may be enforced in the same way as any other similar order in the High Court or a county court.

Attempts to defeat Claims for Maintenance.—A spouse might well try to defeat an application for financial provision by disposing of his property or transferring it out of the jurisdiction. He might do this beforehand in anticipation of an application or order or, alternatively, after an order has been made in order to reduce the property available to meet it. To prevent fraudulent dispositions of this kind, a measure of protection is given to the payee by section 16 of the Matrimonial Proceedings and Property Act 1970.[10] This applies to any order for financial provision made in proceedings for divorce, nullity and judicial separation,[11] any order made under section 6 of the Act on the ground of wilful neglect to maintain,[12] the variation of any of these orders during the payer's lifetime, and the alteration of a maintenance agreement during the parties' joint lives. For the sake of convenience, it will be assumed throughout the following discussion that the wife (or former wife) is applying for or has obtained an order against the husband; it must be appreciated, however, that exactly the same principles apply if the husband is seeking financial provision from the other for himself or the children of the family.

If the court is satisfied that the husband is about to make any disposition or to transfer out of the jurisdiction or otherwise deal with any property with the intention of defeating the wife's claim, it may make such order as it thinks fit to restrain him from doing so and to protect the claim. If it is satisfied that he has already made a disposition with this intention, the court may make an order setting the disposition aside. In this case, however, a wife who has not yet obtained an order must also show that, if the disposition were set aside, the court would make a different order from that which it would otherwise make. Defeating the wife's claim may take the form of preventing her

---

[7]See *Curtis* v. *Curtis*, [1969] 2 All E.R. 207, C.A., where the court ordered the husband to pay the wife £33,600 capitalising an annual sum of £2,400 to enable her to take bankruptcy proceedings if he remained contumacious.

[8]See the definition of " maintenance order " in the Administration of Justice Act 1970, s. 28 and Sched. 8, as amended by the Matrimonial Proceedings and Property Act 1970, Sched. 2, and the Attachment of Earnings Act 1971, Sched. 1, para. 3.

[9]Matrimonial Proceedings and Property Act 1970, s. 10.

[10]The power was originally given by the Matrimonial Causes (Property and Maintenance) Act 1958, s. 2.

[11]*I.e.*, the orders specified on p. 426, *ante.*

[12]See *ante*, p. 428.

from obtaining an order at all, reducing the amount that might be ordered, or impeding or frustrating the enforcement of any order that might be made or has been made.

In many cases it obviously might be difficult to establish what the husband's intention was when he made a disposition. Consequently the Act has introduced a compromise designed to protect in part the interests of the wife, the husband and the transferee. If the husband made the disposition three years or more before the application to set it aside, the wife must prove affirmatively that he had the intention to defeat her claim. If he made it less than three years before or is about to make it, this intention will be presumed if the effect of the transaction would be to defeat her claim or, where the disposition has already taken place and an order is in force, if it has had this effect: the burden then shifts on to him to prove that this was not his intention.[13]

No order may be made with respect to any disposition by will or codicil or to any disposition already made to a *bona fide* purchaser for valuable consideration (other than marriage) without notice of the husband's intention to defeat the wife's claim.[14]

The disposition is voidable, and not void, and consequently, even if it is set aside, this cannot affect any subsequent dealings with the property in good faith. Hence if the husband's immediate transferee is not protected but disposes of the property to a *bona fide* purchaser for value without notice, the latter's title cannot be upset by the order. In *National Provincial Bank, Ltd.* v. *Hastings Car Mart, Ltd.*[15] the husband, who had deserted his wife, conveyed the matrimonial home to the defendant company who immediately charged it to the plaintiff bank. Although the conveyance to the defendants was set aside on the ground that it was made with the intention of defeating the wife's claim to maintenance, it was held by the Court of Appeal that this did not extinguish the plaintiff's mortgage which remained a valid charge.

F. REGISTRATION OF MAINTENANCE ORDERS IN OTHER COURTS

It will readily be seen that if the spouse ordered to pay money duly fulfils his or her obligations, orders made in magistrates' courts have the advantage that payment is made through the clerk of the court; conversely, if he fails to fulfil them, a spouse who has an order made in the High Court or a county court has superior means of enforcing it at his

---

[13]Presumably the transaction can be set aside or restrained if the husband had an intention both to defeat the claim and to benefit the transferee. Otherwise the wife's application could always be defeated by showing that the husband genuinely wanted to benefit his mistress or second wife at her expense.

[14]See Crane, *After the Deserted Wife's Licence*, 29 Conv. 254, at pp. 261-262. Nor may an order be made if the disposition took place before 1st January, 1968, as there was an absolute limitation of three years before the Matrimonial Proceedings and Property Act came into force: see s. 16 (5).

[15][1964] 3 All E.R. 93, C.A.; [1964] Ch. 665. See further the same case in the House of Lords, *National Provincial Bank, Ltd.* v. *Ainsworth, ante,* p. 391. There was no appeal on the point discussed here. Presumably in circumstances such as these the immediate transferee may be ordered to pay over the value of the property.

or her disposal. Consequently the Maintenance Orders Act of 1958 introduced the means of registering in one court a " maintenance order "[16] made by another. Under this Act a person entitled to payments under a maintenance order made by the High Court or a county court may apply to the court that made the order to have it registered in a magistrates' court; whether or not the application is granted lies completely in the discretion of the court.[17] A person entitled to payments under a maintenance order made by a magistrates' court may apply to that court to have it registered in the High Court; in this case the court *must* grant the application if it is satisfied that there is due and unpaid an amount equal to not less than four payments in the case of an order for weekly payments and not less than two payments in other cases.[18]

If the application is granted, no proceedings may be begun or continued to enforce the order in the original court and any attachment of earnings order already in force .ceases to have effect.[19] Once the order has been registered, it may be enforced only as though it had been made by the court in which it is registered.[20]

An order may be varied, revoked, suspended and revived only by the original court except that, in the case of orders made by the High Court or a county court and registered in a magistrates' court, variation of rates of payment (as distinct from a variation of other provisions and complete revocation, suspension and. revival of the

---

[16]The following are " maintenance orders " for the purpose of these provisions (s. 1 (1A), added by the Administration of Justice Act 1970, s. 27 (3) and Sched. 8, and amended by the Matrimonial Proceedings and Property Act 1970, Sched. 2, and the Guardianship of Minors Act 1971, Sched. 1):

> Orders for periodical or other payments made under Part I of the Matrimonial Proceedings and Property Act;
> Orders for the payment of money made under the Matrimonial Proceedings (Magistrates' Courts) Act;
> Affiliation orders;
> Orders made under the following statutory provisions:
>> Guardianship of Minors Act 1971, ss. 9 (2), 10 (1), 11 and 12 (2) *(ante,* p. 327, and *post*, p. 478);
>> Family Law Reform Act 1969, s. 6 *(post*, p. 479);
>> Ministry of Social Security Act 1966, ss. 23 and 24 *(ante,* p. 413, and *post*, pp. 478 and 487);
>> Children and Young Persons Act 1933, s. 87 (contribution orders) *(ante,* p. 298);
>> Children and Young Persons Act 1963, s. 30 (arrears orders) *(ante*, p. 298);
>> Children Act 1948, s. 26 *(post*, p. 485);
> Maintenance Orders made in other parts of the United Kingdom or Commonwealth and registered in or confirmed by an English court under the Maintenance Orders Act 1950 or the Maintenance Orders (Facilities for Enforcement) Act 1920.

[17]Ss. 1 (1) (a), 2 (1).

[18]Ss. 1 (1) (b), 2 (3).

[19]S. 2 (2), (4); Attachment of Earnings Act 1971, s. 11 (1) (a), (2). But a warrant of committment remains in force if the defendant is *already* detained under it: s. 2 (4) (b).

[20]S. 3. This includes the power to remit the whole or any part of arrears due. In the case of an order registered in a magistrates' court, payment must be made through the clerk unless the court orders otherwise. In the case of an order made under the Matrimonial Proceedings (Magistrates' Courts) Act and registered in the High Court, the leave of that court must be obtained to enforce arrears which have been due for more than twelve months: see the Matrimonial Proceedings (Magistrates' Courts) Act 1960, s. 13 (5), (6) and (7) (added by the Matrimonial Proceedings and Property Act 1970, s. 32).

order) may be made only by the magistrates' court in which it is registered[1] if both parties are in England.[2]

The party entitled to payments under a registered order may give notice to have the registration cancelled. This has a similar effect to an application to have the order registered in the sense that no proceedings may be begun or continued to enforce the order in the court of registration[3] and any attachment of earnings order is automatically discharged. The court in which the order is registered must then cancel the registration provided that no process for the enforcement of the order is in force and, in the case of an order registered in a magistrates' court, no proceedings for variation are pending in that court. If the court that originally made an order registered in a magistrates' court varies or discharges it, it may itself direct that the registration be cancelled; if a magistrates' court discharges an order registered in the High Court, it *must* direct that the registration be cancelled if there are no arrears remaining to be recovered.[4]

---

[1] Or any other magistrates' court having jurisdiction in the place where the complainant is for the time being: Magistrates' Courts (Maintenance Orders Act 1958) Rules 1959, r. 9.

[2] S. 4, as amended by the Administration of Justice Act 1970, Sched. 11. But the magistrates' court has a discretion to remit the application to the original court and the original court may vary the rate of payment in proceedings to vary other provisions of the order.

[3] Save that a warrant of commitment remains in force if the defendant is *already* detained under it.

[4] S. 5; Attachment of Earnings Act 1971, s. 11 (1) (b).

CHAPTER 16

Rights in Property Affected by the Relationship of Parent and Child and Financial Provision for Children

A. RIGHTS IN PROPERTY

I. GENERAL

Rights in property are not greatly affected by the relationship of parent and child. A parent, it seems, has no rights as such in the property of a child of any age; thus in the absence of any agreement he has no claim on a child's wages,[1] and even an arrangement by which the child promises to pay his father or mother a weekly sum for his board and lodging is probably unenforceable on the ground that the parties never intended to create any legally binding obligation.[2] Similarly, property bought by a child out of his income will remain exclusively his own. With respect to gifts to a child the position is not so clear. Obviously in the case of clothes bought for a young child the property and therefore the right of disposal remain in the parent or parents; clothing bought for an older child presumably belongs to the child: at what stage this transition is effected must be a question of fact in each case. In whom the property (and therefore the right of disposal) vests in the case of other types of presents given to a young child is even more doubtful. Normally they will be of such slight value that the question is of no practical importance; if the chattel is of greater value and the child is too young to have the necessary intention of receiving the gift, it is arguable that the legal interest will vest in the parents who will hold it on trust for the donee.

It is because a minor is rarely the legal owner of property of any value that this problem is usually of no more than academic interest. If he has an interest of any value, he will normally derive it under a settlement or will or on an intestacy, and the legal ownership will therefore usually vest in trustees. His parents may be able to make a claim on the fund for his maintenance and education; the extent of this will depend on the terms of the instrument creating the interest and the provisions of the Trustee Act 1925 and the Administration of

---

[1] *Cf. Williams* v. *Doulton,* [1948] 1 All E.R. 603.
[2] *Cf. ante,* p. 120. But if a child has a sufficient income to keep himself, presumably the father could not be guilty of wilful neglect to maintain him. For the liability of a child engaged in remunerative full-time work to contribute towards his own maintenance when he is in the care of a local authority, see *ante,* p. 298.

458

Estates Act 1925—matters which belong rather to the general law of property and impinge only indirectly upon family law.[3]

But three subjects require particular attention.

Presumption of Advancement.—If a father has property conveyed into the name of his legitimate child, this raises a presumption of advancement, so that, unless the presumption is rebutted, the child takes the whole beneficial interest and there will be no resulting trust in favour of the father.[4] The basis of this presumption is the recognition by equity of the father's obligation to provide for his children and to advance them, but it would seem to arise in every case of father and child and has even been applied where a father aged 92 transferred property to his son with whom he was living and who was looking after him.[5]

On the other hand there is no automatic presumption of advancement if property is purchased by a mother in the name of her child or by either parent in the name of an illegitimate child, since the obligation to maintain in these cases is not one that equity recognises. In all other cases a resulting trust in favour of the purchaser will be presumed unless he has put himself *in loco parentis* to the child, that is, unless he has intentionally taken upon himself a father's duty to make provision for the other.[6] Whether or not one person is *in loco parentis* to another is a question of fact. Little evidence will be required to establish the relationship between a mother and her child (particularly if the mother is widowed)[7] or probably between a parent and an illegitimate child, but it may arise in other cases as well, for example, grandfather and grandchild,[8] uncle and nephew,[9] stepfather and stepchild,[10] and other strangers in blood. If the child is living with his father, this may be evidence that another is not *in loco parentis* to him but it is by no means conclusive.[11]

Undue Influence.—If a transaction between parent (whether father or mother) and child or a transaction entered into by the child at the instance of either parent involves a sum so large that it cannot be reasonably accounted for on the ground of affection, there is a presumption that the parent has exercised undue influence over the other. Hence if the child later seeks to have such a contract or gift set aside for this reason, the burden shifts on to the party wishing to uphold it to prove that there was in fact no such influence. The difficulty of discharging a negative burden is obvious: as was stated in *Re Pauling's*

---

[3]See Snell, *Equity*, 26th Ed., 285 *et seq.*

[4]So held in a series of cases from *Dyer* v. *Dyer* (1788), 2 Cox Eq. Cas. 92, to *Shephard* v. *Cartwright*, [1954] 3 All E.R. 649, H.L.; [1955] A.C. 431. On the question of the evidence admissible to rebut the presumption, see *Shephard* v. *Cartwright*.

[5]*Hepworth* v. *Hepworth* (1870), L.R. 11 Eq. 10.

[6]*Per* LORD COTTENHAM, L.C., in *Powys* v. *Mansfield* (1837), 3 My. & Cr. 359, 367, and JESSEL, M.R., in *Bennet* v. *Bennet* (1879), 10 Ch.D. 474, 477.

[7]*Bennet* v. *Bennet*, (*supra*), at pp. 479-480. See also *Re Ashton*, [1897] 2 Ch. 574.

[8]*Ebrand* v. *Dancer* (1680), 2 Cas. in Ch. 26.

[9]*Powys* v. *Mansfield*, (*supra*).

[10]*Re Paradise Motor Co. Ltd.*, [1968] 2 All E.R. 625, C.A.

[11]*Powys* v. *Mansfield*, (*supra*), at p. 368.

Settlement Trusts[12] it must be shown that the child acted spontaneously and with knowledge of his rights; it is desirable, though not essential, that he should have had independent advice given with knowledge of all the relevant circumstances and such as a competent and honest adviser would give if he were acting solely in the child's interest. The advice must be genuinely independent, and hence the burden is not discharged by showing that the child was advised by a solicitor who was acting for the parent or another interested party at the same time.[13]

The presumption of influence does not cease when the child comes of age or is "emancipated" by marriage: there must be many cases when the natural influence which most parents are bound to have over their children continues after this. The question is purely one of fact, although the presumption will normally last for only a short time after the child attains his majority.[14] These points are well illustrated by *Lancashire Loans, Ltd.* v. *Black*.[15] In this case a daughter, who had come of age and who had left her parental home on marriage, was persuaded by her mother to charge a reversionary interest under her grandfather's will in order to pay off the mother's debts. Later at the mother's instigation she signed a promissory note for £775 plus interest at 85% *per annum* and made a second charge on the reversion. The necessary instruments were drawn up by a solicitor who was also acting for the mother and the moneylenders concerned and who did not give the daughter a full explanation of the true nature and effect of the guarantee and the consequences of entering into it. It was held that the transactions must be set aside, as the moneylenders had full knowledge of all the facts from which undue influence could be inferred and could therefore be in no better position than the mother.

As in the case of all other transactions which are voidable in equity, the child will lose his power to have the contract or gift set aside by laches or by affirming the transaction after he has ceased to be under the parental influence. But, subject to this, it may be avoided against anyone save a *bona fide* purchaser for value without notice of the circumstances surrounding it.[16]

Family Arrangements.—Family arrangements are transactions which " tend to the peace or security of the family, to the avoiding of family disputes and litigation, or to the preservation of family property ".[17] Common examples are agreements between members of the family to divide the property of a deceased member or to compromise claims

---

[12][1963] 3 All E.R. 1, 10, C.A.; [1964] Ch. 303, 336. See also *Lancashire Loans, Ltd.* v. *Black*, [1934] 1 K.B. 380, C.A.; *Powell* v. *Powell*, [1900] 1 Ch. 243.

[13]*Lancashire Loans, Ltd.* v. *Black*, (*ante*); *Powell* v. *Powell*, (*ante*); *Bullock* v. *Lloyds Bank, Ltd.*, [1954] 3 All E.R. 726; [1955] Ch. 317.

[14]*Re Pauling's Settlement Trusts*, (*supra*), at pp. 10 and 337, respectively. At the time this case was decided the age of majority was 21. Will the courts now accept that the reduction of the age of majority to 18 implies greater maturity and judgment on the part of a person over that age and give correspondingly less weight to the presumption?

[15][1934] 1 K.B. 380, C.A. See also *Bainbrigge* v. *Browne* 1881), 18 Ch.D. 188, where the three children were all over the age of 21.

[16]*Bainbrigge* v. *Browne*, (*supra*). In *Re Pauling's Settlement Trusts*, (*supra*), it was held that children acting under parental influence could compel trustees to return money paid out in breach of trust when the latter knew (or ought to have known) of the undue influence.

[17]*Per* ROMILLY, M.R., in *Hoghton* v. *Hoghton* (1852), 15 Beav. 278, 300.

under disputed wills. In arrangements of this sort the parents as heads
of the family are bound to exercise some influence over the judgment
of their children entering into the agreement, and consequently a strict
application of the presumption of undue influence would make many
such transactions voidable. A special rule has therefore been developed
that family arrangements may be set aside on this ground only if a
parent derives some benefit from the agreement which he did not
formerly possess.[18] In addition it should be borne in mind that family
arrangements are contracts *uberrimae fidei* and may therefore be avoided
by any party on the ground that another party failed to disclose a
material fact of which he was aware but of which the complaining party
was ignorant.[19]

Life Assurance Policies in Favour of Children.—As we have
already seen, if either parent takes out a policy of assurance on his or
her own life expressed to be for the benefit of any or all of his or her
children, this will create a trust in favour of the child or children.[20]

2. DISPOSITIONS IN FAVOUR OF CHILDREN

The Position at Common Law.—The common law knew nothing
of legitimation or adoption and regarded a bastard as *filius nullius*.
Consequently it became settled law that the term " children " in any
instrument (whether testamentary or made *inter vivos*) *prima facie*
must be construed as *legitimate* children. The same rule applied to any
other relationship, and a bequest, for example, to the testator's
nephews would normally confer a benefit only on the legitimate sons of
his legitimate brothers and sisters.[1]

This was purely a rule of construction and the presumption could
therefore be displaced if the instrument indicated a contrary intention
on the part of the person executing it. It was rare for this to happen
in the case of a deed, but in a number of reported decisions illegitimate
children have succeeded in taking under a will. But in such a case
it must be proved that the testator *must* have meant an illegitimate
child to take the benefit: it is not sufficient that he probably intended
this. Thus, where a testator married a woman by whom he had
already had two illegitimate children and by his will made on the
day following his marriage he left property to his children by her, it
was held that, since the spouses might still have legitimate children, the
presumption was not rebutted and the two illegitimate children could
not take even though no legitimate children were ever born.[2]

---

[18] *Hoghton* v. *Hoghton*, (*supra*); *Hoblyn* v. *Hoblyn* (1889), 41 Ch.D. 200, 206;
Turner v. *Collins* (1871), 7 Ch. App. 329 (where the son's action to have the deed set
aside was in any case defeated by his own laches).
[19] *Gordon* v. *Gordon* (1819), 3 Swan. 400 (failure to disclose an earlier secret marriage
between the parents, as a result of which the eldest son, believed to be illegitimate, was
in fact legitimate); *Greenwood* v. *Greenwood* (1863), 2 De G. J. & Sm. 28 (failure to
disclose the true value of property). *Cf. Re Roberts*, [1905] 1 Ch. 704, C.A. (compromise
effected on a false assumption of the party's rights).
[20] See *ante*, pp. 372-373.
[1] See *Sydall* v. *Castings, Ltd.*, [1966] 3 All E.R. 770, C.A.; [1967] 1 Q.B. 302 (illegitimate daughter not a " descendant " for the purpose of the trusts of a pension scheme).
[2] *Dorin* v. *Dorin* (1875), L.R. 7 H.L. 568, H.L.

The problem was considered by the House of Lords in *Hill* v. *Crook*,[3] where LORD CAIRNS specified two cases where illegitimate children could take an interest under a gift to the testator's children. This will occur, first, if he names them or expressly states that illegitimate children are to take under a class gift,[4] and secondly if the facts known to the testator are such that it is possible for illegitimate children but not legitimate children to take.[5] Although the will speaks from the death of the testator, the important facts for the purpose of interpretation are those known to him at the time the will was made. Hence it has been held that illegitimate or reputed children must have been intended as the beneficiaries when at the time of the execution of the will the legatees' parent had no legitimate children and was, to the testator's knowledge, dead,[6] or a woman beyond the age of child bearing,[7] or a man incurably impotent.[8]

As gifts tending to encourage or reward sexual immorality are regarded as contrary to public policy, gifts to illegitimate children to be procreated in the future are void at common law.[9] This is a rule of law and not of interpretation and consequently applies only to children conceived after the deed or will *takes effect*: children born after a will was made and even those *en ventre sa mere* at the testator's death may take.[10]

Legitimated Children.—The first exception to the common law rule was made by the Legitimacy Acts. They followed the principle that legitimation shall have the effect of giving the child the rights of a legitimate child but that it shall not operate retrospectively, and they virtually enacted that a claim to property can be made only if the title is subsequent to, and not prior to, the date of the legitimation. As will be seen, a different rule now applies in the case of an instrument made after 1969, but under the Legitimacy Acts a person legitimated under the Act of 1926 or the Act of 1959[11] is entitled to take an interest as if he had been born the legitimate child of his parents only

(a) under a disposition coming into operation after the date of his legitimation; or

(b) by descent under an entailed interest created after that date.[12]

---

[3](1873), L.R. 6 H.L. 265, 282-283, H.L.

[4]See *Owen* v. *Bryant* (1852), 2 De G. M. & G. 697.

[5]In *Re Jebb*, [1965] 3 All E.R. 358, C.A.; [1966] Ch. 666, it was held that it was sufficient that it was highly improbable that the parent would have legitimate children. But this is inconsistent with the decisions of the House of Lords in *Dorin* v. *Dorin* and *Hill* v. *Crook*, (*supra*), and must be regarded as wrongly decided. See Morris, *Palm-Tree Justice in the Court of Appeal*, 82 L.Q.R. 196.

[6]*Lord Woodehouselee* v. *Dalrymple* (1817), 2 Mer. 419.

[7]*Re Eve*, [1909] 1 Ch. 796. Contrast *Re Dicker*, [1947] 1 All E.R. 317; [1947] Ch. 248.

[8]*Re Herwin*, [1953] 2 All E.R. 782, C.A.; [1953] Ch. 701.

[9]*Hill* v. *Crook*, (*supra*), at pp. 278, 285-286; *Re Shaw*, [1894] 2 Ch. 573 (deed).

[10]*Occleston* v. *Fullalove* (1874), 9 Ch. App. 147; *Crook* v. *Hill* (1876), 3 Ch.D. 773. Some relaxation of the rule has been seen in recent years and in *Re Hyde*, [1932] 1 Ch. 95, it was held that a power to appoint amongst X's children could be exercised in favour of an illegitimate child conceived after the death of the testator by whose will the power was given. This distinction is difficult to justify logically. See further Theobald, *Wills*, 12th Ed., 267 *et seq.*; Jarman, *Wills*, 8th Ed., c. XLV.

[11]For legitimation generally, see *ante*, pp. 239-241. For claims by persons legitimated otherwise than under the Acts (*e.g.*, under the law of his father's domicile) see *post*, pp. 464-465.

[12]Legitimacy Act 1926, ss. 1 (3) and 3 (1). For succession on intestacy, see *post*, p. 507.

It will be observed that, in either case, the disposition must come into operation after the date of the legitimation. A disposition is defined as " an assurance of any interest in property by any instrument whether *inter vivos* or by will ":[13] hence if A bequeaths property to B's children and C claims it as B's legitimated son, he will succeed if A died after C was legitimated even though he executed the will before that event. In the case of a *special* power of appointment the disposition for this purpose is the instrument under which the power was granted and not that by which it was exercised, for the property is disposed of by the donor of the power who merely leaves the donee the power to select the ultimate beneficiary out of the persons designated by himself.[14] Consequently a power to appoint among X's children can be exercised in favour of X's legitimated child only if he was legitimated before the instrument granting the power came into operation.

It is of course always possible for the person making the disposition to express a contrary intention in the instrument and thus exclude legitimated children who would otherwise take an interest under it or include those who would otherwise be left out.[15] In any event a legitimated person may not succeed to any dignity or title of honour or to any property which would, but for the operation of the Act, have devolved along with a dignity or title of honour.[16]

Where any right to property depends upon the relative seniority of a person's children (as it might do, for example, in the case of the descent of an unbarred entailed interest), then legitimated persons rank as if they had been born on the date of their legitimation, and if more than one child is legitimated at the same time, they rank *inter se* in order of seniority.[17]

In order to preserve the rights of a person's spouse and issue if he is not legitimated because he happens to die before his parents' marriage, there is one exception to the general rule. Section 5 of the Act of 1926 enacts:

" Where an illegitimate person dies after the commencement of [the Act by virtue of which he would have been legitimated had he survived] and before the marriage of his parents leaving any spouse, children or remoter issue living at the date of such marriage, then, if that person would, if living at the time of the marriage of his parents, have become a legitimated person, the provisions of this Act with respect to the taking of interests in property by, or in succession to, the spouse, children and remoter issue of a legitimated person . . . shall apply as if such person as aforesaid had been a legitimated person and the date of the marriage of his parents had been the date of legitimation."

It will be seen that this section has no application unless a number of conditions are satisfied. In the first place, it will not apply unless the

---

[13]*Ibid.*, s. 11. For the operation of s. 33 of the Wills Act 1837, see *post*, p. 493, n.[7].
[14]*Re Wicks' Marriage Settlement*, [1940] Ch. 475; *Re Hoff*, [1942] 1 All E.R. 547; [1942] Ch. 298. A *general* power of appointment gives the donee the complete power to dispose of the property so that the only disposition that will have to be considered is the instrument by which the power is *exercised*.
[15]See the Legitimacy Act 1926, s. 3 (4).
[16]*Ibid.*, ss. 10 (1), 3 (3).
[17]*Ibid.*, s. 3 (2).

person, who would have been legitimated but for his prior death, dies after 1926 (or 28th October, 1959, if either of his parents was married at the time of his birth), so that there can be no question of shifting interests that have already vested.[18] Secondly, his spouse or at least one of his issue must still be alive at the date of the parents' marriage, for the policy of the section is to ensure that they are not prejudiced rather than to confer rights on any other person who might claim through them. Thirdly, it will be further observed that the effect of the section is not only to enable them to take an interest in property but also to enable others to take in succession to them.

An illustration may show its operation more clearly. F and M have a child, X, born in 1930. X dies in 1960, leaving a legitimate child, G. F and M intermarry in 1965, and F dies in 1968, having bequeathed a sum of money on trust for his grandchildren. Section 5 enables G to claim. X died after the Act came into force and left a child, G, who was alive when F and M married; consequently G can take such interest as he could have taken had X been legitimated on his parents' marriage.

Persons Legitimated by Foreign Law.—A person recognised as legitimated by section 8 of the Legitimacy Act 1926[19] is regarded as a person legitimated by that Act and consequently he can claim an interest in property only in the circumstances mentioned above. But if his legitimation is recognised at common law,[20] it would seem that he can establish a claim to property provided that he was legitimated before the interest vested, even though the disposition under which he claims took effect before the date of his legitimation. A clear example of this can be seen in the case of *Re Hurll*.[1] A testator died in 1939, having left a third of his residuary estate on trust for his daughter for life with remainder to her children. The plaintiff was born to the daughter in 1943. In 1949 the daughter married the plaintiff's father, who was at all material times domiciled in Italy, and by Italian law the plaintiff was thereby legitimated. The question then arose whether he was an object of the trust established by the will. Obviously he could not claim under the Act because the disposition under which he claimed (the will) took effect ten years before his legitimation. Nevertheless HARMAN, J., held that he could still claim under the trust because his legitimation was recognised at common law and the Act had done nothing to cut down these rights.

At common law a legitimated person could not claim realty as heir at all because of the rigid application of the rule that an heir must be legitimate by the common law rules.[2] Hence a legitimated person seeking to inherit an entailed interest can still do so only if the interest

---

[18]But hardship can still be worked, for if the illegitimate person died before the commencement of the relevant Act, his spouse and issue can claim nothing even though the instrument did not come into operation till after the commencement of the Act: see *Re Lowe*, [1929] Ch. 210.

[19]See *ante*, p. 243.

[20]See *ante*, p. 243.

[1][1952] 2 All E.R. 322; [1952] Ch. 722. See also *Re Grey's Trusts*, [1892] 3 Ch. 88; *Re Askew*, [1930] 2 Ch. 259.

[2]*Birtwhistle* v. *Vardill* (1826), 5 B. & C. 438, K.B.; *Doe d. Birtwhistle* v. *Vardill* (1835), 2 Cl. & F. 571, H.L.; *Birtwhistle* v. *Vardill* (1840), 7 Cl. & F. 895, H.L.

was created after his legitimation so that he can rely on the provisions of the Act.[3]

Illegitimate Children.—The common law presumption that " children " in any disposition *prima facie* means legitimate children only has been reversed by section 15 of the Family Law Reform Act 1969. This provides that in any disposition *made* on or after 1st January, 1970, any reference to a child of any person shall be construed as including an illegitimate child and any reference to a person related to another in some other manner shall include a person who is illegitimate or whose relationship is traced through an illegitimate person. In each case the term " illegitimate " includes a person who has been legitimated. The section also abolishes the rule prohibiting an illegitimate child not in being when a disposition takes effect from claiming under it. Thus if a deed or will executed in 1971 settles a fund on X for life with remainder to his children in equal shares, all X's children can take whether they are legitimate, legitimated or illegitimate, and neither the date of their birth nor the date of the legitimation is relevant. Similarly a bequest made in 1971 to X's nephews will include the illegitimate sons of X's legitimate brothers and sisters and the legitimate sons of his illegitimate brothers and sisters.[4] Similarly a gift to X's eldest son can now be claimed by that person even though he is illegitimate and the seniority of legitimated children no longer dates from their legitimation.

A disposition includes a disposition made *inter vivos* (whether oral or in writing) and a will or codicil. But a codicil executed after the section came into force is not to be treated for this purpose as republishing a will or codicil made before that date. Hence if a testator dies in 1971 but his will was made in 1968, it must still be construed according to the old law and section 15 has no application.

The operation of the section is subject to three limitations. First, it does not apply if a contrary intention is shown in the disposition itself. A gift to X's legitimate children will still pass an interest only to those born legitimate or legitimated before the disposition takes effect (unless the context indicates that legitimated children are also excluded). Secondly, it does not affect the construction of the word " heir " or the devolution of an entailed interest which can still descend only to those born legitimate at common law or legitimated before the entail was created. Thirdly, it does not affect the devolution of property which would (apart from this section) devolve along with a title or dignity of honour. It must also be remembered that the section in no way affects the operation of the Adoption Act. Thus a gift to X's

---

[3]A strict interpretation of the Act would result in his being unable to claim an entailed interest as heir at all if his legitimacy is recognised at common law, for s. 3 applies only if he is legitimated *under the Act* (see s. 11), and if his legitimacy is recognised at common law, he does not seem to come within this category: *Re Hurll, (supra)*.

[4]It is more doubtful whether the illegitimate sons of illegitimate brothers and sisters can take. The section applies to persons who would be so related if he *or* some other person through whom the relationship is deduced had been born legitimate. If the word " or " is to be given a disjunctive meaning, the section does not apply if both were born illegitimate.

S

children will also include any children adopted by X before the disposition comes into operation but will exclude any of his children adopted by somebody else before that date.[5]

Trustees and personal representatives are not bound to ascertain whether there are any persons who could take an interest by virtue of the operation of this section and they will not be personally liable for distributing property if they have no notice of their existence. But this does not prevent the beneficiary from following the property (or any property representing it) in the hands of a recipient.[6]

It is too early to say whether in the end the new rule will work any greater justice than the old one. The section was passed despite the views of the Russell Committee on the Law of Succession in Relation to Illegitimate Persons[7] who were of the opinion that its introduction might well force a testatrix who wished to exclude her illegitimate children to disclose by implication that she had some, or a father to offer his daughter a gratuitous insult by expressly limiting a gift to her legitimate children. These fears seem a little exaggerated: the testatrix can name the children she wishes to benefit, and the father can exclude the operation of the section in general terms if he wishes to do so. But many testators, unaware of the existence of others' illegitimate children, may unwittingly give them an interest which they do not wish them to take.[8]

Adopted Children.—Under the Adoption of Children Act of 1926, an adopted child was not deemed to be the child of the adopters but remained the child of his natural parents for the purposes of the devolution of interests in property. This anomalous rule was altered by the Adoption of Children Act 1949 with respect to dispositions made after 1949 or, in the case of an intestacy, where the intestate died after 1949. Now as regards interests in property, the general principle is the same as that relating to personal rights and duties: *i.e.*, from the date of the adoption order an adopted child is deemed to become the legitimate child of the adopter or adopters and ceases to be regarded as the child of his natural parents or, if he has been previously adopted, of his former adopters,[9] and therefore is no longer considered as related to any other person through his natural or former adoptive parents.

Section 16 (2) of the Adoption Act of 1958 accordingly provides that in any disposition of property made *inter vivos* after the date of an adoption order or by a will or codicil of a person dying after the making of an adoption order:[10]

---

[5]See *infra*.

[6]Family Law Reform Act 1969, s. 17.

[7]1966, Cmnd. 3051, paras. 57-58.

[8]It should be noted that the powers of trustees in relation to protective trusts under s. 33 of the Trustee Act 1925 have been similarly extended to enable them to hold the income on trust for the illegitimate children or remoter issue of the principal beneficiary: Family Law Reform Act 1969, s. 15 (3). For a discussion of the operation of s. 15 generally, see Morris, *The Family Law Reform Act 1969, sections, 14 and 15*, 19 I.C.L.Q. 328; Samuels, *Succession and the Family Law Reform Act 1969*, 34 Conv. 247, at pp. 249 *et seq.*

[9]Adoption Act 1958, s. 17 (4).

[10]But if a will or codicil was executed before 1st April, 1959, this provision applies only if the adoption order was made before its execution unless it was confirmed by codicil after that date: *ibid.*, s. 17 (2) and Sched. 5, para. 4 (3).

(a) any reference (whether express or implied) to the child of the adopter shall, unless the contrary intention appears, be construed as, or as including, a reference to the adopted person;

(b) any reference (whether express or implied) to the child or children of the adopted person's natural parents[11] or either of them shall, unless the contrary intention appears, be construed as not being, or as not including, a reference to the adopted person; and

(c) any reference (whether express or implied) to a person related to the adopted person in any degree shall, unless the contrary intention appears, be construed as a reference to the person who would be related to him in that degree if he were the child of the adopter born in lawful wedlock and were not the child of any other person.[12]

As in the case of a legitimated child, an adopted child may not take any interest in property limited to devolve along with a dignity or title of honour.[13] Strangely enough, there is no express provision in the Act to determine the relative seniority of the adopters' natural and adopted children—a matter which may be of importance in the descent of an unbarred entail created after the adoption order was made or in other claims to property. By analogy with the provisions of the Legitimacy Act, it is suggested that an adopted child should rank as though he had been born on the date of his adoption.

Foreign Adoption Orders.—As we have already seen, a child adopted in Scotland, Northern Ireland, the Isle of Man or the Channel Islands is in precisely the same position as a child adopted in England. This rule will also apply to a child who has been the subject of an " overseas adoption " specified by the Secretary of State when the Adoption Act 1968 comes into operation.[14] But quite apart from these statutory provisions, it is clear that the courts are prepared to recognise that some foreign adoptions can confer rights to claim property on the children in question. Two decisions of the Court of Appeal must be considered.

In *Re Marshall*[15] T, who was domiciled in England, died in 1945. By his will made in the same year he bequeathed a part of his estate to W for life and on her death to X with the proviso that, if X predeceased W, the remainder should be divided amongst X's issue. X, who was domiciled in British Columbia, had adopted C in that province before T made his will. X predeceased W and the question was whether C was X's issue for the purpose of the will. The Court of Appeal held that he could not take because under the law of British Columbia in force at the time of T's death, C's rights of succession were virtually limited to his adopters, and as T was not the adopter, C could not claim as X's child under the law by which he was adopted.

---

[11]Or former adoptive parents: s. 17 (4).

[12]In order to see whether there is any contrary intention, the court may look at the surrounding circumstances as well as at the instrument in question: *Re Jones's Will Trusts*, [1965] 2 All E.R. 828 (contrary intention inferred from testator's conversations with other members of the family). *Cf. Re Jebb*, [1965] 3 All E.R. 358, C.A.; [1966] Ch. 666.

[13]Adoption Act 1958, s. 16 (3). Although there is no express provision to this effect, the inference is that an adopted child cannot claim the dignity or title of honour.

[14]See *ante*, pp. 261-262.

[15][1957] 3 All E.R. 172, C.A.; [1957] Ch. 507.

The case seems to be authority for the proposition that English courts will recognise a foreign adoption only if its effect is substantially to confer upon the child the status of a legitimate child.[16] Hence C's claim failed because his rights of succession were so much more limited than those of a legitimate child. Similarly, it is in the highest degree unlikely that we should recognise a foreign order which does not place the adopter *in loco parentis* to the person adopted, for example an order by which a husband adopts his wife or a man of 82 adopts another man of 57 in order to give financial advantage to the latter.[17]

The emphasis in *Re Marshall* on C's rights under the law of British Columbia *at the time of T's death* is peculiar. Had C been adopted in England, he could have claimed nothing because T made his will before the Adoption of Children Act of 1949 came into operation; had T died in 1957 (when the case was heard) and C been adopted in England, the relevant date would still have been the date of T's will. This implies that a child adopted abroad may have wider rights to succession than a child adopted in England.

This case is not easy to reconcile with the later decision of the Court of Appeal in *Re Valentine's Settlement*.[18] By a deed executed in 1946 the settlor had settled a fund on her son's children. The son and his wife had adopted two children in 1939 and 1944. At all relevant times they had been domiciled and resident in Southern Rhodesia and both adoption orders had been made by a court in the Union of South Africa where the children were resident. The question was whether the children could claim under the settlement. LORD DENNING, M.R., held that the English courts would recognise a foreign order only if the court making it assumed a jurisdiction on the same ground as English courts:[19] in other words, the adopters must be domiciled in that country and the child ordinarily resident there. As the first condition was not satisfied, the orders in this case would not be recognised here. DANCKWERTS, L.J., held that, as status is governed by the *lex domicilii*, it is sufficient if the adopters are domiciled in the country where the order is made, and consequently in his opinion also these orders could not be recognised. SALMON, L.J., dissenting, held that English courts should always recognise an order if the court making it had jurisdiction over the child in question (as it obviously had in this case) provided that the principles applied by the court are basically the same as those applied in England and the same safeguards exist to ensure that the order will be for the benefit of the child. It is to be regretted that this view was not generally accepted. If spouses domiciled in England but ordinarily resident abroad adopt a child in the country where they are resident, it seems absurd that English courts will not recognise this adoption, for the only way in which a valid adoption can now be made is for the parties to go

---

[16]See the extra-judicial views of SCARMAN, J., *English Law and Foreign Adoptions*, 11 I.C.L.Q. 635.

[17]See Dicey and Morris, *Conflict of Laws*, 8th Ed., 466-467, and the cases cited *ibid.*, n. 71.

[18][1965] 2 All E.R. 226, C.A.; [1965] Ch. 831.

[19]*Cf.* the recognition of foreign divorces (*ante*, p. 219). See also *Re Wilson*, [1954] 1 All E.R. 997; [1954] Ch. 773, where VAISEY, J., held that a child could not claim on the intestacy of an adoptive parent, domiciled in England, who had obtained an adoption order in Montreal, even though this was valid by Quebec law.

to the expense of applying for an order under the English Act. In any case, even accepting the test of domicile, it should be sufficient if the courts of the adopters' *lex domicilii* recognise the adoption themselves.[20]

LORD DENNING, M.R., also expressed the view (which was strictly *obiter*) that children adopted abroad could acquire no greater rights than those adopted in England, which meant that the claims of the two adopted children would fail on this ground too, for, as the law stood when the settlement took effect in 1946, adopted children in this country could claim nothing as the children of their adoptive parents. SALMON, L.J., would have admitted their claim, apparently on the ground that the South African statute, by virtue of which they were adopted, conferred full proprietary rights on them. Here one feels he may have gone too far: the main question is whether the order can be recognised at all and, given that it will be, there seems no justification for according to children adopted abroad any greater rights than they would have had if they had been adopted here.

Accepting the principle that by English law status is basically determined by the parties' *lex domicilii*, it is suggested that we should recognise a foreign adoption if it is effected or recognised by the law of the adopters' and the child's domicile (or if the child has a different domicile from the adopters, by the laws of both domiciles).[1] If they have different domiciles and the two laws are not in agreement on this question, we must fall back on the further principle that we will recognise the validity of legal acts in other countries if *mutatis mutandis* we should assume jurisdiction: this is the basis of LORD DENNING's judgment in *Re Valentine's Settlement*. We must then add the proviso that we will not in any event recognise a foreign adoption unless its effects are substantially similar to those of an English adoption. If a child is to be regarded as an adopted child by these tests, he spould be put in the same position as a child adopted in this country and his rights to claim property should be exactly the same as if his adoption had been made by an order of an English court.[2]

B. FINANCIAL PROVISION

At common law a father was under a duty to maintain only his legitimate minor children and to provide them with food, clothing, lodging and other necessaries. But the duty was wholly unenforceable. A child has never had an agency of necessity[3] and a father is under no legal obligation to reimburse one who has supplied his child with necessaries. Unless he constituted the child his agent, the only way in

---

[20]*Cf.* the recognition of foreign divorces in similar circumstances (*ante*, p. 219). LORD DENNING, M.R.'s views are even more surprising in view of his strictures on the artificiality of the concept of domicile in the comparable jurisdiction relating to wards of court: *Re P. (G.E.)*, [1964] 3 All E.R. 977, C.A.; [1965] Ch. 568.

[1]This appears to be the view of HARMAN, J., at first instance in *Re Marshall*, [1957] 1 All E.R. 549; [1957] Ch. 263.

[2]*Cf.* the conclusions of Dicey and Morris, *op. cit.*, 461-476. See also Cheshire, *Private International Law*, 8th Ed., 451-456; Scarman, *loc. cit.*; Cowen, *English Law and Foreign Adoption*, 12 I.C.L.Q. 168; Jones, 5 I.C.L.Q. 205; Lipstein, 12 I.C.L.Q. 835; North, 28 M.L.R. 470.

[3]*Mortimer* v. *Wright* (1840), 6 M. & W. 482.

which he could be compelled to fulfil his obligation was through the wife's agency of necessity, which extended to the purchase of necessaries for the children of the marriage as well as for herself.[4] With the abolition of the wife's agency of necessity, the common law position is now of purely historical interest.[5]

On the breakdown of a marriage there are a number of ways in which financial provision can be claimed for children. The mother may also claim maintenance for an illegitimate child from the father to whom she has never been married at all. The provisions are now all statutory and present a veritable " chaos of enactments ".[6] It will be convenient to deal with them under three heads: those relating to children of the family, those relating to legitimate, legitimated and adopted children only, and those relating to illegitimate children only. In the first place, however, we must consider the entitlement to benefit under legislation relating to social security.

Concurrent Orders.—As in the case of orders for custody or for financial provision for a spouse, two orders for financial provision for a child should not be in force at the same time. As we shall see, a mother may obtain maintenance for a child in a county court or a magistrates' court under the Guardianship of Minors Act or in a magistrates' court under the Matrimonial Proceedings (Magistrates' Courts) Act. If she later petitions for a divorce, she may wish to obtain an order for financial provision in a divorce county court or the High Court. It seems that she should first have the earlier order discharged.[7] The facts that should be borne in mind in deciding which method of obtaining maintenance a party should pursue are the same as in the case of orders for financial provision for a spouse and for custody of the children.[8]

I. BENEFITS UNDER LEGISLATION RELATING TO SOCIAL SECURITY

Family Allowances.—The Family Allowances Act of 1945 was one of the first of a series of statutes passed after the end of the Second World War to give effect to the system of social security recommended in the Beveridge Report.[9] Its provisions (as amended) were consolidated in the Family Allowances Act 1965. Its object is to relieve one of the causes of poverty and to help parents to perform their social and legal

---

[4]*Bazeley* v. *Forder* (1868), L.R. 3 Q.B. 559.

[5]For the abolition of the wife's agency of necessity, see *ante*, p. 402. There is an old authority at nisi prius for the proposition that a father is also liable for necessaries supplied for the use of his children at the request of a servant who has charge of them: *Cooper* v. *Phillips* (1831), 4 C. & P. 581. Today the courts might require proof of an ostensible authority.

[6]Cretney, *The Maintenance Quagmire*, 33 M.L.R. 662, at p. 676, *q.v.* for a trenchant criticism of the present position.

[7]But in the case of an order made under the Matrimonial Proceedings (Magistrates' Courts) Act 1960, the High Court or divorce county court can discharge the magistrates' order: see *ante*, p. 407.

[8]See *ante*, p. 290. The fact that a woman already has an order for herself under one Act does not prevent her from applying for maintenance for her children under another: *Re Kinseth*, [1947] 1 All E.R. 201; [1947] Ch. 223. For the reciprocal enforcement of maintenance orders within the three jurisdictions in the United Kingdom, see the Maintenance Orders Act 1950, Part II.

[9]1942, Cmd. 6404.

duty of maintaining their children by providing money payments by the state in respect of the children of the family who are not yet earning their own living. The scheme is administered by the Department of Health and Social Security and allowances are payable weekly through the Post Office.[10]

The allowance is intended to be for the benefit of the family as a whole.[11] For this purpose a family consists of either (a) a man and his wife living together, the issue of both or either of them and any children being maintained by them, or (b) a man or woman not having a spouse or not living with his or her spouse,[12] his or her issue and any children being maintained by him or her. " Issue " in this context means issue of the first generation, and if a child is not living with its parents or parent, no allowance may be claimed in respect of it unless the claimants or claimant contributes at least eighteen shillings a week towards it maintenance.[13]

Once the child is earning its own living, it should help to swell the family funds rather than be a drain upon them. Consequently a person will be treated as a child for the purpose of the Act only

(a) during any period whilst he is under the upper limit of the compulsory school age[14]; and

(b) during any period before he attains the age of nineteen whilst he is undergoing full-time instruction in a school or is an apprentice; and

(c) during any period before he attains the age of sixteen whilst he is by reason of illness or disability of mind or body incapacitated, and likely to remain for a prolonged period incapacitated, for regular employment.[15]

Moreover the larger the family, the greater risk of poverty, and so no allowance is payable in respect of the eldest child coming within this definition.[16] Hence no allowance will ever be payable in respect of the eldest child of the family, and once the eldest child ceases to come within the definition, no allowance is payable for the second child, and so on.

At present the allowance is eighteen shillings a week for the first child in respect of whom an allowance may be claimed and twenty shillings a week for each other such child.[17] If the husband and wife are living together, the allowance belongs to the latter, for she is generally the member of the family by whom it will be needed to maintain the

---

[10]For further details, see Aikin, *Social Insurance and the Family*, 8 J.S.P.T.L. 167.

[11]Family Allowances Act 1965, s. 1.

[12]*I.e.*, permanently living in separation either by agreement or under a court order or where one has deserted the other: *ibid.*, s. 17 (1).

[13]Family Allowances Act 1965, ss. 3, 11, 17, 19 (1) and Sched., as amended by the Family Allowances and National Insurance Act 1968, s. 1 (1), and the Children and Young Persons Act 1969, Scheds. 5 and 6. For the meaning of " living with ", see *Hill* v. *Minister of Pensions and National Insurance*, [1955] 2 All E.R. 890. Detailed provisions relating to nationality, residence and membership of a family are contained in the Schedule to the Act and in the Family Allowances (Qualifications) Regulations, S.I. 1969, No. 212.

[14]See *ante*, p. 300.

[15]Family Allowances Act 1965, ss. 2 (1), (2) and 19 (1).

[16]*Ibid.*, s. 1.

[17]*Ibid.*, s. 1, as amended by the Family Allowances and National Insurance Act 1968, s. 1 (1).

children and there is the danger in some families that, if it were paid to the husband, it would never reach the wife at all. But the husband is empowered to give a valid receipt for it. It will be appreciated that in some cases even this might be inadvisable, whilst in others the husband might be anxious to keep the money out of the hands of a spendthrift wife. In order to guard against these contingencies, power is given to either spouse to apply to a magistrates' court for an order that the allowance shall be receivable by the applicant only to the exclusion of the other.[18]

National Insurance.—The benefits that an insured person (or his widow) can claim under the National Insurance Acts are increased for every child included in his family.[19] The same principle applies to death benefits payable under the National Insurance (Industrial Injuries) Acts.[20] The detailed statutory provisions are far too complex to be considered here, but it should be noted that, if a child's deceased parent was insured, payment may be made to a guardian in certain circumstances.[1]

Supplementary Benefit.—No person under the age of 16 may apply for supplementary benefit himself, but in calculating the requirements of anyone over that age the Commission must take into account the requirements of any child under 16 who is a member of the same household.[2] For the purpose of the Ministry of Social Security Act 1966, both parents are liable to maintain their legitimate, illegitimate and adopted children under the age of 16, and if benefit is given in respect of such a child, the Commission may take steps to recover it from either or both parents. The question of recovery will be considered later.[3]

2. CHILDREN OF THE FAMILY

Matrimonial Proceedings (Magistrates' Courts) Act.—Under this Act a magistrates' court can order either or both spouses to pay such weekly sum as it thinks fit for the maintenance of any child of the family *for the purpose of this Act* who is a dependant.[4] A " dependant " is one

---

[18]*Ibid.*, s. 4. The allowance is inalienable and any assignment of it or charge on it or agreement to assign or charge it is void. On the bankruptcy of the recipient, the allowance does not pass to the trustee in bankruptcy or any other person acting on behalf of the creditors: *ibid.*, s. 10.

[19]See the National Insurance Act 1965, Part II, and the National Insurance Act 1969, Sched. 2. The term " child " has the same meaning as it has under the Family Allowance Act: National Insurance Act 1965, s. 114 (2).

[20]National Insurance (Industrial Injuries) Act 1965, s. 21, and National Insurance Act 1969, Sched. 5.

[1]See the National Insurance Act 1965, ss. 29 and 42, and the National Insurance Act 1969, Sched. 2. At the moment the benefits payable with respect to a child vary from 55p to £2.45 a week according to the circumstances and the number of children.

[2]Ministry of Social Security Act 1966, s. 4 and Sched. 2. Only in special circumstances will benefit be given to a person over 16 who is still at school or receiving instruction of a type normally given in a school (s. 9); he will normally be regarded as a dependant of the person in whose family he is living. For the Ministry of Social Security Act generally, see *ante*, p. 413. Further assistance is now given by the Family Income Supplements Act 1970.

[3]*Post*, pp. 478 and 487.

[4]S. 2 (1) (h), as amended by the Maintenance Orders Act 1968.

" (a) who is under the age of 16 years; *or*

(b) who, having attained the age of 16 but not of 21 years, is either receiving full-time instruction at an educational establishment or undergoing training for a trade, profession or vocation in such circumstances that he is required to devote the whole of his time to that training for a period of not less than two years; *or*

(c) whose earning capacity is impaired through illness or disability of mind or body and who has not attained the age of 21 years ".[5]

The meaning of " child of the family " has already been discussed,[6] and it will be seen from the definition that one spouse may be ordered to pay maintenance for a child of the other spouse of which he is not the parent if he accepted it as one of the family. In these circumstances the court must have regard to the extent[7] to which he has assumed responsibility for the child's maintenance on or after accepting it as one of the family and also the liability of any other person to maintain it.[8] Even if, for example, a husband accepts his wife's children by a previous marriage as members of the family, the court might well conclude that no order for their maintenance should be made against him if he had made it clear when he married her that he was accepting no financial responsibility for them and their own father was quite capable of providing for them.[9]

If the child is under the age of 16, an order for maintenance may be made and remain in force only so long as there is also in force an order committing him to the custody of one of the spouses or to a third person[10] or to the care of a local authority. If the custody order is in favour of one of the spouses, naturally only the other may be ordered to pay maintenance; in other cases both spouses may be ordered to make payments. If the child is over the age of 16 (or when a child in respect of whom an order has already been made attains that age), the order may be made or (if already made) remain in force so long as he is under the age of 21 and a dependant and the court may direct the payments to be made to any person (including the child himself) or to the local authority in question.[11]

It will be recalled that an order for the custody and maintenance of a child of the family can be made even though the complaint is dismissed.[12] If the order directs one spouse to make the payments to the other, it will not be enforceable so long as they are cohabiting and will cease to have effect if they continue to cohabit for three months or, if they separate, they subsequently resume cohabitation.[13] In other cases neither the continuation nor the resumption of cohabitation will affect the order.[14] The court is not precluded from making an order

---

[5] S. 16 (1).   [6] *Ante*, pp. 283-285.

[7] *I.e.*, the amount, not the length of time: *Roberts* v. *Roberts*, [1962] 2 All E.R. 967; [1962] P. 212. See Samuels, 26 M.L.R. 92.

[8] S. 2 (5). This includes the potential liability of a parent against whom proceedings have not yet been brought: *Caller* v. *Caller*, [1966] 2 All E.R. 754; [1968] P. 39 (proceedings adjourned to give the wife an opportunity to seek an order against the father of her illegitimate child).

[9] See *Bowlas* v. *Bowlas*, [1965] 3 All E.R. 40, C.A.; [1965] P. 450.

[10] Whether the order is made by the magistrates' court or by any other court in England. In an interim order maintenance may be made payable to either party or a parent having custody of the child.

[11] S. 2 (1) (h).   [12] See *ante*, p. 149.

[13] *Cf. ante*, p. 200.

[14] Ss. 7 (1), (2) and 8 (2). *Cf. ante*, p. 200.

for maintenance (whether the payments are to be made to a spouse or to a third person) by reason of the fact that the complainant has been guilty of adultery or, where the ground of complaint is the defendant's adultery, that the complainant has condoned it, connived at it or conduced to it by his own wilful neglect or misconduct,[15] nor is it bound to discharge the order if the complainant later commits adultery.[16]

In other respects—variation, revocation, revival and enforcement—orders (including interim orders) in respect of a child are governed by the same rules as orders for the maintenance of a spouse.[17]

Matrimonial Proceedings and Property Act.—The High Court or a divorce county court has various powers under this Act. In each case they can be exercised for the benefit of a child of the family *for the purpose of this Act*. The meaning of this term has already been explained.[18]

Divorce, Nullity and Judicial Separation.—In proceedings for divorce, nullity and judicial separation, the court may make an order for periodical payments (which may be secured or unsecured) and for a lump sum payment. The order may be made before the decree is granted, when it is granted, or at any time afterwards; alternatively, to avoid a party's having to take fresh proceedings for financial provision for the children if the petition is unsuccessful, an order may be made on the dismissal of the petition or within a reasonable time thereafter. Normally, the sums will be payable by one spouse (or former spouse) to the other, but either (or presumably both)[19] of them may be ordered to make payments to a third person, if the child is in that person's custody or care and control, or to the child himself in an appropriate case (as might happen if he were over 18).[20] As in the case of provision for a spouse, a lump sum may cover any liabilities or expenses already incurred by the child or for his benefit; it may also be made payable by instalments, which may be secured.[1]

It will also be recalled that the court has power to order the transfer and settlement of property and the variation of ante-nuptial and post-nuptial settlements to or for the benefit of any child of the family. This can be exercised, however, only if a decree is pronounced.[2]

Wilful Neglect to maintain.—Under section 6 of the Act either spouse may apply for an order on the ground that the other has wilfully

---

[15] See s. 2 (3).
[16] S. 8 (2).
[17] See *ante*, pp. 420-426. This includes the power to have the order registered and enforced in the High Court.
[18] See *ante*, p. 287.
[19] The court had power under previous legislation to make an order against both spouses: *Freckleton* v. *Freckleton*, [1966] C.L.Y. 3938.
[20] Consequently an application for an order may be made by a guardian, anyone with custody or care and control of the child, a local authority and the Official Solicitor as guardian *ad litem*: Matrimonial Causes Rules 1968, r. 69.
[1] S. 3. For payments to the other spouse, see *ante*, pp. 430-434.
[2] S. 4. See *ante*, pp. 434-443.

neglected to provide, or make a proper contribution towards, reasonable maintenance for a child of the family to whom the section applies. Apparently neither spouse can contract out of the duty to maintain children; consequently if the husband and wife have separated on the understanding that the wife will support all the children herself or that the husband will pay only a limited sum towards their maintenance, she will not be precluded from alleging that he is guilty of wilful neglect to maintain them.[3] On the other hand, this section applies only to children for whose maintenance it is reasonable in the circumstances to expect the respondent to provide or contribute.[4]

If the court is satisfied that the grounds alleged have been made out, it may order the respondent to make secured or unsecured periodical payments and a lump sum payment for the benefit of any child to whom the application relates.[5] As in the case of similar orders made on divorce, the sums may be payable to the applicant, the child or a third person, and a lump sum may be made payable by instalments, which may be secured.[6]

Assessment.—In the case of divorce, nullity and judicial separation, section 5 (2) directs the court

" . . . to have regard to all the circumstances of the case including the following matters, that is to say—
(a) the financial needs of the child;
(b) the income, earning capacity (if any), property and other financial resources of the child;
(c) any physical or mental disability of the child;
(d) the standard of living enjoyed by the family before the breakdown of the marriage;
(e) the manner in which he was being and in which the parties to the marriage expected him to be educated or trained;
and so to exercise those powers as to place the child as far as it is practicable and, having regard to the spouses' income, earning capacity, property and other financial resources and their financial needs, obligations and responsibilities, just so to do, in the financial position in which the child would have been if the marriage had not broken down and each of the spouses had properly discharged his or her financial obligations and responsibilities towards him."

These provisions largely reflect the principles which the courts applied before 1971. But it will be seen that the very wide definition of the term " children of the family " gives the court power to make an order against a spouse who is under no other legal obligation to make financial provision for the child and who may have assumed no responsibility for its maintenance. Consequently a measure of protection is

---

[3] See *Northrop* v. *Northrop*, [1967] 2 All E.R. 961, C.A., at pp. 965 and 978-979; [1968] P. 74, at pp. 97 and 116. The point was left open in *Starkie* v. *Starkie (No. 2)*, [1953] 2 All E.R. 1519, 1522.
[4] See *ante*, pp. 427-428. For the facts to be taken into account in deciding whether it was reasonable to expect the respondent to provide for a child, see *infra*.
[5] If the court finds the respondent guilty of wilful neglect to maintain the applicant but not the child, it may take into account the cost to her of looking after the child in assessing financial provision for her: *Ridley* v. *Ridley*, [1953] 1 All E.R. 798; [1953] P. 150.
[6] S. 6 (1), (3), (6) and (7). An interim order for periodical payments may also be made: s. 6 (5).

necessary and, in deciding whether to make an order against a party to
the marriage in favour of a child who is not his natural or adopted
child and, if so, how much to award, the court must have regard
(among the other circumstances of the case) to the extent to which he
assumed responsibility for the child's maintenance, the basis upon
which he did so, the length of time for which he had discharged it,
whether he knew that the child was not his own, and the liability of
any other person to maintain the child.[7] The same questions must also
be asked when determining the question whether it was reasonable to
expect the respondent to provide for such a child's maintenance in an
application under section 6.[8]

It should also be appreciated that the spouses may not oust the
jurisdiction of the court by agreeing between themselves what maintenance should be paid. Any agreement between the parties containing
provisions relating to the maintenance or education of any child will
be a " maintenance agreement " for the purpose of section 13 of the
Act provided that it is in writing. This means that any term restricting
the parties' power to apply to a court for an order containing financial
arrangements will not be binding but the agreement will not thereby
be rendered void: the covenantee may prefer to hold the spouse to his
contract and may also apply to the court to have the agreement
altered.[9] If the agreement is not in writing, any such restrictive term is
contrary to public policy at common law on the ground that the right to
apply to the court is given for the child's benefit and therefore cannot
be surrendered even for valuable consideration.[10] Consequently either
spouse may apply for an order and, if the undertaking not to do so is
the sole or main consideration for the other party's promise to pay
maintenance, the whole contract will be void and cannot be enforced.[11]

Duration of Orders.—Section 8 of the Act imposes a further limitation
on the court's power to make financial provision for a child. No order
for periodical payments (secured or unsecured), a lump sum payment
or the transfer (as distinct from the settlement) of property may be
made in favour of a child over the age of 18, and periodical payments
may not continue after his eighteenth birthday. To both limbs of this
rule, however, there are two exceptions: there is no age limit to the
making or continuation of orders so long as the child is in receipt of
education or training (whether or not he is also gainfully employed) or,
in any event, if there are special circumstances justifying this. It will
be seen therefore that the court has power, at least in theory, to
compel a spouse to provide for, say, a mentally handicapped child for
the rest of his life if he will never be able to earn his own living: it
remains to be seen whether they will be prepared to exercise it.

---

[7]S. 5 (3).
[8]S. 6 (4).
[9]See *ante*, pp. 408-410.
[10]*Bishop* v. *Bishop*, [1897] P. 138, 165, C.A.; *Bennett* v. *Bennett*, [1951] 1 All E.R.
1088; [1951] 2 K.B. 572 (affirmed on other grounds, [1952] 1 All E.R. 413, C.A.; [1952]
1 K.B. 249).
[11]*Bennett* v. *Bennett*, (*supra*). But this does not apply to an agreement to oust the
jurisdiction of a foreign court: *Addison* v. *Brown*, [1954] 2 All E.R. 213. *Cf.* agreements
relating to the maintenance of one of the parties to the marriage, *ante*, p. 409.

Unless the court otherwise orders at the time, the term for which periodical payments are to last is not to extend in the first instance beyond the child's birthday next following his attaining the upper limit of compulsory school age. In any case unsecured periodical payments will cease on the payer's death but, as in the case of maintenance for a spouse, this rule does not apply to secured periodical payments.

Variation and Discharge of Orders.—As in the case of orders for the benefit of a party to the marriage, there is a general power to vary, discharge, suspend and revive orders for periodical payments. The court may also vary an order relating to the terms on which a lump sum is payable by instalments but not the total sum payable. On an application for variation the court has no power to order the transfer or settlement of property or the variation of an ante-nuptial or post-nuptial settlement, but it can order the payment of a lump sum—a power that it does not possess on an application to vary an order in favour of a spouse. The reason for the difference is that a lump sum may be valuable to a child long after the marriage has broken down, for example to enable him to pay admission fees to an Inn of Court. No application to vary an order for secured periodical payments after the payer's death may be made more than six months after representation to his estate was first taken out except with the leave of the court.

In exercising its powers to make a variation, etc., the court must have regard to all the circumstances of the case including any change in the matters which it was expressly directed to take into account while making the order originally. It must also take into account any change in circumstances resulting from the death of the party against whom the order was made.[12]

Enforcement.—An order can be enforced in exactly the same way as a similar order made for the benefit of either party to the marriage. This includes the power to remit arrears, to restrain and set aside dispositions made with the intention of defeating the claim, to register the order in a magistrates' court and to recover overpayments after a change of circumstances.[13]

3. LEGITIMATE, LEGITIMATED AND ADOPTED CHILDREN

As we have already seen, an order may be sought against either parent to recover the cost of supplementary benefit given in respect of a legitimate child. Maintenance may also be obtained under the Guardianship of Infants Acts and for wards of court. In each of these cases the term " legitimate child " includes a child who has been legitimated and a child who has been adopted.

---

[12]Matrimonial Proceedings and Property Act 1970, s. 9. For variation, etc., of an order in favour of a spouse, see *ante*, pp. 449-452.

[13]See *ante*, pp. 452-457. Similarly arrears of periodical payments and the payment of a lump sum cannot be enforced more than twelve months after they fall due without the leave of the court.

Supplementary Benefit.—If benefit is given in respect of a child under the age of 16, the Supplementary Benefits Commission may apply to a magistrates' court for an order against either parent. In determining what order to make, the court must have regard to all the circumstances and particularly to the parent's resources. Any payments ordered must be made to the Secretary of State in so far as they represent reimbursement of benefit given and to the person named in the order (who will normally be the person with custody or care and control of the child) in so far as they represent maintenance for the future. All orders may be subsequently varied or revoked, and they are enforceable like other maintenance orders made by a magistrates' court.[14]

Guardianship of Minors Act.—If any court makes an order under this Act for the custody of a *legitimate* child in favour of the mother, it may further order the father to pay her periodical sums for the child's maintenance and education.[15] As regards variation and discharge and the accrual of liability if the mother resides with the father, maintenance orders are governed by the same rules as custody orders.[16]

It will be recalled that a magistrates' court cannot make an order if the child is over the age of 16 unless he is physically or mentally incapable of self-support, although an order once made may remain in force after he reaches that age.[17] Although a custody order made in any court cannot now extend beyond the child's eighteenth birthday, maintenance provision may remain in force until he reaches the age of 21 (in which case the sums may be made payable to him personally). If a *legitimate* person over the age of 18 was the subject of *any* order under the Act whilst he was a minor, the court, on the application of *either* parent or of the child himself, may order *either* parent to make periodical payments for his maintenance for any period not extending beyond his twenty-first birthday. The sums may be made payable to the other parent, a third person or the child himself. Parents are, however, given a measure of protection against the possibility of applications being made, particularly by the child himself: no fresh order may be made if the parents are residing together, and if they subsequently reside together, no liability will accrue under such an order whilst they are doing so and the order will automatically cease to have effect if they reside together for three months. The order may be varied or discharged on the application of any person by or to whom payments are to be made.[18]

---

[14]Ministry of Social Security Act 1966, s. 23. For enforcement, see *ante*, pp. 422-426. See further *ante*, p. 472, and Brown, *National Assistance and the Liability to maintain one's Family*, 18 M.L.R. 110.

[15]Guardianship of Minors Act 1971, ss. 9 (2), (3), (4), 14 (2) and 20 (2).

[16]See *ante*, p. 282.

[17]See *ante*, p. 282. The limitation formerly imposed on the amount that a magistrates' court can order was removed by the Maintenance Orders Act 1968.

[18]Guardianship of Minors Act 1971, ss. 12 and 14 (4).

In assessing the amount to be ordered, the first question that the court must ask is: what does the infant need? All his circumstances must be taken into account, including his age, the type of education he is receiving, the standard in which he has been brought up and any other money available for his maintenance. Secondly, of course, the means of both parents must be taken into consideration.[1]

The usual means of enforcement are open if the order is made in the High Court or a county court; an order made in a magistrates' court is enforceable in the same way as an affiliation order.[2] In all cases the order may be registered and enforced in another court and an attachment of earnings order may be made.

Wards of Court.—We have already seen what rights generally a guardian has to claim maintenance for his ward from the surviving parent. If the child is a ward of court, the parents' liability has been considerably extended by the provisions of section 6 of the Family Law Reform Act 1969. The court may now order either parent to pay to the other such periodical sums towards the maintenance and education of the ward as it thinks reasonable having regard to the means of the parent against whom the order is made. If the ward is in the care and control of a third person, either or both parents may be required to make periodical payments to that person. Such an order may remain in force until the child reaches the age of 21 and, if he is over the age of 18, the sums may be made payable to him personally. Furthermore, so long as a former ward of court is between the ages of 18 and 21, either parent or the child himself may apply for an order requiring either parent to pay maintenance to the other parent, a third person or to the child himself. Except for an order requiring a parent to pay maintenance for an existing ward of court to a third person, no order can be made if the parents are residing together at the time, and if they subsequently reside together, no liability will accrue so long as they do so, and the order will cease to have effect if they reside together for a period of three months. There is no power at all to make an order for maintenance if the child is illegitimate. All orders can be varied and discharged by the court and may be enforced in the same way as other orders for payment in the High Court.

4. ILLEGITIMATE CHILDREN: AFFILIATION ORDERS

At common law neither the father nor the mother is liable to maintain an illegitimate child.[3] Although the Poor Law legislation cast upon the mother the obligation of maintaining her illegitimate child, she could

---

[1] See *Re T.*, [1953] 2 All E.R. 830; [1953] Ch. 787; *Re W.*, [1956] 1 All E.R. 368 C.A.; [1956] Ch. 384, where it was pointed out that the fact that the mother is working will not necessarily go in diminution of the claim if the court is of the opinion that it is not in the children's interest that she should do so.

[2] Guardianship of Minors Act 1971, s. 13 (3). See *ante*, pp. 422-426.

[3] *Ruttinger* v. *Temple* (1863), 4 B. & S. 491. In *Hesketh* v. *Gowing* (1804), 5 Esp. 131, the father was held liable if he adopted the child as his own, but today it would probably be necessary to establish an authority to incur expenses on the child's behalf by the person seeking reimbursement.

still not recover the expenses of maintenance from the father in the absence of any contract to that effect between them.[4] A statute of 1576 empowered Justices to make an order on the putative father for the maintenance of an illegitimate child charged on the parish,[5] but it was not until the Poor Law Amendment Act of 1844 that the mother was given the power to apply for an order for maintenance to be paid to herself. The law was amended and consolidated in the Bastardy Laws Amendment Act of 1872 and again in the Affiliation Proceedings Act 1957. The principle of the Act of 1957 is that a "single woman" who is with child or who has been delivered of an illegitimate child may apply to a magistrates' court for a summons to be served on the man she alleges to be the father; if the court adjudges him to be the putative father, it may make a further order (known as an affiliation order) that he shall pay her maintenance in respect of the child.

If a man has been adjudged to be the father of a child in affiliation proceedings, this is *prima facie* evidence (which may be rebutted) of the fact of his paternity in any subsequent *civil* proceedings, whether or not he is a party to them.[6]

Who may apply for an Order.—In order to apply for an order the mother must prove that she was a " single woman ".[7] It is obvious that an unmarried woman—whether she is a spinster, widow or divorced—comes within this category.[8] In addition, a married woman may also be a " single woman " for the purposes of the Act, provided that she is living apart from her husband and has lost the right to be maintained by him. The reason for this apparently anomalous rule is that, since the woman can no longer look to her husband for maintenance, she is entitled to turn to the putative father at least for maintenance of the child. A clear example of this is to be found in the decision of the King's Bench Division in *Jones* v. *Evans*.[9] The applicant's child was conceived and born whilst her husband was absent overseas in H.M. Forces. On becoming aware of the facts, the husband wrote and told her that he had decided to forgive her to a certain extent until he returned home. It was held that, since the wife was not living with her husband and had committed the uncondoned offence of adultery which had deprived her of her right to be maintained by him, she was a " single woman " within the meaning of the Act.

It will be observed that two conditions have to be satisfied. First, there must be a *de facto* separation between the applicant and her husband, for clearly, if they are still cohabiting, the right to maintenance will not be lost.[10] The separation may be due to desertion or

---

[4] As to agreements to pay maintenance, see *post*, p. 488.
[5] 18 Eliz. I, c. 3.
[6] Civil Evidence Act 1968, s. 12.
[7] Affiliation Proceedings Act 1957, ss. 1 and 2 (2).
[8] If *Newbould* v. *A.-G.* is correctly decided (*ante*, p. 69), this must also include a woman who is married at the time of the child's birth but whose voidable marriage is subsequently annulled.
[9] [1945] 1 All E.R. 19; [1944] K.B. 582.
[10] The test of cohabitation is probably the same as in the case of desertion (see *ante*, pp. 162-164): cf. *Watson* v. *Tuckwell* (1947), 63 T.L.R. 634, followed in *Whitton* v. *Garner*, [1965] 1 All E.R. 70, and *Giltrow* v. *Day*, [1965] 1 All E.R. 73.

to any other cause which prevents their living together—for example, the husband's absence on military service in *Jones* v. *Evans*[11] or their living apart under a court order[12] or perhaps even under a separation agreement.[13] Secondly, the wife must have lost the right to be maintained by her husband. In this connection it must be remembered that the birth of the child means that she must have committed adultery, so that, unless this has been condoned, the second condition is automatically satisfied.[14] On the other hand, however, if the husband condones the adultery and the parties resume cohabitation, the wife's right to maintenance revives and consequently she is precluded from applying for an affiliation order.[15]

Earlier legislation required the mother to be a " single woman " at the time she made her application. This worked hardship on a woman who was " single " at the time of the child's birth but who had married or become reconciled with her husband before applying for an order. Consequently section 4 of the Legitimacy Act 1959 now provides that such a woman can apply for an order: in other words the complainant must show that she was a " single woman " at the time of the child's birth or at the time of the application (or, of course, on both occasions).[16]

Effect of Adoption.—As the effect of adoption is to put the child in the position of the legal child of the adopters and to discharge all existing parental rights and duties, no application for an order may be made if the child has been adopted. This does not apply, however, if the child is adopted by the mother alone for otherwise she would lose the only claim for financial provision that she probably has.[17]

Jurisdiction.—The jurisdiction to make affiliation orders (like magistrates' jurisdiction generally) is based upon the parties' residence, and as a general rule the court cannot make an order unless both the mother and the defendant are resident in England.[18] The difficulties which occur when one of them has moved to another country have been partly alleviated by the provisions of section 3 of the Maintenance Orders Act 1950 provided that both of them are resident in the United Kingdom. If the defendant resides in England, the mother can apply for an order here if she resides in Scotland or Northern Ireland; if she resides in England, she can apply for an order here if the defendant resides in Scotland or Northern Ireland *and* the act of intercourse

---

[11]See *Mooney* v. *Mooney*, [1952] 2 All E.R. 812; [1953] 1 Q.B. 38. In this case LORD GODDARD, C.J., left open the question whether the wife would be a " single woman " if her husband were serving a long sentence of imprisonment, although he apparently thought that she would be. In *R.* v. *Pilkington* (1853), 2 E. & B. 546, it was held that an affiliation order could be made when the applicant's husband was serving a sentence of transportation in Van Diemen's Land.

[12]*Kruhlak* v. *Kruhlak*, [1958] 1 All E.R. 154; [1958] 2 K.B. 32; *Boyce* v. *Cox*, [1922] 1 K.B. 149.

[13]But not if the separation is purely colourable in an attempt to give the court jurisdiction to make an order: *Jones* v. *Davies*, [1901] 1 Q.B. 118.

[14]*Jones* v. *Evans*, (*ante*); *Hockaday* v. *Goodenough*, [1945] 2 All E.R. 335.

[15]*Jones* v. *Davies*, (*supra*).

[16]*Gaines* v. *W.*, [1968] 1 All E.R. 189; [1968] 1 Q.B. 782.

[17]Adoption Act 1958, s. 15 (2).

[18]Affiliation Proceedings Act 1957, s. 3; *Berkley* v. *Thompson* (1884), 10 App. Cas. 45, H.L.

resulting in the child's birth (or any act of intercourse which might have had this effect) took place in England.[19]

For years the question of jurisdiction was bedevilled by the historical connection between affiliation proceedings and the old Poor Law which turned largely on the settlement of the person seeking relief. The effect of this was that the mother's power to apply for an order was limited if the child was not born in this country. Whatever justification there may have been for this rule a century ago, the position has been changed by rapid international transport and the presence in this country of a large immigrant population. Consequently the Court of Appeal seized the opportunity of overruling a number of old cases in *R.* v. *Bow Road Domestic Proceedings Court, Ex parte Adedigba*[20] and laid down the principle that, provided the residence qualification is satisfied, the place of the child's birth is completely irrelevant.

Time Limit upon Application for Summons.—In order to prevent the mother from commencing proceedings some time after the birth of the child, when the defendant might find it difficult to adduce rebutting evidence, the summons must be applied for within one of the following periods:[1]

(1) Before the birth of the child; *or*

(2) Within twelve months of the child's birth; *or*

(3) At any time if the defendant has paid money for the child's maintenance within twelve months of its birth;[2] *or*

(4) Within twelve months of the defendant's return to England, if he ceased to reside in England either before the child's birth[3] or within twelve months after the birth.

But even if the applicant relies on period (3) or (4), it would seem that she cannot obtain an order if the child is over the age of 13 years.

Procedure.—The application is heard before a magistrates' court sitting as a domestic court.[5]   The applicant must herself give

---

[19]Scottish and Northern Irish courts have a similar jurisdiction.

[20][1968] 2 All E.R. 89, C.A.; [1968] 2 Q.B. 572. The case raises two questions. Is normal residence necessary or is physical presence sufficient? On this point, see von Landauer in 17 I.C.L.Q. 1015. Does the child also have to be present in this country? SALMON, L.J., implied that this was not necessary (at pp. 94 and 581, respectively): the residence of the child seems irrelevant if the mother is remitting money for its maintenance elsewhere.

[1]Affiliation Proceedings Act 1957, ss. 1, 2. There is no time limit if the mother and the defendant were parties to a marriage which would have been valid but for the statutory provisions making it void because one of them had not attained the age of 16, provided that the defendant had access to the mother within the twelve months preceding the birth: *ibid.*, s. 2 (2).

[2]Payment by the father's agent will bind him if he authorised it: see *G. (A.)* v. *G. (T.)*, [1970] 3 All E.R. 546, C.A.; [1970] 2 Q.B. 643. Provision of maintenance in kind paid for out of money coming from the father (*e.g.*, when the child is living in the father's household) is equivalent to the payment of money for this purpose: *Roberts* v. *Roberts*, [1962] 2 All E.R. 967; [1962] P. 212.

[3]*R.* v. *Evans*, [1896] 1 Q.B. 228. Presumably this applies equally if the child was conceived abroad and the defendant has never resided in England.

[4]Under s. 6 of the Act the Court may order that payments under the order shall *continue* after the child's thirteenth birthday, which implies that the order must originally be made before that date. For a criticism of the present state of the law, see Lasok, *Time Factor in Affiliation Proceedings*, 120 New L.J. 679.

[5]Legitimacy Act 1959, s. 5.

evidence, which must be corroborated in some material particular.[6] This may be by an admission of paternity by the defendant or circumstantial evidence that he had intercourse with the mother. Of more importance now is the court's power to direct blood tests;[7] but it must be remembered that the burden of proving paternity is upon the applicant, so that if there are two or more men, any of whom might be the father, an affiliation order may be made against none of them. A furthet injustice results from the fact that the mother must herself give evidence, for if she dies before the application is heard or if she cannot give evidence for some other reason, no order can be made at all, despite the fact that her death does not discharge an order once it has been made.[8]

Appeals.—Either party may appeal to Quarter Sessions or, on a point of law only, by a case stated to the High Court. An appeal to Quarter Sessions is virtually a rehearing of the case, and the mother again has to give evidence which must be corroborated.[9] Consequently, if she were to die before the appeal were heard, it would seem that Quarter Sessions is bound to find for the defendant, which suggests that the latter may always obtain the discharge of an order made against him if the mother dies within fourteen days of the hearing by the simple expedient of giving notice of appeal.[10]

Subsequent Applications.—Before the passing of the Criminal Justice Administration Act in 1914 the mother had no power to appeal if the court dismissed her application. This, coupled with the fact that the court may not declare that the defendant is not the putative father of her child in such circumstances, led the Court of Queen's Bench in *R.* v. *Machen*[11] to hold that it could not have been the Legislature's intention that a magistrates' court should finally adjudicate against the mother and that consequently a dismissal of the application—even on the merits of the case—did not prevent the mother from making a second application within the statutory time limit. Although it is no longer true that the mother has no right of appeal, the court still cannot finally adjudicate against the mother in the sense that it may not declare that the defendant is not the putative father, and the Queen's Bench Division therefore held in *Robinson* v. *Williams*[12] that a dismissal is in the nature of a non-suit and that consequently a second application may still be made provided that the mother produces some evidence other than that led before, for the court cannot be asked to

---

[6]Affiliation Proceedings Act 1957, s. 4 (1), (2).
[7]For the nature of corroborative evidence, see Cross, *Evidence*, 3rd Ed., 177-182. For a detailed examination of the cases on affiliation, see Chislett, *Affiliation Proceedings*, 27-32. For blood tests, see *ante*, pp. 235-237.
[8]*R.* v. *Armitage* (1872), L.R. 7 Q.B. 773.
[9]Magistrates' Courts Act 1952, s. 87; Affiliation Proceedings Act 1957, s. 8. The putative father may also apply to the High Court for an order of *certiorari* to quash the affiliation order.
[10]But see Chislett, *op. cit.*, 59-61. This point was deliberately left open in *R.* v. *Armitage*, (*supra*).
[11](1849), 14 Q.B. 74.
[12][1964] 3 All E.R. 12; [1965] 1 Q.B. 89, following *R.* v. *Sunderland Justices*, [1945] 2 All E.R. 175; [1945] K.B. 502.

come to a different conclusion on identical evidence.[13]   On the other hand, however, it has been held that if a magistrates' court makes an order and the father appeals to Quarter Sessions which quashes the order *on the merits of the case*, the mother may not then make a second application to a magistrates' court,[14] but if Quarter Sessions allows the appeal on a technical point and not on the merits, this does not prevent the mother from making a fresh application.[15]   As Quarter Sessions has no more power to make a declaration that the defendant is not the father of the applicant's child than a magistrates' court has, this distinction is quite illogical and indefensible.

Orders that may be made.—If the court adjudges the defendant to be the putative father of the child, it may further order him to make various payments.[16]   He may be ordered to pay the expenses incidental to its birth and also the funeral expenses if the child has died before the making of the order;[17] in addition he may be ordered to pay such weekly sum as the court thinks fit for its maintenance and education.   Presumably the court may take into account expenses incurred by the mother over and above that of feeding and clothing the child, for example increased rent due to her having to live in more expensive accommodation and the loss of income caused by the birth of the child and the necessity of having to look after it.[18]   The removal of the former limit on the maximum sum that magistrates can award has raised a new problem of assessment: should the court be guided by the standard of living of the father or the mother?   Suppose, for example, that the mother is a woman who is never likely to enjoy a high income and the father is a " pop star " earning a very high salary.   Although one feels that the child (for whose benefit the order is being made) ought not to be prejudiced by his mother's position, it might be equally unwise to drive a wedge between him and any brothers and sisters he might have later by giving him an undue advantage over them.   In such a case it is regrettable that, as only magistrates have jurisdiction, it is impossible to order periodical payments to be secured and thus safeguard the child's position should the father become penniless in a few years' time.

---

[13]But this need not be " fresh evidence " in the sense of evidence that could not have been obtained with reasonable diligence at the first hearing: *Robinson* v. *Williams*, (*supra*).   The application of this rule to a paternity issue arising in proceedings under the Guardianship of Infants Acts in *Re F. (W.)*, [1969] 3 All E.R. 595; [1969] 2 Ch. 269, seems wholly misconceived.   (The second application was in fact dismissed because the evidence was identical.)

[14]*R.* v. *Howard*, [1938] 3 All E.R. 241; [1938] 2 K.B. 544.

[15]*R.* v. *May* (1880), 5 Q.B.D. 382.   If Quarter Sessions quashes the order because of insufficiency of corroborative evidence, this is a decision on the merits and the mother may not make a fresh application: *R.* v. *Howard*, (*supra*).   Presumably if the *mother* appeals to Quarter Sessions from a dismissal of the application and her appeal is dismissed on the merits, she may not then make a second application to a magistrates' court.

[16]Affiliation Proceedings Act 1957, s. 4 (2), as amended by the Maintenance Orders Act 1968.

[17]But the child must have been born alive.   No order may be made at all if it was still-born: *R.* v. *De Brouquens* (1811), 14 East 277.

[18]*Cf. Northrop* v. *Northrop*, [1967] 2 All E.R. 961, C.A.; [1968] P. 74 (*ante*, p. 416).

Unless the court fixes a shorter period, the order will remain in force till the child reaches the age of 16, but payments under it are not required to be made after the child's thirteenth birthday unless the court directs that they are to continue (as in practice it usually does).[19] The order may be extended on the mother's application for one or more periods of two years after the child reaches the age of 16 if it is engaged in a course of education or training, provided that the order does not extend beyond the date when the child reaches the age of 21.[20]

Normally money due under an affiliation order is payable to the mother and, unless the court otherwise orders, payments will be made through a magistrates' clerk.[1] After the mother's death or whilst she is of unsound mind or confined in prison, the court may grant the custody of the child to any other person, to whom payments under the order then become due, or, if the child is over the age of 18, payments may be made to him personally.[2] In addition, the court may, upon the application of any person for the time being having the custody of the child, make or vary an order so as to provide that the payments shall be made to the applicant[3] and the latter may apply to have them continued beyond the child's sixteenth birthday in the same circumstances as the mother.[4] Although the word " make " suggests that a person other than the mother may apply for an order in the first instance, this, it is submitted, is not possible, for all affiliation proceedings must be commenced by her; the hardship of this can be seen in the case where the mother leaves her child to be brought up by someone else and then refuses to apply for an affiliation order so that that other person has no means of getting the father to contribute to the child's maintenance.

There is, however, in certain circumstances a power vested in local authorities to apply for an affiliation order even though the mother has not done so, for if an illegitimate child is in the care of the authority either under a care order or under section 1 of the Children Act 1948[5] the authority may apply for an order.[6] Apart from the fact that an application may be made within three years of the making of the order or of the child's being taken into the authority's care, the procedure is the same as when the mother herself applies, and consequently no order can be made if she herself does not give evidence.[7] Moreover, if

---

[19]Affiliation Proceedings Act 1957, s. 6. The sum may be calculated from the birth of the child if the application for the affiliation order was made before the birth or within two months after it: *ibid.*, s. 4 (3).

[20]*Ibid.*, s. 7. *Cf.* the provisions of the Matrimonial Proceedings (Magistrates' Courts) Act 1960 (see *ante*, p. 473).

[1]Magistrates' Courts Act 1952, s. 52 (1), (2). *Cf. ante*, p. 420.

[2]Affiliation Orders Act 1957, s. 5 (4); Family Law Reform Act 1969, s. 5 (2). A child over 18 may himself apply for an extension of the order in these circumstances.

[3]*Ibid.*, s. 5 (3). The applicant must either have a custody order in his favour or have custody by virtue of an arrangement approved by the court.

[4]*Ibid.*, s. 7 (6).

[5]See *ante*, pp. 294 and 296. A contribution order (see *ante*, p. 298) can also be made against the mother.

[6]Children Act 1948, s. 26, as amended by the Children and Young Persons Act 1969, Scheds. 5 and 6.

[7]But presumably an order may be made even though the mother was not a " single woman ", for the Affiliation Proceedings Act merely requires that the *applicant* shall be a " single woman ". *Cf. post*, p. 487 (supplementary benefit).

an affiliation order is already in force, it may be varied in similar circumstances so as to make the sums payable to the local authority concerned.[8] In one respect, however, the liability of the putative father is less if the child is in the care of a local authority, for no application can be made to extend the duration of the affiliation order beyond the child's sixteenth birthday unless he is permitted to reside with the mother.[9]

Variation and Discharge of Orders.—The court which made the order has a general power to revoke, revive or vary it.[10] Two specific cases of the variation of an order have already been noticed—the extension of it after the child has reached the age of 16 and a direction that payments under it shall be made to someone other than the mother. Changes in the financial circumstances of either the mother or the putative father may well, of course, lead either of them to ask for the amount payable to be increased or decreased.

The death of the child automatically discharges the order[11] as does the death of the putative father, whose liability upon it is purely personal.[12] The order will also be discharged if the child is adopted unless the adopter is his mother and she is a "single woman".[13] On the other hand, as we have already seen, the order is not discharged by the mother's death; nor does liability upon it cease if she subsequently marries[14] or resumes cohabitation with her husband[15] although the fact that the latter is quite capable of supporting the child might well be relevant if the putative father applied for a variation of the order. Just as the mother cannot deprive herself of the power to apply for an order by entering into an agreement with the putative father,[16] an existing order will not be discharged by any agreement between them.[17]

Enforcement of Affiliation Orders.—The methods by which affiliation orders may be enforced have already been discussed when dealing with maintenance orders made under the Matrimonial Proceedings (Magistrates' Courts) Act which are enforceable in the

---

[8]Children and Young Persons Act 1933, s. 88; Children Act 1948, s. 23; Criminal Justice Act 1961, Sched. 5; Children and Young Persons Act 1969, Scheds. 5 and 6.
[9]Affiliation Proceedings Act 1957, s. 7 (4), (5), (6). The parents of a legitimate child are not required to contribute to his maintenance in such circumstances after he has reached the age of 16: see *ante*, p. 298.
[10]Magistrates' Courts Act 1952, s. 53. But the Act refers only to "periodical payment of money", so that there is no power to revoke, revive or vary the order in so far as it relates to the adjudication of paternity: *Colchester* v. *Peck*, [1926] 2 K.B. 366; *R.* v. *Copestake*, [1927] 1 K.B. 468, C.A. There is no power to make a variation on the application of either party if the other is out of the jurisdiction, but in such circumstances magistrates may effectively vary the order in the putative father's favour by remitting arrears on proceedings for enforcement: *R.* v. *Gravesend Justices, Ex parte Doodney*, [1971] 2 All E.R. 364.
[11]Affiliation Proceedings Act 1957, s. 6.
[12]*Re Harrington*, [1908] 2 Ch. 687.
[13]Adoption Act 1958, s. 15 (1).
[14]But if she marries the father, the legitimation of the child may be a ground for applying for the order to be discharged.
[15]*Hardy* v. *Atherton* (1881), 7 Q.B.D. 264; *R.* v. *Pilkington* (1853), 2 E. & B. 546.
[16]See *post*, p. 488.
[17]*Griffith* v. *Evans* (1882), 46 L.T. 417.

same way.[18] As in the case of other orders, magistrates hearing proceedings for enforcement may remit the whole or any part of the arrears. An affiliation order may also be registered and enforced in the High Court.[19]

Recent research into the whole question of affiliation orders fills one with grave disquiet. Comparatively few orders are made, they are usually for small sums, and they tend to lapse after a few years.[20] Many of the problems are personal and social, for example the mother's reluctance to invoke the law, the poverty of many fathers (who will often be young men earning very little), and the tendency of the parties to lose touch with each other. In some cases, however, it is the procedure which needs to be revised. There is a great deal of proper public concern about the use and availability of information collected by official bodies, but one feels that the Department of Health and Social Security could probably do much more in helping mothers to trace the whereabouts of fathers who have disappeared.

5. ILLEGITIMATE CHILDREN: OTHER FINANCIAL PROVISIONS

Family Allowances.—For the purposes of the Family Allowances Act an illegitimate child is regarded as the issue of the mother only.[1]

Supplementary Benefits.—Under the Ministry of Social Security Act 1966, the mother of an illegitimate child and a man adjudged to be its putative father are liable to maintain it until it reaches the age of 16.[2] If the Supplementary Benefits Commission gives assistance by reference to the requirements of an illegitimate child, it may recover the cost from the mother in the same way as it could in the case of a legitimate child; if (as will be more likely) it wishes to recover the cost from the putative father, it must apply to have the affiliation order varied so that the sums under it are made payable direct to the Commission. If no affiliation order is already in existence,[3] the Commission may itself apply for one within three years of giving assistance. This power is quite independent of the mother's, so that the Commission may obtain an order even though the mother could not apply because her application would be out of time or she was not a " single woman ", and even though Quarter Sessions have already dismissed an appeal by her on its merits; but all the provisions of the Affiliation Proceedings Act relating to evidence must be complied with, as in the

---

[18]See *ante*, pp. 422-426 For the power to deduct sums due under an affiliation order from the pay of a serving member of the armed forces, see *ante*, p. 407.

[19]Maintenance Orders Act 1958, s. 21. See *ante*, pp. 455-457.

[20]See McGregor, *The Social Effects of the Exercise of the Matrimonial Jurisdiction of Magistrates*, 118 New L.J. 41.

[1]Family Allowances Act 1965, s. 17 (5). For family allowances, see *ante*, pp. 470-472.

[2]S. 22 (1).

[3]*I.e.*, no order requiring payments to be made to the mother. An order adjudging the defendant to be the putative father *simpliciter* does not prevent the Commission from applying: *Oldfield* v. *National Assistance Board*, [1960] 1 All E.R. 524; [1960] 1 Q.B. 635.

case where a local authority applies for an order under the power given to it by the Children Act 1948.[4]

An order in favour of the Commission may be varied in favour of the mother.[5] It will thus be seen that the mother of an illegitimate child who is out of time to apply for an order herself may nevertheless obtain the benefit of one if she receives a supplementary benefit and the Commission takes proceedings against the father.

Maintenance Agreements.—As early as 1842 it was recognised that an agreement between the mother and father of an illegitimate child that the latter should pay the former maintenance for the child was actionable.[6]   The consideration for the father's promise has been variously stated: it is usually recognised as a counter-promise on the mother's part either to maintain the child herself (notwithstanding her liability to do so under the Ministry of Social Security Act)[7] or to refrain from taking affiliation proceedings.[8] If there is no agreement as to the time for which the father is to remain bound, it would seem that either side may terminate the contract by giving the other reasonable notice.[9] The father's liability will automatically terminate on the mother's death unless the parties otherwise agree, for her personal representatives cannot claim the benefit of the agreement without at the same time accepting the burden of maintaining the child—an obligation which will not normally have been contemplated.[10] On the other hand, since the father's obligation is not personal but can be met out of his estate, there seems to be no reason why his personal representatives should not be bound.[11]

In one respect agreements of this type seem singular, for it was held in *Follitt* v. *Koetzow*[12] that although the mother may sue the father on his promise to pay her maintenance made in consideration of her counter-promise not to take affiliation proceedings, this does not prevent her from commencing proceedings to obtain an affiliation order. Like the power to award maintenance in a matrimonial cause, the power to order the putative father to pay maintenance under an affiliation order is not given for the benefit of the mother alone and consequently she cannot by agreement deprive herself of the right to apply for it. Unlike agreements made in consideration of the wife's undertaking not

---

[4]Ministry of Social Security Act 1966, s. 24;   Affiliation Proceedings Act 1957, s. 5; *National Assistance Board* v. *Mitchell,* [1955] 3 All E.R. 291; [1956] 1 Q.B. 53; *National Assistance Board* v. *Tugby,* [1957] 1 All E.R. 509; [1957] 1 Q.B. 506; *Clapham* v. *National Assistance Board,* [1961] 2 All E.R. 50; [1961] 2 Q.B. 77.   For local authorities' powers under the Children Act see *ante,* p. 485.

[5]Ministry of Social Security Act 1966, s. 24 (6); *Payne* v. *Critchley,* [1962] 1 All E.R. 619; [1962] 2 Q.B. 83.

[6]*Jennings* v. *Brown* (1842), 9 M. & W. 496.

[7]*Ward* v. *Byham,* [1956] 2 All E.R. 318, C.A. Whilst this decision is in accordance with the merits of the case, it can be criticised on the ground that DENNING, L.J., held that the performance of an existing obligation can be valuable consideration (contrary to earlier authorities) and MORRIS and PARKER, L.JJ., did not discuss this point at all.

[8]*Jennings* v. *Brown, (supra); Linnegar* v. *Hodd* (1848), 5 C.B. 437.

[9]*Knowlman* v. *Bluett* (1873), L.R. 9 Exch. 1, Ex.; *ibid.,* 307, Ex. Ch.

[10]*James* v. *Morgan,* [1909] 1 K.B. 564.

[11]This was apparently accepted in *Jennings* v. *Brown, (supra).* In each case, of course, it will be a question of the construction of the particular contract. For the effect of an adoption order on the agreement, see *ante,* p. 260.

[12](1860), 2 E. & E. 730.

to apply for maintenance in a matrimonial cause, however, these agreements are valid in so far as the mother may sue the father upon them: they therefore present what is probably a unique example of a promise which is valid for one purpose but contrary to public policy for another. But if the mother takes affiliation proceedings, this will obviously entitle the father to treat himself as discharged on his promise to pay maintenance and he could also presumably sue the mother for damages for breach of the contract. Moreover, the existence of the agreement is one of the factors which the court should take into consideration in determining the amount of maintenance to award.[13]

---

[13]*Follitt* v. *Koetzow, (supra)*.

CHAPTER 17

Property and Financial Provision on the Death of a Member of the Family

A. TESTATE SUCCESSION

The law relating to wills and testate succession generally presents few problems peculiar to family law. Until the beginning of this century the most important question was the testamentary capacity of a married woman. At common law she had virtually no power to make a will at all,[1] although she could always devise and bequeath property held to her separate use in equity even if it were subject to a restraint upon anticipation.[2] When the equitable concept of separate property was extended to legal separate property by the Married Women's Property Act 1882, her power to dispose of it by will was likewise extended, so that her testamentary incapacity remained only with respect to property acquired by her during coverture before 1883. Now by the Law Reform (Married Women and Tortfeasors) Act 1935 she has full power to dispose of all her property as if she were a feme sole.

Today the most important aspect of family law with respect to testate succession is family provision, which, together with the transmission of statutory tenancies under the Rent Act, will be considered separately.[3] One or two other matters, however, should be noted.

Revocation of Wills by Marriage.—By section 18 of the Wills Act 1837 every will made by a man or woman is revoked by his or her marriage.[4] This clearly will not apply if the marriage is void;[5]

---

[1]She had no power at all to dispose of realty and leaseholds, although she could exercise a power of appointment by will. With the consent of her husband copyholds could be surrendered to the use of her will. Although all her choses in possession vested in her husband, she could bequeath personalty if there were an ante-nuptial contract to that effect or if her husband assented to the bequest and did not revoke his consent before probate was granted. For further details, reference must be made to the editions of standard works on property, wills and married women published in the late nineteenth and early twentieth centuries.

[2]But until the passing of the Married Women's Property Act 1893, s. 3, a will made by a woman during coverture would not pass property acquired after the marriage was terminated unless it was republished after the termination of coverture.

[3]*Infra*, secs. C and D.

[4]But this will not be a breach of an ante-nuptial contract not to revoke a will already made: *Re Marsland*, [1939] 3 All E.R. 148, C.A.; [1939] Ch. 820. A decree of divorce or nullity does not affect a will made during the marriage; this may obviously work an injustice and consequently the Morton Commission recommended that in such a case a gift to, or appointment in favour of, a former spouse should lapse unless the testator expressly directs to the contrary (1956, Cmd. 9678, paras. 1187-1191).

[5]*Mette* v. *Mette* (1859), 1 Sw. & Tr. 416.

whether it applies if the marriage is voidable and is subsequently annulled must depend upon how far a decree of nullity is retroactive.[6] It has been held that this section applies only to persons domiciled in England at the time of the marriage. Hence, if by the testator's *lex domicilii* his will was not revoked by his marriage, it will not be revoked if he acquires an English domicile after the celebration of the marriage;[7] but if a woman domiciled in such a country marries a man domiciled in England, her will will be revoked because she will automatically acquire an English domicile herself.[8]

There are two exceptions to this rule. First, section 18 itself provides that a will shall not be revoked insofar as it is made in exercise of a power of appointment if the property thereby appointed would not pass in default of appointment to the testator's heir, executor, administrator or statutory next-of-kin.[9] The reason for this exception is obvious: the marriage cannot conceivably affect the devolution of the property appointed. Secondly, in order to fulfil the intention of the testator who makes his will on the eve of his wedding, section 177 of the Law of Property Act 1925 now provides that " a will expressed to be made in contemplation of a marriage shall . . . not be revoked by the solemnisation of themarriage contemplated ". In order to bring this section into operation t wo conditions must be satisfied: the testator must express the fact that he is contemplating marriage with a particular person and the ensuing marriage must be to that person. The section has been liberally construed: in *In the Estate of Langston*,[10] for example, it was held that a will by which the testator devised and bequeathed his whole estate " unto my fiancée M.E.B." was not revoked by his marriage to that lady two months later. But the mere fact that the will is expressed to be made in contemplation of marriage will not save it unless there is a reference to the particular marriage by which it is followed.[11]

Mutual Wills.—Although mutual wills are rare, they are still occasionally made, and they are of particular interest in family law since mutual testators are almost invariably husband and wife. They usually take the form of a gift to the second testator provided that he survives the first with identical remainders over on the death of the survivor; alternatively (and this will have the same effect) each gives an absolute interest to the other with identical provisions in case the

[6]See *ante*, pp. 69-71.
[7]*In the Goods of Reid* (1866), L.R. 1 P. & D. 74; *In the Estate of Groos*, [1904] P. 269.
[8]*Re Martin*, [1900] P. 211, C.A. Conversely it has been held in Scotland (where marriage does not automatically revoke a will) that the will of a woman domiciled in England is not revoked by her marrying a domiciled Scotsman: *Westerman's Executor v. Schwab* (1905), 8 F. (Ct. of Sess.) 132.
[9]Hence the will may be revoked in part but not insofar as the power is exercised: *In the Goods of Russell* (1890), 15 P.D. 111. See also *In the Goods of Gilligan*, [1949] 2 All E.R. 401; [1950] P. 32; Mitchell, *The Revocation of Testamentary Appointments on Marriage*, 67 L.Q.R. 351.
[10][1953] 1 All E.R. 928; [1953] P. 100.
[11]*Sallis* v. *Jones*, [1936] P. 43. In *Pilot* v. *Gainfort*, [1931] P. 103, the testator made a will by which he bequeathed his personalty to " D.F.P. my wife ". Although he was living with her at the time, he did not marry her until 18 months later. It was held that the will was made in contemplation of this marriage and was therefore not revoked. *Sed quaere?* On the face of the will it appeared that the testator was *already* married.

beneficiary predeceases the testator.[12]   The peculiarity of mutual
wills is that, provided certain conditions are satisfied, the survivor is
bound by the provisions of his or her own will after the death of the
other testator and cannot revoke it—the property of both, in other
words, becomes subject to a trust in favour of the remaindermen.

The trust arises out of the agreement between the testators. Hence,
in the first place it must be affirmatively proved that the wills were made
in pursuance of an agreement: whilst their very execution is some
evidence of an agreement to that effect, it is by no means conclusive.[13]
Secondly, it is clear that the trust does not take effect until one of the
two testators dies, and if either revokes his or her will before then, the
other is not bound and is free to make any other disposition before or
after the death of the first. But what is not clear is whether the party
revoking is bound to give notice of this to the other. The basis of the
doctrine is that the survivor, having let the other die in the belief that
he will not go back on the bargain, will not be permitted to do so after
the will of the first takes effect. Now let us suppose that A and B are
the testators and that A secretly revokes his will before B's death. If
A dies first, B is bound to know of the revocation and may make a
fresh will: hence the mutual wills create no trust.[14] But if B dies first
unaware of the revocation, it seems contrary to the whole basis of the
rule to permit A to take the benefits under B's will without at the same
time being bound by the bargain.[15]

Thirdly, it is still not clear whether the survivor is bound by the
agreement if he disclaims the gift to himself. The dicta are conflicting,[16] but since the trust arises from the prior agreement, the better
view is that it is automatically impressed on the property on the first
party's death and the survivor's accepting the gift is therefore
immaterial.[17]

If these conditions are satisfied, the trust takes effect from the
moment the first testator dies.[18] Consequently the remaindermen have
a vested interest from this time, and the gifts to them will not lapse if
they die after this date but before the surviving testator.[19] But even
now it is not settled whether any property acquired by the survivor
after the first party's death is also subject to the trust or whether this
will attach only to the property which he has at that time.[20]   Since

---

[12]But since the apparent intention to make an absolute gift is inconsistent with
the life interest that will result, it will probably be easier to rebut the presumption of
a trust in such a case: see *Re Oldham*, [1925] Ch. 75, 88.

[13]*Re Oldham*, *(supra)*; *Gray* v. *Perpetual Trustee Co. Ltd.*, [1928] A.C. 391, P.C.

[14]*Stone* v. *Hoskins*, [1905] P. 194.

[15]See LORD CAMDEN, L.C., in *Dufour* v. *Pereira* (1769), 1 Dick. 419, 420-421;
2 Hargr. Jurid. Arg. 304.

[16]See the different interpretations placed on LORD CAMDEN's judgment in *Dufour*
v. *Pereira*, *(supra)*, by LORD HAILSHAM, L.C., in *Gray* v. *Perpetual Trustee Co., Ltd.*,
(supra), at p. 399, and by CLAUSON, J., in *Re Hagger*, [1930] 2 Ch. 190, 195. See Mitchell,
Some Aspects of Mutual Wills, 14 M.L.R. 136.

[17]If this were not so and the survivor were the widow or widower of the other, he
or she might disclaim the legacy and take the estate on intestacy, thus obtaining the
benefit whilst going back on the agreement: Mitchell, *loc. cit.* See also Burgess, *A Fresh
Look at Mutual Wills*, 34 Conv. 230, at p. 240.

[18]*Re Hagger*, *(supra)*; *Re Green*, [1950] 2 All E.R. 913; [1951] Ch. 148.

[19]*Re Hagger*, *(supra)*.

[20]See Mitchell, *loc. cit.*, for a fuller discussion of this and other difficulties

the beneficiaries may not know that the wills were mutual until the death of the surviving testator, not the least of the practical difficulties is to see how he can effectively be prevented from disposing of the trust property *inter vivos*.[1]

Gifts to the Testator's Wife or Husband.—Provided that this was obviously the testator's intention, a gift to the testator's wife (or husband) will take effect in favour of a woman (or man) with whom he (or she) is living as husband and wife even though they are not legally married.[2] Such a gift will even be valid if it is directed to be held on trust during widowhood; in this case it will be construed as being determinable upon the other's contracting a valid marriage after the testator's death.[3]

It will be observed that, unlike the position on intestacy,[4] the surviving spouse cannot demand that the matrimonial home or personal chattels should be appropriated as part of a gift (for example, a residuary bequest). If they have not been specifically disposed of by the will, the only thing a widow or widower wishing to retain such property can do is to ask the personal representatives to exercise their power of appropriation in this way.[5]

Gifts to Children.—The only problem that arises here is over the power of illegitimate, legitimated and adopted children to take under a testamentary disposition. This has already been discussed.[6]

Testamentary Gift to a Deceased Child.—In the normal way if a devisee or legatee predeceases the testator, the gift lapses and either it drops into residue or the testator is deemed to die intestate with respect to it. But by section 33 of the Wills Act 1837, if the beneficiary is a child or other issue of the testator, the gift does not lapse but takes effect as if the beneficiary had died immediately after the testator, provided that the interest is not determinable at or before the beneficiary's death and provided also that the beneficiary leaves issue living at the testator's death.[7] Just as the testator may prevent the usual rule from operating, a gift to issue will not be preserved if a contrary intention appears in the will.

It is not essential that the issue surviving the testator should be

---

[1]Mitchell, *loc. cit.*
[2]*Re Brown* (1910), 26 T.L.R. 257. *A fortiori* if he names her (*e.g.*, " to my wife E.A.S."): *Re Smalley*, [1929] 2 Ch. 112, C.A.
[3]Even though the " wife " is already married to another man: *Re Wagstaff*, [1908] 1 Ch. 162, C.A.; *Re Hammond*, [1911] 2 Ch. 342. Contrast *Re Boddington* (1884), 25 Ch.D. 685, C.A., where it was held that a wife who had obtained a decree of nullity after the will was made but before the testator's death was not entitled to an annuity payable during widowhood. Neither can a divorced husband or wife be regarded as a *surviving* spouse: *Re Allan*, [1954] 1 All E.R. 646, C.A.; [1954] Ch. 295. See Theobald, *Wills*, 12th Ed., 255-258.
[4]See *post*, p. 504.
[5]For the personal representatives' powers-of appropriation, see the Administration of Estates Act 1925, s. 41.
[6]*Ante*, pp. 462-469.
[7]The section operates even though the beneficiary had died before the will was made: *Wisden* v. *Wisden* (1854), 2 Sm. & G. 396. It always applied if the beneficiary was legitimated: *Re Brodie*, [1967] 2 All E.R. 97; [1967] Ch. 818. If the testator died on or after 1st January, 1970, it will apply if the beneficiary or his issue was illegitimate or legitimated or is descended through such a person: Family Law Reform Act 1969, s. 16.

alive when the devisee or legatee died. Thus, suppose that A by his will made in 1960 bequeathed property to his son, B, and that B died in 1963 leaving a son, C, who in turn had a son, D, born in 1966. If C died in 1968 and A died in 1971, the legacy would not lapse, because D, who is issue of B, would be living on A's death even though he was not born till after B's death.[8] But it has been doubted whether a child *en ventre sa mere* is " issue living " for this purpose,[9] although it is submitted that it would be more in keeping with the spirit of the Act to include them in this class.

But this rule does not apply to class gifts, for it is always presumed that the testator intends the benefit to be taken by those members of the class alive at his death. Hence if the testator has three children, X, Y and Z when he makes his will and X predeceases him, a gift to the testator's children in general terms will pass the whole interest to Y and Z even though X leaves issue.[10] Further, although the testamentary exercise of a *general* power of appointment in favour of a child or other issue will not lapse if the person in whose favour the donee has exercised it predeceases him, the provision does not apply to the exercise of a *special* power which is not technically a devise or bequest for the purpose of the section and which will therefore lapse.[11]

Whilst it might appear that the purpose of the section is to enable the gift to be taken by the issue instead of the beneficiary named in accordance with the testator's presumed wish, this in fact is not so, and the gift forms a part of the deceased beneficiary's estate. Hence if the latter died an undischarged bankrupt, the gift passes directly to his trustee in bankruptcy.[12] Furthermore, all the modern cases (admittedly all at first instance) have followed the rule that the fiction that the child or other issue survives the testator is to be applied solely for the purpose of preventing the lapse and that for all other purposes the property must be dealt with on the assumption that the beneficiary in fact died when he did.[13] Hence a gift to the testator's daughter, who had covenanted to settle all property acquired during coverture and who predeceased the testator, was not caught by the covenant for it did not form a part of the daughter's estate until the coverture had been terminated by her death.[14] Again in *Re Basioli*,[15] where the

---

[8] *In the Goods of Parker* (1860), 1 Sw. & Tr. 523.

[9] In *Re Griffiths' Settlement*, [1911] 1 Ch. 246, JOYCE, J., held that such a child was " issue living ", but this was doubted by LORD TOMKIN and LORD RUSSELL in *Elliot* v. *Joicey*, [1935] A.C. 209, H.L., at pp. 216, 230.

[10] Even though in the event the class consists of only one member: *Re Harvey's Estate*, [1893] 1 Ch. 567. *Secus* if the gift had been to the children *by name* as tenants in common.

[11] *Eccles* v. *Cheyne* (1856), 2 K. & J. 676 (general power); *Holyland* v. *Lewin* (1883), 26 Ch.D. 266, C.A. (special power).

[12] *Re Pearson*, [1920] 1 Ch. 247.

[13] Some of the cases are discussed by UPJOHN, J., in *Re Basioli*, [1953] 1 All E.R. 301; [1953] Ch. 367. In *Re Mason's Will* (1865), 34 Beav. 494, it was questioned whether this was the right construction; *Re Hone's Trusts* (1883), 22 Ch.D. 663, is clearly inconsistent with the rule as stated in the text.

[14] *Pearce* v. *Graham* (1863), 32 L.J.Ch. 359. *Cf. Re Wolson*, [1939] 3 All E.R. 852; [1939] Ch. 780.

[15] [1953] 1 All E.R. 301; [1953] Ch. 367, following *Re Hurd*, [1941] 1 All E.R. 238; [1941] Ch. 196. A curious case of circuity arose in *Re Hensler* (1881), 19 Ch.D. 612, where a father devised realty to his son who predeceased him having devised all his realty to his father. HALL, V.C., held that the son's son took as the *son's* heir; *quaere* whether he should not have taken as the *father's* heir: see *Re Basioli*, at pp. 304 and 375-376, respectively.

testatrix's daughter died intestate in 1929 and the testatrix died in 1940, it was held that a devise and bequest to the daughter must be distributed on the assumption that she died in 1929 and not in 1940.

The Rule against Double Portions.—This rule is a direct application of the equitable presumption that a father or other person *in loco parentis* intends to favour none of his children at the expense of the others and in particular intends to divide his estate or fortune amongst them all equally. They may obviously take a share of this in two ways: by payments made to the child by the parent during the latter's lifetime, and by a gift to the child in the parent's will.[16] Consequently in certain circumstances, unless the presumption that all the children were to share alike can be rebutted, they must bring into account what they have received during the testator's lifetime before they can take the gift under the will. Hence equity is said " to lean against double portions ".

But it is not every gift that the child received from the testator while he was alive that must be brought into account. Like the presumption of advancement, this rule applies only to gifts and payments made by his father or other person *in loco parentis* to him.[17] Further, it would clearly be impractical to make the beneficiary account for every penny received, and consequently he must bring in only such gifts as may fairly be called advancements by way of portion, that is, something given to the child to establish him in life. Whether or not this is the purpose of any particular payment must be a question of fact in each case: payments made to a child on his marriage always come into this category, and the gift of a substantial sum raises a presumption that it was intended as an advance by way of portion.[18] On the other hand, a mere bounty is not a portion,[19] nor is a payment made to extricate a child from financial embarrassment;[20] and a gift will not *prima facie* amount to an advancement by way of portion unless it is made early in life.[1] An instructive case is *Taylor* v. *Taylor*.[2] A father had two sons, A and B. A originally intended to go to the Bar and his father paid (1) his fees to enter the Middle Temple and (2) his fees to enter the chambers of a special pleader. Later A joined the army and the father then paid for (3) his commission, (4) his uniform, and (5) his outfit and his wife's passage when his regiment went to India. Whilst he was there, he became financially embarrassed and his father paid (6) his debts to the tune of £650. Finally A decided to go into mining in Wales and the father gave him (7) £850 to buy plant and materials. B on the other hand went into the

---

[16]Or, of course, by the child's taking a benefit on the latter's intestacy: see *post*, p. 506.

[17]For the meaning of " person *in loco parentis* ", see *ante*, p. 459.

[18]*Re Hayward*, [1957] 2 All E.R. 474, C.A.; [1957] Ch. 528.

[19]*Re Livesey*, [1953] 2 All E.R. 723; *Re Vaux*, [1938] 4 All E.R. 703, 709, C.A.; [1939] Ch. 465, 481.

[20]*Taylor* v. *Taylor* (1875), L.R. 20 Eq. 155; *Re Scott*, [1903] 1 Ch. 1, C.A.

[1]*Re Hayward*, (*supra*), at pp. 479 and 538, respectively.

[2](1875), L.R. 20 Eq. 155. This case reminds one of the parable of the prodigal son who, it will be recalled, asked his father " for his portion ". See also *Re George's Will Trusts*, [1948] 2 All E.R. 1004; [1949] Ch. 154 (*post*, p. 499) (gift of live and dead stock with which son was to set up as a farmer held to be a portion).

Church and the father made several payments to him (on one occasion of £200) to assist him in his housekeeping. Of these sums it was held that (1), (3), (4) and (7) were all obviously portions. It was held that (2) was not as it " appeared to be rather in the nature of a payment for preliminary education ", although it is submitted that a court today might hold otherwise.[3]   (5) was not a portion as it clearly did nothing to set A up in any sort of career, nor was (6) as this was a payment made to extricate the son from financial embarrassment. Similarly the payments made to B were not portions, as they came into the category of casual payments intended as temporary assistance.

For brevity, an enforceable obligation to make an advancement by way of portion is known as a " portion debt ". Thus, if a father on his daughter's marriage settles £5,000 on her, this will be a portion; if in consideration of her marriage he covenants to do so, his covenant will be a portion debt.

It will be seen that the rule against double portions may arise in three different situations.

(1) *Satisfaction of Portion Debts by Portions.*—This can be illustrated by *Re Lawes*.[4]   The putative father of an illegitimate youth executed a bond whereby he bound himself to pay his son £10,000 on a certain day.   A month before this day he took his son into partnership and brought in capital of £37,500, of which £19,000 was to be considered as belonging to the son.   The £10,000 was never paid and when the son sought to claim it from the father's personal representatives after the father's death, it was held that the debt had been satisfied by the gift of the capital.

But the debt and the gift must be *ejusdem generis* if the latter is to satisfy the former.   In *Re Lawes* all the members of the Court of Appeal were agreed that the father had in effect given his son a gift of the sum of £19,000; but had he given him a share of the partnership property without putting a value on it or, say, given him a gift of land without specifying its value, it seems clear that this would have been essentially different from the sum of £10,000 which the father was bound to pay and therefore would not have satisfied the debt.[5]

It will be seen that the child is not bound to take the gift: it is his voluntarily doing so that extinguishes the contractual obligation.   If the portion is of the same value as the debt or of greater value, the latter will be satisfied entirely.   If it is of less value, it will presumably be satisfied *pro tanto*.[6]

---

[3] If payment for preliminary education is not to be regarded as advancement by way of portion, some anomalous results follow.   Why should a son who becomes a barrister have to bring into account money payable before and on call, whilst another, who receives a professional training at a university, may not have to do so?   If on the other hand money received for educational purposes is a portion, further anomalies arise.   If the student lived away from home and were given, say, £1,000 to see him through the university, he would presumably have to bring it in; but if he lived at home and received pocket money from time to time, he would not have to do so.

[4] (1881), 20 Ch.D. 81, C.A.

[5] See *Re Lawes*, at pp. 87-89, and *Re Jaques*, [1903] 1 Ch. 267, C.A.

[6] By analogy with satisfaction by a legacy and ademption (*infra*).   But see *Re Lawes*, at pp. 84, 89.

(2) *Satisfaction of Portion Debts by Legacies.*—Let us suppose that a father, in consideration of his daughter's marriage, covenants to pay her the sum of £5,000. He later makes a will by which he gives her and her brother a legacy of £5,000 each. The rule against double portions comes into play and *prima facie* she is entitled to only one sum of £5,000. She is immediately put to her election. She may decline to take the legacy, in which case she gets only the £5,000 on the covenant; but if she wishes to take the legacy, she may do so only on condition that she will not enforce the covenant. The legacy in short satisfies the portion debt.

Since the father is no longer alive to make the satisfaction of the debt an express condition of the receipt of the gift, satisfaction by a legacy will be more easily presumed than satisfaction by a subsequent portion. It is obvious that the contracting of the debt must precede the *making* of the will or codicil by which the legacy is given, for it is presumed to be the testator's intention at the time he makes the will that the legatee shall take the gift in place of the debt, and he cannot intend the satisfaction of a debt which is not yet in existence. If the legacy is of less value than the debt, it can satisfy it *pro tanto*,[7] and the gift of the residue of the testator's estate (or a part of the residue) may on valuation have the same effect.[8]

But there must be a substantial similarity between the terms of the contract and the provisions of the legacy. A slight difference between the two will not prevent the presumption from arising, but a marked difference will do so. How thin the line between these may be can be shown by contrasting two decisions of the House of Lords in the nineteenth century. In the first, *Thynne* v. *Glengall*,[9] the testator, on his daughter's marriage, agreed to give her a portion of £100,000. He transferred stock of a third of this value to the four trustees of the settlement and gave them a bond for the transfer of the balance on his death. The stock was to be held on trust for the daughter's separate use for her life, with remainder to such of the children of the marriage as she and her husband should jointly appoint or as the survivor of them should appoint, and in default of appointment in trust for the child or children of the marriage. By his will, which was made after he had entered into this covenant, the father devised and bequeathed the whole of his residue to two of these trustees on trust for sale and investment and as to one half of it to hold it on trust for the daughter for life for her separate use, with remainder to such of her children as *she* should appoint, and in default of appointment in trust for *all* her children in equal shares. The residue was worth about £185,000, and it was held that she was not entitled first to claim the £66,000 odd that was still owed to her on the covenant and then, having depleted the residue by this amount, to claim half the balance, but that she must take her half of the £185,000 as satisfaction of the portion debt.

In the second case, *Chichester* v. *Coventry*,[10] the father on his

---

[7]*Thynne* v. *Glengall* (1848), 2 H.L. Cas. 131, 154, H.L.; *Chichester* v. *Coventry* (1867), L.R. 2 H.L. 71, 95, H.L.

[8]*Thynne* v. *Glengall*, (*supra*).   [9](1848), 2 H.L. Cas. 131, H.L.

[10](1867), L.R. 2 H.L. 71, H.L.   See also *Re Tussaud's Estate* (1878), 9 Ch.D. 363, C.A.

T

daughter's marriage covenanted to pay to trustees £10,000 within three
months of their demanding it, and in the meantime to pay 3% interest
on this sum together with £1,700 a year to make up £2,000 a year. The
income and capital (when assigned) were to be held on trust to pay £200
a year to the daughter for her life and to pay the residue to the husband
for life. After the death of either, the trustees were to hold the fund on
trust for the survivor for life, with remainder on certain trusts for their
children, and in default of children for the wife absolutely or, if she
predeceased the husband, for such persons as she should by will appoint
and in default of appointment on trust for her next-of-kin. By his will
made 15 years later, the father gave certain specific devises and
bequests to his two daughters (who were his only children) and then
directed that his residue should be divided into two equal shares each
of which was to be held on trust for one of the daughters for her life,
with remainder to such *persons* as she should appoint, and in default
of appointment in trust for his nephew, C. He expressly directed that
no part of his estate should go to his daughters' husbands, and that, if
this should happen either by construction or by operation of law, the
interest should immediately go over to C. It was held that this gift
did not satisfy the covenant (which was still unfulfilled on the father's
death) and that the daughter could consequently claim first her £10,000
and then half the reduced residue.

It will be seen that the difference between the two limitations was
much more marked in *Chichester* v. *Coventry* than in *Thynne* v. *Glengall*.
In the latter case the chief difference was that under the testamentary
disposition the husband was given no power of appointment and the
objects of the power and the ultimate beneficiaries in default of appointment were all the daughter's children and not merely those of that
particular marriage. In *Chichester* v. *Coventry* not only were the ultimate remainders completely different, but the husband, who was given
a life interest under the settlement, was expressly excluded from taking
any interest under the residuary gift. Furthermore (although this alone
would hardly be enough to rebut the presumption against double
portions) the testator in *Chichester* v. *Coventry* had expressly directed
that all his debts should be paid and the portion debt was apparently
the only debt that he had. No general rules can be laid down to determine whether or not there is a sufficient difference to prevent the
presumption from arising: the trial judge must exercise his own
discretion in the matter[11] and his task is clearly not an easy one.

Just as there can be satisfaction *pro tanto* if the debt is greater than
the legacy, there may be satisfaction of some interests and not others
if the beneficiaries under the covenant are different from those under
the will. The fact that the latter do not include all the former is
strong evidence that there is no intention of satisfaction anyway;[12]
but assuming that the court is satisfied that a question of satisfaction
is raised, a covenant to settle property on a daughter for life with

[11]*Chichester* v. *Coventry*, (*supra*), at p. 83.
[12]*Re Tussaud's Estate*, (*ante*), at p. 380. In *Chichester* v. *Coventry* LORD ROMILLY
denied that there could ever be a case of satisfaction when the parties were not the
same (at p. 91).

remainder to her children, followed by a legacy to the daughter absolutely, can be satisfied only with respect to the daughter's life interest.
She alone therefore is put to her election; her children may claim only
under the covenant and have no interest in the legacy.[13]

(3) *Ademption of Legacies by Portions and Portion Debts.*—Ademption
in a sense is the converse of satisfaction, for here the making of the will
precedes the giving of the portion or the creation of the portion debt.
Thus if a father executes a will in which he gives a legacy of £2,000 to
his son and then he gives him £3,000 to set him up in business, he will
once more be presumed to have intended that the son should not take
both sums and therefore the legacy is *prima facie* adeemed by the
portion.

It will be seen that ademption differs from satisfaction in another
important respect. As we have already seen, a beneficiary can never
be compelled to take a gift or legacy; consequently in satisfaction he is
strictly put to his election and he can take the gift only on condition
that he does not enforce his debt. But the testator is always free to
vary and revoke the provisions of his will, so that if the presumption
is raised and not rebutted, it will adeem the legacy automatically: the
child may not claim it at all. The revocable nature of the will makes
it easier to infer an intention that a legacy should be adeemed than it
does to infer an intention that a legacy shall be taken in satisfaction
of a portion debt.[14]

Like satisfaction, there may be ademption *pro tanto*[15] or with
respect to only one beneficiary's interest.[16] It would also seem to apply
even though one or both of the gifts have been made in pursuance of
the exercise of a special power of appointment.[17] But the two gifts
must still be *ejusdem generis;* thus it has been held that a devise is not
adeemed by a portion,[18] nor in the usual way would a pecuniary
legacy probably be adeemed by a gift *in specie*. But if a value is put
on the gift, then, as in the case of satisfaction, the legacy may be
adeemed. In *Re George's Will Trusts*[19] a farmer devised and bequeathed his residuary estate on trust for sale and conversion as to
two-thirds for his son, Ernest, and as to the other third for his son,
Robert. Ernest, unlike Robert, was also a farmer and he had worked
two farms with his father for some years; consequently the testator
directed that Ernest might take his share of the residue *in specie*. A
few months later the County War Agricultural Committee threatened
to evict the father (who was already over 80 years of age) on account
of his inefficient farming, but they eventually withdrew their notice on

---

[13]See *Re Blundell*, [1906] 2 Ch. 222, and the observations of LORD ROMILLY on
Thynne v. *Glengall* in *Chichester* v. *Coventry*, at pp. 93-94. Similarly, beneficiaries who
acquire a derivative interest are not put to their election: *Re Blundell*.
[14]*Chichester* v. *Coventry*, (*ante*), at pp. 82, 87; *Re Tussaud's Estate*, (*ante*),
at p. 380.
[15]*Montefiore* v. *Guedalla* (1859), 1 De G. F. & J. 93.
[16]*Durham* v. *Wharton* (1836), 3 Cl. & F. 146, H.L., as explained in *Chichester* v.
Coventry, (*ante*).
[17]*Re Peel's Settlement*, [1911] 2 Ch. 165.
[18]*Davys* v. *Boucher* (1839), 3 Y. & C. (Ex.) 397. But *quaere* whether the *ratio
decidendi* is still good law.
[19][1948] 2 All E.R. 1004; [1949] Ch. 154.

his virtually handing over the farms to Ernest. Under this arrangement he assigned all his live and dead stock (valued at more than £2,000) to his son together with a share in the tenancy of one of the farms (of which he and Ernest were joint lessees). He also granted to him a lease of his other farm (of which the father was tenant in fee simple) at a rent of £172 *per annum* and made arrangements with his bank to secure adequate financial resources to enable Ernest to run the farms. At the time the father had an overdraft of £151, but, as a result of the son's successful management, within two years this had been converted into a credit balance of over £529. After the father's death the question arose whether Ernest's share of the residue had been adeemed (at any rate *pro tanto*) by this arrangement, and JENKINS, J., held that it was. Since the assignment of the farm amounted to a portion, it was immaterial that it had been carried out on pain of eviction; and the fact that Ernest received the half share of the tenancy in the first farm negatived any inference that this was no more than a business transaction that might be drawn from his taking a lease in the second farm. In view of the fact that under the will Ernest was to be permitted to take the stock *in specie*, the assignment and the testamentary gift were clearly *ejusdem generis*; but even had this not been so, JENKINS, J., would have been prepared to hold that the latter was adeemed because a value had been placed upon the stock at the time of the transfer.[20] Hence the value of the farm (*viz.* the value of the stock transferred less the £151 overdraft which had to be off-set) had to be brought into account in calculating the interest which the two sons took in the residue.

Although the presumption is more difficult to rebut in the case of ademption, it will nevertheless not apply where the circumstances obviously indicate that the testator had no intention that the legacy should be adeemed. Thus in *Re Vaux*[1] the testator gave his residue to trustees on trust to apply it for his children and the issue of his deceased children at their absolute discretion. He subsequently settled £10,000 on each of his four children. It was held by the Court of Appeal that he could not have intended that the trustees' discretion should be fettered by his own act in settling the property and therefore the rule against double portions could not apply. But as it will be seen from *Re George's Will Trusts*, the mere fact that the estate is to be divided in unequal shares does not of itself prevent the rule from being applied.

It need hardly be added that, if the portion is larger than the legacy, there is no question of the beneficiary's having to pay a part of this back. Thus suppose that a father has bequeathed his residue (valued at £10,000 on his death) to his two sons, A and B, in equal shares and that he later gives A a portion of £4,000. A must bring this sum into account, so that he will take £3,000 from the residue (giving him £7,000

---

[20] *Cf. Re Lawes, ante,* p. 496.

[1] [1938] 4 All E.R. 703, C.A.; [1939] Ch. 465. See also *Re Lacon,* [1891] 2 Ch. 482, C.A. In *Re Vaux* the Court of Appeal left open the question whether the rule against double portions could apply where there was a partial intestacy. SIMONDS, J., had held that it could in the court below ([1938] 2 All E.R. 177; [1938] Ch. 581); but as he was overruled on the main question in the Court of Appeal, this point did not have to be considered.

in all) and B will take £7,000 from the residue. If the father had given A a portion of £12,000, he would keep this and B would take all £10,000 of the residue. Moreover, the purpose of the rule is to secure equality between children and no other person may benefit from its operation. Let us suppose now that the testator has directed that his residue is to be divided equally among his two children, A and B, and his widow, W. He later gives a portion of £2,000 to A, and the residue is worth £12,000. W can take no more than a third of this, that is £4,000; in distributing the other £8,000 between A and B, account must now be taken of the £2,000 already received by A. Hence A takes £3,000 of this (which with his £2,000 will give him £5,000 in all) and B takes the other £5,000.[2]

Extrinsic Evidence to rebut the Presumption.—The rule that the testator did not intend any child to take a double portion is rebuttable by evidence *dehors* the will as well as by intrinsic evidence. But if the construction of the will and contract or gift does not give rise to a presumption of satisfaction or ademption, no extrinsic evidence may be led to raise the presumption.[3]

B. INTESTATE SUCCESSION

Intestate Succession before 1926.—Before the Administration of Estates Act 1925 came into force, there was a considerable difference between the descent of realty and the descent of personalty.

Succession to Realty.—All inheritable estates of freehold still descended to the heir at law subject to the husband's curtesy and the wife's dower.[4]

Succession to Personalty.—Until 1857 the granting of letters of administration with respect to personalty fell within the jurisdiction of the ecclesiastical courts. Although in the Middle Ages the Ordinary would try to ensure that the deceased's dependants were provided for out of the estate, the law became chaotic. It was put on a less confused and more rational footing by the three Statutes of Distributions passed in 1670, 1677 and 1685, the policy of which was to make provision for the deceased's dependants and to ensure that the property descended in much the same way as a thoughtful testator would have directed. We have already seen that on the death of a married woman her husband

---

[2] *Meinertzagen* v. *Walters* (1872), 7 Ch. App. 670. Any person claiming a deceased child's share must bring the advances to the child in as well, for they can obviously claim no more than the child: *Re Scott*, [1903] 1 Ch. 1, 9, C.A. (*per* VAUGHAN WILLIAMS, L.J.).

[3] See Snell, *Equity*, 26th Ed., 558-559. There is still some doubt what effect the execution of a codicil has. If a father gives a legacy to his son and then gives him a portion and subsequently republishes the will by executing a codicil, may the son take the legacy? The portion will *prima facie* have adeemed the original legacy, and there is authority for the proposition that a legacy once adeemed cannot be revived by a republication: *per* LORD COTTENHAM, L.C., in *Powys* v. *Mansfield* (1837), 3 My. & Cr. 359, 376; but if the testator republishes the will without *expressly* revoking the legacy, common sense dictates that he intends the son to take it in addition to his portion. See also *Re Scott*, (*supra*).

[4] See *ante*, pp. 347 and 348. See works on real property for a fuller discussion.

took all her personalty at common law.[5]   On the death of a married
man his widow took one third of his estate if there were issue of the
marriage alive; in other cases she took a half.   The remainder of the
estate was divided amongst the issue *per stirpes* or, in default of issue,
amongst the deceased's next-of-kin as defined in the Statutes.[6]

Married Women's Separate Property.—If a married woman predeceased her husband without having disposed of her separate property
inter vivos or by will, the whole interest vested in her husband as at
common law.   This rule still applied to statutory separate property after
the Married Women's Property Act 1882.

The Intestates' Estates Act 1890.—This Act was passed in order to
give an intestate's widow a larger provision than she had had under the
old law.   Under this Act if a person died wholly intestate leaving a
widow but no issue, she was in future to take the whole of the real and
personal estate if the total value did not exceed £500.   If the value
exceeded this sum, the estate was to stand charged with the payment
to her of £500.

The Administration of Estates Act 1925.—This Act radically
overhauled the law relating to intestate succession in two respects.
First, the law relating to realty and personalty has been put on exactly
the same footing; and secondly the distribution of estates has been
completely changed.   The principal effect of this Act has been to give
the surviving widow a much greater interest than she had before 1926
and to give the surviving widower the same rights as the surviving
widow.   The details of this have been modified by the Intestates'
Estates Act 1952 and the Family Provision Act 1966, which have given
the surviving spouse an even larger share of the estate and, as will be
seen, have made him or her in most cases the universal successor.[7]

It must be remembered that the general law of intestate succession
does not apply to entailed interests, which still descend according to
the old laws of intestate succession applicable to entailed realty.[8]   For
the rest, the whole of the intestate's estate vests in his personal representatives on trust for sale and conversion, and after the payment of
all expenses and debts they must then distribute it in the way about to
be described.[9]   It must also be borne in mind that the distribution
is liable to be upset by claims of dependants under the Inheritance
(Family Provision) Act (as amended) and under section 26 of the
Matrimonial Causes Act 1965.[10]

The Rights of the Surviving Spouse.—The surviving widow or
widower now takes the following interests.[11]

---

[5]*Ante*, p. 349.   [6]See, further, works on the law of personal property.
   [7]Ss. 46–49 of the Administration of Estates Act, as amended by the Intestates'
Estates Act, are now set out in the 1st Sched. to the latter Act.   References to these
sections " (as amended) " are to the sections as set out in that schedule.
   [8]The widower of a deceased female tenant in tail is still entitled to a life interest
by the curtesy, see *ante*, p. 354.
   [9]Administration of Estates Act 1925, s. 33.
   [10]See *post*, section C.   For criticisms of the present state of the law, see Stone, *The
Economic Aspects of Death in the Family*, 8 J.S.P.T.L. 188.
   [11]Administration of Estates Act 1925, s. 46 (as amended); Family Provision Act 1966,
s. 1.

Personal Chattels.—The surviving spouse is always entitled to the personal chattels (provided that the estate is solvent), and personal representatives may not sell them unless this is necessary to pay debts and expenses.[12] Personal chattels are defined as:[13]

> Carriages, horses, stable furniture and effects (not used for business purposes), motor cars and accessories (not used for business purposes), garden effects, domestic animals, plate, plated articles, linen, china, glass, books, pictures, prints, furniture, jewellery,[14] articles of household or personal use or ornament, musical and scientific instruments and apparatus, wines, liquors and consumable stores, but [they] do not include any chattels used at the death of the intestate for business purposes[15] nor money or securities for money.

Residuary Interests.—The interest which the surviving spouse takes over and above the personal chattels depends upon what other relatives the intestate leaves surviving.

If he leaves any children or remoter issue, the spouse takes £8,750 free of death duties and costs with interest at £4% *per annum* until it is paid and a *life* interest in half the residue.

If he leaves no issue but a parent or a brother or sister of the whole blood or issue of such a brother or sister, the surviving spouse takes £30,000 free of death duties and costs with interest at £4% *per annum* until it is paid and an *absolute* interest in half the residue.

If he leaves neither issue nor any of the above relations, the surviving spouse takes the whole of the residue absolutely.

In view of the large interest which the surviving spouse takes in the other's estate, the rule that, where it is uncertain which of two persons died first, the younger shall be deemed to have survived the elder does not apply as between a person dying intestate and his or her spouse.[16] Where there are no issue, it is obviously not desirable that the presumption should operate so as to put £30,000 or more at the disposal of a man's parents-in-law rather than at the disposal of his own parents.

Redemption of Life Interest.—The spouse may, if he wishes to do so, insist on the personal representatives' redeeming his life interest by paying the capital value to him.[17] He must elect to do so within 12 months after representation is taken out, but the court may extend this period if it considers that the limit will operate unfairly because a previous will was revoked or invalid, or because the interest of some person in the estate has not been determined when representation was taken out, or because of any other circumstances affecting the administration or distribution of the estate.[18]

---

[12] Administration of Estates Act 1925, s. 33 (1).

[13] *Ibid.*, s. 55 (1) (x). This section has been widely construed and has been held to include a 60-foot motor yacht: *Re Chaplin*, [1950] 2 All E.R. 155; [1950] Ch. 507. The mere fact that the property might be regarded as an investment does not prevent it from being a personal chattel too: *Re Reynolds' Will Trusts*, [1965] 3 All E.R. 686 (valuable stamp collection, which was deceased's principal hobby, held to be an article of personal use). See R.E.M. in 82 L.Q.R. 18.

[14] Including cut but unmounted jewels: *Re Whitby*, [1944] 1 All E.R. 299, C.A.; [1944] Ch. 210.

[15] See *Re Ogilby*, [1942] 1 All E.R. 524; [1942] Ch. 288.

[16] Administration of Estates Act 1925, s. 46 (3) (as amended).

[17] *Ibid.*, s. 47A (as amended).   [18] *Ibid.*, s. 47A (5) (as amended).

Rights with respect to the Matrimonial Home.—The Act of 1952 has given the surviving spouse a right within certain limits to retain the matrimonial home *in specie.*[19] Where the intestate's estate comprises an interest in a dwelling-house in which the surviving spouse was resident at the time of the intestate's death, the survivor may require the personal representatives to appropriate the house in or towards satisfaction of any absolute interest that the survivor has in the estate,[20] and if the value of the house exceeds the value of the survivor's interest, he may exercise this option if he pays the excess value to the representatives.[1]   He must exercise this option within 12 months of representation being taken out, but this period may be extended by the court as in the case of an application to have a life interest redeemed.[2]   Consequently the personal representatives are forbidden to sell the house within this period without the written consent of the surviving spouse unless this is necessary for the payment of expenses or debts.[3]

There are two limitations upon this power. First, these provisions do not apply if the house is held upon a lease which had less than two years to run from the date of the intestate's death or which could be determined by the landlord within this period.[4]   This means that many houses (for example, those held on weekly tenancies) come outside these provisions, but to off-set this it must be remembered that, if the tenancy is protected under the Rent Act, the surviving spouse will usually automatically become a statutory tenant whether or not the deceased was one.[5] Secondly, the spouse cannot require the personal representatives to appropriate the house in the following cases except on an order of the court which must be satisfied that the appropriation is not likely to diminish the value of assets in the residuary estate (other than the interest in the house) or make these assets more difficult to dispose of.[6] This is where

(a) the dwelling-house forms part of a building and an interest in the whole of the building is comprised in the residuary estate[7]; or

(b) the dwelling-house is held with agricultural land and an interest in the agricultural land is comprised in the residuary estate; or

(c) the whole or part of the dwelling-house was at the time of the intestate's death used as a hotel or lodging house; or

(d) a part of the dwelling-house was at the time of the intestate's death used for purposes other than domestic purposes.

Judicial Separation.—By section 40 of the Matrimonial Proceedings and Property Act 1970, if either spouse dies wholly or partially intestate whilst a decree of judicial separation is in force and the separation is

---

[19]Intestates' Estates Act 1952, 2nd Sched.

[20]*Ibid.*, para. 1 (1). An absolute interest includes a redeemed life interest: *ibid.*, para. 1 (4).

[1]*Ibid.*, para. 5 (2).

[2]*Ibid.*, para. 3. It cannot be exercised after the surviving spouse's death by his or her personal representatives: *ibid.*, para. 3 (1) (b).

[3]*Ibid.*, para. 4. But if they fail to observe this provision, the spouse has no right to claim the house from the purchaser: *ibid.*, para. 4 (5).

[4]*Ibid.*, para. 1 (2).

[5]See *post*, pp. 517 *et seq.*

[6]Intestates' Estates Act 1952, 2nd Sched., para. 2.

[7]*E.g.*, if the house is attached to a shop and the owner would normally live in it.

continuing, his or her property is to devolve as though the other were dead. The reason for this provision is that the rules of intestate succession are intended to reflect the testamentary dispositions the deceased might reasonably be expected to have made, and as judicial separation almost always marks the *de facto* end of the marriage, it is highly unlikely that either would have left anything to the other. On the other hand, this is not necessarily true of separation orders made by magistrates which may well be followed by a reconciliation. Consequently it is expressly provided that a magistrates' order is not to have the same effect as a judicial separation for this purpose and the ordinary rules of intestate succession apply even though such an order is in force.[8]

Interests taken by the Intestate's Children and Remoter Issue.—If the intestate leaves a surviving spouse, the personal representatives must hold one half of the residue (after taking out the personal chattels and the spouse's £5,000) on the statutory trusts for the intestate's issue and the other half on the same trusts subject to the surviving spouse's life interest. If the intestate leaves no surviving spouse, the personal representatives must hold the whole of the residue on the statutory trusts for the issue.[9]

The Statutory Trusts.—The property is to be held on trust for all the children alive at the intestate's death who reach the age of 18 or marry under that age in equal shares. But if any of his children has predeceased him, that child's share is held upon the same trusts for his own children or remoter issue.[10]

Thus suppose that the intestate had four children, A, B, C and D. The first three are alive at their parent's death but D is already dead. D had two children, K and L, of whom K is still alive but L is also dead, leaving two children, X and Y. By applying the above rules, we see that A, B and C each take one quarter; K takes half of D's share (*i.e.*, one-eighth) and the other half of D's share goes to X and Y, who thus get one-sixteenth each. If the share of any of the above fails to vest because he dies a minor and unmarried, his share will go over to the others as if he had predeceased the testator.[11] Thus if A were to die in such circumstances, B and C would each take one third of his share, K would take a sixth, and X and Y would each take a twelfth. If K were to die, his share would pass to X and Y equally; and if X were to die, his share would go to Y.

Until a beneficiary obtains a vested interest by attaining his majority or marrying, the trustees may use the whole of the income of the part to which he is contingently entitled for his maintenance, education or benefit, and they may use one half of the capital to which he is con-

---

[8]S. 40 (2). See further Law Com. No. 25, pp. 107-109. This section replaces earlier legislation going back to 1857 which applied only to certain property with respect to which the wife died intestate.

[9]Administration of Estates Act 1925, s. 46 (1) (as amended); Family Provision Act 1966, s. 1.

[10]*Ibid.*, s. 47 (1) (i) (as amended); Family Law Reform Act 1969, s. 3 (2).

[11]*Re Young*, [1950] 2 All E.R. 1040; [1951] Ch. 185.

tingently entitled for his advancement.[12] Subject to this they must accumulate the income at compound interest.[13] They may also at their discretion permit him to have the use of any personal chattels.[14]

Hotchpot.—The Administration of Estates Act expressly brings the rule against double portions into operation by enacting that any portion or portion debt must be brought into account in satisfaction in whole or part of that child's share of the intestacy unless a contrary intention on the part of the intestate can be inferred.[15] This is frequently known as " bringing into hotchpot ".

Interests taken by other Members of the Family.—If the intestate dies leaving a surviving spouse but no issue, the other half of the residue (after taking out the personal chattels, the £30,000 and the half interest which has gone to the surviving spouse) is to be held on trust for the intestate's parents in equal shares (or for one parent absolutely if only one parent survives the intestate), and if neither of his parents survives him, on the statutory trusts for his brothers and sisters of the whole blood and their issue.

If the intestate leaves neither a spouse nor issue surviving, his whole estate must be held on trust for the persons coming into the first of the following classes that can be satisfied. In other words, if neither of the parents (who come in class (1)) is alive, then the persons coming into class (2) will take and so forth. If none of these classes is filled, the whole estate will go to the Crown as *bona vacantia*.[16]

(1) For the intestate's parents (if they are both alive) in equal shares, or, if one only is still alive, for that parent absolutely.

(2) On the statutory trusts for the brothers and sisters of the whole blood of the intestate and their issue.

(3) On the statutory trusts for the brothers and sisters of the half blood of the intestate and their issue.

(4) For the surviving grandparents of the intestate in equal shares.

(5) On the statutory trusts for the uncles and aunts of the intestate (being brothers or sisters of the whole blood of one of his parents) and their issue.

(6) On the statutory trusts for the uncles and aunts of the intestate (being brothers or sisters of the half blood of one of his parents) and their issue.

The statutory trusts are exactly the same in the above cases as the statutory trusts for the intestate's children and issue except that the hotchpot rule does not apply. Hence the members of each class take *per capita* and the issue of any deceased member of the class take *per*

---

[12]Administration of Estates Act 1925, s. 47 (1) (ii) (as amended); Trustee Act 1925, ss. 31 (1), 32 (1).
[13]Trustee Act 1925, s. 31 (2).
[14]Administration of Estates Act 1925, s. 47 (1) (iv) (as amended).
[15]*Ibid.*, s. 47 (1) (iii) (as amended).
[16]Administration of Estates Act 1925, s. 46 (1) (as amended). If all the members of a particular class are dead but one or more have left issue, the issue will take in preference to the members of a more remote class: *Re Lockwood*, [1957] 3 All E.R. 520; [1958] Ch. 231. Thus, *e.g.*, issue of a brother or sister of the whole blood will take before a brother or sister of the half blood.

stirpes. All the interests are contingent upon the beneficiary's attaining his majority or marrying, and if no member of any class takes a vested interest, the members of the next class will take.[17]

Illegitimate, Legitimated and Adopted Children.—Originally,
in accordance with the general rule at common law, only legitimate persons and those claiming a relationship through legitimate persons could participate in intestate succession. A claim may now be made by or through a person legitimated before the intestate's death as though he had been born legitimate[18] as well as by the issue of a person who would have been legitimated had he not died before his parents' marriage.[19] Similarly if a legitimated person or his issue dies intestate, his estate is to be distributed as though he were born legitimate.[20] The same principles now apply to adopted children, and if after the making of an adoption order the adopted child, his adopters (or sole adopter) or any other person dies intestate, the estate is to be distributed as though he were the legitimate child of his adopters and not the child of any other person.[1] If he was adopted by two spouses jointly, he is deemed to become the brother (or sister) of the whole blood of any other child or adopted child of both the adopters and the brother of the half blood of any child or adopted child of one of them; if he was adopted by one person only, he becomes the brother of the half blood of any other child or adopted child of his adopter.[2]

The position of illegitimate persons who have been neither legitimated nor adopted is now governed by section 14 of the Family Law Reform Act 1969.[3] The principle underlying this section is that illegitimate children and their parents should be entitled to succeed to each other. Thus on the death of a person intestate his illegitimate child (or, if the child has predeceased the intestate, his *legitimate* issue) may now participate in the intestacy on exactly the same terms as though he were legitimate, and on the death of an illegitimate child without issue, his parents have the same claims as they would have on the death of a legitimate child. But it should be noted that claims to succeed by, to or through an illegitimate person are limited to these two cases; thus he can claim nothing on the intestacy of a grandparent or any collateral relative, nor can they claim on his intestacy.[4] Furthermore the section does not affect the devolution of an entailed interest and an illegitimate person cannot take as heir.

---

[17] *Ibid.*, s. 46 (4), (5) (as amended).
[18] Legitimacy Act 1926, s. 3 (1) (a). But he may claim by descent under an entailed interest only if it was *created* after his legitimation: *ibid.*, s. 3 (1) (c). *Cf. ante*, pp. 462-463.
[19] *Ibid.*, s. 5. See *ante*, pp. 463-464.
[20] *Ibid.*, s. 4.
[1] Adoption Act 1958, s. 16 (1). He may claim by descent under an entailed interest only if the instrument creating it took effect after his adoption: see *ante*, pp. 466-467. For the recognition of foreign adoption orders, see *ante*, pp. 467-469.
[2] *Ibid.*, s. 17 (1).
[3] This implements the recommendations of the majority of the Committee on the Law of Succession in Relation to Illegitimate Persons 1966, Cmnd. 3051. It applies if the intestate died on or after 1st January, 1970. Any reference to statutory next of kin in an instrument taking effect on or after this date is to be likewise construed: s. 14 (6).
[4] Nor can a legitimate person succeed on the death of his legitimate cousin if the relevant parent of either of them is illegitimate.

One difficulty that may well arise is that of establishing the relationship of the claimant to the deceased: unlike some systems that permit succession by or to illegitimate persons, we have no means by which paternity can be formally acknowledged.[5] A more cogent criticism that has been levelled against the section is that it permits a father to take advantage of the relationship on the child's death even though he did nothing to support him or even recognise him during his lifetime. Because of the difficulty in tracing the fathers of many illegitimate children, whose identity might well not be known, an illegitimate child is to be presumed not to have been survived by his father unless the contrary is shown.[6] Nor are personal representatives bound to ascertain whether there are illegitimate children (or fathers of illegitimate children) who could take on an intestacy and they will not be personally liable for distributing the estate if they have no notice of their existence.[7]

Partial Intestacy.—These rules apply equally to a partial intestacy. But in this case if the deceased devises or bequeaths property to the surviving spouse (other than personal chattels or under the exercise of a special power of appointment), the spouse must take this in partial or whole satisfaction of the £8,750 or £30,000 to which he is entitled under the intestacy.   Similarly a child *or any remoter issue* of the deceased must bring into hotchpot any beneficial interests acquired by him under the will (except those acquired by virtue of the exercise of a special power of appointment).[8]

C. MAINTENANCE OUT OF THE ESTATE OF A DECEASED SPOUSE OR PARENT

I. FAMILY PROVISION

By permitting a husband to extinguish his wife's right to dower, the Dower Act 1833 abolished the last vestige of family provision in English law.[9]   After that there was nothing to stop a man (or a

---

[5]*Cf.* claims to testamentary gifts to children: *ante*, p. 466.

[6]Family Law Reform Act 1969, s. 14 (4).

[7]*Ibid.*, s. 17. But the beneficiary may follow the property, or other property representing it, into the hands of a recipient. See further Morris, *The Family Law Reform Act 1969, sections 14 and 15*, 19 I.C.L.Q. 328. For a comparison with other systems, see Stone, *Illegitimacy and Claims to Money and other Property: a Comparative Study*, 15 I.C.L.Q. 505, at pp. 520-527.

[8]Administration of Estates Act 1925, s. 49 (as amended). In *Re Young*, [1950] 2 All E.R. 1040; [1951] Ch. 185, and *Re Grover's Will Trusts, National Provincial Bank Ltd.* v. *Clarke*, [1970] 1 All E.R. 1185, it was held that, if the will confers a life interest on the testator's child with remainder over to his children, the capital value of the *whole* fund must be brought into account if the child also claims on a partial intestacy. This is based on the principle that the interest taken by the whole *stirps* must be regarded as a gift to the testator's issue. *Quaere* whether the child should not have to bring into account only the capitalised value of the life interest which is all that *he* takes under the will: *cf. Re Morton*, [1956] 3 All E.R. 259; [1956] Ch. 644. See further Scott, *Hotchpot and Intestacy*, 120 New L.J. 848, where the writer contends that if the child and grandchildren together take an absolute interest, the whole must be brought into account, but that in other cases the interests must be separately valued.

[9]See *ante*, p. 348; Unger, *The Inheritance Act and the Family*, 6 M.L.R. 215.

woman with respect to her separate property) from devising and
bequeathing his whole estate to a charity or a complete stranger and
leaving his widow and children penniless. It was to prevent this evil
that in 1938 the Legislature passed the Inheritance (Family Provision)
Act. This Act does not cast upon the testator any positive duty to make
reasonable provision for his dependants—indeed it would be impossible
to enforce any such obligation—but provides that, if he fails to do so,
the court may order such reasonable provision as it thinks fit to be
made out of the estate to those dependants defined in the Act.

The Act of 1938 was amended by the Intestates' Estates Act 1952.
In addition to making certain modifications in the detailed provisions
of the principal Act, the Act of 1952 made a most important change by
extending the Act of 1938 to cases of intestacy. It is easy to see that
the general law of intestacy may in fact leave a child inadequately
provided for; one may take the case of the widower who leaves two
children, a daughter married to a rich man and a minor son whose
education is as yet incomplete. Obviously the latter's need is greater
than his sister's. Further important modifications of detail were made
by the Family Provision Act 1966 and the Family Law Reform Act
1969. The Act of 1938 as amended up to 1966 is now set out in the
Third Schedule to the Family Provision Act 1966, and references in this
book to sections of the Inheritance (Family Provision) Act should be
read as references to the amended Act as there set out.[10]

Deceased's Domicile.—The Act applies only if the person against
whose estate the claim is being made died domiciled in England.[11]

Who are Dependants.—Applications for provision may be made
only by or on behalf of the deceased's " dependants ". These are
defined as:[12]

(a) the deceased's wife or husband;

(b) a daughter who has not been married[13], or who is, by reason of some
mental or physical disability, incapable of maintaining herself;

(c) a son under the age of 21;

(d) a son who is, by reason of some mental or physical disability, incapable
of maintaining himself;

(e) the surviving party to a void marriage with the deceased.

" Sons " and " daughters " include adopted children, children *en ventre
sa mere*,[14] legitimated and illegitimate children.[15]

The fifth category of surviving party to a void marriage was added
by section 6 of the Law Reform (Miscellaneous Provisions) Act 1970,
which defines such a person as one who " had in good faith entered into
a void marriage with the deceased ". The reason for this addition is

[10]For criticisms of the Act, see Stone, *The Economic Aspects of Death in the Family*,
8 J.S.P.T.L. 188. See generally Tyler, *Family Provision*.
[11]S. 1 (1); Law Reform (Miscellaneous Provisions) Act 1970, s. 6 (1).
[12]S. 1 (1), as amended by the Family Law Reform Act 1969, s. 5 (1) (a), and the Law
Reform (Miscellaneous Provisions) Act 1970, s. 6 (1).
[13]Including a daughter whose voidable marriage has been annulled: *Re Rodwell*,
[1969] 3 All E.R. 1363; [1970] Ch. 726. See further *ante*, p. 70, n. [15].
[14]S. 5 (1).
[15]Family Law Reform Act 1969, s. 18 (1).

that such a person may not discover that the marriage is void until it is too late to take proceedings to have it annulled[16] and, by abolishing actions for breach of promise of marriage, the Act of 1970 took away the survivor's only possible remedy. The section imposes three express limitations on the court's power to make an order in favour of such a person: the marriage must not have been the subject of annulment or dissolution recognised as valid in England; the survivor must not have entered into a later marriage (whether valid, voidable or void); and in any event the court must be satisfied that it would have been reasonable for the deceased to make provision for the survivor's maintenance.

A comparison with the relevant provisions of the Matrimonial Proceedings and Property Act 1970 will show how much more limited are the claims of dependants under the Inheritance (Family Provision) Act. A child of the family for the purpose of the Act of 1970 cannot be a dependant if he is not a child of the deceased; maintenance can be claimed for a son over the age of 21 who is still in receipt of education or training under that Act but not by way of family provision; and the parent of a daughter who has been married can be ordered to provide for her under the Act of 1970 even though she is capable of self-support —a provision which may be of importance, for example, if she marries before she finishes her education and is widowed very shortly afterwards. On the other hand, the middle aged unmarried daughter who has given up a career to look after an aging parent can make a successful claim under the Inheritance (Family Provision) Act although no order with respect to her would ever be made under the Matrimonial Proceedings and Property Act.

Reasonable Provision.—In order to succeed, the dependant must show that the provisions of the deceased's will or the law relating to intestacy (or a combination of both where there is a partial intestacy) is not such as to make reasonable provision for him; and the court is not to assume that the law relating to intestacy necessarily make reasonable provision in all cases.[17] So far as the provisions of the deceased's will are concerned, the earlier cases indicate that it is not sufficient that the court, if placed in the position of the testator, would have made other provisions; the test is subjective, and it must usually be shown that the latter has acted unreasonably. Obviously this must be judged, *prima facie* at all events, by the circumstances existing at the time of the deceased's death, which must of course include all eventualities which he ought reasonably to have foreseen. This is illustrated by *Re Howell*.[18] The testator, who had divorced his first wife, left his whole estate, which was valued at about £2,500, to his second wife. He had been given the custody of the two children of the

---

[16]In which case he or she would be entitled to apply for an order as a former spouse: see *post*, p. 516.

[17]S. 1 (1), (8). See *Sivyer* v. *Sivyer*. [1967] 3 All E.R. 429, where the whole estate went to the intestate's widow to the exclusion of his daughter, aged 14, by a previous marriage.

[18][1953] 2 All E.R. 604, C.A. See also *Re Styler* [1942] 2 All E.R. 201, 204; [1942] Ch. 387, 389; *Re Pugh*, [1943] 2 All E.R. 361, 365; [1943] Ch. 387, 395; *Re Inns*, [1947] 2 All E.R. 308, 311; [1947] Ch. 576, 580-581; *Dun* v. *Dun*, [1959] 2 All E.R. 134, P.C.; [1959] A.C. 272.

first marriage and had appointed his second wife their testamentary guardian. After his death, she had been taken seriously ill, and as a result the children had had to return to their mother. It was held that the testator had acted eminently reasonably in giving his property to his second wife, who in the normal course of events would have provided the children with a home, as he could not have foreseen her illness. Consequently it could not be argued that he had failed to make reasonable provision for the children and therefore an application on their behalf under the Act must fail.

This approach was not followed, however, in *Re Goodwin*.[19]   The testator provided for his children by making specific bequests in their favour and for his widow, their stepmother, by a legacy and the bequest of the residue of his estate. He acted reasonably in that he expected the residue to be worth over £8,000 whereas it turned out to be worth about £1,500. MEGARRY, J., took the view that the true test was an objective one, *viz.*, whether in the event the provision made for the dependant was reasonable, irrespective of the reasonableness or unreasonableness of the testator's actions. In the circumstances he held that he had jurisdiction to make an order. This principle is much to be preferred as it looks at the reality of the dependant's financial position, but it is doubtful how far it can stand with the decision of the Court of Appeal in *Re Howell*. It has been suggested that the cases can be reconciled by postulating that the court will interfere only if the testator acted unreasonably unless he acted under a mistake; if, however, he made dispositions on a mistaken view of the facts, or has failed to revise his will in the light of changed facts, or has failed to appreciate the effect of the dispositions he has made, the court can interfere even though, subjectively, he acted perfectly reasonably.[20] It remains to be seen whether this compromise will be accepted.

The objective approach also means that the court can look at events which occur after the deceased's death. Thus, in *Re Goodwin* MEGARRY, J., took into account the fact that a large part of the residue left to the widow consisted of an interest free loan which the testator had made to her son but which he was unlikely to be able to repay owing to illness which had occurred after the testator's death. A similar approach is to be seen in the case of *Re Clarke*.[1] The testator, who had no children, left the whole of his estate to his mother. She died a fortnight after him, having left the whole of her estate to him. The result was that her bequest lapsed and his estate was divided amongst cousins. Bearing in mind the ultimate destination of the property (which could not be known on the testator's death) an order was made in favour of his widow.

In determining whether reasonable provision has been made, the

---

[19][1968] 3 All E.R. 12; [1969] 1 Ch. 283. See also *Re Franks*, [1947] 2 All E.R. 638; [1948] Ch. 62 (order made in favour of son although testatrix, his mother, died only two days after his birth).
[20]See WINN, L.J. in *Re Gregory*, [1971] 1 All E.R. 497, 502, C.A.; Cretney, 85 L.Q.R. 331.
[1][1968] 1 All E.R. 451.

court must obviously look at a number of things: the size of the estate,[2] the standard at which the applicant lived whilst the deceased was alive,[3] the dependant's financial resources,[4] the financial claims that the dependant made on the deceased during his lifetime,[5] and the relations of the parties and the conduct of the dependant towards the deceased.[6] But probably the most important consideration is the extent to which the testator was under a moral obligation to make provision for the applicant.[7] So if the deceased's estate came largely from a former spouse, the children of that marriage may have a stronger claim to it than the deceased's widow.[8] Again it has been held that a father is under no obligation to provide for his unmarried daughter who has lived with a married man as his wife for 42 years[9] or for a daughter who is incurably insane and may be expected to take advantage of free hospital facilities under the National Health Act.[10] Now that the difference between the spouses' earning capacity is becoming less, it may be unreasonable for a woman not to make provision for her widower, particularly if his earning capacity is reduced.[11] The moral dilemma that a testator may find himself in is well illustrated by *Re Joslin*.[12] The testator had left his wife and under a separation deed had covenanted to pay her £1 a week during their joint lives. He had subsequently gone to live with another woman who had borne him two children. He left his whole estate (which was worth only £370) on trust for this woman for her life with remainder to the two illegitimate children. The wife, who had an income of about £190 a year, then made an application under the Act. It was held that the testator had acted reasonably in making provision for the mother of his children (who was now in receipt of Poor Relief) and consequently the wife's application failed.

---

[2]The estate may be too small to make any effective contribution to the dependant's maintenance: *Re Vrint*, [1940] 3 All E.R. 470; [1940] Ch. 920; *Re Clayton*, [1966] 2 All E.R. 370.

[3]*Re Inns*, (*ante*), at pp. 311 and 581, respectively. The provision which a husband made for his wife while he was alive may be relevant but is by no means conclusive: contrast *Re Charman*, [1951] 2 T.L.R. 1095, with *Re Borthwick*, [1949] 1 All E.R. 472; [1949] Ch. 395.

[4]S. 1 (6). This includes any state aid that the dependant can claim: *Re E.*, [1966] 2 All E.R. 44; *Re Clayton*, (*supra*).

[5]*Re Clarke*, (*supra*).

[6]S. 1 (6); *Re Inns*, (*ante*), at pp. 311 and 581, respectively. The mere fact that a man has been bullied into marrying a woman does not relieve him of his legal and moral duty to maintain her: *Re Watkins*, [1953] 2 All E.R. 1113.

[7]*Per* WYNN-PARRY, J., in *Re Andrews*, [1955] 3 All E.R. 248, 249.

[8]*Re Styler*, (*ante*); *Re Sivyer*, (*ante*).

[9]*Re Andrews*, (*supra*). But in an appropriate case the court may make an order in favour of an adult unmarried daughter who has chosen to follow an unremunerative career: *Re Ducksbury*, [1966] 2 All E.R. 374.

[10]*Re Watkins*, [1949] 1 All E.R. 695. *Cf. Re Catmull*, [1943] 2 All E.R. 115; [1943] Ch. 262, and the observations of STAMP, J., in *Re E.*, (*supra*).

[11]*Re Clayton*, (*supra*) (widower crippled and earning only £10 a week); *Re Wilson* (1969), 113 Sol. Jo. 794 (widower aged 92). The opposite view was expressed in earlier cases: see *Re Silvester*, [1940] 4 All E.R. 269; [1941] Ch. 87 (especially at pp. 271 and 89, respectively); *Re Styler*, [1942] 2 All E.R. 201; [1942] Ch. 387 (especially at pp. 204 and 389, respectively).

[12][1941] 1 All E.R. 302; [1941] Ch. 200. *Cf. Re Charman*, (*supra*).

Evidence.—Section 1 (7) of the Act enacts:

" The court shall . . . have regard to the deceased's reasons, so far as ascertainable, for making the dispositions made by his will (if any), or for refraining from disposing by will of his estate or part of his estate, or for not making any provision, or any further provision, as the case may be, for a dependant, and the court may accept such evidence of those reasons as it considers sufficient including any statement in writing signed by the deceased and dated, so, however, that in estimating the weight, if any, to be attached to any such statement the court shall have regard to all the circumstances from which any inference can reasonably be drawn as to the accuracy or otherwise of the statement."

This provision fell to be discussed in *Re Smallwood*.[13] An application for an order made by the deceased's widow was opposed by his son, who gave evidence that his father had told him that he got on badly with his wife because she drank too much, had had an affair with another man and had social aspirations which did not interest the testator, and that she had nagged the father, had quarrelled with him and had once assaulted him. Clearly this evidence was not admissible at common law because it was merely hearsay, but ROXBURGH, J., held that the statement was admissible under the Act. The wide wording of the section lets in any relevant evidence and the specific reference to written statements signed by the deceased does not automatically preclude all other evidence. Further, ROXBURGH, J., held that this section makes admissible not only direct evidence of the deceased's reasons for failing to make further provision for the dependant but also of facts from which the court may infer the reasons itself.[14]

Time in which the application must be made.—In order to enable the personal representatives to distribute the estate, an application for provision may not be made more than six months after the date on which representation is first taken out without the permission of the court.[15] Personal representatives may be personally liable if they distribute the estate within six months;[16] they will not be personally liable for distribution after this time if no application is then pending, but property may be recovered from the beneficiaries to whom it has been transferred if it is needed to make provision for a dependant to whom the court gives leave to make a late application.[17]

---

[13][1951] 1 All E.R. 372; [1951] Ch. 369, following *Re Vrint*, [1940] 3 All E.R. 470; [1940] Ch. 920.

[14]But a statement that the deceased proposed to alter his will in the dependant's favour is not admissible, because this is a statement of intention, not of fact or of the deceased's reasons: *Re Pugh*, [1943] 2 All E.R. 361; [1943] Ch. 387. If the statement is clearly inspired by malice, it may help the dependant as showing that the deceased was acting out of spite and therefore unreasonably: *Re Borthwick*, [1949] 1 All E.R. 472, 476; [1949] Ch. 395, 402.

[15]S. 2 (1), (1C). The court's discretion is unfettered and an extension should be granted whenever " it is reasonably clear that [it] is required in the interests of justice ": *per* UNGOED-THOMAS, J., in *Re Ruttie*, [1969] 3 All E.R. 1633, 1637.

[16]*Re Simson*, [1949] 2 All E.R. 826, 829; [1950] Ch. 38, 43. But see also *Re Ralphs*, [1968] 3 All E.R. 285.

[17]S. 2 (1B).

Orders that may be made.—The court may order " such reasonable provision as it thinks fit " to be made out of the deceased's estate.[18] Presumably the standard of reasonableness is the same as that which we have already discussed.[19] There are three types of order that the court can make.

(1) If a dependant is in immediate need of financial assistance and property forming part of the net estate can be made available to meet his needs but it is not yet possible to make a final order, the court may make an interim order. This may take the form of one payment or of periodical payments, and the court may later direct that any sum paid under an interim order shall be treated as having been paid on account of the final order. As far as possible, the same matters should be taken into account in making an interim order as in making a final order.[20]

(2) In a final order the court usually provides for maintenance by way of periodical payments which become a charge on the income of the estate.[1] It may impose conditions and restrictions on the order[2] and must provide for the termination of the payments not later than:

(a) in the case of the surviving spouse, his or her remarriage;
(b) in the case of a daughter, her marriage or the cesser of her disability, whichever is the later;
(c) in the case of a son under the age of 21, his reaching that age;
(d) in the case of a son under a disability, the cesser of his disability;
(e) in the case of a surviving party to a void marriage, his or her remarriage;

or in any case the dependant's earlier death.[3]

(3) The court also has power, if it sees fit, to make an order for a lump sum payment, either along with or instead of periodical payments.[4] This is particularly valuable if the estate is small because an order for periodical payments might well prove to be valueless. In other cases it is submitted that it should be made only in exceptional circumstances to avoid the appropriation of capital.

---

[18]S. 1 (1). The court has a complete discretion to determine which beneficiaries are to bear the burden of the award but it is usually thrown on to the residuary estate: *Re Preston*, [1969] 2 All E.R. 961.

[19]The effect of social security legislation should also be considered if the dependant is in receipt of benefit: *Re Canderton* (1970), 114 Sol. Jo. 208 (dependant given a lump sum award so that benefit should not be reduced).

[20]S. 4A.

[1]S. 1 (2). These may be of a specified amount or may be equal to the whole or part of the income of the net estate (or any part of the net estate appropriated or set aside for this purpose) or may be of an amount to be determined in some other way: s. 3 (1A). This can take into account increases in the value of the estate after the order has been made. The court must not order a realisation that would be improvident having regard to the dependants and others interested in the estate: s. 1 (5).

[2]S. 1 (1). For examples of conditions, see *Re Lidington*, [1940] 3 All E.R. 600; [1940] Ch. 927 (condition that widow should maintain minor children of the marriage); *Re Hills*, [1941] W.N. 123 (condition that applicant should inform the trustees of the will if she became entitled to any property worth £100 or more).

[3]S. 1 (2), as amended by the Family Law Reform Act 1969, s. 5 (1) (b); Law Reform (Miscellaneous Provisions) Act 1970, s. 6 (2), (4). In the last case it is expressly provided that " remarriage " includes a marriage that is void or voidable; in the other cases it presumably does not: *cf. Re Rodwell* [1969] 3 All E.R. 1363; [1970] Ch. 726. In *Re Lidington, (supra)*, the order was made in the first instance until the dependant's children came of age.

[4]S. 1 (4).

The court can only make an order to take effect on property which the deceased had power to dispose of by will.[5] Hence an obvious way of getting round the Act is for a person to make an *inter vivos* settlement on himself for life with remainder to the person whom he wishes to benefit after his death. Although the settlement could be attacked during the settlor's lifetime if it was intended to defeat a claim for financial provision, it is unassailable after he dies.[6]

Variation of Orders.—Since a certain part of the estate will have been appropriated for the purpose of raising provision for dependants, no variation can be ordered which would have the effect of increasing the total amount of property affected.[7] The Act expressly provides for variations in two cases. First, the order may be varied on the ground that a material fact was not disclosed to the court when the order was made[8] or that a substantial change has taken place in the circumstances of the dependant or of some other person beneficially interested in the deceased's estate.[9] Since the total provision cannot be increased, a dependant may not ask that the periodical payments payable to him be increased on the ground that his own circumstances have changed for the worse except at the expense of another dependant already in receipt of payments; but there is no reason why a beneficiary, A, should not have payments to B decreased on the ground that A is now in financial straits or that B's circumstances have changed substantially for the better. Secondly, the order may be varied by a further order making provision for another dependant.[10] Again this could be done only at the expense of a dependant already in receipt of payments; and it will be seen that, if no order is in force, a dependant whose circumstances change after the end of the statutory six months has no power to apply at all without the permission of the court to extend the time limit as no order is in force which can be varied.[11] A variation may provide for periodical payments, the payment of a lump sum, or both.[12]

The court may also give consequential directions at the time the order is made, but once more the second order may not affect a greater part of the deceased's estate than that already appropriated.[13] If it appears that a dependant, who is not in need at the moment, may require financial aid in the future, the only thing the court can do is to appropriate a large part of the estate and direct the trustees or personal representatives to pay the income to those beneficially entitled under the will or intestacy until the dependant actually

---

[5] See the definition of " net estate " in s. 5 (1).
[6] See Albery, *Inheritance (Family Provision) Act 1938*, App. D. For transactions intended to defeat a claim for financial provision, see *ante*, pp. 454-455.
[7] S. 4 (1).
[8] But presumably evidence may not be adduced which the party could have put before the court at the time the order was made: *cf. ante*, p. 451.
[9] S. 4 (1) (a).
[10] S. 4 (1) (b).
[11] See *Re Dorgan*, [1948] 1 All E.R. 723; [1948] Ch. 366.
[12] This is made clear by the Family Provision Act 1966, s. 4 (1).
[13] S. 3 (2).

requires provision. This point arose in *Re Franks*.[14] Here a married woman had given her husband a legacy of £1,000 and had given the residue of her estate (worth £16,000 odd) to her son by a previous marriage. An application was made on behalf of her younger son who had been born only two days before his mother's death. No provision was needed for him at the moment because his father was capable of maintaining him, but clearly he might well need maintenance later. The elder son was by this time aged 18 and was hoping to go up to Oxford after completing his military service. WYNN-PARRY, J., resolved the problem by ordering that provision should be made for the younger son and then standing the application over till just before the elder son came of age, when the questions of the quantum of the provision and the date from which it should be paid would have to be decided. In the meantime the elder son would not be prejudiced because the trustees could still use the income for his benefit, and liberty to apply to all parties protected both sons in the event of the circumstances of either changing in the meantime.

2. MAINTENANCE OF A FORMER SPOUSE

The principle underlying the Inheritance (Family Provision) Act was extended by the Matrimonial Causes (Property and Maintenance) Act 1958 (in provisions now contained in the Matrimonial Causes Act 1965), to enable a former spouse of a person who has died domiciled in England to apply for provision to be made out of that person's estate. A former spouse for this purpose is one whose marriage to the deceased had been annulled or dissolved and who has not re-married.[15] The court[16] must be satisfied that it would have been reasonable for the deceased to make provision for her or him and that no such reasonable provision has been made, and must have regard to the income and capital, past, present and future, of the applicant, her (or his) conduct in relation to the deceased or otherwise, any order or application made for financial provision after the decree of nullity or divorce or the reasons why no order or application was made, and to any other matter which may be relevant whether in relation to the applicant or other persons interested in the estate.[17] The fact that the applicant is in receipt of secured periodical payments after the former spouse's death is not conclusive and does not prevent a further application: if her needs and other means remain the same, it is reasonable that she should continue to receive the same amount as she did during his lifetime, provided that the estate is sufficient for the purpose bearing in

---

[14] [1947] 2 All E.R. 638; [1948] Ch. 62. See also *Re Borthwick*, [1949] 1 All E.R. 472; [1949] Ch. 395 (widow given £750 a year, daughter given £100 a year with liberty to apply for further provision on her mother's death).

[15] A spouse is to be regarded as having re-married even though the second marriage is void or voidable: Matrimonial Causes Act 1965, s. 26 (5A) (added by the Matrimonial Proceedings and Property Act 1970, s. 36).

[16] *I.e.*, the High Court or, if the net estate does not exceed £5,000, a county court: Family Provision Act 1966, s. 7.

[17] Matrimonial Causes Act 1965, s. 26 (1), (2), (4), (6). The right to apply to the court is not extinguished by an agreement entered into during the former spouse's lifetime not to apply after the deceased's death even if this is embodied in a court order: *Re Minter*, [1967] 3 All E.R. 412; [1968] P. 174.

mind the needs of others beneficially entitled.[18] As in the case of applications under the Inheritance (Family Provision) Act, the court must have regard primarily to the extent of the former spouse's moral claim upon the estate.[19] Other provisions are similar to those of the Inheritance (Family Provision) Act: the application must be made within six months after the date on which representation was taken out (unless the court permits an application to be made later); the order will usually take the form of periodical payments terminating not later than the applicant's remarriage or death but, if the court sees fit, it may order the provision to be made wholly or in part by a lump sum payment; and interim orders may be made.[20] The court must also have regard to the nature of the deceased's estate and must not make any order that would be imprudent having regard to the interests of the applicant, those who are dependants for the purpose of the Inheritance (Family Provision) Act and those beneficially entitled to the estate.[1]

In the light of changed circumstances the court may at any time vary or discharge any order made in favour of a former spouse or suspend any of its provisions or revive any provisions that have been suspended. An application to have the order varied, etc., may be made by the person in whose favour it was originally made, by any other former spouse or dependant of the deceased, by the trustees of any property affected by the order or by any person who is beneficially entitled to the property. As in the case of orders made under the Inheritance (Family Provision) Act, the variation may affect only the capital or income that was the subject of the original order.[2]

D. THE TRANSMISSION OF STATUTORY TENANCIES

We have already seen that the Rent Act prevents a landlord from arbitrarily evicting a tenant under a controlled or regulated tenancy.[3] In addition to protecting the tenant and his (or her) spouse, this must necessarily give security to members of the tenant's family so long as they are living with him. This secondary purpose of the Act would be completely defeated if it were possible for the landlord to evict the

---

[18] *Eyre* v. *Eyre*, [1968] 1 All E.R. 968.

[19] *Roberts* v *Roberts*, [1964] 3 All E.R. 503. *Cf. Re Bellman*, [1963] 1 All E.R. 513; [1963] P. 239. In *Re Harker-Thomas*, [1968] 3 All E.R. 17; [1969] P. 28, it was held that the court must be satisfied that the deceased acted unreasonably in failing to make provision for the former spouse. This follows earlier cases under the Inheritance (Family Provision) Act, but see *ante*, p. 511.

[20] Matrimonial Causes Act 1965, ss. 26 (1), (3), (5A), 28 and 28A, as amended by the Family Provision Act 1966, ss. 3 (2), 4, 5 (3), 6 and Sched. 1, and by the Matrimonial Proceedings and Property Act 1970, s. 36. " Remarriage " includes a marriage that is void or voidable. The court may make the order retrospective to the date of death: *Askew* v. *Askew*, [1961] 2 All E.R. 60. For the liability of personal representatives and the recovery of property already distributed from beneficiaries, see s. 28 (1).

[1] *Ibid.*, s. 26 (5).

[2] *Ibid.*, s. 27.

[3] *Ante*, pp. 394 *et seq*.

members of the tenant's family immediately the tenancy was ended by the tenant's death. Consequently the Act provides that, subject to certain conditions, security shall be given to members of the deceased tenant's family by vesting a statutory tenancy in them. It is, of course, open to the landlord to grant a fresh contractual tenancy to the person remaining in possession. Whether or not he has done so must be a question of fact in each case, but a contractual tenancy cannot be inferred from the mere receipt of rent as the landlord is bound to accept the new tenant.[4] If he does not do so, the new tenant has all the protection given by the Act to the person who becomes a statutory tenant by remaining in possession after his contractual tenancy has ended.

To whom the Tenancy may be transmitted.—There are two classes of persons to whom a statutory tenancy may be transmitted.[5]

(1) *The Tenant's Widow.*—There is an automatic transmission to the widow of the tenant provided that she was residing with him at the time of his death. She remains a statutory tenant even though she subsequently remarries and thus ceases to be the former tenant's widow.[6] It will be observed that the residence qualification precludes the deserted wife, who has remained on the premises by virtue of her husband's tenancy, from claiming the benefit of the Act.[7]

(2) *Members of the Tenant's Family.*—If the tenant leaves no widow residing with him at the time of his death or is a woman, there is a transmission to any member of his or her family who has been residing with the tenant for not less than six months immediately before the death. Such a tenancy can vest in only one person;[8] consequently if there are more members of the family than one, they should decide amongst themselves to whom it is to be transmitted. If they cannot come to an agreement, the question must be determined by the county court.[9]

The words " residing with " must be given their ordinary and popular meaning.[10] As EVERSHED, M.R., said in *Edmunds* v. *Jones*,[11] the successor must have " lived [in] and shared for living purposes the whole of the premises to which he or she claims to have succeeded ". Hence, as in that case, there will be no transmission of the tenancy if the successor was in fact the sub-tenant of the deceased tenant.

---

[4]*Dealex Properties, Ltd.* v. *Brooks*, [1965] 1 All E.R. 1080, C.A.; [1966] 1 Q.B. 542.
[5]Rent Act 1968, s. 3 and Sched. 1.
[6]*Apsley* v. *Barr*, [1928] N.I. 183.
[7]The wife's obtaining an order that her right of occupation should continue after the husband's death (see *ante*, p. 391) would presumably give her no protection because the statutory tenancy and therefore her right would come to an end on his death.
[8]*Dealex Properties, Ltd.* v. *Brooks*, (*supra*).
[9]The court must take into account th merits of the rival claims, the claimants' needs and perhaps the wishes (or probable wishes) of the deceased tenant: see *Williams* v. *Williams*, [1970] 3 All E.R. 988.
[10]*Morgan* v. *Murch*, [1970] 2 All E.R. 100, C.A.
[11][1957] 1 W.L.R. 1118, n., 1120, C.A. See further *Foreman* v. *Beagley*, [1969] 3 All E.R. 838, C.A. (son living in mother's flat whilst she was in hospital not " residing with " her); Megarry, *Rent Acts*, 10th Ed., 212-214.

The expression "member of the tenant's family" is not easy to define and has given rise to a spate of litigation. It is not a term of art and must be construed in a very broad and popular sense.[12] It is not sufficient that the claimant and the deceased should have been members of the same family; the former must show that he was a member of the latter's family.[13] The test really is: would an ordinary man aware of the facts so describe the claimant?[14] Nevertheless some judicial limit has been placed upon the term. Servants and lodgers apparently do not come within the definition, for it could hardly have been the intention of the Legislature to protect them.[15] In *Gammans* v. *Ekins*[16] ASQUITH, L.J., suggested that the decisions limited the membership of the family to three relationships: children of the deceased, relationships constituted by marriage (for example, husband and wife) and those where the deceased stood *in loco parentis* to the claimant. There is no doubt that the tenant's widower comes within this category.[17] So do legitimate children, together with their husbands or wives;[18] and in *Brock* v. *Wollams*[19] the Court of Appeal held that a child who had been *de facto* adopted by the tenant came within the definition even though there had never been a formal legal adoption. It has also been suggested that the class includes illegitimate children and step-children,[20] and this seems to be in keeping with the trend of the decided cases.

But it is clear that ASQUITH, L.J.'s classification cannot be regarded as exhaustive. In *Jones* v. *Whitehill*[1] the Court of Appeal held that a niece who had gone to look after her elderly aunt and uncle in their declining years was a member of their family (although it is easy to see here the resemblance of the niece's position to that of a daughter). But it is difficult to see how to fit into ASQUITH, L.J.'s classification the earlier decision of WRIGHT, J., in *Price* v. *Gould*[2] that the tenant's brothers and sisters were members of her family. With this one exception, however, the decided cases appear to fall into these three groups. Consanguinity is not the sole test and the parties' conduct must be

---

[12]*Price* v. *Gould* (1930), 143 L.T. 333, 334; *Brock* v. *Wollams*, [1949] 1 All E.R. 715, 717, C.A.; [1949] 2 K.B. 388, 394; *Jones* v. *Whitehill*, [1950] 1 All E.R. 71, 72, C.A.; [1950] 2 K.B. 204, 207; *Gammans* v. *Ekins*, [1950] 2 All E.R. 140, 143, C.A.; [1950] 2 K.B. 328, 333; *Langdon* v. *Horton*, [1951] 1 All E.R. 60, C.A., at pp. 60, 61, 62; [1951] 1 K.B. 666, at pp. 669, 671, 672; Megarry, *op. cit.*, 214-216.

[13]*Langdon* v. *Horton*, (*supra*), at pp. 60, 61, and 669, 671, respectively.

[14]*Brock* v. *Wollams*, (*supra*), at pp. 718 and 395, respectively; *Standingford* v. *Probert*, [1949] 2 All E.R. 861, 864, C.A.; [1950] 1 K.B. 377, 383; *Hawes* v. *Evenden*, [1953] 2 All E.R. 737, 738, C.A.

[15]Per COHEN, L.J., in *Brock* v. *Wollams*, (*supra*), at pp. 718 and 394, respectively.

[16][1950] 2 All E.R. 140, 141, C.A.; [1950] 2 K.B. 328, 331; followed by SINGLETON, L.J., in *Langdon* v. *Horton*, (*supra*), at pp. 62 and 672, respectively.

[17]*Salter* v. *Lask*, [1925] 1 K.B. 584; approved by EVERSHED, M.R., in *Gammans* v. *Ekins*, (*supra*), at pp. 143 and 333, respectively.

[18]*Standingford* v. *Probert*, (*supra*).

[19][1949] 1 All E.R. 715, C.A.; [1949] 2 K.B. 388.

[20]*Brock* v. *Woollams*, (*supra*), at pp. 717 and 394 (*per* BUCKNILL, L.J.), 718 and 396 (*per* DENNING, L.J.), respectively.

[1][1950] 1 All E.R. 71, C.A.; [1950] 2 K.B. 204. See further EVERSHED, M.R.'s remarks on this case in *Langdon* v. *Horton*, (*infra*), at pp. 61 and 669, respectively.

[2] (1930), 143 L.T. 333. SINGLETON, L.J.'s view that they came within this classification because they are children of the same parents is, with respect, unconvincing: *Langdon* v. *Horton*, (*infra*), at pp. 62 and 672, respectively.

taken into account as well as their relationship:[3] thus in *Langdon* v. *Horton*,[4] where two sisters had gone to live with their widowed cousin and had stayed with her until she died 29 years later, the Court of Appeal held that they were no more members of her family than would be two strangers to the blood who shared a flat for their convenience.

The same problem arises when a man and woman, who are not married to each other, live together outwardly as husband and wife. This arose in *Gammans* v. *Ekins*,[5] where the Court of Appeal held that the man was not entitled to be treated as a member of the woman's family. If, as he alleged, their relationship had been purely innocent and they had taken the same name to avoid a scandal, the position was the same as in *Langdon* v. *Horton* and could be no different from that of two persons of the same sex who shared premises for their convenience; had it not been innocent, it would be anomalous if fornication could give the claimant a right which he did not otherwise possess.[6]

In *Gammans* v. *Ekins* the court left open the question whether the result would have been the same if the couple had had children. This fell to be decided by the Court of Appeal in *Hawes* v. *Evenden*,[7] where the tenant, his mistress and their child had all lived together for some years. The court had no difficulty in deciding that in the popular sense the mistress was a member of the tenant's family. But the mere birth of the child is not sufficient: where the man claims to be a member of the family of the woman who was his mistress and mother of his child, he will fail if he cannot show that he has put himself *in loco parentis* to the child by maintaining it and adopting it at least *de facto*.[8]

Limitations on Transmission.—There are two important limitations on transmission. First, the statutory tenancy must still be in existence. Hence, if the tenancy has been terminated by the tenant's vacating the premises or by the landlord's obtaining an order for possession against him before his death, the landlord is entitled to possession against the members of his family remaining on the premises.[9]

Secondly, there must obviously be some limitation upon the number of times that a statutory tenancy can be transmitted, for otherwise it

---

[3]*Ross* v. *Collins*, [1964] 1 All E.R. 861, 865, C.A.
[4][1951] 1 All E.R. 60, C.A.; [1951] 1 K.B. 666.
[5][1950] 2 All E.R. 140, C.A.; [1950] 2 K.B. 328.
[6]At pp. 141-142, 143 and 331, 334, respectively.
[7][1953] 2 All E.R. 737, C.A.
[8]*Perry* v. *Dembowski*, [1951] 2 All E.R. 50, C.A.; [1951] 2 K.B. 420. In this case the Court of Appeal left open the interesting question whether a child of four or five years of age could be a member of his deceased parent's family for the purpose of the Rent Act.
[9]This is so even though the court has suspended the execution of an order for possession and the tenant dies before the order takes effect: *American Economic Laundry, Ltd.* v. *Little*, [1950] 2 All E.R. 1186, C.A.; [1951] 1 K.B. 400. The Court of Appeal left open the question what the position would be if a conditional order had been made (at pp. 1190 and 406, respectively), but they have subsequently said that, in order to prevent this difficulty from arising, courts should not make orders suspended indefinitely or for a long period of time: *Mills* v. *Allen*, [1953] 2 All E.R. 534, C.A., at pp. 544, 547; [1953] 2 Q.B. 341, at pp. 357, 364.

could be tied up in the family in perpetuity and the landlord could never obtain possession. Consequently it is provided that there cannot be more than two transmissions and the second can operate only if the person who became the statutory tenant by the first continues to occupy the premises as his or her residence.[10] The rules and limitations relating to the second transmission are exactly the same as those relating to the first except that, whether the tenancy was originally controlled or regulated, the second transmission will always produce a regulated tenancy.[11] Thus, if on the death of a statutory tenant there is a transmission to his widow., there may be a second transmission on her death to any member of her family who had been residing with her for not less than six months immediately beforehand. There cannot be any further transmission after the death of that person, however.

Nature of a Transmitted Tenancy.—The new tenant takes the tenancy on the same terms as his predecessor, with all the rights and liabilities, advantages and disadvantages unaltered.[12] Thus the burden of paying the same rent, of repairs, or of restrictive covenants will fall on him as it fell on the deceased tenant.[13] Similarly he may exercise any power the statutory tenant had to sub-let a part of the premises, and consequently, as the Court of Appeal held in *Lewis* v. *Reeves*,[14] his sub-tenant is protected by the Act. Thus if the tenant under a second transmitted tenancy wishes to give further security to a member of his family, his best plan is to grant a sub-tenancy to that person provided that he may lawfully do so.[15]

Contractual Tenants.—Up till now we have been considering the position where the deceased tenant was a statutory tenant. Originally it was held that there could be no transmission if the deceased tenant was a contractual lessee, with the result that the protection given to the widow of a statutory tenant would not be accorded to the widow of a protected tenant if he chose to bequeath his interest to someone else. It was partly because of this anomaly that the House of Lords held in *Moodie* v. *Hosegood*[16] that the widow or other member of the family is entitled to the same protection whether the deceased was a statutory or protected tenant provided, of course, that the dwelling-house is held on a controlled or regulated tenancy. Statutory effect has now been given to this rule by the Rent Act 1968.[17] Thus suppose

[10]Rent Act 1968, s. 3 and Sched. 1.
[11]*Ibid.*, Sched. 2, para. 5. If the court vests a statutory tenancy in the tenant's husband or wife on divorce or nullity (see *ante*, p. 400), this does not affect the total number of transmissions that can take place: Matrimonial Homes Act 1967, s. 7 (3), as amended by the Rent Act 1968, Sched. 15.
[12]*Bolsover Colliery Co., Ltd.* v. *Abbott*, [1946] K.B. 8, 12, C.A.; *Tickner* v. *Clifton*, [1929] 1 K.B. 207, 211.
[13]*Bolsover Colliery Co., Ltd.* v. *Abbott*, (*supra*), followed in *American Economic Laundry, Ltd.* v. *Little*, [1950] 2 All E.R. 1186, C.A.; [1951] 1 K.B. 400. But the new tenant is not liable for arrears of rent owed by his predecessor: *Tickner* v. *Clifton*, (*supra*), and therefore could not have a possession order made against him on this ground, since the rent is not due *from the tenant*.
[14][1951] 2 All E.R. 855, C.A.; [1952] 1 K.B. 19.
[15]See the remarks of DENNING, L.J., at pp. 859 and 26, respectively. He could not do so, *e.g.*, if the terms of the tenancy forbade sub-letting.
[16][1951] 2 All E.R. 582, H.L.; [1952] A.C. 61.
[17]S. 3 (1) (b).

that a husband, H, dies leaving a widow, W, and a son, S, to whom he has bequeathed the balance of the lease on which H held the matrimonial home. The contractual lease passes to H's personal representatives who must then vest it in S, whilst at the same time a statutory tenancy vests in W. It seems impossible that there should be two adverse tenancies in existence at the same time; the true position is that the contractual tenancy is in abeyance until the statutory tenancy is determined. The result was thus described by LORD MORTON OF HENRYTON in *Moodie* v. *Hosegood*:[18]

> " If a contractual tenancy is still subsisting at her husband's death and devolves upon someone other than the widow, it is not destroyed, but the rights and obligations which would ordinarily devolve upon the successor in title of the contractual tenant are suspended so long as the widow retains possession of the dwelling-house.
>
> " If the contractual tenancy is determinable by notice, the landlord or the contractual tenant can determine it by giving the appropriate notice, but such notice will not affect the widow's rights and obligations . . . and, if no notice is given, the contractual tenancy will come into full operation when the widow gives up possession. . . . If the contractual tenancy is a lease for years, it will remain in being, but so long as the widow remains in possession she, and not the contractual tenant, is bound to observe the terms and conditions of the lease and has the benefit thereof. . . . At no time are there two tenants, each one entitled to the benefit and subject to the burden of the contractual tenancy. The so-called statutory tenant is not a tenant in the true sense. He or she is merely a person who is given certain protection by the Acts. . . ."

But whilst *Moodie* v. *Hosegood* removes one anomaly, it creates a score of injustices and difficulties. Thus if H were to devise another house to W with the intention that she should live in that and that S should live in the house bequeathed to him, his intentions can be completely defeated, for W can claim the beneficial interest in the former as devisee and remain in the latter as statutory tenant, and S cannot obtain a possession order against her as he is not the landlord. Moreover, if the lessor determines the contractual tenancy by giving notice to S, S is deprived of the protection of the Rent Act as he is not a contractual tenant in possession. There is little incentive for the landlord to obtain a possession order since this could enure only for the benefit of S whose contractual tenancy will then resume its full force. Furthermore, when the widow dies, there can be a second transmission to a member of her family residing with her. It is obviously difficult to predict the full effects of this decision with certainty.[19]

---

[18]At pp. 586 and 74, respectively.
[19]For a fuller criticism of *Moodie* v. *Hosegood* and the difficulties which it raises, see Megarry, *Rent Acts*, 10th Ed., 221-224, and in *The Rent Acts and the Invention of New Doctrines*, 67 L.Q.R. 505, 512 *et seq.*

APPENDICES

SUMMARY OF CONTENTS

Business Assigned to the Family Division of the High Court

(The Administration of Justice Act 1970, First Schedule)

Busines at first instance

Proceedings for a decree of divorce, nullity, judicial separation, presumption of death and dissolution of marriage, or jactitation of marriage.

Proceedings under section 6 of the Matrimonial Proceedings and Property Act (wilful neglect to provide reasonable maintenance).

Proceedings for a declaration—

(a) under section 39 of the Matrimonial Causes Act 1965, as to a person's legitimacy, or the validity of a marriage, or a person's right to be deemed a British subject; or

(b) with respect to a person's matrimonial status.

Proceedings in relation to the wardship of minors.

Proceedings under the Adoption Acts 1958 and 1968.

Proceedings under the Guardianship of Minors Act 1971 and otherwise in relation to the guardianship of minors, except proceedings for the appointment of a guardian of a minor's estate alone.

Proceedings under section 3 of the Marriage Act 1949 for obtaining the court's consent to the marriage of a minor.

Proceedings under section 17 of the Married Women's Property Act 1882 (determination of title to property in dispute between spouses).

Proceedings in which a parent or guardian of a minor applies for a writ of habeas corpus ad subjiciendum relative to the custody, care or control of the minor.

Proceedings under the following enactments:-

(a) the Maintenance Orders (Facilities for Enforcement) Act 1920 (enforcement in England and Wales of orders made overseas for periodical payments to a man's wife or dependant);

(b) Part II of the Maintenance Orders Act 1950 (enforcement in England and Wales of certain maintenance and other orders made in Scotland or Northern Ireland);

(c) the Maintenance Orders Act 1958 (registration and enforcement of certain maintenance and other orders);

(d) the Attachment of Earnings Act 1971.

Proceedings under section 1 of the Matrimonial Homes Act 1967 (means whereby a spouse can continue in occupation of, or obtain entry to, a dwelling-house which is, or has been, the matrimonial home).

Appellate business

Proceedings on appeal under—

(a) section 16 (2) of the Guardianship of Minors Act 1971 (appeal to High Court from order of county court under that Act);

(b) section 16 (3) of the Guardianship of Minors Act 1971 (corresponding appeal from a magistrates' court);

(c) section 11 of the Matrimonial Proceedings (Magistrates' Courts) Act 1960 (appeal from certain decisions of a magistrates' court under that Act).

Proceedings on appeal from a magistrates' court under section 10 of the Adoption Act 1958 against the making of, or refusal to make, an adoption order.

Proceedings on appeal from a magistrates' court under section 4 (7) of the Maintenance Orders Act 1958 against the variation of, or refusal to vary, an order registered in accordance with the provisions of that Act.

Proceedings on appeal under section 13 of the Administration of Justice Act 1960 (appeal in cases of contempt of court) from an order or decision of a magistrates' court under section 54 (3) of the Magistrates' Courts Act 1952 where the order or decision was made to enforce an order of such a court under the Guardianship of Minors Act 1971 or the Matrimonial Proceedings (Magistrates' Courts) Act 1960.

Proceedings on appeal by case stated against an order or determination of a court of quarter sessions, or a magistrates' court, made or given in affiliation proceedings.

Proceedings on appeal by case stated against an order or determination of a magistrates' court with regard to the enforcement of—

(a) an order for the payment of money made by virtue of the Matrimonial Proceedings (Magistrates' Courts) Act 1960;

(b) an order for the payment of money registered in a magistrates' court under the Maintenance Orders Act 1958 or registered in a court in England and Wales under Part II of the Maintenance Orders Act 1950 or the Maintenance Orders (Facilities for Enforcement) Act 1920 or confirmed by a magistrates' court under the last-mentioned Act.

Proceedings on appeal by case stated against an order or determination of a magistrates' court under section 24 of the Matrimonial Causes Act 1965 (alteration of maintenance agreement between spouses).

Prohibited Degrees of Kindred and Affinity

(The Marriage Act 1949, First Schedule, as amended by the Marriage (Enabling) Act 1960)

Mother
Daughter
Father's mother
Mother's mother
Son's daughter
Daughter's daughter
Sister
Wife's mother
Wife's daughter
Father's wife
Son's wife
Father's father's wife
Mother's father's wife
Wife's father's mother
Wife's mother's mother
Wife's son's daughter
Wife's daughter's daughter
Son's son's wife
Daughter's son's wife
Father's sister
Mother's sister
Brother's daughter
Sister's daughter

Father
Son
Father's father
Mother's father
Son's son
Daughter's son
Brother
Husband's father
Husband's son
Mother's husband
Daughter's husband
Father's mother's husband
Mother's mother's husband
Husband's father's father
Husband's mother's father
Husband's son's son
Husband's daughter's son
Son's daughter's husband
Daughter's daughter's husband
Father's brother
Mother's brother
Brother's son
Sister's son

APPENDIX C

Consents Required to the Marriage of a Minor by Common Licence or Superintendent Registrar's Certificate

(The Marriage Act 1949, Second Schedule)

I. Where the Minor is Legitimate

Circumstances	Person or Persons whose consent is required
1. Where both parents are living:	
(a) if parents are living together;	Both parents.
(b) if parents are divorced or separated by order of any court or by agreement;	The parent to whom the custody of the minor is committed by order of the court or by the agreement, or, if the custody of the minor is so committed to one parent during part of the year and to the other parent during the rest of the year, both parents.
(c) if one parent has been deserted by the other;	The parent who has been deserted.
(d) if both parents have been deprived of custody of minor by order of any court.	The person to whose custody the minor is committed by order of the court.
2. Where one parent is dead:	
(a) if there is no other guardian;	The surviving parent.
(b) if a guardian has been appointed by the deceased parent.	The surviving parent and the guardian if acting jointly, or the surviving parent or the guardian if the parent or guardian is the sole guardian of the minor.
3. Where both parents are dead.	The guardians or guardian appointed by the deceased parents or by the court under section 3 or 5 of the Guardianship of Minors Act 1971.

II. Where the Minor is Illegitimate

Circumstances	Person whose consent is required
If the mother of the minor is alive.	The mother, or if she has by order of any court been deprived of the custody of the minor, the person to whom the custody of the minor has been committed by order of the court.
If the mother of the minor is dead.	The guardian appointed by the mother.

528

APPENDIX D

Orders Relating to Financial Provision and Children under the Matrimonial Proceedings and Property Act

Nature of Provision	Proceedings in which it can be ordered	Whether it can be secured	Whether it can be varied	Whether repayment can be ordered	
				(1) after change of circumstances	(2) after remarriage
Maintenance pending suit	Divorce, nullity, judicial separation, wilful neglect	No	Yes	Yes	No
Periodical payments for spouse	Divorce, nullity, judicial separation, wilful neglect	Yes	Yes	Yes	Yes
Lump sum payment for spouse	Divorce, nullity, judicial separation, wilful neglect	Yes, if payable by instalments	Payment by instalments only	No	No
Transfer and settlement of property	Divorce, nullity, judicial separation	—	Only order for settlement made on judicial separation	No	No
Variation of settlements	Divorce, nullity, judicial separation	—	Only if made on judicial separation	No	No
Custody of children of the family	Divorce, nullity, judicial separation, wilful neglect	—	Yes	—	—
Education of children of the family	Divorce, nullity, judicial separation	—	Yes	—	—
Periodical payments for children of the family	Divorce, nullity, judicial separation, wilful neglect	Yes	Yes	Yes	—
Lump sum payment for children of the family	Divorce, nullity, judicial separation, wilful neglect	Yes, if payable by instalments	Payment by instalments only	No	—

APPENDIX E

Pending Legislation

At the time of writing (April, 1971) there are two Bills before Parliament which are almost certain to receive the Royal Assent and which introduce changes of some importance. Their main provisions are summarised below.

I. NULLITY OF MARRIAGE BILL

This Bill implements the recommendations contained in the Report of the Law Commission on Nullity of Marriage (Law Com. No. 33). It is to come into force one month after receiving the Royal Assent (clause 7 (5)).

Void Marriages.—By clause 1 a marriage celebrated after the commencement of the Act will be void only if either party lacked capacity, or if the parties knowingly and wilfully failed to comply with certain provisions of the Marriage Act 1949 (see *ante*, p. 72), or if the parties are of the same sex.[1] The law on these three subjects remains unchanged.

Voidable Marriages.—By clause 2 a marriage celebrated after the commencement of the Act will be voidable only on the following grounds:

(a) Either party's incapacity to consummate it. This reproduces the existing law.

(b) The respondent's wilful refusal to consummate it. This also reproduces the existing law.

(c) Absence of consent. The circumstances in which consent will be regarded as lacking remain unchanged but the marriage will be undoubtedly voidable and not perhaps void, as at present.

(d) Mental disorder. A marriage will be voidable on this ground only if

" at the time of the marriage either party, though capable of giving a valid consent, was suffering (whether continuously or intermittently) from mental disorder within the meaning of the Mental Health Act 1959 of such a kind or to such an extent as to be unfitted for marriage."

It will be seen that this makes a number of changes in the law (see *ante*, p. 78). References to " unsoundness of mind ", " insanity " and " fitness for the procreation of children " disappear; epilepsy ceases to be a ground for nullity; and it is made clear that the mental disorder may be continuous or intermittent.

(e) The respondent's venereal disease. This reproduces the existing law.

(f) The respondent wife's pregnancy *per alium*. This also reproduces the existing law.

Bars and Defences.—The bars of approbation, ratification, lack of sincerity and the like will be abolished (clause 3 (4)) and replaced by a new statutory bar contained in clause 3 (1). This provides that the court shall not pronounce a decree in the case of a voidable marriage if the respondent establishes

" (a) that the petitioner, with knowledge that it was open to him to have the marriage avoided, so conducted himself in relation to the respondent as to lead the respondent reasonably to believe that he would not seek to do so; *and*

---

[1] A marriage will also be void if the Royal Marriages Act 1772 is not complied with: clause 7 (4).

(b) that it would be unjust to the respondent to grant the decree."

This largely reproduces the existing law except that it will no longer be a bar that the decree would be contrary to public policy.

In all cases of voidable marriages except those based on inability and refusal to consummate, the petition must be brought within three years (clause 3 (2)). It will be seen that in cases (d), (e) and (f) this extends the present period from one year (see *ante*, p. 79) and also applies the same provision to marriages where one party lacked consent which will, therefore, no longer be open to challenge at a remote time in the future. In cases (e) and (f) the petitioner will not be able to obtain a decree unless he was ignorant of the ground at the time of the marriage (clause 3 (3)). This reproduces the existing law (see *ante*, p. 79) except that knowledge of the ground at the time of the marriage will no longer be a bar in the case of unsoundness of mind. The fact that the petitioner has had sexual intercourse with the respondent after discovering the existence of the ground will cease to be a bar altogether.

Collusion will also cease to be a bar in proceedings for nullity and *ex abundanti cautela* it is declared that neither collusion nor any other conduct on the part of the petitioner is to be a bar to the granting of a decree for presumption of death and dissolution (clause 6).

Effect of Decree.—Clause 5 provides that in the case of a voidable marriage a decree

" shall operate to annul the marriage as respects any time after the decree has been made absolute, and the marriage shall, notwithstanding the decree, be treated as if it had existed up to that time."

This represents a compromise between the two conflicting judicial views about the effect of a decree (see *ante*, p. 70). Under the Bill a second marriage contracted by either party before decree absolute will be void and will remain so after the decree has been pronounced (*cf. Wiggins* v. *Wiggins, ante*, p. 70) and neither party will be able to give evidence against the other if he or she would have been incompetent to do so had the marriage been dissolved (*cf. R.* v. *Algar, ante*, p. 70). On the other hand, after the decree has been pronounced the parties will revert to their status before the marriage and, subject to the law relating to concluded transactions, either will be able to claim, for example, a legacy payable so long as the beneficiary remains unmarried (*cf. Re D'Altroy's Will Trusts, ante*, p. 70).

Foreign Marriages.—The Bill purports to deal solely with English marriages. Consequently clause 4 expressly provides that nothing in the Bill is to affect any question which by the English conflict of laws is to be determined by foreign law. Similarly, a marriage celebrated under the Foreign Marriages Acts 1892 to 1947 or allegedly valid as a common law marriage may still be void through failure to comply with the statutory provisions or common law rules.

2. RECOGNITION OF DIVORCES AND LEGAL SEPARATIONS BILL

This Bill implements the proposals of the Law Commission and the Scottish Law Commission (Cmnd. 4542) that effect should be given, in a somewhat modified form, to the Hague Convention on the Recognition of Divorces and Legal Separations signed in 1968. If it is passed, it will come into operation on 1st January, 1972. It will apply to decrees of divorce and legal separation obtained before the date of commencement unless their validity has already been decided by a competent court in the British Isles, but it will not affect any rights to property to which anyone has already become entitled (clause 9 (4), (5)).

British Decrees.—Subject to what will be said below about exceptions, clause 1 provides that any decree pronounced in any part of the British Isles (*i.e.*, the United Kingdom, the Channel Islands and the Isle of Man) shall be recognised in any other part. Hence it will no longer be open to an English court to refuse to recognise a Scottish decree on the ground, for example, that the parties were not domiciled there.

Overseas Decrees.—Overseas decrees (that is, decrees obtained by judicial or other process outside the British Isles) will be recognised if any of the following conditions is satisfied.

(a) That the decree was obtained in the country of the spouses' domicile (clause 6 (a)).

(b) That the decree is recognised by the spouses' *lex domicilii* (clause 6 (a)). This will give statutory recognition to the decision in *Armitage* v. *A.-G.* (see *ante*, p. 219).

(c) That either spouse was habitually resident in the country where the decree was obtained. In the case of countries (like the U.S.A.) comprising territories with different legal systems, each territory is to be regarded as a separate country, and if the law of the country in question bases jurisdiction on domicile, " habitual residence " for this purpose includes domicile within the meaning of that law (clause 3).

(d) That either spouse was a national of the country where the decree was obtained (clause 3 (1) (b)).[2] It will be seen that, if a spouse possesses dual nationality, we shall recognise a decree obtained in either country.

No other decree of divorce or legal separation is to be recognised (clause 6). It is improbable that a party with a real and substantial connection with the country in question will be neither a national of it nor habitually resident there, but the decision in *Indyka* v. *Indyka* (*ante*, p. 221) will be abrogated insofar as it is wider than the provisions contained in the Bill.

Miscellaneous Matters relating to Residence and Nationality.—If recognition is sought on the ground of a party's habitual residence or nationality, the relevant condition must be satisfied at the date of the institution of the proceedings or, if there were cross-proceedings, at the commencement of either the original proceedings or the cross-proceedings (clauses 3 (1) and 4 (1)). Any finding of fact made in the proceedings on the basis of which jurisdiction was assumed (for example, in relation to a spouse's residence, nationality or domicile) will be binding on an English court if both parties appeared in the proceedings and in other cases may be treated as sufficient evidence of the fact if the court thinks fit (clause 5). The reason for this distinction is, of course, that a spouse who appeared in the original proceedings will have had the opportunity of challenging the jurisdiction then. If a legal separation recognised on ground (c) or (d) is converted into a divorce in the country in which it was obtained, the divorce will be recognised in this country even though the conditions relating to residence or nationality were not satisfied at the time of the conversion (clause 4 (2)).

Exceptions from the General Rule.—No decree of divorce or legal separation (whether obtained in some other part of the British Isles or overseas) is to be recognised if by English law (including the English rules of private international law and the provisions of the Bill) there was no valid marriage between the parties at the time. An English court will also have a discretion to refuse recognition of an overseas decree of divorce or legal separation if

(a) reasonable steps were not taken to give notice of the proceedings to the other party; *or*

(b) for any other reason the other party was not given a reasonable opportunity of taking part in the proceedings; *or*

(c) its recognition would manifestly be contrary to public policy (clause 8).

This probably does no more than embody the existing rules under which recognition may be refused (see *ante*, pp. 223-224). In any event, an English court will not be bound to recognise or give effect to any finding of fault or any ancillary order (clause 8 (3)).

---

[2] For nationality in the case of British colonies and dependencies, see clause 10 (3).

Remarriage of Divorced Persons.—If a decree of divorce is recognised in this country, neither party to the marriage dissolved will be precluded from remarrying here on the ground that the decree is not recognised in some other country (clause 7). It therefore follows that, if the Bill becomes law, a case with facts similar to *Ex p. Arias* (*ante*, p. 17) will be differently decided. As the applicant in that case was domiciled in Switzerland, we shall still recognise the Swiss decree of divorce. It was held that he could not remarry here because by his *lex domicilii* his capacity to remarry was to be determined by his *lex patriae* (which was Italian) and the Swiss decree was not recognised in Italy. It seems that we shall have to disregard the Italian refusal to recognise the decree under clause 8 and thus hold that he will be able to marry here. As this will have the effect of creating a limping marriage which will not be recognised by the husband's *lex domicilii*, it is doubtful whether, in this situation at least, it effects any improvement in the law.

U

Index

535

CHILDREN—*continued*
  local authority—*continued*
    duties of authorities, 290, 291 *et seq.*
    maintenance, contribution to, 298
    powers and duties, 297
    reception into care, 296
    wards of court, 338
  magistrates' courts, powers of, 266, 270, 282. *And see* MAGISTRATES' COURTS
  maintenance of, 472 *et seq. And see* MAINTENANCE
  marriage of—
    common licence, 32, 528
    consent to—
      conflict of laws, 23
      dispensed with, 29, 33, 32
      inferred, 32
      required, 28, 31, 528
      minimum age, 23
        below, recognition, 44
      parental rights after, 263
      procured by fraud, 29
      ward of court, 336, 338
      widow or widower, 31
  married, appointment of guardian for, 324, 325
  mental disease, suffering from, order in case of, 294
  moral protection of, 276, 292, 308
  name, change of, 305
    injunction against, 305
  nationality of, 317
  neglect of—
    civil liability for, 308
    criminal liability for, 306, 307
    guardian's responsibility, 327
    powers of juvenile court in case of, 292 295
  offence against as ground for order, 182
  order for benefit of, effect of cohabitation of parents, 200
  portions for, 495. *And see* PORTIONS
  posthumous, nationality of, 318
    right to damages on death of relative, 108
  property of, rights of parents, 458
  protection of, duty of guardians, 327 parents, 263, 305
  provision on death of parent, 509 *et seq.*
    And see FAMILY PROVISION
  religion of. *See* RELIGION
  rights and duties of parents—
    assumption by local authority, 290, 291 *et seq.*, 296
    at common law, 263, 268
    by statute, 265, 269
    in equity, 263, 269
  safety, detention in place of, 295
  security for good behaviour of, 311
  services of—
    action for loss of, 313 *et seq.*
      by person having custody, 320
      due to tort, 314, 316
      proposed abolition, 316
    right to, 304
    to which parent due, 315

CHILDREN—*continued*
  settlement for. *See* MARRIAGE SETTLEMENT; SETTLEMENT
  suffocation in bed with drunken person, 307
  supervision of, 320
    order, power to make, 293
  supplementary benefits for, 412, 472, 477, 478
  surname, change of, 305
    injunction against, 305
  tort committed against, action by parent, 314, 316
  undue influence of parents, 460
  ward of court, application to have child made, 264, 281, 299, 336. *And see* WARD OF COURT
  welfare of, in equity, 264
    paramount, 267, 280, 288
    witholding decree to safeguard, 288
  wilful neglect to maintain, 474

CHURCH OF ENGLAND
  marriage according to rites of, 33, 37

CLERGYMAN
  refusal to marry divorced person, 208

COHABITATION. *And see* CONSORTIUM
  agency, presumption arising from, 121
  bilateral intention essential, 192
  cessation of, as element in desertion, 104
  condonation, as element in, 192
  duty of, 102, 169
    breach of, 102
    partial, 103
    polygamous marriage, 50
  evidence of marriage, as, 52
  intention to bring to an end, 174
  judicial separation, effect of, 144
  maintenance order, effect on, 200, 418
    made during, 200, 282
  non-cohabitation clause, order, in, 198
  presumption, condonation, as to, 192
    sexual intercourse, as to, 232
  prevented by foreign law, nullity proceedings, 74
  ratification of voidable marriage by, 61
  reconciliation provisions, 214
  refusal to resume, 179
  residing with distinguished from, 200
  resumption of—
    desertion terminated by, 177
    discharge of separation order, 200
    effect on judicial separation, 145
      separation agreement, 137, 139
    evidence of, 178
    in relation to condonation, 192
    three-month period, for, 193
  separation order during, 200
  temporary withdrawal form, 169

COITUS INTERRUPTUS
  insistence on, justifying separation, 169

CRUELTY—*continued*
 sexual intercourse, condonation, as, 193,
   194
    refusal of, as, 78, 96,
     157, 169
  offences as, 156, 157
  perversion as, 156
 threats as, 157
 what amounts to, 151

CUSTODY
 children, of, 283 *et seq.* *And see*
  CHILDREN
 wife, of, 92

CURTESY
 tenancy by, 348, 354

DAMAGES
 action between spouses, 357
 adultery, for, 103
 breach of separation agreement, for, 142
 Carriage by Air Act, under, 117
 consortium, for loss of, 103 *et seq.*
 expectation of life, relevance of, 112
 fatal accident, in respect of, 108 *et seq.*
   And see FATAL ACCIDENT
 loss of services of children, for, 313 *et
  seq.*
  proposed abolition, 316
 measure of—
  death of passenger on aircraft, 117
  fatal accident, 112
  loss of consortium, 106
  pecuniary loss as, 109
 offence of child, for, liability, 311, 329
 remoteness of possibility as bar, 109

DEATH. *And see* FATAL ACCIDENT
 action for damages, limit of time, 110
 child, of, action for loss of services, 315
    responsibility for, 306
    testator, of, 493
 damages for, effect of wife's adultery,
   109
 discharge of matrimonial order after,
   201
 effect on—
  action for loss of consortium, 106
  affiliation order, 483, 485, 486
  income tax, liability of husband, 374
  maintenance agreement, 412
     order, 201
  separation order, 201
 family provision, 508 *et seq.* *And see*
  FAMILY PROVISION
 guardian, of, 331
 husband, of, effect on wife's agency, 124
 illegitimate child, of, before marriage of
  parents, 463
 intestate, 501 *et seq. And see* INTESTATE
  SUCCESSION
 maintenance agreement, effect on, 412
     order, effect on, 201
 marriage, termination by, 202
 married woman, of, effect on action for
  tort, 124, 125

DEATH—*continued*
 matrimonial home, provisions as to, 385
 mother, of, effect on affiliation proceedings, 483
 order for provision out of estate of
  former spouse, 517
 parent, of—
  custody of child after, 263, 323
  declaration of unfitness, effect of, 289
  guardianship of children after, 319.
   And see GUARDIAN
 party to voidable marriage, of, 59
 passenger on aircraft, of, 117
 periodical payments, effect on, 430, 450
 posthumous child, legitimacy of, 228,
   229
 presumption of, 53, 54
  dissolution of marriage on, 202
  domicile of parties, 203
 spouse, of, effect on joint account, 362
     separation order,
      201
   matrimonial home, provisions
    as to, 385
   right to damages, 108. *And see*
    FATAL ACCIDENT
 statutory tenancy, transmission of, 518
  et seq. And see RENT ACTS
 testate succession, 190 *et seq. And see*
  WILL
 ward, of, effect on guardianship, 331

DECLARATION OF LEGITIMACY, 244

DECLARATION OF UNFITNESS, 289

DECLARATORY JUDGMENT
 validity of marriage, as to, 56

DECREE NISI
 application to make absolute, 208

DEED POLL
 change of child's name by, 305n.

DEFAMATION
 claim to be wife of person, by, 95n.
 communication between spouses, 127
 loss of consortium due to, 104

DEFENCE FORCES. *See* ARMED FORCES

DELAY
 marriage, in solemnization of, 73
 nullity proceedings barred by, 64, 79

DELUSION
 desertion, as defence for, 165

DEPENDANT. *See* FAMILY PROVISION;
  FATAL ACCIDENT

DESERTION
 animus deserendi, loss of, 179
 change of domicile, effect of, 219
 child, of, custody on, 279
 cohabitation—
  duty of, 169
  resumption of, 177

DIVORCE—*continued*
desertion—*continued*
  reconciliation provisions, 214
domicile, provisions as to, 218 *et seq.*
education, order as to, 304
financial provisions. *See* FINANCIAL
  PROVISIONS
five years separation as fact establishing
  marriage breakdown, 213
  children, protection of, 217
  financial protection of respondent, 216
  hardship to respondent in case of, 215
  reconciliation provisions, 215
foreign decree, recognition of, 218
  pending legislation, 531
ground for, 206, 209 *et seq.*
  facts establishing, 209 *et seq.*
    adultery, 209
    behaviour of respondent, 210
    desertion, 211
    five years separation, 213
    two years' separation, 212
historical development, 143
illegitimate children, custody of, 271
income tax, effect as to liability, 374
insane respondent, in case of, 211, 213
jurisdiction of English courts, 218, 220
legitimacy of child born after, 228, 230
maintenance of children, 286
        spouse, 414 *et seq.*
  And see FINANCIAL PROVISIONS;
  MAINTENANCE
matrimonial home, rights to, 95, 375,
  400 *et seq. And see* MATRIMONIAL
  HOME
name, use of husband's after, 95
nationality, based on, 219
non-compliance with restitution decree,
  on, 103
nullity of marriage, distinguished from, 58
polygamous marriage, 47, 50 51
        designed to termi-
        nate, validity, 51
presumption of death, 202
previous decree as evidence, 207
      proceedings, after, 207
proceedings pending, application for
  separation order, 198
reconciliation provisions, 213 *et seq. And
  see* RECONCILIATION
reform, 205, 206
  Royal Commission on, 205
  working of 1969 Act, 217
remarriage, refusal to officiate, 208
residence, jurisdiction based on, 219
restraint on anticipation, effect on, 351
royal commission on, 1850....204
            1951....205
Scottish degree, recognition of, pending
  legislation, 531
separation—
  fact establishing marriage breakdown,
  as, 212, 213
  children, protection of, 217
  financial protection for respondent,
  216
  five years, for, 213
  hardship to respondent, 215
  reconciliation provisions, 215

DIVORCE—*continued*
separation—*continued*
  two years, for, 217
settlement of property on, 434 *et seq.*
  And see SETTLEMENT
sexual misconduct after, irrelevance of,
  451
termination of marriage by, 203 *et seq.*
three years of marriage, within, 206
tort, effect on action for, 125
two years separation as fact establishing
  marriage breakdown, 212
  children, protection of, 217
  financial protection for respondent,
  216
  hardship to respondent, 215
  reconciliation provisions, 215
undefended petitions, 206, 217
will, effect on, 490

DOMICILE
adoption, as basis of, 248, 259, 261
  effect on, 10
affiliation proceedings based on, 393
capacity to marry governed by, 17
change of, by deserting husband, 219
    effect on validity of mar-
    riage, 49
choice, of, 8, 219, 222
concept of, 6, 7
dependent, 8
family law, importance in, 6, 7
  provision, relevance to, 509
fraudulent misrepresentation, 223
infant, of, 9
jurisdiction—
  declaration of legitimacy, 244
  divorce, 218
  judicial separation, 143
  nullity of marriage, 84
  problems as to, 56
law of—
  capacity to marry governed by, 17, 18,
  19
  declaration of divorcement under, 48
  divorce proceedings, effect on, 218 *et
  seq.*
  polygamy not permitted by, 47, 48
    permitted by, 43 *et seq.*
  property rights of spouses under 36on.
legitimacy in relation to, 7, 49
legitimation by marriage, 240, 243
  not by marriage, 244
  whether retrospective
    effect, 7n.
marriages invalid by English law, effect
  on, 43 *et seq.*
married woman, of, 8
matrimonial proceedings before magistrates, 147, 148
minor, of, 9
nature of, 7
origin, of, 7
pending legislation, 531 *et seq.*
polygamy, in relation to, 43 *et seq.*
presumption of death, in case of, 203
residence, distinguished from, 6
wife, of, where marriage invalid, 86

FAMILY DIVISION OF HIGH COURT
appeal to, 526
business assigned to, 525
establishment of, 3
jurisdiction, 3

FAMILY PROVISION
application for—
limitation on, 510
time for making, 513
dependents, who are, 509
domicile, relevance to, 509
evidence in support of application, 513
former spouse, for, after divorce,
nullity, 516
lump sum, order for payment of, 514
moral obligation of deceased, 512
object of legislation, 509
orders that may be made, 514
variation of, 515
personal representatives, liability for
distribution within six months,
513
reasonable provision, 509, 510 *et seq.*
termination of, 514
void marriage, in case of, 510

FATAL ACCIDENT
action for damages, 108 *et seq.*
against whom lies, 111
death of child, on, 108, 315
for whose benefit, 108
guardian, by, 329
limit of time for, 111
personal representative, by, 110
adopted child, in respect of, 108, 261
aircraft, death of passenger, 117
contracting out of liability, 111
contributory negligence, effect of, 116
Crown, liability of, 111
damages—
apportionment of, 116
assessment of, 112
business loss, 109
mental suffering, 112
protection from creditors, 115n.
reduction by value of benefit, 114, 115
defence of *volenti non fit injuria*, 111
dependants, legitimated children, 241
parents and children, 108,
317

FATHER. *See* PARENT

FINANCIAL PROVISIONS. *And see*
MAINTENANCE; MAINTENANCE
ORDER
ante-nuptial settlements, 436 *et seq. And
see* SETTLEMENT
assessment, principles of, 443 *et seq.*
age of parties, 447
children, interests of, 445, 447
conduct of parties, relevance of, 444,
448
contributions to welfare of family, 447
duration of marriage, 447
financial needs and liabilities, 447
resources, 445
future benefits, loss of, 448

FINANCIAL PROVISIONS—*continued*
assessment—*continued*
National Insurance benefits, loss by
wife, 448
pension, loss by wife, 448
standard of living before breakdown,
443, 444, 447
children, for, 474 *et seq.*
assessment, 475
orders relating to, 529
duration, 476
enforcement, 477
variation and discharge, 477
wilful neglect to maintain, in case of,
474
claims for, attempts to defeat, 454
consent orders, 431
variation of, 451
fraudulent disposition to defeat claim,
454
income tax provisions, 432
lump sum payments, 433
bankruptcy, in case of, 454
enforcement of, 454
variation of orders, 449 *et seq.*
maintenance pending suit, 426, 428 *et seq.*
variation of orders, 449 *et seq.*
nullity, position as to, 449
orders as to, 426 *et seq.*
discharge of, 449 *et seq.*
enforcement of, 452 *et seq.*
nominal, 43
revival of, 449 *et seq.*
suspension of, 449 *et seq.*
variation of, 449 *et seq.*
discretion of court, 451
when made, 426
periodical payments—
arrears—
death, effect of, 453
instalments, payment by, 452
judgment summons in case of, 452
recovery of, 452
remission of, 452
assessment of, 432
consent orders, 431
enforcement of, 452
income tax provisions, 432
overpayments, recovery of, 453
pending suit, 428
secured, 430
death of party, effect of, 430, 450
unsecured, 430
termination on death, 430
variation, etc. of orders, 449 *et seq.*
post-nuptial settlements, 436 *et seq. And
see* SETTLEMENT
property, transfer or settlement of, 434
et seq. And see SETTLEMENT
protection of payee, courts' power as to,
455
remarriage, effect of, 427, 441
settlements, 434 *et seq. And see* SETTLE-
MENT
sexual misconduct after decree not
relevant, 451
transfer of property, power to order, 434
et seq.
wilful neglect to maintain, in case of, 427

FINE
offence of child, for liability, 311, 329

FOREIGN DECREE
divorce, of, recognition of, 18, 50, 218
judicial separation, of, recognition of, 203

FOREIGN MARRIAGE
invalid by English law, provision as to, 43 *et seq.*
member of forces, by, 19 *et seq.*
common law marriages, 21, 22
non-Christian monogamous, validity of, 43, 49
nullity proceedings, cohabitation prevented by foreign law, 74n.
jurisdiction of English courts, 85
recognition of, 4
void, pending legislation, 531

FOSTER PARENTS
boarding child with, 297
child made ward of court by, 299
disputes as to care and control of child, 298
duty to protect child, 305
guardian distinguished from, 319

FRAUD
action between spouses in respect of, 125n.
condonation procured by, 195
declaration of legitimacy obtained by, 245
enticement of child by, 312
foreign nullity decree obtained by, 89
marriage induced by, 82
of infant procured by, 29
separation agreement voidable for, 136

FUNERAL EXPENSES
affiliation order for, 484
damages, included in, 112

FURNITURE
housekeeping savings, bought with, 363
husband and wife, respective rights, 389
ownership in case of bankruptcy, 366

GAMBLING
cruelty, as, 156

GIFT
husband and wife, as between, 365
by, avoidance by creditors, 366
illegitimate child, to, effect of, 459
parent to child, effect of, 458
rule against double portions, 495
will, by. *See* WILL

GUARDIAN
ad litem, adoption proceedings, for, 255
appointment by court, 325
parent, 322
care and control, right of, 328
corporal punishment by, 304
costs payable by ward, liability for, 329
county court, appointment by, 325

GUARDIAN—*continued*
Court of Chancery, appointment by, 264
criminal liability for neglect, 327
custody of child, right to, 328
damages payable by ward, liability for, 329
death of, effect of, 331
ward, effect of, 331
discharge of, 332
education, duty as to, 328
fatal accident, action in respect of, 329
fine of ward, liability for, 329
foreign, recognition in England, 326
foster parent distinguished from, 319
High Court, appointment by, 325
ill-treatment of child by, 306
jurisdiction of High Court over, 321
liability for acts of ward, 311, 329
magistrates' courts, appointment by, 325
jurisdiction over, 321
maintenance of ward, 327
majority of ward, effect of, 331
marriage of ward, consent to, 31, 528
effect of, 331
married child, in respect of, 324, 325
meaning of, 319
more than one, disputes, 329
parental rights resolution, notice to, 297
protection of child, duty as to, 327
religion, duty as to, 328
relevance to appointment, 325
removal of, by court, 332
revocation of appointment of, 323
rights and duties of, 327
of, liability for interference with, 329
security for good behaviour of child, 311
termination of guardianship, 331
testamentary—
acting with surviving parent, 319, 324
assignment of office of, 324n.
power to appoint, 322
review of Acts, 269, 322
trustee, compared with, 321
of ward's property, as, 330
undue influence by, 330
ward of court, of, 332

GUARDIANSHIP ORDER
juvenile court, power to make, 294

HABEAS CORPUS
custody of child, to obtain, 281

HEIR
legitimated person, 462 *et seq.*
by foreign law, 243
succession to realty by, 501

HIGH COURT
application to, while magistrates' order in force, 289, 406
children—
adoption of, jurisdiction as to, 255, 257
marriage of, consent to, 32

HIGH COURT—*continued*
  children—*continued*
    proceedings as to, clash in jurisdiction, 289
  declaratory judgments, jurisdiction as to, 56
  Family Division—
    appeal to, 526
    business assigned to, 525
    establishment of, 3
    jurisdiction, 3
  financial provision, power to make orders as to, 426 *et seq.*
  guardians—
    disputes between, 329
    jurisdiction over, 322
      to appoint, 325
        remove, 332
  jurisdiction, 2
    history of, 2
  matrimonial orders made by, 197
  nullity of marriage, jurisdiction in, 60
  settlement of property, 434
  transfer of proceedings to, 4

HOMOSEXUALITY
  cruelty, as, 156

HOSPITAL ORDER
  juvenile court, power to make, 294

HOTCHPOT, 506

HUMILIATION
  cruelty, as, 157

HUSBAND AND WIFE
  absence, presumption of death, 202
  actions for damages between, 357
    in tort, between, 125, 357
  adoption by, 248
  arrest, spouse, of, impending, 128
  bill of sale, validity of, 367
  civil proceedings, evidence in, 98
  communication between—
    breaking of confidence, 97
    privilege, 99
      abolition, 99
  conspiracy between, 127, 129
  corporal punishment, right to administer, 92
  crime, marital coercion, 128
  criminal proceedings, evidence in, 99
  death of spouse, damages for, 108. *And see* FATAL ACCIDENT
  matrimonial home, provisions in case of, 385
  defamation, communication between, 127
  desertion, effect of change of domicile, 89
  equality of rights of, 93
  evidence—
    civil proceedings, in, 98
    criminal proceedings, in, 99
    incriminating spouse, 99
    sexual intercourse, as to, 231
  family allowance, to whom payable, 471
    provision for, 508 *et seq. And see* FAMILY PROVISION

HUSBAND AND WIFE—*continued*
  gift between, validity of, 365
    by husband, avoidance by creditors, 366
  husband's earnings, attachment of, 422 *et seq.*
  income tax, 373. *And see* INCOME TAX
  injunction, action for, by wife, 357
  insurable interest in each other, 371
      matrimonial home, 372
  intestacy, rights on, 501 *et seq. And see* INTESTATE SUCCESSION
  loan by one to other, 371
  maintenance. *See* MAINTENANCE
  marital coercion, 128
  marital confidences—
    breaking of, 97
    civil proceedings, in, 98
    criminal proceedings, in, 99
    privilege, 99
      abolition, 99
  matrimonial home. *See* MATRIMONIAL HOME
  mutual wills by, 491
  nationality after marriage, 130
  partnership contract between, 121
  property rights, 343 *et seq.*
    actions between spouses, 125, 126, 344, 356
    bankruptcy of one, in case of, 344, 367, 368
    breakdown of marriage, on, 344
    creditors, protection of, 367, 368
    death of one, effect of, 344, 363
    deserted wife, of, 353n.
    disputes between one spouse and stranger, 344, 359
      spouses, 125, 126, 344, 356
    formulation of, need for, 344
    furniture, as to, 363, 389
      bankruptcy, in case of, 366
    gifts to spouses, 365
    housekeeping allowance, savings from, 362
    income from spouse, 360
    insolvency of one, on, 344
    investment from joint account, 360, 361
    joint savings, 360
    judicial separation, effect of, 352
    law of domicile, effect of, 360n.
    maintenance, relation with, 345
    Married Women's Property Act 1964, under, 362, 363
    matrimonial home, 344, 375 *et seq. And see* MATRIMONIAL HOME
    property at time of marriage, 359
    purchase by one spouse, 363
      in name of other, 364
    separate estate, development of, 352 *et seq.*
    settlements, bankruptcy, in case of, 367 *et seq.*
    transfer with intention to defraud, 367
    under common law—
      copyholds, 349
      disposition before marriage, 350, 353

NATIONALITY
children, of, 317
citizen, status of, 317
divorce based on, 219
domicile distinguished from, 7
dual, 318
marriage, effect on, 130

NAVY
custody of child, 271
maintenance of dependents of members, 407
marriage of member of, 19 *et seq.*, 30, 42

NECESSARIES
husband's duty to provide, 402
meaning of, 401
wife's authority to purchase, 401

NEGLECT
child, of, liability for, 309
cruelty, as, 157

NEGLIGENCE
action between spouses for, 125
contributory, reduction of damages, 115
death due to, damages for, 108 *et seq.*
And see FATAL ACCIDENT
failure to prevent child causing damage, 310, 329
injury to child, action by parent, 316
loss of consortium due to, 104
neglect of child, liability for, 309

NON-CONSUMMATION
marriage, of, 74. *See also* CONSUMMATION OF MARRIAGE

NON-MOLESTATION CLAUSE, 136, 139

NORTHERN IRELAND
adoption orders made in, 261
jurisdiction of magistrates' where party residing in, 148
publication of banns in, 33

NOTICE
banns, by, 33. *See also* BANNS
marriage, of, not duly given, 74
with licence, of, 38
without licence, 37

NULLITY OF MARRIAGE
action between spouses after decree, 126
adoption of child, effect of, 63
approbation as defence, 60
child—
born after decree, legitimacy, 239
custody of, orders as to, 286, 287
made ward of court, 336
provision as to, 287
withholding decree, welfare, to safeguard, 288
collusion bar to petition, 66
death after, order for provision for former spouse out of estate, 516
decree nisi, 60

NULLITY OF MARRIAGE—*continued*
decree of—
avoidance of transactions on, 69
by foreign court, recognition of, 84, 88
distinguished from divorce, 58
effect of, on—
concluded transactions, 71
legitimacy, 69
separation agreement, 137, 141
order, 201
status, 58
will, 490
grounds for. *See* VOID MARRIAGE; VOIDABLE MARRIAGE
jurisdiction to grant, 59, 84
nature of, 58
obtained by fraud or collusion, 89
retrospective effect, 58, 69
tax allowance after, 71n.
variation of settlement on, 436, 443
when necessary, 58, 59
delay, effect of, 64, 79
education of children, order as to, 304
estoppel, 67
evidence of wife against husband after, 70
financial provisions, 426 *et seq. And see* FINANCIAL PROVISIONS
foreign decrees, recognition of, 88
income tax, effect as to, 375
insincerity of petitioner, 61
maintenance—
arrangements, danger of collusion in case of, 67
children, of, 472 *et seq.*
wife, of, 404, 445, 447, 474 *et seq.*
And see FINANCIAL PROVISIONS; MAINTENANCE; MAINTENANCE ORDER
matrimonial home, right to occupy after decree, 400
transfer of tenancy on, 400
pending legislation, 530
polygamous marriage, 49
proceedings barred by delay, 64, 79
public policy in relation to, 65
separation agreement, effect on, 137, 141
settlement, of property on, 434 *et seq.*
And see SETTLEMENT
undefended petitions, 60

PARENTAL RIGHTS RESOLUTION, 297

PARENTS
adoption, termination of rights on, 260
advancement to children, 458 *et seq. And see* ADVANCEMENT; PORTIONS
children, liability for acts of, 310, 311
welfare as paramount consideration, 267, 270
custody of children, 267 *et seq. And see* CHILDREN
death of child, damages for, 317. *And see* FATAL ACCIDENT
defence by or of children, 308
duty to protect child, 305
equality of rights of, 270

REGISTERED BUILDING
marriages, for purpose of—
forces chapel as, 42
not duly certified, 72
registration of, 39

REGISTRAR OF BIRTHS, DEATHS
AND MARRIAGES
certificate to marry, issue of, 29, 36
with licence, 38
without licence, 37
creation of office of, 29
solemnization of marriage by, 39

REGISTRATION
High Court order, of, in magistrates'
court, 456
maintenance order, of, 455
order under Guardianship of Infants
Acts, of, 479

REGULATED TENANCY
meaning, 395. *See also* RENT ACTS

RELIGION
adoption, condition as to, 252
appointment of guardian, relevance to,
325
change of, polygamous marriage after,
47
child, of—
agreement as to, 303
changing, 302, 329
disputes as to, 301
father's rights, 263
parents' right to determine, 300
custody of child, relevance to 277, 278,
302
discrimination between faiths, 301
duties of guardians as to, 328
parents as to, 300

RENT ACTS
contractural tenancy, protection in case
of, 521
controlled premises, meaning of, 394
tenancy, 394
deserted spouse—
rights of, 398
transmission of tenancy, 517, 518
owner-occupier, temporary letting by,
398
purpose of, 394
recovery of possession, 397
regulated tenancy, meaning, 395
recovery of posses-
sion, 398
release from rent regulation, 395
statutory tenancy—
member of tenant's family, 518
remarriage of widow, 518
residing with, meaning of, 518
surviving spouse, of 504, 518
transmission on death, 517 *et seq.*
limitations
on, 520
transmitted tenancy, nature of, 521
statutory tenant, meaning of, 395
temporary absence of tenant, 396
wife of tenant in occupation, 396

RESCISSION
divorce decree, of, effect of, 208

RESIDENCE
adoption, for purpose of, 248, 261
as basis of jurisdiction in—
application for maintenance, 148
divorce, 219
ecclesiastical courts, 143
judicial separation, 143
matrimonial orders, 148
nullity of marriage, 85
domicile, distinguished from, 6
elements of, 6
family law, importance in, 6
meaning of, 6, 33, 36, 85, 86n.
requirements for purpose of marriage—
by banns, 6, 33
certificate with licence, 36, 38
without licence, 36
common licence, 35, 37
failure to comply with, 72
in registered building, 39, 40
residing with compared with cohabiting,
200
meaning of, 518
temporary absence from, 6, 7
two or more places of, 6

RESTITUTION OF CONJUGAL
RIGHTS
decree for, abolition, 102
ecclesiastical courts, in, 203
enforcement of consortium by, 93
injunction to restrain proceedings, 142

RESTRAINT ON ANTICIPATION
abolition of, 355
effect of, 351
preservation of, 353
property subject to, settlement of, 441

RING
engagement, ownership on termination
of engagement, 15

ROYAL COMMISSION
marriage and divorce, on, 1951...205
matrimonial offences, on, 1850...204

SATISFACTION
portions, of, 496, 497

SCOTLAND
adoption orders made in, 261
jurisdiction of magistrates where party
residing in, 148
publication of banns in, 33

SECURITY
good behaviour of child, for, 311

SEDUCTION
action for, 315 *et seq.*
parent encouraging, 308

SEPARATION. *And see* JUDICIAL
SEPARATION; SEPARATION AND
MAINTENANCE AGREEMENTS;
SEPARATION AND MAINTENANCE
ORDERS
adoption by one spouse after, 249
of child of marriage after, 249
conduct justifying, 168 *et seq.*, 103
consent to, 180
withdrawal of, 166
consortium terminated by, 101
deed of, 134
divorce, fact establishing ground for,
212, 213
income tax, effect as to, 374
insanity as justifying, 169
justification, 168 *et seq.*
matrimonial home, disagreement as to
location, 95
misconduct as justifying, 101
rape of wife by husband after, 97
refusal to have sexual intercourse as
justifying, 169
reasonable belief in grounds for, 171
sexual practices justifying, 96, 169
theft between spouses after, 129
wife's authority to pledge husband's
credit after, 401

SEPARATION AGREEMENTS. *And see*
SEPARATION
consideration, 134, 408
covenant not to apply for maintenance,
138, 413
custody of children, legality of provisions, 138, 270
desertion negatived by, 138
discharge by—
bankruptcy, 142
breach, 140
cohabitation, 139
subsequent matrimonial proceedings,
141
terms of agreement, 139
discharge of, effect of, 139
divorce, effect of, 141
dum casta clause, 137
education, terms as to, 303
effects of, 138
enforcement against husband's estate,
137
form of, 134
indemnity against wife's debts, 138
injunction to restrain breach, 142
judicial separation, effect of, 141
legality of, 134
liability for supplementary benefits, 413
maintenance, of wife, 137
non-molestation clause, 136, 139, 142
periodical payments, covenant to make,
409
property, provisions as to, 138
religion, terms as to, 303
remedies for breach, 142
specific performance, 142
subsequent change of law, 141
void and voidable, 135

SETTLEMENT
ante- and post-nuptial—
meaning, 437 *et seq.*
variation, divorce, nullity or judicial
separation, in case of, 436 *et seq.*
power of appointment, of, 441, 442
remarriage, on, 441
restraint upon anticipation, 441
retrospective, 443
ultimate remainders, destruction of,
443
bankruptcy, avoidance on, 368
fraudulent, avoidance of, 367
property, of, divorce, nullity or judicial
separation, in case of, 405, 434
et seq.
absolute transfer, 436
limitation on, 435, 436
matrimonial home, provisions as to,
435
meaning of property, 435
power to order, 434 *et seq.*
property situated abroad, 435
wife's right to, in equity, 350

SEX
change of, capacity to marry, effect on,
24

SEXUAL INTERCOURSE
action by spouse for loss of, 105
condonation by, 193
consummation of marriage by, 74. *And
see* CONSUMMATION OF MAR-
RIAGE
contraception, disagreement as to, 96
effect on consummation
of marriage, 75, 77
desertion, whether terminated by, 178
drunkenness, during, 150
evidence as to, 231 *et seq.*
insistence on, as cruelty, 96
ground for order, 182
legitimacy, in relation to, 231
loss of daughter's services due to, 366
matters justifying separation, 169
offer to resume cohabitation without,
180
physical inability, effect of, 75
presumption as to, between spouses, 231
et seq.
rape. *See* RAPE
refusal of—
as conducing to adultery, 189
separation, 169
cruelty, 78, 96, 157, 169
desertion, 162
delay in proceedings, 64
justifying separation, 169
non-consummation by, 77
right of spouse to, 96
taking girl for purpose of, 313
venereal disease, spouse suffering from,
96n., 182

SEXUAL OFFENCE
application for order on ground of, 182
cruelty, as, 156

SINGLE WOMAN
meaning of, 480

SODOMY
cruelty, as, 156
ground for judicial separation, 143, 203

SOLICITOR
acting for parent and child, 460
costs of. *See* COSTS

SPECIAL LICENCE, 36. *See also*
MARRIAGE LICENCE

SPECIFIC PERFORMANCE
separation agreement, of, 142

STATUS
marriage, created by, 12

STATUTORY TENANCY, 516 *et seq. And
see* RENT ACTS

STATUTORY TRUSTS
intestacy, on, 505, 506. *And see* IN-
TESTATE SUCCESSION

STERILITY
legitimacy, in relation to, 233

SUPERVISION ORDER
juvenile court, power to make, 293

SUPPLEMENTARY BENEFIT
adopted child, for, 477, 478
children, claims for, 472
neglect to obtain for, 307
recovery of cost of, 413

SURNAME
child's, change of, 305
deed poll, by, 305n.
wife's right to husband's, 95

TENANCY
by curtesy, 347, 354
entireties, 348, 354
controlled, 394
regulated, 395, 398
statutory. *See* RENT ACTS

THEFT
husband and wife, between, 129

THIRD PARTY
nullity decree, bound by, 60
validity of marriage, contesting, 60
wedding present by, recovery of, 15

THREATS
cruelty, as, 157

TORT
action between spouses, 124, 125 *et seq.*,
357
divorce, after, 126
nullity, after, 126
child, of, liability of parents, 310

TORT—*continued*
depriving parent of child's services, 314,
316
vicarious liability for spouse's, 125
ward, of, liability of guardian, 329
wife, committed against, 124
by, 124

TRESPASS
action between spouses, 357

TRUST
child, for, maintenance from, 458
payments to guardian, 327
guardian as trustee for ward, 321, 330
insurance policy, created by, 372, 461
mutual wills, created by, 491
statutory, on intestacy, 505, 506. *And
see* INTESTATE SUCCESSION

UNCHASTITY
whether marriage voidable because of, 81

UNDUE INFLUENCE
between engaged couple, 15
guardian and ward, 330
parent and child, 16n, 459
separation agreement voidable for, 136

UNNATURAL OFFENCE
adultery aggravated by, 204
as ground for judicial separation, 143,
203
cruelty, as, 156

VENEREAL DISEASE
application for matrimonial order on
ground of, 182
insistence on sexual intercourse when
suffering from, 96n., 182
nullity, as ground for, 78

VOID MARRIAGE. *And see* MARRIAGE;
NULLITY OF MARRIAGE; VOID-
ABLE MARRIAGE
ancillary relief, 59
declaration as to, 56
distinguished from voidable, 58
domicile, provisions as to, 8, 84, 87, 88
estoppel as to validity of, 67
financial provisions in case of, 426 *et seq.*
And see FINANCIAL PROVISION
grounds rendering void—
age of party, 25
consanguinity and affinity, 25, 527
drunkenness, 81
fear and duress, 82
formal defects, 28, 72, 85, 86
fraud or misrepresentation, 82
infant marrying without consent, 28,
29
under sixteen, 24, 72
insanity of party, 80
lack of capacity, 71
consent, 79
mistake as to identity, 81
nature of ceremony, 81
jurisdiction of English courts, 84
maintenance in case of, 404, 421